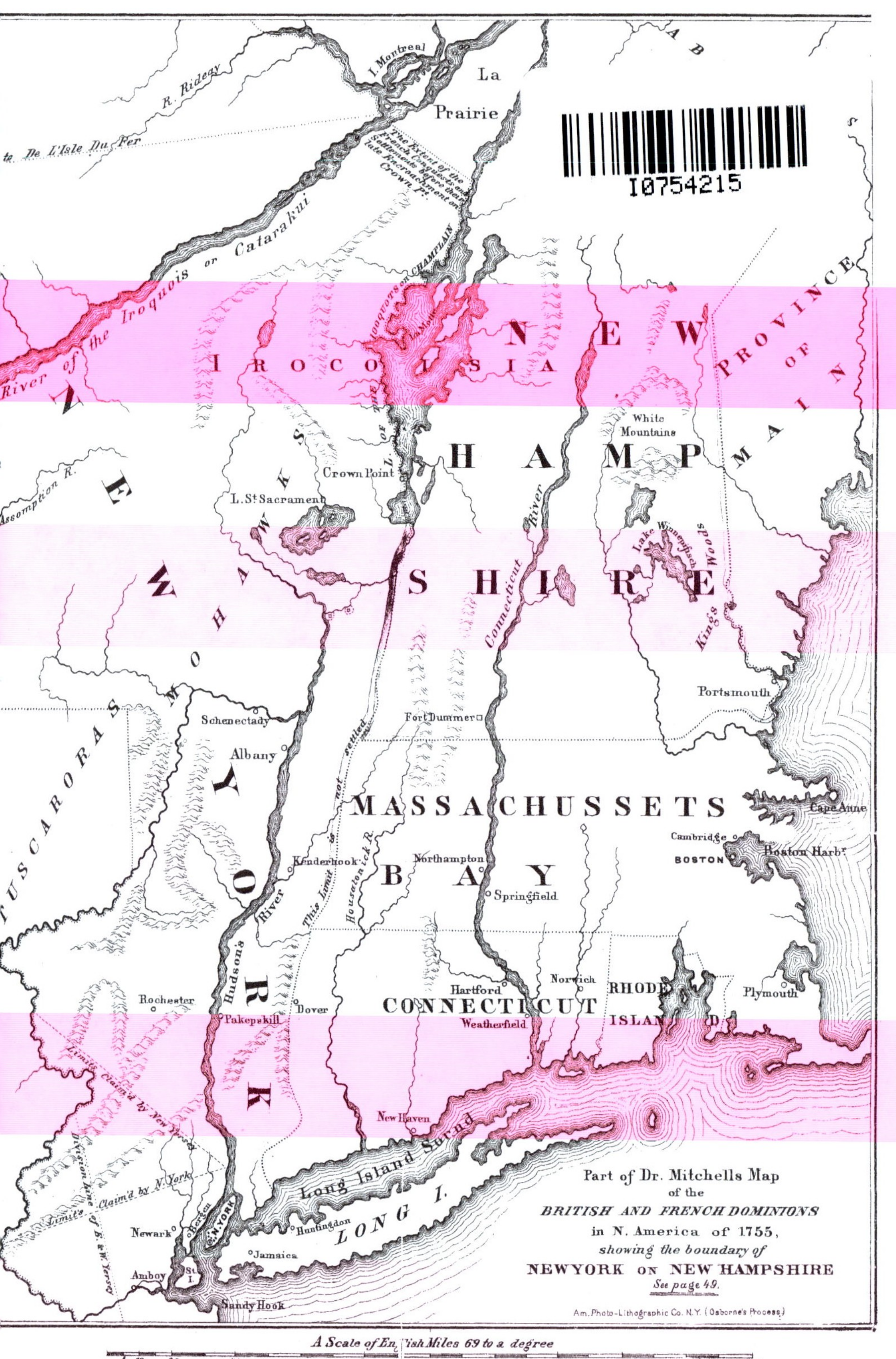

I. Montreal
La Prairie
R. Rideau
to De L'Isle Du Fer
The Extent of the French Conquests and Settlements before their late Encroachment on Crown Pt.
River of the Iroquois or Catarakui
L. CHAMPLAIN
IROCOISIA
NEW HAMPSHIRE
PROVINCE OF MAIN
White Mountains
Crown Point
L. St Sacrament
Assumption R.
NEW YORK
MOHAWKS
TUSCARORAS
Lake Winnepisseoke
Kings Woods
Connecticut River
Portsmouth
Schenectady
Albany
Fort Dummer
This Limit is not settled
MASSACHUSSETS BAY
Cape Anne
Cambridge
BOSTON
Boston Harbr.
Kinderhook
Northampton
Springfield
Housatonick R.
Hudsons River
Rochester
Pakepskill
Dover
Hartford
Weatherfield
CONNECTICUT
Norwich
RHODE ISLAND
Plymouth
Limits Claim'd by New Jersey
Limits Claim'd by N. York
Division line of E. & W. Jersey
New Haven
Long Island Sound
LONG I.
Huntingdon
Jamaica
Newark
Bergen
N. YORK
Amboy
St. I.
Sandy Hook
Part of Dr. Mitchells Map of the BRITISH AND FRENCH DOMINIONS in N. America of 1755, showing the boundary of NEWYORK ON NEW HAMPSHIRE
See page 49.
Am. Photo-Lithographic Co. N.Y. (Osborne's Process)
A Scale of English Miles 69 to a degree
5 10 20 40 60 100 200

THE

HISTORY OF VERMONT,

FROM ITS

DISCOVERY TO ITS ADMISSION INTO
THE UNION IN 1791.

BY

HILAND HALL.

ALBANY, N. Y.:
JOEL MUNSELL.
1868.

TO THE

VERMONT HISTORICAL SOCIETY,

THIS VOLUME

IS

RESPECTFULLY DEDICATED

BY

THE AUTHOR.

PREFACE.

The purpose of the author is to treat more fully than has yet been done by any writer, of the discovery, exploration and settlement of Vermont; of the adverse claims to the lands occupied by the settlers, and of the origin and character of those claims; of the necessity under which the early inhabitants were placed of forming themselves into a separate and distinct community, in order to maintain their titles and preserve their property; of their earnest and valuable services against the common enemy during the revolutionary war; and of the obstacles they encountered in organizing a new state government, and in establishing and maintaining its independence. His aim is to embody facts, and to state them with his views in intelligible language, without making any pretensions to literary merit.

Among those to whom the author is indebted for information and ready access to papers and documents on the subjects of his inquiries, his acknowledgments are specially due to Benjamin H. Hall, Esq., of Troy, author of the *History of Eastern Vermont;* to E. B. O'Callaghan, LL.D., of Albany; the Hon. J. Hammond Trumbull, of Hartford; the Rev. Pliny H. White of Coventry, President of the Vermont Historical Society; the Hon. Charles Reed, of Montpelier; the Hon. James H. Phelps, of Townshend; Henry Hall, Esq., and Henry Clark, Esq., of Rutland.

NORTH BENNINGTON,
September, 1868.

CONTENTS.

APPENDIX NO. I.

APPENDIX NO. 2.

APPENDIX NO. 3.

APPENDIX NO. 4.

APPENDIX NO. 5.

APPENDIX NO. 6.

APPENDIX NO. 7.

APPENDIX NO. 8.

APPENDIX NO. 9.

APPENDIX NO. 10.

APPENDIX NO. 11.

APPENDIX NO. 12.

APPENDIX NO. 13.

EARLY HISTORY OF VERMONT.

CHAPTER I.

Settlement of Vermont and Conflicting Claims to its Territory.

1609-1665.

Approach of civilized men — The Dutch, the French and the New England Puritans—Fort Dummer—Territorial claims of Massachusetts—Boundary dispute of that province with New Hampshire — Lands granted by Governor Wentworth — French war — Settlements under New Hampshire — Transfer of jurisdiction to New York — Lands regranted by New York, and under what claim.

THE state of Vermont, as an independent commonwealth, struggled into existence through a double revolution. The early inhabitants of the state revolted against the province of New York, to which the territory had been annexed by the arbitrary will of the king, and they united with their brethren of the other colonies in their armed resistance to the demands of the mother country. It is my purpose to inquire into and state the causes which produced the former revolution, and to take some notice of its progress, from its commencement to its final consummation in the acknowledgment of the independence of the state by New York, and its consequent admission as a member of the federal union.

At the close of the French war which terminated in the conquest of Canada in 1760, the territory now the state of Vermont, with a trifling exception, was an uninhabited wilderness. Civilization, however, had long been gradually, though slowly, approaching it.

In 1609, Henry Hudson had sailed up the river which bears his name, and as early as about the year 1620, the Dutch had established themselves at Albany. That place had, however, been occupied principally as a post for carrying on trade with the western Indians, and so tardy had been the progress of settlement, that at the end of one hundred and forty years the northern frontier of the province of New York, east of the Hudson, was along the banks of the Hoosick river, within about thirty miles of that city.

Simultaneously with the first visit of the Dutch to Hudson's river, Champlain the French governor at Quebec, had ascended the St. Lawrence and Sorel into the lake which bears his name, and as early as 1646, the French Jesuits had discovered that beautiful body of water now known as Lake George, and had given it the name of St. Sacrament. In 1730, a few individuals or families, came up the lake from Canada, and established themselves at Chimney point in the present township of Addison, and built a block house and wind mill. The next year troops were sent out who erected on the opposite side of the lake Fort Frederick, afterwards known as Crown Point. At a later date the French built a fort at Ticonderoga. They claimed that the territory of New France, by rights of discovery and exploration, included both lake St. Sacrament and Champlain, and the governors of Canada made extensive grants of land along both shores of the latter lake. It does not, however, appear that settlement, for purposes of cultivation were made by the French other than in the vicinity of those forts. They were not very extensive and were abandoned on the approach of the English under General Amherst in 1759.[1]

Southerly and easterly of the territory of Vermont were the Puritan settlements of New England. As early as 1636, these enterprising pioneers had commenced a settlement at Springfield on the Connecticut river; eighteen years later they had begun a town at Northhampton; by the year 1670 had founded Deerfield; and in 1714, a previous settlement which had been made at Northfield and broken up by the Indians, was permanently renewed. Northfield embraced both sides of Connecticut river, and bordered on the present states of New Hampshire and Vermont.

Westerly from Springfield the progress of the Massachusetts emigrants had been less rapid. Although they had founded Westfield, ten miles west of Connecticut river by the year 1666, it was as late as 1730, that they had crossed the range of mountains and established themselves in the valley of the Housatonic at Sheffield, and Stockbridge, near the western border of the province. In the year 1744, the government of Massachusetts had erected a fort on the Hoosick river between the present villages of North Adams and Williamstown, called Fort Massachusetts, and sometimes Hoosick fort, and before the close of the French war in 1760, some progress

---

[1] Swift's, *History of Addison County*, chap. IV.

had been made in the settlements of Pittsfield and Lanesborough, and perhaps of one or two other towns in the northerly part of the present county of Berkshire.[1]

The first permanent occupation of any of the territory of Vermont by civilized men was in 1724, when a block-house, named Fort Dummer, was built on the Connecticut river at Brattleboro. It was erected by the colony of Massachusetts for the better protection of the settlers at Northfield and its vicinity against the incursions of the French and Indians from Canada, and garrisoned by a few men, their number varying from five to thirty or more, as the proper security of that section of the province seemed from time to time to demand. It was supported principally, if not wholly, by Massachusetts, and was occupied as a military post during the continuance of the Indian and French wars.

The government of Massachusetts had always claimed that the province extended much further north than the present limits of that state, and included a large portion of the territory now in New Hampshire and Vermont; and, in accordance with that claim, had early in the eighteenth century made grants of land on both sides of Connecticut river within such territory. In 1715 a tract of about forty-four thousand acres, covering a portion of the present Vermont townships of Putney, Dummerston and Brattleboro, had been granted to the colony of Connecticut, as an equivalent for lands which had been previously granted by Massachusetts, and which on running the line between the two provinces were found to fall within the limits of Connecticut, which "equivalent lands," as they were called, were, the succeeding year, sold and transferred by Connecticut to Wm. Dummer, afterwards lieut. governor of Massachusetts, Anthony Stoddard, Wm. Brattle and John White. On the 19th of Nov., 1736, in pursuance of a vote of the general court of Massachusetts, a township, designated as number one, was laid out between the great falls and the equivalent lands, comprising the present township of Westminster. Vernon, which formed a portion of Hinsdale, and also Guilford, and perhaps other townships, were likewise granted by Massachusetts, at an early day.[2]

In 1740, a long pending controversy between Massachusetts and New Hampshire, about their respective limits, was decided by the crown in favor of the latter, by the establishment of the present

---

[1] Holland's *History of Western Massachusetts.*

[2] Hall's *Eastern Vermont,* chap. I. *Statistics of the American Association,* vol. I, p. 13–21.

northern line of Massachusetts, as the boundary between them; of which controversy and decision, a more full account will be given hereafter. The next year Benning Wentworth was appointed governor of New Hampshire, and in his commission from the king, his province was declared to extend westerly until it should meet his majesty's other governments.[1]

The western boundary of New York had always, both in England and America, been generally understood to be a line running from the western limits of the colony of Connecticut on Long Island sound, northerly to Lake Champlain; and upon the determination of the boundary controversy before mentioned, it was not doubted in New England, that New Hampshire, as well as Massachusetts, was bounded westerly by that line, and that the former thus included the territory now Vermont. In accordance with this understanding Governor Wentworth, in 1749, granted the township of Bennington six miles square situated six miles North of Massachusetts line, and twenty miles east of Hudson's river; and he subsequently, from time to time, made other similar grants west of Connecticut river up to the year 1764, when the whole number of townships which had been granted by him was about one hundred and thirty.[2] But the exposure of the territory to Indian depredations had prevented very extensive settlements until after the conclusion of the French war, which terminated in the month of September, 1760, by the capture of Montreal and the formal surrender of the province of New France to the English arms. With the exception, indeed, of a few small tracts which had been cleared and partially cultivated, under the immediate protection of Fort Dummer at Brattleboro and of some private block houses on the banks of the Connecticut in the towns of Hinsdale (now Vernon), Putney and Westminister, the territory still remained an unbroken forest. It had, however, been frequently traversed by the men of New England in their expeditions to the theatre of war in the vicinity of Lakes George and Champlain, and the fertility of its soil had become familiarly and favorably known to them. No sooner, therefore, was the territory opened for safe occupation by the conquest of Canada, than a strong desire pervaded the New England colonies to emigrate to it. Several townships were accordingly occupied under the New Hampshire charters, in the spring of 1761, and settlements continued thereafter to be rapidly made.

[1] *Belknap,* Farmer's Edition, p. 257. *American Statistics,* vol. I, p. 26. Iowa of Cang, Oct. 8, 1787. *Doc. Hist. New York,* vol. 4, p. 532.

[2] Slades' *Vermont State Papers,* p. 13.

On the 20th of July, 1764, the king by an order in council placed the settlers under the government of New York, by declaring "the western bank of the river Connecticut, from where it enters the province of Massachusetts bay, as far north as the forty-fifth degree of northern latitude, *to be* the boundary line between the two provinces of New Hampshire and New York." [1] This change of jurisdiction, which had been made without the consent or knowledge of the settlers, though not pleasing to them, would no doubt have been quietly submitted to, if nothing further had been demanded. But the lieutenant governor of New York and his council held that the king's order, not only conferred on them the powers of government as far eastward as Connecticut river, but was in effect a declaration of the crown that such had always been the rightful extent of their jurisdiction. As a consequence of this retrospective interpretation of the order in council, they declared that all the grants which had been made by Wentworth, as governor of New Hampshire, having been of lands not within his province, were absolutely null and void. They thereupon treated the settlers as trespassers upon the king's domain, and the lieutenant governor proceeded to grant the lands anew to others. This conduct of the New York government towards the settlers and claimants under New Hampshire, was the sole cause of the long and bitter controversy which followed, and which ended in the separation of the territory from that province. The grounds, therfore, on which the rulers of New York sought to justify their measures against the settlers, will deserve a particular and careful examination.

That the words "to be the boundary," in the connexion in which they were used in the king's order, were designed to have any further meaning, than that such should be the boundary from that time forward, must at best be very doubtful. Indeed, the construction that would limit the operation of the order to the future, would seem to be the most natural. But its true construction could be of very small importance, for the declaration, even of the king, could not alter the fact of history, whatever it might have been. The New York rulers did not in truth appear to place much reliance upon their critical exposition of the words "to be," but asserted an earlier title to the territory, under the charter of King Charles the second to the Duke of York, in 1664, which title they declared to be "clear and undoubted." A particular examination of the character of this charter claim, will therefore be necessary, and the subject will be pursued in a future chapter.

---

[1] *Doc. Hist. N. Y.*, vol. 4, p. 574, Appendix, No 4.

CHAPTER II.

GRANTS AND COLONIZATION OF TERRITORY.

1497-1662.

Colonization by the Dutch and English — Their conflicting claims to territory — The English claim from Labrador to Florida, and deny any right in the Dutch — Different classes of English colonial governments — Grant of the first and second colonies of Virginia in 1606 — Of New England to the council of Plymouth in 1620 — Grant by that company to Massachusetts in 1627 with territory extending to the Pacific — Colonies of Plymouth, Connecticut and New Haven — New England confederacy — Boundary treaty between their commissioners and the Dutch governor of New Netherland at Hartford in 1650, and its ratification by the States General of Holland — Charter of Connecticut by King Charles in 1662, including New Haven and reaching west to the Pacific.

NEW York was originally settled by the Dutch under the name of New Netherland, and was conquered by the English in 1664. The charter of King Charles, by virtue of which the territory of Vermont was afterwards claimed by the rulers of New York to constitute a part of that province, had been issued to the Duke of York, a few months previously, in contemplation of such conquest. The charter was undoubtedly designed to embrace the Dutch colony as it then existed, and without any intention of the king to interfere with existing rights under previous grants of the English crown. A knowledge of the extent of that colony, at that time, will therefore be necessary in order to determine the proper effect to be given to the language of the charter in regard to boundaries, and in deciding what were subsequently the extent and limits of the province of New York. A proper understanding of this matter, will require some account of the origin and progress of colonization by both the Dutch and English, prior to that period.

It has been previously stated, that Henry Hudson, sailing under the authority of the Dutch, had, in 1609, discovered and partially explored the river which bears his name. That enterprising commercial people soon opened a trade for furs with the natives along that river, and about the year 1614, established a trading post on an island near the present site of Albany, and another on Manhattan island. This trade gradually increased in activity and importance, and in 1623, settlements for purposes of cultivation were commenced near the ocean, under the direction of the Dutch West India company, to which, by a charter from the United Netherlands, had been granted a monopoly of trade to the African and American continents. The Dutch from Manhattan, which afterwards bore the name of New Amsterdam, and subsequently that of New York, made an early exploration of Long Island sound, and of the coast further eastward; and they claimed that New Netherland extended from Delaware bay to Cape Cod, especially embracing the river Connecticut, which they named Versch, or, Fresh river. This claim was always denied by the English government, who as early as 1621 "having been informed that within the year past the Hollanders have entered upon some parts of North Virginia, by us called New England, and there left a colony, and given new names to the several ports appertaining to that part of the country, and are now in readiness to send for their supply six or eight ships," instructed Sir Henry Carlton, their embassador at the Hague, to represent to the States General that his majesty had "many years since by patent granted the quiet and full possession of the whole precinct unto particular persons," and to require of them "that as well those ships as their further prosecution of that plantation be stayed." Which representation and request were accordingly made, but without any other apparent result, than information from the States General that the matter had been properly referred, and would be inquired into. The English, however, ever afterwards insisted that the Dutch of New Netherland were intruders upon territory which belonged to them,[1]

The English claimed the whole of North America, from Labrador to Florida, by virtue of its prior discovery by the Cabots under their authority in 1497, and of subsequent explorations and efforts to colonize it, though their claims had to some extent been interfered with by the occupation of Canada by the French, and New Netherland by the Dutch. By the English constitution, the title to all the lands belonging to the natives was vested in the king, who might grant them at pleasure. The king also exercised the power of creating corporations by charter, and prior to this grant of King Charles to the duke, extensive portions of North America had been granted by the crown, either to individuals or to corporations thus constituted. The charters to corporations not only passed the title of the crown to the lands they described, but also conferred on the grantees certain powers of government over the people that should thereafter inhabit them. Some of the king's charters to individuals also con-

[1] *Colonial Hist. N. Y.*, vol. 3, p. 678, and vol. 1, p. 27, 28. *Brodhead's N. York*, vol. 1, p. 140, 142.

ferred on them powers of government, while others only conveyed the title to the soil.

These charters were irrevocable by the king, who while they remained in force had no authority to recall the titles or the political privileges with which he had thus parted. The charters might, indeed, be declared forfeited for a violation by the grantees of some of their express or implied conditions, but this forfeiture could not be taken at the pleasure of the crown. It could only be ascertained and declared by a judicial proceeding instituted in the courts of law or equity for that purpose; the usual mode being by what was termed a writ of *quo warranto*. The grants of the king with corporate powers constituted what was denominated *charter governments*. To this class belonged those of Massachusetts, Connecticut and Rhode Island, and also some of the more southern colonies. Where the lands of a province with political authority were granted to an individual the government thus constituted was termed a *proprietary government*. Of this character were the grants of Maryland to Lord Baltimore, of Pennsylvania to Mr. Penn, and also the grant now under consideration, that of New Netherland to the Duke of York.

There was still another class of English colonial governments which were styled royal governments, of which it is necessary that special notice should be taken. Those were governments in which the king, untramelled by charter grants of the soil or of political privileges retained over them all his original authority. They were presided over by a governor, assisted by a council, appointed by the crown, and removable at his pleasure. The governor had a negative upon the proceedings of any assembly of the people which he might convene, with power to prorogue or dissolve it, whenever he saw fit. To the governor also was committed authority to grant, for and in the name of the king, any unchartered lands in his province. The king retained full power over the boundaries and extent of these royal colonies, and might enlarge on or contract them at pleasure. These changes in the limits and extent of royal provinces were not unfrequently made, sometimes by creating new charter governments in portions of the territory, sometimes by the adjudication of boundary disputes between provinces, at others by descriptions of territory in commissions to governors, and sometimes by mere informal recognition or usage. To this class of royal provinces belonged both New Hampshire and New York at the time of the territorial controversy between them in relation to Vermont; for although the latter province had originally been chartered to the Duke of York, with political authority, yet on his accession to the throne in 1685 his title merged in the crown, and the colony was ever afterwards governed as a royal province.

Owing perhaps to the imperfect knowledge in England of the geography of this country, and especially of its interior; or to the small value which was placed upon its remote and uncultivated lands, or to the carelessness or dishonesty of draughtsmen or transcribers of patents or others, many of the descriptions of territory in the early English charters were confused and of uncertain meaning, so much so, that new grants were frequently found to clash with others of previous date, or to be of very indefinite and doubtful extent.

Thus the grant of New Hampshire to Mason in 1629, which reached southerly to the middle of the river Merrimack plainly clashed with that of Massachusetts, which had been made two years previous, and which extended northerly to a line three miles to the northward of every part of that river. The descriptions of their boundaries were also so confused in other respects as to produce a long and tedious controversy which was finally settled by the king in council, by establishing an arbitrary line that neither of the parties claimed. So likewise there was a direct conflict between the two charters of Connecticut and Rhode Island, the former granted in 1662 and the latter, the year after. By the first charter Connecticut was bounded east by Narragansett river and bay, and by the latter Rhode Island included the whole of that river and bay, and extended west twenty miles farther to Pawkatuc river. Notwithstanding the priority of the Connecticut charter, the disputed territory, after a tedious controversy, was retained by Rhode Island by the final decision of the king.[1] Indeed there were scarcely any two of the original English colonies adjoining each other, between which serious controversies did not arise, growing out of the ambiguous or contradictory language of the evidences of their title under the crown.

The charter of King Charles to the Duke of York when brought into comparison with those of adjoining colonies, was found from its indefinite language to be peculiarly exposed to disputes of this character. Not only did it occasion sharp and tedious controversies with the several New England colonies, of which full accounts will be given hereafter, but also with the two adjoining provinces of New Jersey and Pennsylvania, which bounded it to the west and south.

In pursuance of the English claim to the whole northern part of this continent, King James the second, in 1606, granted in one

[1] Story's *Com.*, vol. 1, p. 75, 83. *Hutchinson,* vol. 2, p. 313.

charter to two separate companies, the one denominated the London and the other the Plymouth company, the right to colonize any part of North America between the latitudes of thirty-four and forty-five degrees north. The London company, whose settlement was to be distinguished as the first colony of Virginia, might plant any where between the thirty-fourth and forty-first degrees of north latitude, or between cape Fear and the east end of Long Island. The Plymouth company, whose settlement was to be called the second colony of Virginia, might plant any where between the thirty-eighth and forty-fifth degrees of north latitude, or in other words between Delaware bay and Halifax; but neither company was to begin its settlement within one hundred miles of any spot previously occupied by the other. Each colony was to extend along the coast fifty miles each way from the spot first occupied, and one hundred miles inland. Under this charter the first permanent English settlement on this continent was made at Jamestown in Virginia, the following year. In 1609, the London company obtained from the crown a new charter, with powers of government, comprising a territory which reached two hundred miles south and the same distance to the north of Old Point Comfort; that is, from about latitudes thirty-four to forty degrees north, and extended west to the Pacific Ocean. This charter was however vacated in England, in 1624, by writ of *quo warranto*, and Virginia becoming thereby a royal colony, several new provinces, and among them Maryland and North Carolina, were subsequently carved out of its territory, by charters from the king.

The early operations of the Plymouth company were not of an encouraging character. Attempts were made in 1607, 1610, and 1616, to establish colonies on the coast of "North Virginia," the latter under the famous Capt. John Smith, but all of them proved unsuccessful. The company however, under date of Nov. 3, 1620, obtained from the crown a new charter, incorporating them by the name of "the council established at Plymouth in the county of Devon, for the planting, ruling, ordering, and governing of New England in America," by which there was granted them in full property with exclusive jurisdiction, settlement and traffic, all that part of America "lying in breadth from 40 to 48 degrees north latitude, and in length by all the breadth aforesaid, throughout the main land from sea to sea." The whole of North America, as claimed by the English, was thus divided into the two provinces of Virginia and New England, by a line very nearly corresponding with that which now separates the late slaveholding from the non-slaveholding states, the charter of the Plymouth company comprehending the whole of New York as well as New England.[1]

This Plymouth company was not however, destined to plant the first English colony within the territory which had thus been granted them. At the date of their charter, Nov. 3, 1620, a small band of men with their families, in a frail bark, were approaching its wild and inhospitable coast, seeking amidst peril and suffering, a place in which they might enjoy in peace and quiet their peculiar religious opinions. Such a place they found a few weeks afterwards, and named it New Plymouth, after the port from which they had last embarked in England. This settlement was made without any authority from the king or his patentees, and it was not until nine years afterwards, that they obtained a grant from the council of Plymouth, of a territory including their settlement, and covering most of the south-east part of the present state of Massachusetts. Plymouth constituted a separate and distinct colony from Massachusetts, until 1691, when it was made a part of that province, by charter from King William and Queen Mary.[2]

Of the New England colonies, Massachusetts was the next in the order of time. The council of Plymouth by their deed of indenture, duly executed under their common seal, and bearing date March 19, 1627, conveyed to "Sir Henry Roswell, Sir John Young, Thomas Southcott, John Humphreys, John Endicott, and Simon Whitcomb, their heirs and assigns and their associates forever, all that part of New England in America," lying between the Merrimack and Charles rivers and three miles to the south of Charles river, "and lying and being within the space of three English miles to the northward of the said river, called the Monomack alias Merrimack, or to the northward of any and every part thereof, and all lands and hereditaments whatsoever lying within the limits aforesaid north and south in latitude and in length and longitude all the breadth aforesaid, throughout the mainland there *from the Atlantic and western sea and ocean on the east part to the south sea on the west parts.*"

King Charles, by letters patent, dated March 28, 1628, confirmed to the said Roswell, Young, Southcott, Humphreys, Endicott and Whitcomb and their associates by name, being eighteen in number, all the lands before conveyed to them by the council of Plymouth by the same descriptive words, and also created the said Roswell, Young, Southcott, Humphreys, Endicott and Whitcomb and their

---

[1] *Haz.*, vol. 1. *Brod. N. Y.* 138.

[2] *Story on the constitution*, Book 1, chap. iii.

associates, a body politic by the name of "the governor and company of Massachusetts Bay in New England," with extensive powers of government. The southern line of the territory thus conveyed and confirmed, which was run three miles south of the southernmost part of Charles river, is identical with the present north line of Connecticut extended due east to the Atlantic and west to the Pacific ocean. The northern boundary was long the subject of controversy. Of the Merrimack river, little could have been known at the time of the grant. It is now understood to be formed in the interior of New Hampshire, by the junction of the Pemigewasset and the Winnipiseogee rivers, in latitude about forty-three and a half degrees north. After running from thence nearly south about sixty miles it turns rather abruptly towards the east and pursuing that direction for about thirty miles empties into the Atlantic. It was claimed by Massachusetts that what is now known as the Winnipiseogee branch constituted a part of the Merrimack, which if correct would carry its source some twenty or thirty miles farther north than the junction of that river with the Pemigewasset.

There would seem to be little, if any, doubt from the language of the charter of Massachusetts that the northern boundary of the territory would be a line drawn from a point three miles north of the mouth of the Merrimack and thence following up the course of that river at three miles distance from "any and every part thereof," until it reached another point three miles north of its source or termination, and from thence due west to the Pacific ocean. Whether this west line should start from the junction of the Pemigewasset with the Winnipiseogee, or at the head waters of the latter river, it will be readily seen, by reference to a map of the Northern States, that between it and the southern boundary line there would be comprised a large portion of the present states of New Hampshire and Vermont, and more than half of the territory of New York, including all the western part of it, which lies to the southward of Lake Ontario. Massachusetts further claimed, though without apparent reason, that the north line also extended east from the three mile point north of the head waters of the Merrimack, thus including much of the residue of New Hampshire, and a great part of Maine.[1]

In 1635 the council of Plymouth, after distributing among its members a large portion of the residue of its territory, surrendered its charter to the crown. The previous grant of the company, to Sir

---

[1] *Haz.*, vol. 1, p. 239, 564, 572. *Story, book* I, chap. iv. *Records of Massachusetts,* vol. 3, p. 288, 321. *Hutchinson,* vol. 1, p. 1.

Henry Roswell and his associates, of the territory of Massachusetts, and the King's confirmatory charter of it, were left unimpaired and were in full force at the time of the issuing of the charter of King Charles to the Duke of York, in 1664.

Originally, and until 1662, there were two separate colonial organizations in Connecticut, one of which was called Connecticut, and the other New Haven. The boundary between them was not very definitely fixed, but the former colony was understood to include the towns to the eastward of Connecticut river, and those along the river on both sides of it. It was at first occupied at Winsdor in 1633, by a few settlers from Plymouth, who were followed the next and succeeding years, by larger bodies of emigrants from Massachusetts, who settled at Wethersfield, Saybrook, Hartford and other places.

New Haven was first colonized in 1638, by emigrants who came directly from England, and in the course of ten or twelve years their plantations had extended along the Long Island sound, some sixty miles to the westward of Connecticut river, and to within less than twenty miles of the Hudson. Several English settlements had also been made on the easterly portion of Long Island, under the protection, of either the Connecticut, or the New Haven governments. These settlements of the colonies of Connecticut and New Haven were made in disregard of the before mentioned claims of the Dutch, who, in fact, had occupied a post on Connecticut river, in the vicinity of the present site of Hartford, which they called Fort Good Hope, a few months prior to the English settlement at Windsor, in 1633. The Dutch continued to occupy a few acres of land in the vicinity of this fort until it was surrounded by English settlements, and until about the year 1654, when during the war between Cromwell and the Netherlands, it was declared forfeited to the English at Hartford, who took possession of it. This is believed to have been the only settlement of the Dutch, on the main land to the eastward of Greenwich, with which the English plantation had come in collision. The Dutch had, however, long possessed a portion of the west end of Long Island.[1]

The Dutch and English were rivals for the Indian trade, and a feeling of jealousy and distrust had always existed between them, producing many controversies of a serious character in regard to their trade and intercourse with the natives and with each other; and also in relation to boundaries.[2]

---

[1] *Brodhead's N. Y.* *Bancroft,* vol. 2, chap. xv.

[2] *Brodhead's N. Y.*, 247, 257, 260, 293 – 4. *Hutchinson,* vol. 1, p. 148.

In 1643, a confederacy, known as the united colonies of New England, was entered into between delegates from Plymouth, Connecticut, New Haven and Massachusetts, by which commissioners from each colony were to meet annually and oftener, if necessary, to consider and determine matters relating to the general interest. In order to consider and adjust the various disputes existing between the English and Dutch it had been arranged that Governor Stuyvesant should attend a meeting of the commissioners to be held at Hartford in the month of September 1650. Accordingly the governor accompanied by his secretary and a large suite embarked at Manhattan and reached the place appointed, by way of the sound and Connecticut river. The negociation being opened, a long correspondence ensued in which the points of controversy were reviewed and explained in detail, and it was finally agreed that "all differences" should be referred to two delegates, from each side, who should prepare satisfactory articles of agreement. On their part, the New England commissioners appointed Simon Bradstreet of Massachusetts and Thomas Prence of Plymouth; and Governor Stuyvesant on his part delegated Captain Thomas Willett and Ensign George Baxter. These representatives of the respective parties after duly considering the matters committed to them, on the 19th of September 1650, made an award or agreement in writing under their hands, which was afterwards known as the Hartford treaty. This treaty, so far as it related to boundaries, was in the following words, viz:

1. That upon Long Island, a line run from the westermost part of the Oyster Bay, south and in a straight and direct line to the sea, shall be the bounds between the English and Dutch there; the easterly part to belong to the English, the westermost part to the Dutch.

2. The bounds upon the mainland to begin at the west side of Greenwich Bay, being about four miles from Stamford, and to run a northerly line twenty miles up into the country, and after, as it should be agreed by the two governments of the Dutch and of New Haven; provided the said line come not within ten miles of Hudson's river. And it is agreed that the Dutch shall not at any time hereafter, build any house or habitation within six miles of the said line. The inhabitants of Greenwich to remain, till further consideration thereof be had, under the government of the Dutch.

3. That the Dutch shall hold and enjoy all the lands in Hartford that they are actually possessed of, known or set out by certain marks or bounds; and all the remainder of the said land on both sides of Connecticut river to be and remain to the English there. And it is

agreed that the aforesaid bounds and limits, both upon the island and main, shall be observed and kept inviolate, both by the English of the United Colonies and all the nation, without any encroachment or molestation, until a full and final determination be agreed upon in Europe by the mutual consent of the states of England and Holland."

It will be noticed that by this treaty about two-thirds of Long Island was left to the English, and that the boundary line on the main land commenced very near what is now the south west corner of Connecticut, and running northerly so as not to approach nearer than ten miles to the Hudson river, gave some territory to the English which was afterwards relinquished to New York.

This treaty boundary was formally approved and ratified, under the seal of the States General of the United Netherlands, February 22, 1656, as "The line of division between New Netherland and New England;" and the English remained in the undisturbed possession of the territory thus agreed upon, until the surrender of New Netherland to the forces of King Charles September 8, 1664. This boundary line was not only respected and admitted by the Dutch as the eastern limit of New Netherland until the time of its surrender to the English in 1664, but also nine years afterwards, when they retook it from the English and held it for a few months. In the commission which on that occasion was issued to Anthony Colve as governor of the conquered province, dated August 12, 1673, the eastern boundary on the main land is described as running from Greenwich northerly "conformable to the provisional settlement made in 1650 and afterwards ratified by the States General, February 22, 1656, and January 23, 1664."[1]

It is scarcely necessary to add that the territory of Vermont was wholly unknown to the Dutch during the time of their jurisdiction over New York; that they had no settlements eastward of the banks of the Hudson river as far northerly as the twenty mile line agreed upon by the Hartford treaty would extend, and that it was only to the country bordering on the southern portion of the Connecticut river that they had ever made any specific claim. The relinquishment of this claim under an agreement that their eastern boundary line of twenty miles in length, might be indefinitely prolonged northerly so that it did not approach the Hudson river nearer than ten miles, was a full and complete abandonment of all claim to the

---

[1] *Haz.*, vol. 2, p. 172. *Hutch.*, vol. 1, 447. *Brodh.*, 518, 621, 654. *Col. Hist. N. Y.*, vol. 1, p. 611, vol. 2, p. 228–609.

whole of Connecticut river, and of all territory to the eastward of said prolonged line, whatever may have been their original pretensions. And this treaty agreement by the Dutch must be conclusive to show that New York could have no ground whatever for claiming to extend eastward to Connecticut river by virtue of succeeding to the rights of New Netherland.

Soon after the news of the restoration of Charles the second to the throne reached the colonies, John Winthrop governor of Connecticut, was sent to England as agent of that colony, and he succeeded in obtaining from the crown, with liberal powers of government, a charter to "the governor and company of the English colony of Connecticut," covering all the territory between the Massachusetts south line on the north, and the sea on the south, and Narragansett bay on the east, and the Pacific ocean on the west, by the following descriptive words, viz:

"All that part of our dominions in New England, in America, bounded on the east by Narragansett river, commonly called Narragansett bay, where the said river falleth into the sea; and on the north by the line of Massachusetts plantation; and on the south by the sea; and in longitude in the line of the Massachusetts colony, running from east to west, that is to say, from the said Narragansett bay on the east to the South sea on the west part, with the islands thereunto adjoining."

This charter bore date April 22, 1662, two years prior to the grant of New Netherland to the Duke of York, and in terms included the southern portion of the Dutch colony. Whatever may be thought to have been its legal effect upon the territory in actual possession of the Dutch, there can be no possible doubt that it granted to Connecticut all the lands east of the boundary line previously established by the Hartford treaty, and that the king by this charter deprived himself of all right and title to it, and of all power and authority to regrant it to the Duke of York, or any other party.[1]

---

[1] *Conn. Public Records*, vol. 2, p. 10. *U. S. Land Laws*, vol. 1, p. 80. *Brodh.*, p. 702. *Bancroft*, vol. 2, p. 52-56.

CHAPTER III.

THE CHARTER OF KING CHARLES TO THE DUKE OF YORK.

1662-1683.

The Dutch commercial rivals of the English — Hostile feeling towards them of King Charles and his brother the Duke of York — They resolve upon a secret expedition for the conquest of New Netherland — Grant of it to the Duke — Is not described as New Netherland, but in vague terms as English territory and why — Commissioners appointed by the King to Superintend the expedition and visit the New England colonies — They determine upon a line twenty miles east of the Hudson, as the boundary between the Duke's patent and Connecticut, which is afterwards confirmed by the crown.

IT has been already intimated that the conquest of New Netherland had been agreed upon in the councils of King Charles, prior to his granting the charter of it to the Duke of York. During the period of the civil war in England the commerce of the Dutch was in a prosperous condition, and in the time of the commonwealth they had become formidable rivals of the English. This rivalry produced a naval war between the two countries, which terminated unfavorably to the Dutch. Towards the close of this war an expedition against New Netherland had been prepared by Cromwell with the concurrence of the New England colonies, but the territory was saved to the Dutch for a few years longer by the conclusion of a general peace in the spring of 1650.[1]

When King Charles came to the throne in 1660 he found the Dutch commerce recovered from the shock of the previous war, and in a flourishing condition. In fact the Dutch had become successful commercial competitors of the English in all parts of the world. They had trading establishments in the East Indies, on the coast of Africa and in America; and by their industry and frugality were enabled to undersell the English in every market, and to retain possession of the most lucrative branches of commerce. This success naturally produced a hostile feeling among the English merchants. The directors of the East India company complained of their formidable Batavian rivals. The African company of which the king's brother, James Duke of York, was governor, denounced the Dutch West India Company, which had striven to secure its trade on the

---

[1] *Brodh.*, p. 582-6. *Ling.*, vol. 10, 379-87, and vol. 11, 30-34.

Gold coast from the participation of the English. James, a man of narrow mind and unforgiving temper, had been libeled in Holland, and he became the advocate of his African company with the king and with parliament, and in February 1664, without any declaration of war, an expedition, with the consent of the king, was secretly dispatched by the duke against the Dutch possessions in Africa.

There were special grounds of complaint against the Dutch of New Netherland. Their right to the territory they occupied, had always been denied. They were complained of as intruders at the north by Connecticut, and at the south by Lord Baltimore, the proprietor of Maryland. And recently the Duke of York had become personally interested in opposition to their territorial claims, by the conveyance to him from Lord Stirling, of a supposed title to Long Island, which title the Dutch had resisted. The Dutch were also accused, and doubtless justly, of evading the navigation acts which prohibited all foreign trade with the English colonies. The farmers of the revenue complained that traders to Virginia, New England, Maryland and Long Island, were constantly conveying great quantities of tobacco to the neighboring Dutch plantations, by which they alleged the revenue was defrauded "to the amount of ten thousand pounds per annum and upwards."

To remedy all these evils at once, and at the same time to strike a blow at the prosperity of a rival, the conquest of New Netherland was resolved upon. A charter designed to include the Dutch possessions comprising Long Island, and also other lands which had been released by Lord Stirling, was issued by the king to the Duke of York, under date of March 12, 1664, and the duke as lord high admiral was authorized to employ the necessary force to make his grant available. He accordingly detached for that service, four vessels of war, having on board about four hundred and fifty soldiers. The command of the expedition was entrusted to Colonel Richard Nicolls who had served with James on the continent and was one of the gentlemen of his bed chamber. Nicolls was also appointed to be the duke's deputy governor, after the Dutch possessions should have been reduced. With Nicolls, were associated Sir Robert Carr, Col. George Cartwright and Samuel Maverick, as royal commissioners to visit the several colonies of New England. These commissioners, or any three of them, of whom Nicolls was to be one, were clothed with extensive powers, among which was authority to ascertain the limits of the several colonies and adjust disputes between them in regard to boundaries. They were furnished with detailed instructions in regard to those and other matters, and the New England governments were required by royal letters "to join and assist them vigorously" in reducing the Dutch to subjection.[1]

The expedition left England early in May, but the vessels were separated on the way, and owing to a variety of causes, which it is unnecessary to detail, the squadron was not united and ready to attack the Dutch possessions until late in the summer. On the 31st of August, Col. Nicolls, having been joined by Gov. Winthrop of Connecticut with a body of volunteers from that province, appeared before New Amsterdam and made a formal demand of Gov. Stuyvesant for its surrender to the English crown. After a negociation of several days commissioners were mutually appointed, who agreed upon terms of submission, highly favorable to the Dutch, and New Amsterdam, with its immediate dependencies, was formally surrendered into the possession of the English on the 8th of September, 1664. Expeditions were sent up the Hudson, and also to the South river, and on the 24th of September Fort Orange, now Albany, capitulated, and the Dutch possessions on the Delaware were captured on the first of October, by which the conquest of New Netherland was completed.[2]

It is proper here to state that prior to the surrender of the charter of the council of Plymouth to the crown in 1635, that company in the distribution of its favor to its members, had conveyed to the Earl of Stirling, the territory between the Kennebeck and St. Croix rivers in the present state of Maine; and also Long Island, Martha's Vineyard and Nantucket. The earl's title had been purchased by the Duke of York, and the charter of King Charles to the duke, of March 12, 1664, was designed to confirm this purchase to him, as well as to embrace the Dutch possessions of New Netherland.[3]

The operative words of the charter were as follows, viz:

"Charles the Second by the grace of God king etc. * * * to all to whom these presents shall come greeting. Know ye that wee for divers good causes and considerations us thereunto moving have etc. * * * and by these presents etc. * * * do give and grant unto our dearest brother James Duke of York, his heirs and assigns all that part of the main land of New England begin-

---

[1] *Col. His. N. Y.*, vol. 3, 41-66. *Brodh.*, chap. xx.

[2] *Ling.*, vol. 11, p. 271. *Hume*, vol. 6, p. 36. *Col. Hist. N. Y.*, vol. 3, p. 42-65.

[3] Pemaquid papers in *Maine His. Col.*, vol. 5. *N. Y. His. Col.*, vol. 3, p. 606. *Williamson's Maine*, vol. 1, p. 256-8, and 407. *Massachusetts His. Col.*, vol. 6, 185-189. *Thompson's Long Island*, vol. 1, p. 117-121.

ning at a certain place called or known by the name of St. Croix, next adjoining New Scotland in America, and from thence extending along the sea coast unto a place called Potuaquine or Pemaquid, and up the river thereof to the farthest head of the same as its breadth northwards; and extending from thence to the river Kinebequi, and so upwards by the shortest course to the river Canada northwards, and also all that island or islands called by the several name or names of Mattowacks or Long Island situate lying and being towards the west of Cape Cod, and the Narrow Highgansetts, abutting upon the main land between the two rivers there called or known by the several names of Connecticut and Hudson's river *together also with the said river called Hudson's river, and all the land, from the west side of Connecticut river to the east side of Delaware Bay ;* and also all those several islands called or known by the names of Martin's Vineyard and Nantukes or otherwise Nantucket."[1]

It will be perceived that nearly all this long description is applicable to territory to which the Duke of York claimed to have a previous title under the crown, which the charter was designed to confirm to him; and that the only words which purport to convey to him such territory are the following viz: *"together with the said river called Hudson's river, and all the land from the west side of Connecticut river to the east side of Delaware bay."*

Whether this language be supposed to have been intended to comprise all the land westward from every part of Connecticut river, that is, westward from its whole length, as was afterwards contended by New York, corresponding with the length of Delaware bay, or only from the lower portion of it, it will be readily seen, from what has been before shown, that the grant must be inoperative and void for a very great portion of it, for the reason that the king had already parted with his interest in it, by granting it to Massachusetts and Connecticut; both their charters extending west to the Pacific ocean. Even if it should be admitted that these grants of Massachusetts and Connecticut could not legally take effect upon territory, which at the time of making them was in the possession of the Dutch, the difficulty with the charter to the duke would not be thereby removed, for there can be no pretence whatever, that the Dutch, at the dates of either of these prior grants, had any possessions as far eastward as Connecticut river, or even as far as twenty miles east of the Hudson, where the eastern line of New York was subsequently established.

---

[1] *Col. His. N. Y.*, vol. 2, p. 295. *U. S. Land Laws*, vol. 1, p. 80.

But in addition to the improbability that the king would designedly grant to the duke, a large extent of territory which had already been granted to others, a great portion of it, that of Connecticut, only two years previous, and actually occupied under the charter, there are other strong, if not conclusive reasons for believing, that the river Connecticut was not intended to be a definite boundary line, but rather an outer limit within which New Netherland, the object of the grant, was supposed to be included. Upon this point the following facts and observations are submitted.

1. The language of the description in the duke's charter is so imperfect and uncertain, that it is impossible to mark out from it any definite extent of territory. It has no interior boundary to the northward, and no two persons would be likely to agree in conjecturing what it should be. This uncertainty does not arise from an erroneous or mistaken description of such boundary, but from the absence of all attempt to designate any. A line drawn from the source of Connecticut river to the head of Delaware bay, according to the most natural import of the language, would include "all the land between" the two, but by reference to a map it will be seen that it would cross the Hudson river some sixty or seventy miles below Albany, and would form a territory of such extreme length, narrow width, and irregular shape, as to render it quite absurd to suppose that any such boundary could have been designed. It would be much more reasonable to think it was expected that the inner boundary would be a line drawn from the head of Delaware bay to the Connecticut river, as nearly as might be, parallel to the sea coast. Such a conjecture would be favored by the fact that, little or nothing, was then known in England of the interior of the country, or of Connecticut river, and that the possession and control of the bays, mouths of rivers and lands on the coast, was the great and leading object of the crown, as well as of its grantees.[1] If it be said that

---

[1] In a letter of instructions from the colonial assembly of New York, to Mr. Charles, the assembly's agent in England, in 1750, it is claimed that the northern boundary of New Jersey at the most was the head of Delaware bay and not at latitude 41 degree 40 minutes, north, as described in the grant of the duke of York to lords Berkley, and Carteret, "because," to use the language of the letter, "the said duke could not extend his grant to them higher on Delaware bay or river, than was granted to him by his brother King Charles the second, the north boundary of which grant from King Charles we take to be at Reedy island, or the head of Delaware at that place where that river divides itself into two branches, commonly called the Forks of Delaware," Reedy island, which was thus properly

"Hudson's river" formed a part of the grant and that the interior boundary should be modified by that part of the description, the difficulty will, if possible, be still further increased. How, it may be asked, shall it be modified? Can any one tell? Can any one mark out the lines of modification? The natural inference from the confused language of the charter as well as from all the circumstances attending its issue, is, that the description was designed to point out New Netherland as the object of the grant, leaving its extent and limits, then imperfectly known to the crown, to be afterwards ascertained and determined. It may be added that under this view of the charter to the duke his grant may be made to extend westward to Lake Erie and northward to Ontario and Canada, covering territory which was claimed by New Netherland under the Dutch, and which now forms a large portion of the state of New York, but which, upon any construction depending on the language of the charter, would be excluded from its limits.

2. But there was an all powerful reason for not describing New Netherland, as such, in the charter. The English government had never formally admitted the right of the Dutch to any part of their American possessions, but had always insisted that they were unlawful intruders upon English territory. This claim of the wrongfulness of the Dutch possessions, was strongly declared on the king's instructions to his commissioners and made the ground upon which the expedition against the Dutch was to be justified. The king could not, therefore, recognize the existence of their territory in his grant without abandoning the habitual pretensions of his government and depriving himself of the best excuse he could possibly make for taking forcible possession of it. He was consequently under a controlling necessity to treat New Netherland in his charter as English territory, and this was accordingly done.[1]

3. But if the king had desired in his grant to designate a line as the western boundary of the New England provinces, he would have found great difficulty in accomplishing it, in a definite and satisfactory manner. A line had indeed been agreed upon at Hartford, in 1650, by treaty between the Dutch governor and the New England commissioners, which had been ratified by the States General of Holland, and was admitted by the Dutch to be their eastern boundary. They made no claim beyond it; but the line had not been recognized

---

claimed as the head of Delaware bay, is about 25 miles above Cape May, and 20 below Philadelphia.—*Smith's New York*, vol. 2, p. 159, 160, 161.

[1] *Col. His. N. Y.*, vol. 3, p. 52, 57, 178.

by the English government; by which government the existence of any Dutch territory and consequently of its having any boundary whatever, was denied. The line of that treaty could not therefore be adopted in the charter, even by the use of new and indirect language, without impliedly conceding a right in the Dutch to the westward of it, which concession was by all means to be avoided. There was no river or other natural object between the Connecticut and the Hudson, which could be referred to as a proper boundary, and for these reasons there appears to have been an imperious necessity of adopting some such comprehensive description as that found in the charter. The Dutch, by their possession of the Hudson river, had acquired a monopoly of the trade with the northern and western Indians, which was deemed of much importance, and hence the charter, so far as regards the main land, first grants "Hudson's river," and then to cover any other possessions the Dutch might have, specifies "all the land from the west side of Connecticut river to the east side of Delaware bay," leaving the limits of New Netherland towards New England, to be adjusted by the commissioners to be sent west with the expedition for its conquest.[1] Such adjustment it will be found was accordingly made by them.

On the 13th of October, 1664, within less than two weeks after the conquest of New Netherland had been completed, the assembly of Connecticut appointed five commissioners, at the head of whom was Governor Winthrop, who had been a party to the surrender of the Dutch, to agree upon and settle with the king's commissioners the boundary line between that colony and the new province granted to the duke. These commissioners soon afterwards repaired to New York, and the king's commissioners after a full hearing made their decision and award in regard to the conflict of boundaries in the two charters, which was formally accepted and agreed to by the commissioners of Connecticut. This award is deemed of sufficient importance to justify its insertion at length. It is as follows, viz:

---

[1] The Dutch possessions on the west side of the Delaware were treated by the Duke of York as covered by his grant though clearly beyond its limits and within the previous grant of Maryland to Lord Baltimore. They were also subsequently, in 1681, included in that of Pennsylvania. Penn purchased of the duke his right to the territory in order to strengthen his claim. This claim of the duke and the importance which seems to have been attached to it, is additional evidence that the possessions of the Dutch, rather than the indefinite territory in the charter was understood to be the object of the grant, *Douglass's Summary*, vol. 2, p. 297. *Hildreth*, vol. 2, p. 65, 71. *Bancroft*, vol. 2, 385, 386. *Col. His. N. Y.*, vol. 3, p. 290, 340, 341.

"By virtue of his Majesty's commission we have heard the difference about the bounds of the patents granted to his royal highness the Duke of York and his Majesty's colony of Connecticut; and having deliberately considered all the reasons alleged by Mr. Allyn Senior, Mr. Gold, Mr. Richards and Capt. Winthrop appointed by the assembly held at Hartford the 13th of October, 1664, to accompany John Winthrop, Esq., the governor of his Majesty's colony of Connecticut, to New York, and to agree upon the bounds of the said colony, why the said Long Island should be under the government of Connecticut (which are too long to be here recited). We do declare and order that the southern bounds of his Majesty's colony of Connecticut is the sea, and that Long Island is to be under the government of his royal highness the Duke of York as is so expressed in said patents respectively.

And also by virtue of his Majesty's commission and by the consent of both the governors and the gentlemen above named, we also order and declare that the creek or river called Mamaroneck which is reputed to be about thirteen miles to the east of Westchester, and a line drawn from the east point or side where the fresh water falls into the salt, at high water mark, north-northwest to the line of the Massachusetts, be the western bounds of the said colony of Connecticut; and all plantations lying westward of that creek and line so drawn to be under his royal highness's government, and all plantations lying eastward of that creek and line to be under the government of Connecticut.

Given under our hands at James Fort in New York on the island of Manhattan, this 4th day of December, 1664.

RICHARD NICOLLS.
GEORGE CARTWRIGHT.
S. MAVERRICK.

We the governor and commissioners of the general assembly of Connecticut, do give our consent to the limits and bounds above mentioned as witness our hands.

JOHN WINTHROP.
ALLYN SENIOR.
RICHARDS.
GOLD.
JOHN WINTHROP JR.[1]

At the time of the conquest of New Netherland its whole population was probably less than ten thousand, fifteen hundred of

[1] *Documents of the N. Y. Senate*, 1857, vol. 4, No. 165, p. 102. *Smith's, N. Y.*, vol. 1, p. 36.

of which might have been upon Manhattan, now New York island. The population of the colony of Connecticut exceeded that of New Netherland, more than three quarters of which would have been within the duke's patent, if it had been held to extend eastward to Connecticut river.

This early adjudication and agreement, by which any claim on the part of New York to extend eastward to the main part of Connecticut river was foreclosed and abandoned, is confirmatory of the reasons before given to show that that river was not named in the duke's charter as a definite boundary, but merely as a limit which would make its description include the Dutch possessions, and that the actual extent of his territory towards New England was intentionally left to be ascertained by the commissioners under whose superintendence its conquest was to be made.

But whatever may have been the design of the duke's patent, it was found by such commissioners upon taking possession under it, that a large portion of the territory described by its language had been long held by others under previous grants and to which the duke could have no valid claim; and that, therefore, his interest, as well as the demands of justice, required that the Connecticut river should be relinquished as an eastern boundary and a line established towards the Hudson river; and that such commissioners having full authority from the king and the duke to adjudicate upon the matters, proceeded at once to determine upon such line, corresponding very nearly with that which had been formerly claimed on behalf of New Netherland, as its eastern boundary.

The government of the Duke of York over the conquered territory was entirely despotic. It was exercised through the instrumentality of deputy governors appointed by him and removable at his pleasure. Col. Richard Nicolls, his first governor, was succeeded at the end of about three years by Sir Francis Lovelace, whose administration was brought to an abrupt termination in July 1673, by the reconquest of the province by the Dutch. Up to this period the boundary question seems to have rested where it had been left by the king's commissioners. The commission of the Dutch Governor Colve, as has been already seen, recognized the boundary described in the Hartford treaty of 1650, and thus no practical change was made in the eastern limits of the province. By the treaty of peace between the Dutch and English, New York was to be restored to the latter, and the duke, to obviate any objections which might be raised against his title in consequence of the reoccupation of the territory by the Dutch, procured from the king a second charter

(June 20, 1674), describing it in precisely the same language which was used in the former charter. He appointed Edmund Andros, afterwards famous for his tyrannical conduct in New England, his new governor, who arrived in New York and received the surrender of the province in October following. The commission of Andros described the territory over which he was to preside in the words of the duke's charter, thus in terms constituting him governor over "Hudson's river, and all the land from the west side of Connecticut river to the east side of Delaware bay," disregarding alike the boundary which had been fixed upon with Connecticut by the king's commissioners, and the duke's own solemn grant of the territory of New Jersey made ten years previous, to Lord Berkley and Sir George Carteret. It is not improbable that the language of the commission was considered by the duke as merely formal. It was however interpreted by Andros according to the letter, and he proceeded to demand of the deputy of Carteret the jurisdiction over New Jersey, and on his refusal to surrender it, sent a file of soldiers who arrested him and carried him a prisoner to New York, for which act he was said to have incurred the displeasure of the duke. He also sent a copy of his commission and of the duke's charter to Connecticut, and demanded "of the general court that part of his royal highness's colony in their possession," which embraced more than one half the territory and not less than three-fourths of the then population of the colony. This demand not being complied with, Andros hearing of the breaking out of King Philip's war and thinking it a favorable time to enforce his claim, sailed with an armed force from New York, and appearing before Saybrook at the mouth of the Connecticut, summoned the place to surrender. But being prevented from publicly reading his commission and the duke's charter, and finding he was likely to meet with serious resistance, he retired. He afterwards falsely pretended his visit was to offer his friendly assistance to the inhabitants in their warfare with the Indians, adding that his proffers were not only refused but "a severe protest made against him as an invader of the country." The duke on being notified of this demand on the government of Connecticut, which it would seem was made without his direction or knowledge, informed his governor that he was unwilling to have him proceed further in the matter at that time, for though the boundary agreed upon by Nicolls in 1664, had never been confirmed by him, yet he approved of his prudence in not admitting Connecticut to come nearer than twenty miles to Hudson's river, adding his satisfaction with the demand Andros had made, as a means of saving his rights for the future.

This appears to have been the last and indeed only claim ever made in behalf of the duke to extend his province eastward to Connecticut river. Controversies however afterwards arose in regard to the precise position of the boundary line, to which position little importance had been attached so long as it divided the settlements of the respective provinces. At the time the line had been fixed upon in 1664, the only plantation under New York on the main land east of the Hudson, is believed to have been in the vicinity of Westchester on Long Island sound, and this embraced but few inhabitants. But when the settlements from the two colonies began to approach and interfere with each other, conflicting claims were found to exist; and it was seen that there had been an evident mistake in the language by which the boundary had been described in 1664, and especially in the direction of the northern line which running "north-northwest" would cross Hudson's river instead of being parallel to its general course, as had been designed. And the king's commissioners declaring they had not intended the line should come nearer than twenty miles to that river, it was afterwards by further negotiations surveyed and established as a twenty mile line from the Hudson, the colony of Connecticut being extended westward along the sound to a less distance than twenty miles to include the English settlement made in conformity to the boundary treaty, with the Dutch in 1650, before mentioned, New York receiving other territory farther north as an equivalent.

This final establishment of the Connecticut boundary line was effected under the administration of Gov. Thomas Dongan, who on his appointment in 1683 was specially instructed by the duke "with all convenient speed after his arrival in New York, to endeavor to ascertain and agree upon the boundaries of his territories towards Connecticut." The following authentic account of the establishment of this boundary line is given in a report of the English board of trade to king William, dated March 3, 1700.[1]

"In order to the settling a division line between the said province [of New York] and colony [Connecticut] commissioners were appointed by his late Majesty King Charles the second who in the year 1664 having heard the allegations on both sides did by the mutual consent of both parties agree upon and sign a report by which those boundaries were to be settled; but it being afterwards found that some places named in the said report for boundaries, were not at that

[1] *Smith's N. Y.*, vol. 1. p. 4, 15, 41 – 49, 51. *Trumbull's Conn.*, vol. 1, p. 330. 3 *Col. His. N. Y.*, 216, 235, 247, 264, 333. 4 *Col. His.*, 628.

distance from other places which had been agreed upon (as the commissioners for New York declared) to be the rule and measure of their proceeding, and that the towns of Rye and Bedford which by the supposed distance of the aforesaid places named for boundaries would have been included in the province of New York, were by the mistake about that distance made to fall within the colony of Connecticut; another agreement was afterwards made and concluded in the month of November 1683 between Colonel Dongan then governor of the province of New York for the then duke on the one side, and the governor of Connecticut, Robert Treat, Esq., with three others in commission with him, on the other side, by which last agreement the division line between the said province and colony is more exactly expressed and settled, from place to place, so as to answer *the true intention of the first agreement*, and to remove all future controversy about the towns of Rye and Bedford by including them undoubtedly in the province of New York."

This report of the board of trade concludes by recommending the confirmation by the king of the agreement of 1683, which was accordingly done the next day. The line thus authoritatively established had been partially surveyed in 1684, but controversies from time to time arising in regard to the proper location of portions of it a new and more perfect survey was made and completed in 1731, and sanctioned by an agreement of indenture executed by commissioners of the respective provinces.[1]

---

[1] *Col. His. N. Y.*, vol. 4, p. 625-6. *Smith's N. Y.*, vol. 1, p. 38, 285-8. *N. Y. Senate Doc.*, 1857, No. 165.

CHAPTER IV.

The Eastern Boundary of New York and Massachusetts.

1664 - 1786.

Massachusetts supposed to reach north to Canada until 1740 — Evidence that the eastern boundary of New York was understood to be a twenty mile line from the Hudson from 1664 — Established by agreement as such in 1773 — Adjustment with New York in 1786, of the claim of Massachusetts territory west of the Hudson.

THE boundary adjustment between the king's commissioners and those of the colony of Connecticut, was in terms, made only with the Connecticut colony. It was however the withdrawal from the outlet and main body of a navigable river as a boundary, and the substitution for it of another, parallel to its general course and under the circumstances would, without explanation, be naturally regarded as an abandonment of the whole river as a limit. There is strong evidence that the new line, twenty miles from the Hudson, was understood at the time, as applicable to the whole of the duke's patent. Indeed, there can be no doubt that such was the case.

It should be borne in mind that there was not, at the time of the original adjustment of the boundary between New York and Connecticut, and for nearly a century afterwards, any established northern boundary of New York; that no dividing line had been ascertained or agreed upon between the French and English; that it was not until the year 1763, three years after the surrender of New France to the English, that the line of the 45th degree of latitude running from the river St. Lawrence across Lake Champlain to Connecticut river, was designated by proclamation of King George the third, as the southern limit of Canada; and that this line was fixed upon after the whole country had become British territory as a convenient line of division between the king's provinces, without any reference whatever to any previous boundary. Until the conquest of Canada the respective claims of the English and French were conflicting. Sir Henry Moore, who had attended to the survey of the proclamation line on the part of the province of New York, in writing to Lord Hillsborough on the subject, under date of October 24, 1768, says, "No line of jurisdiction having ever been settled between this province [New York] and Quebec till that which was fixed by general Carleton, and myself and approved by his majesty, each of the provinces have endeavored to extend their claims as far as they possibly could; the English to the river St. Lawrence, and the French to the southward of lake George." The French were, beyond doubt, the first discoverers and explorers of both lake Champlain and lake George, and they were the first to take possession of the former lake, if not of the latter. Some of the bloodiest battles between the forces of the contending nations were for the possession of the southern borders of those lakes, and it was not until late in the summer of 1759 that Ticonderoga and Crown Point were abandoned by the French and occupied by the English. Up to that time, both lakes had been claimed as being within the limits of New France, and upon the principle, then acknowledged, that prior discovery and occupation constituted a good European title to American territory, it is difficult to see how their claim, especially to lake Champlain, could be successfully controverted. Practically, the south end of those lakes was the northern limit of New York, though the pretensions of the province went farther north. The northern limits of New England also being unknown and undetermined, it was not until after the determination of the boundary line between Massachusetts and New Hampshire in 1740, before mentioned, universally understood that the province of Massachusetts, as well as that of New York, reached northward to the undefined limits of Canada.[1]

Among the facts to show that the settlement with Connecticut was intended and understood to apply to the whole eastern boundary of New York; are the following, which, indeed seem to be quite conclusive.

1. In the decision of the King's commissioners in 1664, before recited, the Connecticut western line is declared to extend from the sound northerly "to the line of Massachusetts," thus clearly indicating that the latter province reached at least as far west as the line established for the former.

2. Col. Nichols in giving an account to his master, the duke, of that adjudication and agreement speaks of it as an act of justice to Connecticut to be followed towards the other colonies, whose prior charters, he says, were of forty years standing. He gave the duke distinctly to understand that the boundary between the territory held by him under his patent and the whole of New England, was a line twenty miles east of Hudson's river. This appears by the following extracts from a letter written by him to the duke, dated November 1665.

---

[1] *Col. His. N. Y.*, p. 121, 126, vol. 6. *Doc. Hist. N. Y.*, p. 552, vol. 4.

"I have formerly rendered account of the decision and settlement of bounds between your royal highness and the patent of Connecticut made by his majesty's commissioners, and the governor and council of Connecticut, wherein five towns were relinquished to Connecticut by virtue of their precedent grant from his majesty, although the same tracts of land were given to your royal highness to the utter ruin of that colony, and a manifest breach of their late patent, which determination was a leading case of equal justice, and of great good consequence in all the colonies, and we are therefore assured would be an acceptable service to your royal highness, though to the diminution of your bounds. *So that to the east of New York and Hudson's river*, nothing considerable remains to your royal highness except Long Island and *about twenty miles from any part of Hudson's river.* I look therefore upon all the rest as only empty names and places possessed forty years by former grants, and of no consequence to your royal highness, except all New England could be brought to submit to your royal highness's patent."[1]

3. After attending to the affairs of the conquered territory of New Netherland, the king's commissioners proceeded to New England, where they had a long and bitter controversy with the authorities of the province of Massachusetts. Among the complaints made by the commissioners against the government of that colony was their alleged extravagant claims of territory under their charter, the limits of which territory they say, "the commissioners find to be Seconnett brook on the south west and Merrimack river on the north east, and two right lines drawn from each of those two places *till they come within twenty miles of Hudson's river ; for that is already planted and given to his royal highness.*" This determination of the commissioners was so far approved by the king that the governor and council of Massachusetts were, in April 1666, instructed in an admonitory letter from secretary Morrice, that it was his majesty's pleasure "that all the determinations of his commissioners upon the bounds and limits of the several colonies should continue and be observed till upon a full representation of all pretences, his majesty shall make his own final determination."[2]

---

[1] *N. Y. Col. Hist.*, vol. 3, p. 106, and vol. 8, 597. That it would have been "to the utter ruin" of Connecticut to have the Connecticut river for the duke's boundary is very plain, three-fourths of the population of that colony being west of that river. The former grants "of forty years" were undoubtedly those of Massachusetts.

[2] *Col. Hist. N. Y.*, vol. 3, 52 – 53, 110, 117, 170 – 240 ; vol. 7, 597.

4. That Massachusetts was understood in New York to extend as far westward as Connecticut, is further shown by the agreement made in 1683, between the duke's governor Dongan and the commissioners from Connecticut, before mentioned, in relation to the boundary line of that province with New York, and the report by the commissioners of the two provinces, of the survey of that line made in 1684, in both of which the northern termination of the Connecticut line is declared to be "the south line of the Massachusetts colony."[1]

The authority of the Duke of York as lord proprietor continued until February 1685, when upon the death of King Charles he succeeded to the throne and his title under his charter became extinct by merger in the crown. Of all this Gov. Dongan was soon afterwards officially informed by letter from the new king, in which it is recited that "by the decease of the late king our most dearly beloved brother, and our accession to the imperial crown of this our realm, our province of New York, the propriety whereof was, by letters patent of his said majesty vested in us, has now wholly devolved upon our royal person and annexed to our other dominions."[2] From this date the charter to the duke ceased to have any effect whatever, in regard, either to the powers of government which it had conferred, or to the extent of territory conveyed by it, other than as furnishing historical evidence of the past. Thence forward, New York became a royal province subject to such government and such limits as the king might prescribe.

In the commission of the Duke of York to Governor Dongan, bearing date Sept. 30, 1682, the territory over which he was to preside is described in the language of the charters to the duke as comprehending "Hudson's river and all the lands from the west side of Connecticut river to the east side of Delaware bay," excepting out of it, however, East and West Jersey, which are recited to have been released to Sir George Carterett and others. Accompanying this commission, it will be remembered, were instructions from the duke to make a speedy adjustment of his limits with Connecticut, which was the only colony whose settlements had approached the Hudson river. This adjustment had been made prior to his accession to the throne, as has already been seen. Under date of June 10, 1686, the same person as king issued a new commission to Dongan, in which the charter boundaries are wholly omitted, the commission constituting him "our captain general and governor in chief in and over

[1] *Col. Hist. N. Y.*, vol. 4 p. 628–630.

[2] *Col. Hist. N. Y.*, vol. 3, p. 359.

our province of New York and the territories depending thereon in America." [1]

This change in the language of the commission which was ever afterwards followed in commissions to other governors, must be considered as an adoption, in lieu of the charter boundary, of the actual extent of the colony as then understood, which to the eastward, we have seen, was limited by a twenty mile line from the Hudson. From this date for a period of over sixty years, nothing, after a very thorough search, has been found in the New York or English documents indicative of a belief that the province extended eastward to any part of the Connecticut. On the contrary the language used in the official, and other papers connected with the New York government, is in accordance with the understanding that it only reached to the twenty mile line before mentioned.

Among the public documents of this period which have more or less bearing upon this boundary question, the following may be mentioned.

Gov. Dongan, under date of Feb. 22, 1687, in answer to an enquiry of the lords of trade and plantations, as to what were the boundaries, and longitude and latitude of the colony of New York, refers to a map sent with his answer, of which no copy is given in the published report, from which map he says: "you will see in what narrow bounds we are cooped up." He also says of the land of the province that "what was good and did lie convenient to the sea, for the most part is taken from us by Connecticut and East and West Jersey," and that "what is left is pretty well settled," which is inconsistent with the idea that New York to the northward of the colony of Connecticut, extended eastward to Connecticut river,[2] on which river there were no settlements whatever.

Governor Sloughter in a circular to the governors of the other colonies, asking for aid against the French and Indians, dated 11th July, 1691, says: "I doubt not that you are very sensible of the many branches that have been lopped off from this government in the late reigns, and that it is now confined to great narrowness, having only Hudson's river and Long Island for the bounds."[3]

In the year 1720 the lords of trade and plantations, addressed certain questions in writing to Brigadier Robert Hunter, who was then in England, and who had been governor of New York, from 1710 to 1719, in regard to the condition of the province. Among them

---

[1] *Col. Hist. N. Y.*, vol. 3, p. 328, 377.

[2] *Col. Hist. N. Y.*, vol. 3, p. 397.

[3] *Col. Hist. N. Y.*, vol. 3, p. 745.

he was asked "what were the reputed boundaries thereof? To this he returned the following answer, viz:

"Its boundaries east, a parallel twenty miles distant from Hudson's river, to the west, the New Jersey patent, here on record must determine."[1]

Although a line twenty miles to the eastward of the Hudson, extending northerly to Lake Champlain, was generally understood to be the eastern boundary of New York, no survey had been made of it, and its exact position was unknown until a late period. Massachusetts made pretensions under her conveyance from the council of Plymouth in 1627, and also by virtue of her charters from the crown, to extend westward to the Pacific ocean, and denied the authority of the king to regrant any part of the territory to others. The uncertainty of the true position of the line, together with this claim of Massachusetts to extend beyond it, furnished occasions for controversies which were not terminated until a short time prior to the commencement of the American revolution. Some notice of them should now be given.

At the time of the conquest of New Netherland by the English in 1664, the Dutch had made no settlements on the east side of the Hudson river to the northward of Manhattan Island, and their progress to the westward of any part of that river was extremely slow. In Massachusetts the English had already occupied Springfield, Northampton, Hadley, and Hatfield, on both sides of the Connecticut river, and two years later they had begun a settlement at Westfield ten miles farther towards the Hudson. Their settlements gradually extended along the valley of the Connecticut, and before the close of that century reached northward to the present northern boundary of the state. In 1722, the general court of Massachusetts granted two townships situated on the Housatonic river, and under this grant a settlement was commenced at Sheffield in 1725, which appears to have been temporarily suspended in consequence of some disturbance by claimants under New York. The difficulty was, however, in some way obviated, and the town reoccupied in 1730. The surveyors in laying out these townships are said in a letter of Lt. Gov. Clark of New York, to have come within sixteen miles of the Hudson river, and to claim lands which had been granted by that government as early as 1688; alluding no doubt to Livingston's patent. Two years after the grant of the Massachusetts townships, in 1724, the proprietors made a purchase and took a deed from the Indians of a tract bounded south on the divisional line between

[1] *Col. Hist. N. Y.* vol. 5, p. 555.

Massachusetts and Connecticut; west by the colony of New York; eastward by a line four miles from the Housatonic river, and extending northward "to the north mountain." This purchase included the two townships which had been granted by Massachusetts and covered several others in the southwestern part of the present county of Berkshire. In 1736, the Indian Mission was founded at Stockbridge, under the patronage of the government of Massachusetts, and soon afterwards lands were surveyed and occupied under that province, which were claimed to be within the manors of Livingston and Rensselaerwick, in the colony of New York, and which were probably within less than twenty miles of the Hudson. Prior to the year 1744 quite a number of towns distant from twenty to forty miles to the westward of Connecticut river, had been granted by Massachusetts, and occupied under her grants, and during that year several forts for their protection had been erected and garrisoned; among which was one on the Hoosick river about three miles to the eastward of the present site of William's College. It was called fort Massachusetts, and in 1746 after a brave defence was captured by an army of French and Indians and partially destroyed; but it was soon repaired and reoccupied. By the year 1753, when the government of Massachusetts appears to have been first notified by that of New York that the latter claimed, under the charter to the Duke of York, to reach eastward to the Connecticut, the territory, thus claimed, had been nearly covered by townships granted by Massachusetts, and a large portion of them had been occupied. Several of the border towns, besides Sheffield and Stockbridge, had been settled.[1]

That it had not occurred to the government of New York up to the year 1738 to claim for that colony an extent eastward to the Connecticut river under the old charter to the duke, seems to be incontrovertibly shown by an official report then made by the surveyor general of the province. The lords of trade in England, having addressed certain inquiries in regard to the state of the colony of New York to the governor, they were by him laid before the council, and a portion of them by that body referred to that officer. Cadwallader Colden, who had been for over fifteen years surveyor general and a member of the council, under date of February 14, 1738 in his answer to one of the inquiries referred to him, gives the boundaries of the province in much detail, in which he does not mention Connecticut river, or follow or profess to follow the description in the

---

[1] *Brodhead's N. Y. Holland's E. Mass.*, vol. 1, chap. x and xi, and vol. 2. *Berkshire Co. Col. Hist. N. Y.*, vol. 6, p. 143. *Doc. Hist. N. Y.*, vol. 3, p. 734 – 738 and 754.

charter to the Duke of York. That charter, it will be remembered, only purported to grant to the duke "Hudson's river and all the lands from the west side of Connecticut river to the east side of Delaware bay." Surveyor general Colden not only extends the province a long distance to the northward of Delaware bay towards the head waters of the river of that name which falls into the bay, but also westward to lake Erie, more than two hundred miles beyond that bay and river, thus including a very large territory which could by no possibility be embraced by the language of the duke's charter. He makes no mention of the Connecticut river as a boundary, but bounds the province to the eastward by the colonies of Massachusetts and Connecticut, using language quite inconsistent with the supposition that New York reached eastward to any part of that river. His account of the northern limit of New York evidently proceeds upon the idea, that the undetermined line with Canada would run from the east end of lake Ontario in such direction as to strike the Massachusetts west line in the vicinity of the south end of Lake Champlain.

The following is Mr. Colden's description of the boundaries of the whole province.

"The province of New York is bounded to the southward by the Atlantic Ocean, and runs from Sandy Hook including Long Island, and Staten Island, up Hudson's river till the forty-first degree of north latitude be completed, which is distant twenty miles above the city of New York, East Jersey lying for that space on the west side of Hudson's river; from the forty-first degree of latitude on Hudson's river, it runs northwesterly to forty-one degrees forty minutes latitude on the most northerly branch of Delaware river, which falls near Cashiektunk, an Indian settlement on a branch of that river called the Fishkill. Thence it runs up that branch of Delaware till the forty-second degree of latitude be completed, or to the beginning of the forty-third degree, Pennsylvania stretching along the west side of Delaware river, so far northward as to this parallel of latitude. From the beginning of the forty-third degree, New York runs westerly, on a parallel of latitude, along the bounds of Pennsylvania to Lake Erie, or so far west as to comprehend the country of the Five Nations (the French having by the treaty of Utrecht, quitted all claims to those Five Nations). Then it runs along lake Erie, and Cadarackuy [Ontario] lake, and along Cadarackuy lake to the east end thereof. From thence it continues to extend easterly along the bounds of Canada *to the colony of Massachusetts bay; then southerly along the boundaries of Massachusetts bay, and of the colony of Connecticut, to the sound between Long Island and the main*, and then easterly along that sound to the Atlantic ocean."

If Mr. Colden had conceived that Connecticut river could, by any possibility, have been the eastern boundary of any part of New York, he would most certainly have so stated. Instead of which he describes its eastern boundary as a straight line running southerly along the western bounds of the two provinces of Massachusetts and Connecticut, without taking any notice of the river, or of the line of fifty or sixty miles on the north bounds of the latter province running directly west instead of south, which on the supposition that New York reached to Connecticut river, would become a part of its boundary.

Mr. Colden was also asked whether any of the reputed boundaries of New York "are in any parts thereof disputed, what parts and by whom."

To this inquiry he answered to the effect that disputes existed between proprietors of lands near the New Jersey line, and that similar disputes were likely to arise near the Pennsylvania line, when the lands should be settled; that the boundaries between New York and Canada were undetermined, that the French had built a fort at Crown Point, and made large claims of territory which should be opposed, etc., etc.

In regard to the eastern boundary he declares that the line with Connecticut is "entirely settled by agreement," and relative to the line with Massachusetts, uses the following language:

"The boundary between Massachusetts bay and New York is every where disputed. By the Massachusetts bay charter, that colony is to extend as far west as Connecticut. The question is whether it shall extend as far west as to Connecticut, or extend as far west as Connecticut does. The difference is so considerable, that it takes in near as great a quantity of land, as the whole of what is not disputed. *It is probable, they may at last make their claim good, by the numerous settlements they have already, and are daily making upon it.*"

Without noticing at present the language or construction of the Massachusetts charter, to which Mr. Colden refers, it may be remarked that the disputes to which he alludes, are doubtless, those which have been mentioned, as existing between the border settlers, and that he seems to admit that the Massachusetts claim to go west as far as Connecticut does, is likely to prevail. He makes no claim to lands to the northward of Massachusetts.[1]

---

[1] *Doc. Hist. N. Y.*, vol. iv, p. 171, 177-179. *Col. Hist. N. Y.*, vol. 6, p. 121-125.

As early as the year 1731 the assembly of Massachusetts passed an act to provide for the adjustment of the boundary question, which was communicated to the governor of New York and by him laid before the assembly of that province; and after that, several proposals were made by one government or the other, and conferences were held or attempted by their agents for the purpose of settling it, but for a long period without success. At length the disturbances on the borders became so serious that the attention of the Board of Trade was called to the subject, who summoning before them the agents of the respective provinces, then in England, and having heard what they had to offer, on the 25th of May 1757, made a representation of the case to the king, in which they say, that "upon a full consideration of the matter and of the little probability there is that the dispute will ever be determined by any amicable agreement between the two governments, it appeared to us, that the only effectual method of putting an end to it and preventing those further mischiefs which may be expected to follow, so long as the cause subsists, would be by the interposition of your majesty's authority to settle such a line of partition, as should upon a consideration of *the actual and ancient possession* of *both provinces*, without regard to the exorbitant claims of either, appear to be just and equitable." The board further say "We were of opinion, that a line to be drawn northerly from a point on the south boundary line of Massachusetts bay, twenty miles due east from Hudson's river, to another point twenty miles distant due east from the said river, on that line which divides the province of New Hampshire and the Massachusetts bay, would be a just and equitable line of division between your majesty's provinces of New York and the Massachusetts bay." They therefore recommend the establishment of such boundary line by his majesty's order in council. This they think, may be properly done by the consent of the agent of Massachusetts already given, though the soil and jurisdiction of that province had been granted by royal charter.[1]

The line thus recommended by the Board of Trade not being quite satisfactory to either of the provinces, and the right of the crown to interfere with the boundary of Massachusetts, which was held by royal charter, not being admitted, no authoritative determination of it was made by the king. The question still remaining open and the border disturbances continuing, the Earl of Shelburn, by command of the king, on the 11th of Dec. 1766, addressed letters to the governors of the respective colonies, earnestly recommending that "ef-

[1] *Col. His. N. Y.*, vol. 7, p. 223 – 4. *Smiths, N. Y.*, vol. 2, p. 303 – 9.

fectual measures be taken to settle every difference relative to their boundaries, by commissioners appointed from each for that purpose." [1]

In accordance with this recommendation the assemblies of both provinces appointed agents or commisioners for that purpose, who met at New Haven, in the colony of Connecticut, Oct. 1, 1767, and continued in conference on the subject for several days, but separated without coming to an agreement.

The claims of the respective parties were however, stated in writing with the grounds on which they rested, and several proposals for an adjustment were made on each side, of which it may be worth while to take some notice.

The claim of New York to extend east to Connecticut river, was based upon the charter of King Charles the second, to the Duke of York in 1664, which purported, as has been before seen to grant him "Hudson's river and all the lands from the west side of Connecticut river to the east side of Delaware bay."

The Massachusetts commissioners made a claim to extend westward from the Atlantic ocean to the South sea, under the charter of King William and Queen Mary, of Oct. 7, 1691; but the language of that part of the charter specially appropriated to the description of the territory granted, only made it reach "towards the South sea, or westward as far as the colonies of Rhode Island, Connecticut and the Narragansett country." If they had been content to claim under this charter that it covered the Massachusetts territory westward to within twenty miles to the Hudson, by making it *reach as far westward as the colony of Connecticut did*, there would have been plausibility at least in the interpretation; for though its language is confused, that seems to have been its most probable meaning. But by claiming farther than Connecticut extended they were obliged to rely on the recitals and general scope of the charter, which though strongly favoring their construction, might yet be considered as leaving the matter in doubt.

The principal reliance of the Massachusetts commissioners was, however, upon their title under the grant of King James the first to the council of Plymouth, of November 3, 1620, of New England, extending from the fortieth to the forty-eight degree of north latitude, and from the Atlantic ocean on the east to the Pacific on the west; and the sale and conveyance, on the 19th of March, 1627, by the said council of Plymouth to Sir Henry Roswell and his associates of a portion of that territory. This sale and conveyance was of all

[1] *Col. Hist. N. Y.*, vol. 7, p. 879.

that part of America between the Atlantic ocean on the east and the Pacific ocean on the west which is situated between two lines of latitude, the one running from a point three miles to the south of Charles river and the other from a point three miles to the north of the Merrimac, which comprehended all the territory in controversy.

The charter of King Charles, of 1628, constituting Roswell and his associates a corporation with powers of government, by the name of the governor and company of Massachusetts Bay, and confirming the grant from the council of Plymouth, had indeed, been vacated in Chancery in England in 1684; yet, as the sale and conveyance from Plymouth company was clearly valid without the assent of the king and needed not his confirmation, it was still left in full force.[1]

The New York commissioners sought to avoid the effect of this conveyance of the Plymouth company, by refering to a proviso in the king's charter to that company, that the lands described "were not then" (1620) "actually possessed or inhabited by any other christian prince or state," and by arguing therefrom that the grant, at least so far as it regarded New Netherland, was inoperative. But as there could be no pretence that the Dutch at that time "actually possessed or inhabited" more that a fractional part, if any, of the territory in dispute, the argument did not appear to be entitled to much consideration.

At this conference after offers by the Massachusetts commissioners to agree first upon a line twelve miles and then upon one sixteen miles from the Hudson, and by the commissioners of New York of a thirty and then a twenty-four mile line, the commissioners of Massachusetts finally offered to adopt the line which in 1757, had been recommended by the board of trade, viz.

"That a straight line to be drawn northerly from a point on the south boundary of the Massachusetts bay, twenty miles due east from Hudson's river, to another point twenty miles distant due east from the said river, on that line which divided the province of Massachusetts bay from New Hampshire, be the eastern boundary of the province of New York."

To this line the commissioners from New York objected, asserting their belief that the board of trade fixed upon the line under the supposition that the course of the Hudson was due north and south, whereas its course was considerably to the east of north, and that therefore the line they proposed would come nearer to the river than

---

[1] For the descriptive language of these grants, see *ante*, chap. II, p. 29 – 31.

they intended; and they proposed in lieu of it, a line twenty miles from the Hudson measured by lines at right angles to the general course of the river, instead of upon east and west lines.

Upon this small difference the commissioners separated without coming to an agreement.[1]

The question remained open between five and six years longer when commissioners appointed and duly authorized by the respective provinces met at Hartford, and, on the 18th of May 1773, executed in presence, and with the approval, of the governors of the two provinces, an agreement by indenture, by which it was declared that "A line beginning at a place fixed upon by the two governments of New York and Connecticut, in or about A. D. 1731, for the north west corner of a tract of land commonly called the Oblong, or equivalent land; and running from the said corner north 21 degrees 10 minutes and 30 seconds east, as the magnetic needle now points, to the north line of the Massachusetts bay, shall at all times hereafter be the line of jurisdiction between the said province of Massachusetts bay and the said province of New York, *in all and every part and place where the said province of New York on its eastern boundary, shall adjoin on the said province of the said Massachusetts bay.*"[2]

This line though described in different language, is believed to be substantially the twenty mile line from the Hudson, which had been recommended by the board of trade in 1757 as the ancient eastern boundary of New York, and which had been understood to be such from the time of the action of the king's commissioners who accompanied the expedition for the conquest of New Netherland in 1664. The antiquity and high authority of this line, though well known both in New York and Massachusetts, was not mentioned by the commissioners of either in any of their arguments, for the very plain reason that each of the parties desired to go beyond the line and thus to gain additional territory.

Thus the long pending controversy in regard to the eastern boundary of New York, so far as that province bordered on Massachusetts, was finally terminated. But the Massachusetts commissioners were not authorized to compromise any right which that province might have to territory west of Hudson's river, and hence, as will have been noticed, the agreement only designates the line fixed upon as the *eastern boundary of New York*, and not as *the western boundary of Massachusetts*.

---

[1] *Journal N. Y. Assembly*, Nov. 25, 1767.

[2] *Jour. N. Y. Assembly*, Jan. 12, 1774. *Jour. Congress*, Sept. 29, 1785.

After the close of the revolution in 1784, the state of Massachusetts presented a petition to the congress of the United States alleging that the state of Massachusetts under the charter of King James, in 1620, to the council of Plymouth, and the sale and conveyance in 1627, by said council to Sir Henry Roswell and his associates and successors were entitled to all the territory between the line of latitude of forty-four degrees and fifteen minutes, and that of forty-two degrees and two minutes north, and extending west from the rivers Merrimack and Charles to the Pacific ocean, that a portion of said territory was claimed by the state of New York, and praying that a court might be constituted agreeably to the articles of the confederation for the trial and decision of their claim.

In answer to this petition, commissioners were agreed upon and appointed, and a time and place was fixed for a hearing of the controversy, but before any trial, the commissioners from the two states being duly authorized for that purpose, met at Hartford, and on the 4th of December, 1786, agreed upon the terms of a compromise, by which Massachusetts relinquished all claim of jurisdiction as a government over the lands claimed by the state of New York, and the state of New York ceded and granted to Massachusetts the right of property to and in over two hundred and thirty thousand acres between the Oswego and Chenango rivers. New York also granted the right of soil to Massachusetts in all that part of the state of New York lying west of a line beginning at a point on the north line of Pennsylvania, eighty-two miles west of the north-east corner of that state, and running from thence due north, through Seneca lake to Lake Ontario, excepting therefrom one mile in width along the eastern branch of Niagara river. This cession of New York, covered about six millions of acres of land, and comprised a territory equal in extent to the present entire state of Massachusetts.[1]

This relinquishment by New York of so great an extent of territory is very conclusive evidence of the strong apprehension entertained by her statesmen, that the claim of Massachusetts was likely to prevail if brought to a legal determination — and tends to confirm the correctness of the view which has been hereinbefore taken of the weakness of the claim of that colony to reach eastward to the Connecticut river.

In the next chapter the eastern boundary of New York, against New Hampshire will be considered.

---

[1] *Jour. Cong.*, June 3, 1784, June 9, 1785, and Oct. 8, 1787. *Turner's Holland Purchase*, p. 325. *Street's N. Y. Council of Revision*, p. 153 - 156, in note.

CHAPTER V.

The Eastern Boundary of New York on New Hampshire.

1741-1764.

New Hampshire in 1741, declared by the king to extend westward to New York — New York bounded east by a twenty mile line from the Hudson and Lake Champlain — Action of the king and the officers of his government in relation to it — Fort Dummer — Lands granted by Massachusetts west of Connecticut river — Official acts and declarations recognizing the western extent of New Hampshire — Maps and geographical descriptions prior to the king's order of July 20, 1764, showing New Hampshire to reach westward to within twenty miles of the Hudson and to Lake Champlain.

THE extent westerly of the province of New Hampshire was not claimed, like that of Massachusetts, to be founded upon a royal charter, but upon the fact that by order of the crown it reached westward from the Atlantic to his majesty's province of New York, and that the eastern boundary of New York when the king's order was made, was a line running from Long Island sound parallel to the Hudson, to Lake Champlain. Many historical facts have already been adduced to show that such was understood to be the boundary of New York, and others more particularly applicable to its limits upon New Hampshire, will be presented hereafter. But it will first be proper to take some notice of the origin and progress of the colony of New Hampshire, prior to the commencement of its boundary controversy with New York.

In November 1629, the next year after the confirmation of the grant by the council of Plymouth to Sir Henry Roswell and his associates of the province of Massachusetts, before mentioned, Captain John Mason, secretary to the council of Plymouth, obtained from that company a patent under its common seal of all that part of New England "lying upon the sea coast, beginning from the middle part of Merrimack river, and from thence to proceed northwards along the sea coast to Piscataqua river, and so proceeds up within the said river and to the farthest head thereof; and from thence north westwards until three score miles be finished from the first entrance of Piscataqua river; and also from Merrimack through the said river and to the farthest head thereof, and so forwards up into the lands westward, until three score miles be finished; and from thence to cross over land to the three score miles end accounted from Piscataqua river, together with all islands and islets within five leagues distance of the provinces."[1]

This territory, after the name of the county in England in which Mason resided, was called New Hampshire. A portion of it came in direct conflict with the charter of Massachusetts of earlier date, being bounded on the south by the river Merrimack, while that of Massachusetts reached "three miles to the northward of any and every part" of that river. Upon any construction of Mason's grant its inland breadth could not exceed sixty miles, and by reference to a map it will at once be perceived that it would fall some twenty or thirty miles short of reaching westward even to Connecticut river. All lands lying west of this grant to the Pacific ocean as far northward as a line of latitude running through a point three miles north of the source of the Merrimack, in latitude about forty-three and a half degrees north, was claimed to be within the charter limits of Massachusetts, and indeed, seem to be embraced by its language. Massachusetts also claimed with much less apparent reason, that her territory extended eastward to the Atlantic ocean and northward to the same line of latitude. This eastern extension of territory, if admitted, would include nearly all of Mason's grant in Massachusetts. At the time of this grant there were several detached settlements within it, and a large portion of the settlers favoring the claim of Massachusetts, she succeeded in establishing jurisdiction over it, and maintained it for about forty years. In 1679 the matter having been brought before the king in council, the claim of Massachusetts to extend its northern boundary line from the source of the Merrimack eastward to the Atlantic was declared to be unfounded, and the four towns of Portsmouth, Dover, Exeter, and Hampton, were determined to be without the bounds of that province. It being admitted that Mason, under his grant from the council of Plymouth, had no right to exercise any powers of government, a commission was issued by the crown for the government of the colony, and from that time down to the period of the revolution, New Hampshire continued to be governed by commissioners as a royal province.[2]

In 1737 a controversy which had long existed between Massachusetts and New Hampshire in regard to their boundaries was heard at Hampton, in the latter province, by commissioners appointed by the crown from other colonies. On the part of Massachusetts it was contended that her northern boundary should be a line running

[1] *Haz.*, vol. 1, p. 289. *Story on the Constitution*, vol. 1, 64. *Belknap*, 8, *Farmer's ed.*

[2] *Farmer's Belknap*, chap. iv, and p. 449-452. *Story*, 65-68.

three miles to the northward of the mouth and of every part of Merrimack river to a point three miles north of the crotch where the rivers Pemigewasset and Winnipiseogee unite and form the Merrimack, and from thence due west to the South sea; while on the part of New Hampshire it was claimed that the boundary line should commence three miles north of the mouth of the Merrimack and thence run directly west until it should meet with his majesty's other governments. The commissioners instead of deciding the question made an evasive and conditional report, declaring in substance that if the charter of King William in 1691, granted all the lands which had been granted by King Charles the first, then the commissioners found that the line claimed by Massachusetts was the true line; but if otherwise, then that line should be as claimed by New Hampshire, referring the question of the construction of the charters to the decision of the king in council. An appeal being taken to the king and heard by him in council, a decision was made in 1740, which, disregarding the question contested before the commissioners and submitted by them, declared the northern boundary of Massachusetts to be "a similar curve line pursuing the course of the Merrimack river, at three miles distance, on the north side thereof beginning at the Atlantic ocean, and ending at a point due north of Patucket falls, and a straight line drawn from thence due west until it meets with his majesty's other governments." This decision was highly favorable to New Hampshire, carrying much the greater part of her southern line about twelve miles farther south than had ever been claimed by that province, and cutting off from Massachusetts a strip of territory of that width along nearly the whole of her northern boundary.

For the previous forty years the governor of Massachusetts, under the direction of the crown, had also acted as governor of New Hampshire, each of the two provinces having distinct colonial councils and assemblies; but on the adjustment of the boundary question, Benning Wentworth was appointed to the sole governorship of New Hampshire. His commission, which bore date June 3, 1741, described "our province of New Hampshire, within our dominions of New England in America," as extending westward until it should "*meet with our other governments.*"[1]

At the date of the commission to governor Wentworth, and for a long time before and ever afterwards until the period of the revo-

[1] *Belknap* chap. 17 and 18. *Doc. His. N. Y.*, vol. 4, p. 532. For governor Wenthworth's commission, see Appendix No. 2.

lution, both New Hampshire and New York were royal colonies, whose limits and extent by the English constitution were subject to the pleasure of the king. He might fix or alter them whenever he thought proper and in such manner as he chose. The boundaries of such royal colonies were sometimes pointed out in specific and intelligible language by a formal and express order. But such was not always the case. So little value was placed by government officials upon wild and uncultivated territory in a distant country, that the importance of definite descriptions of it was seldom properly appreciated, and the will of the monarch in regard to the limits of a province was often left to be ascertained and determined by evidence of a circumstantial character, such as acts of the crown and its officers indicating that certain territory was either within or without the jurisdiction and government of a particular colony; or by the recognition or even acquiesence of the king in the exercise of acts of jurisdiction over such territory. A colony whose early boundaries had been particularly specified by charter or in some other manner, might be shown to have been enlarged or contracted by such indirect historical evidence.

The colony of New York itself furnishes a striking example of this character. The only direct action of the crown describing the western boundary of New York, is that which is found in the charter to the Duke of York, granting him, as we have seen, "Hudson's river, and all the lands from the west side of Connecticut river to the east side of Delaware bay." Now if it should be conceded that by "Delaware bay" was intended the whole of the river of that name which empties into it, which is giving the language the most liberal construction possible, there is still beyond that river, and between it, and the lakes Erie and Ontario—a territory of more than fifteen thousand square miles in extent, which sometime before the revolution was considered as forming a portion of New York and was claimed as such, and which now constitutes a part of the state. And yet, for this extension of territory beyond the charter language no declaration of the king can be found. It rests solely upon circumstantial evidence, relating mainly to the acquiescence of the crown in claims and acts of supervision by the province over the Indians inhabiting such territory.

The historical evidence to show the contraction of New York, throughout its whole eastern extent on New England, is much more direct and explicit than that in favor of its enlargement to the westward. It has already been seen that the object of the grant of King Charles to the Duke of York, in 1664, was to cover the Dutch colony of New Netherland; that prior to the conquest of that colony by the English, its whole eastern extent had been limited by the Dutch, to less than twenty miles from the Hudson river; that immediately after its conquest the king's commissioners who accompanied the expedition, agreed with commissioners from Connecticut, upon a twenty mile line from the river, as the eastern boundary of the duke's patent; that this agreement had the sanction and approval of Col. Nichols, the duke's governor of the new province, who wrote to his master, that it was a favorable adjustment for him to be followed with the whole of New England; that the king's commissioners a few months later declared the western boundary of Massachusetts, which was then understood to extend north to the French territory, to be a line twenty miles from the Hudson, and bounded there by the duke's grant; that the change in the language of the commission to the governor, when, in 1686, the province became public, instead of private property, by the duke's accession to the throne, was in effect a disclaimer of the Connecticut river as a boundary; that the official documents and correspondence of the crown officers in New York, down to about the year 1750, and of those in England, to a still later period, uniformly recognize the existence of a parallel line to the Hudson, as the eastern boundary of the province on New England, and are wholly inconsistent with the supposition on the part of such officers that it reached eastward to any part of Connecticut river.

The claim of New York to extend eastward beyond a twenty mile line from the Hudson, rests solely on the charter to the Duke of York, and must consequently reach to Connecticut river or stop at such twenty mile line. There is no ground whatever for any claim to an intermediate boundary. Any evidence therefore which shows New Hampshire to extend west of that river is also evidence that it is bounded west by the twenty mile line.

By the survey of the boundary line between New Hampshire and Massachusetts, as established by the decision of the crown in 1740, Fort Dummer situated on the west side of Connecticut river in the present township of Brattleboro, which had been built by Massachusetts in 1724, and afterwards garrisoned and supported by that colony, was found to be without its limits, and, as was not doubted, within those of New Hampshire.

When the French and Indian war of 1744 commenced, the governor of Massachusetts complained to the English ministry of the hardship of requiring that colony to maintain a fort which was no longer within its territory, and the matter having been duly considered, an order of the king in council was thereupon made directing that it should thereafter be garrisoned and maintained by New Hampshire; that the governor of that province, should move the assembly to make a proper provision for that service; and further "that he should at the same time inform the assembly in his Majesty's name that in case they should refuse to comply with such proposal, his majesty would restore the fort and a proper district contiguous thereto to Massachusetts."[1] Gov. Wentworth at the next meeting of the assembly, in compliance with the king's order, recommended that they should make provision for the future maintenance of the fort. But the assembly, by a considerable majority, declined to make such provision, alleging, among other reasons, that the fort was at a great distance from their settlements and not necessary for their protection, but only for that of Massachusetts, which province would without doubt provide for its support. Upon this, Governor Wentworth dissolved the assembly, and immediately called another, to which in the most pressing terms, he recommended the same measure. A resolution was passed to provide for a garrison of a few men, which being deemed insufficient by the governor and council of Massachusetts, the maintenance of the fort was continued by the latter province.

In consequence of the neglect of the assembly of New Hampshire to make suitable provision for maintaining the fort in compliance with the king's order, the subject was brought before the board of trade, and their committee to whom the matter was referred, reported, on the 3d of August 1749, that New Hampshire ought to reimburse Massachusetts for maintaining the fort, and advised that the governor of New Hampshire should be directed to recommend to the assembly of his province, a permanent provision for it. New Hampshire, however, through the skill and adroitness of their agent in England as it is said, succeeded in evading both the support of the fort and the reimbursement of Massachusetts for its maintenance. But the repeated action of the king in council and the board of trade through a series of years, in which Fort Dummer and the territory contiguous to it on the west side of Connecticut river were declared to be within the province of New Hampshire, is conclusive proof, that neither the king nor the officers of his government who had the management of his colonial affairs, had yet as late as 1749, conceived the idea that New York had any claim to extend eastward to Connecticut river.[2]

---

[1] For a copy of the order to support Fort Dummer, see Appendix No. 3.

[2] *Belknap,* 285-6, 303, 305, 312. *Hall's Eastern Vt.,* 28-32, 79. *Mass. Archives,* vol. 72, p. 698.

The same delusion of the English government on the subject — if it were a delusion — continued until a much later period, and, indeed, seems never to have been removed, of which the proofs are numerous.

In 1752, a question in relation to the legal effect of the establishment of the boundary between Massachusetts and New Hampshire, upon the title to certain lands situated north of the boundary line, and west of Connecticut river, was referred by the crown to the attorney and solicitor generals, the first of those offices then being held by Sir Dudley Ryder, and the second, by Mr. Murray, afterwards Lord Mansfield. From their report, which was dated August 14th of that year, the following is extracted:

"There are also about 60,000 acres of land situated on the west side of Connecticut river, which were purchased by private persons from the government of Connecticut, to which that land had been laid out by the government of the Massachusetts bay, as an equivalent for two or three townships which the Massachusetts bay purchased from the Connecticut government. This tract of land, by the determination of the boundary line in 1738, *is become a part of New Hampshire*, but the proprietors of it are subject to no conditions of improvement, and the land lies waste and uncultivated."[1]

Although the precise position of the boundary line of New York on Massachusetts and New Hampshire had not been actually ascertained and settled, like that with Connecticut, yet it appears to have been well understood, in England, that it was a continuous parallel line to the Hudson, extending from the northwest corner of Connecticut to Lake Champlain. That such was the understanding of the British government, is decisively shown by the authoritative map of Dr. Mitchell of the British and French American provinces, published in London in 1755. (See a copy of this map fronting the title page.)

It is a well engraved map about six feet in length and nearly the same in width, and is entitled on its face as follows, viz:

"A map of the British and French dominions in North America, with the roads, distances, limits and extent of the settlements, humbly inscribed to the Right Honorable the Earl of Halifax and the other Right Honorable the lords commissioners for trade and plantations, by their lordship's most obliged and humble servant.

JNO. MITCHELL."

---

[1] *Doc. His. N. Y.*, vol. 4, 547–8. *New Hampshire Records. Stevens's Papers*, 1730–1775, p. 14, 17. *Mass. Archives*, vol. 20, p. 536.

On the map is engraved the following certificate:

"This map was undertaken with the approbation and at the request of the lords commissioners for trade and plantations, and is chiefly composed from draughts, charts, and actual surveys of different parts of his majesty's colonies and plantations in America; great part of which have been lately taken by their lordship's orders and transmitted to this office by the governors of said colonies and others.

Plantation office, February 13, 1755. JOHN POWNAL,
Secretary."

On this map the boundary between New Hampshire and New York, is a distinctly dotted line, running northerly from the northwest corner of Massachusetts to lake Champlain—New Hampshire extends northerly to Canada, and easterly from said line and Lake Champlain to the Atlantic Ocean, including the territory now occupied by both New Hampshire and Vermont. The name of the province—New Hampshire—is engraved in capitals in three lines across the Connecticut river, the letters N of *New*, H A of *Hamp*, and S H of *Shire* being placed to the west of the river, and the other letters on the east side.

This map was used by the British and American commissioners, in settling the limits of the United States at the treaty of peace in 1783, and upon it was marked by them the boundary line then agreed upon, and it has always been regarded as possessing the very highest authority. Mr. Smith in his history of New York, published in 1757, speaking of it, in reference to the boundaries of the British and French American territory, calls it "the most authentic map extant." [1]

Another map partaking of an official character is strongly indicative of the understanding of the English government in regard to the boundary in question. Under the treaty of Aix La Chapelle, of 1748, commissioners were appointed by France and England to adjust the disputed boundaries of their American possessions. A report of the English commissioners entitled, "Memorials of the English and French commissioners concerning Nova Scotia or Acadia," published in London in 1755, contains a map of the English colonies upon which the divisional line between New York and New Hampshire is designated precisly as in that of Dr. Mitchell,

---

[1] *Exec. Doc.* 25 *Cong.*, vol. 11, No. 451, p. 124, 77–8, and 112–13. *Smith's N. Y.*, ed. 1757, p. 136, note; and *Hist. Society Ed.*, vol. 1, p. 226. Mitchell's map is found in the N. Y. State Library at Albany, and in other libraries.

the province of New Hampshire embracing the whole territory now included in both that state and Vermont.

Besides these there were numerous other maps published in England prior to the order of the king in council of July 20, 1764, severing the present territory of Vermont from New York, on which the eastern boundary of New York is marked. Not a single map has been found which extends the province eastward to Connecticut river, and all concur in separating it from New England by a line running from Long island sound parallel to the Hudson. Of the maps bearing an earlier date than those of Dr. Mitchell, and of the treaty commissioners, on which the twenty mile line from the Hudson is made the eastern boundary of New York, and the western boundary of New England, a few will be mentioned.

In Morden's Geography of the World, published in London in 1688, at page 606 is a map of "New England and New York," which has a dotted line for the boundary between the two, beginning on Long Island sound with "Rye" on one side of it and "Greenwich" on the other, extending north beyond Albany, but not having Lake Champlain upon it.

A large quarto "Geography of the Earth, London 1709" (the name of the author not given), contains a map of North America, on which New England is separated from New York by a line running near the Hudson to Lake Champlain and along that lake to Canada.

In Oldmixon's "British Empire in America," London, 1741, is a map of "New England, New York, New Jersey and Pennsylvania," on which, for the eastern boundary of New York is a dotted line, about one-third of the distance from the Hudson to the Connecticut river, running from Long island sound nearly to the top of the map in latitude about forty-three degrees and a half north. In the body of the work (vol. 1, p. 238), the boundaries of New York are given thus: "On the south it is bounded by Long island and on the east by New England. Hudson river divides it from the Jerseys and a line drawn between Rye and Greenwich separates it from New England. Thus the whole province on the continent is not above twenty miles over, but is one hundred and twenty miles in length."

In the volume of the Gentlemen's Magazine for 1754, is a small map of "the British American Plantations," which only extends north to latitude forty-three degrees, on which the boundary line between New York and New England is a dotted line parallel to the Hudson, and reaching from Long island sound to the top of the map. The same magazine for each of the years, 1755, 57, 62, and

63, contains maps of the British colonies, on all of which New Hampshire is distinctly marked as extending westward to lake Champlain and to a line reaching northward from Long island to that lake.

From the year 1755 the English maps on which the limits of the several American colonies are designated, become very numerous, and all of them until several years after the king's order of July 1764, correspond with that of Dr. Mitchell in giving lake Champlain and the twenty mile line from the Hudson as the boundary between New York and New Hampshire.

That the officers of the king's goverment in England well understood that New Hampshire extended west to the line designated on Mitchell's and other maps of the period, is also shown by their uniform language whenever they speak of the extent of the province.

Thus, in the report of the lords of trade to the king, of the 25th of May, 1757, in which they recommend the authoritative establishment of a twenty mile line from the Hudson as the boundary between New York and Massachusetts, they describe it as running northerly to a point twenty miles east of Hudson's river "on that line which divides the province of New Hampshire and the Massachusetts bay," indicating very clearly, that New Hampshire extended as far west as the northern termination of the proposed line. And even Mr. De Lancey, lieutenant governor of New York, writing afterwards to the board of trade, speaks of the proposed line as reaching northerly *to the line of New Hampshire.*

Lord Hillsborough, the English secretary for the colonies, in his official correspondence with the governors of New York, uses language of a similar character. Thus, in addressing Lieut. Gov. Colden, under date of December 9, 1769, he says: "I think fit to send you a copy of his majesty's order in council of the 24th of July 1767, forbidding any grants to be made *of the lands annexed to New York*, by his majesty's determination of the boundary line, between that colony and New Hampshire," and he uses similar language in a despatch to Governor Moore under date of Feb. 25, 1768. So in a letter to Governor Tryon of December 4, 1771, he says: "I have long lamented the disorders which have prevailed on the lands *heretofore considered as a part of New Hampshire but which were annexed to New York* by his majesty's order in council of the 20th of July, 1764." And again, in another letter to Governor Tryon, of the 18th of April, 1772, he speaks of "that country which has been *annexed to New York*, by the determination of the boundary line" with New Hampshire.

So Lord Dartmouth, after he became colonial secretary, writing to Gov. Tryon, Nov. 4th, 1772, speaks of "the wisdom of the royal instructions by which you [Gov. Tryon] were forbid to make any grants within the *district annexed to New York* by the determination of the boundary with New Hampshire." And in the representation of the board of trade to the king of the 3d of December, 1772, the first object of consideration is stated to be, "the propriety or impropriety of *reannexing* to New Hampshire the lands west of Connecticut river."[1]

It also appears to have been understood in New York that New Hampshire, prior to the king's order of July, 1764, extended westerly to the twenty mile line, and to lake Champlain. Sir William Johnson, long a member of the New York council, and superintendent of Indian affairs, having been requested to point out a suitable place in the province for the location of a grant of land to which his friend, Commissary Gen. Leake, was entitled from the king, wrote him, under date of August 16, 1765, on the subject, saying, "for my part I know of no better at present *than that part of New Hampshire lately made part of this province.*"[2]

From all which, it seems very clear that, if New York, prior to the determination of the king in council of July, 1764, extended eastward to Connecticut river, it was not only unknown to the public in England and America, but also to the government officials in both countries.

---

[1] *Smith's N. Y.*, vol. 2, p. 305. *Col. Hist. N. Y.*, vol. 7, pp. 224, 334; vol. 8, pp. 12, 193, 285, 295, 318.

[2] *Doc. Hist. N. Y.*, vol. 2, p. 821.

CHAPTER VI.

THE EASTERN BOUNDARY OF NEW YORK ON NEW HAMPSHIRE.

1749 - 1765.

The origin of the claim of New York to reach to Connecticut river, to the northward of the colony of Connecticut, in 1749, and its history — The king's order in 1764, making that river the boundary with New Hampshire — Lands chartered by Governor Wentworth, of New Hampshire — Claim of the New York government, that the grants of the governor of New Hampshire were void, and the granting of the lands anew to others.

FOR more than three quarters of a century after the conquest of New Netherland by the English, the boundary adjustment then made between the king's commissioners and those of the colony of Connecticut, had been considered and treated as applicable to the whole eastern boundary of New York, and during all that time nothing had been heard of any claim of that province to reach eastward to Connecticut river, to the northward of that colony. It was not until some years after the determination of the crown, made in 1740, fixing upon the present northern line of Massachusetts as its boundary with New Hampshire, that it appears to have occurred to the rulers of New York to set up a claim under the old charter to the Duke of York, to extend eastward to that river. The rise and progress of the claim will now be considered.

Under date of Nov. 17, 1749, Gov. Wentworth of New Hampshire, wrote to Gov. Clinton of New York, that he had it in command from his majesty to make grants of unimproved lands within his government to such persons as would oblige themselves to improve the same; that applications were making for some townships to be laid out in the western part of it, and that wishing to avoid as far as he could interfering with the government of Gov. Clinton, he enclosed a copy of his own commission from the king, and desired to be informed "how far north of Albany and how many miles east of Hudson's river to the northward of Massachusetts line his (Gov. Clinton's) government *by his majesty's commission* extended."

This letter being laid before the New York council by Gov. Clinton, they advised him to acquaint Gov. Wentworth "that this province is bounded eastward by Connecticut river — the letters patent from King Charles the second to the Duke of York expressly granting all the lands from the west side of Connecticut river to the east side of Delaware bay."

This advice of the New York council being communicated to Gov. Wentworth, several letters subsequently passed between the two governors, the one claiming to the Connecticut river, and the other to a twenty mile line from the Hudson, and it was finally agreed to refer the matter to the decision of the king, and mutually to exchange the representations they should make to the crown on the subject.[1]

The letter of Gov. Clinton to Gov. Wentworth, of April 9, 1750, communicating the foregoing advice of the New York council, was so far as can be discovered, the first announcement ever made in behalf of the government of New York, that any part of that province to the northward of Connecticut extended eastward to Connecticut river.

It is evident from the correspondence, that the claim was entirely new to Gov. Wentworth; that when informed of it he was taken completely by surprise. The claim to extend eastward to the Connecticut river had never been made, except against the colony of Connecticut, and that not seriously persisted in; the twenty mile line having been agreed upon and accepted in behalf of the Duke of York in 1664, within three months after the conquest of the country by the Dutch. After having lain dormant for nearly a century it is not matter of great wonder that Gov. Wentworth had never heard of it, and should have been at a loss what to say in regard to it.

It is quite apparent also, that the claim was but a recent idea in New York. In July following the receipt of Gov. Wentworth's first letter, the subject of the claim of New Hampshire was referred by the governor and council to the attorney general. That office had then been held by Richard Bradley for over twenty-five years, and he ought to have known something of the claim, if it had been long in existence. And yet it was evidently new to him; his report concluding as follows, viz:

"I am very sensible, may it please your excellency, that the above representation, relating to the eastern bounds of this government, is very imperfect, being framed only on the few papers and materials I have been able to collect, at this time; relating to a matter, which I must confess myself much unacquainted with. But hope these few hints, may be of some use in the affair, and doubt not but his majesty's surveyor general, who I suppose is much better acquainted

---

[1] See the correspondence at length in *Doc. History of N. Y.*, vol. 4, p. 531 – 537, and in *Slade's Vt. State Papers*, p. 9 – 13.

with the bounds of this government, than I can pretend to be, will give your excellency much further light relating to them." But Mr. Colden, his majesty's surveyor general, having some twelve years previous, described the bounds of New York in great detail, without making any mention of Connecticut river, was not then ready to shed "further light" on the ancient existence of a new and more extended boundary. On the contrary when the attorney general's report was referred to him, he contented himself with stating, in substance, that the soil of the two governments, being vested in the crown, the king might fix the boundaries as he pleased; and with offering some suggestions, showing why, in his opinion, it would be for the interest and convenience of those who should inhabit the territory, to be connected with the province of New York. Some years later, however, on a nearer view of the personal advantages that might accrue to himself, by establishing the fact of the early extension of the province to Connecticut river, he made up his mind to advocate it, with great zeal.

Not long after the foregoing report of Attorney General Bradley, the boundary question came before the New York council, on the petition of the proprietor of Livingston's manor, who complained of intrusions of Massachusetts people on his lands; and the council thereupon, adopted a labored report in which it was declared, that the Connecticut river to the northward of the colony of Connecticut had always been the eastern boundary of New York. This report in March, 1753, was transmitted to the governor of Massachusetts, and was, so far as can be ascertained, the first notice given to that province of the existence of such claim.

When the New York assembly met in June following, their attention was called to the subject of the Massachusetts intrusions, and a joint committee of the two houses having reported that they were "humbly of opinion that the ancient Dutch records lodged in the secretary's office of the colony might give them some light into the eastern boundaries of the colony," an act was thereupon passed appointing commissioners to examine such records, and to prepare a representation of "all such matters and things as should come to their knowledge relating to the eastern boundaries of the colony, and of the encroachments made thereon by the neighboring colonies" [1] The representation was accordingly made in November following,

[1] It has already been seen that the "ancient Dutch records," which the assembly were desirous of having examined, furnished conclusive proof that New Netherland, at the time of its conquest by the English, did not reach eastward beyond a twenty mile line from the Hudson.

and together with the previous reports and proceedings of the New York authorities in relation to the matter, was transmitted to England to be laid before his majesty, as evidence that the province extended eastward to Connecticut river.[1]

These representations do not, however, appear to have had much effect upon the English board of trade, who, in May, 1757, after duly considering the same, made their report to the king, declaring it as their opinion that a twenty mile line from the Hudson should be fully established by his majesty as the boundary between the two provinces of New York and Massachusetts, as has already been seen.

In February, 1761, Cadwallader Colden, having by the death of Lieut. Gov. DeLancey, become acting chief magistrate of the colony, wrote to the lords of trade that he was "clearly *convinced* the province of New York extended eastward to Connecticut river, and that New Hampshire could have no pretence to the westward of that river," and he earnestly urged that the river should be established as the boundary. But notwithstanding the zeal of Mr. Colden and others, in favor of the eastern extension of New York, the officers of the province were by no means unanimous on the subject, as appears by a formal representation made by the council to Gov. Monckton, on the 25th of June, 1763. At the head of the council, at that time as its president, was Mr. Horsmanden, who had been one of its members for thirty years, and who was afterwards chief justice of the colony. The report referred to the adjustment of the boundary by the king's commissioners, with the assent of those of Connecticut in 1664; to the letter of Col. Nichols to the Duke of York, approving such adjustment, and also to the action of the king's commissioners, in 1665, declaring a twenty mile line from the Hudson to the western boundary of Massachusetts; and it expressed the belief of the council, that a twenty mile line from the Hudson was understood at an early day to be applicable to the whole eastern boundary of New York, and that it would, therefore, be an equitable line with both Massachusetts and New Hampshire. The council accordingly advised Gov. Monckton that in order to prevent further tumults and controversies on the border, it would be proper to agree to its establishment as such.[2]

Upon the return of Governor Monckton to England, the administration of the affairs of the province devolved upon Lieut. Gov.

---

[1] *Doc. Hist. N. Y.*, vol. 4, pp. 537–547; vol. 3, p. 734. *New York Assem. Jour.*, June 14, 1753; Law of July 4, 1753.

[2] *Col. Hist. N. Y.*, vol. 7, pp. 562–5. *Colden's Letter Book* in N. Y. Hist. Soc. Library, Sept. 25, 1763.

Colden, who, in numerous communications to the lords of trade, prosecuted the boundary claim with great industry and skill; and, as before stated, succeeded in July, 1764, in obtaining an order of the king in council declaring "the western banks of the river Connecticut from where it enters the province of Massachusetts bay, as far north as the forty-fifth degree of northern latitude, to be the boundary line between the two provinces of New Hampshire and New York." (For a copy of this order See Appendix No. 4.)

The reasons for making this order are not stated in the order, and must, perhaps to some extent, be matter of conjecture. The transfer of the territory from New Hampshire to New York, could not have been founded upon any considerations of public necessity or convenience. It weakened a small province to increase the power and extent of a larger one; was made without consulting the feelings or interest of the people who were the subject of the transfer, and was contrary to their wishes.[1]

That the order was not understood by the English government as establishing an old boundary, but as making a new one, may be fairly inferred from the letters of the lords of trade of July 13, 1764, to Lieut. Gov. Colden, written some days before the date of the order, in which they say that "as the reasons you assign *for making* Connecticut river the boundary line between the two provinces appear to us to have great weight, we have adopted and recommended that proposition." These reasons of Lieut. Gov. Colden are to be sought in his letters to the board of trade of Sept. 26, 1763, and of January 20, February 8, and April 12, 1764; all of which will be found in the seventh volume of the *Colonial History of New York.*

Besides the claim of right which he made under the old charter to the Duke of York, the lieutenant governor urged several considerations of expediency in favor of the Connecticut river boundary. The king's revenue, he stated, would be increased by having the lands granted under the government of New York, the quit rent in that province being two shillings and sixpence sterling for each hundred acres, and but one shilling in New Hampshire. A great number of reduced officers and soldiers, he said, who were entitled to bounties, under the king's proclamation of 1763, were desirous of locating their land in New York, and would not accept of grants

[1] It was for a long time believed by the settlers that fraudulent petitions had been presented to the crown in their names, falsely stating that they wished to be annexed to New York. See *Ira Allen's Vt.*, p. 18. But no evidence to sustain such belief has been found, and it was probably erroneous.

under New Hampshire. But these reasons seem hardly sufficient to justify so important a measure. Lieut. Gov. Colden further alleged that it would be more convenient for the inhabitants of the territory in question to be connected with New York, for the reason that their commerce and business would naturally be with Albany and along the Hudson river. This must have been understood to have been but partially true, it being evident that the business of the largest part of the territory would be likely to take other directions. Lieut. Gov. Colden also made loud and earnest complaints against the conduct of Gov. Wentworth for granting numerous townships of land without any expectations, as he alleged, that the grantees would occupy and improve them, but to enable them "to make jobs" by selling out their claims to others; as evidence of which he, among other things, stated that "a man no better in appearance than a pedler had lately traveled through the provinces of New Jersey and New York, hawking and selling his pretended rights of thirty townships on trifling considerations." He also complained of Gov. Wentworth's violation of an engagement with the governor of New York in regard to his granting lands, and of his selfishness in reserving a farm to himself in each of the numerous townships he had patented. But however strong and weighty reasons such conduct of Gov. Wentworth might furnish the king for removing him from office and placing another in his stead, it could not possibly be any ground for dismembering the province over which he temporarily presided. The period was, however, favorable to the success of the New York claim. The English ministry had announced their intention to tax the colonies and were preparing their measures for that purpose. They were desirous of circumscribing within as narrow limits as possible, the stubborn republican spirit of New England, from which they anticipated the most determined opposition. Lieut. Gov. Colden was favorably known to the ministry for the high-toned tory principles which he had manifested in advocating the taxation of the colonies by parliament, the establishment of fixed salaries for the crown officers, and "an hereditary council of privileged landholders, in imitation of the lords of parliament," to curb and control the popular features in the colonial governments. In urging the claims of New York he did not overlook the political aspect of the question, but presented it in the following characteristic language, viz:

"The New England governments," he says, "are founded on republican principles, and these principles are zealously inculcated on their youth, in opposition to the principles of the constitution of

Great Britain. The government of New York, on the contrary, is established as near as may be, after the model of the English constitutions. Can it be good policy to diminish the extent and jurisdiction in his Majesty's province of New York to extend the power and influence of the others?"

It is well known that the measures of the English ministry at this period were adopted with entire reference to the great object of establishing an unlimited power over the colonies, and there can be little doubt that this political argument of Lieut. Gov. Colden — founded as it was upon undeniable facts — exerted a controling influence in the councils of the king, and decided the controversy in favor of the more aristocratic province.

Although the order of the king, annexing the New Hampshire grants to New York, bore date July 20, 1764, yet for some reason, which has not been explained, it was not made known to the settlers until the spring of 1765.

It appears from the minutes of the New York council that it was laid before that body by Lieut. Gov. Colden on the 10th of April of that year, and in pursuance of their advice, a proclamation was issued bearing that date, giving notice of the same "to the end that all his Majesty's subjects within the province might conform thereto and govern themselves accordingly." The proclamation recited the order in council at length, and will be found in full in the Appendix, No. 3.

The territory annexed to New York by virtue of this order of the king, comprised the whole of the present state of Vermont. It had until then, as has been seen, been considered as a part of New Hampshire, and a large portion of it had been granted in townships of six miles square by Gov. Wentworth of that province. The charters of these townships had been issued under the great seal of the province in the name of the king, George the Third by the grace of God, of Great Britain, France and Ireland, king defender of the Faith, etc.," being the grantor, "by and with the advice of our trusty and well beloved Benning Wentworth, Esq., our governor and commander in chief, of our said province of New Hampshire, in New England," etc. The land covered by each charter was usually divided into seventy shares of which sixty-four were granted to that number of individuals whose names were entered on the back of the charter; upon which was also an indorsement disposing of the remaining six shares as follows, viz:

"His Excellency Benning Wentworth, Esq., a tract of land to contain five hundred acres, marked BW on the plan, which is to be accounted two shares, one whole share for the incorporated society for the propagation of the gospel in foreign parts, one share for a glebe for the church of England, as by law established, one share for the first settled minister of the gospel, and one share for the benefit of schools in said town."

By these charters there were reserved to the crown "all the white and other pine trees fit for masting our royal navy" and also a yearly rent for the first ten years of one ear of corn if demanded, and after the expiration of that time a rent of one shilling, proclamation money for every one hundred acres, payable at the council chamber at Portsmouth, on the 25th of December, annually.[1]

Prior to the king's order, making Connecticut river the boundary, the number of those charters which had been issued by Gov. Wentworth was about one hundred and thirty, sixteen of which had been granted before the breaking out of the French war in 1754, and the residue after its close — from 1760 to 1764. The grantees in these charters were exclusively inhabitants of New England, largely those of Massachusetts and Connecticut, though many were from New Hampshire and Rhode Island. Little or nothing, indeed, was known of the territory by the people of the other colonies. It had, however, long occupied the attention of New England. Separating its frontier settlements from those of the French and Indians of Canada, its dark points had for several generations been frequently passed through by New England people, either as hunters, prisoners to the Indians, fugitives from captivity, or soldiers on expeditions against their enemies. Previous to the last French war, several routes to the lakes and Canada, across different parts of the territory had often been traversed by them, and had become quite well known. That war called to the field in the vicinity of lakes George and Champlain, and finally to Canada, large bodies of New England troops who participated in the bloody contest for supremacy with the French, and in its successful issue. In 1755 the colonies of New Hampshire, Massachusetts, Connecticut and Rhode Island furnished over six thousand men for the expedition to the lakes; in 1757 a still larger number, and probably an equal or greater number in each of the three last years of the war. Early in the summer of 1759, the French abandoned and the English took possession of Ticonderoga and Crown Point, and the next year the conquest of Canada was completed. During the two latter years of the war, a

[1](For the form of a New Hampshire charter, See *Thompson's Vermont*, part 2d, page 224.)

military road was constructed from Crown Point to Number Four, Charlestown, New Hampshire, and other routes from that fortress and Ticonderoga were opened, taking a more southern direction. In passing to and from the military stations on the lakes and in Canada, almost every part of the territory, now Vermont, had been explored and noticed by New England men. Much of the soil appeared rich and of easy tillage, and to possess many advantages over the lands which could be obtained nearer their residences. The desire to possess and improve new lands, which has since distinguished the people of New England, was then as strong among them as it has been since. The dangers from a foreign enemy being happily removed by the termination of the war, the wish to emigrate to this territory extensively prevailed. Particular localities had sometimes been selected by officers and men as they traversed the territory. Such was the case in regard to the township of Bennington, the first that was granted by Gov. Wentworth. Capt. Samuel Robinson of Hardwick, Massachusetts, belonging to the regiment of Col. Ruggles, in returning from the lakes with his company or a portion of it, encamped on its soil over night, and resolved to settle upon it. Finding that it had been granted some years previously, he sought out the original proprietors and with others, his associates, purchased their rights, or a large portion of them, and commenced its occupation in the spring of 1761. Purchases of lands in other townships, by other parties, were made in like manner, and numerous new grants of townships were obtained from Gov. Wentworth by persons who had thus visited the lands for which they sought. It was usual for people residing in the vicinity of each other, in different parts of New England, to associate themselves together to the necessary number of sixty, in order to procure the charter of a township, and to defray the expenses of the charter and survey.

In this manner most of the charters were granted, and thus a very great proportion of the people in all parts of New England became directly interested in the New Hampshire title. In one hundred and thirty townships of sixty proprietors each, they would number nearly eight thousand, each of whom was entitled to about three hundred and thirty acres of land. Some of the names in the charters will doubtless be found repeated in others of a subsequent date; but making liberal allowances for such repetitions, and for cases in which one person obtained more than a single right by the use of the names of others, the number of actual proprietors would still be extremely large. They probably numbered several thousand. Very many of them were persons who obtained grants for speedy settlement, either by themselves, or by members of their families.[1]

At the time of Lieut. Gov. Colden's proclamation in the spring of 1765, announcing the annexation of the lands west of Connecticut river to New York, the settlers under the New Hampshire charters had spread themselves over a considerable extent of country, and were constantly receiving accessions to their numbers from Massachusetts, Rhode Island and Connecticut, in all of which colonies extensive preparations were making for further emigration. The settlers had cleared lands, erected dwellings, outhouses and mills, laid out and opened roads, established schools and organized churches. Their several charters had conferred on them all the "privileges and immunities" of other corporate towns in New Hampshire, in conformity to which they had organized themselves, chosen their town officers and passed local ordinances and regulations for their government, and were in short enjoying many of the advantages of well ordered and cultivated society, with favorable prospects for future improvement and prosperity.

This change of jurisdiction, which had been made without the knowledge of the settlers, was displeasing to them. A jealousy, to call it by no harsher name, had always existed between the colonies of New England and the colony of New York, and the people of the former were not favorably inclined towards the institutions and government of the latter province. A large portion of the lands in New York had been granted in very extensive tracts, the cultivators of the soil occupying the position of tenants to landlord owners, who were dignified with the lordly titles of patroons. This tenancy was looked upon by the independent farmers of New England as a species of degrading servitude. The government of New York, as had been represented by Lieut. Gov. Colden, was also of an aristocratic character, in which the body of the people appeared to have but little participation. Nearly all the officers, from the highest to the lowest, from the judges of the superior courts down to overseers of the poor and of highways, were appointed, either directly or indirectly by the central executive authority; the town meeting, that school and nursery of republican equality and instruction, in which the men of New England were accustomed to elect their inferior

---

[1] *Hildreth's U. S.*, vol. 2, chap. 26 and 27. *Belknap*, chap. 22. *Hall's Eastern Vt.*, Index Roads. *Slade's State Papers*, p. 13.

officers and to consult and legislate upon their important local affairs being an institution scarcely known in that province.[1]

But notwithstanding the aversion of the settlers to the New York system of laws, the new jurisdiction would have been quietly submitted to if nothing further had been demanded. But the New York government not only claimed to extend its laws over the territory, but insisted that the titles of the settlers under New Hampshire were absolutely void, and proceeded at once to grant the lands anew to others, which occasioned the long and bitter controversy that followed. Before however, giving an account of that controversy it will be necessary to take some notice of the land system of the province of New York and of the manner in which it was administered by those in authority.

---

[1]Mr. Sabine in his *American Loyalists*, vol. 1, p. 28, appropriately designates and describes the political and social condition of New York at the commencement of the revolution in a few words, as follows: "To say that the political institutions of New York formed *a feudal aristocracy*, is to define them with tolerable accuracy. The soil was held by a few. The masses were mere retainers and tenants as in the monarchies of Europe. Nor has the condition of society entirely changed, since "anti-rent" dissentions of our own time arose from the vestige which remains."

CHAPTER VII.

General Character of New York Colonial Land Grants.

1664-1775.

Early authority of New York governors to grant lands — Their selfish conduct — A portion of their extravagant grants annulled — New regulations of the crown to prevent abuses, made, and evaded — The province parceled out into large tracts to favorite persons — The governors by exacting exorbitant fees and reserving lands for themselves, in the names of others, acquired immense fortunes — When Lieut. Gov. Colden came into office in 1761, most of the vacant lands in the province had been granted — Hence his anxiety to extend its boundary to the Connecticut, and his disregard of the titles of the settlers.

THE authority to grant lands, which the king had conferred on the governors of his royal colonies, had been very generally exercised by them with less regard to the interests of the crown and its subjects than to their own individual emolument, and in none of them had this disregard of the public good been carried to so great excess as in the province of New York.

The principal object of the crown in allowing the governors to grant lands was declared to be to promote the settlement of the country, and thereby to increase the strength and wealth of the colonies. Lands were not to be sold by the crown for a consideration to be paid, but a small rent was to be reserved, payable annually, termed a quit rent, which it was anticipated might eventually yield some revenue to the government. Nothing was therefore to be paid by the subject on receiving the grant, except a compensation to the governor and other officials for their time and labor in preparing and issuing the patent.

When by the accession of James, duke of York, to the throne in 1686, the colony of New York became a royal province, Gov. Dongan was by his commission, empowered, "with the advice and consent of his council, to agree with the planters and inhabitants of the province concerning such lands, tenements and hereditaments as then were or thereafter might be in his power to dispose of, and them to grant under such moderate quit rents, services and acknowledgments to be thereupon reserved *to us*, as he, by and with the advice aforesaid, should think fit."

This authority in the same terms was continued to succeeding governors, and was by most of them very greatly abused. Instead of granting lands for purposes of settlement and cultivation, as had been intended by the king, they were generally parceled out in very large tracts to such persons as would by their money and influence, best contribute to the immediate wants of the governors, without any regard to the revenue of the crown, or to the improvement of the colony. Little notice of this misconduct appears to have been taken in England until Lord Bellamont became governor of the province in 1698, when he called the attention of the board of trade to the subject, by furnishing them with a list and description of several enormous grants which had then recently been made by Col. Fletcher, his immediate predecessor. This communication having been duly considered, the board made a representation of the matter to the lords justices of England, who administered the government during the absence of King William on the continent, and who directed the Earl of Bellamont "to put in practice all methods whatsoever allowed by law for the breaking and annulling the said grants."

Lord Bellamont, in obedience to these instructions, called the attention of the New York assembly to the subject, and with considerable difficulty, succeeded in procuring the passage of an act entitled "an act for vacating, breaking and annulling several extravagant grants of land made by Col. Benjamin Fletcher, late governor of this province under his majesty." The principal grants which were vacated by this act (passed May 12, 1699), were the following, viz:

1. One to Capt. John Evans of a tract lying on the west side of Hudson's river, comprising a large portion of the present counties of Ulster and Orange, and containing about six hundred square miles, with a reserved rent to the crown, for the whole territory, of twenty shillings per annum.

2. One to Col. Nicholas Bayard, a member of the governor's council, of the valley of Schoharie creek, extending from the mouth of the creek at the Mohawk river about fifty miles toward its source, the rent one otter skin per annum.

3. A grant to the Rev. Godfrey Dellius, minister at Albany and four others, of fifty miles in length by four in breadth along the Mohawk river, two miles wide on each side of it, with a quit rent of one beaver skin per annum for the first seven years, and five beaver skins forever after.

4. Another grant to Godfrey Dellius, of a tract seventy miles in length by twelve in width on the east side of Hudson's river, bounded

on the south by the north bounds of Saratoga, the rent to the crown being one raccoon skin per annum. By the same act the Rev. Mr. Dellius for alleged fraud in deluding the Indians to execute a grant of the Mohawk lands to him and his associates, and for other fraudulent practices, was declared suspended from his clerical functions.

This act was not however passed without considerable opposition, especially in the council, where the vote stood three and three, and was only carried by the casting voice of the governor, the three opponents of the bill holding some of the largest remaining grants in the province." They were *Stephen Van Cortland*, who had a patent for eighty-six thousand acres in the present county of Westchester; constituting the tract into a manor or lordship, with a hereditary right of representation in the colonial assembly; *Robert Livingston*, proprietor of the manor of Livingston, situated on the east side of Hudson river in the present county of Columbia, covering as it was afterwards surveyed and held over one hundred and sixty thousand acres, who also had the right of representation in the assembly; and *William Smith*, who had a patent of all the vacant land on Long Island lying between the bounds of former grants, supposed to be not less than fifty square miles.

Besides these, there were several other grants of a most extraordinary character, which were not included in the annulling act, some of them patented by Gov. Fletcher and some by other governors. Among these the following may be mentioned, viz:

One tract to Col. Peter Schuyler and Herman Ganzevort, four miles in breadth along the east side of Hudson river by twenty in length. Another to Col. Henry Beekman, of a tract of the same breadth and length along the east side of the same river. And a third tract to Col. Caleb Heathcote, also on the east side of the Hudson, twenty miles in length along the river by five in breadth. Among these extraordinary grants must also be reckoned that of the princely manor of Rensselaerwick, granted by Gov. Dongan in 1685. This was originally understood to be twenty-four miles square, with Albany at the centre; but it was finally construed to extend twenty-four miles east and as many west of Hudson's river, and to include a tract forty-eight miles in length by twenty-four in breadth, with an area of eleven hundred and fifty-two square miles, embracing most of the land in the present counties of Albany and Rensselaer. This manor had also the right of representation in the assembly.

The passage of the act vacating a portion of these extravagant grants aroused a strong opposition to Lord Bellamont among the large landed proprietors, who had great influence in the colony, and efforts were immediately made to prevent its approval by the king, for which purpose Mr. Dellius and others repaired to England. The Earl of Bellamont dying, was succeeded in 1702, by Lord Cornbury, who though of noble descent and cousin to Queen Anne, was one of the most profligate and corrupt, as well as tyrannical of colonial governors. He is said to have exceeded all of his predecessors in the extent and improvidence of his grant, and it is stated on apparently good authority, that he had contracted with two gentlemen, to grant them all the lands in the province in a lump, and that the only thing which prevented the grants from passing the seals, was the fear of the intended grantees, that it would create so many enemies that they should not be able to hold it.

The first assembly which Lord Cornbury had called, in 1702, had passed an act, with his connivance, repealing the annulling act of 1699. Neither of those acts, however, was effective without the approval of the crown; both remained in the colonial office without being acted upon until after Lord Cornbury was removed from the government, when, in 1708, the subject was brought before the queen in council and the Earl of Bellamont's annulling act was thereupon confirmed and the act repealing it disapproved.

The selfish and profligate conduct of the king's governors in disposing of the public lands solely for their own individual emolument was productive of many apparent evils besides that of depriving the crown of an anticipated resource. These extravagant grants were objectionable, not only on account of their immense extent, but for being situated for great distances along the banks of rivers, with comparatively narrow widths into the interior, thus comprising and monopolizing the most convenient and desirable lands in the colony, and leaving only those of difficult access and less value, to be afterwards disposed of. The grants being made without any condition for their cultivation or improvement, and being in the hands of a few men who desired to people them with a dependent tenantry, but not in general to sell them, were almost completely locked up from settlement, by which the growth of the colony was greatly obstructed. It was another serious evil that the boundaries of these grants were frequently so vaguely described as to render their real position and extent quite uncertain, and to make it difficult if not impossible to determine what land had been actually granted and what remained to the crown.

When Lord Bellamont's annulling act was approved by the queen, in compliance with the recommendation of the board of trade, efforts appear to have been made to prevent the recurrence of the like abuses in future. By instructions to Lord Lovelace, Cornbury's successor, he was directed to make no grants of more than two thousand acres to any one person, and always to reserve a yearly quit rent to the crown of two shillings and six pence for every one hundred acres, and also to insert in his patents a condition of forfeiture if at least three acres in every fifty were not cultivated within three years. And in order to prevent a monopoly of all the good lands in the hands of the first patentees, it was provided that the governor, the collector of the customs, the secretary of the province and the surveyor general, or any three of them, of which the latter officer was to be one, who were to "set out all lands should constitute a board, to be thereafter granted and that therein they should have regard to the profitable and unprofitable acres, so that each grantor may have a proportionable number of one sort and the other, as likewise that the length of each tract to be hereafter granted do not extend along the banks of any river, but into the mainland, that thereby the said grantees may have each a convenient share of what accommodation the said rivers may afford, for navigation or otherwise." These instructions were continued to all succeeding governors, the only material change being that in 1753 the quantity which might be granted to any one individual was reduced from two thousand to one thousand acres, and so it ever after remained.[1]

This effort of the crown to effect a reform in the granting of lands was but partially successful. The peremptory direction in regard to the reservation of quit rents appears to have been complied with by subsequent governors, though their payment was very generally in some way evaded by influential proprietors. The governors also caused to be inserted in their patents a condition of forfeiture for nonimprovement within three years, agreeably to their instructions; but this provision was seldom or never enforced, and was thus practically a nullity. Under these instructions surveys of lands previous to the issuing of patents seem to have been required, thus rendering less uncertain the boundaries of the tracts granted. The provision in relation to the granting of lands in strips along rivers, and of a proportionable share of good and poor lands was but little regarded, and that which was designed to prevent the accumulation of large tracts in the hands of a few persons, was wholly inoperative, both under the first limitation of two thousand

---

[1] *Col. Hist. N. Y.*, vol. 3, 381; vol. 4, 397, 510, 622, 813; vol. 5, 21-26, 54, 141, 650-4; vol. 6, 790; vol. 7, 743. *Doc. Hist. N. Y.*, vol. 1, 377-381. *Van Schaick's Statutes*, p. 32.

acres to a single person, and of one thousand at a subsequent date. If an individual desired to obtain a tract to himself of twenty or thirty thousand acres or more, he had only to apply for it in the name of himself and such number of other individuals, with whom he had previously contracted for that purpose, as might in the whole be entitled to receive the required quantity, and *provided he had access to the granting ear of the governor*, he would readily obtain a patent of the whole to the applicants as tenants in common, the only remaining thing to be done to complete his title being to have a conveyance made to himself by his nominal associates, in accordance with their previous agreements. This mode of obtaining extensive tracts of land through the instrumentality of nominal grantees continued through the whole colonial period, and was practised with the knowledge and connivance of most if not all of the governors, many of them thus openly and shamefully obtaining for themselves princely estates, in plain violation of the spirit of their instructions, and in fraud of the crown and the public, as will hereafter be more fully seen.[1]

A more direct and legitimate source of revenue to the governors, derived from the granting of lands, was the money received on issuing the patents, termed patent fees. Until after the approval by the crown of the New York act annulling the Dellius and other extravagant grants, there does not appear to have been any attempt to regulate the amount which might thus be taken. The governors seem to have made the best terms they could with the grantees, in effect selling them the fee of the king's land for their own personal benefit, and reserving to the crown the mere nominal quit rent of a beaver, an otter, or a raccoon skin for an almost unlimited number of acres. It is impossible to ascertain with any degree of accuracy what sums were secured by the governors during this period. Gov. Dongan admitted that he received two hundred pounds for the grant of the manor of Rensselaerwick before mentioned. It was estimated by Lord Bellamont that his predecessor, Col. Fletcher, during

[1] A large map of the province of New York, prepared under the direction of Gov. Tryon, showing the state of the province at the beginning of the revolution, was published in England in 1779, of which there is a copy in the New York State Library, and also, on a reduced scale, in the first volume of the *Documentary History of New York*. It purports to exhibit the division of its territory into "counties, manors, patents and townships," and also "all the private grants of lands in the province." An examination of this map will show that a great portion of the territory was covered by these private grants, and that those which ranged from ten to one hundred thousand acres each were quite numerous.

his term of office, had received not less than four thousand pounds for his grants; and there is no doubt that Lord Cornbury received and squandered all he could possibly obtain.

Soon after Gov. Hunter's appointment in 1710, a bill of fees to be taken on the granting of lands, was under instructions from the crown adopted by ordinance of the governor and council, which is believed to have been the only authoritative regulation ever made on the subject in New York during the colonial period.

This regulation was, however, soon departed from, and the allowances specified were enormously increased. By the council minutes of Feb. 5, 1772, the following bill of fees is admitted to have been usually exacted on the issuing of a patent for 1,000 acres.

By the Governor,	$31.25
Secretary of the Province,	10.00
Clerk of the Council,	10.00
Auditor,	4.62
Receiver General,	14.38
Attorney General,	7.50
Surveyor General,	12.50
Total amount for 1,000 acres,	$90.25

And the same amount was taken for any additional thousand acres included in the same patent. Thus, if the patent was for two thousand acres the fees would be twice that sum, and at that rate for any larger quantity. The fees were not, however, reduced in the like proportion for a smaller quantity of land, but they amounted to nearly the same, however small the grant, and they exceeded eighty dollars for a patent of one hundred acres. The progressive increase of fees for every thousand acres included in the same patent was defended by Colden on the ground that the fees were not intended merely as a compensation for actual services, but as perquisites of office.[1]

By the adroit exercise of this power of granting lands most of the governors previous to the time of Mr. Colden, had contrived to amass large fortunes. Mr. Smith in his history of New York (vol. 2, p. 82), says of Mr. Clarke who had held office many years, and was lieutenant governor from 1736 to 1743, that "by his offices of secretary, clerk of the council, councilor and lieutenant governor, he had every advantage of inserting his own name, or the name of some other person in trust

[1] *Council Minutes*, vol. 26, p. 275–7. *Col. Hist.*, vol. 7, p. 921–7. 2 *Smith's N. Y.*, 366. *Colden's Letter to the Lords of Trade*, Oct. 13, 1764.

for him in the numerous grants, which he was in a condition for near half a century to *quicken or retard;* and his estate, when he left us, by the rise of his lands and the population of the colony, was estimated at one hundred thousand pounds." Of Gov. Clinton, whose term extended for ten years from 1743, the assembly, in an address to the crown, offered to prove "that he granted extravagant tracts of land, and exacted twelve pounds and ten shillings, for every thousand acres, in the remote parts of the colony, besides reserving considerable shares in the grants to himself, by inserting fictitious names." And Mr. Smith (vol. 2, p. 191–2, and 202) says of him that "he set the precedent for the high fees since demanded for land patents, and boldly relied upon the interests of his patrons to screen him from reprehension," and that "it was supposed he returned to England with a fortune very little less than eighty-four thousand pounds sterling."

The policy of treating the charters issued by the governor of New Hampshire as nullities began under the administration of Cadwalader Colden, then holding the office of lieutenant governor. He was of Scotch birth, and by profession a physician, had emigrated to Philadelphia, and afterwards removed to New York, where, in 1720, he was appointed surveyor general of the province, and two years later a member of the executive council, both of which offices he held for over forty years. On the death of Lieut. Gov. De Lancey in August, 1761, he was called to administer the government, by virtue of being the senior member of the council, and was soon afterwards appointed lieutenant governor, and as such continued at the head of the affairs of the province, with the exception of about a year, while Gen. Monckton was governor, until November, 1765, when he was superseded by the arrival of Sir Henry Moore from England. On the death of Gov. Moore in Sept. 1769, he again came into power, and exercised the office of chief magistrate for over a year until he was succeeded by Lord Dunmore in October, 1770. He held his commission as lieutenant governor until his decease in 1776, and once more occupied the position of chief magistrate during the absence of Gov. Tryon in England, from April, 1774 to July, 1775. Mr. Colden was possessed of considerable talent, learning and industry, and for a large portion of his time had much influence in the colony, which was often exercised for beneficial purposes. He was, as has been before stated, of high tory principles, sustaining with all his might the most odious measures of the British ministry for establishing an unlimited power of the crown and parliament over the colonies. Nor could he be said to have been destitute of that keen love of money and office, which Junius declared to be peculiarly characteristic of his countrymen. He was always, indeed, quite willing to enrich himself and his numerous family at the expense of the public, and not a little ingenious in devising ways to accomplish it. From the zeal with which, while urging the establishment of Connecticut river as the boundary of his province, he had declaimed against the selfishness and favoritism of Gov. Wentworth, in making his land grants, it might perhaps have been inferred that he himself was wholly above being influenced by such paltry personal considerations. Such an inference would, however, have been quite erroneous. It will, indeed, be found that he was no less greedy of the gains to be derived from the granting of lands, than was his New Hampshire rival, and that in fact, his avaricious cupidity, coupled with his desire of power and patronage, laid the foundation for the long and bitter controversy which followed, and for the consequent independence of the territory of Vermont, which might otherwise have formed a part of New York.

At the time Mr. Colden came to the head of affairs, the official income from the granting of lands had much decreased. Nearly all of the desirable lands in the colony which were not subject to the Indian title, had been covered by patents of former governors, and even the territory of the natives had been largely encroached upon. Taking advantage of their ignorance and credulity, the land speculators had often induced them to execute what were dignified with the name of "Indian deeds," which, under the interpretation of the grantees, sanctioned by the ruling authorities of the province, who were the recipients of the patent fees, and often of a considerable portion of the lands, were found to embrace territory of immense extent, and frequently to include Indian plantations and cherished hunting grounds — lands with which the Indians never had a thought of parting.[1] These fraudulent encroachments had been so numerous as to create extensive dissatisfaction among the Mohawks and other tribes of the six nations, and greatly to weaken the hold of the English upon their friendship. In fact many of the Indians, influenced mainly by these intrusions, had emigrated to Canada and put themselves under the protection of the French, while those who remained were in a state of uneasiness and irritation. The disaffection occasioned by these oppressive practices was viewed with appre-

[1] It would appear from representations made to Lieut. Gov. DeLancey in 1753, that it was customary for the governors to have as their share, one-third of the lands purchased of the Indians. *Col. Hist.*, vol. 6, p. 818.

hension and alarm in England as well as in New York. The conduct of the rulers of the province in allowing them was not only severely censured by the board of trade, but they had made it one of the standing instructions to the governors to put in requisition every means in their power to break and annul several of the most obnoxious of them, either by acts of the assembly or by judicial proceedings. But as governors, legislators, and judges were all either directly or indirectly interested, to maintain the sanctity of the grants, the instructions were of course inoperative.[1]

Such being the character and position of Lieut. Gov. Colden, it is not perhaps matter of great wonder that he should, on coming into power, have abandoned his former views of the limited extent of the province of New York to the eastward, and under the influence of anticipated patent fees, and power to be derived from the annexation to New York of the territory, now Vermont, should have obtained new light on the subject, and to use his own language, should have become "clearly convinced that the province of New York extends eastward as far as Connecticut river;" nor that when he had obtained a decision of the crown making that river the boundary, he should have been willing to construe it as annulling all previous grants made in the territory by New Hampshire."

---

[1] *Doc. Hist. N. Y.*, vol. 2, 1821. *Col. Hist. N. Y.*, vol. 4, p. 720, 345; vol. 5, p. 569, 650, 549, 472; vol. 6, p. 851, 962; vol. 7, p. 77, 87, 117, 130, 169, 260, 301, 677, 701, 576.

CHAPTER VIII.

THE SETTLERS AND CLAIMANTS UNDER NEW HAMPSHIRE.

1763-1766.

Colden's proclamation against the settlers of December, 1763 — Counter proclamation of Wentworth — Notice to the settlers of the annexation of the territory to New York in April, 1765 — Colden issues patents of lands which had been previously granted by New Hampshire — Nearly all of them on the west side of the Green mountains, and why — His further issue of patents suspended by the stamp act, Nov. 1, 1765 — Also suspended by Sir Henry Moore — His character and measures in regard to the New Hampshire grantees.

WHILE Lieut. Gov. Colden was urging the British ministry to make Connecticut river the eastern boundary of his province, the territory of which he desired to obtain jurisdiction was being rapidly occupied by New England men, who were fast transforming the wilderness into cultivated fields, and making it their permanent habitation. This excited his alarm for the success of the measure he had so ardently at heart, and he determined to do all in his power to prevent the further settlement of the country. For this purpose he issued a proclamation, bearing date December 28, 1763, setting forth in strong and positive language the claim of New York to extend eastward to Connecticut river by virtue of the charter of king Charles the second to the Duke of York, declaring that the government of New Hampshire without having any jurisdiction whatever to the westward of that river, had granted lands beyond it and within the jurisdiction of the government of New York, and that "sundry persons, ignorant that they could not derive a legal title under such grants had attempted a settlement of lands included therein;" warning all persons against purchasing titles or making settlements under the charters of that province; commanding "all judges, justices and other civil officers within the same to continue to exercise jurisdiction in their respective functions as far as to the bank of Connecticut river;" and enjoining the high sheriff of the county of Albany to return to him the names of all persons who under the grants of New Hampshire, did or should hold the possession of any lands westward of Connecticut river, "that they might be proceeded with according to law."[1]

[1] For a copy of this proclamation see *Doc. Hist. N. Y.*, vol. 4, p. 558. See also *Slade's Vt. State Papers*, p. 16.

Whatever may be thought of other portions of this proclamation, there is no doubt of the truth of that part of it which affirms that the settlers under New Hampshire "were ignorant that they could not derive a legal title" under their grants. They fully believed their titles to be good, and there is no reason to doubt that this proclamation gave them the first information they received that the validity of their charters would be called in question. It is true that the claim of New York had been asserted to Gov. Wentworth by letter from Gov. Clinton, in 1750, as has been before mentioned, but the correspondence which had taken place between the two governors does not appear to have been published, and was wholly unknown to the settlers.[1]

One of the noticeable features of this proclamation is the formal and apparently serious manner in which the lieutenant governor commands and requires civil officers "to *continue* to exercise jurisdiction as far east as the banks of the Connecticut river," when no New York officer whatever had as yet begun to exercise any jurisdiction over the people of that territory. The New Hampshire charters had conferred corporate authority on the inhabitants of the townships, and they had organized themselves and appointed their local officers in conformity to the laws of that province. No New York judge, justice of the peace, or other officer had ever been appointed within the territory, or had attempted to exercise any authority therein. By New Hampshire these town organizations had been authorized and recognized, and the necessary machinery for the exercise of judicial authority had been provided by the appointment of justices of peace on both sides of the Green mountain.[2]

Prior to this proclamation, one hundred and twenty four of the one hundred and thirty charters granted by Gov. Wentworth had been issued; only six of the whole number bearing date after December, 1763.

---

[1] In the narrative of proceedings on the New Hampshire grants published in behalf of the New York patentees in 1773, a proclamation of Gov. Clinton of July 28, 1753, is referred to as having been a public warning to claimants under New Hampshire; but that proclamation was occasioned by intrusions on Livingston's manor by people from Massachusetts, and it makes no mention of Connecticut river, or of any claim of New York to the eastward of a twenty mile line. It related to riotous proceedings between that line and the Hudson. See *Doc. Hist. N. Y.*, vol. 3, 751, and vol. 4, 753. *Col. Hist. N. Y.*, vol. 8, p. 381.

[2] Samuel Robinson, of Bennington, was one of the justices under New Hampshire, his commission bearing date Feb. 8, 1762.

This proclamation of Lieut. Gov. Colden exciting apprehension and alarm among the settlers, Gov. Wentworth, on the 13th of March following, issued a counter proclamation denying the right of New York to the territory, and affirming that of New Hampshire. It declared the patent to the Duke of York to be obsolete, as a description of the boundaries of New York, and referred to the well known limits of that province and those of Connecticut and Massachusetts as proof that it was inoperative, claimed for New Hampshire the like extent of those two provinces to the westward, denied that the government of New York had ever at any time exercised any jurisdiction eastward to Connecticut river, and stated that if it should be his majesty's pleasure thereafter to alter the jurisdiction, there could be no doubt that "all grants made by New Hampshire that should be fulfilled by the grantees would be confirmed to them." The proclamation of the governor of New Hampshire concluded by exhorting the grantees under that government "to be industrious in clearing and cultivating their lands agreeably to their charters," and by requiring and commanding "all civil officers within the province, of what quality soever, as well those that are not as those that are inhabitants of said lands, to continue and be diligent in exercising jurisdiction in their respective offices, as far westward as grants of land had been made by that government, and to deal with any person or persons, that might presume to interrupt the inhabitants or settlers on said lands, as to law and justice appertained, the pretended right of jurisdiction mentioned in the aforesaid [New York] proclamation notwithstanding." [1]

The proclamation of Gov. Wentworth restored, in a great degree, the confidence of the settlers and grantees under New Hampshire in the soundness of their titles, and rapid emigration from the New England colonies continued until after the proclamation of Lieut. Gov. Colden in the spring of 1765 had announced the king's order, changing the jurisdiction. This latter proclamation contained a copy of the order in council, making Connecticut river the boundary, but was silent in regard to land titles, and the settlers would not at first give credit to rumors that came floating over the territory that the change was to be treated by the government of New York as annulling their charters. The appearance, however, among them of New York surveyors running lines across their cultivated fields and setting up new land marks soon convinced them that their all

[1] *Doc. Hist. N. Y.*, vol. 4, p. 570. *Slade*, 17.

was at stake.[1] And before they could take any steps to propitiate the favor of the New York government, they found most of their valuable lands granted, not to persons who desired to occupy their possessions, but to New York city gentlemen, who wished to make or increase their fortunes by compelling them to purchase their homesteads over again, or by disposing of them to others.

After the assumption by New York of jurisdiction over the New Hampshire grants, under Lieut. Gov. Colden's proclamation of April 10, 1765, the first New York patent of lands which was ostensibly within the limits of the new territory, was that of twenty-six thousand acres called Princetown. This incipient grant bore date May 21, 1765, and being important in itself, as well as characteristic of those which followed, deserves particular notice.

The patent was issued nominally to Isaac Vrooman and twenty-five others for one thousand acres each as tenants in common, but a few weeks after its date all the patentees except Robert Colback (who was perhaps a myth), conveyed their shares to John Taber Kempe, James Duane and Walter Rutherford, all of the city of New York, Kempe being attorney general of the province, Duane a prominent lawyer, and Rutherford a merchant speculator. They were no doubt the real parties for whose benefit the grant was originally made. The tract covered by the patent was one of the most valuable in the territory, comprising the rich valley of the Battenkill. It extended from about a mile west of the present village of Arlington north-easterly through the township, across the corner of Sunderland and through Manchester into Dorset, being about twelve miles in length by an average width of a little more than three miles. It was of irregular shape and had no less than nine angles, the lines being run along the base of the mountains which bounded it on each side, leaving it narrow in the middle where the mountains approached each other, and widest at the ends where the valley is broadest. At the time of this grant there were a large number of settlers occupying lands under the New Hampshire title, in the several townships through which it reached, which

[1] It should be borne in mind that the early grants of New York were not, like those of New Hampshire, in a square or rectangular form, but were made to the patentees in such shape as they chose; the desired quantity of land being run around by the surveyor in such manner as to include the best land, without regard to regularity of form, leaving outside the tract, wherever practicable, all mountains and rocky or other undesirable soil. By this mode of making grants, numerous ill-shaped spaces or gores of unpatented lands were left between different grants.

fact was well known to the granting authority, the description of the land in the patent itself commencing its boundaries "one hundred and six chains to the westward of John Holley's house," one of the settlers, and included the house within its limits. Not only were the rights of the New Hampshire occupants thus insultingly disregarded, but the instructions of the crown, regulating the granting of lands, were also violated in order to enhance the value of the grant to the favored patentees. Those instructions, as has been before seen, required the land commissioners, of whom Mr. Attorney General Kempe was one, to certify that in setting out the tract they had regard to "the profitable and unprofitable acres, so that each grantee might have a proportionable number of one sort and the other, as likewise that the *length of each tract did not extend along* the banks of any river." This certificate was given, though it appeared upon the face of it, copied into the patent, that the tract was in the vicinity of mountains, and that it extended twelve miles in length on both sides of the Batten kill, by about three miles across it.[1]

Besides grants of this class there were others denominated Military grants which were made in compliance with the proclamation of the king, of the 7th of October, 1763. By this proclamation the reduced officers and soldiers of the regular army who had served in America in the late war with France, were to be entitled to grants of land in such of the king's royal provinces as they might prefer in quantities as follows, viz: to one having the rank of a field officer five thousand acres; to a captain, three thousand acres; to a subaltern or staff officer, two thousand acres; to a non-commissioned officer, two hundred acres; and to a private, fifty acres. A large portion of the troops entitled to this bounty were disbanded in New York city, and being principally from Europe, and desirous of returning there, were in general, very ready to dispose of their claims on such terms as were offered them, and nearly all of them went into the hands of speculators. It appears from the report of the New York commissioners for distributing among the land claimants the sum paid by Vermont on the final adjustment of the controversy, that of three hundred and twelve claims presented for military patents, covering over one hundred and seven thousand acres, only five of them, embracing seven thousand four hundred, were in the names of the original patentees or their representatives, the remaining three hun-

[1] *Ante*, p. 167–8. *Albany Records* Patents, vol. 14, p. 66, and *Report of New York Commissioners on Land Claims in Vermont*, 1797, p. 42.

dred and seven claims being brought forward by assignors. Few, if any of the patentees ever undertook to settle personally on their lands.[1]

Other grants immediately followed that of Princetown, and thenceforward patents were issued by Colden, with great rapidity, and with little or no regard to the claims under New Hampshire, until the first day of November following, when their further issue was suddenly stopped by an event which cannot well be passed over without notice.

At nearly the same time with the reception of the order of council annexing the territory of the New Hampshire grants to New York, news arrived in this country of the passage by the British parliament of the famous stamp act. By this act, all important written instruments, including warrants of survey, and grants and conveyances of land, in order to be valid, were required to have affixed to them government stamps, which stamps were to be prepared in England, and distributed and sold by government agents in each of the colonies. This act, which was considered by the colonists as an infringment of their liberties, met with determined opposition and caused great agitation throughout the country. In Massachusetts, Connec-

---

[1] *Ms. Report of N. Y. Coms.*, 1797. *Mrs. Grant's American Lady*, 232–233. Among those who obtained military grants was Duncan McVicar, a staff officer of the fifty-fifth regiment of Scotch Highlanders of the rank of lieutenant, and father of Mrs. Grant, author of an entertaining book entitled *Memoirs of an American Lady*. While her father was in the army during the French war, and for several years afterwards, Mrs. Grant, a child, was an inmate of the family of a worthy aristocratic lady at Albany, whom she designates as "Aunt Schuyler," and to whose memory her book is an affectionate and admiring tribute. Her father was entitled as such officer to two thousand acres of land, and by purchasing, as she says, "for a trifle" the claims of two brother officers, he became the proprietor of four thousand acres more, all of which he caused to be located in a body partly in the township of Shaftsbury and partly in what is now White Creek, N. Y., "the twenty mile line," according to her account, "running exactly through the middle of his property." Her father thus becoming, as his daughter expresses it, "a consequential land holder," resolved, as soon as circumstances would permit, to seat himself upon the tract, and surrounding himself with a dependent tenantry, to found a baronial establishment after the manner of European society. He called his property a township, and gave it the name of Clarendon. Determining "at his leisure to let his lands out on lease," preparatory to his removal to it, he anticipated great enjoyment on his baronial estate. His daughter in her childish fancy, pictured her future home upon it as a real paradise, talking of it as "a sylvan scene," "the vale of bliss"— was constantly "dancing on air" at the thoughts of it, and dwelling on "the simple felicity which was to prevail among the amiable and innocent tenants," of the Manor of Clarendon. But these

ticut and other colonies, the stamp officers were induced by the threats and violence of the people to give up their stamps, and they had then been placed where they were secure against being used. The first day of November 1765 was the time appointed for the act to go into operation. In New York the first day of November came and went, and the stamps were still withheld from the control of the people. On their arrival from England, the stamp distributor, following the example of those in the other provinces, had resigned, refusing to receive them, but Lieut. Gov. Colden had taken them into Fort George, and had obtained a detachment of marines from a ship of war in the harbor, resolving to preserve them by force if necessary, and cause them to be distributed. In the evening of that day a vast torch light procession carrying a scaffold and two images, one of the governor and the other of the devil whispering in his ear, came from the fields, now the park, down Broadway to within eight or ten feet of the fort, knocked at its gate, broke open the governor's coach house, took out his chariot, carried the images upon it round town and returned to burn them with his carriages and sleighs, before his eyes, on the Bowling Green, under the gaze of the garrison on the ramparts, and of all New York gathered about. The next day, it becoming evident that the people were too strong to be successfully

---

fascinating anticipations were not destined to be realized. The people who were rushing to settle on the lands in that region, she says, were "fierce republicans," who refused to become tenants to any one, and insisted on owning the lands they should occupy, whose "whole conversation was tainted with politics — Cromwellian politics," who talked about "slaves to arbitrary power," and whose "indifference to the mother country, and illiberal opinions and manners" were extremely offensive to all loyal subjects of the king. Her father becoming disgusted with the surroundings of his property, unable to obtain a suitable tenantry and alarmed at the spread of republicanism and disloyalty, embarked in the summer of 1770, with his daughter, then about fifteen years old, for his native Scotland. Mrs. Grant carried with her the most embittered feelings towards "the drawling New England republicans" who had blotted out her "paradise of Clarendon," and she vents her indignation against the subsequently formed state of Vermont and its inhabitants, in no measured terms. Lieut. McVicar, his daughter says, "entrusted his lands to the care of John Munro, Esq., then residing near Clarendon, and chief magistrate of that newly peopled district, a very worthy friend and countryman of his own, who was then "in high triumph on account of a fancied conquest over the supporters of the twenty mile line." This triumph, which was probably the decision of the Albany courts against the New Hampshire title, as will appear in the sequel, was but fancied — not real.

Albany Records, Land Papers, vol. 18, p. 111, 139; vol. 19, p. 97. *Mrs. Grant's American Lady*, Appleton's edition, 1846, p. 3, 232-3, 235-7, 239, 241, 247, 255-7, 267, 274, 275, 276.

resisted, Colden gave way, and the stamps were deposited in the City Hall, in the custody of the mayor and corporation.[1]

As all land patents were to be void unless stamped, and as no stamps could be obtained, their issue was necessarily suspended. Up to this time the patents issued by Colden, of lands within the disputed territory, now Vermont, covered over one hundred and seventy-four thousand acres, nearly all of which had been previously granted by New Hampshire. Of this quantity, it is worthy of special notice, that only four thousand acres were lands on the east side of the Green mountain, the remaining one hundred and seventy thousand acres being on the west side. This quantity of four thousand acres comprised the rights of Gov. Benning Wentworth of five hundred acres each in the eight townships of Barnard, Bridgewater, Hartford, Hartland, Pomfret, Springfield, Weathersfield and Woodstock, and was all of it unoccupied.

A sufficient reason for this difference in the location of New York patents on the two sides of the mountain may perhaps be found in the fact that the lands on the east side were at a greater distance from New York, and were much less familiarly known to the city speculators than those on the west side, and were therefore rarely sought for. But there appears also to have been another reason for this difference, of a somewhat peculiar character, which is not undeserving attention.

In 1764, a daughter of the Earl of Ilchester, a British nobleman closely connected with the ministry, to the great disgust of her family, made a clandestine match with one O'Brien, a play actor. To rid themselves as far as possible of the continued mortification of this unfortunate affair, it was deemed advisable by the bride's aristocratic friends, to send the happy couple to America, and to provide for them at the public expense. Orders of the king in council were therefore obtained directing the governor of New York to grant to Lord Ilchester, Lord Holland and a Mr. Upton, sixty thousand acres of land for O'Brien's benefit, and he was also recommended for an important appointment in the New York customs. The place in the customs appears to have been too strongly held by the incumbent to be made available, and O'Brien seems to have been further disappointed in not being permitted to locate his land in the rich valley of the Mohawk, and to have complained of the conduct of Lieut. Gov. Colden in that respect to the lords of trade. In answer to the letter of the board on that subject, Colden wrote to Lord Hillsborough, under date of June 7, 1765, averring that

[1] *Col. His. N. Y.*, vol. 7, p. 771. *Bancroft*, vol. 5, p. 355.

there were no unpatented lands on the Mohawk that could be granted; and after stating that there were large tracts of good and valuable lands on and near Connecticut river subject to grant, added as follows: "I have put off the granting of land in that part of the country until October that I may know my Lord Ilchester and Lord Holland's pleasure as to the location of the king's grant to them." He did accordingly postpone the granting of any of those lands until the close of October, the patents of the four thousand acres, before mentioned, bearing date the 30th of that month. History furnishes numerous instances in which great and important events appear to flow from remote and trifling causes, and perhaps it is not possible to aver with absolute certainty that the settlers under New Hampshire on Connecticut river might not, like those on the Batten kill, have waked up some morning and found the lands they occupied had been granted to others by Gov. Colden, but for the lucky union of a female sprig of the British aristocracy with a vagabond play actor.[1]

It will at all events be perceived that, while the New York government was rapidly disposing of the property of the settlers and grantees of lands on the west side of the Green mountain, those on the other side of the mountain were as yet unmolested; up to this time the injury to them was only prospective.

On the 12th of November, ten days after Colden had surrendered the stamps to the mayor of New York, Sir Henry Moore arrived from England and superseded him in the government of the province. Sir Henry had been lieutenant governor of the Island of Jamaica, where he had shown considerable skill and energy in suppressing a dangerous slave insurrection; in reward for which the order of knighthood and the office of governor of New York had been conferred upon him. Mrs. Grant, who at the time was an inmate of the Schuyler family at Albany, where Governor Moore visited, says of him in her *American Lady* that "like many of his predecessors he was a mere show governor," that "he had never thought of business in his life, but was honorable so far as a man could be who always spent more than he had, was gay, good natured, and well bred, affable and courteous in a very high degree, and if the business of a governor was merely to keep the governed in good humor none was fitter for that office than he."

It may justly be said of him that though well meaning he was indolent and frivolous and addicted to social pleasures and amuse-

---

[1] *Col. Hist. N. Y.*, vol. 7, pp. 741–745. *Calendar of N. Y. Land Papers*, p. 344.

ments, and was consequently in the ordinary affairs of his government influenced and led by those about him.

On learning of the arrival of a new governor, the settlers in the townships of Pownal, Bennington, Shaftsbury, Arlington, Sunderland, Manchester and Danby, resolved to apply to him for relief against the New York claimants. They accordingly appointed Samuel Robinson of Bennington, and Jeremiah French of Manchester, their agents for that purpose, who repaired to New York in the month of December and laid their case before him. He gave them pleasant language, but offered them no protection against the patents of their lands which had already been issued by Colden, nor any effectual security against future grants.

On a change of ministry in England, the stamp act had been repealed in the month of March 1766, information of which reached New York the ensuing May. So much complaint had been made to Sir Henry Moore by the settlers under New Hampshire, of the conduct of his predecessor in granting their lands to others, and so much difficulty seemed likely to arise in consequence, that he thought it advisable to have an order of his council made and published, allowing three months from the 6th of June, for persons claiming under such grants to appear and produce evidence of their titles, in which order it was declared that on their failure to do so their claims were to be rejected, "and the petitions already preferred for said lands forthwith proceeded on." [1]

In consequence of this order, petitions were presented to Gov. Moore by the proprietors of a considerable number of the townships granted by New Hampshire, for a confirmation of their charters, and verbal negotiations were entered into in relation to many more. But the expense of obtaining the confirmation of a township charter, which included not only enormous patent fees but also the cost of a new survey which was always required, was found to be so great as to render it impossible for most of them to comply. This was the more difficult and oppressive on the west side of the Green mountain, where there was scarcely a township in which grants of more or less extent had not already been made by Colden and generally of the best lands, leaving only the poorer and less valuable subject to confirmation. The settlers had in general, been farmers and mechanics at their former homes, in moderate circumstances, or the sons of such persons. They had expended their small fortunes in acquiring the New Hampshire title, in preparing for the settlement, and in improvement of their lands, and they were absolutely unable to meet this additional demand.

[1] *N. Y. Doc. Hist.*, vol. 4, p. 584, 587. *N. Y. Land Papers*, vol. 19, p. 28.

CHAPTER IX.

Application of the Settlers to the Crown for Relief, and Order in Council in their Favor.

1766 - 1767.

Samuel Robinson agent of the settlers to present their petition to the king — Copy of their petition — Their case stated more in detail by one from Samuel Robinson prepared in England — Another presented by the society for the propagation of the gospel — Letter of censure from Lord Shelburne to Gov. Moore, enclosing the two petitions — Gov. Moore's reply — Order of the king in council of July 24, 1767, forbidding further grants by New York of the controverted lands — Mr. Robinson's death in London — End of Gov. Moore's administration.

THERE being no longer any hope of relief from the government of New York, the claimants under New Hampshire resolved to appeal for redress of their grievances to the conscience of the king. A petition was accordingly prepared and signed by over one thousand of the settlers and grantees, and Samuel Robinson, Esq., was appointed their agent to repair to England and lay it before his majesty. Mr. Robinson had emigrated from Hardwick, Mass., to Bennington, in 1761, and had held the office of justice of the peace under New Hampshire from February, 1762. He had served as captain in the troops of Massachusetts in the French war during several campaigns, and was at the head of his company in the battle of lake George, in September, 1755, when the French were defeated by Generals Johnson and Lyman. Although about sixty years of age, he was active, intelligent, enterprising and energetic, and of an unblemished moral and religious character, and he could not be considered as wholly unsuited to the responsible position to which he had been assigned.

William Samuel Johnson, an eminent lawyer and statesman of Connecticut, was then preparing to leave for England, as agent for that colony to the home government, and the petitioners employed him to assist Mr. Robinson in his mission. They sailed in the same vessel from New York, the 25th of December, 1766, and landed at Falmouth, England, the 30th of January following, and reached London a few days afterwards.[1]

---

[1] Mr. Johnson's Manuscript Diary, in possession of his grandson and namesake at Stratford, Conn.

The petition of which Mr. Robinson was the bearer was couched in the following terms :

" *To the king's most excellent majesty. The humble petition of the several subscribers hereto, your majesty's most loyal subjects, sheweth to your majesty :*

" That we obtained at considerable expense of your majesty's governor of the province of New Hampshire, grants and patents for more than one hundred townships in the western parts of the said supposed province ; and being about to settle the same, many of us, and others of us, having actually planted ourselves on the same, were disagreeably surprised and prevented from going on with the further intended settlements, by the news of its having been determined by your majesty in council that those lands were within the province of New York, and by a proclamation issued by Lieut. Gov. Colden in consequence thereof, forbidding any further settlement until patents of confirmation should be obtained from the governor of New York. Whereupon we applied to the governor of said province of New York to have the same lands confirmed to us in the same manner as they had been at first granted to us by the governor of the said province of New Hampshire ; when, to our utter astonishment, we found the same could not be done without our paying as fees of office for the same at the rate of twenty-five pounds New York money, equal to about fourteen pounds sterling, for every thousand acres of said lands, amounting to about three hundred and thirty pounds sterling at a medium, for each of said townships, and which will amount in the whole to about thirty-three thousand pounds sterling, besides a quit rent of two shillings and sixpence sterling for every hundred acres of said lands ; and which being utterly unable to do and perform, we find ourselves reduced to the sad necessity of losing all our past expense and advancements ; and many of us being reduced to absolute poverty and want, having expended our all in making said settlements.

" Whereupon your petitioners beg leave most humbly to observe.

" 1. That when we applied for and obtained said grants of said lands, the same were and had been at all times fully understood and reported to lie and be within the said province of New Hampshire, and were within the power of the governor of that province to grant ; so that your petitioners humbly hope they are equitably entitled to a confirmation of the said grants to them.

" 2. The said grants were made and received on the moderate terms of your petitioner's paying as a quit rent *one shilling* only, proclamation money, equal to *nine pence* sterling per hundred acres ; and which induced us to undertake to settle said township throughout, and thereby to form a full and compacted country of people, whereas the imposing the said *two shillings* and *six pence* sterling per hundred acres will occasion all the more rough and unprofitable parts of said lands not to be taken up; but pitches, and the more valuable parcels only to be laid out, to the utter preventing the full and proper settlement of said country, and in the whole to the lessening your majesty's revenue.

"3. Your humble petitioners conceive, that the insisting to have large and very exorbitant fees of office to arise and be computed upon every thousand acres in every township of six or perhaps more miles square, and that when one patent, one seal and one step only of every kind, towards the completing such patents of confirmation respectively is necessary, is without all reasonable and equitable foundation, and must and will necessarily terminate in the totally preventing your petitioners obtaining the said lands, and so the same will fall into the hands of the rich, to be taken up, the more valuable parts only as aforesaid, and those perhaps not entered upon and settled for many years to come; while your petitioners with their numerous and helpless families, will be obliged to wander far and wide to find where to plant themselves down, so as to be able to live.

"Whereupon your petitioners most humbly and earnestly pray, that your majesty will be graciously pleased to take their distressed state and condition into your royal consideration, and order that we have our said lands confirmed and acquitted to us on such reasonable terms, and in such way and manner as your majesty shall think fit.

"*Further*, we beg leave to say, that if it might be consistent with your majesty's royal pleasure, we shall esteem it a very great favor and happiness, to have said townships put and continued under the jurisdiction of the government of the said province of New Hampshire, as at the first, as every emolument and convenience both public and private, are in your petitioners' humble opinion, clearly and strongly on the side of such connection with the said New Hampshire province. All which favors, or such and so many of them as to your majesty shall seem meet to grant, we humbly ask; or that your majesty will in some other way, grant relief to your petitioners; and they, as in duty bound, shall ever pray.

"*Dated* in New England, November, 1766; and in the seventh year of his majesty's reign." [1]

---

[1] *Doc. Hist. of N. Y.*, vol. 4, p. 1027. The original petition with most of the signatures, found among the papers of Mr. Johnson, is preserved in the office of the secretary of state at Montpelier.

After the arrival of Mr. Robinson in England, it was deemed advisable to present the case of the New Hampshire claimants to his majesty in greater detail than it had been stated in the foregoing petition. A new petition was therefore drawn up by Mr. Johnson, giving a more particular statement of their grievances, which being subscribed by Mr. Robinson "in behalf of himself and more than one thousand other grantees," was delivered to Lord Shelburne, principal secretary of state for the colonies, the 20th of March, to be laid before his majesty in council. A petition was also presented about the same time by "the society for the propagation of the gospel in foreign parts," to which one right of three hundred and fifty acres had been granted in each of the charters of Gov. Wentworth, and which also had an indirect interest in another right in each township "for a glebe for the church of England." [1]

The New York grants not being by townships, but to individuals in *pitches*, as they were termed in New England, did not reserve any right to the society, or indeed for any public or charitable purpose whatever.

The immediate action of the king in council upon these petitions is stated in a letter of sharp rebuke from Lord Shelburne to Gov. Moore, which is as follows:

"White Hall April 11, 1767.

"Sir: Two petitions having been most humbly presented to the king in council, one by the incorporated society for the propagation of the gospel, and the other by Samuel Robinson, of Bennington, in behalf of himself and more than one thousand other grantees of lands on the west side of Connecticut river, under certain grants issued by Benning Wentworth, Esq., governor of New Hampshire, and praying for redress in several very great grievances therein set forth, lest there should be any further proceedings in this matter till such time as the council shall have examined into the grounds of it, I am to signify to you his majesty's commands that you make no new grants of those lands, and that you do not molest any person in the quiet possession of his grant, who can produce good and valid deeds for such grant under the seal of the province of New Hampshire until you receive further orders respecting them.

"In my letter of the 11th of December, I was very explicit upon the point of *former grants*. You are therein directed 'to take care that the inhabitants lying westward of the line reported by the board

[1] *Mr. Johnson's Diary* and *ante*.

of trade as the boundary of the two provinces be not molested on account of territorial differences, or disputed jurisdiction for *whatever province* the settlers may be found to belong to, it should make no difference in their property, provided that their titles to their lands should be found good in other respects, or that they have long been in the uninterrupted possession of them.

"His majesty's intentions are so clearly expressed to you in the above paragraph, that I cannot doubt of your having immediately upon receipt of it removed any cause of those complaints which the petitioners set forth. If not, it is the king's express command that it may be done without the smallest delay. The power of granting lands was vested in the governors of the colony, originally for the purpose of accommodating, not distressing settlers, especially the poor and industrious. Any perversion of that power therefore, must be highly derogatory, both from the dignity of their stations and from the disinterested character which a governor ought to support, and which his majesty expects from every person honored by him with his commission. The unreasonableness of obliging a very large tract of country to pay a *second time* the immense sum of thirty-three thousand pounds in fees, according to the allegations of this petition, for no other reason than its being found necessary to settle the line of boundary between the colonies in question, is so unjustifiable that his majesty is not only determined to have the strictest inquiry made into the circumstances of the charge, but expects the clearest and fullest answer to every part of it.

I am, etc.,

SHELBURNE." [1]

Sir Henry Moore, Bart.

With this letter were transmitted copies of the petitions of Mr. Robinson and of the propagation society, which however are not preserved in the public archives at Albany, nor have copies been found in print. Our only knowledge of their contents is derived from the replies made to them by Gov. Moore, contained in several elaborate letters to Lord Shelburne dated the 9th and 10th of June, and published in the 7th volume of the Colonial History of New York, and also in the 4th volume of the Documentary History.

Gov. Moore in his reply expresses much "concern and astonishment" at his lordship's letter, and great indignation at the presumption of Mr. Robinson, in making "free with the characters of his

[1] *Col. Hist. of N. Y.*, vol. 7, p. 917. *Doc. Hist. N. Y.*, vol. 4, p. 589.

12

majesty's governors," a man, he says, whose "service in the late war was nothing more than that of driving an ox cart for sutlers," and who thus following "one of the lowest and meanest occupations, at once sets himself up for a statesman, and from a notion that the wheels of government are as easily managed as those of a waggon, takes upon himself to direct the king's ministers in their departments." And he adds in the way of irony, "as for my part I have been taught to treat with so much respect, those whom his majesty is pleased to honor with his confidence, that I am persuaded they will do that which is best for his service and the good of the people, without standing in need of such able counselors as *Mr. Robinson*, or myself."

In regard to Mr. Robinson, it is unnecessary to repeat what has already been stated in the beginning of this chapter. His character was without reproach, and his standing highly respectable. The muster rolls now in the office of the secretary of the commonwealth of Massachusetts, for 1755 and 1756, show that he was a captain of a company in Col. Ruggles's regiment of provincials, and served as such on the frontier in both of those years, and that he was in the battle of Lake George. The rolls of his company also contain the names of several of those who, afterwards, emigrated with him from Hardwick to Bennington.

In preparing his answer to Mr. Robinson's petition, Sir Henry Moore availed himself of the assistance of James Duane, Esq., who he says "is a barrister at law here, and a man of so good character, that his testimony carries the greatest weight with it." As we shall often have occasion hereafter to mention the name of Mr. Duane, it is proper to say of him now that he was a prominent lawyer of New York city — that at the commencement of the troubles with the mother country, he belonged to the class of New York conservative whigs, was a member of the Continental congress, from that state during most of the revolutionary period, was afterwards mayor of the city of New York, and a judge of the United States district court, and died in 1797. He had married in early life, the daughter of Robert Livingston, the proprietor of Livingston's manor, and he thus became associated in interest and feeling with the landed aristocracy of the province, whose leading ideas in regard to the soil of the country, appear to have been, that it was formed by the Creator, to be subdued and worked by the mass of mankind for the benefit of a class of lordly proprietors, and that the ownership by an individual of only so much of the earth as he could actually cultivate, would be an infringement of the laws of the divine economy. We have already seen that he was the proprietor of one third of twenty-six thousand acres in the first grant made by Colden in Vermont. He afterwards became the owner under the New York title of nearly fifty thousand acres more, thirty-nine thousand acres of which were the military claims of officers and soldiers of which he had by purchase become the assignee. He was the acknowledged leader and champion of the New York speculators in Vermont lands, was their attorney and counselor in the institution and prosecution of the numerous ejectment suits brought against the settlers, and was the author of most of the official and unofficial papers and documents in favor of the New York title during the whole period of the controversy. He could therefore, be considered in any other light, than that of an impartial adviser of the governor in relation to the character and rights of the New Hampshire claimants.[1]

With the aid of Mr. Duane, Gov. Moore was enabled to make a somewhat plausible, but by no means a very clear and satisfactory answer to Mr. Robinson's petition. In relation to the grants which had already been made of lands in the occupation of the settlers, he referred to an order of the New York council of the 22d of May, 1765, requiring the surveyor general not to return surveys of lands thus occupied to other persons than the occupants; but neglected to state, as the truth was, that the order had been wholly disregarded. He also referred to two instances of large grants to New Yorkers in which the lands possessed by several New Hampshire claimants had, as he said, been excepted out to the extent of two hundred acres to each person.

In regard to the application for confirmation of the charters of ninety-six townships he disposes of twenty-one of them in quite a summary manner, by declaring that "they were deemed to be within this government before his majesty's order in council fixing the limits on Connecticut river, as they were within twenty miles of Hudson's river *and within the same distance of the waters of South bay and Lake Champlain*," thus marking out an eastern boundary line for New York between Lake Champlain and Connecticut river, which had never before been heard of. The twenty mile line, whether recognized as a boundary or not, had always been treated as having its northern termination at the south end of the lake. Having thus shown, as he would be understood, that these townships situated on the west side of the Green mountain are not entitled to

[1] *Memoir of Duane, in Doc. Hist. N. Y.*, vol. 4, p. 1061. *Ms. Journal of N. Y. Coms.*, p. 1797. *Life of John Adams*, vol. 2, p. 349, 354, 357. *Gordon's Am. Rev.*, vol. 2, p. 119, 120, London edition.

confirmation on any terms, he speaks of the residue as mostly unoccupied, and of those that were occupied, as having fewer settlers on them than had been stated by Mr. Robinson. He also undertakes to weaken the equity of the claims of the New Hampshire grantees by affirming that their expenses in obtaining their charters, were much less than they pretended.

Upon the important subject of patent fees the governor is very far from being explicit. He does not assert that the New Hampshire charters would have been confirmed on the payment of any less sum than that stated in the petition, though he evidently wishes it to be so inferred. He declares that he had "never made a *demand* for fees of any kind either from Mr. Robinson or any person living," but had always "thought himself happy in having an opportunity in remitting them," to those he "apprehended would be distressed in paying them." This was however a mere evasive flourish. He admits that he had received fees for the six patents of the New Hampshire lands which he had already passed, which, if according to the bill he had transmitted to the lords of trade the preceding February, must have been at a still higher rate than that stated by Mr. Robinson. According to Mr. Colden, Sir Henry exceeded him in the pertinacity with which he exacted the payment of fees. In relation to the six patents, before mentioned, he says, in a letter to the colonial secretary of the 4th of January, 1770, that he, Colden, had prepared patents for the confirmation of several townships, and had agreed with the proprietors to accept such proportion of the regular fees as they might choose to pay, which induced them "to take the necessary steps for obtaining the new grants," but that he "was prevented from putting the seal to any of them by the arrival of Sir Henry Moore." He then says that Sir Henry "afterwards took his full fees for one of those grants which had been very near ready for the seals before he came," and he was told "refused to pass any without his full fees were paid." This he says, "gave great disgust to the people, and occasioned those applications which have since been made to the king on the subject." Upon this point there is indeed no doubt of the truth of the statement in Mr. Robinson's petition.[1]

The residue of Gov. Moore's reply to Lord Shelburne is principally taken up in an account of measures which he had adopted for the benefit of the newly acquired territory, among the most prominent of which was a plan he had "determined to engage in personally,"

---

[1] *Doc. Hist. N. Y.*, vol. 4, p. 590 to 608, and 620-1. *Col. Hist. N. Y.*, vol. 7, p. 921-926.

for the encouragement of a settlement in the north eastern part of that district. His plan, which he says had been approved by the council, was "to have a township laid out to himself and some others associated with him, at twelve miles distance from the north line of the new county of Cumberland, and on a spot neither granted by New Hampshire nor claimed by any persons whatever, to be distributed out to poor families in small farms, on condition that they should begin upon the manufacture of potash and the culture of hemp," and upon the production of certain quantities of these articles yearly, "the fee of the land was to be rested absolutely in the possessors with no rents or profits reserved to himself." He says that as soon as these terms were made known "applications were made by different persons for grants, and no less than fourteen families were already settled on it, and that he had had proposals for ten more then living in town (New York) who would settle there in the course of the summer, besides several others, as well from Connecticut as Massachusetts bay, so that there was the greatest probability of a considerable settlement being made there in a very short space of time." "But," he continues, "as the giving of lands alone to those people was not sufficient without other assistance, I have at their request ordered a saw mill and grist mill to be built for their use, and as there is no building in that part of the country yet appropriated for divine worship, I have directed a church to be built at my sole expense in the center of the township, and shall set apart a large farm as a glebe for the incumbents." "Those measures" he adds "will contribute greatly to the peopling of that part of the province," etc., etc. Now all this, no doubt, appeared very well when read by the lords of trade in London, but like many settlements of more modern date the improvements were only *on paper*. The township described was situated on Connecticut river, and is now known as Bradford. Its settlement had been commenced as early as 1765, prior to the arrival of Governor Moore in New York; but either from dislike to the terms imposed by him on the settlers, or from distrust of his promises, its progress was so tardy that the township six years afterwards, in 1771, contained only ten families. A large portion of the "fourteen families already settled on it," if ever there, had departed; the ten families from New York city as well as "the several others from Connecticut and Massachusetts," had remained at home, and neither the saw mill, the grist mill or the church which Governor Moore was "at his sole expense" to build, had ever been erected; and the "large farm" which was to be "set apart for a glebe for the incumbent" was never more heard of. On the 3d of May, 1770, after Governor Moore's death, the township by the name of Mooretown, containing twenty-five thousand acres, was granted by Colden to William Smith the historian, in the name of himself and twenty-four others, he agreeing to convey three thousand acres of it to persons in the occupancy of some of its lands. The residue of the township was afterwards deeded by Smith to his son-in-law John Plenderleaf of Scotland, perhaps as his wife's marriage portion, by which he was enabled to obtain about eleven hundred dollars of the thirty thousand paid by Vermont to New York, on the final settlement of the controversy. There is no doubt that the course taken by Governor Moore was of serious injury to the prosperity of the town. Most of the land was taken up by pitches, and troublesome contentions arose and continued among the settlers for many years, which were only terminated in 1791, by a grant by Vermont of the township to three trustees to be conveyed by them to those persons they should deem entitled to the ownership.[1]

Governor Moore also in a separate letter comments at some length upon the petition of "the society for the propagation of the gospel," but his answer to it is very general in its terms, and contains nothing requiring special attention.

These elaborate replies to the petitions of Mr. Robinson and the society, did not produce any change in the determination of the crown, expressed in Lord Shelburne's letter of the 11th of April; and on the 24th of July following, upon a report of the case by the lords of trade, a formal order of the king in council was made, commanding the governor of New York, "upon pain of his majesty's highest displeasure" to make no grant whatever of any part of the controverted lands, "until his majesty's further pleasure should be known concerning the same." [2]

---

[1] *Doc. Hist. N. Y.*, vol. 4, pp. 595, 596. *Ms. Journal of N. Y. Coms.*, 1797, *Thompson's Gazetteer of Vt., Bradford. Demming's Vt., Bradford. Smith's Hist. N. Y.*, vol. 1, p. xx. *Journal Vt. Assembly*, Oct. 23, 1781. *Hall's E. Vt.*, 123. According to Hall's Eastern Vermont (p. 123–4) the town was patented to John French and others, Nov. 7, 1766, and afterwards on the death of French to Mr. Smith and his associates. This is an error. There was no patent to French. He merely petitioned for the land for himself and associates without naming them, estimating the quantity at twenty-four thousand acres. Smith and his associates in their petition March 28, 1770, state that French is dead and that "the petitioners were the persons intended to be chiefly benefited by French's application." Thus it seems the settlers under Governor Moore, if there were any, had no title but only his promise. *Albany Land Papers*, vol. 22, p. 39, and vol. 27, p. 4. *Patent Records*, vol. 14.

[2] *Doc. Hist. N. Y.*, vol. 4, p. 609. For a copy of the order, see also Appendix, No. 5.

These measures of the king and his ministry were highly favorable to the New Hampshire grantees and settlers, recognizing as they did, in the fullest manner the equity and justice of their claims, and strongly condemning the oppressive conduct of the New York government towards them. Still their New Hampshire titles remained unconfirmed, and the New York grants of their lands, which had already been made, had not been declared inoperative. It was evident that no certain remedy for the past or security for the future had been obtained, though there was much ground of hope for both. Mr. Robinson, in a letter to his family, written in August, appears confident that the whole of the privy council were of opinion that the New Hampshire grantees ought not to be disturbed by New York patents, though they differed in regard to the mode in which a remedy should be furnished. Lord Shelburne, the colonial secretary, John Pownal, secretary of the board of trade, and the Archbishop of Canterbury, were active and firm friends and willing to grant speedy relief by the action of the crown; but Lord Northington, the president of the council, who was old, gouty and irritable, and averse to any further hearing before that body, insisted that the parties should be left to seek their remedy at law, by instituting suits in the New York courts, with perhaps an ultimate appeal to the king in council. This opposition of Lord Northington, together with the interference of other matters, in which the council was almost constantly engaged, seemed likely to prevent the further consideration of the subject for a long period; and Mr. Robinson, who began to feel seriously the want of pecuniary means to continue his stay in London, and to prosecute his business with advantage, determined to return home, leaving the interests of his constituents in the charge of Mr. Johnson. But before he was ready to embark he was so unfortunate to take the small pox, from which he died in London, the 27th of October. Mr. Johnson, in communicating the intelligence of his decease to his widow, under date of November 2, 1767, says of him: " He is much lamented by his friends and acquaintances which were many. You may rest assured no care or expense was spared for his comfort and to save his life, had it been consistent with the designs of Providence. After his death, as the last act of friendship to his memory, I took care to furnish him a decent funeral, at which General Lyman and other gentlemen here from America attended with me as mourners. He is interred in the burial ground belonging to Mr. Whitefield's church, where he usually attended public worship."

There is no doubt that a serious obstacle in the way of a speedy and successful prosecution of Mr. Robinson's mission, was the want of pecuniary means, which from the poverty and scattered situation of the New Hampshire claimants, they were not in a condition to furnish. In his letters to his family, he speaks of "the great expense of living in London," of his being in want of money, and being obliged to borrow; and says, "it is hard to make men believe the truth where there is ready money on the other side." Mr. Johnson in a letter to John Wendell dated the next month after Mr. Robinson's death, attributes the failure of complete success principally to this cause. He says, "the real poverty of those who joined Capt. Robinson, rendered them unable to give the cause that effectual support, which was necessary to give it proper weight, and render the application to the crown as regular and respectable as its importance and the usual course of proceedings in cases of this kind justly required. Money has, in fact, been wanting to do justice to this cause. It came here rather in *forma pauperis*, which is an appearance seldom made or much regarded in this country; and is by no means an eligible light in which to place an affair of this kind."

Mr. Johnson remained in England as agent for the colony of Connecticut until 1771, and some further applications from the New Hampshire claimants to the crown were made through him, but without important results.

Before Mr. Robinson died, he obtained, he says, in one of his letters, the best advice in his power in regard to the conduct to be pursued by the settlers, which he proceeds to say was "to fulfill the duty required in your grants made by Wentworth that are not yet meddled with by New York, for if Wentworth's charters should not be held good, then the land would be the king's, and he never dispossessed any settlers. And where New York has made grants, give up no possession till they come in course of law, and then apply for a special jury for the trial of each case, and if the request is refused, it will be better for us here to have the application made to both the judges and the governor." This advice was made to the settlers and was the guide of their future conduct.

Gov. Moore, in obedience to the king's order in council, ceased at once to make grants of lands within the territory which had been claimed by New Hampshire, and ever afterwards complied with its requirements. This order of the king forbidding in such strong and decided terms the further interference of the New York government with the New Hampshire charters, inspired additional confidence of the grantees in their titles, and operated to promote the extension of their settlements. On the other hand it tended greatly to discourage the claimants under the New York patents, and though some of them brought suits in ejectment against the settlers, few, if any, of them were brought to trial, and the occupants remained in quiet possession of their lands during the continuance of Gov. Moore's administration, which, however, terminated abruptly by his death the 11th of September, 1769.[1]

---

[1] Mr. Johnson's Diary and his Manuscript letters — also Manuscript letters of Mr. Robinson to his family. Petition of the widow Robinson to Vermont assembly, Oct. session, 1780. *Journal of Assembly,* Nov. 2, 1780.

CHAPTER X.

VIOLATION OF THE KING'S ORDER OF JULY, 1767, BY THE NEW YORK GOVERNORS.

1769-1775.

New and erroneous construction of the king's order in council of July 24, 1767, by Colden. The order incorporated into the standing instructions to the governor and in force till the revolution — Colden's grants violating it — Gov. Dunmore — His character and quarrel with Colden — His fraudulent grant to himself — Gov, Tryon, his character and his grants, including one to himself — His visit to England, and Colden's grants in his absence — All the governors disregard the king's order and instructions, and are repeatedly censured therefor by the Board of Trade and the ministry — Quantity of Vermont lands granted by New York — Tryon's proceedings in England, and his return after the commencement of the revolutionary war.

THE decease of Sir Henry Moore brought Mr. Colden again to the head of affairs, and he immediately adopted new measures in regard to the controverted territory. The order of the king in council, of the 24th of July, 1767, had been construed by Sir Henry Moore, to forbid the making of any grants whatever, within the district of country which had been formerly claimed by New Hampshire, and such was its natural construction. The petition of Mr. Robinson, in behalf of his constituents to the king, had not only asked for relief against against New York patents, but also to have the jurisdiction of the territory restored to New Hampshire, the object of the crown being to prevent any further complication of the controversy until the whole subject should be fully investigated and determined. The subject of the report of the board of trade, on which the order was founded, was "the lands lying on the west side of Connecticut river," which "on the 20th of July, 1764, had been declared by his majesty to be within the government of New York," and the order prohibited the making "*of any grants whatever of any part* of the land described in said report." Mr. Colden, however, under the temptation of increased patronage and fees, did not hesitate to give it a different construction.

On the 20th, of October 1769, a few weeks after the death of Governor Moore, a formal opinion from his council was obtained that the order prohibited only the granting of such lands as had actually been granted by the government of New Hampshire, and did not extend to any part of the said lands which had not been granted by that government." He was, however soon apprised that he had mistaken the sense of the order, as intended and understood by his superiors in England, by a letter from Lord Hillsborough, the colonial secretary, dated December 9, 1769, in which he says: "I likewise think fit to send you a copy of his majesty's order in council, of the 24th, of July 1767, forbidding *any grants to be made of lands annexed to New York* by his majesty's determination of the boundary of that colony and New Hampshire," adding an injunction that he should not "on any pretence, presume to act contrary thereto." The receipt of this letter was acknowledged by Colden under date of the 24th, of February following. Indeed, he must have been previsously aware that the order was designed to embrace the whole territory, for his predecessor had repeatedly written to the colonial secretary on the subject, and had forwarded him petitions from applicants for grants of land within the district, that did not interfere with claims under New Hampshire, but without effect, of which Mr. Colden was, no doubt well informed.[1]

The intentions of the king in making the order and the earnest injunctions of his ministry were however disregarded by Mr. Colden, and he proceeded at once to make grants of the prohibited lands, as fast as applicants were ready to pay the patent fees; and his successor, if not himself, made grants, indiscriminately, as well of lands which were embraced in New Hampshire charters as those were not, the order being thus wholly disregarded, as will be more fully seen hereafter.

As this order of July 1767 has an important bearing upon the whole controversy which followed, it is proper to state here, that it remained in force during the whole colonial period, though very generally violated by all the governors. That there might be no excuse for disregarding the order, or any doubt about its construction, it was, on the 7th of February 1771, incorporated into the standing instructions of the king to his New York governors, being the 49th article of those instructions, in the following words, viz:

"49th. Whereas we thought fit by our order in council, of the 20th of July, 1764, to declare that the western banks of the river Connecticut, from where it enters the province of Massachusetts bay as far north as the forty-fifth degree of northern latitude should be the boundary between the provinces of New York and New

---

[1] *Col. Hist. N. Y.* vol. 8, p. 193, 106. *Doc. Hist. N. Y.* vol. 4, p. 609, 610, 611, 612. Appendix No. 4.

Hampshire; and whereas we have further thought fit by our order in council of July 24, 1767, to declare that no part of the lands lying on the western side of the Connecticut, *within that district heretofore claimed by our province of New Hampshire*, should be granted until our further pleasure should be known, concerning the same. It is therefore our will and pleasure that you do take effectual care for the observance of said order in council, and that you do not upon pain of our highest displeasure, presume to make any grant whatever, or pass any warrant of survey of any part of the said lands, until our further will and pleasure shall be signified to you concerning the same." [1]

These instructions were laid before the New York council, the 24th of July, 1771, by Gov. Tryon, and entered on its minutes.

This period of Lieut Gov. Colden's administration, which began in September, 1769, continued a little more than a year, terminating the 18th of October, 1770, by the arrival of Lord Dunmore, the new governor. During this time Mr. Colden had so industriously prosecuted the business of making land grants, that his patents covered not less than six hundred thousand acres of government lands. During the whole period of nearly four years of Sir. Henry Moore's administration, his patents, besides those which were in confirmation of the New Hampshire charters, did not exceed twenty thousand acres. Besides the vast amount of fees which Colden had derived from these grants, he had contrived to reserve to himself, in the names of others, over twenty thousand acres of the lands he had granted, and had moreover provided liberally in lands for the several members of his family.[2]

The new governor, John Murray, Earl of Dunmore, was a needy Scottish peer, passionate and unscruplous in rapacity, who had come to this country to amass a fortune, and during his whole administration every other consideration appears to have been sacrificed to that object. Immediately on his arrival in the colony a quarrel arose between him and Colden, which is quite charactristic of both.

Colden had hurried through his office, the land patents before mentioned and others of lands in other parts of the province, in order that the premature arrival of a successor might not deprive him of the office fees, and had thus obtained the large sum of not less than ten thousand pounds, New York currency, equal to $25,000.

---

[1] *New York Council Minutes* for July 24, 1771. *Col. Hist. N. Y.*, vol. 8, p. 331.

[2] *Albany Records Land Patents* vols. 14 and 15. *Military Grants*, vol. 2. *Report of N. Y. Com.*, 1797, p, iii, -113.

This sum, which had been thus clutched by Colden, was equally craved by Dunmore; and in order to secure it, or at least a portion of it, he had procured from Lord Hillsborough an order, directing Colden to account for and pay over to him one-half of the emoluments of his office, from the date of his, (Dunmore's) commission, which was Jan. 2, 1770, nearly ten months prior to his arrival in the colony. Colden declined to pay and applied to Lord Hillsborough by letter, to reconsider and reverse the order. Whereupon Dunmore caused a suit to be instituted before himself as chancellor, in the name of the king, for its recovery for his own benefit. He had the shameless effrontery to hear the case solemnly argued by counsel and to prepare for deciding it in his own favor, but after one or two postponements of the time which he had fixed for that purpose, finding that his decree would be appealed from, to the king in council, where it was sure that the case would be dismissed, on the ground that he as chancellor had no jurisdiction, he finally left it undecided, and fortunate Colden continued to pocket the money.[1]

Dunmore had been but a few weeks in the colony, before he was appointed to the governorship of Virginia, but he had acquired a knowledge of the New York fee bill, and was too well pleased with his lucrative position to abandon it in haste; and he continued to exercise the offiee of chief magistrate of that colony until the arrival of Sir Wm. Tryon, his successor, in July, 1771. He, indeed, lingered in the province some months longer probably endeavoring to exchange governments with Tryon, for which he seems to have had the assent of the ministry, but Tryon and he failed to agree on the terms of the trade, and the bargain fell through. During the eight months of Dunmore's administration, he had been able to grant to speculators four hundred and fifty thousand acres of Vermont lands and to receive the fees for the same, and also by his own grant to himself, in the names of others, to become the proprietor of fifty-one thousand acres more. This grant will serve to show the cool, unblushing manner in which the instructions of the king were violated, by the New York governors, and how readily their frauds on the public were countenanced and participated in by the officers of government and other prominent individuals. The land appears to have been petitioned for by one Alexander McLure, in behalf of himself and fifty associates, not naming them, stating that there was a vacant tract of land near Otter creek, of fifty-one thousand

---

[1] *Judge Daley's Sketch of New York Judicial Proceedings*, p. 45. *Col. Hist. N. Y.*, vol. 8, p. 209, 249, 256, 257.

acres of which he and his associates were desirous of obtaining a patent "intending to cultivate and improve the same." The application being laid before the council, and approved, a patent was issued to McLure and fifty other persons by name on the 8th day of July, 1771, the very day on which Dunmore surrendered his office to Tryon his successor. Five days afterwards, on the 13th of the same July, every one of the patentees conveyed their shares to Dunmore who in the name of the king had issued the patent to them. Among the patentees who thus voluntarily united in the fraud were Alexander Colden, son of Lieut. Gov. Colden, and surveyor general of the province, Andrew Elliot the receiver general, Hugh Wallace and Henry White, members of the council, Edward Foy, Dunmore's private secretary, Goldsbrow Banyer, clerk of the council and deputy secretary of the province, Hugh Gaine, the public printer, Whitehead Hicks, mayor of the city of New York, and a long list of land speculators holding patents for, from fifteen thousand to one hundred thousand acres each, among whom were Simon Metcalf, John Bowles, John Kelly, Crean Brush, and James Duane. The land described in the patent was situated in the present county of Addison, and was a tract some twelve or thirteen miles in length from north to south, by six or seven in width, lying principally in the east side of Otter creek, in the townships of Leicester, Salisbury, and Middlebury, embracing within its limits the lake which bears the name of the grantor; but reaching across the creek into the townships of Whiting and Cornwall. All the land included in the patent had been previously granted by New Hampshire. The granting of the land, as has been seen, was prohibited by the king's order of the 24th of July, 1767, even upon the limited construction given it by Colden; and the grant being thus made without authority of the crown, was unquestionably void in law for that reason, and would have been declared so by any competent and impartial judicial tribunal having power to determine it.[1]

It may be added in further notice of Lord Dunmore, that he went to Virginia in 1772, where he was charged with seeking to weaken the colonies in their resistance to the arbitrary measures of the mother country, by promoting a territorial controversy between

[1] *Col. Hist. N. Y.*, vol. 8, p. 278, 209, 323, 221, 148, 149, 188, 694. *Report N. Y. Com.*, 1797. *Albany Records Patents*, vols. 15 & 16. *Military grants*, vol. 2. *Deeds*, vol. 19, p. 3. That Lord Dunmore was well aware that the prohibitory order was still in force is apparent from several letters of his to Lord Hillsborough, vainly asking to have it rescinded. *Col. Hist. N. Y.*, 252, 259, 261, vol. 8.

Virginia and Pennsylvania, and by exciting a slave insurrection and an Indian attack upon the back settlements. When hostilities began in New England, he fled from his capital, on board the Foway man of war, and for several months amused himself by committing depredations about the harbors and rivers of his province, ending his achievements by the burning of Norfolk, whence he retired with his plunder to St. Augustine, Florida. He is said to have died in England in 1809.[1]

Sir William Tryon, the successor of Dunmore, had spent his early life in the army, and was fond of parade and display. His manners and address were dignified and pleasing, wearing the appearance of sincerity and candor; but he was artful, treacherous and cruel. Bancroft sums up his moral qualities in a few words, calling him "selfish Tryon who under a smooth exterior concealed the heart of a savage." He came to the province from North Carolina, where he had been the king's governor for the previous six years. He had there exhibited his love of pomp and display, by numerous military parades at the public charge, and by the erection at an enormous expense for his own occupation, of "a governor's house, worthy the residence of a prince of the blood," and when he had dexterously procured the assent of the assembly to a tax to cover his extravagant expenditures, he caused its collection to be enforced with rigor, and to the serious oppression of the people, producing an insurrection which he put down with a strong hand, and with vindictive and unfeeling cruelty.[2]

But notwithstanding the unfavorable rumors which had preceded Tryon's arrival in New York, he seems to have been well received there, and by his plausible and conciliatory manner, coupled with a skillful use of his power of granting lands, and a judicious distribution of favors and promises in influential quarters, he acquired much popularity, especially with the colonial assembly, which he kept far behind those of the other colonies in their opposition to the tyrannical measures of the king and parliament.

Although Gov. Tryon was well aware of the king's prohibitory order of July, 1767, and of the new instructions including the forty-ninth article, forbidding him from granting any lands within the territory formerly claimed by New Hampshire, having laid those instructions before his council a few weeks after his arrival in the colony, he did not long obey them. He continued to administer the

---

[1] *Col. Hist. N. Y.*, vol. 8, p. 209. *Allen's Biog. Dic.*

[2] *Martin's North Carolina*, vol. 2, chap. vii and viii.

government until in April, 1774, when he departed for England in obedience to the direction of the ministry, leaving the government in the temporary charge of Lieut. Gov. Colden. During this period of Tryon's administration, besides confirming the New Hampshire charters of several townships on the east side of the Green mountain, he issued patents to new applicants, for over two hundred thousand acres of land, within the prohibited territory, a considerable portion of which had been previously granted by New Hampshire. Besides this, after the fashion of his predecessor, he provided himself with a township of thirty-two thousand acres, by the name of Norbury, situated in the present county of Washington, in the vicinity of the towns of Calais and Worcester. The patent bore date April 14, 1772, and was issued to thirty-two individuals, among whom were his son-in-law, Edmund Fanning, Receiver General Elliott, Secretary Banyar, James Duane, Col. John Reid, John Kelly, Crean Brush, and other noted land speculators. On the 16th day of April, the second day after the date of the patent, all the patentees conveyed their shares to the governor.[1]

The last patent issued by him during this term of his administration bore date in June, 1772, from which time till his leaving for England, a period of nearly seventeen months, there appears to have been a total suspension of grants of Vermont lands. Perhaps the reason for Gov. Tryon's ceasing to make grants at that time, may be found in a new movement which the New Hampshire settlers were making to carry their complaints again to England. On the 25th of November, 1772, a few days after the date of his last patent, the governor communicated to his council, "intelligence he had received from Major Philip Skene, informing him that the deputies of Bennington and the adjacent towns, at a meeting at Manchester, on the 21st of October, had appointed Jehiel Hawley and James Brackenridge their agents, who were immediately to repair to London, to solicit their petition to his majesty, for a confirmation of their claims under the grants of New Hampshire."[2] Serious disturbances had arisen within the controverted territory, accounts of which had from time to time been sent to England, by the New York government, and the whole subject had for some time been under the consideration of the board of trade. It is not improbable that Tryon may also have received intimations that his conduct towards the New Hampshire grantees was not viewed in a favorable

[1] *Albany Records Land Papers. Patents,* vol. 16. *Deeds,* vol. 19, p. 97.
[2] *Doc. Hist. N. Y.,* p. 802.

light by that body. That his deliberate violation of the king's prohibitory order, of July, 1767, as well as his general disregard of the regulations of the crown, respecting the granting of lands, met the strong disapprobation of the board of trade and of the ministry, he not long afterwards had very full evidence.

As early as Dec. 4, 1771, Lord Hillsborough had written to Tryon, asking for a full report "of the method of proceeding upon application for grants of land, in order that his majesty may be informed whether such method does or does not correspond with the letter and spirit of the royal instructions given for that purpose; for," he adds, "if it should turn out that grants are made to persons by name who never personally appear at the council board, or who are examined as to their ability to cultivate and improve the land they petition for, and that the insertion of names in a patent under pretence of their being associates or copartners is only a color for giving to any one person more than he is allowed by the king's instructions, it is an abuse of so gross and fraudulent a nature as deserves the severest reprehension, and it is highly necessary both for the interest of the crown, and for the dignity of his majesty's government that some effectual measures should be taken to put a stop to it." In his answer to this letter of the colonial secretary, Gov. Tyron, after stating that it would be extremely difficult to prevent the application for lands "under borrowed names," undertakes to show that such grants deserve encouragement rather than censure. "I conceive it my lord," he says, "good policy to lodge large tracts of land in the hands of gentlemen of weight and consideration. They will naturally farm out their lands to tenants; a method which will ever create subordination, and counterpoise, in some measure, the general leveling spirit, that so much prevails in some of his majesty's governments." It may be worth while to mention that this answer to Lord Hillsborough's instructions against fraudulent grants to nominal grantees bears date April 11, 1772, three days prior to that of the patent which Tryon had issued for himself of thirty-two thousand acres in the names of that number of his dependants and friends. Under date of the 18th of the same April, Lord Hillsborough again wrote to Tryon, enjoining him "to pay strict attention to the instructions that had been given him," in regard to the lands "in that country which had been annexed to New York by the determination of the boundary line" with New Hampshire; to which injunction it is scarcely necessary to state that he paid no attention. It should now be understood that Gov. Tryon, in July,

1772, attended a congress of Indians at the residence of Sir Wm. Johnson, where he assented to the purchase from the Mohawks, by a few individuals, of more than a million of acres of their lands, and promised to issue patents for the same to the purchasers.[1] On hearing of this proceeding, Lord Dartmouth, the new colonial secretary, under date of Nov. 4, 1772, wrote to Tryon, saying that "the engrossing of lands on the Mohawk on pretence of purchases from the Indians had been repeatedly and justly complained of," and forbidding him to take any steps to confirm the purchases, until the Indian deeds were transmitted to him and "the king's pleasure signified thereupon." Lord Dartmouth also complained of his conduct in granting lands "annexed to New York, by the determination of the boundary with New Hampshire," which, he says, makes it necessary for the board of trade to resume again the consideration of the whole subject.

On the 3d of December 1772, the board made a representation of the whole matter to the committee of the privy council, in which they submitted several propositions for the adjustment of the land controversies; which propositions and the proceedings thereon, will be noticed hereafter. In this representation the board speak of the difficulties which had arisen from the disregard by the New York governors of the king's order of July, 1767, of "the great injury and oppression suffered by the settlers from the irregular conduct of the governor and council of New York, in granting warrants of

[1] The Indian deeds there obtained were as follows: the lands lying on the upper waters of the Hudson and between that and the Mohawk river.

To John Glen and others,	9,000 acres.
Jellis Fonda and associates,	120,000
John Bergen and associates,	24.000
Thos. Palmer and associates,	133,000
Ebn. and Edward Jessup and others,	40,000
Joseph Totten and Stephen Crossfield,	800,000
Total,	1.126,000

Col. Hist. N. Y., vol. 8, p. 304–310. *Albany Records, Land Papers*, vol. 32, p. 40 to 45. Gen Philip Schuyler in a private letter to a friend written in September, after this, says that Tryon's fees for the grants made on this visit to the Indians exceeded £22,000, being equal to $55,000, and he adds, "a large premium is offered by the land jobbers at New York to any ingenious artist who shall contrive a machine to waft them to the moon; should Ferguson, Martin, or any eminent astronomer, report that they had discovered large vales of fine land in that luminary, I would apply to be a commissioner for granting the lands, if I knew to whom to apply for it." — *Lossing's Life of Schuyler*, vol. 1 p. 263.

survey for lands under their actual improvement," and of the exorbitant fees demanded on the granting of lands, which they say are by the ordinance of 1710 "considerably larger than what are at this day received for the same service in any other of the colonies;" and yet, the representation proceeds, "the governor, the secretary, and the surveyor, have taken and do now exact *more than double what that ordinance allows*, and a number of other officers do upon various pretences take fees upon all grants of land insomuch that the whole amount of these fees upon a grant of one thousand acres of land, is in many instances not far short of the real value of the fee simple, and we think we are justified in supposing that it has been from a consideration of the advantage arising from these exorbitant fees, that his majesty's governors of New York have of late years taken upon themselves, upon the most unwarrantable pretences, to elude the restrictions contained in his majesty's instructions with regard to the quantity of land to be granted to any one person, and to contrive by the insertion in one grant of a number of names either fictitious or which, if real, are only lent for the purpose, to convey to one person in one grant from twenty to forty thousand acres of land, an abuse which is now grown to that height as well to deserve your lordship's attention."

In a letter from Lord Dartmouth to Governor Tryon, dated the 9th of the same December, he says: "I am further to acquaint you that the sentiments, expressed in Lord Hillsborough's letter to you of the 4th of December, 1771, concerning the unwarrantable and collusive practice of granting lands in general are fully adopted by the king's servants, and I was exceedingly surprised to find that such an intimation to you on that subject had not had the effect to restrain that practice, and that the same unjustifiable collusion had been adopted in a still greater extent in the liences you have granted to purchase lands of the Indians." In a letter of March 3, 1773, Lord Dartmouth again expresses his dissatisfaction with the conduct of Governor Tryon, in relation both to the licences granted to the purchasers of land from the Indians, and to the grants under New Hampshire.

The report of the board of trade, of December 3, 1772, before mentioned, having been approved by the king in council, was transmitted to Governor Tryon, with instructions to have it carried into effect; and he, in reply, addressed a long communication to the colonial secretary, insisting that the plan therein proposed was unjust to the New York patentees and impracticable. He also in another letter, attempted a defence of his conduct in relation to the purchases of the lands of the Indians. In reply to this last letter Lord Dartmouth, under date of the 4th of August, 1773, says: "I have read and considered your letter with great attention, and still remain of opinion, that a license given without the king's previous consent and instruction, to private persons to make purchases from the Indians of above a million of acres of land, accompanied with an engagement to confirm their titles by letters patent under the seal of the colony, was contrary to the plain intention of the royal proclamation of 1763,[1] incompatible with the spirit of the king's instructions, and an improper exercise of the power of granting lands, vested in the governor and council." * * * Lord Dartmouth further declares, that he cannot advise the king to confirm the purchases, but intimates that the purchasers may perhaps be entitled to some reasonable compensation for their expenses; and he then adds, "but I must be better informed of many circumstances before I can judge in what mode it can be given; and it is for this reason, as well as from a consideration of the want of a more ample and precise explanation of the state of the province in general respecting those different claims to lands that have been a source of so much disquiet and disorder, that I have humbly moved the king that you may be directed to come for a short time to England, and his majesty has been graciously pleased to approve thereof."

The receipt of this letter was acknowledged by Tryon early in October, but as it allowed him considerable latitude in regard to the time of his departure, he postponed it until the ensuing spring.

When the colonial assembly met in January, the governor in his speech, announced his intended visit to England, in such a manner as did not imply (as we have seen the truth was) that dissatisfaction of the king's advisers with his own conduct in the granting of lands was one of the principal causes of his recall. His language in his speech was as follows:

"The contests which have arisen between the New York grantees and the claimants under New Hampshire, and the outrages committed on the settlers under this government, having been productive of much confusion and disorder, and requiring immediate consideration, his majesty has been graciously pleased to command me to repair to

---

[1] This proclamation after declaring that great frauds and abuses had been committed in the purchase of lands from the Indians, etc., prohibited all such purchases by private persons, and declared that all purchases should be by the governors for the crown only.— *U. S. Land Laws,* vol. 1, p. 87.

England for a short time to attend to the discussion of this important matter." [1]

The absence of Gov. Tryon continued from the 7th of April, 1774, to the first of July, 1775, during which time the government of the province was administered by Lieut. Gov. Colden. Notwithstanding the strong condemnation which the conduct of the New York governors in granting lands in the prohibited territory had repeatedly received from the ministers of the crown, Mr. Colden continued the issue of patents so freely, that during the absence of Tyron in England, about four hundred thousand acres of Vermont lands were covered by them, the patent fees for which could not have been less than ten thousand dollars. The whole quantity of Vermont land patented by New York, up to the period of the revolution, besides that embraced in confirmatory charters, exceeded two millions of acres, more than three quarters of which had been granted in direct violation of the king's order of July 1767, and of the 49th article of the standing instructions of the crown. These grants, in the hands of those who were aware of the want of authority in the governors to make them, as was the case with most of the patentees, were, in point of law, absolutely null and void.[2]

The mission of Gov. Tryon to England, so far as it related to the controversy with the New Hampshire claimants, was without result. The matter appears to have been discussed before the board of trade the 2d of March, 1775, when upon the proposal of Gov. Tryon, it was agreed that a case should be stated in relation to the conflicting grants, and "an action brought thereupon in the supreme court of New York, upon such grounds that either by special verdict or upon some plea of error an appeal might lie from the judgment of said court, to the governor and council, and from them to his majesty in his privy council; or otherwise that the matter should be settled by arbitration in any mode that should be satisfactory to the different parties." But at a meeting of the board a week afterwards, Col. Reid, who held a grant of seven thousand acres, made in violation of the king's prohibitory order of July, 1767, and who was also agent of Lord Dunmore, in relation to his grant to himself, appeared, and having stated that he had material evidence and information to lay before their lordships, touching this matter, it was agreed to reconsider the propositions stated in the minutes of the 2d instant,

---

[1] *Col. Hist. N. Y.*, vol. 8, p. 313, 330, 336, 339, 350, 342–6, 359, 373, 380–7, 392. *Assembly Jour. of Jan.* 12, 1774.

[2] *Albany Records, Patents*, vol. 14, 15, & 16, and *Military Grants*, vol. 1, 2, and 3.

when Gov. Tryon, who was going to Bath on account of his health, should return from thence." It would seem from these minutes of the board, that Col. Reid was unwilling to have the legality of his own grant and that of Lord Dunmore, tested by judicial proceedings, and doubtless not without good reason.

The troubles between the mother country and the colonies were now approaching a crisis, and engrossed the principal attention of the British ministry. It is not probable that any further action was taken by the board in relation to this local controversy. Lord Dartmouth, however, on the eve of Gov. Tryon's departure, in a letter bearing date May 4, 1775, assured him that their lordships were actively engaged in examining the subject, and that he should soon be able to send him his majesty's orders in regard to it. He then instructs him as follows: "In the mean time, it will be your duty to take no further steps whatever regarding those cases, and to avoid, in conformity to the instructions you have already received, making any grants or allowing any surveys or location of lands in those parts of the country which are the seat of the present disputes."[1]

On the 25th of June, Gov. Tryon reached New York harbor from England, to find the country involved in civil war. Information of his arrival was communicated to the provincial congress, then in session in that city, and on the same day a letter was received from Gen. Schuyler, that Gen. Washington, who had just been chosen commander in chief of the American army, was on his way with his suit from Philadelphia to Boston, and would reach New York before night. The provincial congress, composed largely of secret tories and timid and hestitating whigs, were in great trouble how to act in case both Gov. Tryon and Gen. Washington should reach the city at the same time. Tryon was, however, several hours behind Washington, and public receptions were given to both, the welcome of the general being the most earnest and hearty. Gov. Tryon had, however, a strong hold on the aristocratic element in the province, of which the land speculators composed an important part. He was thereby enabled to make his residence in the city for several months, and to exert a very unfavorable influence on the patriot cause. Gen. Washington, as well as most of the ardent whigs in the province, would have been glad to have him siezed and confined. A motion to that effect was made in the continental congress, but

[1] *American Archives*, 4th series, vol. 2, p. 136, 137. *Col. Hist. of N. Y.*, vol. 8, p. 373.

being earnestly opposed by Mr. Duane, was unsuccessful. But early in October a resolution, aimed principally at Tryon, was adopted, recommending to the several provincial assemblies and committies of safety, "to arrest and secure any person in their respective colonies, whose going at large might, in their opinion, endanger the safety of the colony, or the liberties of America." The movers of the resolution, says Gordon, "had little or no expectation that the New York convention would secure Tryon, but they hoped the sons of liberty at large would effect the business." But, continues Gordon, "Mr. Duane's footman went off to Gov. Tryon in season to give him information of what was resolved," which enabled him to escape on board a vessel in the harbor and eventually to continue his intrigues and outrages against the people he was sent to govern.

No further proceedings in relation to the New Hampshire grants took place under the administration of Gov. Tryon, except that in accordance with his chronic habit of violating the king's prohibitory orders against granting lands in that territory, he issued a patent the 28th of October, 1775, to Samuel Avery and others for forty thousand acres of land, and in June 1776, another to Samuel Holland, and associates, for twenty-three thousand acres more; the former tract lying on the west side of the Green mountain, and the other on the east side. Both of these patents bear date after the governor had taken refuge from his indignant people on board the king's man of war.[1]

---

[1] *Sparks's Washington*, vol. 3, p. 8. *Irving's Washington*, vol. 1, p. 493. *Gordon's American Revolution*, vol. 2, p. 94, 119, 120. *Jour. Cong.*, Oct. 6, 1775. *Bancroft*, vol. 8, p. 32. *Albany Records, Patents*, vol. 16 and 17.

CHAPTER XI.

Collisions between the New York and New Hampshire Claimants.

1766-1771.

Brief summary of the preceding chapters — The settlers but little annoyed during the administration of Governor Moore — much troubled when Colden comes again into power in 1769, and also under Dunmore — The patent of Walloomsack, and disturbances in regard to it — Trials of ejectment suits at Albany in June 1770 — John Munro Esq., a New York justice and agent of Messrs Kempe and Duane — He assists the sheriff in his attempts to arrest rioters and to execute writs of possession — Silas Robinson arrested and carried off to Albany — The militia of Albany county marched to Bennington to aid the sheriff in taking possession of the farms of James Breakenridge and Josiah Fuller — Their discomfiture and its effects.

In the preceding chapters, we have given an account of the origin and character of the respective claims of the governments of New York and New Hampshire, to the soil and jurisdiction of the territory now constituting the state of Vermont. We have seen that the continent of America, from Labrador to Florida, was originally claimed by the English by right of prior discovery; that the Dutch were the first to explore the Hudson river, and to occupy the lands in its vicinity; that they claimed that their territory, under the name of New Netherland, extended from Delaware bay on the south to Cape Cod on the north; that their right to any part of the territory they claimed was disputed and denied by the English, that the settlements of the Dutch in New Netherland and the English in New England commenced about the same time, that their settlements gradually approached and they began to encroach upon each other; that in consequence of such encroachments a treaty was entered into in 1650, between the Dutch governor and the commissioners of the New England colonies, by which a temporary boundary line was agreed upon, extending from a point on Long Island sound indefinitely to the north, so that it should not come nearer than ten miles to the Hudson river; that such line was ratified by the States General of Holland as the permanent eastern boundary of the Dutch territory; that the English government did not so recognize it and could not without abandoning the ground it had always maintained that the Dutch were intruders and had no rightful territory whatever; that in 1664 King Charles the second granted the territory claimed by the Dutch to his brother, James Duke of York, and sent across the Atlantic, a naval and military force, to which New Netherland was surrendered in the autumn of that year; that New Netherland at that time contained less than ten thousand inhabitants, fifteen hundred of whom were upon Manhattan, now New York island; that the population of Connecticut was then fully equal to that of New Netherland, more than three quarters of which was west of Connecticut river, the settlements extending on Long Island sound more than seventy miles west of that river and reaching within less than twenty miles of the Hudson; that two years previously the same king Charles had granted the charter of Connecticut extending from Narragansett bay on the east to the South sea or Pacific ocean on the west, disregarding any claim of the Dutch to New Netherland; that the charter of Massachusetts had been granted thirty years earlier, also reaching westward to the Pacific ocean; that the descriptive language of the charter to the Duke of York was necessarily vague; that it could not consistently with the long cherished pretensions of the English government be otherwise; that the territory could not be described in the grant to the duke in general terms as New Netherland without impliedly admitting the right of the Dutch who had settled it, and given to it its name; that a description bounding it by the temporary line which had been acknowledged by the States General of Holland as its eastern extent toward New England, was equally inadmissible, for the same reason; that there being no river or range of mountains or other natural object for a boundary between the settlements of the English and the Hudson river, that could be fixed upon, a description was necessarily adopted which, treating the grant as covering only English territory used language sufficiently comprehensive to include the Dutch possessions; leaving any apparent interference with previous grants to be adjusted when the territory should be reduced to possession by conquest; that accordingly the grant to the duke was nominally of Hudson's river and all the land from the west side of Connecticut river to the east side of Delaware bay;" that in accordance with this intention of the crown to embrace only the Dutch possessions in the duke's grant, the boundary on the east, was within six weeks after the conquest of New Netherland, curtailed to within twenty miles of the Hudson by the king's commissioners who accompanied the expedition, of whom the duke's governor of the province, then named New York, was one; that this twenty mile line reaching northerly to Lake Champlain is designated as the eastern boundary of New York on all the English and American maps up to the period of the revolution, including that of the celebrated geographer Dr. Mitchell, published in 1755, under the authority of the English board of trade; that such line was recognized by New York as such boundary for more than three quarters of a century, the first public claim set up by the government of that province, either against Massachusetts or New Hampshire, that its territory reached east to Connecticut river was made by Gov. Clinton in 1750, after the grant by Wentworth of the charter of Bennington; that even Cadwallader Colden, who eventually under the temptation of a rich harvest of patent fees, became a zealous advocate of the ancient right of New York to reach eastward as far as the Connecticut, had as late as 1738, while surveyor general of the province, in an elaborate official report for the information of the crown, given the boundaries of the province on all sides of it, in great detail, without making any mention whatever of that river; and that although the Dutch at the time of the conquest of New Netherland, made no claim to reach eastward beyond the before mentioned treaty line of 1650, yet that they did claim by reason of their trade with the Mohawks and other tribes of the six nations of Indians and of their protecting care over them, to extend westerly to lakes Ontario and Erie, in virtue of which claim continued by their English successors western New York became a part of that province and state, though by no construction whatever could the language of the duke's charter be made to include it.

We have further seen, that by the accession of the Duke of York to the throne, in 1685, his charter title merged in the crown making New York a royal province; that its eastern boundary, being a twenty mile line, from the Hudson extended northerly to lake Champlain, the king, in 1741, commissioned Benning Wentworth, governor of New Hampshire, describing his province as reaching westward *until it met his other governments*, thus bounding it westerly on New York; that the country thus included in New Hampshire, lying to the westward of Connecticut river, was then an uncultivated wilderness; that Gov. Wentworth, with authority from the king to grant his lands, issued charters of over one hundred townships each of six miles square, within such territory; that while settlements of the country under these charters were rapidly making, the government of New York procured an order of the king in council, bearing date July 20, 1764, fixing upon Connecticut river as the boundary between the two provinces; that up to that time the territory, thus severed from New Hampshire, had been repeatedly and uniformly recognized by the king's government as belonging to that province, and never to that of New York; that the reasons for this change of jurisdiction were those of state policy, a preference of the crown for the aristocratic institutions of New York, to the more democratic institutions of New England, and a desire to extend the area of the former by curtailing that of the latter; that upon the receipt of the king's order in council annexing the territory west of Connecticut river to New York, lieutenant governor Colden proceeded at once to grant the lands to others than the New Hampshire claimants, and when the latter applied to the New York governors for a confirmation of those not thus granted, such enormous patent fees were demanded as to make it impossible for them to comply; that the New Hampshire claimants then appealed directly to the crown for relief; that the conduct of the New York governors in regard to their lands was severely censured by the colonial secretary, and an order of the king in council made, bearing date July 24, 1767, forbidding in the most positive terms, under the penalty of his majesty's highest displeasure, the granting of any more lands whatever within that territory "until his majesty's further pleasure should be known concerning the same;" that the New York governors, notwithstanding this peremptory order of the king, proceeded to grant the lands within the disputed territory, and continued making such grants up to the period of the revolution, having granted more than a million and a half of acres in direct and palpable violation of such order.

We are now to treat of the controversies which arose between the settlers and the New York claimants in regard to the possession of the lands thus covered by conflicting grants.

It has already been seen that Lieutenant Governor Colden's operations in the issuing of patents were suddenly brought to a close, the 1st of November, 1765, in consequence of his inability to procure stamps to authenticate them, as required by the English stamp act. The same difficulty also put a stop to further surveys, warrants for that purpose also requiring stamps. Mr. Colden had patented nearly all the lands for which surveys had been ordered, and when in the summer of 1766 the obstacle occasioned by the stamp act was removed by its repeal, Sir Henry Moore found that it would require considerable time to make the necessary preparations for future grants; and before his patent granting machinery could be put in active operation, the letter of the Earl of Shelburne, of the 11th of April, 1767, came forbidding him in the most peremptory manner, from making any further grants in the disputed territory. This was soon followed by the king's prohibitory order of the 24th of July, 1767, to which, we have already seen, Governor Moore paid due obedience.

This stoppage of further grants, accompanied as it was by the decided condemnation by the crown of the past conduct of the New York governors, greatly discouraged the patentees of the lands already granted, and for some time seemed to paralyze their operations. During the remaining two years of Governor Moore's administration, little occured to disturb the quiet industry of the New Hampshire occupants. The grantees under that province were inspired by the friendly action of the crown, with new confidence in the validity of their titles, and the numbers and strength of the settlers were largely increased by new arrivals in the territory from the New England colonies, whose people were then, as they have been since, constantly emigrating to new and uncultivated lands.

Upon the decease of Sir Henry Moore, which took place September 11, 1769, Lieutenant Governor Colden came again to the head of the government, and a new era in the affairs of the territory commenced. We have already seen that Mr. Colden, under color of a new construction of the king's prohibitory order, proceeded at once to violate it. His restoration again to power also aroused to increased activity the claimants under the patents which had been previously issued. Numerous ejectment suits were immediately brought against the settlers, and other steps were taken to make their grants available.

There was a tract of land in the north-westerly part of Bennington, which stood upon a different footing from any other New York grant; being embraced in a patent issued prior to the charter of the township by New Hampshire. It contained twelve thousand acres, called Walloomsack, which had been granted in 1739, the greater portion of which was within the acknowledged bounds of New York. In the patent, no natural boundaries of the land were mentioned. The description began at a certain marked tree, which must have been in the province of New York near the present village of North Hoosick, and its boundary lines ran by ten different courses and distances around the tract to the place of beginning. It was granted in an awkward and unseemly form, to correspond with the windings of the Walloomsack river, in order to include the rich alluvial land along its banks, and was thus made in violation of the king's standing instructions prohibiting the granting of any tract "whose length should extend along the banks of any river." The patent contained the usual proviso declaring it to be void if the patentees "should not within three years from its date, settle and effectually cultivate at least three acres of every fifty of the land granted," which they had not done.[1]

It was claimed by the patentees that this tract crossed the south-west corner of Shaftsbury and extended in a south-easterly direction some three miles or more into the township of Bennington; and thus included the farm of James Breakenridge. At the time of the settlement of Bennington it is believed none of the lands embraced by the patent, had been occupied, certainly none of it within the the township; and it was not until several years after Mr. Breakenridge had settled upon it, and had made extensive and valuable improvements, that the existence of a New York claim was made known to him.

The New Yorkers, considering this a favorable patent under which to carry on their attacks upon the settlers, not only demanded of Breakenridge the possession of his farm, and served upon him a writ of ejectment, but procured the appointment of commissioners under the quit rent law of the province, for the puropse of dividing his land among the New York claimants. The commissioners, with surveyors and chainmen, made their appearance on his possessions, October 19, 1769, where they found a considerable number of men collected, some of them having arms and employed mainly in harvesting corn. The commissioners and their attendants, not relishing the presence of so great a number of people, called on them to disperse, which request not being complied with Justicc Munro, of whom we shall learn more hereafter, advanced and read the riot act, but without much effect. No actual violence appears to have been offered, but the New Yorkers believing they had cause to apprehend resistence if they continued their survey, became intimidated and gave up their undertaking. They made report of their proceedings to Lieutenant Governor Colden, who in pursuance of the advice of his council, issued a proclamation for apprehending the offenders as rioters, naming as "the principal authors and actors in the riot," James Breakenridge, Jedediah Dewey (the clergyman of the town), Samuel Robinson, Nathaniel Holmes, Henry Walridge and Moses Robinson. They were soon afterwards indicted as rioters in the court of sessions at Albany, but none of them were ever arrested or brought to trial.[2]

---

[1] *Ante,* p. 69. *Albany Records.* Lands Patent, *Allen's Narrative,* 1774, p. 131–2.

[2] *N. Y. Council Minutes,* 12 Dec., 1769. *Doc. Hist. N. Y.,* vol. 4, pp. 615–619. *N. Y. Narrative of* 1773. *Allen's Narrative,* 1774, pp. 131–134. *Docket Min. of Court of Sessions.*

The actions of ejectment which were pending before the Supreme Court of the province were to be tried at the term, to be held at Albany, in June 1770. Among these suits were two for lands in Shaftsbury, claimed under a patent to John Small, dated October 22, 1765, four for lands under the patent of Princetown before mentioned, and two for lands in Bennington, patented to Michael Slaughter, May 30, 1765, all of which patents had been issued by Lieut. Gov. Colden, covering lands which had been previously granted by New Hampshire and occupied under its charters. Besides which, there was an action against James Breakenridge, for land in Bennington, claimed under the before described patent of Walloomsack.

Although the settlers had little confidence in the New York courts, they resolved to appear and defend the suits. Proper documents to show their titles under the grants of Gov. Wentworth were obtained from New Hampshire, and Jared Ingersol, an eminent counselor of New Haven, Connecticut, was employed for their defense, to be aided by Mr. Silvester, an Albany lawyer. The trial was presided over by Judge Robert R. Livingston, with whom was associated Judge Ludlow, who were two of the king's justices of the province, Attorney General John Taber Kempe and James Duane appeared as council for the plaintiffs. The first case for trial was that of John Small against Isaiah Carpenter, for land in Shaftsbury. The patent of the plaintiff having been produced, and the defendant shown in possession of the land, the counsel for the defendant offered in evidence, the New Hampshire charter of the township, bearing date August 20, 1761, four years prior to the plaintiff's patent, together with authentic copies of Gov. Wentworth's commission, and the king's instructions authorizing him to grant lands, but the judges took judicial notice that New York had always extended eastward to Connecticut river, and holding the New Hampshire charter to be null and void, refused to allow it to be read to the jury. A verdict was consequently taken for the plaintiff; and as the ruling in this case precluded all defense in the others, judgment was rendered for the plaintiffs in all of them without further opposition.[1]

Ethan Allen, who afterwards became famous in the annals of the state and nation, is first heard of on the New Hampshire grants, in connexion with these trials. He had resided in Salisbury, Connec-

---

[1] *New York Narrative of* 1773. *Allen's Narrative of* 1774, p. 6. *Ira Allen's Hist. of Vt.*, p. 23. *Doc. Hist. N. Y.*, 681 - 689. *Bill of Exceptions*, Small vs. Carpenter, Appendix No. 6.

ticut, and came to Bennington about this time, was a proprietor under some of the New Hampshire charters, and had taken an active part in preparing the cases for trial. It is related of him that after the trials were over, Attorney General Kempe, with two or three other gentlemen, interested in the New York grants, called upon him and advised him to return to his Green mountain friends and persuade them to make the best terms they could with their new landlords, intimating that however fair their claim might be, it had certainly become desperate, and reminding him of the old proverb, that "might makes right." To this proposal Allen merely replied "that the gods of the valleys were not the gods of the hills." This laconic figure of speech he left to be interpreted by his visitors, adding, only when an explanation was asked by the king's attorney, that "if he would come to Bennington the meaning should be made clear to him." [1]

That the judgments thus obtained were inequitable, and if carried into effect would inflict great injustice and oppression upon the settlers, was too plain for argument. The *legality* of the decision may also be very seriously questioned. If, as we think, as has already been shown, the jurisdiction of New Hampshire, prior to the king's order of July 1764, fixing upon Connecticut river as the boundary, extended westerly to the twenty mile line between New York and Massachusetts prolonged northerly to lake Champlain, then Wentworth's grants were unquestionably valid, having been made within territory which he had clear authority to grant. But, conceding that the jurisdiction was disputed and unsettled, which is the most that could be claimed in behalf of New York, how then stands the decision? By the principles of the English constitution, the lands in both New York and New Hampshire were vested in the king, both being royal provinces. Their boundaries, also, might be fixed and changed by him at pleasure. It could not be material to him or to the public, through which of his servants his grants were made, and it would be difficult to find a reason why a grant obtained in good faith from the government of one province, should be declared void, merely because the land by the subsequent settlement of a disputed boundary should happen to fall within the newly established jurisdiction of the other.

There is high English authority against the *legality* as well as the injustice of these New York decisions. We have seen that Lord Shelburne in his letter to Governor Moore, copied on a pre-

[1] *Ira Allen's Vermont*, p. 24.

ceding page gives it as distinctly his opinion that to whatever province the settlers of lands might be found to belong, on the adjustment of the disputed boundary, "it should make no difference in their property, provided that their titles to their lands should be found good in other respects," and such also appears to have been the opinion of the subsequent colonial secretary. In 1773, Governor Tryon, in addressing Lord Dartmouth, in relation to certain French grants, referred to these Albany trials, saying that "on the footing of original right, our courts determined that the New Hampshire grants were void for want of legal authority in that government," to which the secretary replied as follows: "With regard to the grants heretofore made by the governors of Canada adjacent to Lake Champlain, and by the governor of New Hampshire to the west of Connecticut river, I do not conceive the titles of the present claimants or possessors, ought to have been determined upon any argument or reason drawn from a consideration of what were or were not the ancient limits of the colony of New York. Had the soil and jurisdiction within the province of New York been vested in proprietaries as in Maryland, Pennsylvania, Massachusetts Bay, or other charter governments, it would have been a different question; but when both the soil and jurisdiction are in the crown, to limit that jurisdiction and to dispose of the property in the soil in such manner as shall be thought most fit; and after what had passed, and the restrictions which had been given respecting the claims, as well on Lake Champlain, *as in the district to the west of Connecticut river*, by which the king had reserved to himself the consideration of those claims, I must still have the misfortune to think, that no steps ought to have been taken to the prejudice of the claimants under the original titles." To the same purport was a previous letter of Lord Dartmouth, of December 9, 1772.[1]

By the settlers the justice and legality of these decisions were not only denied, but the integrity of the court in making them was seriously distrusted. It was well known that the lieutenant governor, several members of his council, and also many other leading men of the province, were either patentees of lands or favored petitioners for grants, within the disputed territory. Attorney General Kempe and Mr. Duane, two of the most noted lawyers in the colony by whom the suits were prosecuted, were, as proprietors of Princetown, interested parties in four of the actions in which judgments had been obtained; and Judge Livingston, who presided at the trials,

[1] *Col. Hist. N. Y.*, vol. 8, pp, 330, 343 - 4 and 356 - 7.

had, the previous month of November, obtained a patent to himself, his friends and members of his family, of thirty-five thousand acres of land within the disputed district of which he was believed to be the principal, if not the sole owner. Under these circumstances it was perhaps not unnatural that they should have looked upon the forms of trial which had been allowed them as a mere mockery — as the result of a prior determination to annul their titles and deprive them of their possessions; and that they should have felt that the court of law was but a part of the machinery selected and prepared for that purpose. It has been truly said that "there is no kind of injustice so hard to be borne as that which is inflicted in the name of the law:" and when the purity of the judicial fountain from which it flows is distrusted, the wrong becomes doubly intolerable. It need not therefore be matter of surprise that the settlers should have earnestly endeavored to find some mode of escape from the threatened injury.[1]

In Bennington, then the largest settlement, a town meeting was called to determine what should be done. It was plainly a matter in which all was at stake. The decision of the judges, in effect, annulled all the charters which had been granted by the governor of New Hampshire throughout the territory. If the judgments were suffered to be executed, the settlers would be cast beggars upon the world, and their possessions, which many of them had for years been improving, would pass into the hands of mercenary strangers. On the other hand it would be assuming a fearful responsibility to resist the authority of the law — to brave the power of a government from which little mercy was to be expected. The king had indeed seen and acknowledged the injustice of the conduct of their enemies, in regranting their lands; they had by petitions, through their agent in London, kept him informed of the hostile measures with which they had been pursued since the decease of Gov. Moore; of the survey of their possessions by New York claimants, and of the numerous suits in ejectment which had been brought against them. Was there not reason to hope that when this new outrage upon their rights was made known to him, his power and authory would be interposed to stay the hands of their oppressors? On consideration of the whole subject it was determined, that *until a final decision of the controversy by the king*, the possessions of the defendants should not be surrendered to the plaintiffs, that the

[1] For Livingston's grant of Camden, see *Albany Records, Land Papers*, vol. 22, pp. 45, 61; vol. 26, p. 12; vol. 30, p. 4, and *Patents*, vol. 14, Nov. 13, 1869.

execution of writs of possession should be resisted by force if necessary, and that the farms of Mr. Breakenridge and Mr. Fuller, against whom judgments had been rendered, should be taken under the special protection of the town. A committee was accordingly appointed to see that those farms were properly and effectually defended.[1]

It is stated in the New York narrative of 1773, that Allen, when at Albany, becoming satisfied that the New York title would prevail, promised to go home to his constituents and advise their submission to the judgments, and that in this town meeting he did so, but was successfully opposed by Mr. Dewey, who advocated the claims of New Hampshire. There is no doubt that Mr. Dewey, the reverend clergyman of the town, was earnestly in favor of the measures adopted, though the statement in relation to Mr. Allen, so inconsistent with all his other known conduct, seems at least very questionable.

Encouraged by the successful issue of the Albany trials, the New York claimants of the Walloomsack patent, in the month of September following, made a second attempt to divide the lands of Mr. Breakenridge between them, but met with quite as decided opposition as before; whereupon Lord Dunmore, then governor of the province, "issued his proclamation for the arrest of the 'rioters,' Simeon Hathaway, Moses Scott, Jonathan Fisk and Silas Robinson being designated as 'the principal authors and actors in the riot and breach of the peace.'" The sheriff of Albany county, with his under officers, aided by John Monro, soon afterwards succeeded in arresting one of their number. This John Monro, under a New York military patent, which he had purchased or contracted for, had seated himself on Little White creek, just within the limits of the western boundary of Shaftsbury, under the patronage of Messrs. Duane and Kempe, the noted New York speculators, with whom he kept up an active correspondence. These friends had procured for him from the governor, a commission as justice of the peace for the county of Albany, and he was not only ready to exercise his judicial functions against the New Hampshire claimants, but also, when occasion offered, to act in the capacity of constable or sheriff's assistant in arresting them, and being a bold, active and meddling person, he was for a long time quite troublesome to the settlers. Silas Robinson, one of those named in the proclamation, resided about two miles to the north of the village of Bennington, and

[1] Petitions of Oct., 1769, and Feb. 22 and Oct. 3, 1770, in papers of the old congress, state department, Washington. *Ira Allen's History,* p. 25.

early in the morning of the 29th of November, the sheriff, accompanied by Munro and others, succeeded in arresting him, and by returning with great speed before notice could be given to his neighbors, were enabled to carry him off to Albany. Sheriff Ten Eyck appears to have been greatly elated with this exploit, and immediately wrote to Gov. Dunmore, informing him of his successful expedition to Bennington, at the same time telling him, " that from the advice of said Munro and other information he received, he judged it best to return with his prisoner (especially as he was reported to be one of the principal among them), rather than risk his being rescued." The governor wrote a complimentary letter to the sheriff, highly approving his conduct, and directed him to hold his prisoner in custody until he should be released in due course of law. The governor also instructed the king's attorney general to prosecute Robinson for the matter charged against him. Mr. Robinson, with fifteen others, were indicted for a riot before the Albany court of sessions, but none of the others were arrested. He was kept in jail until the following October, when he was released on bail.[1]

During the following winter, attempts were made by the plaintiffs in the ejectment suits, to obtain possession of the lands which had been adjudged them by the Albany court, but with only partial success. The sheriff, accompanied by Munro and some twelve or fifteen others, succeeded, during the absence of Samuel Rose of Manchester, in entering his house, but seeing a large number of his neighbors approaching, apparently to oppose them, departed, directing Mrs. Rose to hold the premises as tenant to the plaintiffs. The party were able to turn Mr. Carpenter of Shaftsbury, out of possession, but the plaintiffs' tenant soon became alarmed for his personal safety, and fled. Against James Breakenridge and Josiah Fuller, the two Bennington defendants, not even a nominal possession was gained. When the sheriff went to execute his writs, he was, says Munro, " opposed by a number of armed men who had shut themselves up in the defendants' houses, and threatened to blow his brains out if he proceeded." It had became apparent that the judgments of the plaintiffs could not be made available to them without invoking the extraordinary power of the country. It was therefore resolved that the *posse comitatus*, the militia of the country, should be called to the aid of the sheriff.

---

[1] *N. Y. Council Minutes*, Dec. 18, 1770. *Doc. Hist. N. Y.*, vol. 4, p. 651-3, 671 and 687. *Manuscript Letters of Munro to Duane.*

Now came on the great trial at Bennington, which was to determine the strength of New York laws, and the fate of the settlers. Sheriff Ten Eyck made a general summons of the citizens of Albany, and when he left the city for Bennington on the morning of the 18th of July, 1771, he found himself at the head of about three hundred variously armed men of different occupations and professions; among whom, of the gentry of the town, was the mayor, several aldermen, and four eminent counsellors at law, viz: Mr. Silvester, Mr. Bleecker, Robert Yates and Christopher Yates. The party halted for the night at Sancock, a place situated on the Walloomsack creek, a little west of the present village of North Hoosick, and having received some additions to its numbers, by new levies on the way, took up its line of march the next morning for the residence of Mr. Breakenridge, some six or seven miles distant.

The settlers had received notice of the approach of the sheriff and his *posse*, and had prepared themselves for their reception. Mr. Breakenridge's house was situated about a mile from the New York line, at the foot of a slight ridge of land running east and west, then covered with woods; along the southerly side of which ridge ran the road, by which the *posse* would naturally come. In the woods so far behind the ridge as to allow only their heads and the points of their muskets to be obscurely seen among the trees from the road, were posted nearly one hundred well armed men. Across a cleared field to the south-east of the house in sight, and within gunshot of it, was another somewhat smaller body of armed men. The house itself had been prepared against an assault by strong barricades for the door, and loop holes in the walls from which to fire upon the assailants, and within it were eighteen resolute men, well supplied with the proper means of defense, and provided with a red flag to be hoisted from the chimney, to notify their friends without, whenever their assistance should be needed. The family of Mr. Breakenridge had taken up their temporary abode at a neighbor's, and in this condition the settlers calmly waited the approach of their adversaries.

When the advance of the sheriff's party reached the bridge across the Walloomsack, half a mile to the northwest of Breakenridge's, they found it guarded by "six or seven men in arms who said they had orders to stop them." However after some conversation it was agreed that a few of the party might pass for the purpose of seeing Mr. Breakenridge, upon condition that no more should cross until their return. These, headed by mayor Cuyler, were then conducted near Mr. Breakenridge's house, where they found some twenty or thirty others. On being inquired of why so many men were assembled with the apparent design of opposing the sheriff, Mr. Breakenridge gave them for answer that he had no further concern with the farm, "and that the township had resolved to take the same under their protection and that they intended to keep it." This the mayor told him was a mere evasion, which would not excuse him from the consequences that might ensue; "but that whatever blood should be spilled in opposing the king's writ would be required from his hands." After more discourse it was agreed that Mr. Breakenridge should have some further communication with his friends; that the mayor and his party should return to the bridge where they should be informed in half an hour of the result of his conference.

At the end of half an hour the sheriff, who had now reached the bridge with his whole party, was notified by a message from the settlers that the possession would not be given up, "but would be kept at all events." Whereupon the sheriff gave order for the *posse* to march forward to the house. But only a small portion of them could be persuaded to move, and most of those with much apparent reluctance. The men comprising the sheriff's party had by this time obtained an inkling of the kind of reception they were likely to meet, and were unwilling to expose their lives in a cause in which they had no interest, and of the justice of which they were not well assured. In fact a majority of them disapproved of the conduct of the speculators, and sympathized with the settlers, in their defense of their possessions.

The sheriff and those who accompanied him, on approaching the house held a parley with the leaders of the settlers in which Counsellor Robert Yates endeavored to persuade them to desist from any opposition to the execution of the writ. He told them, in substance that the jurisdiction of the government of New York over them was undoubted, and that although the king had power "to allow, establish or change the jurisdiction as often as he pleased, yet that when once his majesty had divested himself of the right of soil, any dispute that should arise between subject and subject about the right could only be determined by the courts of justice where such controversies arose." Mr. Yates says, they readily acknowledged that they were under the present jurisdiction of New York and that they were the king's loyal subjects, but insisted that they had been very ill used in the trials for their lands by reason that the proofs they offered were rejected by the court," and declared that "they had lately received from their agent in England the strongest assurance that their differences would soon be determined in their favor, and that he had advised them in the meanwhile to hold their possessions until such decision, which they were resolved to do." It appearing evident that the New York arguments, however plausible, were not to be accepted by the Bennington tribunal, the sheriff seized an axe and going towards the door of the house threatened to break it open. Immediately the party in the field perceiving his movement presented their pieces towards him, upon which he came at once to the conclusion that in his position "discretion was the better part of valor," and retired. On returning to the bridge the sheriff, doubtless to save himself from blame, made a formal demand of the *posse* to accompany him five miles further into the township of Bennington to aid him in taking possession of the farm of Mr. Josiah Fuller, but as no one seemed inclined to venture farther in that direction, it was concluded to omit that part of the *programme* of the expedition from Albany. "The power of the county" was allowed to evaporate, and the men composing it dispered with all commendable speed to their several homes, thus leaving the settlers in the quiet occupation of their property, and illustrating the truth of the quaint apothegm of Allen, after the trials at Albany, "that the gods of the valleys were not the gods of the hills." [1]

It is scarcely possible to overestimate the importance, in the New York controversy, of this discomfiture of the sheriff and his *posse*. It not only gave confidence to the New Hampshire claimants in their ability to defend their possessions, but served to convince their opponents, that the feelings of the body of their own people were in unison with those of the settlers, and that any attempt to gain possession of the disputed lands by calling into public action the civil power of the province, would necessarily prove unavailing. This defeat of the New York claimants was the entering wedge that eventually severed the New Hampshire grants from a province to which they had been without their knowledge, annexd by the arbitrary will of the crown. Here, in fact, on the farm of James Breakenridge, was born the future state of Vermont, which, struggling through the perils of infancy, had by the commencement of the general revolution, acquired the activity and strength of adventurous youth; had by its close reached the full stature of manhood, and which not long afterwards became the acknowledged equal of its associate American republics.

---

[1] *Manuscript Letter of Robert Yates to Kempe and Duane of July* 20, 1771. *Ira Allen's Vt.*, p. 23 – 31. *Doc. Hist. N. Y.*, p. 732 – 742. *Connecticut Courant*, March 24, and April 21, 1772, Nos. 379, 383, and May 5, No. 384.

CHAPTER XII.

COLLISIONS BETWEEN NEW YORK AND NEW HAMPSHIRE CLAIMANTS — *continued.*

1771-1772.

Town committees of safety meet in general convention and resolve to stop New York surveys, and settlements on lands granted by New Hampshire — Military organization of Green Mountain Boys — Surveyor Cockburne prevented from surveying Socialborough, and other lands — Surveyor Stevens driven off — New York military grants in Rupert, Pawlet, and Dorset, for the benefit of Duane and other speculators — New York claimants prevented from occupying lands in those towns — Seizure of Remember Baker at Arlington by John Munro, and his rescue — Formidable character of the opposition to the New York claims — Cannon brought from Fort Hoosick for defense against an apprehended attack by Gov. Tryon with regular troops — Tryon by letter to Rev. Mr. Dewey proposes negotiation — Agents by his invitation sent by the settlers to New York — Terms of reconciliation proposed by the governor and council, and approved, with great rejoicing, by a public meeting of the settlers at Bennington.

THE resolve of the Bennington town meeting, to resist the execution of the Albany judgments, and hold the possessions of the defendants by force, if necessary, until the final decision of the crown upon their titles, was very generally approved by the inhabitants of the other townships. It was also readily seen that, upon the principles adopted by the New York courts, judgments would at once be rendered against the settlers in all actions that had been or might be brought by the New York patentees, and that it was perfectly useless to appear in court and contest them. Nor could the settlers gain anything by waiting to have the claims of their adversaries prosecuted. The opposition to them seemed indeed more likely to be made effectual by resisting at once, all the efforts of the claimants towards perfecting their titles.

The inhabitants of the several townships, as fast as they had become sufficiently numerous, had organized themselves into municipal communities in conformity to their charters, and had adopted rules and regulations for their local government. The maintenance of the possession and title to their lands against the New York claimants, soon became an absorbing interest, and town committees were appointed, whose special duty it was to attend to their defense and security. The committees of the different townships, as occasion seemed to demand, met in general convention to consult upon and adopt measures for their common protection. Few records of the proceedings of these conventions remain, though sufficient accounts of them have been preserved to show that they exercised a general supervision over the affairs of the settlers, and that their decrees in regard to their land title controversy, were received and obeyed as laws.

At these general conventions, the resolve of the people of Bennington to resist the execution of the Albany judgments was not only approved, but in conformity to the policy above indicated of meeting their adversaries at the threshold, it was further determined that New York claimants should not be permitted either to take possession or make surveys of lands which had been granted by New Hampshire, and that New York officers should be prevented from serving writs of ejectment on the settlers and from arresting any of them for riots or other offences connected with their land controversy.

At first the execution of these resolves seems to have been left to individual and neighborhood efforts. But subsequently as the attempts to intrude upon the settlements increased and became more formidable, a military organization was resorted to. This consisted of several companies of volunteers, of which Seth Warner, Remember Baker, Robert Cochran and some others were captains, the whole being under the command of Ethan Allen with the title of colonel. These eventually assumed the name of Green Mountain Boys, in derision and defiance it is said, of a threat of Gov. Tryon, to drive the settlers from their possessions into the Green mountains. This name, by the bravery and military exploits of those who bore it during the revolutionary period, became an honorable appellation, and has often been used to designate all the troops of the state and sometimes the whole people.

This military organization of the settlers appears to have been commenced towards the close of the year 1771, some months after the expedition of the *posse* of Albany county to Bennington. The resistance on that occasion was doubtless made by the militia of the town, of which a company had been formed as early as October, 1764, aided probably by volunteers from the neighboring towns. The first notice which has been found of the volunteer organization for opposing " the Yorkers," as they were styled, is in a letter from John Munro, Esq., to Governor Tryon, dated in February, 1772, and in an affidavit of one Benjamin Gardner, taken by Munro three days afterwards and forwarded to the governor. From the letter and affidavit it appears that a company, commanded by Seth Warner (Munro erroneously has it *John* Warner), met on the preceding new year's day and "reviewed and continued all day firing at marks." Gardner in his affidavits says: "he was present on the first day of January last when a number of men were under arms at the house of Seth Warner of Bennington, when the men honored said Warner as their captain, Tubbs as their lieutenant, and Nathaniel Holmes as ensign, by firing about his house, etc., and drinking good success to Governor Wentworth and all his grants, and damning the Yorkers; and deponent heard often that they were enlisting men and putting each recruit under oath to be true in maintaining the New Hampshire Grants."[1]

The duties of these men were to watch, and detect in their several neighborhoods, any hostile movements of their adversaries, and to hold themselves in readiness to repair to any part of the territory to which the general convention or its executive committee should require them to go for the proper defence of the persons or lands of the settlers. It was not often that occasion was found for calling them out in large numbers, but they were always prompt and efficient in every emergency.

In carrying into execution the resolves of the general convention collisions with the New York officers and claimants were not unfrequent, and they occured occasionally through a series of years. Some of those which their adversaries most loudly complained of, will now be noticed.

We have a pretty full account of the manner in which the New York claimants were sometimes prevented from making surveys of their "interfering grants," in a letter from Mr. Cockburn, a deputy of the surveyor general, to James Duane, dated at Albany, in September, 1771, on his return from an attempt to survey, and divide into lots the lands included in the patent of Socialborough. Of this patent a full account will be given hereafter. For the present it is sufficient to say that it was issued by Governor Dunmore, in 1771, in violation of the king's prohibitory order of July, 1767, that it covered the two townships of Rutland and Pittsford, which had been chartered ten years previously by New Hampshire, and that the lands were already occupied under those charters. The patentees of Socialborough were all New York city speculators, among the most prominent of whom was Mr. Duane. Notwithstanding the illegality of their patent the patentees seemed determined to enforce it, and to deprive the settlers of their possessions. The following extracts comprise all the material parts of Surveyor Cockburn's letter.

[1] *Doc. Hist. N. Y.*, vol. 4, p. 762. *Allen Papers*, in Vermont secretary of state office, p. 15.

"ALBANY, Sept. 10, 1771.

Sir: Your favor of the 16th of August, and the £60. 2s. 9d. of Mr. Robert Yates, I received on my return here, after being the second time stopped in Socialborough by James Meads and Asa Johnson in behalf of the settlers in Rutland and Pittsford. I have *run out* lots from the south bounds to within about two miles of the Great Falls. I found it in vain to persist any longer, as they were resolved at all events to stop us. There have been many threats pronounced against me. Gideon Conley who lives by the Great Falls was to shoot me, * * * * and your acquaintance Nathan Allen was in the woods with another party blacked and dressed like Indians, as I was informed. Several of my men can prove Townshend and Train threatening my life, that I should never return home, etc. * * * * * The people of Durham, [now Clarendon] assured me, these men intended to murder us if we did not go from thence, and advised me by all means to desist running. * * * * I found I would not be allowed to go to the northward as they suspected I would begin again, and therefore intended to convey us to Danby and so on to the southward, and by all accounts we should not have been very kindly treated. I was advised by no means to go that road. * * * * On my assuring them I would survey no more in those parts, we were permitted to proceed along the Crown Point road, with the hearty prayers of the women, as we passed, never to return. * * * I have not been able to fix Kier's location and Danby people have been continually on the watch always. * * * * Since I have been here several have visited me, asking questions, no doubt to be able to know us, should we venture within their territories, and at the same time warning us of the danger, should we be found there. Marsh's survey is likewise undone as I did not care to venture myself that way. I shall be able to inform you more particularly at our meeting, and am Sir your most obedient servant,

WILL. COCKBURN."

In this case no actual violence appears to have been used, but the surveyor was deterred from continuing his work by the apprehension of personal injury from men who he believed designed to shoot him, some of whom disguised as Indians, he supposed, were prowling in the woods for that purpose. It is not probable that his life was at any time in actual danger, though it was doubtless the object of the settlers to make him think so and thus by intimidation to frighten him away, in which they were successful. There is no doubt however that force would have been applied to expel him from the territory and perhaps to inflict personal chastisement upon him, if it had been found necessary.

The threatening demonstrations of the settlers appear to have prevented him from making further attempts under the patent of Socialborough. The next summer however, he was found with a number of assistants at Bolton on Onion river, and was arrested by Remember Baker, Seth Warner, and others, who after breaking his compass and chain took him and his party to Castleton for trial before a court of the settlers, but on learning that negotiations for arranging their difficulties had been entered into at New York between Governor Tryon, and agents of the people of Bennington, he was allowed to proceed to Albany without further molestation.

A few weeks afterwards, another surveyor, by the name of Benjamin Stevens, was discovered in the same section of the country, and was taken into custody by Baker, Ira Allen, and others; and, according to the New York account of the affair was still more roughly handled than Corkburn had been. By the activity and perseverance of the settlers, the New York claimants were prevented from making much progress in the location of their grants, and the operations of the speculators were greatly obstructed.[1]

Nor were the efforts of the New York claimants to obtain and hold possession, without process of law, of lands under their interfering grants, more successful than their attempts to make surveys. The settlers were continually on the alert, and whenever an intrusion on their chartered territory was made, the invaders were pretty sure to be met and either by intimidation or force were compelled to remove. Some of the early personal contests of this character occurred in Rupert and its vicinity.

Rupert and the adjoining towns of Pawlet on the north and Dorset on the east had been chartered by New Hampshire in 1761. In 1771 ten years afterwards, military patents were issued by Lord Dunmore, governor of New York, covering a great portion of the most desirable land within the limits of these towns. These claims of officers and soldiers had long previously been purchased by New York city speculators, and were located by them for their own benefit in detached parcels, without regard to regularity of form, the sole object being to obtain the specified quantity of good land, rejecting the poor. These military grants were principally included in two patents, the

---

[1] *Allen Papers* in the office of the Vermont secretary of state, p. 3, 36, 63. *Ira Allen's Vermont,* 37-40. *Slade,* 29-33. *Doc. Hist. N, Y.,* 799, 803, and *N. Y. Nar.* of 1773.

patentees and those who might occupy adjoining lands being incorporated into two townships, by the names of Chatham and Eugene. The patentees of Chatham were Lieut. John Cruikshank and four other commissioned officers, thirteen non commissioned officers, and three privates, to whom were granted in the whole twelve thousand seven hundred and fifty acres, ten thousand acres of which belonged to James Duane. These lands were principally in Dorset. The patentees of Eugene were two commissioned officers, forty-seven non commissioned officers, and thirty-nine privates, to whom were granted fifteen thousand three hundred and fifty acres, all of which belonged to Mr. Duane. These lands were mainly in Rupert and Pawlet.

The patent of Chatham bore date March 14, and that of Eugene June 14, 1771, and both were in plain violation of the king's order of July 1767, even upon the limited construction which had been given it by Colden, all the lands having been previously granted by New Hampshire. Mr. Colden, indeed, declined to patent them, and in regard to the lands in Chatham, Mr. Duane made an appeal to the sympathies of the king and his ministry by petition in the name of Lieut. Cruikshank and the other ostensible claimants, urging the hardships of their case in not being allowed to obtain the lands they had sought for, which petition was transmitted to Lord Hillsborough, the colonial secretary, by Lieut. Gov. Colden in Jan., 1770. In his letter to the secretary, Mr. Colden after stating that he was forbidden to grant the lands by the king's order before mentioned, and arguing in favor of the justice of the application, added that "the *petitioners* had been at considerable expense in exploring and surveying their lands, and had hitherto been prevented from receiving the benefit of his majesty's bounty." It is difficult to conceive how Mr. Colden could have been ignorant of the fact that the patentees had parted with all interest in their claims long before an exploration or survey of the land had been made, and that they had already received all "the benefit of his majesty's bounty," which they could ever possibly obtain. No favorable answer was returned to the petition, but patents for this and the other township were issued by Gov. Dunmore, as before stated, in direct violation of the order and instruction of the king, which patents were consequently null and void, for want of authority in the governor to make them.[1]

The shameless manner in which the commands of the king in relation to the granting of these lands were disregarded by Gov.

[1] *Albany Land Papers*, vol. 21, p. 88, vol. 23, p. 138. *Albany Military Patents*, vol. 2. *Col. Hist. of N. Y.*, vol. 8, p. 196, 206, 272. *Rep. of N. Y. Com. of* 1797, p. 42, 44, 85.

Dunmore, was not calculated to inspire in the New Hampshire settlers and grantees respect for his own authority; and we accordingly find them resisting with spirit and determination, every attempt of the New York patentees to encroach upon their territory. As early as June, 1771, efforts appear to have been made by claimants under military grants to occupy some lands in the western part of Rupert, but the intruders were attacked by a large party under Robert Cochran, who claimed the lands by the New Hampshire title, and driven off. Other attempts to make settlements in Rupert and Pawlet were made under New York claims in October following, but with no better success.

It seems that two brothers of the name of Todd, claiming under a New York patent to one Lieut. Farrant had commenced work on a lot, near the west line of Rupert, which was claimed by Robert Cochran under the New Hampshire charter, and which, it is said, he had partly cleared; that another New York claimant of the name of Hutchinson had begun to build a log house on another lot belonging to a New Hampshire grantee, the logs being laid and rafters fixed for a roof; and that further to the northward one Reid had begun an improvement on a piece of land in Pawlet, and had erected there a shelter, having four crotches driven in the ground with boughs for a covering. Cochran with a party of seven armed men from Rupert, accompanied also by Ethan Allen and Remember Baker, went to the Todds, drove them from their work, declaring they would never suffer any man to be seated there who held under a New York title. The party then went to Hutchinson's place, took down the logs and rafters of his house and placing them in piles "burned them with fire." The house or shelter of Ried was afterwards destroyed in the same manner, all the claimants being required to depart immediately from the lands granted by New Hampshire, and threatened with barbarous usage if they returned. According to the affidavit of Hutchinson, taken before justice McNaughton, his assailants conducted in a rough, swaggering, and boisterous manner, declaring that they had "that morning resolved to offer a burnt sacrifice to the gods of the woods in burning the logs of his house," with oaths boastingly telling him to go his way and complain to his "scoundrel governor," that they had hundreds of New Hampshire men to prevent any soldiers or others settling on their lands, defying the New York council, assembly and laws, and affirming that if any New York constable attempted to arrest them they would kill him, and that if any of them should be put in Albany jail they would break it down and rescue him.

Complaint of these violent proceedings having been made to Gov. Tryon, who had succeeded Lord Dunmore as chief magistrate of the province, he, by advice of his council, issued a proclamation bearing date Dec. 9, 1771, offering a reward of twenty pounds each for apprehending and securing Cochran, Allen, Baker, and the six others concerned with them, "that they might be proceeded against as the law directs." Two days afterwards, on the 11th of December, Gov. Tryon issued another proclamation in which he maintained at considerable length by argument and authority, what he called "the ancient and incontrovertible right of New York to extend to Connecticut river as its eastern boundary," and warned all persons that his government would adopt the most rigorous measures for suppressing all opposition to its authority.[1]

These threatening proclamations served to increase rather than to allay the ill feeling of the settlers. That of the 11th was answered in detail, in two communications in the *Connecticut Courant* of the 24th of March and April 28th, 1772. These articles, which were undoubtedly from the pen of Ethan Allen, were written with considerable ability, were extensively read, and exerted much influence in forming a friendly public opinion towards the settlers.

The proclamation for the arrest of Allen, Baker and Cochran, was treated by them with defiant contempt, by issuing and circulating extensively, over their signatures, a printed burlesque proclamation, offering a reward of fifteen pounds for the apprehension and delivery at "Landlord Fays," in Bennington, of James Duane, and ten pounds for Attorney General Kempe, who are described as common disturbers of the public peace.[2] It appears

---

[1] *Doc. Hist. N. Y.*, vol. 4, pp. 720, 745–755. *New York Narrative. Allen's Narrative*, pp. 149 150.

[2] The following is a copy of the proclamation:

£25 REWARD.

Whereas, James Duane and John Kempe, of New York, have by their menaces and threats greatly disturbed the public peace and repose of the honest peasants of Bennington, and the settlements to the northward, which peasants are now and ever have been in the peace of God and the king, and are patriotic and liege subjects of George III. Any person that will apprehend those common disturbers, viz, James Duane and John Kempe, and bring them to Landlord Fays, at Bennington, shall have £15 reward for John Duane and £10 for John Kemp, paid by

ETHAN ALLEN,
REMEMBER BAKER,
ROBERT COCHRAN.

Dated Poultney,
Feb. 5, 1772.

See *Allen's Papers*, pp. 1, 39. *Letter from Peter Yates to James Duane*, Albany, April 7, 1772.

from a letter of Justice Munro to Gov. Tryon, dated in February following, and from affidavits which accompanied it, that the excitement of the settlers was much increased by the offering of rewards for Allen and the others, and by what they termed the "grand falsehoods" in the governor's proclamation in relation to the New York title, and that violent and threatening language was in common use against Tryon and his government. Munro in his letter speaks of the military organization which they had entered into, and says "he finds that any act of indulgence which the government offers is treated with disdain," and that by the best information he could get, the settlers were determined to oppose the authority of the government, "assigning for reason that should they comply it would weaken their New Hampshire title, and they should lose their lands; for this reason they should fight till they died." Sheriff Ten Eyck of Albany, who went to Rupert and Pawlet to endeavor to arrest the parties named in the governor's proclamation, reported to him his inability to find any of them, and added "that from the conduct and behavior of those who were at home, though not particularly mentioned or concerned in the riot, he finds the greatest appearance of a determined resolution not to submit to the government, and this he found particularly verified by the conduct of eight or nine who were armed with guns and clubs, in which manner they came to the house of one Harmon, on Indian river,[1] where he then was, and from their conduct it appeared what they intended."

Justice Munro, who, as we have before seen, was an agent of Mr. Duane and his associate land claimants, and who resided near the west line of Shaftsbury, ambitious to serve his principals and to stand well with the government, resolved to make a serious effort to capture Remember Baker and take him to Albany jail. Baker's residence was a mile or more to the eastward of the present village of Arlington, some ten or twelve miles distant from Munro's. Munro, by means of a spy, having learned the precise position of things at Baker's house, with his constable Stevens and a party of ten or twelve others, surrounded the house a little before daylight on the 21st of March, 1772, and after a desperate struggle, in which Baker was severely wounded, and his wife and little son also much injured succeeded in arresting him. He was immediately bound and placed in a sleigh, which was driven off toward Albany. Caleb Henderson and John Whiston, two of Baker's neighbors, attempted to stop the sleigh but failed, and Whiston was taken prisoner and carried

---

[1] Indian river is a small stream that runs through Rupert and Pawlet.

off by the party, but Henderson escaped. A messenger was immediately dispatched to Bennington to carry the news. Munro and his party drove about sixteen miles to Sancoik, where they stopped several hours to rest. In the mean time, ten men had been rallied at Bennington who rode with all speed to the ferry across the Hudson, where the city of Troy is now situated. On arriving there, they found, as they had hoped, that they were ahead of Munro and his party, and they accordingly turned back on the road to Arlington, and after traveling six or seven miles, met them. Most of the party on coming in sight of the Green Mountain Boys fled to the woods, but Munro and his constable were captured and detained until the rescuers were well on their way with Baker to Bennington when they were released. Baker was so exhausted by loss of blood and by hard usuage, that he was almost helpless, and he was held on his horse by a man riding with him. The rescuers reached Mr. Breakenridge's in the north-east part of Bennington at two o'clock the next morning, having traveled more than sixty miles in twenty-four hours. It appears from several contemporaneous accounts of this affair that Baker and his family were treated in a very barbarous manner by Munro and his party. Munro, in his letter to Duane giving an account of Baker's rescue, complains of the want of spirit of his neighbors, and says "that if he had had but ten men that would have stood by him when the Bennington mob met him he should have had Baker in Albany jail, but all run for it only the two constables," and in a letter to Gov. Tryon, he makes complaint, that the men with him would not obey his orders "but all run into the woods when they ought to have resisted." [1]

---

[1] *Rural Magazine*, Aug. 1795. *Connecticut Courant* of April 21 and June 2d, 1772. *Doc. Hist. N. Y.*, vol. 4, p. 776. *Munro to Duane*, March 28, 1772. *Allen's Nar.*, 1776, p. 59. *Ira Allen's History*, p. 31. *Miss Hemenway's Vt. Magazine*, No. 2, p. 124. *N. York Narrative*, 773. In the *Documentary History of New York*, vol. 4, p. 777, a list of fourteen names is given as of "persons who rescued Baker" stated to have been produced in council, 26 May, 1772. The persons designated were all from Arlington and Sunderland, and could not have been the actual rescuers. Uniform tradition has always ascribed the rescue to Bennington men. Munro, as stated in the text, calls them "the Bennington mob." Ira Allen in his history says, "an express was sent to Bennington with the tidings; instantly on the news ten men mounted their horses and pursued them," etc., etc. In a biographical notice of Remember Baker published in the *Rural Magazine* for August, 1795, when many who were actors in the affair were living, a detailed account of the whole transaction is given with the names of the rescuers, as follows (the men being designated by their subsequent titles), viz: Gen.

This attack upon Baker heightened the animosity of the settlers against the Yorkers, and strengthened their determination to resist their encroachments at all hazards. Soon after this, Surveyor Campbell went with Hugh Munro, whom Ira Allen calls an "old offender," to survey a tract of land for him in Rupert, when, according to the New York account, the party were seized as prisoners by Cochran and others, who "conducted them to their tribunal as if they had really been malefactors, where after deliberating upon their fates it was resolved to chastise them severely. Sergeant Munro and the chain-bearers were beat with clubs unmercifully; but to the deputy surveyor they shewed a little more lenity, and he received only three blows from Cochran." The account further states that Cochran boasted of his exploits, saying he was a son of Robin Hood and would follow his mode of life, which sentiment was received with great applause by his party, and that "after this treatment, and every species of derision, Mr. Campbell and his assistants were conducted in triumph several miles, and then dismissed with a solemn denunciation that death would be their doom if they presumed to return." [1]

More stringent measures were also adopted by the settlers against the few men among them, who from timidity or some other cause, were willing to purchase the New York titles. Some of them gave doleful accounts to the New York governor, of the state of affairs in their neighborhood. Other statments of an alarming character came to him from other quarters. Justice Munro wrote him "that the rioters were enlisting men daily, offering fifteen pounds bounty to every man who joined them; that they struck terror into the whole country; that his house was surrounded every night by rioters,

---

Isaac Clark, Col. Joseph Safford, Major Wait Hopkins, Col. David Safford, and Messrs Timothy Abbott, Stephen Hopkins, Elnathan Hubbel, Samuel Tubbs, Ezekiel Brewster and Nathaniel Holmes. This is doubtless a correct list. The account in the *Rural Magazine* states that on the return of the rescuers with Baker, they met in the night at the crossing of Hoosick river, "another party of men from the Grants in quest of Baker, and that the two parties having joined, proceeded on to Bennington. The list in the *Documentary History* probably gives the names of the men comprising this party, who were from Baker's neighborhood.

A brief account of the attack upon Baker, was published in the *Connecticut Courant* of April 28, 1772, and another in greater detail in that of June 9. In both the conduct of Munro and his party is represented as most unfeeling and barbarous.

[1] Ira Allen in his history (pp. 27), states that Hugh Munro was whipped with bush twigs until he fainted.

firing their guns, so that he was already worn out with watching, and that nothing saved him but the figure he made about his house with arms, etc., and that he hoped his excellency would lose no time in affording him relief." Counselor Yates at Albany, in a letter to Mr. Duane of the 7th of April, expressed his decided opinion that the civil power of the province was insufficient to subdue the rioters. "You," he says, "will stand in need of military force to bring these people to a proper sense of their duty, and obedience to the laws of the country, and until this happens you will, I presume, never recover the possession of your lands." But a still more formidable demonstration of the power and determination of the settlers occurred. Information, supposed to be reliable, had been received at Bennington that Gov. Tryon was on his way from New York to Albany by water, with a body of British regulars, to reduce them to submission. Upon which a general meeting of the committees of safety and military officers was speedily held, at which, after due deliberation, it was unanimously resolved, "that it was their duty to oppose Gov. Tryon and his troops to the utmost of their power, and thereby to convince him and his council that they were punishable by the Green Mountain Boys for disobeying his majesty's prohibitory order of July 1767." A plan of action was agreed upon. Two pieces of cannon and a mortar were brought from the old fort at East Hoosick (Williamstown), with powder and ball, the military were warned to be in readiness, and every preparation for a vigorous defence was made. It proved, however, to be a false alarm. The troops were destined for Oswego and other western posts, and the governor was not with them.[1]

This warlike demonstration of the settlers, following their other late hostile proceedings, seems to have produced some alarm in the mind of Gov. Tryon, and to have suggested to him the expediency of trying what could be done with the rioters by negotiation. On the 19th of May, he laid his information in regard to this military display before his council, together with the draft of a letter he had prepared to forward to some of the rioters, which was approved by the council. The letter was addressed "to the Rev. Mr. Dewey and the inhabitants of Bennington and the adjacent country, on the east side of Hudson's river." It complained of "the many illegal acts they had lately committed against the peace and good order of the province," expressed a desire "to avoid compulsive measures while lenient

---

[1] *Ira Allen's Vermont*, 32-35. *Allen Papers*, 37. *Doc. Hist. N. Y.*, vol. 4, p. 776-778.

methods might prove successful," invited them, "by the advice of his council, to lay before the government the causes of their illegal proceedings," and expressed a disposition "to examine into the grounds of their behavior and discontent, with deliberation and candor, and as far as in him lay to give such relief as the nature of their situation and circumstances would justify." In order to enable them to lay before him and his council, a fair representation of their conduct, the governor engaged "full security and protection to any person whom they should choose to send on that business to New York, from the time they leave this town until they return," except Allen and the other persons named in his proclamation of the 9th of the previous December, and Seth Warner, "whose audacious behavior to a civil magistrate," he says, "has subjected him to the penalties of the laws of the country." [1]

In pursuance of this invitation the committees of Bennington and adjacent townships met and appointed Captain Stephen Fay, and his son, Dr. Jonas Fay, their agents to repair to New York to represent them before the governor and council. They were the bearers of a letter signed by Mr. Dewey and some others, in which their grievances were briefly stated, and another from Ethan Allen, Seth Warner, Remember Baker, and Robert Cochran, whose appearance in New York had been proscribed in Governor Tryon's letter, in which a more particular account of the condition of the settlers, in their relations to the New York government, was given. Both acknowledged that they were under the lawful jurisdiction of New York by the king's order in council of 1764, but complained of the oppression of that government in regranting to others the lands which had before been granted to them, and in aiding an artful

[1] The offence of Warner, here alluded to, occurred under the following circumstances. In Munro's expedition to Arlington he had succeeded in carrying off Baker's gun, which had not been recaptured with its owner. Soon after Warner with a single companion rode to Munro's house and in the name of Baker demanded the gun. Munro refused to deliver it and seizing Warner's horse by the bridle commanded a constable and several other bystanders to arrest him. Warner immediately drew his cutlass and striking the pugnacious magistrate over the head felled him to the ground, and then rode off. The injury though severe was not dangerous. This exploit was looked upon in a different light by the Green Mountain Boys from that in which it appears to have been viewed by Gov. Tryon. Warner was in fact complimented for it by the proprietors of Poultney, with a pitch of 100 acres of land in that township. The vote is still found on the proprietors' records May 4, 1773, declaring it to be "for his valor in cutting the head of Esquire Munro the Yorkite." *New York Narrative*, and *Allen Papers*, p. 43. *Ira Allen's Vt.*, p. 35. *Slade*, p. 26.

and mercenary set of speculators in their efforts to deprive them of their possessions, to their utter ruin. In regard to their alleged illegal proceedings, they averred that they had done nothing more than was justified by the great law of self preservation, in the defence of their liberty and property. "If," says the latter communication, "we do not oppose the sheriff and his *posse*, he takes immediate possession of our houses and farms; if we do, we are immediately indicted as rioters; and when others oppose officers, in taking such their friends, so indicted, they are also indicted, and so on, there being no end of indictments against us, so long as we act the bold and manly part, and stand by our liberty." [1]

The Messrs. Fay accordingly repaired to New York and presented the letters from the settlers to Gov. Tryon, who laid them with other papers relating "to the disorders and disturbances in Bennington and the townships adjacent thereto," before his council, and they were referred to a committee of that body, of which Mr. Smith, the historian, was chairman. On the 1st of July, the committee made a long report on the subject in which the great lenity and kindness which it was claimed had ever been shown by the New York government towards the grantees and settlers under New Hampshire, were elaborately and ingeniously set forth, the committee coming to the conclusion that "the right of the New York patentees was incontrovertible," and that the settlers had no real grounds of complaint. Nevertheless the committee "in great tenderness for a deluded people" add, "we are desirous that your excellency should afford the inhabitants of those townships all the relief in your power by suspending until his majesty's pleasure shall be known, all prosecutions on behalf of the crown, on account of the crimes with which they stand charged by the depositions before us, and to recommend to the owners of the contested lands under grants of this province to put a stop during the same period to all civil suits concerning the lands in question." This report was adopted by the council and entered on its minutes, and with a copy from the minutes of so much of it as is given above together with a letter from Gov. Tryon approving of the same, the messengers returned to their constituents. These terms on their first view were thought by the settlers to furnish them complete relief, as is shown by an article published in the *Connecticut Courant*, bearing date August 22d, 1772, in which an account is given of their proceedings on the re-

[1] This correspondence was published is the *Connecticut Courant*, of July 14, 1772, by request of Ethan Allen, as stated in that paper. It is found in full, in *Slade*, pp. 22-29.

turn of their agents. The article was evidently from the pen of Ethan Allen, and it concluded as follows:

"After our agents received copies of the minutes of council and also a letter from his excellency, purporting his approbation and compliance therewith, they returned to Bennington with great joy, warned a meeting of that town and the adjacent country, which was held on the 15th of July ultimo, and before a large auditory of people, the copy of the minutes of council was read and also his excellency's letter of compliance with the same, which diffused universal joy through the country of the New Hampshire Grants; and the people were at strife in doing the most exalted honor to Governor Tryon. And having at Bennington a cannon, it was discharged sundry times in honor of his excellency and his majesty's honorable council, and after the report of the cannon each several time, the whole audience gave a huzza in acclamation, good will, gratitude and vocal honor to Governor Tryon. And Captain Warner's company of Green Mountain Boys under arms, fired three volleys of small arms in concert and aid of the glory. His majesty's health, also a health to his excellency and his majesty's honorable council was drunk, with full flowing bowls, and confusion to Duane and Kempe and their associates, hoping peace and plenty may abound."

CHAPTER XIII.

Negotiations, Publications and Collisions; Right of Revolution against Oppression.

1772-1773.

The supposed reconciliation a failure — Collisions of claimants continued — Col. Reid's tenants at Panton and New Haven dispossessed — His patent in violation of the king's order of July 1767, and void — The New Hampshire claimants, the first to occupy the land, had been previously driven off by him — Correspondence between Gov. Tryon and Allen and the others who had dispossessed Reid — Surveyor Stevens attacked and sent out of the territory — The New York claimants few in number and with their own people against them, are no match for those under New Hampshire, who flock into the territory and occupy the lands — Breakenridge and Hawley agents to London — "The state of the right of New York," etc., reported to the assembly, and published with an Appendix giving a highly colored account of the violent and tumultuous proceedings of the settlers — Their conduct compared with that of the people in the early stages of the American revolution and defended as a justifiable revolt against governmental oppression.

THE rejoicing of the settlers, over the supposed arrangement of their difficulties, was premature and of short continuance. The engagement of the governor and council might be considered as furnishing sufficient security against public prosecutions for past violations of New York laws, but the resolve in relation to the suspension of civil suits concerning the contested lands was advisory only, and left it at the option of the claimants to comply or not as they should think proper. Besides the language of the treaty was not sufficiently comprehensive to embrace all the occasions of dissention and tumult. Some of them at least still remained, of which an example was soon furnished.

It has been already mentioned that Surveyor Cockburn had been arrested on Onion river by Baker, Warner and others, brought to Castleton and there discharged, on learning the favorable result of the negotiation with Tryon, of which they had till then been ignorant. During their absence the party had also forcibly expelled some tenants of Col. John Reid from their possessions on Otter creek. On being informed of these proceedings, Gov. Tryon addressed a letter of sharp rebuke "to the inhabitants of Bennington and the adjacent country," charging that such conduct "during the very time their commissioners were at New York waiting the determination of the government on their petition, was a breach of faith and honor," and requiring their immediate assistance in reinstating the expelled parties in their former possessions.

This letter of Gov. Tryon was taken into consideration, and an answer returned to him by a meeting of the committees of Bennington and ten other townships, held at Manchester, on the 25th of August. The answer denies that there was any breach of faith in the acts complained of, for the reason that the messengers who went to New York were not authorized to complete any arrangement, that the binding force of the treaty could only commence on its ratification by the public meeting at Bennington on the 15th of July; but that if there could be any breach of faith during the pendency of the negotiation, Surveyor Cockburn was first guilty of it by invading their territory; that it was understood by them to be implied in the terms of the arrangement "that no further settlements or locations on their lands, granted under the great seal of New Hampshire should be made until his majesty's pleasure should be obtained as to the validity of the grants;" that if such was not the understanding, they begged to be undeceived by him, "declaring that such locations and settlements on their lands, would be incompatible with friendship, and had all along been the bone of contention." The expulsion of the tenants of Col. Reid was justified on the ground that it was only a restoration to the real owners of property, of which Col. Reid had previously deprived them by force. The following is the language of the committee on that point.

"Our people having notice of Mr. Cockburn's intrusion on our borders, rallied a small party, and pursued and overtook him and his party; and in their pursuit, passed the towns of Panton and New Haven, near the mouth of Otter creek; dispossessed Col. Reid of a saw-mill, in said Panton, which by force and without color, or even pretence of law, he had taken from the original owners and builders, more than three years before, and did, at that same time, extend his force, terrors and threats into the town of New Haven; who, by the vicious and haughty aid of Mr. Benzel, the famed engineer, with a number of assistants under their command, so terrified the inhabitants (which were about twelve in number), that they left their possessions and farms to the conquerors, and escaped with the skin of their teeth, although they had expended large sums of money in cutting roads to, and settling in that new country, as well as fatigued, and labored hard in cultivating their farms. Col. Reid,, at the same time, and with the same force did take possession of one hundred and thirty saw logs, and fourteen thousand feet of pine boards, which boards were made in the same mill, and all lying thereby, all which he converted to his own use. Not long after, the original proprietors of said mill did reenter and take possession thereof, but were a second time attacked by Col. Reid's steward, with a number of armed men, under his (supposed) instructions and by their superior force and threats, obliged to quit the premises again — all which tenements, said Reid occupied and enjoyed until dispossessed, as your excellency's letter complains of."

The committees therefore declined to aid in restoring the possession to Col. Reid's tenants and expressed the conviction that if his excellency had known by what unlawful means he had originally obtained possession, he would not have required it. This answer of the settlers was received by Gov. Tryon, and laid before his council the 8th of September, and by that body treated as "highly insolent and deserving of sharp reprehension." The council advised him that, in their opinion, the opposition to the government had become so formidable that it "could not be effectually suppressed without the aid of regular troops." From this time it was evident that the negotiation was a failure, and no further regard appears to have been paid to it on either side.

The strife between Col. Reid and the grantees under New Hampshire occupies a prominent position in the New York controversy, and as it was not yet ended some further account of its origin seems necessary.

Col. Reid held a patent for seven thousand acres of land situated on both sides of Otter creek in the townships of New Haven and Panton, both of which townships were chartered by New Hampshire in 1761. Reid's patent was ten years later, bearing date June 7, 1771, and having been issued by Gov. Dunmore in violation of the king's prohibitory order of July, 1767, was consequently illegal and void.[1] He seems to have obtained from Gov. Moore as early as 1766, an order of survey and from that time to have claimed the land as his own, though destitute of any show of title till 1771, as before stated. In answer to the foregoing statement in behalf of the

[1] Col. Reid's was not a military but a civil grant made to him in the name of himself and six nominal associates, after the usual manner of conferring lordly domains on favored individuals. He does not appear to have been a "reduced officer," and could not, therefore, have been entitled to the bounty under the king's proclamation, though he applied to the governor in 1771 for such a grant of five thousand acres, but no patent for it is found. He had probably obtained the rights of some officers to additional tracts which he expected to locate adjoining his seven thousand acres and obtain patents for them. *Col. Hist. N. Y.*, vol. 8, p. 312. See also Land Papers referred to in *New York Calender Index,* title John Reid.

settlers made by Col. Reid to the New York council, he admitted that the New Hampshire claimants were the first occupants, and that treating them as unlawful intruders upon his land he had dispossessed them of the saw mill and the adjacent improvements, and had forcibly prevented them from regaining and holding possession, substantially as related by them. He claimed that during his occupancy of the premises he had erected a grist mill and made other expensive improvements, of which by the recent dispossession of his tenants, he was now deprived. We shall hear more of this claim of Col. Reid's hereafter.

Gov. Tyron, in giving an account to the colonial secretary of the unfavorable answer of the settlers to his letter, requiring them to reinstate Col. Reid in his former possessions, informed him that the opposition to the government appeared to be daily increasing in strength, and was likely to become too formidable "for militia forces to encounter." In reply to this letter Lord Dartmouth under date of December 9, 1772, after imforming the governor of his expectation that the "question which had occasioned the disturbances, would shortly be determined in a manner that would be more effectual to restore quiet than the interposition of any military force, which," he adds, "ought never to be called in to the aid of the civil authority, but in cases of absolute and unavoidable necessity, and which would be highly improper if applied to support possessions, which after the order issued in 1767, upon the petition of the proprietors of the New Hampshire townships, may be of very doubtful title."[1]

Soon after the termination of the abortive attempt at reconciliation, Benjamin Stevens a New York surveyor with several assistants was met near the mouth of Onion river by a party composed of Remember Baker, Ira Allen and four or five others, and according to the account laid before the New York council, "stript of their property and effects, insulted and threatened, and John Dunbar thrown into the fire, bound and burned and otherwise beat and abused in a cruel manner." For this unlawful conduct the council advised the governor that "it be recommended to Mr. Chief Justice Horsmanden to issue his warrant to apprehend the said Baker and Allen for the offence with which they stood charged, and that his excellency should promise a reward of one hundred pounds for apprehending each of the offenders, to be paid to the person or persons by whom they should be appre-

---

[1] *Slade* 28–33. *Doc. Hist.*, vol. 4, 793–799, 815. *Albany Land Patents* vol. 15. *Land Papers*, vol. 28, p. 139. *Col. Hist. N. Y.*, vol. 8, p. 312, 338-9. *J. D.* Smith's History of Panton in *Vt. Quarterly Magazine* No. 1, p. 78-79. *Thompson's Vt. Gazetteer*, New Haven and Panton.

hended and brought before the chief justice." A proclamation to that effect was issued, but it is scarcely necessary to say that neither of the offenders was apprehended.[1]

It was evident that in a personal contest for the possession of the disputed lands, the New York claimants had no reasonable prospect of success against those under New Hampshire. They were composed of quite different classes of people. The New York claimants were few in number and mainly residents of New York city. They had obtained patents for large tracts, not to occupy the lands themselves, but for the purpose of making or increasing their fortunes by disposing of them to others, or perhaps in a few instances, like that of Col. Reid, with a view of peopling them with a dependant tenantry. On the other hand, the lands under New Hampshire had been chartered in townships to numerous persons, holding some three hundred and thirty acres each. The grantees were scattered throughout the New England provinces, almost every neighborhood having one or more of these proprietors who had generally become such, either with the intention of removing to the lands, or of providing homes for members of their families. The territory as before stated had long been familiarly known to New England people, many of them had already removed to it, and the desire to settle upon it was very general. From New York to this territory there was no emigration or wish to emigrate. The people there knew little or nothing of its lands, and the surplus population found more convenient and desirable situations to the westward, in New Jersey and Pennsylvania.

Besides, the New Hampshire claimants had the popular side of the controversy even in the province of New York. John Munro, who was one of the most bitter and active enemies of the settlers, and who was frequently and almost constantly threatened, and often harshly treated by them, in a letter to Mr. Duane in the spring of this year says: "The rioters have a great many friends in the county of Albany, and particularly in the city of Albany, which encourages them in their wickedness, at the same time hold offices under the government and pretend to be much against them, but at heart I know them to be otherwise; for the rioters have often told me, that be it known to me, that they had more friends in Albany than I had, which I believe to be true." But there was no need of this direct evidence of the prevailing feeling of the New York people. The fact that the sheriff's *posse*, when called to Bennington, were unwilling to act; the numerous rewards offered for the apprehension

[1] *Doc. Hist. N. Y.*, vol. 4, 799. *N. Y., Nar.* *Ira Allen's Hist. Vt.*, p. 39.

of rioters, and the perfect security with which the proscribed parties remained at their homes and attended to their ordinary business, as well as the frequent declarations of the governor and his subordinate officers that the civil power of the province was insufficient to overcome the opposition to the laws, together with their frequent calls for the aid of regular troops, furnish satisfactory proof that the heart of their own people was against them.

The following extract of a letter from Gov. Tryon to Lord Hillsborough, dated Sept. 1, 1772, indicates the material direction from which emigration came to the territory, and proves that the foregoing is a correct view of the strength of the contending parties, and of the public feeling on the subject.

"Proclamations," he says, "have often issued to prevent the grantees under New Hampshire and others from making any settlements in those parts [between Connecticut river and Lake Champlain] all which have been treated with more or less neglect or contempt. I am under the firmest persuasion, no effectual measures at present, *less than military force*, can prevent the entire colonies *pouring in their inhabitants* between the river and the lake, especially into Bennington and the adjacent townships, in order to strengthen themselves, that they may be the better able to maintain their possessions. * * * * As property and not mere delusive opinion is the object of dispute, it is natural to believe the contest will be mantained with great obstinacy."

Although the settlers under New Hampshire were determined to defend their grants, against invasion by the New York claimants, until the controversy should be decided by the king, they were extremely anxious to be able to enjoy their homes in peace, and for that purpose to obtain the speedy determination of the crown. Petitions to the king for immediate relief were numerously signed, and at a convention of the several townships on the west side of the Green mountain, held at Manchester on the 21st of October 1772, James Breakenridge of Bennington and Jehiel Hawley of Arlington had been appointed their agents to repair to London to solicit his majesty to confirm their claims under the New Hampshire charters.[1]

This new application to the crown, which was believed to be countenanced by the government of New Hampshire, to which the settlers had asked to be restored, together with the colonial secretary's severe rebukes of Gov. Tryon, for his disregard of the king's instructions, had the effect to stop the issuing of further patents for a con-

[1] *Col. Hist. N. Y.*, vol. 8, p. 310. *Doc. Hist. N. Y.*, vol. 4, p. 800-804.

siderable period. They appear also to have produced in the New York claimants serious apprehensions, that they might be permanently prevented from making their grants available. Under these circumstances it was considered very important to the government and its patentees, to place their cause before the British authorities and the public, in its strongest and most imposing light, and under the sanction of the colonial assembly. Accordingly a petition subscribed by some of the prominent land claimants was presented to that body on the 16th of February, 1773, of which the following notice is found on its journal.

"A petition of Col. John Maunsell and a number of other persons interested in lands to the westward of Connecticut river was presented to the house and read, praying that this house will adopt such measures as to them shall seem expedient, as well to prevent the success of the solicitation and interposition of the government of New Hampshire, in prejudice of the ancient limits of this province, and of the right of the petitioners and those claiming with them, as of the unreasonable claims set up under the late French government of Canada, to lands on both sides of lake Champlain." This petition is not now found among the colonial archives at Albany, and its further purport or who were its other signers has not been ascertained. It is worthy of remark however that the patent under which Maunsell, who headed the petition claimed, bore date March 7th, 1771, and was issued by Lord Dunmore in violation of the king's prohibitory order of July, 1767, and was for land situated in the township of Wells which had been chartered by New Hampshire Sept. 15th, 1761, nearly ten years previously.

On consideration of the petition, resolutions were adopted by the house affirming the right of New York against New Hampshire, to extend eastward to Connecticut river, denying the validity of the French claims and providing for the appointment of a committee to prepare a statement of the rights of the colony in these respects. Upon which, in the language of the journal, an order was made as follows:

"Ordered, that Col. Schuyler, Mr. De Noyellis, and Mr. Brush, be a committee to prepare a draft of a representation to be transmitted to the agent of this colony at the court of Great Britain, pursuant to the foregoing reslution, and that they report the same to this house with all convenient speed."

On the 6th of March, Mr. Brush from the committee made a report which two days afterwards was adopted by the house, and ordered to be entered on the journal. It consisted of two parts, one relating to the French claims, and the other entitled, "A state of the right of the colony of New York with respect to its eastern boundary on Connecticut river, so far as it concerns the late encroachments under the government of New Hampshire."

Crean Brush, who presented this report to the house, was a member from the county of Cumberland, which had been constituted by the government of New York, on the east side of the Green mountain, and was at this session first represented in the assembly. He was a lawyer by profession, who had emigrated from Dublin to the city of New York, where he had resided for a few years, extensively engaged in land speculations. Besides large tracts in other parts of the province, he held claims for over twenty thousand acres, under New York patents, in the district of the New Hampshire Grants. He had recently taken up his residence at Westminster, the county seat of Cumberland county, where in addition to his membership of the assembly, he held the offices of county clerk and surrogate. He was a fluent speaker, possessed of some shrewdness as a politician, and had considerable influence in the assembly. This he always exerted in favor of the government, sustaining with great zeal all the most arbitrary and tyrannical demands of the mother country, as well as the most oppressive measures of the provincial authorities against the settlers under New Hampshire. He was wholly destitute of principle, and though at first a favorite, he eventually became unpopular and troublesome to the people of the new territory in which he had settled. This, however, he abandoned in 1774, and returned to New York. He was afterwards at Boston with the British army, fled with it on the evacuation of that town, was captured, brought back to the city and imprisoned for fraud, peculation and robbery, escaped from prison and fled to New York, where he became a confirmed sot and ended his career by committing suicide.[1]

---

[1] *Assembly Journal N. Y. Com. Report*, pp. 120, 121. *Thompson's Vt. Gaz., Wells.* For an interesting biographical notice of Crean Brush, see *B. H. Hall's Eastern Vt.*, p. 603. A daughter of Mr. Brush, who became the wife of Thomas Norman, was allowed in 1797 by the New York commissioners appointed to distribute the $30,000 paid by Vermont on the settlement of the controversy, the sum of $718.60, for the loss of title to fourteen thousand five hundred and fifty acres of Vermont land, granted her father by the New York government. Brush's claims were still more extensive, but the above is all that were held sufficiently proved. It appears from the journal of the commissioners (p. 3), that Brush had a conveyance of ten thousand acres, being the whole of Snyder's patent of land in Bennington and Pownal, and had transferred one thousand two hundred and twenty-two acres to Goldsbrow Banyar. His heirs were not allowed for the residue of it, and what was done with it does not appear.

Mr. Brush had little or nothing to do in the preparation of this report, though he was doubtless ready and competent to advocate its adoption by the house. It was an elaborate paper, covering eighteen folio pages of the assembly journal, and had been drawn up with great labor and care by Mr. Duane, who, prompted by his own deep interest in the success of the New York patents and his employment as counsel for the other claimants in the ejectment suits, had made the subject his peculiar study.[1] The object of the report was to show that Connecticut river was the eastern boundary of the province of New York prior to its being declared so by the crown in 1764; that it had in fact always been such boundary, and that the charters of the governor of New Hampshire, though previous to that date, were void, because they granted lands which were not within that province. It embodies all the arguments that have at any time been adduced in favor of the New York title, and presents the title in its most plausible and imposing character. It shows much historical research, and evinces the skill and adroitness of a learned professional advocate. By ingeniously giving prominence to historical events of trifling consequence, and by either discoloring and distorting or entirely suppressing others of real importance to the question discussed, the author succeeded in constructing an argument not ill calculated to make a favorable impression on a cursory reader. As a historical document it is, however, deceptive and unreliable. It would occupy too much space to enter into a critical examination of this report in the body of this work, but such a review of it will be found in the Appendix (No. 6). One or two, however, of its prominent errors will here be pointed out.

As a basis for his argument that New York originally extended eastward to Connecticut river, Mr. Duane undertakes to convey the idea that such was the extent of New Netherland at the time of its conquest by the English in 1664, thereby having it understood that

[1] In Mr. Lossing's *Life of Gen. Schuyler*, vol. 1, page 265, the preparation of this report is ascribed to him, perhaps from the fact that he was chairman of the committee. It was not reported to the house by him, and there is no doubt whatever that Mr. Duane was the author. It is so stated in his biography by Hon. S. W. Jones published in the fourth volume of the *Documentary History of New York*, page 1065. John Adams in his diary for August, 1774, written on his way to the congress at Philadelphia, of which both he and Mr. Duane were members, says John Morin Scott told him that the document "was principally drawn by Mr. Duane who had unhappily involved almost all his property in the lands;" and that "he had purchased patents of government and claims of soldiers to the amount of a hundred thousand acres."

New York, by succeeding to the rights of the Dutch, would be of equal extent. In support of the assumption that such was the extent of New Netherland, he quotes the letter of Gov. Stuyvesant of Sept. 2, 1664, in answer to the summons of Col. Nicolls to surrender his province to the English, when in that very letter Gov. Stuyvesant refers, as of binding force on the Dutch, to the treaty of Hartford in 1650, by which the eastern boundary of New Netherland on New England was declared to be a line running from the west side of Greenwich bay on Long Island sound, indefinitely to the northward, so "that it came not within ten miles of Hudson's river;" which line, we have already seen, had been ratified by the States General of Holland, and had been declared in the commission of the Dutch governor, on the reconquest of the province from the English in 1673, to be their eastern boundary. The existence of this treaty boundary is not mentioned by Mr. Duane for the very good and sufficient reason that it would overthrow at once his whole argument on that most important point.[1]

In order to make it appear that the government of New York had always claimed jurisdiction over the disputed territory of the New Hampshire grants, Mr. Duane refers to several ancient patents of land by the governors of that province which he claimed were situated, not indeed upon Connecticut river or very near it, but which reached towards that river, and beyond the line as claimed by New Hampshire. The most important of those grants, and indeed the only one which on close examination seemed to favor such a claim of jurisdiction, was one made to Godfrey Dellius in 1696, which was alleged to embrace a territory of twelve miles in width and about sixty miles in length along the eastern shore of Lake Champlain, and within the present limits of Vermont. An examination of the description in the grant makes it very plain that not a single acre of the land could possibly be situated within the disputed territory. These two examples of error in this New York document must suffice for the present.[2]

Soon after the adoption of this legislative manifesto, it was published and extensively circulated, together with an appendix of still greater length, entitled "A narrative of the proceedings subsequent to the royal adjudication, concerning the lands to the westward of Connecticut river, lately usurped by New Hampshire, with remarks on the claim, behavior and misrepresentations of the intruders under that government."

[1] For the letter of Gov. Stuyvesant, see *Smith's Hist. N. Y.*, vol. 1, p. 20.

[2] For the descriptive language of the patent, see Appendix No. 7.

This narrative, after a weak apology for the regranting of the disputed lands by New York, relates, in much detail and in highly colored language, the various threatening and violent acts of the settlers before mentioned, together with some others of similar character, but of less importance; and represents them as the lawless and unjustifible proceedings of a tumultuous unfeeling mob, deserving the decided condemnation of all friends of order and good government. If considered without reference to the cause which produced them, they should doubtless be viewed in that light. The conduct of the settlers was in opposition to the laws of the province, and might therefore be termed "lawless." The actors were not directed in their operations by an established and recognized government, and might consequently be denominated "a mob." But it should be remembered that such is always the character of the uprising of a people against government oppression. The American Revolution was initiated and largely aided in its early progress by "tumultuous mobs." The famous stamp act was prevented from being put in execution by what has often been styled "mob law." The officers of the crown who were appointed to distribute the stamps were in all the colonies prevented from doing so, either by threats of injury to their persons or property, or by actual violence. In New York, Lieut. Gov. Colden was only induced to give up the stamps by the pursuasion of a mob, which had first broken open his coach house and made a bonfire of its contents, together with his own effigy, amid the plaudits of a surrounding populace. The British armed schooner Gaspee, at Rhode Island, was captured and destroyed by "a mob," and "a lawless mob," disguised as Indians, seized by force and emptied into Boston harbor, three hundred and forty-two chests of tea, thereby in connection with similar irregularities in other parts of the country rendering the odious tax on that article inoperative. But there can be no need of enumerating instances of such unauthorized demonstrations. Such irregularities inseparably belong to every forcible opposition of a people to the tyranny of an established government. The question in such case is whether there shall be submission, or irregular or in other words mob resistance, for that is the only resistance which it is possible to make.

The point to be determined in relation to the New Hampshire settlers and claimants, is whether the measures attempted and threatened by the New York government were such as to excuse and justify resistance.

If we consider the instances in which those who have revolted against established governments, have been justified by the tribunal of history, we shall rarely find a case stronger than that of the New Hampshire claimants. Our American revolution can scarcely be said to furnish so clear an example of rightful resistance to oppression. The American people revolted from the mother country because of the imposition of taxes, which though small in amount, were founded on a principle that would allow the extortion of any further sum the parliament might at any time think proper to demand; thus destroying the security of the residue of their property, and leaving it at the mercy of the government. In the case of the inhabitants of the New Hampshire grants the principle of government exaction was carried at once by New York to its utmost extent by requiring not a fraction of their property, but demanding as a right the immediate surrender of the whole. If revolution were justifiable in the former case, as is now universally admitted, it must be deemed at least equally so in the latter. It should also be remembered that the New York oppression was rendered peculiarly hateful and odious by the fact that the motives which prompted it were of the most selfish and mercenary character; and that it was moreover inflicted by a subordinate government contrary to the declared opinion and express command of the king, its acknowledged superior.

The New Hampshire settlers were freemen, intelligent, hardy and brave. They had, in general, expended their all in the purchase, in good faith, of the lands which they occupied, and in transforming them into comfortable homes for themselves and families. Is it surprising that they should have resisted the attempts of the New York rulers to deprive them of their possessions? Would it not, indeed, have been craven and unworthy of manly heroism to do otherwise?

CHAPTER XIV.

CONDITION OF AFFAIRS ON THE EAST SIDE OF THE GREEN MOUNTAIN; SECOND APPEAL TO THE KING, AND FAVORABLE REPORT OF THE BOARD OF TRADE.

1772-1773.

Treatment of the settlers east of the Green Mountain by the New York government — Counties of Cumberland and Gloucester formed —Smothered discontent with the New York government — Outbreaks at Windsor and Putney — Grant by Tryon of ten thousand acres of land in Hinsdale to Col. Howard — Breakenridge and Hawley in England — Favorable Report of the Board of Trade and Protest against it of Gov. Tryon — The terror inspired by the threats of the Green Mountain Boys a principal weapon of defense against their adversaries — Corporal punishment by whipping, a common mode of punishment in New York and other colonies prior to the revolution.

WHILE the controversy in relation to their land titles was producing serious disturbances among the inhabitants on the west side of the Green mountain, those on the east side had remained comparatively quiet. It has already been seen that Lieut. Gov. Colden's patents in 1765, for peculiar reasons, had been confined to lands on the west side of the mountain. The numerous complaints made to Sir Henry Moore, his successor, of the great injustice of Colden's interfering patents, the application of the settlers to the king for relief, and the order of the crown consequent thereon, forbidding any further grants, operated to protect the lands of the inhabitants on the east side from the grasp of the speculators. As late as March 4th, 1771, Alexander Colden, surveyor general of the province, certified and doubtless truly, "that he had not made any return of the survey of any lands known to be held under the government of New Hampshire eastward of the ridge of the Green mountains," except of the rights allotted to Gov. Wentworth before mentioned. As these were not occupied, regranting of them did not injure the inhabitants. In fact, the formidable opposition occasioned by Colden's interfering grants made it for the interest of the New York government to strengthen itself with the crown and also at home, by conciliating the good will and obtaining the aid of the eastern settlers, in their controversy with those at the west, and that was the policy early adopted by that government. The New Hampshire titles were confirmed to the original proprietors in several of the townships on Connecticut river, and in some instances with liberal deductions from the customary patent fees. As a further means of winning the favor of the eastern inhabitants, new counties were formed, creating a variety of offices to be filled by influential individuals. A county by the name of Cumberland was constituted by act of the assembly in July, 1766, embracing territory nearly identical with the present counties of Windsor and Windham. Among the officers immediately appointed were a sheriff, a surrogate, a county clerk and a coroner, three judges of the court of common pleas, seven assistant judges of the same court and fifteen justices of the peace. This act of the assembly was repealed and annulled by the king, and his order was laid before the assembly by the governor the 2d of December, 1767. The county consequently became extinct. It was however revived and reestablished by ordinance of the governor and council, bearing date February 10th, 1768.[1] By ordinance of the governor and council adopted in March, 1770, another county was constituted, by the name of Gloucester, comprising all the territory north of Cumberland county and east of the Green mountain, of which Kingsland, now Washington in Orange county, was made the county seat. There were no inhabitants within many miles of the place, but a log hut, dignified with the name of a jail was erected in the wilderness and left without a keeper or tenant, but in which the courts were directed to be held. For this county the governor at once appointed a sheriff, a county clerk, four commissioners to administer oaths, three judges of the court of common pleas, four assistant judges and nine justices of the peace. The population within the limits of the county was probably less than six-hundred, and it is difficult to conceive what motive there could have been for its formation, other than that of gratifying the taste of persons ambitious for office and titles. An attempt to hold the court of common pleas in February, 1771, proved abortive. The officers after travel-

[1] Mr. B. H. Hall, in his *History of Eastern Vermont* (p. 2), treats the reestablishment of Cumberland county as the *personal* act of the king in consequence of "numerous applications and representations made to the crown." In point of fact the king knew nothing whatever of the ordinance. The New York governor and council were the sole actors. The charter of the county issued by the governor, like his land patents, was in the name of the king, but the king knew no more of it than he did of the patent of Socialborough and that to Col. Reid, both of which were issued by the governor without the king's knowledge and in violation of his express order.

ing from Mooretown, now Bradford, during parts of two days in the woods on snow shoes, not being able to find the court house, gave up the search and returned.[1]

But notwithstanding the marked distinction made by the New York government between the settlers on the two sides of the Green mountain, there always extensively existed among the inhabitants on the east side, a lurking, though partially smothered dissatisfaction with that government. So strong indeed, as occasionally to break out in open resistance to its authority. The requirement that the New Hampshire claimants should obtain, at a serious expense, and much trouble, confirmatory charters, in order to quiet their titles, was very generally thought to be an unnecessary hardship, only demanded for the sake of the fees of office, and the emoluments of the surveyor general, new surveys being insisted on. The New York system of organization and laws was also different from those to which they had been accustomed, and of a less democratic character. All county officers were appointed by a distant governor, and they in turn appointed inferior officers to perform duties which their town meetings and town officers had previously regulated and executed. The New York officers and courts were accused of corruption, and some of the officers were very unpopular. Some knowledge of the state of feeling which was very prevalent on the east side of the mountain, may be gathered from a statement made under oath by Simon Stevens, an intelligent friend of New York, then residing in Charlestown, and afterwards in Vermont. His affidavit was sworn to at New York, March 2, 1771, before Chief Justice Horsmanden, in which he says, "That by the law of New Hampshire, every township chooses annually selectmen, and a variety of other public officers, and are authorized to hold town meetings, all which are on the plan of the like regulations in the province of Massachusetts

---

[1] The following is from the record of the expedition entered by the clerk. "Feby. 25, 1771. Set out from Mooretown for Kingsland, traveled until night, there being no road and the snow very deep — we traveled on snow shoes or rackets. On the 26th we traveled some ways and held a council, when it was concluded it was best to open the court. As we saw no line it was not known whether in Kingsland or not. But we concluded we were far in the woods, we did not expect to see any house unless we marched three miles within Kingsland, and no one lived there when the court was ordered to be opened on the spot." It appears from the record that the persons present on this memorable occasion, were John Taplin, judge, John Taplin, Jun., sheriff, John Peters of the Quorum and John Peters, clerk, the two latter being doubtless but one person. See *Doc. Hist. N. Y.*, vol. 4, p. 1033, and *Deming's Vt. Officers*, p. 119.

Bay. And that the public taxes are levied by warrant from the selectmen." He then adds, "that since his majesty's determination of the boundary in 1764, many of the townships within the province of New York to the eastward of the Green mountains, had continued to regulate themselves and to elect their town officers, and levy their town taxes in conformity to the New Hampshire patents, and the laws of that province, and not agreeable to the laws of New York, which have not been the rule of their conduct." This attachment to their favorite town republics, and dislike of the province and county government substituted by New York, extensively prevailed on the east as well as on the west side of the mountain, throughout the whole provincial period.

In June 1770, a large body of men from Windsor, who complained of the New York jurisdiction and denied the authority of that government to constitute the county of Cumberland, declaring "its formation a sham," repaired to Chester where the court of common pleas was to be held, and by their violent proceedings prevented it from transacting business, and seized an obnoxious attorney, whom they carried to Windsor where they held him under keepers for several days. The state of feeling in the county was such that there was little prospect of his obtaining compensation for the injury. Nor do the rioters appear to have been dealt with criminally for their conduct. In fact the principal leaders seem to have been afterwards appeased and reconciled to the New York government by appointments to office and by becoming favored petitioners for land patents. Out-breaks of a similar though of less formidable character against the New York authority, occurred in Putney, and in some other towns.[1]

Although the New Hampshire claimants on the east side of the mountain were not in general disturbed by interfering patents from New York, yet there was not wanting an example of sufficient importance to call their attention to the oppressive conduct of that government toward their brethren on the other side. On the 23d of November, 1771, Gov. Tryon issued to Col. Thomas Howard a patent for ten thousand acres of land in Hinsdale, now Vernon, and the patentee soon afterwards repaired to that town to take possession. The land had first been granted at an early day by Massachusetts, which grant was afterwards, in 1753, confirmed by charter of New

[1] *New York Assembly Journals and Council Minutes. Doc. Hist. N. Y.*, vol. 4, p. 694. *Index,* titles, Cumberland and Gloucester. *Hall's Eastern Vt.*, p. 1–6, 142, 161–168, 172–173. *Ira Allen's Vt.*, 22. *Deming's Vt. Officers,* p. 119.

Hampshire, and was some of the richest and best land on Connecticut river, much of which had been occupied and cultivated for many years. This patent was the occasion of much excitement and comment, not only in the immediate vicinity of its location, but in the neighboring colonies of Massachusetts and New Hampshire. The *Essex Gazette* of Dec. 24, 1771, published at Salem, contains letters from Putney, dated the 11th and 14th of that month, giving an account of the grant and of Col. Howard's visit to that section of the country, in which all parties connected with the transaction are very severely handled. One of the letters states that the writer had had a conversation with Howard at the house of Judge Wells, and that Howard told him "he had a mandamus from the king for ten thousand acres of land to be laid out in the province of New York, where it had not been granted before by that province. He, upon information at York of the value of the town of Hinsdale, made a pitch of said place by plan, obtaining a charter under the province seal of the same, signed by Gov. Tryon." "Immediately upon which," the letter adds, "he comes here with two livery servants, his attendants, tells Hinsdale people of it, makes them an offer, viz., to lease the lands to them they now enjoy for five years for one penny sterling per acre, another five years for one shilling per acre, and at the expiration of said time to come to a new agreement. Hinsdale people have got the same now under consideration, they are in great perplexity, not knowing what to do; many of them are wealthy men, but persons of no liberal education, and I am afraid they will do something prejudicial to themselves on that account." These terms, which would have furnished an income to the patentee of over two hundred dollars annually for the first five years, and of about two thousand five hundred each year for the last, and at the end of that time leave him the owner of the land with all its intermediate improvements, do not appear to have been accepted; for an application was afterwards made to the crown for relief against the patent. Gov. Tryon when complained of for this unjust and oppressive grant to his friend Howard, sought to excuse himself on the ground that the grant was made in obedience to the mandamus of the crown, arguing that having the king's command to grant that quantity of unpatented land, Colonel Howard had the right to select it wherever he pleased within the province, and that he was obliged to issue his patent for it, although it was already occupied under previous charters from Massachusetts and New Hampshire, and notwithstanding the king's prohibitory order forbidding him to make any grants whatever within that territory. But this plea, which was really frivolous, was unsatisfactory to the English board of trade, who severely condemned his conduct in making it. Though Gov. Tryon, after the loud complaints made against him, expressed some regret for the act, yet he does not appear to have had any proper sense of its injustice, for in a letter to Lord Dartmouth in defence of his conduct, he denies the legality of the settlers' title under both the Massachusetts and New Hampshire charters, and adds "that the offer Col. Howard made to the occupants when he became acquainted with their circumstances, was too generous to leave room for complaint."[1] It does not appear that Col. Howard was ever able to derive any benefit from his patent.

When Messrs. Breakenridge and Hawley, agents of the New Hampshire claimants, reached England in the winter of 1772–3, they found the subject of their mission had already been considered by the board of trade, and that they had made a report to the king in council, bearing date Dec. 3, 1772, proposing terms for the adjustment of the controversy, as favorable to their constituents as they could expect to obtain. They, therefore, soon returned home. The report was not, however, confirmed by order of the king in council till the ensuing April, when it was transmitted by the Earl of Dartmouth to Gov. Tryon, with a recommendation that it should be carried into effect. The report, as has been before seen, censured in the strongest language the avaricious and oppressive conduct of the New York governors in regranting the lands in controversy, and proposed terms for accommodating the disputes. The most material of those terms were, in substance, that all actual settlers should be quieted in the possession of the lands they occupied, without regard to the origin of their titles; and that the charters of the New Hampshire townships which had not been occupied by claimants under New York should be confirmed to the original proprietors and those claiming under them, without reference to any subsequent New York patents of the land; and that such subsequent patentees should be indemnified for their losses by grants of other lands. The report was not in the nature of an order or command, but was a proposition to the New York government, which being deemed just and equitable by the king in council, it was hoped would be assented to and carried into execution by that government. This hope was, however, fallacious. The plan, if adopted, would annul most of the New York patents and send the patentees in search of

[1] *Albany Records, Land Patents,* vol. 16. *Col. Hist. N. Y.*. vol. 8, pp. 321, 346, 381. *New York Narrative. E. Allen's Narrative,* 1774. *Hall's Eastern Vermont,* pp. 171, 172. *Duane's MS. Plea before Congress,* p. 17.

other lands, and it could not be expected to meet their approbation. Governor Tryon, who was one of them and a fair representative of the others, protested against the proposed plan in a letter of great length, and in the most earnest and vehement terms, declaring it to be in a high degree unjust to the New York claimants and altogether impracticable. He proposed as a substitute that all the New Hampshire charters should be declared void and all New York patents valid. This favorable report of the board of trade, with its approval by the king, soon became known to the settlers and increased their confidence in the ultimate success of their cause.[1]

The territory in controversy had now acquired the distinctive name of The New Hampshire Grants, the claimants under the charters of that province, being familiarly designated as "Hampshire men," and their opponents as "Yorkers." The active defenders of the New Hampshire title were beginning to be known as "Green Mountain Boys," though they continued by the New Yerk government, to be usually styled "the Bennington mob." They had become well satisfied that the only means of preserving their possessions from the grasp of the New York claimants was to prevent their acquiring a foot hold in their territory by the occupation of lands under their patents, and to the accomplishment of that object, their subsequent efforts were mainly directed. Their position was such that not only bravery, but also great discretion was required. They were under the dominion of Great Britain, whose king they acknowledged as their sovereign, and to whom they had appealed for relief against the oppressions of his subordinate government of New York. Their appeal had been favorably received, and by the interposition of the crown they had strong expectations of eventual protection. If they had been disposed, they were too weak to brave the power of the king, though they felt able to compete successfully with that of New York. But by opposing the subordinate government they were in danger of incurring the serious displeasure of its superior, and of thereby forfeiting all hope of a successful termination of the controversy. They saw that excessive injuries to the persons, or wanton destruction of the property of their adversaries, would be likely to excite against them the displeasure of the king and his ministry. Sound policy therefore required that the resistance to the New York government should assume as mild a form as

[1] For the report of the board of trade, Lord Dartmouth's letter and Tryon's reply, see *Col. Hist.*, vol. 8, p. 330, 359, 360, and *Doc. Hist.*, vol. 4, p. 803, 827, 831. See also *Slade*, p. 33. *Ira Allen's Vt.*, p. 47, 48. *E. Allen's Nar. of* 1774, p. 167, 174.

was possible. In order that it should be effectual a system of terrorism, if it may be so called, seems to have been early adopted and steadily pursued.

Violence, which was resorted to, when deemed necessary, was always accompanied by threats of much greater for any repetition of the offense, and the threats were made in such an earnest and defiant manner as to produce the belief that they were likely to be executed. The minutes of the New York council are full of the complaints of patentees and surveyors that their lives were in danger from the armed bands of the Green Mountain Boys, and they furnish abundant evidence of the terror which their threatenings inspired, and of their great efficacy in deterring invasions of the disputed territory. And yet, during the whole controversy not a single life was taken, not a person was permanently maimed, and there is no evidence that a gun was ever aimed and discharged at any one. Surveyors and claimants were not unfrequently told that their lives would be taken if they attempted certain forbidden things and that armed men were prowling in the woods to shoot them. Shots were sometimes fired by way of intimidation, of which the case of Justice Munro is an instance. Guns were frequently discharged about his residence, and sometimes into the roof of his house to frighten him away, and though he might any day have been taken and punished in any manner his opponents chose, he was, from policy, if not from humanity, suffered to remain in fear of his life until he chose to retire. The mysterious quaintness with which the threatnings of the Green Mountain Boys were sometimes clothed, served to increase the terror they were otherwise calculated to inspire. One of the penalties to which those suspected of being friendly to the Yorkers, were told they were exposed, was that of being "*viewed*." Precisely what that meant was not defined. It was understood to import that the conduct of the suspected party would be examined by a committee of the settlers, and that if found delinquent he would be dealt with as they might direct, even to the punishment by the *beech seal*. That was defined by Allen to be a chastisement of the New York claimants "with the twigs of the wilderness, the growth of the land they coveted." It was termed a seal in allusion to the great seal of New Hampshire, affixed to the grants made by the governor of that province, on which there was a fancied representation of a tree, of which the beech rod well laid on the naked backs of the Yorkers and their adherents, was humorously considered a confirmation.

This mode of punishment by the *beech seal*, though much talked of and abundantly threatened, was not often executed. There are in fact not more than two or three well authenticated instances in which it appears to have been inflicted, one or two in the earlier part of the controversy, and the other on Benjamin Hough, a New York justice, at a later period, of which an account will hereafter be given. The fear of it, however, added much to the strength of the New Hampshire men in the controversy, and was a cause of weakness in their opponents.

In judging of the conduct of the Green Mountain Boys in inflicting corporal punishment upon their adversaries, it should be borne in mind that such punishment was then in common use throughout the colonies, and was looked upon in a very different light from what it would be at the present day. The colony of New York was by no means an exception to that practice. It was there adopted early and continued late. In the description of New Amsterdam by Montanus in 1671 he says " on the river side stood the gallows and whipping post," and in his picture view of the city they occupy quite a prominent position. Until after the commencement of the revolution there was an officer of the city of New York denominated " the public whipper," whose duty it was to inflict such corporal punishment as the proper tribunals directed. By an act of the New York assembly in 1744, for any offence under grand larcency, the mayor and aldermen at the quarter sessions were authorized to inflict " such corporal punishment (not extending to life and limb) as they in their discretion should think proper," the sentence, in the language of the act, to be put in execution " by the public whipper of said city." Two justices in other parts of the province had the same power, and their sentence was to be executed by the constable. By an act passed December 11, 1762, " a person obtaining goods in the city of New York by false pretences," might be punished in the same discretionary manner, the sentence as in the former case was to be executed " by the public whipper." Both these acts were in force at the time of the application of the said beech seal upon the Yorkers, and the courts of New York had like power to inflict corporal punishment for other and higher crimes. Punishment by whipping was in use in New York and the other states during the revolutionary period and for many years afterwards, and was indeed continued in the army and navy of the country until far into the present century. This mode of punishment being sanctioned by the universal practice of the period when it was inflicted by the New Hampshire claimants, is not, therefore, of itself, evidence of any peculiar want of civilization or humanity on their part. It was doubtless used as the most effectual punishment " short of life and limb " which was within their power, the disgrace, which was supposed to attach to it, forming one of the elements that commended it to their favor.[1]

---

[1] *Doc. Hist. N. Y.*, vol. 4, p. 116. *Livingston and Smith's N. Y. Statutes*, p. 339, 340, 297. *Act of* 1785, chap. 40 and 47. *Col. Hist. N. Y.*, vol. 8, p. 445. *Articles of War of* 1776, sec. 18, art 3. *Jour., Cong.* Sept. 20, 1776. *Army Regulations*, article 24. *Jour. Cong.*, May 31, 1786.

CHAPTER XV.

Conflicts of the Green Mountain Boys with Colonel Reid's Tenants, and with the Claimants under the Patent of Socialborough and Durham.

1773.

Attempts of Col. Reid to occupy and maintain the possession of the disputed land on Otter Creek by force—His tenants dispossessed with a strong hand—Capt. David Wooster and his patent in Addison—Application of Gov. Tryon for regular troops to put down the rioters, refused—County of Charlotte constituted and officers appointed—The illegal and void New York patents of Socialborough and Durham, with an account of the grounds of the controversy in regard to them. Violent proceedings of the Green Mountain Boys.

NOTWITHSTANDING the formidable demonstrations of the Green Mountain Boys, some of the Yorkers were determined to maintain their titles by force, and to keep out the New Hampshire men. In the month of June, 1773, Col. Reid engaged several Scotch emigrants, then recently arrived at New York, to occupy as his tenants, the lands of which he had been dispossessed the previous autumn, and he went with them to Otter creek. On entering on the lands they found several persons settled on them, claiming under the New Hampshire charters. These Col. Reid compelled by threats to leave, making however, as he claimed, compensation for the growing crop of one of the principal occupants. He caused the grist mill to be repaired and several log huts to be erected, and then returned to New York. It appears from the affidavit of one of the tenants, that they were informed on their way to Otter creek, that the title to the land was in dispute and desired to return to New York, but that the colonel assured them there was no question about the title, that he would put them in possession and protect them there. This second invasion of the territory by Col. Reid, called out the Green Mountain Boys in considerable force. On the 11th of August, Allen, Warner and Baker appeared on the ground with over one hundred armed men, informed the Scotchmen that they had been imposed upon by Col. Reid, and that the land did not belong to him, and warned them to depart. A short time was given them to remove their effects, when the huts were set on fire and burnt to the ground. The grist mill could not be thus disposed of without endangering the saw mill which had previously been erected by New Hampshire men. It was therefore pulled down, and the mill stones, after being broken, were thrown down the falls into the creek. The land being within a few miles of Crown Point, the New Hampshire men were apprehensive Col. Reid might, by aid from there, attempt to regain the possession. The destruction of the property was therefore deemed necessary as a warning to him that any further improvements he might make would be sure to share a similar fate.

According to the affidavits of several of the tenants, the party of Green Mountain Boys conducted in a very boisterous and swaggering manner, boasting that they were a mob, and defying the authority and power of the New York government: that Baker said "he lived out of the bounds of law, that his gun was his law;" that "he despised everything the New York government could do; that they were resolved never to allow any person claiming under New York to settle in that part of the province;" that he "tore the bolting cloth belonging to the mill in peices, and distributed it among the mob to wear in their hats as cockades, or trophies of their victory," and that, when asked for his commission for doing the work he was then about, Baker held up his thumb which had been cut off in his encounter with Justice Munro, at Arlington, saying "that was his commission;" that Allen when asked for his name in order that it might be given to Col. Reid, declared that "his name was Ethan Allen, captain of that mob; that his authority was his arms, pointing to his gun; that he and his companions were a lawless mob, their law being a mob law; that if any of Col. Reid's settlers offered thereafter to build a house and keep possession the Green Mountain Boys would burn their houses and whip them into the bargain;" and when one of the tenants who had said that he meant to build a house and keep possession for Col. Reid was brought before him, Allen with an oath told him if he attempted such a thing he would have him "tied to a tree and skinned alive;" and that Allen and several others declared "that if they could but catch Col. Reid they would cut his head off."

The largest portion of this party of Green Mountain Boys was from the southern part of the territory, but they had been joined by others from several of the neighboring towns. A number were from the adjoining town of Addison, which had been chartered by New Hampshire, in 1761. David Wooster, who had been a captain in the French war, had subsequently obtained a New York patent for three thousand acres within that township, but had found it occupied by settlers under the New Hampshire charter, who refused to remove or acknowledge his title. "On the return home of the Addison men, thirteen in number, from the expedition against Col. Reid's tenants, they found Capt. Wooster, with his sheriff serving writs of ejectment on those that were on the land which he claimed. Their indignation rose to the highest pitch, that while they had been driving off the Yorkers for their neighbors, their own homes had been invaded. They finally took him and his sheriff and tied them to a tree, and threatened to give them the beech seal. After blustering a good deal, Wooster saw they were in earnest, and that his threats of New York law did not intimidate them; he gave in, sent off his sheriff and took up his copies of the writs he had left, and promised not to disturb them again. The whole was sealed over a stiff mug of flip; and in the morning the captain left. He was afterwards a major general in the revolutionary army, and was mortally wounded, April 27, 1777, at Ridgeford, on Tryon's invasion of Danbury, Conn.[1]

Information of the attack upon Col. Reid's settlement being laid before the New York council, they unanimously advised the governor to request Gen. Haldimand, then in command of his majesty's forces, "to order a sufficient number of troops to occupy the posts of Ticonderoga and Crown Point, to give such aid to the civil magistrate as he should from time to time require for the preservation of the public peace, and the due execution of the laws." This advice was at once communicated by the governor to Gen. Haldimand, by whom it was not received with favor. In his answer he observed "that Crown Point being entirely destroyed and unprovided for the quartering of troops, and Ticonderoga being in a most ruinous state, such troops as might be sent thither, would not be able to stay a sufficient time at those posts to render them of much utility." In conclusion, however, he desired to know, (if the request for troops was persisted in) the number that would be required, and asked to have provision made for the expenses of their transportation. The council being of opinion that a body of two hundred troops would be necessary, and the general declaring that no more than fifty could be provided with winter quarters, the council came to the conclusion that the season was too far advanced for the troops to be of any essential service, and that the aid required must be necessarily postponed. Lord Dartmouth, the colonial secretary, being informed of this appli-

[1] *Doc. Hist.*, vol. 4, p. 842, 846. *Allen's Nar. of* 1774, p. 152-6. *Ira Allen's Vt.*, p. 41. *Swift's Hist. Addison Co.*, p. 67. *Miss Hemenway's Vt. Magazine*, Addison, p. 4, also p. 32, 69, 79.

cation for troops, promptly wrote Gov. Tyron that the requisition "was not under all the circumstances approved." Thus ended this second attempt of the New York claimants to enforce their titles by military power.[1]

The New York government and claimants failing in their open attempts to get possession of the disputed lands, sought to gain a foothold in the territory by sowing the seeds of jealousy and division among the settlers. Some of them who were supposed to possess influence over others were induced, by favorable offers, to accept conveyances of the New York title to their lands in confirmation of that under New Hampshire, thereby separating their interest from that of their neighbors, while others were flattered by appointments to office.

When the New York jurisdiction over the New Hampshire grants had been first assumed in 1765, the whole territory was treated as included in the county of Albany. We have seen that the lands on the east side of the Green mountain had been formed into the counties of Cumberland and Gloucester. By act of the assembly of March 12, 1772, a new county by the name of Charlotte was constituted on the west side of the mountain, reaching from Canada line on the north to the Batten kill and the south line of the New York patent of Princetown on the south, and extending west beyond Lakes George and Champlain. The greatest portions of the towns of Arlington and Sunderland, as well as all the territory to the northward of them, were thus included in the new county, while the lands to the south remained in the county of Albany. The courts of the new county were at first directed to be held at the house of Patrick Smith near Fort Edward, but afterwards Skenesborough, now Whitehall, was made the county seat. The organization of the new county was not completed until the summer of 1773, when a full complement of county officers was appointed. Among them were several who resided in the limits of the New York patents of Socialborough and Durham. Of these patents it is necessary to give some account.

The patent of Socialborough, to which reference has already been made, bore date April 3, 1771, and was issued by Gov. Dunmore in violation of the king's order in council of July, 1767, forbidding any such grant. This prohibitory order, and the consequent want of authority in the governor to make the grant, was well known to the parties for whose benefit it was made, and it was

---

[1] *Col. Hist.*, vol. 8, p. 394, 395, 399. *Doc. Hist.*, vol. 4, p. 843-846, 855-6.

therefore illegal and void. The patent covered forty-eight thousand acres of land, bounded on the south by Clarendon, and was a tract thirteen miles in length from north to south, by over six in width, and was nearly identical with the New Hampshire townships of Rutland and Pittsford. Both of these townships had been granted by New Hampshire ten years previously, and both had been occupied under the New Hampshire charters prior to the date of the New York patent. The nominal grantees in the patent were forty-eight persons, each entitled to one thousand acres, but most of them, a few days after the patent issued, conveyed their shares to a few New York city speculators, for whose benefit the grant had really been made, and who instigated and sustained all subsequent efforts to eject the New Hampshire claimants.[1]

The patent of Durham, which was issued by Gov. Tryon, bore date January 7, 1772, and like that of Socialborough was issued in violation of the king's order in council of July, 1767, as well as of the 49th article of his standing instructions, which Tryon had brought with him from England and laid before his council. It purported to grant thirty-two thousand acres in shares of one thousand acres each to thirty-two individuals by name, and was described as a tract bounded on the north by Socialborough and the

---

[1] From the minutes of the proceedings of the New York commissioners appointed to distribute the thirty thousand dollars paid that state by Vermont on the final adjustment of the controversy, now in the office of the secretary of state at Albany, it appears that allowances were made for the failure of the New York title in Socialborough, as follows, viz, (all the claimants being residents of New York city):

James Duane,	15,000 acres.
Goldsbrow Banyar,	4,000 "
William Walton,	4,000 "
John Watts,	2,000 "
John Kelly,	6,000 "
John DeLancey,	1,000 "
Gerard Walton,	1,000 "
Making	33,000 "
Leaving claims not provided for	15,000 "

These 15,000 acres probably belonged to members of the New York council, or others whose property had been confiscated as loyalists, and who would not therefore be entitled to any allowance.

It is observable that no claim was made by any person who had undertaken to occupy the land in Socialborough in person, for the probable reason that such persons were mere employés or tenants of the New York owners.

New York patent of Newry. It was not in regular square or oblong form, but included most if not all the land in the township of Clarendon, which had been chartered by New Hampshire, September 5, 1761.

The first settlement made in Clarendon was about the year 1768, under a conveyance or lease from one John H. Lydius, an Indian trader and native of Albany. He claimed title to a very large tract of land on Otter creek by virtue of a deed from some Mohawk Indians, dated in 1732, and a pretended confirmation by the king, through Gov. Shirley of Massachusetts, in 1744. When the settlers found their title to be spurious, they were induced by the representation and influence of the New York land adventurers to seek protection against the New Hampshire title by obtaining a patent under the government of New York, although it was well known the king had forbidden the issuing of any such patent. An arrangement was accordingly entered into with Mr. Duane, to procure a patent for them, by which he and his New York friends were to be entitled to fourteen thousand two hundred and twenty-five acres, nearly half of the land, all the persons who were to become patentees executing a covenant under seal, by which they agreed to stand seized of that quantity for Mr. Duane and his associates. By this means the interest of "the Durhamites," as they were afterwards styled by the New Hampshire claimants, became fully indentified with that of the New York speculators.[1]

Among the justices of the peace for the new county of Charlotte, were Jacob Marsh of Socialborough, and Benjamin Spencer of Durham. The latter was also an assistant judge of the court of common pleas. Marsh held under the New York patent, and was prominent in advocating it, and in discrediting the New Hampshire title. Spencer is represented by Ira Allen in his history, as "an artful, intriguing and designing man." He had been an active agent of Mr. Duane and his patentees of Socialborough, in their efforts to get possession of the lands held by the settlers and claimants under the New Hampshire charters of Rutland and Pittsford. His name was at the head of the petition to the governor for the patent of

[1] *Albany Records*, Patents, vol. 16. *Ira Allen's Vt.*, p. 36. *Doc. Hist. N. Y.*, vol. 4, p. 956. *Thompson's Vt. Gaz.*, Clarendon. *Minutes of N. Y. Com. of* 1797, p. 12, 88. By these minutes it appears that Mr. Duane was entitled to four thousand seven hundred and forty-one acres of the Durham land, being one-third the quantity reserved. The other two-thirds were probably for two other persons who by becoming loyalists could not share in the land indemnity paid by Vermont. For a more particular account of Lydius and his title, see Appendix No. 8.

Durham, and he was one of the principal actors in obtaining it. He was in close correspondence with Mr. Duane, and his letters, some of which have been preserved, although they evince a strong feeling of hostility and prejudice against the New Hampshire claimants, throw some light on the nature and character of the controversy, in that section of the disputed district. Under date of April 11, 1772, he had written Mr. Duane from Durham, as follows:

"Sir: The people of Socialborough decline buying of their land, saving four or five, and say they will defend it by force. The people that settled under Lydius's title and those that have come in this spring, have agreed for their land. The New Hampshire men strictly forbid any further survey being made only under the New Hampshire title, which riotous spirit has prevented many inhabitants settling this spring. You may ask why I do not proceed against them in a due course of law, but you need not wonder when I tell you it has got to that the people go armed and guards are set in the roads to examine people, what their business is, and where they are going, and if they do not give a particular account, they are beaten in a most shameful manner, and it has got to that, they say they will not be brought to justice by this province, and they bid defiance to any authority in the province. We are threatened at a distance of being turned off our lands or our crops destroyed. * * * * I hope the survey of our patent may not be stopped on account of this tumult, as we shall labor under a great disadvantage if our lands are not divided this Spring. I look upon it to be dangerous for Mr Cockburn to come into the country until those people can be subdued. * * * One Ethan Allen hath brought from Connecticut twelve or fifteen of the most blackguard fellows he can get, double armed, in order to protect him, and if some method is not taken to subdue the towns of Bennington, Shaftsbury, Arlington, Manchester and those people in Socialborough and others scattered about the woods, there had as good be an end of the government. I am with all due regard your humble servant,

BENJAMIN SPENCER.

The twelve or fifteen "blackguard fellows" mentioned in the letter as being with Allen were doubtless, Baker, Warner, Cochran and their associate Green Mountain Boys, who though many of them were originally from Connecticut, were then residents in the territory, and claimants under the New Hampshire title.

In another letter to Mr. Duane, dated in May following, Spencer says, "The tumults have got to such a height, both in Socialborough and from Bennington to Manchester, that I cannot travel about to do my lawful business, indeed I cannot with safety travel two miles from home. I am threatened daily of having my house burnt over my head, and the rest of the inhabitants driven out of their possessions in Durham. If we are not relieved by government, I know not what our fate must be. The Hampshire people swear that no man shall stay on these disputed lands that favors the government in any shape whatever. The people of Socialborough prevent any settlements at present, swearing they will shoot the first man that attempts to settle under a title derived from New York, although there are many desirous of purchasing."

These threats it is scarcely necessary to say, were never executed, and were doubtless uttered for the purpose of intimidation. The strife however between the respective claimants grew more earnest and severe as new occupations of lands were made or attempted. The continued efforts of the New York claimants to get possession of the lands covered by the patent of Socialborough, aided by Spencer and others residing in Durham, and the determination of the latter to prevent any lands being occupied by New Hampshire claimants under the charter of Clarendon produced bitter controversies that not unfrequently led to violent collisions. The active efforts of the newly appointed officers to exercise and establish their authority over the New Hampshire claimants, in connexion with the advocacy of the New York title by those who had recently been induced to accept it, increased the apprehensions of their neighbors, who held under the New Hampshire charters for the security of their possessions. If the Yorkers could fully establish their jurisdiction and authority over the territory covered by those two New York patents, they would not only deprive the New Hampshire claimants of their lands within the townships of Pittsford, Rutland and Clarendon, but would gain a footing in the district that might enable them to overthrow all the New Hampshire charters.

To counteract these alarming movements of their adversaries, it was resolved in the councils of the Green Mountain Boys that none of the New York officers residing in the disputed territory should be allowed to perform any official acts, and that in order to separate the interests of the inhabitants of Durham from that of their New York city associates, they should be required to acknowledge the validity of the New Hampshire title by purchasing and holding under it, and that if mild measures should not be found sufficient to carry into effect these resolves, forcible means should be resorted to.

In accordance with these resolves, a large body of Green Mountain Boys with Allen and their other leaders visited Clarendon and its vicinity early in the fall of 1773, and invited the compliance of the New York officers and claimants, informing them that unless such compliance took place within a specified time, they must expect force would be used. Justice Spencer having heard of the approach of the party, and being apprehensive of danger kept out of the way and was not to be found. No actual violence against the persons or property of the inhabitants appears to have been used at this time, except that a small dog which had the misfortune to be named Tryon was cut to pieces to show their dislike and defiance of the governor after whom the poor animal had been called. Threats of violence were however, freely used, in case the warning then given them should not be heeded, which threats it was hoped would frighten the New York leaders into submission. In this the Green Mountain Boys were disappointed. The justices still persisted in issuing writs against the New Hampshire men, other New York officers continued to act, and the claimants under that province led by Spencer, Marsh, and Samson Jenny, who held the place of coronor, were loud in their advocacy of the New York title.

A second visit to Durham was accordingly made. In order to be sure of capturing Spencer a party of some twenty or thirty men under the lead of Ethan Allen and Remember Baker went to his house about 11 o'clock on Saturday night, the 20th of November, and took him into custody. He was carried about two miles to the house of one Green, and there kept under the guard of four men, until Monday morning, when he was taken to "the house of Joseph Smith, of Durham, inn keeper." Being informed that he was to be put on trial for his offence against the New Hampshire men, he was asked where he would choose to be tried; to which he replied that he was not guilty of any crime, but that if he must be tried, he would prefer that the place should be at his own door. This favor was readily conceded to him.

By this time the numbers of the Green Mountain Boys had increased to about one hundred and thirty, all armed with guns, cutlasses, etc. The people of Clarendon (*alias* Durham), with many from Socialborough, having notice of what was going on, were also assembled to witness the proceeding. Before commencing the trial Allen addressed the multitude at some length, informing them that "the proprietors of the New Hampshire Grants had appointed himself, Seth Warner, Remember Baker and Robert Cochran to inspect and set things in order, and to see that there should be no intruders on the grants," declaring among other things that "Durham had become a hornet's nest," which must be broken up. After concluding his harangue, the rioters proceeded to erect what they styled "a judgment seat," upon which Ethan Allen, Seth Warner, Remember Baker and Robert Cochran took their places as judges, Spencer was then ordered to stand before them, to take off his hat and listen to the accusations against him. Allen then charged him "with cudling with the land jobbers of New York to prevent the claimants of the New Hampshire rights from holding the lands they claimed, and with issuing a warrant as a justice of the peace contrary to their orders; and Remember Baker charged him with having accepted a commission as magistrate in the colony of New York, and of having acted as magistrate in pursuance thereof contrary to their orders, and of having represented their bad conduct in a letter by him wrote and sent to New York, and of having conveyed a piece of land by title derived under a grant obtained in the colony of New York, and with endeavoring to seduce and inveigle the people to be subject to the laws and government of the colony of New York."

Of all those offences his judges found him guilty, and declaring his house to be a nuisance, passed sentence that it should be burnt to the ground and that he should promise he would not for the future act as a justice of the peace under New York. But upon Spencer's representation that his wife and children would be great sufferers and his store of dry goods and all his property be destroyed if his house was burned, the sentence was reconsidered, and upon the suggestion of Warner it was decided that the house should not be wholly destroyed, but only the roof should be taken off, and might be put on again, provided Spencer should declare that it was put on again under the New Hampshire title, and should purchase a right under the charter of that province. Spencer having promised compliance with these terms, the Green Mountain Boys proceeded to take off the roof "with great shouting and much noise and tumult." Spencer on his further promise not to act again as magistrate was discharged from custody. A company of some twenty or thirty of the "mob party" went to the house of coroner Jenny, and finding him missing and his house deserted set it on fire and burnt it to the ground. Most or all of the other inhabitants of Clarendon who held under the New York patent being visited and threatened, agreed to purchase the New Hampshire title. According to the New York version of this invasion of Durham, which is all the written or printed account of it that has been found, "the men composing the mob," conducted themselves in a coarse, boisterous and blustering manner, using very violent as well as profane language, threatening destruction and death to those who should fail to acknowledge the New Hampshire title and become its advocates.

A number of the men from the southern part of the district, who had visited Clarendon, on their return, met Jacob Marsh, Esq., at Arlington, who was on his way from New York to Socialborough, took him prisoner, and put him on trial for his crimes against the New Hampshire claimants, before Samuel Tubbs, Nathaniel Spencer and Philip Perry as judges. Seth Warner and Remember Baker were his accusers, the latter insisting upon the application of the "beech seal," as a punishment. But his advice did not prevail; the sentence of the judges, which was in writing, and read to him by Warner by direction of the court, was to the effect that he should thereafter encourage settlements of lands under the New Hampshire charters, and discourage those under New York, and that he should not act as a justice of the peace under a New York commission "upon pain of having his house burnt and reduced to ashes, and his person punished at their pleasure." He was then dismissed, his judges furnishing him with a certificate to protect him against further mob punishment for past offences.[1]

It appears from the affidavit of Marsh that on his reaching Socialborough he found that the roof of his house had been publicly taken off by a party of Green Mountain Boys, probably under the idea that when put on again it would be, like that of Spencer, under the New Hampshire title. A day or two after the departure of the mob from Clarendon, Charles Button, a constable residing in that town, was arrested at Pittsford, in the northern part of Socialborough, and a prisoner he had in charge for debt was taken from his custody. Button was put on trial for acting in the office under the New York authority, threatened with the "beech seal," and compelled to give the party six shillings for his damages, and to "promise he would never execute any precept under the province

---

[1] The following is given in the affidavit of Marsh as a literal copy of the certificate.

"Arlington Novr 25th AD 1773. These may Sertify that Jacob Marsh haith ben Examined, and had on fare trial — so that our mob shall not medeal farther with him as long as he behaves

Sartified by us his judges, to wit

SAML TUBS
NATHANIEL SPENCER
PHILIP PERRY"

Teste
CT. Seth Warner

of New York." He was thereupon dismissed and furnished with a certificate as follows:

"These are to certify to all the Green Mountain Boys that Charles Button has had his trial at Stephen Mead's and this is his discharge from us.

PELEG SUNDERLAND,
BENJAMIN COOLEY."

The Durhamites had, indeed, chosen to accept a patent from New York, which they must have known had issued contrary to the order of the king, and was consequently illegal, and they were in active hostility to the New Hampshire claimants. They had nevertheless entered into possession of their lands under a supposed title from Lydius, and it is difficult to justify the violent proceedings of the Green Mountain Boys against them upon any other ground than that the equitable claims of the few should submit to the safety of the many, and that such harsh measures were indispensable to the general security.

But while the Green Mountain Boys were determined to make the settlers in Clarendon purchase and hold their lands under the New Hampshire charters, they were equally decided that they should not be imposed upon by being compelled to pay unreasonable prices for them. Allen, soon after his return from the expedition to Clarendon, being apprehensive that advantage might be taken by the holders of the New Hampshire title to insist upon extravagant rates of compensation from the frightened Durhamites, addressed them a letter, warning them not to submit to any such impositions, and promising them protection against any such oppression. To this letter he procured the additional signatures of Jehiel Hawley, who had been the agent of the settlers in England, and some others of the prominent New Hampshire claimants. The letter was afterwards transmitted to the governor of New York, and laid before his council. It is characteristic of the writer and of the time, and is therefore inserted at length, as follows:

"*To Mr. Benjamin Spencer and Mr. Amos Marsh and the people of Clarendon in general.*

Gentlemen: On my return from what you call the mob, I was concerned for your welfare, fearing that the force of our arms would urge you to purchase the New Hampshire title at an unreasonable rate, though at the same time I know not but that after the force is withdrawn you will want a third army. However, on proviso, you incline to purchase the title aforesaid, it is my opinion that you in justice ought to have it at a reasonable rate, as new lands were valued at the time you purchased them. This with sundry other arguments in your behalf, I laid before Capt Jehiel Hawley and other respectable gentlemen of that place (Arlington), and by their advice and concurrence I write you this friendly epistle, unto which they subscribe their names with me, that we are disposed to assist you in purchasing reasonably as aforesaid; and on condition Col. Willard or any other person demand an exhorbitant price for your lands, we scorn it, and will assist you in mobbing such avaricious persons, for we mean to use force against oppression, and that only. Be it in New York, Willard or any person, it is injurious to the rights of the district.— From yours to serve,

ETHAN ALLEN.
JEHIEL HAWLEY.
DANIEL CASTLE.
GIDEON HAWLEY.
REUBEN HAWLEY.
ABEL. HAWLEY.

Furthermore we are of opinion this letter communicates the general sense of our grants."

A few days after dispatching the foregoing letter, Allen addressed another letter to the inhabitants of Clarendon on the same subject, of which the following is a copy:

"*An Epistle to the Inhabitants of Clarendon.*

"From Mr. Francis Madison of your town, I understand Oliver Colvin of your town has acted the infamous part, by locating part of the farm of said Madison. This sort of trick I was partly apprised of when I wrote the late letter to Messrs. Spencer and Marsh. I abhor to put a staff into the hands of Colvin or any other rascal to defraud your settlers. The Hampshire title must, nay shall, be had for such settlers as are in quest of it, at a reasonable rate, nor shall any villain by a sudden purchase impose on the old settlers.

"I advise said Colvin to be flogged for the abuse aforesaid unless he immediately retracts and reforms, and if there be further difficulties among you I advise that you employ Capt. Warner as an arbitrator in your affairs. I am certain he will do all parties justice. Such candor you need in your present situation, for I assure you it is not the design of our mobs to betray you into the hands of villainous purchasers. None but blockheads would purchase your farms and must be treated as such. If this letter does not settle this dispute you had better hire Capt. Warner to come singly and assist you in the settlement of your affairs. My business is such that I cannot attend to your matters in person, but desire you would inform me by writing or otherwise relative thereto. Capt. Baker joins with the foregoing and does me the honor to subscribe his name with me.

We are gentlemen your friends to serve,

ETHAN ALLEN,

REMEMBER BAKER."[1]

It is believed that a portion of the inhabitants of Clarendon purchased the New Hampshire title in compliance with this requirement of the Green Mountain Boys, and that most of the settlers were eventually, in some way, quieted in their possessions.

---

[1] *Ira Allen's Hist.*, 36, 37. *Doc. Hist. N. Y.*, vol. 4, p. 856 to 869. Spencer's Letters in *Allen Papers*, 39, 63. C. Button's Affidavits, *Allen Papers*, 107. Allen's Letters to the people of Clarendon in *Stevens's Papers*.

CAPTER XVI.

New York Act of Outlawry against Allen and Others.

1774.

Resolutions of the New York Assembly offering rewards for Allen, Baker, Warner, and five others — Act of Assembly declaring them by name, and also any other persons concerned in riots in Albany and Charlotte counties, guilty of felony and punishable with death, without trial, on their neglect to surrender themselves — Public answer of the committee of the settlers, and of the proscribed parties to the provisions of the New York law — Measures of defense against "the Yorkers" — Forts built at New Haven, on Otter Creek, and at Colchester, on Onion river — Application of Colden to Gage, for regular troops, and his refusal.

IN January following the violent proceedings of the Green Mountain Boys against the claimants under the patent of Durham the subject was brought before the assembly of New York by petition of Benjamin Hough of Socialborough, in behalf of himself and others. The petition with accompanying affidavits, was referred to a committee from which Mr. Brush, for Mr. Clinton, the chairman, on the 5th of February 1774, reported resolutions, declaring "that in view of the dangerous and destructive spirit of riot and licentiousness prevalent in part of the county of Charlotte and in the northeastern district of the county of Albany," and in consideration of the exposure of the inhabitants living there to violence and abuse "an humble address be presented to his excellency, desiring that he would be pleased to issue his proclamation offering a reward of fifty pounds for apprehending and securing in his majesty's jail at Albany, any or either of the following named persons:

Ethan Allen, Seth Warner, Remember Baker, Robert Cochran, Peleg Sunderland, Silvanus Brown, James Breakenridge and John Smith; which reward for the apprehension of Allen and Baker was afterwards increased by vote of the assembly, to one-hundred pounds each. The resolution of the assembly further provided that "a bill should be brought in more effectually to suppress the riotous and disorderly proceedings, maintain the free course of justice and for bringing the offenders to condign punishment," and Mr. Brush and Col. Ten Broeck were appointed a committee for that purpose.

These resolutions of the assembly having been published in the *New York Mercury*, reached the people of the district and were taken into consideration: "At a general meeting of the committees of the several townships on the west side of the range of the Green mountains, granted under the great seal of the province of New Hampshire, held at the house of Eliakim Wellers in Manchester, on the 1st day of March, 1774, and afterwards by adjournment at the house of Capt. Jehiel Hawley in Arlington, on the third Wednesday of the same month."

A committee of seven was appointed to prepare an answer to the resolutions, and their report, having been adopted by the convention, was signed by Nathan Clark, chairman, and Jonas Fay, clerk, and published in the *Connecticut Courant*, printed at Hartford, and in the *New Hampshire Gazette*, at Portsmouth.

The answer complained that the resolutions in charging the inhabitants of the New Hampshire Grants with being rioters and disturbers of the public peace "had not mentioned a single word in regard to the title to the land contested for," which their authors very well knew was the sole cause of all the difficulty; averred that they and the people they represented were "loyal subjects of the king of Great Britain," and were the friends of order and good government, and that all they had done was necessary to their protection against the unjust and oppressive attempts of their enemies to deprive them of their property and to make them their tenants and slaves, and was therefore justified by the great law of self preservation. The answer then gave a clear and concise statement of the grounds of the land controversy, claimed that the New Hampshire settlers had a valid title to the lands in dispute under the charters of the king's governor of that province, gave a copy of the order of the king in council of July 24, 1767, prohibiting the New York governors from making any more grants of their lands, which order it was declared had been disregarded and violated by them; that the lords of trade and plantations "having considered and wisely deliberated upon the several circumstances of the controversy, did on the third day of December, A. D. 1772, make their report in favor of the New Hampshire grantees," of which report they were in daily expectation of receiving his majesty's confirmation, and that they were justified in defending their possessions until his final decision. The convention further alleged that those in authority in the New York government were mostly claimants of their lands under patents issued subsequent to the charters of the settlers, that the trials of their titles on writs of ejectments brought by the New York patentees, were before courts "wherein judge and plaintiff were connected in one common interest;" that the judgments were illegal and invalid, and that the settlers ought not to be treated as rioters for opposing their execution.

The convention further declared that they would stand by and defend their proscribed friends and neighbors "at the expense of their lives and fortunes," and in conclusion, resolved as follows; "that, for the future, every necessary preparation be made, and that our inhabitants hold themselves in readiness, at a minutes warning, to aid and defend such friends of ours who for their merit to the great and general cause, are falsely denominated rioters; but that we will not act any thing more or less, but on the defensive, but will always encourage due execution of law in civil cases, and also in criminal prosecutions, that are so indeed, and that we will assist to the utmost of our power, the officers appointed for that purpose." [1]

While the committees of the New Hampshire Grants were preparing their foregoing defence of the conduct of their constituents, Gov. Tryon, in order to carry into effect the views of the assembly, issued his proclamation, bearing date the 9th of March, 1774, offering a reward of one hundred pounds each for the apprehension of Allen and Baker, and fifty pounds each for the six others named in said resolutions. On the same day an act for preventing tumultuous and riotous assemblies in the counties of Charlotte and Albany, and for punishing those concerned in them, passed the assembly; an act, which for its savage barbarity is probably without a parallel in the legislation of any civilized country.

This New York law first specifies several riotous acts, for some of which the penalty was to be imprisonment, and such corporal punishment, short of life and limb, as the court might see fit; and others were declared to be felony, for which the offender was to suffer death without benefit of clergy. The act proceeds to name "Ethan Allen, sometime of Salisbury in the colony of Connecticut, but late of Bennington, in the county of Albany, yeoman; Seth Warner, late of Bennington in said county, yeoman; Remember Baker, late of Arlington in the said county, yeoman; Robert Cochran, late of Rupert, in the county of Charlotte, yeoman; Peleg Sunderland and Silvanus Brown, late of Socialborough in the same county, yeoman; James Breakenridge, late of Walloomsack in the county of Albany, yeoman; and John Smith, late of Socialborough, yeoman;" as the principal ringleaders of the riots and disturbances It then empowers the governor and council to

---

[1] *Jour. N. Y. Assembly*, Febr. 5, 1774. *Slade*, 37-42. *Allen's Narrative*, 11. *Conn. Courant*, June 21, 1774. *N. H. Gazette*, No. 914.

make an order, requiring those persons, or any others who may be indicted for offences within the counties of Albany and Charlotte, to surrender themselves for commitment, to one of his majesty's justices of the peace, within seventy days after the publication of the order in the *New York Gazette* and *Weekly Mercury;* and in case such newspaper summons should not be obeyed, the person neglecting to surrender himself, was, in the language of the act, "to be adjudged, deemed, and (if indicted for a capital offence hereafter to be perpetrated) to be convicted and attainted of felony, and shall suffer death, as in cases of persons convicted and attainted of felony, by verdict and judgment, without benefit of clergy," and the supreme court of the colony, or the inferior courts of oyer and terminer, or of general jail delivery for the said counties of Albany and Charlotte, were authorized and directed "to award execution against such offender so indicted for a capital offence, in the same manner as if he had been convicted or attainted," in said courts respectively. Any person indicted for an offence under the degree of felony, might be summoned to surrender in the same manner, and neglecting to appear was to receive the like punnishment that would have been awarded after trial and conviction.[1]

An appeal to the public, in answer to this act of the assembly and to the governor's proclamation, was soon prepared by seven of the eight prescribed persons, to which their names were appended, and which they caused to be published in the *Hartford Courant* and the *Portsmouth Gazette*, and extensively circulated in hand-bills. It affirmed in clear and forcible, if not uniformly polished language, the justice of their cause, and avowed their determination to maintain it at all hazards. They declared that the title to their lands was the essence of the whole controversy, that if the New York patentees would abandon their claims and quiet them in their possessions, there would be no more disturbances — that the government of New York "had broke over his majesty's express prohibitions in patent-

[1] The resolutions of the assembly, and Gov. Tryon's proclamation offering the rewards, are found in *Doc. Hist. N. Y.*, vol. 4, p. 869–873. For the New York act in full, see *Slade*, p. 42, and *New York Statutes*. It appears from the journal of the assembly, that the clause for hanging offenders without trial, met with some opposition in that body, and that on a vote by yeas and nays, it was carried by fifteen to ten. Among the ayes are the prominent land claimants George Clinton, afterwards governor of the state, and whose persistent obstinacy while in that office, prolonged the controversy and delayed the admission of Vermont into the Union for several years, voted in its favor.—*Assembly Journal*, Feb. 25, 1774. For biographical sketches of the eight proscribed persons, see Appendix No. 1.

ing their lands, and was not therefore entitled to their obedience in respect to them;" they say, "the case stands thus: if we oppose civil officers in taking possession of our farms, we are, by these laws, denominated felons, or if we defend our neighbors, who have been indicted rioters, only for defending their property, we are likewise adjudged felons. In fine, every opposition to their monarchal government is deemed felony, and at the end of every sentence, there is the word DEATH." The charge preferred against them, that they had rescued prisoners for debt, they declared to be false, and to that in regard to their often assembling in arms, they replied as follows: "As to forming ourselves into military order and assuming military commands, the New York *posses* and military preparations, oppressions, etc., *obliged us to it.* Probably Messrs. Duane, Kempe, and Banyar, of New York, will not discommend us for so expedient a preparation; more especially since the decrees of the 9th of March are yet to be put in execution; and we flatter ourselves, upon occasion we can muster as good a regiment of marksmen and scalpers, as America can afford; and we now give the gentlemen above named, together with Mr. Brush and Col. Ten Broeck, and in fine, all the land jobbers of New York, an invitation to come and view the dexterity of our regiment, and we cannot think of a bettor time for that purpose, than when the executioners come to kill us by virtue of the authority their judges have lately received, to award and sentence us to death in our absence." [1]

The latter part of this appeal was addressed "to the people of the counties of Albany and Charlotte, which inhabit to the westward of, and are situated contiguous to, the New Hampshire Grants."

It referred to them as friends and neighbors, who were acquainted with the relation which the settlers sustained towards the New York claimants and government, in language as follows: "your people, in general, cannot but be sensible that the title of our land, is in reality, the bone of contention; and that as a people we behave our-

[1] The persons here named were all prominent leaders among the New York patentees, and deeply interested in the controversy. Duane held patents for over fifty thousand acres; Kempe was attorney general of the colony and held large tracts. Duane and Kempe had been attorneys for the plaintiffs, in all the ejectment suits. Banyar was secretary to the governor's council and had claims for more than one hundred and twenty thousand acres. Crean Brush and Col. Abraham Ten Broeck had large claims, were members of the assembly, and were the committee that reported "the bloody bill" against the settlers, and were active in procuring its passage. Ten Broeck was one of the claimants by purchase of the patent of Walloomsack. *Council Minutes*, Dec. 12, 1769.

selves orderly; and are industrious and honestly disposed, and pay just deference to order and good government; and that we mean no more by that which is called the *mob*, but to defend our just rights and properties. We appeal to the gentlemen merchants, to inform whether our people in general, do not exert themselves to pay their just debts, and whether they have ever been hindered by the country's *mob*, in the collection of their dues. But as to the magistrates, sheriffs, under-sheriffs, coroners, and constables of the respective counties, that hold their posts of honor and profit under our bitter enemies, we have jealousy that some of them may be induced to recommend themselves to those on whom they are dependent, and for the wages of unrighteousness offered by proclamation, to presume to apprehend some of us, or our friends. We therefore advertise such officers, and all persons whatsoever, that we are resolved to inflict *immediate death* on whomsoever may attempt the same; and provided any of us or our party shall be taken and we have not notice sufficient to relieve them, or whether we relieve them or not, we are resolved to surround such person or persons whether at his or their own house or houses, or any where that we can find him or them, *and shoot such person or persons dead.* And furthermore, that we will *kill and destroy* any person or persons whatsoever, that shall presume to be accessary, aiding or assisting in taking any of us as aforesaid; for by these presents we give any such disposed person or persons to understand that although they have a license by the law aforesaid to *kill* us, and "an indemnification" for such murder from the same authority; yet they have no indemnification for so doing from the Green Mountain Boys."

This bold and defiant declaration was signed by Ethan Allen, Seth Warner, Remember Baker, Robert Cochran, Peleg Sunderland, John Smith and Sylvanus Brown, and to it in the published copies both in newspapers and hand bills was appended the following lines, written by Thomas Rowley, a man distinguished in those days among the settlers for wit and poetry.

"When Cæsar reigned king at Rome,
Saint Paul was sent to hear his doom;
But Roman laws, in a criminal case
Must have the accuser face to face,
  Or Cæsar gives a flat denial.
But here's a law made now of late
Which destines men to awful fate,
  And hangs and damns without a trial.
Which made me view all nature through

To find a law where men were ti'd,
By legal act which doth exact
Men's lives before they're tried.
Then down I took the sacred book
And turned the pages o'er,
But could not find one of this kind
By God or Man before. ...... T. R." [1]

This manifesto of the proscribed parties was in accordance with the general feeling of the New Hampshire grantees, the New York law and proclamation being regarded by them as originating in the avarice of a set of speculators, who coveted their lands with their valuable improvements, and as designed to terrify them into submission. They were well aware that the great body of the people of New York felt no interest in enforcing the claims of their adversaries and that the popular sentiment on the contrary, was favorable to those of the settlers, former experience having shown, that the militia of the colony could not be brought to act against them with effect. Under such circumstances, the threatnings of that government, so far from causing terror, were looked upon with utter contempt, and instead of palsying the arm of resistance nerved it to greater vigor.

But while the people of the New Hampshire grants were determined not to submit to the claims of their adversaries, they were not unmindful of the opinions which might be formed of their conduct by the inhabitants of the neighboring colonies.

They were desirous that their position should be fully understood by the people surrounding them, and in addition to other vindications of their conduct, there was published by Ethan Allen, in the year 1774, an elaborate review of "the State of the Right of the Colony of New York with respect to its Eastern Boundary on Connecticut River" etc., which "State of the Right" as has been herebefore mentioned, had been given to the public under the authority of the New York assembly the previous year. This work of Allen was a pamphlet of more than two hundred pages, printed at Hartford, Connecticut, and entitled "A Brief Narrative of the proceedings of the Government of New York relative to their obtaining the jurisdiction of that district of land to the westward of Connecticut river," etc., etc. This narrative was drawn up with considerable ability, and it commented with much severity upon the conduct of

---

[1] *Slade*, 49–54. *Allen's Narrative*, 36–48. *Connecticut Courant*, June 28, 1774. *New Hampshire Gazette*, No. 915.

the New York land claimants towards the grantees under New Hampshire, who were vindicated as purchasers in good faith under one of the king's governors, who had at least a *prima facie* right to grant their charters. Only a portion of the documentary evidence hereinbefore produced in behalf of the New Hampshire title being used, for want of a knowledge of historical and official papers, and of access to them. The pamphlet, however, from the evidence there brought forward of the defects of the New York claim of jurisdiction prior to the king's order of 1764, and of the strength of the title of New Hampshire during the period in which its charters were granted, together with its exposure of the avaricious and inequitable conduct of the New York city speculators, was such as to produce a very favorable impression on the public, especially in New England, where the measures adopted by the New York patentees and government, were very generally viewed with strong disapprobation.

Besides this grave and formal appeal to the public in behalf of the New Hampshire settlers, others of a lighter character were sometimes made, among which may be mentioned certain poetical effusions from the unpolished but popular pen of Thomas Rowley. One of these was entitled "an invitation to the poor tenants under the patroons in the province of New York to come and settle on our good lands under the New Hampshire grants." It is too long for insertion, but a few stanzas may be given as a specimen of its spirit and execution. It began:

"Come all you laboring hands that toil below,
Among the rocks and sands — that plow and sow
Upon your hir'd lands, let out by cruel hands,
'Twill make you large amends — to Rutland go.

Your pataroons forsake, whose greatest care
Is slaves of you to make, while you live there,
Come quit their barren lands, and leave them in their hands,
'Twill ease you of your bands — to Rutland go.

* * * * * *

We value not New York with all their powers,
For here we'll stay and work, the land is ours,
And as for great Duane, with all his wicked train,
They may eject again, we'll not resign.

* * * * * *

In George we will rejoice, he is our king," &c.[1]

[1] *Rural Magazine*, vol. 1, p. 383. *Deming's Vermont Officers*, p. 139.

Notwithstanding the large rewards offered for Allen and his associates, they do not appear to have been in any real danger of being apprehended under the governor's proclamation. The terror which their threats, backed as they were by the known power and determination of the Green Mountain Boys, produced among their adversaries, and the general sympathy felt for them by the people of the province, were sufficient to prevent any serious attempts to capture them.[1] Further protection against invasion of the territory by "the Yorkers" was, however, provided by the erection of two forts near the outskirts of the settlements; one at New Haven falls, on Otter creek, in the neighborhood of Col. Reid's patent, and the other on Onion run, at Colchester. Information of the erection of these fortresses, and of the continued hostility of the settlers being laid before the New York council, that body on the 1st of September, 1774, advised Lieut. Gov. Colden to apply to Gen. Gage, then military commander-in-chief, for the aid of regular troops. With this application Gen. Gage declined to comply, on the ground that a similar application had been previously denied by the British ministry, and also for the reason that Gov. Tryon had been called home to give light on the points in dispute concerning the New Hampshire lands, upon which a final decision might soon be expected. An appeal from this decision of Gen. Gage having been made by Lieut. Gov. Colden to the English ministry, Lord Dartmouth, with strong assurances of regard for the loyal conduct of the New York government, informed him that he did not "at present see sufficient ground for the adoption of such a measure." Thus ended the third and last abortive effort of the New York land claimants to have their titles enforced by the aid of the king's regular troops.[2]

---

[1] Two attempts to arrest Allen were made at an earlier date, under a previous proclamation, for an account of which see biographical notice of Allen, Appendix.

[2] Benjamin Hough's petition and accompanying affidavits and proceedings of the council thereon, and Lieut. Gov. Colden's correspondence with Gen. Gage and Lord Dartmouth.—*Doc. Hist. N. Y.*, vol. 4, p. 875 to 890. *Vermont Quarterly Magazine*, p. 69. *Ira Allen's Hist.*, p. 42.

CHAPTER XVII.

PUNISHMENT OF YORKERS, AND THE WESTMINSTER MASSACRE.

1774-1775.

Ludicrous punishment of Dr. Samuel Adams, a Yorker— Trial and corporal punishment of Benjamin Hough for petitioning the New York Assembly, and advocating the passage of the act of outlawry against Allen and others, and for acting as a magistrate under New York — Uprising of the people of Cumberland county in March, 1775, and the Westminster Massacre — Action of the New York Assembly thereon, and the case of Hough — A convention of Committees of Cumberland and Gloucester counties, resolve to petition the king against the New York government, and to be either annexed to another government, or formed into a new one — Col. Skene's project of a new province — The battle of Lexington gives a new direction to these affairs.

AFTER the passage of the New York act of outlawry, all attempts of the Yorkers to obtain possession under their patents were unsuccessful. Although the Green Mountain Boys were ready, whenever necessity required it, to resort to severe measures against their adversaries, they were not unwilling to try the effect of milder means. Ridicule, as well as violence, was sometimes used. An example of a mixture of both may be found in the case of Dr. Samuel Adams of Arlington. He held lands under the New Hampshire title and up to the close of the year 1773, he had been an advocate of that title. But after the promulgation of the riot act, he for some unexplained reason, began to talk in favor of the New York title and advise his neighbors to purchase it. This open desertion of their cause was very distasteful to the New Hampshire men, and he was repeatedly warned to desist from such discourse. But he persisted in his offensive language, in consequence of which he was arrested and taken to the Green 'mountain tavern at Bennington, for trial. There the committee of safety heard his defence, which not being satisfactory, he was sentenced "to be tied in an armed chair, and hoisted up to the sign (a catamount's skin stuffed, sitting upon the sign post, twenty-five feet from the ground, looking and grinning towards New York), and there to hang two hours, as a punishment merited by his enmity to the rights and liberty of the inhabitants of the New Hampshire Grants." The sentence was executed, to the no small merriment of a large concourse of people. The doctor was then let down and dismissed by the committee, with an admonition to sin no more. "This mild and exemplary disgrace," says Ira Allen, in his history, "had a salutary effect on the doctor and many others."[1]

From this period, there do not seem to have been many occasions for the exercise of violent measures against the New York claimants, they in general, being unwilling by new efforts, to incur the further displeasure of the Green Mountain Boys. To this submission to their power, if not to their authority, a notable exception was found in the case of Benjamin Hough. He not only occupied land under the odious patent of Socialborough, but had, during his residence there, from early in the year 1773, been an open and troublesome advocate of that title, although he claimed to have also agreed for that of New Hampshire. It was on his petition that the resolutions of the assembly, offering the rewards for Allen and the seven others, and the act for hanging them without trial, had been passed. He had spent the winter in New York, advocating their passage, and had come back to his residence with a commission as justice of peace, bearing date the 12th of March, three days after the consummation of those obnoxious measures. He was loud in his denunciation of rioters, and active in the exercise of his office as magistrate. He was formally served with a copy of the resolution of the convention held at Manchester, on the 12th and 13th of April, 1774, certified by Jonas Fay, clerk, by which it was declared that whoever should, in the then situation of affairs, " until his majesty's pleasure in the premises should be further known," presume to take a commission of the peace from the New York government, should "be deemed an enemy to their country and the common cause." He was also verbally warned to desist from the further exercise of his official authority, and threatened with punishment if he persisted. To these warnings he paid no heed, but continued as active and troublesome as ever. The indignation against him became very great, and it was resolved to make such an example of him as would not only effectually silence him, but deter others from the commission of like offences. He was accordingly seized by a body of his neighbors, placed in a sleigh and carried south about thirty miles, to Sunderland, where he was kept for three days under strict guard until Monday, the 30th of January, 1775, when the leading Green Mountain Boys being assembled, he was brought to trial for the offences before mentioned. The court appointed for that purpose, consisted of Ethan Allen, Seth Warner, Robert Cochran, Peleg

[1] *Ira Allen's History*, p. 46. *Vt. Quarterly Magazine*, p. 126. *Slade*, p. 36. B. Hough's affidavit, *Doc. Hist. N. Y.*, p. 897–8.

Sunderland, James Mead, Gideon Warren and Jesse Lawyer. His judges being seated, he was put upon his defence, which being held insufficient, he was found guilty and sentenced "to be tied to a tree and receive two hundred lashes on the naked back, and then as soon as he should be able, should depart the New Hampshire Grants and not return again till his majesty's pleasure should be known in the premises, on pain of receiving five hundred lashes." This sentence was read to him from a paper by Allen, and was put in immediate execution with much severity. For his protection against further punishment for the same offences, and to show their fearless and defiant contempt for the government officers at New York, whither he was going, Allen and Warner gave him a certificate and pass in the following words:

"Sunderland, January 30th, A.D. 1775. This may certify to the inhabitants of the New Hampshire Grants, that Benjamin Hough hath this day received a full punishment for his crimes committed heretofore against this country, and our inhabitants are ordered to give him the said *Huff* free and unmolested passport towards the city of New York, or to the westward of our grants, he behaving as becometh. Given under our hands the day and date aforesaid.

ETHAN ALLEN,
SETH WARNER."

This chastisement of Hough seems to have been the last act of personal violence to which the claimants under New York as such were subjected by the New Hampshire men, during the colonial period; the open resistance to their authority ceasing from that time. It was undoubtedly the most severe and painful injury which had ever been inflicted on any of the Yorkers.

Hough departed the next day for New York, where he made an affidavit before Chief Justice Horsmanden, giving an account in detail of the abusive and cruel manner in which he had been treated, and he petitioned the council for protection against the rioters. The council, after due deliberation, declared they were powerless to furnish such protection; but on his subsequent representation, in connection with one Daniel Walker, Jr., that they had been "expelled from their habitations by the Bennington rioters, and were destitute of the means of support and had been involving themselves in debt for the necessaries of life," it was ordered "that a brief be issued in favor of the petitioners," by which they were allowed to solicit contributions from the public, or in other words were permitted to beg for their livelihood. It would seem that the wealthy New York land claimants, among whom were the lieutenant governor, several members of his council, and other prominent government officers, might have spared this mortification to their friend Hough, who had been so great a sufferer in their behalf.[1]

Before the deliberations of the lieutenant governor and his council on this affair of Hough had terminated, information was laid before them of a most alarming outbreak against the authority of the New York government, on the east side of the Green mountain, no less than that of the breaking up of the session of the county court of the county of Cumberland by mob violence, and the arrest and imprisonment of the sheriff and judges by the rioters. Of this event it is necessary to give some account.

It has been herein before mentioned that the order of the king in council of 1764 for annexing the territory of the New Hampshire Grants to the province of New York, was connected with, and subordinate to the plan then forming by the British ministry for raising a revenue from the colonies by parliamentary taxation. In pursuance of that plan numerous acts of parliament had been passed, which had met with such determined opposition from the inhabitants of the colonies as to render them nearly or quite inoperative. The oppressive character of those acts, and of the means used to enforce them, had served to alienate the affections of the people from the mother country, and to engender a bitter animosity towards the king's government. Riotous resistance to the officers of the crown, as violent and disorderly as any that had been made to those of New York by the New Hampshire settlers, had become common throughout the country; and the whigs concerned in making such resistance were as loudly denounced by the king's government, as the Green Mountain Boys had been by that of New York. In September, 1774, a congress of delegates from twelve of the colonies assembled at Philadelphia, and agreed to suspend all commercial intercourse with the mother country until the obnoxious acts of parliament should be repealed. This and other measures of opposition, were embodied in the form of an agreement or association, subscribed by all the delegates, and recommended for adoption in all the colonies. One of the articles of agreement was that they "would have no trade, commerce, dealings or intercourse whatsoever with any colony or province in North America which should not accede to, or should violate the association, but would hold them unworthy of the

---

[1] *Doc. Hist. N. Y.*, vol. 4, 891-903, 916. *Council Minutes*, 1765-1783, p. 422. *Ira Allen's History*, p. 44.

rights of freemen and as inimical to the liberties of their country." These measures, recommended by congress, were approved and adopted by the assemblies of all the colonies, except New York, where a tory majority steadily defeated every attempt to obtain a vote of approbation; and the assembly also refused, contrary to the action of the assemblies of the other colonies, to appoint delegates to another general congress which was to meet the following May. The whigs of the county of Cumberland, who sympathized with their brethren in the other colonies and approved of the proceedings of congress, very naturally felt that they were under no strong obligations of allegiance to a provincial government with which they had always been dissatisfied, and which had now violated the decrees of the general congress, and had thereby become, in the language of that congress, "unworthy the rights of freemen," and in fact enemies to the liberties of the country.*

By the month of March, 1775, a warlike attack upon the people by the king's troops, which had been collected in force at Boston, was almost daily expected, and preparations for resistance were extensively made, especially in the New England colonies. The business of the inhabitants had become much interrupted, and the courts of justice which had been held under the royal authority were, in general, either shut up or had been adjourned without doing any business. A term of the county court, for Cumberland county, was to be held by appointment at Westminster on the 14th of that month. The conduct of this court had long been complained of as unjust and oppressive, and the judges and other county officers were either known to be advocates of the king's measures, or strongly suspected of being secretly favorable to them. Under these circumstances the whigs of the county, to use their own language, felt it to be "their duty to God, to themselves and posterity, to resist and oppose all authority that would not accede to the resolves of the Continental congress," and especially to prevent the exercise of such authority over themselves, by the holding of a term of such obnoxious court. All efforts to persuade the judges not to hold a session of the court proved unavailing, and the people, to the number of eighty or ninety, assembled at the court house late in the afternoon of the 13th of March, the day previous to the intended session, with the determination to hold possession of it until the hour of opening the court the next morning. Sheriff Patterson, apprehensive of an attempt to stop the court, had industriously collected a body of men, a large portion of whom "were armed with guns, swords and pistols," while those in the house had only staves and clubs. Towards night the sheriff with his posse appeared in front of the court house, and commanded those within to disperse, which demand not being complied with, he caused the king's proclamation against riots to be read, and threatened, with an oath, that "if they did not comply with his demand in fifteen minutes he would blow a hole through them." The sheriff with his party then retired and not appearing again at the appointed time, some negotiations were entered into with one of the judges, by which those in the house were led to believe that they would be suffered to occupy it peacefully until morning, when the negotiation would be renewed. Under this impression a large portion of the party left the house and took lodgings in the village, leaving the residue to keep guard. But a little before midnight the sheriff with his posse again appeared in front of the house, and demanded entrance, which being refused, he commanded his men to fire, and the order being obeyed, and the doorway thereby cleared, the assailants rushed into the house where, after a short hand-to-hand contest, during which several more shots were fired, the sheriff's party obtained a complete victory. Some of the whigs had escaped from the house by a side passage, but ten were wounded, two of them mortally, and seven taken prisoners, who were all thrust into the jail. After a night of revelry by the sheriff and his party, the court was opened at the appointed hour, but no business was transacted. The news of this rash and bloody attack upon the people spread with great rapidity in all directions, and by noon of the 14th, several hundred men, variously armed, and burning with indignation at the conduct of the court party, had collected together at Westminster. The prisoners were at once liberated, and their places in the jail were occupied by the judges and officers of the court as fast as they could be found. William French, one of the wounded, having died, an inquest was held on his body, and a verdict of murder found against the sheriff and several of his assistants. By the morning of Thursday the 16th, says a contemporary account, "five hundred good martial soldiers, well equipped for war," were assembled. Among them were forty or more of the Green Mountain Boys from the west side of the mountain, under Captain Robert Cochran, and a considerable number from the neighboring provinces of New Hampshire and Massachusetts. A committee of those assembled was appointed to pass upon the fate of the prisoners, who, after much deliberation, decided that Noah Sabin and Benjamin Butterfield, two of the judges, Samuel Gale, the clerk, William Patterson, the high sheriff, Benjamin Gorton, a deputy sheriff, and four others, should be taken to Northampton, and there held in jail for trial, and that the others should be released on giving bonds to appear and take their trials at such time as should be appointed. These nine persons, in pursuance of this decision, were escorted to Northampton jail under a guard of twenty-five men, commanded by Captain Cochran and an equal number of men from New Hampshire under Captain Butterfield of that province. The persons thus imprisoned were removed at the expiration of a few weeks by a writ of habeas corpus, issued by Chief Justice Horsmanden, to the city of New York, ostensibly for trial; but they were never prosecuted. This assault of the court or tory party on the people has always been designated as the Westminster Massacre.[1]

Information of this outbreak of the people in Cumberland county, reached New York by messengers from the judges and others of the court party, on the 21st of March. Being embodied in the form of depositions, it was, in accordance with the advice of the council, laid before the assembly by Lieut. Gov. Colden, together with the papers relating to the affair of Hough. Treating the two occurrences as arising from the same causes, the lieutenant governor, in his message to the assembly, used the following language:

"Gentlemen: You will see with just indignation, from the papers I have ordered to be laid before you, the dangerous state of anarchy and confusion which has lately arisen in the county of Cumberland, as well as the little respect which has been paid to the provisions of the legislature at their last session, for suppressing the disorders which have for some time greatly disturbed the north eastern district of the county of Albany and part of the county of Charlotte." The message concluded by recommending that effectual measures be taken "for the protection of his majesty's suffering and obedient subjects," and for the vindication of the honor and dignity of the government.

In the assembly after considerable debate it was finally resolved "that this house will make provision for granting to his majesty the sum of one thousand pounds to be applied in enabling and assisting the inhabitants of the county of Cumberland to reinstate and maintain the due administration of justice and for the suppression of riots in said county." This resolution was carried by a vote of eleven to ten. In the affirmative were the names of Crean Brush and Colonel Wells, the members from Cumberland county, who in

[1] *Slade*, p. 55. *Doc. Hist. N. Y.*, pp. 903-916. *Jour. Congress*, Oct. 20, 1774. *Hall's Eastern Vermont*, chap. 9 and Appendix, pp. 746-755. *Williams's Vermont*, 1st ed., pp. 746-755.

this vote were undoubtedly misrepresenting their constituents. It was also, on motion of the speaker, resolved without a division, that an additional reward of fifty pounds each be voted for "apprehending and confining in any jail in the colony, the following persons, being rioters named in the act of the last session, to wit: Ethan Allen, Seth Warner, Robert Cochran and Peleg Sunderland, and that a reward of fifty pounds be voted for apprehending and securing as aforesaid, James Mead, Gideon Warren and Jesse Sawyer, or either of them so that they can be brought to justice for assisting the first four mentioned persons in committing sundry violent outrages on the person of one of his majesty's justices of the peace for the county of Charlotte."

These proceedings, which took place on the 30th and 31st of March, were the last efforts of the colonial government of New York to exercise jurisdiction over the people of the New Hampshire Grants. It is scarcely necessary to say that the general revolt of the colonies against the king's government, which soon after followed, rendered any attempt to enforce them altogether impracticable.

The uprising of the people of Cumberland county of the 13th of March, was not only an expression of the dislike of the majority of the inhabitants to the measures of the mother country, but also to those of the local government of New York. On the 7th of February a few weeks previous to this outbreak, a convention of the committees of twelve towns, held at Westminster, addressed a memorial to the lieutenant governor, council and assembly, in which they strongly complained of the great expense and heavy burdens imposed on them by the government of that province, particularly in the administration of justice by the county courts, and proposed various radical changes in the colonial laws and in the mode of executing them, as indispensible to the welfare and prosperity of the people. The courts of the county had, in fact, for a long time been extremely unpopular with the masses of the community, as had been shown by previous riotous attempts to interrupt their sittings, and it needed only the supposed countenance of the general congress to prepare the minds of the people to put an end to the proceedings of the courts.

After the hostile action of the assembly in regard to the Westminster massacre, the dissatisfaction of the people with the New York government was shown to be greater than with that of the mother country, by a resolution of the committees of Cumberland and Gloucester counties to petition the king to be relieved from the oppressive jurisdiction of that colony. At a convention of committees from those counties, held at Westminster on the 11th of April, 1775, it was voted:

"That our inhabitants are in great danger of having their property unjustly, cruelly and unconstitutionally taken from them by the arbitrary and designing administration of the government of New York; that the lives of those inhabitants are in the utmost hazard and imminent danger under the present administration," and further "that it was the duty of said inhabitants as predicated on the eternal and immutable laws of self preservation to wholly renounce and resist the administration of the government of New York till such time as the lives and property of those inhabitants should be secured by it, or until such time as they could have opportunity to lay their grievances before his most gracious majesty in council, together with a proper remonstrance against the unjustifiable conduct of that government; with an humble petition to be taken out of so oppressive a jurisdiction, and either annexed to some other government, or erected and incorporated into a new one, as might appear best to the said inhabitants, to the royal wisdom and clemency, and till such time as his majesty should settle the controversy," and Col. John Hazletine, Charles Phelps, Esq., and Col. Ethan Allen were appointed a committee to prepare a remonstrance for that purpose.

It is probable that the contemplated prayer in the proposed petition to the king, in the alternative of being "erected and incorporated into a new government," had reference to a project which had been formed by Col. Allen, William Gilliland and others, in conjunction with Col. Philip Skene, to establish a royal colony, which was to embrace the grants of New Hampshire west of Connecticut river and the country north of the Mohawk and west to Lake Ontario and to reach north to the forty-fifth degree of latitude, of which colony Col. Skene was to be the royal governor. Skene had obtained grants of large tracts of land in the vicinity of Wood creek and Lake Champlain, and had made extensive improvements at Skenesborough, now Whitehall, where he resided. He was then in England and had written home, to Jehiel Hawley of Arlington, who had been one of the agents of the New Hampshire settlers, sent to England in 1772, that he had received the appointment of "governor of Ticonderoga and Crown Point." He is also designated by the title of governor in the *Journal of Congress* of June 8, 1775. What the precise character and extent of his authority was, or what was really in contemplation by him, or by the king's government, is not known. The commencement of the revolutionary struggle by the battle of Lexington on the 19th of April, eight days after the votes of the convention, rendered any petition to the king inexpedient, and the organization of a new government altogether impracticable. That the formation of such new province had been actually ordered by the crown, was long believed by many, and it was thought that, but for the war, full proof of such an order could have been obtained. The existence of such supposed new government, was afterwards earnestly urged in behalf of the inhabitants of the New Hampshire Grants, in opposition to the claim of New York to their territory, the king, it was alleged, having thereby annulled the title of that province.[1]

---

[1] *Doc. Hist. N. Y.*, vol. 4, p. 903 – 916. *Journal of N. Y. Assembly,* March 23, 30, 31. *Brattleboro Eagle,* Dec. 6, 1849. *Slade,* p. 60. *Am. Arch.* 1775, p. 315. In relation to Gov. Skene, see *Ira Allen's Vt.*, p. 53 – 55. *Watson's Champlain Valley,* p. 44, 45. *Williams's Vt.*, p. 224. Dr. Fitch's in *Transactions of N. Y. Agricultural Society for* 1848, p. 964 – 968. *Jour. Cont. Con.*, June 8, 1775, and Jan. 5, 1776. *Sparkes's Washington,* vol. 3, p. 296, 524.

CHAPTER XVIII.

THE CAPTURE OF TICONDEROGA.

1775.

Political situation of the New Hampshire Grants at the breaking out of the revolutionary war — Capture of Ticonderoga and Crown Point by men under Ethan Allen and Seth Warner — Arrogance of Arnold — New Yorkers decline to aid in or approve of the capture — Their strong tory and conservative tendencies — Strange resolve of the Continental congress to abandon those posts and substitute one at the south end of Lake George — Alarm and remonstrance of the New Hampshire Grants and New England — The resolve not executed — A regiment from Connecticut arrives under Col. Hinman and relieves the captors of Ticonderoga and Crown Point — Insubordination of Arnold — He is discharged from service by a committee of the Massachusetts congress.

THE opening of the revolutionary war found the people of the New Hampshire Grants nominally under the jurisdiction of New York, but substantially independent, obeying only the orders and decrees of committees and conventions, and of their cherished town meetings. This had for sometime been their situation on the west side of the Green mountain, and the recent proceedings at Westminster had overthrown the New York jurisdiction on the opposite side, at least for the time being. The people, in general, had been prepared to enter actively into the contest for American liberty, by their natural hostility, as a free people, to the arbitrary measures of the British crown and parliament, by sympathy with their friends in Massachusetts and the other New New England colonies whence they had emigrated; by deep distrust of a monarch who had suffered his greedy servants to grant, in his name, his lands a second time, and to dispossess his first grantees, and to prosecute them as felons and outlaws; by the hesitating and tardy manner in which the province of New York, to which they had been unwillingly annexed, had seconded the patriotie measures of the other colonies, and finally by the massacre by the king's New York officers of two of their number at Westminster.

The approaching struggle with the mother country had for sometime been foreseen, and the provincial congress of Massachusetts on the 15th of February, 1775, to guard against an apprehended attempt of the emissaries of the British ministry to engage the Canadians and Indians in hostilities against the colonies, directed the committee of the town of Boston to open a correspondence with the province of Quebec in such manner as they should think proper. That committee appointed John Brown, Esq., a young lawyer of spirit and intelligence of Pittsfield, to repair to Canada, to obtain information of the state of the province and to endeavor to counteract any unfriendly efforts of their enemies. At Bennington Mr. Brown had a consultation with "the grand committee" of the New Hampshire Grants, and was furnished by them with a guide and assistant, who was an old hunter and familiar with the route and with the Indians on the border. He was no less a personage than Peleg Sunderland, one of the eight outlaws then under the ban of the New York government, with a price set upon his life. After a tedious, as well as dangerous journey of over two weeks, partly by water on the lake, amidst floating ice, they reached Montreal. In a letter written from that place by Mr. Brown to Samuel Adams and Joseph Warren of the Boston committee, dated March 29, 1775, after giving a rather favorable account of the state of feeling among the Canadians and Indians, he speaks of the importance of the fortress of Ticonderoga and of his consultation with the committee at Bennington, as follows: "One thing I must mention to be kept a profound secret. The fort at Ticonderoga must be seized as soon as possible should hostilities be committed by the king's troops. The people on the New Hampshire Grants have engaged to do the business, and in my opinion are the most proper persons for this job. This will effectually curb this province and all the troops that may be sent here." When, therefore, a few days after the battle of Lexington, messengers arrived at Bennington from Connecticut, accompanied by Brown, for the purpose of collecting a force to attack that fortress, they found the leaders of the people with their minds already prepared for the undertaking.[1]

The importance, in the then approaching struggle, of securing Ticonderoga, must have been obvious to others besides Mr. Brown

[1] Brown's letter in *American Archives*, 4th Series, vol. 2, p. 243, *Jour. Mass. Cong.*, Feb. 13 and 15, 1775. *Petition of Peleg Sunderland* to the Vermont Assembly Feb. 26, 1787, and the *Report of a Committee* thereon of March 7, 1787. Sunderland in his petition says, that "in the month of March, 1775, he was called upon by the Grand committee of Bennington to go to Canada to pilot Major John Brown who was sent by the Provincial congress as a delegate to treat with the Indians respecting the then approaching war," and that he was out in that service twenty-nine days, which the committee of the Assembly reported to be true. It also appears from Mr. Brown's letter that his guide was of essential service in his negotiation with the Indians,

and the committee of the Green Mountain Boys, and must, indeed, have been the subject of common conversation among the intelligent whigs of New England. Capt. Benedict Arnold, then of New Haven, appears to have spoken to Samuel H. Parsons, of the Connecticut Assembly of the importance and feasibility of its capture and of his desire to attempt it. But the honor of devising and putting in motion the first expedition to seize it, belongs to some influential gentlemen at Hartford, acting on their individual responbility, of whom Mr. Parsons was one. The orignal parties to the project appear to have been Mr. Parsons, Samuel Wylis, and Silas Deane, who associated with them Christopher Leffingwell, Thomas Mumford and Adam Babcock. Those six gentlemen, for the sake of secrecy and dispatch, without communicating their intention to the assembly then sitting, obtained from the colony treasury on their personal obligations, the sum of three hundred pounds to be used in the undertaking. This was on Friday the 28th of April, and the same day Capt. Noah Phelps and Bernard Romans were dispatched with the money to the northward to obtain men and supplies, and the next day they were followed by Capt. Edward Mott, Epaphras Bull, and four others, and overtaken at Salisbury. Mott, Bull, Phelps and Romans appear to have been intrusted with the disbursement of the money, and with the general conduct of the expedition, they, with such others as they afterwards associated with them in authority, styling themselves "the committee of war." [1] At Pittsfield the party was joined by Col. James Easton and John Brown, Esq., and messengers were sent to Bennington to engage Col. Ethan Allen and his associates on the New Hampshire Grants, in the expedition; who proceeded to raise men with all possible dispatch.

[1] This account of the *origin* of the expedition seems to be well established by contemporaneous documents published in the collections of the Connecticut Historical Society, vol. 1, p. 163–188. In "a letter from a gentleman in Pittsfield to an officer in Cambridge, dated May 4, 1775." (Thursday) it is stated that "the plan was concerted at Hartford last Saturday" (the 29th) by the governor and council, Col. Hancock and Mr. Adams and others from our province being present." This statement has been followed by several historians, but of its correctness there is room for much doubt. John Hancock and Samuel Adams on their way to the congress at Philadelphia did not leave Worcester till the 27th and were not likely to have arrived at Hartford until after the advance party had set out for Ticonderoga. The money was obtained from the treasurer on Friday the 28th, as the receipts show, and the same day Phelps and Romans started for Ticonderoga. It was on the next day, Saturday the 29th, that the Pittsfield letter states "the plan was concocted by the governor and council," etc. Gov. Trumbull in his letter to the Massachusetts congress of May 25, 1775, apparently

On Wednesday the 3d of May, the men from Connecticut, sixteen in number, and forty-one raised by Col. Easton in Jericho (now Hancock), and Williamstown, reached Bennington, where it was agreed that the chief command should be assigned to Col. Allen, and that Castleton, about ten miles from Skenesborough, (now Whitehall), twenty miles from Ticonderoga, should be the place of general rendezvous. Proper measures were taken to prevent a knowledge of the contemplated attack from reaching the fort, and also for procuring information of its condition and means of defense. On Sunday evening the 7th of May the whole party were together at Castleton, and on Monday a council of the committe of war, of which Capt. Mott was chairman, was held to decide upon future operations. It was agreed that a party of thirty men under Capt. Samuel Herrick, of the New Hampshire Grants, should the next day in the afternoon, take into custody Maj. Skene and his party at Skenesborough, and that the residue of the men about one hundred and seventy in number, under the immediate command of Col. Allen should proceed to the lake shore opposite Ticonderoga, cross over in boats and attack the fort. Col. James Easton was second in command to Allen and Capt. Seth Warner, the third, they ranking according to the number of men they had respectively raised.

On the evening of Monday the 8th of May, after the plan of operations had all been settled, the men assigned to their respective duties, and ready to march, Col. Benedict Arnold arrived with a single servant and claimed the chief command, by virtue of a commission which he exibited from the committee of safety of Massachusetts, appointing him "colonel of a body of men not exceeding four hundred," *which he was "directed to enlist," and with them to*

---

disclaims all participation in the origin of the expedition by declaring that it was "an advantage gained by the United councils and enterprise of a number of private gentlemen * * * without public authority to our knowledge." That information of the expedition was, soon after it had been set in motion communicated to Hancock and Adams and to others, in confidence, is doubtless true. Mr. Adams alludes to it in a letter to the president of the Massachusetts congress, dated at Hartford, May 2, four days after the expedition had started, in language as follows: "certain military movements of great importance and with the utmost secrecy, have been set on foot in this colony of Connecticut, while I dare not explain, but refer you to Cols. Foster, Danielson and Bliss." — See *Mott's Journal* and letter of Parsons, and notes of J. H. Trumbull in *Conn. Hist. Collections* above referred to — also *Am. Archives*, vol. 2, 4th series, 507, 706. *Jour. Mass. Cong.*, 527 note. *Wells's Life of Samuel Adams*, vol. 2, p. 297–8. *New York Rev. and Atheneum Magazine*, Feb. 1826, p. 219–220.

proceed to reduce the fort at Ticonderoga. This commission bore date the 3d of May, the day on which the men from Connecticut and Massachusetts arrived at Bennington, and, with the aid of Allen, Warner, and others, were gathering the men of the New Hampshire Grants. Col. Arnold had reached Stockbridge on the western border of Massachusetts, on Saturday the 6th of May, but had scarely begun his attempt to raise men, when learning that a party from Connecticut were in advance of him in the enterprise, he followed with all possible speed in its train, and reached Castleton on Monday evening as before stated. Arnold's commission as colonel was not in the usual general form, but was a special commission for the particular purpose of raising men for the capture of Ticonderoga. By the terms of it he was to "enlist" the men by whom the capture was to be made, and he was authorized to command only those whom he should enlist.[1] The men, among whom he had thus unexpectedly appeared, were already raised; they had in no sense been enlisted by or under him, and he had clearly no right by his commission to assume the command of them, against their wishes. He however, claimed that he had a right to the command, and insisted upon it, with such warmth and pertinacity, that the men, to whom he was an entire stranger, became alarmed lest they should be placed under him, and declared that they would serve under no other officers than those with whom they had engaged, and that if the command was surrendered to him, they would abandon the expedition at once, and return to their homes. Arnold was consequently forced to yield, at least for the time being, but was allowed to serve as a volunteer, with the rank of colonel, but without any command.

The march was pursued according to the original plan, and the party arrived late on the 9th, at Orwell, opposite the fort. With great difficulty a few boats, sufficient only to carry about half the force were procured, on which eighty-three men crossed with Allen and landed near the garrison. The boats were sent back for the rear guard under Capt. Seth Warner, but the day was dawning, and if these men were waited for, the fort could not be taken by surprise. The men were therefore at once drawn up in three ranks and Allen addressed them; "Friends and fellow soldiers; we must this morning quit our pretensions to valor or possess ourselves of this fortress; and inasmuch as it is a desperate attempt, which none but the bravest men dare undertake I do not urge it on any contrary to his will. You that will undertake voluntarily, poise your firelocks." Every

[1]For a copy of the commission see Appendix No. 12.

firelock was poised, and Allen ordering the men to face to the right, and placing himself at the head of the middle file, led them with a quick step up the height on which the fortress stood, and before the sun rose he had entered the gate and formed his men on the parade between the barracks. Here they gave three huzzas, which greatly surprised the sleeping inmates. When Col. Allen had passed the gate a sentinel snapped his fusee at him and then retreated under a covered way. Another sentinel made a thrust at an officer with a bayonet, which slightly wounded him. Col. Allen returned the compliment with a sword cut on the side of the soldiers head, at which he threw down his musket and asked quarter, which being granted, Allen demanded to be led to the apartment of Capt. Delaplace A flight of stairs outside of the barracks was pointed out, which Allen hastily ascended, and with a voice of thunder at the door cried out to the captain to come forth instantly or the whole garrison should be sacrificed. At this the captain came out undressed, with his breeches in his hand. "Deliver to me the fort instantly," said Allen. "By what authority?" asked Delaplace. "In the name of the great Jehovah and the continental congress," answered Allen. Delaplace began to speak again but was peremptorily interrupted, and at sight of Allen's drawn sword near his head, he gave up the garrison, ordering his men to be paraded without arms.

Thus in the gray of the morning of the 10th of May, 1775, the very day of the first assembling of the revolutionary congress, and a few hours prior to the gathering together in the State House at Philadelphia of its illustrious members, was its authority made known and proclaimed by a body of Green Mountain Boys within the walls of Ticonderoga — a fortress which had been acquired by the government from which it was now wrested at the cost of thousands of lives and millions of money. And thus to Allen, with his associate patriots, belongs the honor of compelling the first surrender of the British flag "to the coming republic."

The Americans gained with the fortress fifty prisoners, one hundred and twenty pieces of cannon, also swivels, small arms and stores. To a detachment under Capt. Seth Warner, Crown Point with its garrison of twelve men, with sixty-one good cannon, and fifty-three unfit for service, were surrendered on the first summons. The party which had been sent to Skenesborough was also successful, taking Major Skene the younger prisoner, and seizing likewise a schooner and several batteaux, with all of which they hastened to Ticonderoga.[1]

[1] Papers relating to the expedition to Ticonderoga in *Coll. of Conn. Hist. Soc.*, vol. 1, p. 162–188. *Jour. Mass. Prov. Cong.*, p. 695–726, and *Jour.*

The capture of these two fortresses of Ticonderoga and Crown Point, thus early in the contest, was of great advantage to the struggling colonies, not only protecting them against immediate invasion from Canada, but also furnishing them with a large quantity of the munitions of war, of which they were in great need. Following quickly after the spirited resistance to the king's troops at Lexington and Concord, it increased the confidence and stimulated the enterprise of the Americans, and gave to their enemies further discouraging evidence of the activity and bravery with which they were likely to be resisted. The news of this unexpected event was indeed received by the friends of the king with both astonishment and grief. Lieut. Gov. Colden, who was then, in the absence of Tryon, administering the government of New York, and devoting all his energies to sustain the odious measures of his royal master, gave a doleful account of the misfortune to Lord Dartmouth the British minister. After speaking of sundry violent proceedings of the people of the city of New York, he says, "a matter of greater importance was carried on in the northern part of this province; no less than the actual taking of his majesty's forts at Ticonderoga and Crown Point, and making the garrisons prisoners." The only consolation which he finds in the accounts of the affair that have reached him is, to use his own language, that "the only people of this province who had any hand in this expedition, were that lawless people whom your lordship has heard much of under the name of the Bennington mob." The latter statement of Mr. Colden was true. Of the people of New York, over whom he claimed jurisdiction, it was only the turbulent inhabitants of the New Hampshire Grants that were concerned in the outrage upon his majesty's fortress. The people of the old colony of New York were not prepared for so bold a measure. A great portion of them were either secretly or openly in favor of the crown. Some of these mingled in the deliberations of the whigs and influenced their councils. Isaac Low, chairman of the New York committee, was a loyalist, and was afterwards attainted as such; several of his associates on the commtttee were of the same stripe. Of the twenty-one delegates to the Provincial congress, then recently chosen for the city, no less than one-third were tories, and there were members with like sympathies

---

Mass. Com. Safety for April 29, 30, and May 2, 3, 1775. *Am. Archives*, Allen and Arnold's letters relating to the capture, and letter of May 4. *Allen's Nar. of his Captivity*. *Sparks's Life of Allen* and of *Arnold*. *Gordon's Rev.*, vol. 2, p. 10–13. *Ira Allen's*, *Williams's* and *Thompson's Vt.* *Bancroft*, *Hildreth*, *Lossing* and *Irving's Washington*.

from other parts of the province. Among the whigs in both these bodies, the conservative element, representing the cautious and timid feelings of the wealthy merchants of the city, and the large land holders of the interior, extensively prevailed, and indeed exerted a controlling influence over their proceedings. Their cherished policy was of a mild defensive character, and it was not to be expected that they would countenance an attack upon the king's forts, even though the necessity of their capture to the future security of the country might be quite apparent to others. The movement had consequently been necessarily made by more adventurous spirits from other colonies.

When the party from Connecticut, on their way to Ticonderoga, reached Sheffield, they dispatched two messengers to Albany "to discover the temper of the people at that place," and to endeavor to obtain supplies of provisions for the expedition; but the Albany committee, to whom they applied, declined to interfere, and wrote for advice to Mr. Low's committee at New York, from which, however, no answer appears to have been received. The next day after the capture of Ticonderoga, John Brown was dispatched to Albany with a letter from Col. Allen to the committee at that place, informing them of the surrender of the fort, expressing an apprehension of an attempt to recapture it by Gov. Carlton from Canada, and asking for "immediate assistance both in men and provisions." The committee declined to furnish any aid, but wrote again to the New York committee for advice, sending a copy of Allen's letter, and stating that Mr. Brown was "dissatisfied with their answer, and went away abruptly." These dispatches were received by the New York committee on the 15th of May, and forwarded to the Continental congress, accompanied by a letter signed by their chairman, informing that body that the committee did not conceive themselves "authorized to give an opinion upon a matter of such importance."

The letter from the New York committee, and accompanying papers, reached Philadelphia on the 17th, and were laid before congress the next morning. Mr. Brown who had also arrived from Ticonderoga, was called before that body and gave an account of the capture of the fort, and of the state of affairs in that quarter. Whereupon congress adopted a resolution, which seemingly apologized for the seizure of the fort, "by several inhabitants of the northern colonies residing in its vicinity," as a means of protecting their lives and liberties against "a cruel invasion from the province of Quebec;" and recommended to the committees at New York and Albany, "immediately to cause the cannon and stores to be removed from Ticonderoga to the south end of Lake George, and if necessary, to apply to the colonies of New Hampshire, Massachusetts Bay and Connecticut for such an additional body of troops as would be sufficient to establish a strong post at that place." The resolution also directed "an exact inventory to be taken of all the cannon and stores, that they might safely be returned," on the restoration of harmony between Great Britain and the colonies.

This resolve was not only timid in its character, but illogical, if not absurd in its terms. It sought first, to justify the seizure of the fort as a means of protecting the inhabitants of the colonies in its vicinity against "cruel invasion" from Canada, and then left those inhabitants exposed to the very evils they had thought to avoid by its capture, by directing the fort, and consequently the lake it was designed to command, to be abandoned. The post at the south end of Lake George, which it was proposed to fortify and defend, might furnish some sort of protection to Albany and northern New York, but none whatever to the New Hampshire Grants and the adjoining New England colonies, by whose people the news of the passage of the resolution was received with great surprise and dissatisfaction. Col. Allen, on being informed of the resolution, immediately addressed an earnest remonstrance to the Continental congress, against the contemplated removal, in which he asserted that the abandonment of Ticonderoga and Lake Champlain, and the substitution of a post at the south end of Lake George, "would ruin the frontier settlements, which extended at least one hundred miles to the northward" of the latter place, and which consisted "of several thousand families in that part of country called the New Hampshire Grants;" stated that the people in that territory, by the seizure of Ticonderoga and Crown Point, had "incensed Gov. Carlton and the ministerial party in Canada against them," and declared "that should they after all their good service to the country, be neglected and left exposed, they would be of all men the most miserable." The assembly of Connecticut, and the provincial congresses of Massachusetts and New Hampshire also strongly protested against the removal, and the order was not carried into execution. The proposed measure was so plainly injurious to the cause of the country, as to excite a strong suspicion among the inhabitants of the New Hampshire Grants, that it was the sinister work of their old land speculating adversaries of New York to ruin their settlements; the land claimant interest being strongly represented in the Continental congress by Mr. Duane, the Livingstons and others. This feeling also appears to have extended beyond that district. Capt. Asa Douglass an active and influential whig of western Massachusetts, who at the head of a company which he had aided in raising, was at the taking of Ticonderoga, in a letter to Gen. Washington, dated June 7, 1776, states that after the surrender of the fort, he was sent by the commander to Philadelphia, that on his way there he heard of the order of congress and viewed it "as the finishing stroke to New England;" that when he arrived at Philadelphia he "carefully searched out the cause of it, and found the land jobbers were the foundation and efficient cause of it, and that he gave himself no rest till it was reversed.[1]

But to return to the forces at Ticonderoga, where the trouble with Arnold still continued. No sooner had the fortress surrendered than he again arrogantly claimed the command, but he was obliged to submit to the unanimous opposition of the officers and men; and the committee of war in order to put an end to his annoying assumptions delivered to Col. Allen a certificate, or commission signed by Edward Mott chairman, stating that "by virtue of the power given them by the colony of Connecticut" they had appointed him to take command of the men to reduce the fort, and requiring him "to keep the command and possession of the same for the use of the American colonies until he should have further orders from the colony of Connecticut or the Continental congress." A copy of this commission together with an account of the capture and of the claims of Arnold signed by Mott chairman of the committee of war was immediately transmitted to the provincial congress of Massachusetts by the hand of Col. Easton. Arnold also wrote to the same congress, giving his version of the affair, but his pretensions to the command were not favored by that body. Arnold had however behaved with bravery in the assault upon the fort, marching on the left of Col. Allen and entering the fortress side by side with him, and he seems to have "finally consented to a sort of divided control between Col. Allen and himself, he acting as a subordinate, but not wholly without official consideration."

A few days afterwards Allen and Arnold formed a plan to make a rapid push to St. Johns, take a king's sloop that lay there and attempt

---

[1] *Colden to Lord Dartmouth,* June 7, 1775. Mott's account of the expedition to Ticonderoga, and other papers, in *Conn. Hist. Col.,* vol. 1, p. 165–183. *Am. Archives,* vol. 2, pp. 459, 605, 623, 719, 721, 732–3, 895. *Jour. Cong.,* May 18, and of *N. Y. Cong.,* May 22, 25 and 26. *Sabine's Loyalists,* titles, Low, De Lancey, Folliott, Hallett, Kissam, Walton, Yates. *Stevens paper,* 7776, p. 25–6. *Secret Jour. Cont. Cong.,* vol. 1, p. 19. *Bancroft,* vol. 8, p. 79. vol. 7, p. 79.

a descent on the garrison. For that purpose they armed and manned the schooner and bateaux which had been captured at Skensborough. Arnold, who had been a seaman in his youth, taking command of the schooner and Allen of the bateaux, they both set out together upon the expedition, but a fresh wind springing up from the south, the schooner outsailed the bateaux, and Arnold soon reached St. John's where he surprised and captured the sloop together with a sergeant and twelve men. The wind now shifting to the north Arnold set sail with his prize, and met Allen with his bateaux at some distance from St. Johns. Allen who had with him about one hundred men determined to proceed and make an attack upon that place though informed by Arnold, that large reenforcements were expected there, and that his force was insufficient to hold it. Allen with his party effected a landing, but was attacked by a greatly superior body of troops, and was obliged to retire, leaving three of his men prisoners. By the capture of the king's sloop, which took place the 17th of May, the complete command of the lake was obtained.

The colony of Connecticut having been requested by the Continenal congress and also by the congress of New York to send a force to maintain the posts at Ticonderoga and Crown Point, a regiment of one thousand strong, under Col. Benjamin Hinman, arrived there early in June to whom Allen at once gave up his authority. But Arnold persisted in claiming the command, which tending to produce difficulty and confusion, the Massachusetts congress, under which Arnold claimed to act, sent a committee of their body to inquire into the matter, who on the 23d of June, very much to Arnold's chagrin and mortification notified him that he was discharged from the service.[1]

---

[1] *Jour. Prov. Cong. Mass.*, 696 – 726. *Life of Allen* and also of *Arnold* by Sparks. *Jour. Cont. Cong.*, May 30. *Am. Archives,* vol. 2. 724, 729 – 731, 847, 850, 940.

CHAPTER XIX.

Regiment of Green Mountain Boys and Invasion of Canada.

1775.

Allen and Warner before the Continental Congress and the New York Convention — A battalion of Green Mountain Boys under their own officers to be raised — Coldness of the New Yorkers — Warner chosen lieutenant colonel over Allen — The corps joins Montgomery at the siege of St. Johns, and is posted in advance on the St. Lawrence — Allen sent by Schuyler and Montgomery as a political missionary into Canada — Raises one hundred men, and attempting to surprise Montreal is taken prisoner and sent in irons to England — Gen. Carlton on his way with one thousand men to relieve St. Johns, is attacked by Warner and his Green Mountain Boys, at Longuiel and driven back, which occasions the immediate surrender of that post — Montreal is also abandoned to Gen. Montgomery — Honorable discharge of Warner's corps.

ON the arrival of the Connecticut regiment at Ticonderoga, as before stated, the men from the New Hampshire Grants, who had been hastily collected together for a brief period and a temporary purpose, were discharged, and returned to their homes. Many of them were willing to enter again into the service, but the ill feeling which had long subsisted between them and the governing authorities of New York, to which colony they nominally belonged, was an obstacle in the way, which there was some difficulty in overcoming. On the 2d of June, Col. Allen addressed a long letter to the provincial congress of New York, in favor of the policy of an immediate invasion of Canada, and proposed "to raise a small regiment of rangers," which he thought he could easily do, "mostly in the counties of Albany and Charlotte, provided the congress should think it expedient to grant commissions and thus regulate and put the same under pay." And he added an apology for making the offer as follows. "Probably your honors may think this an impertinent proposal. It is truly the first favor I ever asked of the government, and if it be granted I shall be zealously ambitious to conduct for the best good of my country and the honor of the government." To this letter no answer appears to have been returned, and there was little prospect that a satisfactory arrangement could be made with that body.

Under these circumstances, a council of officers was held at Crown Point on the 10th of June, at which it was recommended to "Col. Ethan Allen, Capt. Seth Warner, and Capt. Remember Baker" to go to Philadelphia and obtain the advice of the Continental congress, in relation to their peculiar position, and that of the men who had served with them. Allen and Warner (Baker not accompanying them), were the bearers of a letter from Maj. Elmore of the Connecticut forces, chairman of the council, to the president of congress, which on the 23d of June, being sent into that assembly, was read; whereupon, "information being given, that two officers who brought the letter were at the door, and had something of importance to communicate, ordered, that they be introducd, and they were introduced." In the presence of this august assembly, Allen and Warner also found themselves standing face to face with their old land claiming antagonist, Mr. Duane, from whom they might have anticipated some opposition to their wishes. But if any were made it was ineffectual. Their manly bearing and intelligent answers to such inquiries as were made of them, evidently produced a favorable impression on the body. When they withdrew, provision was made for the payment of "the men who had been employed in the taking and garrisoning of Crown Point, and Ticonderoga," and a further resolution was adopted as follows:

"*Resolved*, That it be recommended to the convention of New York that they, consulting with Gen. Schuyler, employ in the army to be raised for the defense of America, those called Green Mountain Boys, under such officers as the said Green Mountain Boys shall choose."

With a copy of this resolution and a letter from Pres. Hancock to the convention of New York they repaired to that city. The letter of the president was as follows:

PHILADELPHIA, June 24, 1775.

Gentlemen: By order of the congress I enclose you certain resolves, passed yesterday, respecting those who were concerned in taking and garrisoning Crown Point and Ticonderoga. As the congress are of opinion that the employing the *Green Mountain Boys* in the American army would be advantageous to the common cause, as well on account of their situation as of their disposition and alertness, they are desirous you should embody them among the troops you shall raise, as it is represented to the congress that they will not serve under any officers but such as they themselves choose, you are desired to consult with Gen. Schuyler, in whom the congress are informed those people place a great confidence, about the field officers to be set over them. I am gentlemen your most obedient humble servant,

JOHN HANCOCK, President.

To the members of the provincial congress New York."

In New York, Allen and Warner, as might perhaps have been expected, found a hostile feeling prevailing against them, which there was considerable difficulty in removing. Most of the land claimants, with whom they had been for years in sharp and succesful controversy, resided in New York city, where the convention was sitting, and were strongly represented in that body. The names of Allen and Warner, connected with charges of lawless violence, had there been made familiar by the publication of often repeated official rewards and proclamations for their apprehension and punishment. There was moreover a law on their statute book, enacted only the previous year, declaring them outlaws by name, and consigning them to death on being apprehended. The altered condition of the New York government, together with the eminent services they had recently rendered the colonies by the capture of the northern forts, had made them entirely fearless of this penal law, but the prejudice against them was almost too strong to allow them to participate in the common struggle for the liberties of the country.

After a delay of some days, the resolution of the Continental congress and the letter of its president were, on Saturday the 1st of July, read in the convention, and it was "ordered, that Col. McDougall, Mr. Scott, and Col. Clinton be a committee to meet and confer with Messrs. Ethan Allen and Seth Warner, and report the same with all convenient speed." The journals do not show that this committee made any report, but on Tuesday, the 4th of July, the consideration of the resolve and letter of the Continental congress being resumed, and the congress being informed "that Ethan Allen was at the door and desired admittance," it was moved by Mr. Sears, the early leading radical whig of New York city, that he "be permitted to have an audience of this board." After debate, the question was taken on the motion, when it appeared that nine counties having eighteen votes were in the affirmative, and three counties having nine votes were in the negative, the three negative counties being New York, Albany and Richmond, where the land claimants had the greatest influence.[1] Whereupon Col. Allen was admitted, and Capt. Warner at the same time; who, after being heard, withdrew; whereupon, an order was made by the convention as follows:

"Ordered, that in consequence of a recommendation from the Continental congress, a body of troops not exceeding five hundred men, officers included, be forthwith raised, of those called *Green Mountain Boys;* that they elect all their own officers except field officers; that Maj. Gen. Schuyler be requested to forward this order to them and receive from them a list of such officers as they shall elect, to be communicated to this congress; and that Gen. Schuyler be further requested without delay, to procure the sense of those troops concerning the persons who will be most agreeable to them for field officers; and to make inquiry, and upon the whole advise this congress what persons it will be most proper to be appointed as field officers to command those troops; that the said troops when raised, be considered as an independent body, their field officers taking rank after the field officers of the other troops to be raised by this colony for the continental service; that their corps of officers consist of one lieutenant colonel, one major, seven captains and fourteen lieutenants; and that the general be furnished with blank warrants, to be filled up by him, agreeable to such election, as above mentioned."

Gen. Schuyler, under whose direction this corps of Green Mountain Boys was to be organized, had been chosen a major general, while in attendance on the Continental congress at Philadelphia, and did not reach Ticonderoga until after the middle of July. On the 27th of that month, "the committees of the several townships on the west side of the range of Green mountains," met at Dorset and designated by name two field officers, seven captains and fourteen lieutenants for the battalion, in accordance with the resolve of the New York convention. In the selection of field officers, Allen was left out, Seth Warner receiving the nomination of lieutenant colonel by a vote of forty-one to five, and Samuel Safford was named as

[1] Isaac Sears from the first resistance to the Stamp Act in 1765, to the breaking out of the revolution, was the most active leading whig of the city of New York, but at the election of members of the Provincial congress in April, he was probably thought to be too much in favor of bold measures, to represent the conservative interest of the city and was not chosen. At an election held, however, on the 8th of June, such progress had been made in the public feeling that he was elected by a great majority. *Jour. N. Y. Cong.*, June 9, 1775.

major.[1] By the failure of Allen to receive the nomination as commander of the corps he was much disappointed and mortified. He had been foremost in procuring the necessary action of the congress at Philadelphia and of the convention at New York for raising the battalion, and had left with the latter body a list of officers for it, in which his own name was inserted first and afterwards that of Warner for field officers. In a letter from Allen to Gov. Trumbull, dated at Ticonderoga, August 3d, he speaks of the action of the committees as follows:

"Notwithstanding my zeal and success in my country's cause, the old farmers on the New Hampshire Grants, who do not incline to go to war, have met in a committee meeting, and in their nomination of officers for the regiment of Green Mountain Boys who are quickly to be raised, have wholly omitted me; but as the commissions will come from the Continental congress, I hope they will remember me, as I desire to remain in the service." In a postscript he adds: "I find myself in the favor of the officers of the army and the young Green Mountain Boys. How the old men came to reject me, I cannot conceive, inasmuch as I saved them from the encroachments of New York."

That Allen rendered most important services to the inhabitants of the New Hampshire Grants in their land title controversy is undoubtedly true, and perhaps it was not too much for him to say that "he saved them from the encroachments of New York," for it is impossible to determine what might have been the result of the dispute, without his efficient aid. He had studied into the character of the New York claim of title to the lands in the territory, had collected historical and documentary evidence of its weakness, and had, on various occasions, wielded his rough, unpolished pen against it, with marked and decided effect. In the collisions with the speculating claimants and government officials, he had also acted a prominent, and often a leading part. But Warner had likewise rendered im-

---

[1] The officers of the battalion named by the convention of the committees at Dorset, certified by Nathan Clark, chairman, were as follows:

Seth Warner, Lieut. Col.

Samuel Safford, Major.

Captains—Weight Hopkins, Oliver Potter, John Grant, William Fitch, Gideon Brownson, Micah Vail, Heman Allen.

First Lieutenants—John Fassett, Ebenezer Allen, Barnabus Barnum, Tille Blakely, Ira Allen, Gideon Warren, David Galusha.

Second Lieutenants—John Nobles, James Claghorn, John Chipman, Nathan Smith, Jesse Sawyer, Joshua Stanton, Philo Hard.

portant services, and it might be presumptuous to say that his assistance could have been safely dispensed with. Both Allen and Warner were distinguished leaders in the controversy, but they were different men, and fitted to occupy different positions. The bold and defiant language of Allen in his writings and conversation was well calculated to encourage the timid, confirm the wavering and inspire confidence, and his personal courage cannot be questioned. But his vanity was great, always prompting him to claim at least all the merit he deserved and sometimes rendering his manner overbearing and offensive; and he was not free from rashness and imprudence. Warner, on the other hand, was modest and unassuming. He appeared satisfied with being useful, and manifested little solicitude that his services should be known or appreciated. He was always cool and deliberate, and in his sound judgment, as well as in his energy, resolution and firmness, all classes had the most unlimited confidence. As a military leader he was perferred to Allen. Whatever Allen might have thought on the subject, there is no doubt whatever that the selection of Warner to command the regiment was in accordance with the general feeling of the inhabitants of the New Hampshire Grants. It may also be safely said that the wisdom of their action seems to have been confirmed by subsequent events.

The list of officers selected by the convention of the committees was immediately sent to Gen. Schuyler at Ticonderoga, and by him transmitted to the New York congress, by which body it was ordered that warrants for the captains and lieutenants should be forwarded to him, to be filled up with the names of such as should agree to serve. Gen. Schuyler was also authorized and requested to appoint the field officers, when such a number of men should be raised as in his opinion should make it necessary. This was on the 15th of August. On the 23d, Schuyler wrote the congress from Albany, that Warner had been with him, that he had delivered him six sets of warrants, (one captain declining to serve), and that he could not possibly comply with their request to appoint the field officers, assigning as the reason, that "the peculiar situation of these people and the controversy they had had with this colony or with gentlemen in it, rendered the matter too delicate for him to determine." On the first of September, the letter of Gen. Schuyler was taken into consideration, and after debate the question was put, whether the congress would proceed to nominate any field officers for the regiment of Green Mountain Boys, when it was decided in the affirmative by a vote of fifteen to six, the counties of New York and Queens not voting, for the want of a sufficient number of members present.

Seth Warner was then chosen lieutenant colonel and Samuel Safford major, several members entering their dissent on the journal.

It seems evident from the disposition of both the convention and Gen. Schuyler to shift off the responsibility of confirming the nominations of field officers from the one to the other, as well as from the whole proceedings of the convention and the correspondence of the general in relation to the corps, including his letter above referred to, that the inhabitants of the New Hampshire Grants had a strong feeling against them in the new governing authorities of New York, as well as in the old, and that the corps was organized by them, as expressed in the resolution of the convention "in consequence of a recommendation from the continental congress," rather than from free choice. The cold and hesitating manner in which the raising of the battalion was seconded by the New Yorkers, if it did not cause delay in its organization, could not but tend to increase the distrust of those engaged in it, and to produce mutual ill feeling.

It has already been seen that the policy and necessity of invading Canada had been early urged upon the Continental congress by Col. Allen. If his counsel had been immediately followed, it is quite probable the result would have been more favorable than when attempted with the approbation of that body, at a later day Gen. Schuyler's health not permitting him to continue in the active command on the northern frontier, the American forces were led by Gen. Richard Montgomery, who on the 17th of September, laid siege to St. Johns, a fortified post near the northern outlet of Lake Champlain. The place was garrisoned by the greatest part of two British regiments and contained nearly all the regular troops in Canada. It was also well supplied with artillery, ammunition and military stores. Within two or three days Montgomery was joined by Warner with his corps of Green Mountain Boys, and Warner was sent, with a portion of his men, to the St. Lawrence in the vicinity of Montreal, to watch the motions of the enemy. Col. Allen, when left out of the corps of Green Mountain Boys, had offered his services to Gen. Schuyler as a volunteer, and was employed by him, with the understanding, to use Allen's language, "that he should be considered as an officer the same as though he had a commission, and should as occasion might require, command certain detachments of the army." In the month of August, he was sent by Gen. Schuyler from Ticonderoga into Canada, with interpreters and letters to the Canadians to cultivate their friendship and assure them "that the design of the army was against the English garrisons and not the country, their liberties or religion."

In this mission he appears to have been quite successful. He was afterwards, during the siege of St. Johns, employed by Gen. Montgomery to make a second tour in Canada with the same object. He went through several parishes, "preaching politics," as he says, and mustering recruits for the army. On the 20th of September, he wrote in high spirits to Montgomery from a point some miles east of the river Sorel, that he had two hundred and fifty Canadians under arms, and that they gathered fast as he marched. "You may rely upon it," he said, "that I shall join you in abont three days with five hundred or more Canadian volunteers. I could raise one or two thousand in a week's time, but will first visit the army with a less number, and if necessary will go again recruiting. Those that used to be enemies to our cause come cap in hand to me; and I swear by the Lord I can raise three times the number of our army in Canada, provided you continue the siege." He did not, however, join Montgomery, but after crossing the Sorel towards the St. Lawrence, and while on his way to St. Johns, with about eighty men, mostly Canadians, he on the morning of the 24th fell in with Maj. John Brown, who was at the head of a party of about two hundred Americans and Canadians. Brown proposed an attack upon Montreal, which he thought might be easely taken by surprise, as its inhabitants were not apprehensive of danger. It was then agreed between them, that Allen should cross the St. Lawrence from Longueil, a few miles below Montreal, with his party, and that Brown with his two hundred men should cross at Laprairie above the city. The passage was to be made that night, and early the next morning, on the exchange of three huzzas, which were first to be given by Brown's party, the town was to be attacked. Allen, having added about thirty "English Americans" to his party, crossed over as had been agreed; but daylight appeared, the morning more away, and no signal from Brown was given. He had failed to perform his part of the undertaking. The surprise of the place had become impracticable, and Allen, instead of endeavoring to save himself by a retreat, determined to maintain his ground. A mixed multitude composed of forty regular troops, several hundred English settlers and Canadians, and some Indians, then in Montreal, came out against him. A sharp conflict ensued, which lasted about two hours. Allen appears to have commanded skilfully and to have fought bravely, until most of the Canadians had deserted him, when, overpowered by numbers, he was obliged to surrender. Several were killed and wounded on both sides, and Allen with thirty-eight of his men were taken prisoners. They were immediately loaded with irons, put on board a man of war, and in that condition taken to England. This attempt of Allen, which was without authority from his commanding officers, was censured by both Montgomery and Schuyler, as rash and imprudent, and complained of as having an unfavorable effect upon the cause of the colonies among the Canadians and Indians. The information, however, of the condition of Montreal upon which Allen acted was doubtless in the main correct, and if he had received the cooperation from Brown which he expected, it is quite probable the town might have been captured.[1] Brook Watson, an English merchant, afterwards lord major of London, who by professions of friendship for the colonies had obtained from the New York congress a passport through the American lines into Canada, but who was a bitter enemy, was in Montreal soon after the attempt of Allen; and in a letter from there to Gov. Franklin of New Jersey, under date of the 19th of October, wrote as follows:

"Such is the wretched state of this unhappy province, that Col. Allen with a few despicable wretches, would have taken this city on the 25th ultimo, had not its inhabitants marched out to give him battle. They fought, conquered and thereby saved the province for a while. Allen with his banditti were mostly taken prisoners. He is now in chaines on board the *Gaspeé*. This little action has changed the face of things; the *Canadians* before were ninetenths for the *Bostonians;* they are now returned to their duty."

It is difficult, however, on Allen's own version of the affair, to justify his departure from his engagement to join Montgomery, for the purpose of entering upon this unauthorized expedition. His ambition to distinguish himself and to add to the laurels he had already won at Ticonderoga, probably induced him to engage in the undertaking without sufficiently considering either the chances or the consequences of its failure.

Montgomery, who had been pushing the siege of St. Johns, but under very embarrassing circumstances, for the want of ammunition and other materials of war, had been much aided by the capture of Chambly, a small fortress situated lower down the Sorel, which had

[1] Major, afterwards Col. Brown. was "a soldier of great courage and high moral worth," with a good military record on other occasions. He was killed at Stone Arabia on the Mohawk river, Oct. 19, 1780, in a battle with a body of tories and Indians. In the absence of any testimony to the contrary it is perhaps fair to presume that some unexpected obstacle put it out of his power to perform his part in the attack. See *Allen's Biog. Dic.*, and *Stone's Life of Brant*, vol. 2, p. 115-121.

been effected on the 18th of October, by a party under Majors Brown and Livingston. About one hundred prisoners were taken, and what was of more importance, one hundred and twenty barrels of powder and a large quantity of military stores and provisions were obtained. The garrison at St. Johns consisted of between six and seven hundred men, who in the hopes of being relieved by Gen. Carlton, made a resolute defence. Carlton exerted himself for this purpose, and mustered about a thousand men, including regulars, the militia of Montreal, the Canadians and the Indians. With these he proposed to cross the St. Lawrence from Montreal, and join Col. McLean who had collected a few hundred Scotch emigrants and had taken post at the mouth of the Sorel. With their united forces, he hoped to be able to raise the seige of St. Johns, and relieve the garrison. With this object in view, Carlton embarked his troops at Montreal, intending to cross the St. Lawrence at Longuiel. Their embarkation was observed from the opposite shore by Col. Warner, who with about three hundred Green Mountain Boys and some troops from New York, watched their motions and prepared for their approach. Warner opened upon them a well directed and incessant fire of musketry and grape shot from a four pounder, by which unexpected assault, they were thrown into great confusion and soon retreated in disorder, and gave up the attempt. When the news of Carlton's retreat reached McLean he abondoned his position at the mouth of the Sorel, and hastened to Quebec. Information of Carlton's defeat being communicated to Maj. Preston, the commander at St. Johns, he gave up all hopes of relief, and the garrison laid down their arms on the 3d of November, marched out of the works and became prisoners of war to the number of five hundred regulars, and over one hundred Canadian volunteers.

Col. Warner, having repulsed Gen. Carlton and caused McLean to retire to Quebec, proceeded to erect a battery at the mouth of the Sorel, which should command the passage of the St. Lawrence, and thus block up Carlton at Montreal. In this state of things Montgomery arrived from St. Johns and took possession of Montreal, without opposition, on the 13th of November, Gen. Carlton having abandoned it to its fate, and escaped down the river to Quebec. A large number of armed vessels loaded with provisions and military stores, and Gen. Prescott, with one hundred and twenty British officers and privates, also attempted to pass down the river, but they were all captured at the mouth of the Sorel.

Warner's regiment having served as volunteers, and the men being too miserably clothed to endure a winter campaign in that severe climate, were honorably discharged on the 20th of November, and returned to their homes.[1]

A body of troops under Col. Arnold had been sent from Maine, through the wilderness to attack Quebec. After enduring almost incredible hardships, they reached the vicinity of that place about the time of the abandonment of Montreal by Carlton. Montgomery followed Carlton down the St. Lawrence and, with a few hundred men, joined Arnold before Quebec, taking command of the united forces, which did not number over twelve hundred effective men, including two hundred Canadian volunteers. Though the fortifications of the city were of great strength and the garrison double that of the besiegers, it was finally determined to attempt to carry the place by storm. The attack was made on the 31st of December. The troops fought with great bravery and resolution, but were repulsed with the loss of about sixty in killed and wounded, and over three hundred prisoners. Among the killed was Gen. Montgomery, the heroic commander; Col. Arnold, the second in rank, was severely wounded. Thus closed the year 1775, in the northern department, in disaster and gloom.

---

[1] *American Archives*, vol. 2, pp. 891, 957, 1075, 1255, 1760; vol. 3, pp. 17, 243, 463, 754, 793–801, 952, 953, 954, 973, 1124, 1132, 1342–1344, 1393, 1602. *Jour. Cont. Cong.*, June 23. *Jour, N. Y. Cong.*, June 12, July 1, 4, 15, Sep. 1, 1775. *Thompson's Vermont*, pp. 35, 36. *Allen's Narrative of his Captivity*, pp. 25–30. *Chipman's Life of Warner*, pp. 30–39. *Sparks's Life of Allen*. *Lossing's Life of Schuyler*.

CHAPTER XX.

Military Affairs, and Petition of New Hampshire Grants to Congress.

1776.

Early in January Gen. Wooster in Canada, calls earnestly for reinforcements— Col. Warner raises a regiment of Green Mountain Boys and joins the army before Quebec — Evacuation of Canada — In July Warner is made colonel of a continental regiment, to be raised on the grants — Destruction of the American fleet on lake Champlain, and threatened attack on Ticonderoga — Aid furnished from the grants to Gen. Gates for the defence of that post — Carlton retires into Canada — Civil affairs of the inhabitants of the grants — The revolutionary government of New York equally hostile with the colonial to the New Hampshire land titles — Petition to congress of the convention of January 16, 1776, and proceedings thereon.

BY the sudden death of Montgomery, the command in Canada devolved on Gen. Wooster. He had been left at Montreal in charge of the troops at that place and its vicinity, and he immediately made every effort to obtain reenforcements, from the colonies. On the 6th of Jan. 1776, he wrote to Col. Warner for aid in the most pressing terms. The following are extracts from his letter. After giving a general account of the misfortune at Quebec, he says: "I have not time to give you all the particulars, but this much will show you that in consequence of this defeat our present prospect in this country is rendered very dubious, and unless we can be quickly reenforced, perhaps they may be fatal, not only to us who are stationed here but also to the colonies in general; as in my opinion the safety of the colonies, especially the frontiers, very greatly, depends upon keeping possession of this country. I have sent an express to Gen. Schuyler, Gen. Washington and the congress, but you know how far they have to go, and that it is very uncertain how long it will be before we can have relief from them. You, sir, and the valiant Green Mountain corps, are in our neighborhood. You all have arms, and I am confident ever stand ready to lend a helping hand to your brethren in distress, therefore let me beg of you to raise as many men as you can, and somehow get into this country and stay with us till we can have relief from the colonies. You will see that proper officers are appointed under you and both officers and privates will have the same pay as the continental troops. It will be well for your men to set out at soon as they can be collected. It is not so much matter whether together or not, but let them be sent on by tens, twenties, thirties, forties or fifties, as fast as they can be collected. It will have a good effect upon the Canadians to see succor coming on. You will be good enough to send copies of this letter or such parts of it as you think proper to the people below you. I can but hope the people will make a push to get into this country, and I am confident I shall see you here with your men in a very short time." Gen. Wooster was not disappointed. He did see Warner with his men in Canada "in a very short time." Their promptness and alacrity on this alarming occasion elicited the notice and approval of both Washington and Schuyler. The latter on learning the fate of Montgomery and the consequent unfortunate condition of affairs in Canada, wrote from Albany immediately January 13th, to Washington for reenforcements from the army before Boston. These could not be spared, and Washington, having heard of the patriotic exertions that were making on the New Hampshire Grants, wrote Schuyler on the 18th that he trusted troops from the main army would not be needed, for that "Col. Arnold and his corps would soon be joined by a number of men under Col. Warner, and others from Connecticut, who it was said had marched immediately on getting intelligence of the melancholy affair," and Schuyler on the 22d, wrote Washington, withdrawing his former request for reenforcements, and assigning as the reason therefor that "Col. Warner had been so successful in sending men into Canada;" and that regiments were soon expected from the western part of Massachusetts and from other colonies.

Warner, indeed, had peculiar advantages in the performance of this service. The Green Mountain Boys had long been armed in their own defence against the land claimants under the Colonial government of New York. In that controversy, as well as in the new struggle with the mother country, he had been their trusted and chosen leader, and they had been accustomed to rally at his call. They gathered about him at once, and first among the reenforcements to the troops before Quebec was his regiment. The winter campaign proved extremely distressing; the troops were in want of comfortable clothing, barracks and provisions. Most of them took the small-pox and great numbers of them died. At the opening of the spring, in May, a large body of British troops arrived at Quebec, to relieve the garrison, and the American army was under the necessity of making a hasty retreat. Warner's position was one of the greatest danger, and required the utmost attention and perseverance. He was always in the rear, picking up the wounded and diseased, assisting and encouraging those who were least able to take care of themselves, and he generally kept but a few miles in advance of the British, who closely pursued the Americans from post to post. By his habitual vigilance and care, Warner brought off most of the invalids, and with the corps of the diseased and infirm, reached Ticonderoga late in the month of June, a few days after the main army had taken possession of that post. Canada had been wholly abandoned, but as the Americans were possessed of all the shipping on the lake, no immediate invasion by the enemy was apprehended, and Warner's regiment, with many other troops, were discharged.

The services of Warner and his men were not overlooked. Hitherto his rank had been that of lieutenant colonel, and his corps of a temporary character. On the 5th of July, the day after the declaration of independence, and about two weeks after the return of Warner and his men from Canada, on the report of the board of war, congress resolved to organize, under its own authority, a regiment of regular troops for permanent service, to be under the command of officers who had served in Canada, of which regiment Seth Warner was appointed colonel, and Samuel Safford lieutenant colonel. Most of the other officers were those from the New Hampshire Grants who had served with Warner in Canada, in one or both of the batallions of Green Mountain Boys.

On the evacuation of Canada by the troops of the colonies, Gen. Carlton immediately set about constructing vessels at St. Johns, for the purpose of obtaining the command of Lake Champlain; and such were his advantages of men and means that, at the end of a few months, his naval force greatly exceeded that which the Americans, with their limited resources, had been able to prepare for service. Col. Arnold in command of the American flotilla, on the 11th and 13th of October, made bold and desperate resistance to the attacks of the British fleet, but he was finally overcome. Destroying most of his vessels, he was able to escape with the greater portion of his men.

Gen. Gates, who was now in command at Ticonderoga, apprehending that Carlton would follow up his naval success by an attack upon that post, sought earnestly for reenforcements of both men and supplies. Anticipating this call, Col. Warner had notified "the officers of each regiment of militia on the Grants," that their services would be immediately needed, and on the 20th of October, he wrote Gates from Castleton informing him of the receipt of his orders the previous evening, and that he had in consequence requested the men to march; that Col. Brownson's men were already on the way, that he had sent an express to Col. Robinson who commanded the lower regiment, that he had no doubt they would soon be on the march and that he expected a part of them every moment. The men on the west side of the Green mountain had been organized into three regiments by the committees and conventions of the New Hampshire Grants, and they turned out *en masse*, and joined Gates at Mount Independence. On the 20th, Mr. Yancey, the commissary of that department, addressed a letter to the chairman of the committee at Bennington, informing him that an immediate supply of flour was necessary for the subsistence of the army, and urging the committee in the most pressing terms to collect and forward at once all that was within their power. The next day after the receipt of this requisition, Nathan Clark, the chairman of the committee returned for answer that one thousand bushels of wheat had been collected and was being ground at the mills, and would be forwarded as fast as possible, but saying, "that the militia having left us almost to a man, renders it very difficult to furnish assistance to convey what we have already on hand," and suggesting the propriety of discharging some of the militia for that service. For their promptness and energy in this matter, the committee not only received the very warm thanks of the commissary, but also a dispatch from Deputy Adjutant General Trumbull, in which he says, "The general has seen your letter to Mr. Yancey and directed me to return you his most cordial thanks for the zeal you expressed for your insulted country. Agreeable to the request of the committee, he has ordered one of the companies from your town to return for the purpose of assisting in a work so necessary for the good of the army."

The application of Commissary Yancey to the Bennington committee, a body not recognized as lawful by the governing men of New York, appears to have been quite distasteful to them. A passage in the letter of Mr. Yancy, in which he gave as a reason for his application for flour, "that from the number of disaffected persons in and about Albany there was great danger of too long a delay of the contracted provisions for the army from that place" gave great offence. A committee, which had been appointed under the authority of the New York convention, to repair to Albany and cooperate with Gen. Schuyler, took up the subject with much earnestness, procured a copy of the letter, examined witnesses in regard to the manner in which such information had been communicated to Mr. Yancy, his motives in making the statement, and made a very long report on the subject, censuring the language of Mr. Yancey as calculated to "sow jealousy and distrust at such a critical juncture," and finally concluding with a resolution appointing a sub-committee consisting of Mr. Robert R. Livingston, Mr. Robert Yates and Mr. Duane, to pursue the investigation further. But no additional report is found. It is probable that the real offence of the commissary was in making the application to a body of men who had long been denounced by the old government of New York as enemies to the public peace rather than in the language in which it was couched.

Gen. Carlton landed his forces at Crown Point, but after threatening Ticonderoga for about two weeks retired into Canada for the winter. Thus ending the campaign for the year 1776, in the northern department. The militia which had been hastily collected to re-enforce the garrison were discharged early in November. On dismissing the regiment of Col. Robinson from service the general addressed to him a testimonial as follows:

TICONDEROGA, November 9, 1776.

To Col. Moses Robinson.

SIR: I am to return to you and the officers and men of your regiment my sincere thanks for the spirit and alertness you have shown in marching to the defence of this important pass, when threatened with an immediate attack from the enemy. I now gentlemen dismiss you with honor. I also certify that neither of you nor any of your officers have received any pay from me for your services on this occasion. That I leave to be settled and adjusted between your state and the general congress of all the United States. With sentiments of gratitude and respect.

I am sir your most obedient humble servant,

HORATIO GATES.

A letter of like tenor was also delivered to Col. Brownson.[1]

The civil affairs of the people of the New Hampshire Grants will now demand our attention. Amid the stirring events of the early period of the revolutionary struggle, the controversy with New York seemed for a time to have subsided. The Colonial government of the province had become practically extinct, and no regular authority had been substituted in its place. The people of the old colony were counselled and led rather than governed by committees and

---

[1] *Am. Arch.*, vol. 4, pp. 588. *William's Vt.*, vol. 2, p. 447. *Chipman's Life of Warner*, 39-43. *Sparks's Wash.*, vol. 3, 250-1. *Sparks's Rev. Cor.*, vol. 1, 531-5. *Am. Arch.*, vol. 2, pp. 1146, 1223, 1300—vol. 3, 288-299-623. *Gordon. Thompson. Bancroft.*

conventions. There was no power, and consequently there could be no serious attempt of the New York land claimants to enforce their claims. Criminal prosecutions against the settlers were also at an end. It was hoped that the new government, when it should assume a regular and permanent form, would repudiate the unjust policy of the old in regard to their land titles, and indications were sought for that such would be the disposition of its leaders. But no such indications were given. On the contrary, it gradually became apparent that the old land claiming interest was predominent in the New York convention, and also in the New York delegation to the Continental congress. In both these bodies Mr. Duane, the old antagonist of the settlers, was a leading member, and associated with him were the Livingstons and other aristocratic land holders and claimants, who had long been known as advocates of the New York patents. It was evident that these men possessed a controlling influence over the affairs of the colony, and that no relaxation of former efforts to overthrow the New Hampshire titles was to be expected from them. If the inhabitants of the New Hampshire Grants should submit to have the titles to their farms determined against them by the courts of the new government of New York, as they did not doubt would be the case, if trials should be had before them, and there should be no appeal from the decisions, they would seem to be placed in a worse condition than if they had remained under the crown. The king had repeatedly recognized the equity of their claims, and had denounced the conduct of their opponents as oppressive and unjust; and towards him they had been accustomed to look with some degree of hope for relief. From the land claiming rulers of New York it seemed vain to expect any. In this troubled aspect of their affairs it was judged prudent to ascertain, as far as possible, the feeling with which their cause was likely to be regarded by the Continental congress, and for this purpose, and to obtain the counsel and advice, in regard to their future action, of such members as should be thought friendly to them, some of their leading men, in the fall of 1775, made a visit to Philadelphia. The counsel obtained seems to have been favorable to the continuance of the separate organization by committees and conventions, which they had already formed and which for years had existed among them.

Soon after the return of these gentlemen a notice for a general convention, to be held on the first Wednesday of January, 1776, appears to have been extensively circulated, but in consequence of the absence of Col. Warner and some others whose presence was deemed necessary, the day of the meeting was postponed. A new warrant for the convention was accordingly issued, bearing date at Arlington, the 20th of December, 1775, and signed "by order of Moses Robinson, Samuel Robinson, Seth Warner, Jeremiah Clark, Martin Powell, Daniel Smith, Jonathan Willard, committee." It notified and warned "the inhabitants on the New Hampshire Grants west of the range of Green mountains, to meet together by their delegates from each town, at the house of Cephas Kent, in Dorset, on the 16th day of January next at 9 o'clock in the morning, then and there to act on the following articles, viz:"

1 and 2. To choose a chairman and clerk.

"3d. To see if the law of New York shall have free circulation where it doth infringe on our properties, or title of lands, or riots (so called), in defense of the same.

4th. To see if the said convention will come into some proper regulations, or take some method to suppress all scismatic mobs that have or may arise on the Grants.

5th. To see if they will choose an agent or agents to send to the Continental congress.

6th. To see whether the convention will consent to associate with New York or by themselves in the cause of America."

At the time and place appointed delegates from the towns of Pownal, Bennington, Shaftsbury, Arlington, Sunderland, Manchester, Dorset, Danby, Tinmouth, Clarendon, Rutland, Pittsford, Rupert, Pawlet, Wells, Poultney, Castleton, and Neshobe, now Brandon, assembled and were organized by the appointment of "Capt. Joseph Woodward, chairman, Dr. Jonas Fay, clerk, and Col. Moses Robinson, Samuel McCoon, and Oliver Everts, assistant clerks."

A committee of nine members, was appointed "to report their opinion to the convention, relative to the third article in the warrant"—that is how far the people should submit to the execution of the laws of New York. The convention then adjourned to 3 o'clock in the afternoon.

On reassembling, it was at first voted to make an addition of four persons to the foregoing committee, but it was afterwards resolved to reconsider the two votes relating to the appointment of the committee, and in the language of the journal, "to discourse the matter for which they were appointed, in public meeting." After debate it was voted "to represent the particular case of the inhabitants of the New Hampshire Grants to the honorable Continental congress by remonstrance and petition." Dr. Jonas Fay, Col. William

Marsh and Mr. Thomas Rowley, were appointed to prepare the petition.

The committee reported their draught of a petition in the evening, and the convention adjourned to the next morning, when the petition being a second time read was unanimously adopted, and Lieut. James Breakenridge, Capt. Heman Allen and Dr. Jonas Fay, were appointed to present the petition to congress. It was then voted that Simeon Hathaway, Elijah Dewey and James Breakenridge, be a committee with power "to warn a general meeting of the committees on the Grants when they shall judge necessary *from southern intelligence*," and that Col. John Strong, Zadock Everest and Asahel Ward be a committee, with like power to warn a meeting "when they should judge necessary *from northern intelligence*." The several committees of correspondence which had been appointed by previous conventions, were directed "to continue their duty as usual."

The memorial to congress which was adopted by the convention was entitled :

"The humble petition, address and remonstrance of that part of America being situated south of Canada line, west of Connecticut river, north of Massachusetts Bay and east of a twenty mile line from Hudson's river ; commonly called and known by the name of the New Hampshire Grants."

It stated in substance, that the territory they inhabited was, at the close of the then war with France, "deemed and reputed to be in the province of New Hampshire ;" that the governor of that province granted a large number of townships, of six miles square each, to the petitioners and those under whom they claim ; that "a great number of the petitioners, who were men of considerable substance, disposed of their interest in their native places, and with their numerous families, proceeded, many of them two hundred miles, encountering many dangers, fatigues, and great hardships, to inhabit a desolate wilderness, which is now become a well settled frontier to three governments ;" that the monopolizing land traders of New York "being well apprised of these facts, had, by false representations as the petitioners believed, procured in 1764 an order of the king in council annexing the territory to New York ; that thereupon the land traders obtained patents from the government of that province of much of the same land which had been previously granted by New Hampshire, and threatened to turn the New Hampshire occupants out of possession ; that on the representation of the matter to the king, he on the 24th of July 1767, made a peremptory order in council, forbidding the governor of New York, "on pain of his majesty's highest displeasure" from making any further grants of such lands: that, notwithstanding this order, the several successive governors of the province continued to make grants to the New York land jobbers of the prohibited lands; that upon further representation, made at great expense by the petitioners to the crown, the board of trade had made a report in their favor; that the courts of New York had declared the titles of the petitioners to be invalid, and that they had been compelled for a number of years past, to defend by force their possessions from the grasp of their adversaries.

The petitioners further stated that they were "entirely willing to do all in their power in the general cause of the colonies, *under the Continental congress*, and had been, ever since the taking of Ticonderoga, in which the petitioners were principally active under Col. Ethan Allen, but were not willing to put themselves under the honorable, the Provincial congress of New York, in such manner as might, in future, be detrimental to their private property," which they apprehended would be the case, if they should consent to subscribe the associations and oaths required of those who serve under that congress. As further evidence of their willingness to aid in the common cause, the petitioners said: "We are called on this moment by the committee of safety of the county of Albany, to suppress a dangerous insurrection in Tryon county. Upwards of ninety soldiers were on their march, within twelve hours after receiving the news, all inhabitants of one town, inhabited by your petitioners, and all furnished with arms, ammunition, accoutrements and provisions. Again we are alarmed by an express from Gen. Wooster commanding at Montreal, with the disagreeable news of the unfortunate attack on Quebec, requiring our immediate assistance by troops; in consequence of which, a considerable number immediately marched for Quebec, and more are daily following their example." [1]

---

[1] The exertions of the petitioners on the requisition of Gen. Wooster have already been stated. The application of the committee of Albany was in consequence of an express from Tryon county, giving information that Sir John Johnson, with five hundred tories and a body of Indians, had assembled on the Mohawk with hostile intentions, upon which the militia of the neighborhood were rallied, and calls immediately sent to Berkshire county and the Grants for aid. The ninety men mentioned in the petition were from Bennington, and they joined Gen. Schuyler at Albany, who marched from that place on the 16th for Johnstown. Gen. Schuyler entered into a treaty with Sir John by which, after the arms of his followers had been surrendered, he was allowed to remain at his castle on his parole of honor,

The petition concluded by praying congress to allow the petitioners "to do duty in the Continental service as inhabitants of the New Hampshire Grants, and not as inhabitants of the province of New York, or subject to the limitations, restrictions, or regulations of the militia of that province."

The petition being signed by Joseph Woodward as chairman, and Jonas Fay as secretary, was committed to Heman Allen, one of the committee appointed for that purpose, by whom, on the 8th of May, it was caused to be presented to congress. The petition being read, was referred to a committee consisting of Mr. Rodney of Delaware, Mr. Harrison of Virginia, Mr. Hewes of North Carolina, Mr. Lynch of South Carolina, and Mr. Alexander of Maryland, all being from the southern colonies. After hearing Mr. Allen, the committee, on the 30th of May, reported a resolution as follows, viz.:

"*Resolved*, that it is the opinion of this committee, that it be recommended to the petitioners, for the present, to submit to the government of New York, and contribute their assistance, with their countrymen in the contest between Great Britain and the United Colonies; but that such submission ought not to prejudice the rights of them or others to the lands in controversy, or any part of them; nor be construed to affirm or admit the jurisdiction of New York in and over that country; and when the present troubles are at an end, the final determination of their right may be mutually referred to proper judges."

Although this resolution appeared to recognize the claim of the petitioners as worthy of serious consideration, yet it was apparent that it would furnish them no protection whatever against the New York patents, and before it was acted upon by congress, Mr. Allen, on the 4th of June, was permitted to withdraw the petition, "he representing," as stated in the journal, "that he had left at home some papers and vouchers necessary to support the allegations therein contained." [1]

---

which, however, he violated, and after the recapture of Montreal by the British army, fled to that place. *Am. Archives*, vol. 4, fourth series pp. 682–3, and 818–829. *Stone's Life of Brant*, pp. 119–147.

[1] *Williams's Hist. Vermont*, vol. 2, p. 164. Ms. copy of proceedings of Dorset convention, in the possession of Hon. James H. Phelps, of West Townshend. *Slade*, 61–65. *Jour. N. Y. Cong.*, vol. 1, pp. 337, 360, 364.

CHAPTER XXI.

MEASURES FOR THE FORMATION OF A NEW STATE.

1776.

Convention at Dorset, July 24th, to consider the report of their agent to Congress — and its adjourned meeting at Dorset, looking towards the formation of a separate state — Unfriendly action of Cumberland county towards New York and the action of the assembly thereon — Adjourned Convention of October 30th, and its publications and those of New York on the controversy.

ON the return of Mr. Allen from Philadelphia, another convention was called to hear his report of the proceedings of congress on the petition which he had presented in behalf of the inhabitants of the New Hampshire Grants. The meeting of the convention was notified by warrant signed by James Breakenridge, Simeon Hathaway and Elijah Dewey, the committee appointed at the previous convention "to act upon southern intelligence." It was to be held at "the house of Cephas Kent, innholder in Dorset on Wednesday the 24th of July, 1776."

The objects of the meeting, besides that of hearing the report of their agent, were to consider and determine upon what measures should be adopted in regard to New York, and for the defence of the district against the common enemy.

At the time and place appointed, thirty-one towns on the west side of the Green mountain, and one on the east side, were represented by fifty-one delegates. Capt. Joseph Bowker of Rutland, was chosen chairman, and Jonas Fay of Bennington, clerk. The petition of the former convention, which had been presented to congress by Heman Allen, was read, and Mr. Allen gave an account of the proceedings of congress thereon. In addition to what has been before stated, from the journals of that body, Mr. Allen reported that the motion to withdraw the petition was made in order that the delegates from New York should not have it in their power to bring the matter to a final decision, at a time when the convention of the grants had no proper delegates in the house, the evidence not being at hand at that time.

He further reported that "he had many private conferences with sundry members of congress and other gentlemen of distinction relating to the particular circumstances and situation of the New Hampshire Grants, who did severally and earnestly recommend that the inhabitants of said Grants exert themselves to their utmost abilities to repel by force the hostile invasions of the British fleets and armies against the colonies of America, and that said inhabitants do not by any way or means whatsoever connect or associate with the honorable Provincial congress of New York, or any authority derived from, by or under them, directly or indirectly; but that the said inhabitants do forthwith consult upon suitable measures to associate and unite the whole of the inhabitants of said Grants together."

The convention was in session two days and their proceedings appear to have been conducted with care and deliberation. The question in regard to their future political relations engrossed the principal attention of the members. A proposal to unite the district with New Hampshire was discussed, but met with little favor. A proposition to make application to the inhabitants of "the Grants" to form the whole "into a separate district," was adopted with but one dissenting vote, and a committee was appointed to treat with the inhabitants "on the east side of the range of the Green mountains relative to their association with this convention." A resolution was adopted earnestly recommending the several field officers already nominated in the district "to see that their men be forthwith furnished with suitable arms, ammunition and accoutrements, etc., agreeably to a resolve of the Continental congress."[1]

On the second day of the session the subject of a written association to be subscribed by the members of the convention was considered. As a means of manifesting the sentiments of the people, and of strengthening the cause of the colonies, voluntary associations had been entered into by the members of public bodies in the several colonies, and recommended to be also subscribed by their constituents, by which they engaged to resist by force of arms the fleets and armies of Great Britain. In the month of March, 1776, the form of such an association had been adopted and recommended by the committee of safety of New York, to be subscribed

[1] No record of the committees forming these regiments has been found, though it was doubtless under their direction that they had been organized. From the letter of Col. Warner to Gen. Gates, of the 20th of the following October, referred to in a previous page, it appears that there were three militia regiments on the west side of the Green mountain, of which James Mead of Rutland, Gideon Brownson of Sunderland and Moses Robinson of Bennington were the colonels. *Am. Archives*, vol. 2, p. 1146 and vol. 3, p. 623, 5th series.

by the people of that colony. The inhabitants of the New Hampshire Grants, though they had always shown their readiness to exert themselves to the utmost in the common cause of the country, had generally declined to subscribe the New York association. One was now adopted by the convention, in which the reason for their former neglect was set forth. It was in the following words:

"This convention being fully sensible that it is the will and pleasure of the honorable the Continental congress that every honest friend to the liberties of America in the several United States thereof should subscribe an association, binding themselves as members of some body or community to stand in defence of those liberties; and whereas it has been the usual custom for individuals to associate with the colony or state which they are reputed to be members of. Yet nevertheless, the long and spirited conflict which has for many years subsisted between the colony or state of New York and the inhabitants of that district of land, commonly called and known by the name of the New Hampshire Grants, relative to the title of the land in said district, renders it inconvenient in many respects to associate with that province or state, which has hitherto been the sole reason of our not subscribing an association before this.

"The better therefore to convince the public of our readiness to join in the common defence of the aforesaid liberties, we do publish and subscribe the following association, viz:

"We, the subscribers, inhabitants of the district of land, commonly called and known by the name of the New Hampshire Grants, do voluntarily and solemnly engage under all the ties held sacred amongst mankind, at the risk of our lives and fortunes, to defend by arms the United American States against the hostile attempts of the British fleets and armies, until the present unhappy controversy between the two countries shall be settled."

This association was subscribed by forty-nine of the fifty members of the convention, one member, Thomas Brayton, of Clarendon, who afterwards became an active tory, declining to sign it.

The convention by resolution recommended that the association should be subscribed by all the friends of America in the district, and declared that any persons within that district who should subscribe and return any other association than the above to the committees of safety for either of the counties in the province of New York, should "be deemed enemies to the common cause of the New Hampshire Grants"

A committee of appeals consisting of nine persons was chosen with power to hear and determine all matters that should be brought before them in writing, "by way of proper appeal from the judgment of either of the committees of safety of said Grants, any five of the committee to be a quorum."

The convention then adjourned to meet at the same place on Wednesday the 25th of Sept. following.[1]

It has already been seen that the efforts of the colonial government of New York to maintain its jurisdiction over the inhabitants of the New Hampshire Grants, represented in this convention, had been unsuccessful, and that they had for several years been practically independent of its authority. Their present proceedings made the important declaration and announcement that the managers of the new government of New York, occupied the same position towards the New Hampshire settlers as the old, and were to be equally distrusted and opposed, and that the surest, if not the only way of preserving their property from the grasp of their old adversaries, was to organize for themselves a separate and permanent government.

The people on the east side of the Green mountain though sympathizing with their brethren on the west, had partially submitted to the colonial authority. On the 11th of April, 1775, soon after the Westminister massacre, a convention of the committes of the several towns had resolved, as has been already stated, to renounce and resist the administration of the government of New York "till such time as the lives and property of the inhabitants should be secured by it." No courts had since been held in either of the counties of Cumberland or Gloucester, and the authority of New York in instituting legal proceedings, had not been acknowledged. Attempts had been made by committees from portions of the towns in both counties to nominate officers for organizing a militia under New York authority, but they had met with much opposition, and were only partially successful. On the receipt of circulars from the New York congress inviting the inhabitants to send representatives to that body, meetings of the committees from several towns in Cumberland county, had been held at which delegates were named, who had attended the congress. But these proceedings were not satisfactory to many, and it is doubtful whether they were in accordance with the feelings of the mass of the people.

In consequence of a hand bill from the New York provincial congress, recommending to the inhabitants of Cumberland county "to

---

[1] For the proceedings of this (July) convention see *Ms. Records of J. H. Phelps*, also *Am. Arch.*, vol. 1, 5th series, p. 565. *Conn. Courant* of Feb. 17, 1737. And *Stevens' Papers*, vol, 2, p. 301 and 327.

choose delegates *and invest them with power to establish a form of government,*" the committees of twenty towns met at Westminster on the 21st of June 1776, a month prior to the Dorset convention before referred to, and elected three delegates. Written instructions were given them to use their influence to establish a government "on the principle that all civil power, under God, is originally in the people," and pointing out several important requisites of democratic character which should be provided for in the new government. A letter was then prepared to the New York congress informing that body that "a major part of the people were in favor of instituting civil government according to the exigences of the county," and had elected delegates in conformity to their recommendation, but that the power of their delegates was so limited and restrained that if they broke over their instructions their constituents reserved to themselves full liberty to disavow any and every part of their doings, and also full liberty if they should thereafter deem it expedient, to unite themselves with "that ever respectable and most patriotic government of the Massachusetts Bay province." This communication being signed by the chairman and attested by the clerk was, together with the instructions committed to the delegates and by them laid before the New York convention.[1]

The convention of the New Hampshire Grants assembled, agreably to adjournment at Dorset on Wednesday the 25th of September 1776, and held a session of four days. Capt. Joseph Bowker was again chairman and Dr. Jonas Fay clerk. The convention was attended by fifty-six delegates representing thirty-three towns, about one third of which were situated on the east side of the mountain. Various important measures were adopted which looked forward to the formation of the territory into a separate state, and others to the furnishing aid in the general struggle against the common enemy. Referring to the long continued conflict with New York, in regard to their land titles as still subsisting "by which their property and liberties were greatly endangered," it was voted that no directions or laws of that state should be accepted or obeyed. And a covenant or compact was subscribed by all the members, and recommended for signature by their constituents, which after stating by way of preamble the unwarrantable measures that had been taken by the New York government "to deprive them by fraud, violence and oppression of their property and in particular their landed interest, and that they

[1] *Slade,* p. 60. *Am. Archives,* vol. 1, 5th series, p. 1535, and vol. 3, p. 222. *Hall's Eastern Vt.,* 245-269.

30

had reason to expect a continuance of the same kind of disingenuity;" and considering the great inconvenience of connecting themselves with New York by reason of the distance of its metropolis from their district, concluded as follows, viz:

"We the subscribers, inhabitants of that district of land commonly called and known by the name of the New Hampshire Grants, being legally delegated and authorized to transact the public political affairs of the aforesaid district for ourselves and constituents, do solemnly covenant and engage that, for the time being, we will strictly and regularly adhere to the several resolves of this or a future convention, constituted on said district by the free voice of the friends to American liberties, which shall not be repugnant to the resolves of the honorable the Continental congress, relative to the cause of America."

It was also unanimously resolved "to take suitable measures, as soon as may be, to declare the New Hampshire Grants a separate district." A committee was appointed "to draw up a petition to send to the honorable Continental congress," to be reported at the next meeting of the convention. Measures were taken to have the association entered into at the previous meeting, to resist by force of arms, the fleets and armies of Great Britain, presented for signature to all the inhabitants of the Grants. In regard to those on the west side of the Green mountain, the town committees were specially directed to "faithfully see to it that the association be forthwith signed by every individual male inhabitant of each town, from sixteen years old and upwards, and that the association thus signed, be returned to Dr. Jonas Fay, clerk of the convention, before its next sitting." If any person refused to sign it, the town committees were to take their names and report the reasons they gave for their refusal. It was also resolved that no one should be allowed to act in the choice of committees of safety, but those who had subscribed the association. It was voted to build a jail on the west side of the mountain, "for securing tories," and a committee was appointed to fix upon its location and superintend its construction. It appearing to the convention that one town on the west side of the mountain had not been represented in the convention, and that its inhabitants were principally tories, "the friends of liberty" were directed to choose a committee of safety and conduct their affairs as in other towns, "and if they met with opposition to make application to the committees of the neighboring towns for assistance."

Energetic preparations were made for the common defence against the British forces. A committee of war, consisting of nine members was appointed, who were authorized to issue warrants, or commissions in the name of the convention to the several field officers of the militia, and were invested with the general superintendence of the military affairs of the district. The officers of the militia regiments were to continue in their stations, and those of the regiments on the east side of the mountain were allowed to execute the orders they had received from New York, and were then to be under the direction of the convention. The colonels of the several regiments were directed to give special orders to the captains under them to fill up six companies of rangers for frontier defence. The committee of war were directed on sufficient notice from the Continental congress, or from the commander of the armies of the United States, or on any sudden emergency, to order "the militia to march immediately to such part of the continent as might be required." In case of any neglect to comply with such orders, the officers and men were made subject to heavy fines, of which a schedule for the several ranks of officers and men was prescribed, the committee being empowered to issue their warrant in the name of the convention to enforce their collection.

After the transaction of some other business of minor importance, and the appointment of several committees to make known the proceedings of the convention to the inhabitants of the district, and especially to those on the east side of the Green mountain, that all might have an opportunity to subscribe the association and covenant it had adopted, and to unite in its measures, the convention adjourned to meet at the Court House in Westminster on Wednesday the 30th of October then next.[1]

It appears to have been contemplated that the separation from the government of New York would be consummated at this convention in October. But when the day of meeting came, the inhabitants of the territory were in great confusion and alarm by reason of the defeat and destruction of the American naval force on lake Champlain, and the apprehended attack by Carlton on Ticonderoga, a large portion of the people being in actual service for the defence of that post, as has heretofore been seen. In consequence of this condition of the district, the convention was thinly attended. Capt. Joseph Bowker was again in the chair, but Dr. Fay not being present, Capt. Ira Allen was chosen clerk. On the report

[1] For proceedings of this convention see *Ms. Records of J. H. Phelps. Am. Archives*, vol. 2, 5th series, p. 526-530. *Slade*, p. 66. *Stevens' Papers*, vol. 2, p. 327-336.

of a committee it was voted that the subject of petitioning congress to be formed into a separate jurisdiction, should be postponed to a future meeting. It was resolved that a manifesto should be published in the newspapers, stating briefly the reasons why the inhabitants of the New Hampshire Grants did not choose to connect themselves with the government of New York; and it was also voted that an answer should be prepared to a pamphlet which had been issued by the provincial congress of New York, bearing date October 2d, 1776, in favor of the jurisdiction of that state over the Grants, which answer should set forth the advantages that would arise to the people of the district, by forming themselves into a separate state, and that it be "printed and communicated to the inhabitants as soon as may be."

The convention appointed a large committee to make known its proceedings to their constituents, and to procure their signatures to the association for the defence of American liberty previously adopted, and then without transacting other important business, adjourned to meet again at the same place on the third Wednesday of the ensuing January.[1]

A well written manifesto, setting forth the reasons of the New Hampshire grantees for declining to connect themselves with the government of New York, calculated to make a favorable impression on the public mind towards their cause, was soon afterwards published in the *Connecticut Courant*, and probably in other papers. It was signed by Ira Allen clerk, and bore the character of an official act of the convention. A copy of it is preserved in the *American Archives*, volume second of the fifth series at page 1300.

The New York pamphlet above referred to was the report of a committee of the New York convention upon the letter of the Cumberland county committee of the 21st of June preceding, which had claimed and reserved to the people of the county a right to withdraw from the New York jurisdiction, in case they should not approve the form of government they were preparing for that state. The report had been approved by the New York convention and entered on the journal of October 4, 1776, and is found in the *American Archives*, volume three at page 222. An elaborate answer to this pamphlet was prepared by Ira Allen, embodying the causes, which in the opinion of the writer, justified the withdrawal of the people of the district from the New York government, and also the advantages which would accrue to them by the formation of a separate

[1] For the proceedings of this convention see *Records of J. H. Phelps.*

state. It appears not to have been published until the ensuing spring. It was entitled, *Miscellaneous Remarks on the Proceedings of the State of New York against the State of Vermont;* was printed in pamphlet form at Hartford "by Hannah Watson near the great bridge, A.D. 1777," and was extensively circulated. There is a manuscript copy of it in the *Stevens Papers*, in the office of the secretary of state, at Montpelier. A printed copy of it has not been found.

CHAPTER XXII.

MEASURES FOR ORGANIZING A SEPARATE STATE GOVERNMENT.

1777.

Convention of the New Hampshire Grants at Westminster, Jan. 1777, declare the district a separate state — Proceedings of New York against a new state — The declaration and petition of the New Hampshire Grants, stating the grounds of their claim to independence presented to Congress — Letter of Dr. Thomas Young to the inhabitants of Vermont a free and independent state — Vermont convention at Windsor, of June 4, 1777, and its proceedings. The New York constitution strengthens the friends of the new state — Resolutions of congress of June 30, censuring Dr. Young's letter and disclaiming any participation in the movement of the Vermonters for independence — Debate in Congress on the resolutions — The conduct of Vermont defended by Roger Sherman — The resolutions to be circulated in Vermont by order of the New York council of Safety, and the action of Gouverneur Morris in relation thereto.

THE year 1777 occupies an important place in the history of the New Hampshire Grants. It witnessed a declaration by the inhabitants of their independence and the formation of a state constitution. It was also a period of great peril and suffering, from the invasion of a powerful and cruel enemy, and of commendable energy and valor on the part of the people in effecting his defeat and capture.

The convention of the New Hampshire Grants met agreeably to adjournment at the Court House in Westminster on the 15th of January, 1777, and was in session three days, Capt. Joseph Bowker in the chair, Ira Allen clerk, and Reuben Jones assistant clerk. On Thusday, the second day of the session, a committee was appointed to examine the votes that had been taken among the inhabitants, on the question of separating from the New York government, which committee reported as follows, viz: "We find by examination that three-fourths of the people in Cumberland and Gloucester counties that have acted are for a new state, the rest we regard as neuters." This being understood to be the state of feeling on the east side of the Green mountain, and it being well known that the people on the west side were nearly or quite all for a new jurisdiction, the convention unanimously voted for a separate and independent state. On the morning of Friday the 17th, a committee which had been previously appointed made their report of a form for a public declaration to that effect. The report began by stating that, "whenever protection was withheld by a government no allegiance was due, or could of right be demanded;" that the lives and properties of the inhabitants of the New Hampshire Grants had been manifestly aimed at, for many years past, by the monopolizing land traders of New York and by the legislative and executive authorities of that colony and state, of the truth of which many overt acts were so fresh in the minds of the members as to render it needless to name them. The report then referred to the resolution of congress of May 15, 1776, which had recommended to the respective assemblies and conventions of the United Colonies, "where no government sufficient for the exigencies of their affairs" existed, to form such government, and stating that such new government was necessary "to enable them to secure their rights against the usurpations of Great Britain and also against those of New York and the several other governments claiming jurisdiction of their territory," and offered for the consideration of the convention the following declaration:

"This convention, whose members are duly chosen by the free voice of the inhabitants in the several towns on the New Hampshire Grants, in public meeting assembled, in our own names and in behalf of our constituents, do hereby proclaim and publicly declare, that the district of territory comprehending and usually known by the name and description of the New Hampshire Grants, of right ought to be, and is hereby declared forever hereafter to be considered as a separate, free and independent jurisdiction or state, by the name, and forever hereafter to be called, known and distinguished by the name of New Connecticut,[1] and that the inhabitants that are at present or may hereafter become resident within said territory shall be entitled to the same privileges, immunities and enfranchisements, which are, or that may at any time hereafter be allowed to the inhabitants of any of the free and independent states of America; and that such privileges and immunities shall be regulated in a bill of rights and by a form of government to be established at the next adjourned session of this convention."

This declaration being unanimously adopted, it was voted that it should be published in the newspapers, and a committee of three was appointed to prepare it for the press. At the convention at Dorset the preceding September, Dr. Jonas Fay, Col. William Marsh and Dr. Reuben Jones had been appointed "a committtee to draw a petition to send to the honorable Continental congress," to be reported to a committee to examine the same; and Nathan Clark,

---

[1] In reference to the name given to the state in this declaration, see Appendix No. 9.

Esq., Col. Seth Warner and Capt. Heman Allen had been selected to make the examination. At the present convention, Dr. Jonas Fay, Col. Thomas Chittenden, Dr. Reuben Jones, Col. Jacob Bayley and Capt. Heman Allen were appointed delegates to present the petition to congress. An addition of several members was made to the committee of war. It was recommended to each town in Cumberland and Gloucester counties to choose new committees of safety, where the towns were dissatisfied with the committees, the committees in other towns to remain for the time being. A letter was prepared and signed by the chairman of the convention, addressed to John Sessions and Simon Stevens who had been acting as delegates in the New York convention, informing them of the declaration which had been made for a separate state, and requesting them to withdraw at once from the New York convention, and not to appear again in the character of representatives for that county, adding that they " were not chosen by a majority of the people at large."

The convention was then adjourned to meet at the meeting house in Windsor, on the first Wednesday of June then next.[1]

While the inhabitants of the New Hampshire Grants were preparing to form themselves into a separate state, as related in the preceding chapter, their proceedings had not been unnoticed by the men who administered the New York government.

On the 20th of January, 1777, a committee of the New York convention, to whom the subject had been referred, made a report which was taken into consideration and adopted by that body. It charged the disaffection towards the New York government, principally " to the arts and misrepresentations of certain inhabitants of the county of Charlotte, distinguishing themselves by the name of Green Mountain Boys," who, it was alleged, " made sundry unjust and iniquitous pretensions, anciently set up by the states of Massachusetts and New Hampshire against certain large tracts of land within the known bounds of New York," claiming the lands under grants of those states, and denying the title under New York. It alleged that countenance and encouragement was given to the disaffected by false representations that persons of considerable influence and authority in the neighboring states were favorable to them, and that it was the intention of the Continental congress to aid and assist them in obtaining their independence. It charged that these false statements had "received great weight and authority from the

[1] *Ms. Records of J. H. Phelps. Slade*, p. 68.

appointment of Seth Warner to be colonel of a regiment to be raised in that part of the state, and to appoint his own officers independent of the state of New York, and utterly contrary to the usual mode of appointment in such cases," the said Warner being well known to have been "principally concerned in divers riots, outrages and cruelties committed in direct opposition to the former government." The report concluded with a resolution, declaring that "a pressing application should be immediately made to the Continental congress to interpose their authority, and recommend to the insurgents a peaceable submission to the jurisdiction of that state, and also to disband the said regiment directed to be raised by Mr. Warner."

It may be remarked that if any evidence were wanting to justify the inhabitants of the New Hampshire Grants in regarding the new rulers of New York as equally hostile with the old to their land titles, this report conclusively furnishes it. It styles their claims under New Hampshire "unjust and iniquitous," and their complaints against the late government, as founded only on "frivolous pretenses."

A letter from the president of the convention addressed to the president of congress was prepared, embodying the substance of the foregoing report, to accompany the resolution. It bore date the 20th of January, but it does not appear to have been sent for several weeks afterwards. The delay was probably occasioned by the absence from the Continental congress, of Mr. Duane, who was principally relied upon to present the matter to that body in a favorable light, and who was also a member of the convention. On the first of March, another letter to the president of congress, to enclose the foregoing resolution and letter, was reported to the convention, by Mr. Duane, and adopted. When it was actually forwarded, does not appear. On the 29th of March, the convention by resolution, directed their three delegates then in congress, to come to the convention, and explain certain recent acts of congress, and ordered Mr. Duane and Mr. Philip Livingston, together with Wm. Duer, a newly appointed delegate, to repair immediately to Philadelphia, to attend to the affairs of the state in congress. Mr. Duer presented his credentials on the 7th of April, when the before mentioned resolution and letters were laid before that body, and after being read, were ordered to lie on the table.

The next day the petition in behalf of the New Hampshire Grants, signed by Jonas Fay, Thomas Chittenden, Heman Allen, and Reuben Jones, was presented to Congress. It bore date Jan. 15, 1777, and was entitled "the declaration and petition of that part of North America, situate south of Canada line, west of Connecticut river, north of the Massachusetts Bay and east of a twenty mile line from Hudson's river." It set forth, in clear and direct language, the principal grounds on which the inhabitants of that territory claimed the right to separate from New York and form an independent government. It stated the original granting and settlement of the territory under New Hampshire, the order of the king transferring the jurisdiction to New York, the regranting of the lands by the governors of that province to New York land jobbers; the application of the settlers to the crown for relief, against the New York claimants; the order of the king forbidding further grants and its constant violation by the New York governors; the decisions of the New York courts against the validity of the New Hampshire title, the attempts of the New York officers to enter upon the farms of the settlers by force, "reducing the petitioners to the disagreeable necessity of taking up arms as the only means left for the security of their possessions;" the indictment of the petitioners as rioters and the passage of acts of outlawry by the New York assembly offering rewards for their apprehension and on their neglect to surrender themselves subjecting them to the punishment of death without trial, and the declaration of the New York convention that all quitrents formerly due to the crown were now due to the convention and the future government of the state. It declared that "by a submission to the claims of New York, the petitioners would be subjected to the payment of two shillings and six pence sterling on every hundred acres annually, which compared with the quitrents of Livingston's, Phillips's and Van Rensselaer's Manors, and many other enormous tracts in the best situations in the state, would lay the most disproportionate share of the public expense on the petitioners, in all respects the least able to bear it;" and that "the convention of New York had now nearly completed a code of laws for the future government of the state, which should they be attempted to be put in execution would subject the petitioners to the fatal necessity of opposing them by every means in their power."

The petition then stated that the inhabitants of the district fully represented in convention, had at Westminster in said district made and published a declaration "that they would at all times thereafter consider themselves as a free and independent state, capable of regulating their internal police, in all and every respect whatsoever; and that the people in said described district had the sole right of governing themselves in such manner and form, as they, in their wisdom, should choose; not repugnant to any resolve of the honorable the Continental congress. And that for the mutual support of each other in the maintenance of the freedom and independence of said district as a separate state, the said delegates did jointly and severally pledge themselves to each other, by all the ties that were held sacred among men;" and that they further resolved and declared "that they were at all times ready, in conjunction with their brethren of the United States, to contribute their full proportion towards maintaining the present just war against the fleets and armies of Great Britain."

The petition concluded by praying that the district before described "might be ranked among the free and independent American states, and delegates therefrom admitted to seats in the grand continental congress.[1]

There was evidently a strong disinclination in a majority of congress to take up the subject. Whatever might be the individual opinions of the members in regard to the merits of the application for a new state, there was a general unwillingness to incur the displeasure of the important government of New York, by receiving it with favor, while, on the other hand, it might be no less hazardous to risk the enmity of the petitioners by rejecting it.

There being no prospect of the speedy action of congress on the petition of the New Hampshire Grants, the commissioners who had been appointed to present it returned home, taking with them a printed letter signed by Dr. Thomas Young a distinguished citizen of Philadelphia, bearing date April 11th, and addressed "to the inhabitants of Vermont a free and independent state, bounding on the river Connecticut and lake Champlain." Annexed to the letter was a printed copy, certified by the secretary of congress, of the resolution of that body of the 15th of May 1776, recommending the formation of governments where none were established sufficient for the exigency of their affairs. Among other things in the letter the writer says, "I have taken the minds of several leading members in the honorable the Continential congress, and can assure you that you have nothing to do but send copies of the recommendation to take up government to every township in your district, and invite all your freeholders and inhabitants to meet in their respective townships and choose members for a general convention, to meet at an early day, to choose delegates for the general congress, a committee of safety, and to form a constitution for your state.

"Your friends here tell me, that some are in doubt, whether delegates from your district would be admitted into congress. I tell you to organize fairly, and make the experiment, and I will insure you

[1] *Jour. N. Y. Convention*, January 20 and March 29. *Doc. Hist. N. Y.*, vol. 4, p. 925, 928, 932. *Journal of Congress*, April 7-8. *Slade*, 70. *Stevens Papers*, vol. 3, p. 57, 59, 107, 109. *Ira Allen's History*, 78-85.

success at the risk of my reputation, as a man of honor and common sense. Indeed, they can by no means refuse you. You have as good a right to choose how you will be governed, and by whom, as they had." (See Appendix No. 8).

Soon after the commissioners reached home, the pamphlet which had been prepared by Ira Allen in obedience to the resolution of the October convention before mentioned, in favor of the right of the people, to form a new government, was printed, and together with the letter of Dr. Young, was, to use the language of Mr. Allen, "spread through the state," and they doubtless exerted much influence in fixing the minds of the people on the subject.

In the *Connecticut Courant* of the 14th of April, an official notice of the adjournment of the January convention, to the first Wednesday of the following June, to meet at the Meeting House in Windsor, was published. It was signed by Ira Allen as clerk, and stated that it was the ardent wish of the former convention, that each town in the district, should send a delegate or delegates, and that delegates should be chosen in the towns where none had already been elected. In a note, non-residents who might desire it were invited to attend and witness the proceedings.

The convention assembled on Wednesday, the 4th day of June, and was very fully attended, fifty townships, nearly all in the territory in which settlements had been made, being represented by seventy-two delegates. Twenty-three of the towns represented, were situated on the west side of the Green mountain, and twenty-seven on the east side. Capt. Joseph Bowker, chairman, Dr. Jonas Fay, secretary, and Lieut. Martin Powell, assistant secretary.

This convention was in session three days, but the journal of its proceedings has not been found. We learn from *Ira Allen's History of Vermont*, that the convention "appointed a committee to make a draft of a constitution and passed a resolution, recommending to each town to elect and send representatives to the convention to meet at Windsor, in July following; that William Marsh, James Mead, Ira Allen and Capt. Salisbury, were appointed a committee to wait on the commander at Ticonderoga and consult with him respecting the regulations and defence of the frontiers, and that the convention then adjourned to the 4th day of July, 1777, to meet at the same place." [1]

It will be recollected that at the convention in January it had been voted to publish in the newspapers their declaration for form-

[1] Allen has the date wrong. The adjournment was to the first Wednesday, which was the 2d of July.

ing a new state, and that a committee had been appointed to revise it for publication. The revised declaration was inserted in the *Connecticut Courant* of March 17, 1777. The committee of revision had taken considerable liberty with the language of the original, in some respects improving it, but had strangely omitted to state any reason whatever to justify their separation from the New York government. Principally in consequence of this omission it was deemed necessary and proper for this convention to publish a further declaration. This declaration was dated "In General Convention, Windsor, June 4, 1777," and was officially signed by Jonas Fay, secretary.

It recited the fact that the convention, at its session in the preceding January, had declared the New Hampshire Grants to be a separate and independant state "by the name of New Connecticut," and stated that "by mere accident or through mistake," the declaration alone of that convention had been published in the *Connecticut Courant* "without assigning the reasons which impelled the inhabitants to such separation;" that this convention had been informed that a district of land lying on the Susquehannah river had already been called by the name of New Connecticut, and had in consequence thereof unanimously resolved that the district described in the said declaration should "ever hereafter be called and known by the name of Vermont." The names, with their official titles, of the seventy-two delegates in attendance upon the convention were then given, with the statement that seventy-one of them had answered to their names, and "did renew their pledges to each other by all the ties held sacred among men," to abide by and maintain said declaration, and "in conjunction with their brethren in the United States, to contribute their full proportion towards maintaining the present just war against the fleets and armies of Great Britain." This explanatory document concluded with a detailed assignment of the reasons which had impelled them to a separation from the government of New York, and to the establishment of a new and independent jurisdiction. These reasons were the same in substance with those which had been assigned in the original declaration made at Westminster in January, and more fully stated in the declaration and petition in behalf of that convention which had been presented to the Continental congress, of which accounts have already been given. This further declaration was published in the *Connecticut Courant* of June 30, 1777.

Another act of this convention of which a knowledge has been obtained, and perhaps its last, previous to its adjournment, was the appointment of Wednesday the 18th of the then month of June "to be observed as a day of public fasting and prayer throughout the state," for which a proclamation signed by Joseph Bowker, chairman, and Jonas Fay, secretary, was issued, bearing date in general convention at Windsor, in the state of Vermont, the 7th day of June, A.D. 1777. It was the first proclamation for a fast that was ever issued in Vermont, and is believed to have been very generally and appropriately observed.[1]

On the 8th of May, 1777, the convention of New York had adopted a constitution for the future government of the state which was promulgated in Vermont about the time of the sitting of the June convention at Windsor. Its provisions in connection with an ordinance which accompanied it, increased the dissatisfaction of the people with New York, and greatly strengthened the friends of the new state. The constitution affirmed the validity of all the grants made by the governors of the province during the colonial period, thereby annulling all the grants which had been previously made by New Hampshire, to the certain ruin of a large portion of the inhabitants, if they remained under the jurisdiction of New York; and it left the titles of the residue in uncertainty and doubt. It moreover recognized the hateful annual *quit-rent* as a permanent source of revenue for the support of the state government. This was considered highly unjust, inasmuch as a great portion of the most productive land in the state, which had been granted in large tracts, with but the nominal rent of one or two raccoon or beaver skins or a few shillings in money for several hundred thousand acres, would in effect be exempt from the tax. Probably nine-tenths of the inhabitants of Vermont were emigrants from Massachusetts, Connecticut and Rhode Island, where no such government incumbrance had ever been imposed upon lands, and though they had accepted

---

[1] *Slade,* p. 76. *Doc. Hist. N. Y.* vol. 4, p. 934. *Ira Allen's Hist.*, pp. 85–92. Ira Allen's account against the state in *Thompson's Vermont,* p. 107. List of members of the June convention in papers of J. H. Phelps. For copies of the revised declarations of January, and of the explanatory declaration of June, see *Connecticut Courant,* and *Address of J. D. Butler* before the Vermont Historical Society in 1846, pp. 29–33. A copy of the proclamation for a fast is found in Ms. in vol. 38, p. 54 of *Miscellaneous Papers* in the office of the secretary of state at Albany, and is printed in the *Vermont Record,* published at Brandon July 17, 1863. See also *Rev. Mr. Hutchinson's Sermon* before the Windsor convention of July 2, 1777, p. 37.

In regard to the name of Vermont, and for a notice of Dr. Thomas Young, see Appendix No. 9.

titles under New Hampshire with such rent reserved, yet it had always been looked upon as a badge of servitude, and it became still more objectionable when increased three-fold by the New York government.

The complaints of the people east of the Green mountain in relation to this exaction are stated, probably in softened language, in a report made about this time, by a committee of the New York convention who had been appointed to inquire into their alleged grievances. The committee, after naming the objections of the people to the New York jurisdiction, arising from the defects and uncertainty of their land titles and their distance from the seat of government, used the following language:

"The fourth general inconvenience which furnishes the broadest ground of clamor and complaint is the exaction of heavy *quit-rents* for the lands within the said counties of Cumberland and Gloucester, which they consider an innovation upon the rights of mankind for whose use such lands were given by a bountiful Providence without reservation, and which ought not, in their opinion, to be charged with taxes, other than for the general support and defence of the state and government. Besides this, they observed that the regulation is extremely partial, since thereby lands of the greatest value, both as to quality and situation, pay no part of a tax which falls heavy upon the possessors of a rough or even mountainous country, remote from the means of obtaining large supplies of money for discharging this unequal, and of consequence, inequitable impost. And to this they add, that such quit-rents generally fall heavy upon the poor man who purchases a small farm and who is burthened, not only with paying all the arrearages due upon it, but is liable to be turned out and have his property sold by the laws of this state to pay the quit-rent of a large patent in which he has no other interest than by having purchased a small part."

The constitution, though in its terms emanating from the people, was evidently framed under a strong jealousy and distrust of the popular will. It was, indeed, a piece of complicated machinery, apparently constructed with great care to establish the power and rule of a landed aristocracy, and to perpetuate it by guarding against the future participation of others in the government. It provided for two legislative bodies, styled the assembly and senate, each having a negative on the other, both to be chosen by electors having freehold qualifications, those entitled to vote for senators to be "possessed of freeholds of the value of one hundred pounds over and above all debts charged thereon," a sum which in those days excluded many small farmers from voting. The members of the assembly were to be chosen annually, and the senate for four years, both by *viva voce* vote. The governor was to be chosen by the senatorial electors and to hold his office for three years. Among his powers, was the kingly one of proroguing the two houses. A board was constituted composed of the governor, and four senators selected by the assembly, denominated the council of appointment, who were to appoint all officers civil and military, except some of local and trifling importance. The chancellor, judges of the supreme court and the first judge of each county court were to hold their places during good behavior, and all others "during the pleasure of the council of appointment." It will thus be seen that all the important official positions from the highest in the state down to and including county clerks and justices of the peace, were placed beyond the immediate reach of the people, and under the control of the senatorial representation of land holders. And further, in order to prevent laws from being "hastily and unadvisedly passed," as the constitution expressed it, another board, styled the council of revision was formed, consisting of the governor, the chancellor and the judges of the supreme court, who by a majority were empowered to negative the passage of any bill and prevent its becoming a law, unless it should he again passed by a majority of two-thirds of both houses. The governor being chosen by the land holders who were qualified to elect senators and holding his office for three years, and the other members of the board, in effect, holding theirs for life, must be considered, in connexion with the council of appointment, as constituting a very strong barrier against the ambitious interference of any democratic element in society, that under the pretence of progress or reform, might aspire to change the laws, or share in the offices. The barrier indeed proved impregnable for nearly half a century, but was finally after much agitation, overcome by the adoption of a new constitution in 1821.

At the time of the formation of this constitution of 1777, an ordinance was passed by the convention appointing the times and places in the different counties for holding elections under it, which, reciting that it was impracticable to hold such elections in the southern district of the state, designated and appointed by name nine persons as senators and twenty-two as members of the assembly for that portion of the state. They were to hold their seats until others were elected in their plaees, and in cases of vacancies, those occuring in the senate were to be filled by vote of the assembly, and those of the assembly by vote of the senate. In point of fact this anomalous ordinance representation, comprising about one-third of each branch of the legislature, constituted without any act of the people and having no legitimate constituency, did continue until 1783, a period of over six years.

The constitution, together with the ordinance in which were also inserted the names of the judges of the supreme court, as well as the judges, sheriffs, clerks, and other officers of the various counties, who had been appointed by the convention, was transmitted to the sheriffs of the several counties, including Cumberland and Gloucester; with directions to cause elections to be held for governor, lieutenant governor, senators and members of the assembly; the county of Cumberland being declared entitled to three members, Gloucester to two, and the two counties, together with that of Charlotte, were to form a district for the election of three senators.

Paul Spooner was named in the ordinance sheriff of Cumberland county, but he refused to act and resigned his commission; and the few friends of New York, to use the language they addressed to the council of safety of that state, "being terrified with threats from the people who are setting up a new state, thought it imprudent to proceed to any business," and no election was attempted. Nor was any election held in Gloucester county. Nathaniel Merrill was named in the ordinance as sheriff. Gen. Jacob Bayley who had formerly been a member of New York congress, and who was one of the most influential men in the county, and had been appointed by the convention to administer oaths of office to the sheriff and others, was furnished with a copy of the constitution and ordinance. His letter to the New York council of safety, acknowledging the receipt of these documents, of which an extract is given below, shows what was done in that county in relation to the election, and doubtless fairly represents the feelings of the mass of the people of both counties in regard to the constitution.

"NEWBURY, 14th June, 1777.

Gentlemen: I acknowledge the receipt of an ordinance from you for the election of governor, lieutenant governor and senators and representatives for the state of New York, by the hand of Mr. Wallace. The sheriff and committee gave the proper orders, but I am apt to think our people will not choose any members to sit in the state of New York. The people before they saw the constitution,

32

were not willing to trouble themselves about a separation from the state of New York, but now almost to a man they are violent for it. * * * I am gentlemen, etc.,

JACOB BAYLEY.

To the Council of Safety, Kingston."

In the meantime, the men in authority in New York continued their exertions to obtain the interposition of congress in their behalf. On the 28th of May, the council of safety of that state addressed a letter to the president of congress stating that a report prevailed and was daily gaining credit that "the faction in the north eastern part of the state who had declared themselves independent," were privately countenanced by certain members of that body, and urging congress "by a proper resolution" to vindicate their reputation from "imputations so disgraceful and dishonorable." On the 23d of June this letter was read in congress and on the same day one of the delegates from New York laid before that body the printed address of Dr. Young, before mentioned, to the "inhabitants of Vermont," and those papers, together with all that had been previously received from New York, in relation to the claim of the New Hampshire Grants to independence, and also the declaration and petition of Jonas Fay and others in behalf of the people of that district, were referred to a committee of the whole, and the 25th of June was named for their consideration. After a prolonged discussion, occupying several days, congress on the 30th adopted a series of resolutions on the subject as follows:

"*Resolved*, That congress is composed of delegates chosen by and representing the communities respectively inhabiting the territories of New Hampshire, Massachusetts Bay, Rhode Island and Providence Plantations, Connecticut, New York, New Jersey, Pennsylvania, Delaware, Maryland, Virginia, North Carolina, South Carolina, and Georgia, as they respectively stood at the time of its first institution; that it was instituted for the purpose of securing and defending the communities aforesaid, against the usurpations, oppressions and hostile invasions of Great Britain; and therefore it cannot be intended that congress by any of its proceedings would do or recommend, or countenance anything injurious to the rights and jurisdiction of the several communities, which it represents.

"*Resolved*, That the independent government attempted to be established by the people styling themselves inhabitants of the New Hampshire Grants, can derive no countenance or justification from the act of congress, declaring the united colonies to be independent of the crown of Great Britain, nor from any other act or resolution of congress.

"*Resolved*, That the petition of Jonas Fay, Thomas Chittenden, Heman Allen and Reuben Jones, in the name and behalf of the people, styling themselves as aforesaid, praying "that their declaration, that they would consider themselves as a free and independent state, may be received; that the district in the petition described, may be ranked among the free and independent states, and that delegates therefrom be admitted to seats in congress be dismissed.

"*Resolved*, That congress, by raising and officering the regiment, commanded by Col. Warner, never meant to give any encouragement to the claim of the people aforesaid, to be considered as an independent state, but that the reason which induced congress to form that corps was, that many officers of different states who had served in Canada and alleged that they could soon raise a regiment, but were then unprovided for, might be reinstated in the service of the United States."

The next and concluding resolution after reciting the paragraphs before given of the address of Dr. Young, in reference to the feelings of "leading members of congress," and of the obligations of congress under their former resolution of May 15, 1776, to admit Vermont into the Union, and the readiness of congress to do so, declares "that the contents of the said paragraphs are derogatory to the honor of congress, are a gross misrepresentation of the resolution of congress therein referred to, and tend to deceive and mislead the people to whom they are addressed."

These resolutions indicated, very clearly, that the congress was not ready to recognize the separation of the New Hampshire Grants from New York, and admit the district into the Union as an independent state, and in that respect were calculated to discourage her people in their efforts in that direction; yet they were far from conceding all that had been demanded by New York. While they manifest a disposition in congress, to conciliate the rulers of that state, by disclaiming in strong language any responsibility for the proceedings of the Vermonters, they at the same time cautiously avoid expressing any opinion on the merits of the controversy, evidently intending to leave it, at least for the present, to be determined by the parties themselves, without the intervention of congress. The resolutions of the New York convention had required congress "to recommend to the insurgents a peaceable submission to the jurisdiction of that state," and "to disband the regiment directed to be raised by Mr. Warner," and the letter from the convention to the president of congress enclosing the resolutions, had declared that it was "absolutely necessary to recall the commissions to Col. Warner, and the officers under him as nothing else would satisfy the convention." The resolutions of congress neither recommended submission, nor disbanded the obnoxious regiment. They merely declared that congress had done nothing to encourage the separation of the people of the New Hampshire Grants from the state of New York, that without considering the merits of the claim of the people of that district, their petition should be dismissed, and that Dr. Young was justly censurable for his presumption in undertaking to foreshadow and proclaim the future action of congress on the subject, and for grossly misrepresenting the meaning of a former resolution of congress.

A considerable number of the members of the congress were satisfied that the people of the New Hampshire Grants had just grounds for separating from the government of New York. Among them were Samuel Adams of Massachusetts and Roger Sherman of Connecticut, and probably most of the other New England members, as well as several from the more southern states. There was indeed nothing in these resolves to which the friends of Vermont could not readily subscribe without committing themselves to oppose her admission into the union at any future time.

The congress sat with closed doors during the whole revolutionary period, and until after this time the yeas and nays, if taken were not entered on the journal. We have of course, no account of the state of the vote and no report of the debate which took place on this occasion. In a letter from the New York delegates to the council of safety of that state, dated July 2, enclosing a copy of the resolutions, they state that the greater part of four days was spent in considering the subject, and that "no debate was ever conducted with more deliberation and solemnity." The letter recommended that commissioners should be dispatched at once to commend the resolutions and plead the cause of the state in the insurgent district. "This appears to us the more necessary," they say in conclusion, "as Mr. Roger Sherman of Connecticut, who brought in the petition for those people to congress and has all along acted openly as their advocate and patron, and in the last debate plead their cause with a zeal and passion which he never discovered in any other instance, and which in a judge between a state and some of its own members, was far from being commendable. This gentleman, we say, immediately on passing the resolutions, procured copies, and having obtained leave of absence, is already set out on his journey to the eastward. What may be his views with respect to our dispute, we know not, but to his enmity and officiousness you ought not to be strangers." On the 18th of July, the council of New York wrote their delegates that they had sent printed copies of the resolutions to the revolting district, and had ordered them to be properly published and distributed. How they were received by the people to whom they were sent will be noticed hereafter.

In the meantime it may be safe to say that the reputation of Roger Sherman, for either integrity or discernment, did not greatly suffer from this ill opinion of the New York delegates. Long afterwards Nathaniel Macon of North Carolina said of him that "he had more common sense than any man he ever knew," and Mr. Jefferson pointed him out as a man "who never said a foolish thing in his life." This occasion is not likely to have furnished an exception. An able writer in describing the leading members of the convention which formed the constitution of the United States, speaks of him as follows: "He is no orator, and yet not a speaker in the convention is more effective. The basis of his power is found first in his *integrity*; his countrymen are satisfied that he is a good man, a real patriot, with no little or sinister or personal ends in view; next he addresses the reason, with arguments logically arranged so clear, so plain, so forcible, that as they have convinced him, they carry conviction to others who are dispassionate." Roger Sherman saw and felt that the cause of the inhabitants of Vermont was founded on the principles of justice and equity, and he did not hesitate to declare it. The state may well be proud of an advocate whose name will ever remain among the most illustrious of our revolutionary statesmen.[1]

---

[1] *Slade*, 77, 79. *Doc. Hist. N. Y.*, vol. 4, 941, 944. *Jour. Cong.*, vol. 2, p. 175, 176, 178, 182, 183. *Jour. N. Y. Council of Safety*, for July 16, 18, 23*d*. *Stevens Papers*, vol. 3, p. 203, 319.

CHAPTER XXIII.

VERMONT IN THE CAMPAIGN OF 1777.

Vermont convention at Windsor July 2d — Its efforts to reenforce St. Clair at Ticonderoga — forms a state constitution and appoints a council of safety — Evacuation of Ticonderoga and battle of Hubbardton — Alarm and suffering of the inhabitants — Exertions of the council for the defence of the state — It appeals to New Hampshire and Massachusetts — Confiscates the property of tories who had fled to the enemy, and raises a regiment of rangers — Gen. Stark and his brigade from New Hampshire — His instructions from New Hampshire — Declines to join Schuyler and advises with the Vermont council and Col. Warner — His victory at Bennington and its important consequences — Gen. Lincoln in Vermont — Col. Brown and Vermont rangers at lake George and Ticonderoga — Capt. Ebenezer Allen and his rangers at Mt. Defiance, and in pursuit of the enemy on their flight from Ticonderoga in November, 1777 — Gouverneur Morris about the Vermonters — The convention reassemble in December and revise the constitution — Its provisions.

THE convention of the new state of Vermont met, agreeably to adjournment, at Windsor on Wednesday the 2d day of July, 1777, for the declared purpose of forming a constitution of government. Other objects were also found to require its serious attentention.

Neither the journal of the convention, nor a list of its members has been preserved. Our principal knowledge of its proceedings is derived from a brief account given by Ira Allen in his history, and that which has been gathered from its official orders and correspondence, obtained from other outside sources.

Before proceeding to business, the convention listened to a sermon prepared for the occasion by the Rev. Aaron Hutchinson, of Pomfret. The sermon was published in compliance with a resolve of the convention, and a copy is preserved in the archives of the Vermont Historical Society. Breathing a spirit of Christian love and charity, it nevertheless justifies resistance against the oppressions of Great Britain, and the separation from New York on similar principles; recommends and inculcates firmness in maintaining the independence of the state, wisdom in the formation of its government, and patriotic energy and determined bravery against the common enemy.[1]

---

[1] Mr. Hutchinson was a graduate of Yale College, of respectable talent and literary taste. His sermon which occupies forty printed pages, contains a strong argument in justification of the measures of the inhabitants

At the time of the assembling of this convention the people it represented were in much alarm from the apprehension of an invasion by the British army from Canada, under Gen. Burgoyne; for which great preparations had been made under the directions of the English ministry. An army of ten thousand veterans, one-half of them German hirelings, equipped and furnished with every warlike material that wealth and skill could supply, had been collected in that province, and attended by a formidable body of savages, and a corps of tories, was approaching the American post at Ticonderoga. Its commanding general confidently expected, after an easy conquest of that post, to march triumphantly through the country to the seaboard, crushing out all opposition to British rule. Gen. St. Clair, who commanded at Ticonderoga, had sent Col. Warner to gather reenforcements from the militia; Col. Robinson's regiment was already at Hubbardton, and others from the new state were on the way. On the 2d day of July, Col. Warner wrote from Rutland, "To the hon[ble] the convention now sitting at Windsor in the state of Vermont," that he had just received an express from Gen. St. Clair, who expected an attack every hour, and who had ordered him "to call out the militia of this state, of Massachusetts and New Hampshire, and join him as soon as possible." The letter requested the convention "to send on all the men that could possibly be raised," saying that the safety of the post depended on the exertions of the country; that their lines were extensive and but partially manned, for want of men; and he added, "I should be glad if a few hills of corn unhoed should not be a motive sufficient to detain men at home, considering that the loss of such an important post can hardly be remedied." On the receipt of this letter, the day after its date, president Bowker, by order of the convention, wrote immediately to the assembly of New Hampshire then in session at Exeter, and enclosed a copy of it, saying, "The militia from this state are principally with the officer commanding the Continental army at Ticonderoga, the remainder on their march for the relief of that distressed post," and requesting further aid from that state. The president of the convention also wrote to Gen. St. Clair, informing him of what they had done, and of the exertions they were making to aid him.

---

of the new state in opposition to both Great Britain and New York. Mr. Hutchinson died at Pomfret at an advanced age in the year 1800. He was father of the Hon. Titus Hutchinson, for many years chief justice of Vermont.

By the 5th of July Col. Warner had reached Ticonderoga with nine hundred militia, mostly from Vermont, but the fort, even after this reenforcement, was altogether untenable against the strong and well appointed army of Burgoyne. On the evening of that day a council of war unanimously decided that it should be abandoned before daylight the next morning, which was accordingly done. All the cannon and most of the provisions and military stores fell into the hands of the enemy, and the army retreated rapidly towards Castleton. On the morning of the 7th, the rear guard under Colonels Francis and Warner was attacked at Hubbardton, about fifteen miles from Ticonderoga, by a large pursuing force, when a severe and spirited action ensued. The result for a considerable time seemed doubtful, but a large reenforcement of Germans arriving, the Americans were put to flight. Col. Francis had been slain fighting bravely, many were killed and wounded on both sides, and a considerable number of prisoners were captured by the enemy. Col. Warner ordered his men to take to the woods and to meet him at Manchester, where the remnant of the regiment, mustering about one hundred and fifty effective men, assembled a few days afterwards.

Gen. St. Clair, with the main body of his army, took a circuitous route to the Hudson river by way of Rutland, Dorset and Arlington, and joined Gen. Schuyler at Fort Edward on the 12th.

The efforts of the Vermont convention for the relief of Ticonderoga were duly appreciated by Gen. St. Clair. In a letter dated at Col. Mead's (Rutland), July 7, addressed to the president of that body, he gives a brief explanation of the necessity he was under to evacuate that post, and says: "The exertions of the convention to reenforce us at Ticonderoga merit my warmest thanks, though they have been too late to answer the good purpose they intended." In another letter to the convention, written at Col. Marsh's, in Dorset, on the 9th, he says, "I have just now received a letter from Gen. Schuyler directing that Col. Warner's regiment of your state should be left for the protection of the people." He further informs the convention that he was proceeding to join Gen. Schuyler as fast as possible, and hoped there would be sufficient force collected "to check the progress of the enemy," adding as follows: "Your convention have given such proofs of their readiness to concur in any measure for the public safety, that it would be impertinent to press them now."[1]

---

[1] *Stevens Papers*, vol. 3, pp. 201, 209, 219, 243. *Life of Warner*, pp. 49–52. *Anburey's Travels*, vol. 1, pp. 326–334. *Gordon*, vol. 2, p. 482.

In order to enable the people they represented to offer the more effectual resistance to the common enemy, the convention appointed a committee to procure a supply of arms for the state, with instructions to draw them, if possible, from government stores, but with authority to pledge the credit of the state to the amount of four thousand pounds, if found necessary to purchase them. The convention also voted to establish a loan office, and appointed Ira Allen its trustee, as we learn from an advertisement in the *Connecticut Courant*, of August 18th, 1777, in which Mr. Allen over his signature as trustee informed the public " that agreeably to a resolution of the convention," he had opened a loan office at Bennington, where those disposed to lend any sum amounting to ten pounds might receive security in behalf of the state, payable in one or more years with interest at six per cent per annum.[1]

After due deliberation, the convention adopted a constitution for the government of the new state; directed the first election for state officers to be holden the ensuing December, and the legislature to meet at Bennington the succeeding January. The convention appointed a council of safety to manage the affairs of the state until the government should go into operation under the constitution, and then on the 8th day of July, after a session of six days, adjourned.

Ira Allen's account of the proceedings of the convention is as follows:

" A draft of a constitution was laid before the convention, and read. The business being new, and of great consequence, required serious deliberation. The convention had it under consideration when the news of the evacuation of Ticonderoga arrived, which alarmed them very much, as thereby the frontiers of the state were exposed to the inroads of an enemy. The family of the president of the convention [at Rutland], as well as those of many other members of the convention, were exposed to the foe. In this awful crisis the convention was for leaving Windsor, but a severe thunder storm came on and gave them time to reflect, while other members less alarmed at the news, called the attention of the whole to finish the constitution, which was then reading paragraph by paragraph for the last time. This was done and the convention then appointed a council of safety to act during the recess, and adjourned."

---

[1] No evidence is found that this attempt to borrow money was successful. The state was too young to have an established pecuniary credit, especially when its territory was invaded by a powerful enemy. See *Stev. Papers*, vol. 3, p. 287.

By the retreat of the American army from Ticonderoga, the whole western frontier of the state north of Manchester, comprising more than one half of the inhabitants residing west of the Green mountains, was left wholly unprotected, and was exposed to the immediate ravages of the enemy. Gen. Burgoyne had issued a very boastful proclamation, threatening ruin and destruction to all who should oppose him, but offering protection and security to those who should remain peaceably at their homes; and payment in gold for any provisions they might furnish. Many who were not his well wishers, in the distressed and apparently desperate condition in which they suddenly found themselves, felt it necessary to accept his written protections, while others, either more patriotic or in a better situation to remove, fled to the southward with such of their effects as they were able to take with them. Some of these fugitives stopped with their friends in the south part of the state, while others passed further on. No part of the territory could be considered secure against any rapid incursion of the enemy; especially as a considerable number in their midst were believed to be friendly to the invaders, and alarm and confusion every where prevailed.

Under these trying circumstances, the affairs of the new state came under the administration of the council of safety which had been appointed by the Windsor convention. The most active members of the council, as shown by such minutes of its proceedings as have been preserved, were Thomas Chittenden, president of the body, Jonas Fay, vice-president, Ira Allen, secretary, and Nathan Clark, Paul Spooner and Moses Robinson.[1]

The men of the council were of limited education, and nearly all of them were farmers who had spent their lives in the labors of the field; yet they brought to the task of saving the state from foreign and domestic enemies a comprehensive and discriminating ability,

[1] It appears from a statement of Gen. Stark, published in the *Connecticut Courant* of October 7, 1777, that their original number was twelve. Gen. Jacob Bayley of Newbury was one of the members, but whether he attended the meetings of the council is uncertain. In a letter from the council to him, dated at Bennington, August 11, 1777, requesting his presence at the board, it is said "one of our members, Esquire Spencer, is with our enemies, and an attendance of all the members on this side of the mountain is required to make a quorum." Ira Allen in his history, at page 101, says Heman Allen was a member. Of those already named, six besides Spencer resided west of the mountain, and two, Messrs. Spooner and Bayley on the east side making nine in the whole. If seven were required to make a quorum there was one more on the west side of the mountain and two on the east side,

which in like circumstances, has seldom if ever been exceeded. From the necessity of their situation they were compelled to assume all the powers of government, legislative, executive and judicial, and to exercise them with a strong hand. The general approval of their measures, both at home, and abroad, and the complete success which attended them, furnish the highest evidence of the wisdom and discretion with which they were planned and executed.

The members, who had mostly been at the Windsor convention, repaired to Manchester, whence they forwarded to the committee of safety of New Hampshire the letter of Gen. St. Clair of the 9th of July, and on the 15th addressed the executives of both New Hampshire and Massachusetts, stating fully the distressed condition their people were in from the advance of Burgoyne's army, and expressing the fear that they should be obliged to abandon the whole territory, thus rendering one or both of those states a frontier, unless powerful assistance was speedily furnished them. Col. Warner, who was in consultation with the council, three days afterwards, wrote to the New Hampshire committee to the same effect.

In the mean time, the council adopted the most energetic measures for the defence of their territory. Such of the militia as could be gathered were collected at Manchester under Warner to attempt making a stand at that place, in case a large body of the enemy which Burgoyne had left at Castleton should move in that direction, which for some time was apprehended. The council also issued a brief address to their brethren who had removed their families to the southward of their jurisdiction, and caused it to be published in the *Connecticut Courant*, earnestly inviting and exhorting them to return and aid in defending the state and in securing the growing crops from the ravages of the enemy. As in other parts of the country, there had always been a tory element in their community, composed of men who in sentiment, or from want of confidence in the final success of the Americans, had spoken in favor of the

---

but who they were is uncertain. The deserting member was Benjamin Spencer of Clarendon, the prominent Yorker and justice of the peace under the colonial government of New York before mentioned. He had been a member of the June convention held at Windsor, and had united with the other members of that body in their solemn pledge to stand by the declaration for a new state, and "to resist by arms the fleets and armies of Great Britain." But at the approach of Burgoyne, he had discarded his patriotic engagements and fled to the enemy. He is said to have died at Ticonderoga, a few weeks afterwards. Joseph Fay acted as clerk of the council for some time, and he might have been one of its members, though no other evidence of his membership is found.

measures of the mother country. Their proportion to the whole population was indeed small, when compared with their numbers in many other places, and especially in the neighboring counties of New York. It nevertheless embraced some men of otherwise respectable standing and some who possessed valuable property. Now that British rule seemed about to be established over them, many of them leaving their possessions in the care of their families, took up arms against their country, expecting speedily to return, in triumph over their more patriotic neighbors, under the protection of a victorious army. A permanent volunteer force to patrol the frontiers, and watch these domestic as well as foreign foes, and to stand in readiness to execute the orders of the council, seemed indispensible. But the new state had no funds or established credit, and to raise such a force without pecuniary means, was impossible. The difficulty was at once solved by a resolution of the council that the property of those who had fled to the enemy should be made to pay the expense of defending the persons and property of those that remained. In pursuance of this resolution, the council on the 28th of July appointed "commissioners of sequestration," with directions to seize and dispose of the property, under certain prescribed regulations, of "all persons in the state who had repaired to the enemy." A proper fund for state use being thus secured, a regiment of rangers was soon organized under Col. Samuel Herrick, which did efficient and valuable service to the state and country. "This," says Ira Allen, in his history, "was the first instance in America of seizing and selling the property of the enemies of American independence;" and such is believed to be the fact, though the measure was afterwards pursued in all the states.[1]

The council of safety had now assembled at Bennington, where it remained in permanent session throughout the year. The calls upon New Hampshire for troops had not been unheeded. The assembly at once ordered a large portion of their militia to be organized into a brigade under the command of Gen. John Stark. He had served with reputation as colonel at Bunker Hill, in Canada, and under Washington at Trenton and Princeton, but congress had promoted junior officers over him and he had retired from service, though he retained the same patriotic ardor as before. He knew Gen. Schuyler, who was in command of the northern army; and lacked confidence in his capacity as a military leader, and declined the

---

[1] *Ira Allen's Vt.*, p. 92-108. *Journal of the Council of Safety in Slade*, p. 197-240. *Stevens Papers*, vol. 3, p. 244, 257, 277, 305, 379. *Slade*, p. 79, 80. *Life of Warner*, p. 55.

command of the brigade, unless left with discretionary authority to join the main army or not, as he might deem expedient. His instructions from the president of New Hampshire, dated July 19th, were "to repair to Charlestown, No. 4," and when the troops were collected there "to take the command of them and march into the state of Vermont, and there act in conjunction with the troops of that state or any other of the states, or of the United States, or separately as it should appear expedient to him for the protection of the people or the annoyance of the enemy."

Gen. Stark, crossing the Green mountain from Charlestown, reached Manchester on the 7th of August. Finding that a considerable body of the enemy, which had been for some time in the vicinity of Castleton, threatening to attack Manchester, and to cross over to Connecticut river, had marched to the Hudson, Gen. Stark with his brigade passed on to Bennington where he arrived on the 9th. He was accompanied by Col. Warner, the remnant of whose regiment was left at Manchester under the command of Lieut. Col. Samuel Safford. At Bennington, Stark encamped for several days, collecting information in regard to the position and designs of the enemy, and consulting with the council of safety, and with Col. Warner relative to future operations.

The object of Burgoyne was to march to the Hudson, and at, or below Albany to form a junction with an army from New York, thereby cutting off the communications between the New England and the other states, which it was expected would produce a general submission to the king's authority. But his progress towards Albany had been so retarded by the natural difficulties of the route and the obstructions thrown in his way by the Americans, that it was nearly a month before he had reached the Hudson river. Here he found himself so deficient in provisions, and also in cattle and carriages for transportation, that he was greatly embarrassed about the means of advancing farther. The articles he most needed had been collected in considerable quantities at Bennington, as a convenient depot from which to supply the American forces. These Burgoyne resolved to seize for the use of his own army. He accordingly detached about five hundred German regulars, some Canadians, a corps of provincials (tories), and over one hundred Indians, with two light pieces of artillery, the whole under the command of Col. Baum, a veteran German officer. On arriving within six or seven miles of Bennington, he found it was guarded by a larger force than he had expected; and instead of proceeding to attack the place, he halted on a commanding hill and began to throw up entrenchments, sending back an express to Burgoyne. This was on the 14th of August. The next day was so excessively rainy as to prevent active military operations, though it enabled Baum greatly to strengthen his works of defense. On the 16th, Baum's position was attacked on all sides, by the militia under Stark. The Indians losing two of their number, fled at the commencement of the action. The other troops defended themselves with great bravery, but were finally overpowered, and nearly all either killed or taken prisoners. Among the latter was their commander, mortally wounded, and who died the next day.

This battle was scarcely over and the prisoners sent off, when a reenforcement of British regulars under Col. Breyman, with two pieces of cannon, was found to be approaching. At this juncture Warner's regiment, about one hundred and forty strong, came up fresh from Manchester, when a second distinct and very severe battle ensued, which lasted until sunset, when the enemy abandoned their cannon and fled. They were only saved from capture by the darkness of the night. The enemy lost in these two actions four brass field pieces, several hundred small arms, two hundred and seven men killed, and, including the wounded, about seven hundred were made prisoners. The loss of the Americans was thirty killed and forty wounded. Two of the captured cannon are now in the State House at Montpelier, with the following inscription, anciently engraved on them: "Taken from the Germans at Bennington, August 16, 1777."

In this battle Col. Samuel Herrick led the Vermont militia and his corps of rangers in the attack on the rear of Baum's entrenchments, and greatly distinguished himself; as did also Col. Seth Warner, who went into the battle by the side of Stark, was his counsellor throughout the day, and who, as his associate, is justly entitled to share largely with him in the honors of the victory. Stark in his official account says, "Warner's superior skill in the action was of great service to me." Dr. Thatcher in his contemporaneous journal says, "on the 16th Gen. Stark, assisted by Col. Warner, matured his arrangements for battle;" and Gordon in his history says, "Colonels Warner and Herrick's superior skill in military matters was of service to the general."

The injury to the enemy by this disaster can scarcely be overstated. It was not confined to his actual losses of men and munitions of war, though those were of considerable importance. This victory was the first check given to the triumphant march of Burgoyne from Canada, and was an unexpected example of a successful assault by undisciplined militia, armed with muskets without bayonets, upon an entrenched camp of veteran troops, defended by cannon. By its depressing effect on the spirits of the enemy, and the confidence in their prowess with which it inspired the Americans, the current of success was at once turned from the British to the American arms.

Burgoyne, by the ill success of his expedition to Bennington, was made aware of the resolute determination of the people he was attempting to subdue, and he realized the serious consequences of his defeat. In a private letter to the British minister in London, written four days after the battle, he says: "Had I succeeded, I should have effected a junction with St. Leger, and been now before Albany." And in the same letter in speaking of the spirit of the people he was invading, he pays a high compliment to the patriotism of the people of the new state of Vermont in the following expressive language: "The New Hampshire Grants, in particular," he says, "a country unpeopled in the last war, now abounds in the most active and most rebellious race of the continent, and hangs like a gathering storm on my left." [1]

Gen. Stark from his arrival at Manchester had received the earnest countenance and support of the Vermont council of safety, in all his movements, and he duly appreciated their patriotic services. In a communication over his signature addressed to the *Connecticut Courant*, under date of August 18, 1777, and published in that paper of the 7th of October, he gave a brief account of the active and valuable exertions of that body, for the defence of the frontier, both before and after his reaching the state, concluding his statement as follows: "I cannot therefore in justice omit giving the honorable council the honor of exerting themselves in the most spirited manner in that most critical time."

Gen. Stark's instructions, before mentioned, which in effect authorized him in his discretion, to act for the defence of the frontiers independently of all Continental officers, having been made known to congress, that body on the 19th of August, passed a resolution declaring such instructions to be "destructive of military subordination and highly prejudicial to the common cause," and requesting

---

[1] *Stevens Papers*, vol. 3, p. 307. Stark's letter to Gates, of August 22d, in Archives of N. Y. Hist. Society, copy in *Vt. Quarterly Gazetteer*, No. 2, p. 155. *Hist. Magazine*, vol. 3, p. 268. *Gordon*, vol. 2, p. 536–542. *Thatchers' Jour.*, p. 93. *Memoir of Stark*, p. 47–70. *Everett's Life of Stark, in Sparks' Biog.*, vol. 1, pp. 79–100. *Life of Warner*, p. 58–73. *Burgoyne's Defence in the House of Commons*. Appendix 24 and 25.

the council of New Hampshire at once to revoke them. At Manchester, Stark had met Gen. Lincoln who had been sent from Stillwater by Gen. Schuyler to conduct the militia to the west bank of the Hudson. Stark communicated his instructions and declined obedience on the ground of the dangerous condition in which it would place the people of Vermont, and because he believed Burgoyne would be more embarrassed in his operations by his remaining on his left than by his joining the army in front. That the instructions under which Gen. Stark acted "were destructive of military subordination," need not be denied. Yet there can be no doubt that his refusal to join Schuyler was founded on the soundest views of the actual state of things, and that it was productive of inestimable benefits to the country. But for this refusal, Bennington would probably have been left defenceless on the approach of Baum, and its capture with its depot of provisions and military stores, might have enabled Burgoyne to perform his anticipated speedy march to Albany. It should be here added that congress, on the 4th of October following, did a tardy act of justice to Stark, by passing a unanimous vote of thanks to him, "and the officers and troops under his command, for their brave and successful attack upon, and signal victory over the enemy, in their lines at Bennington," and by appointing him "a brigadier general in the army of the United States."

Three days after the battle of Bennington, Gen. Gates, who had been appointed by congress to supersede Gen. Schuyler, assumed the command of the northern army. Gen. Schuyler had been in charge of the northern department for the greater part of the time from the beginning of the war. His head-quarters had generally been at Albany or Saratoga, and having seldom or never taken the field in person, he had not succeeded in securing the full confidence of the country in his soldierly capacity, and he was particularly distrusted in New England. His aspiring and intriguing successor had greater popularity and larger military experience. Under the inspiriting influence of the recent victory, and the new general's reputed qualifications as a military leader, the militia of the eastern states were speedily rallied to his aid, and after two severe battles, fought and won by his subordinates, he was enabled on the 17th of October following, to compel the submission and receive the surrender of Burgoyne's whole army.

In bringing about this happy result the people of Vermont contributed, in common with their brethren of the other states, their full proportionate share. Besides the aid furnished by the troops which they brought into the field, the council of safety, from their local position, were enabled to render useful and important services to the country in various other ways; such as obtaining for the use of the army early information of the movements and designs of the enemy; in furnishing supplies and means of transportation in sudden emergencies, and in the speedy transmission, by means of a corps of expresses, of intelligence to the army, and orders from it to the neighboring states; for which, and other purposes, the council were in constant communication and correspondence with the commanding general, as abundantly appears by their journal. Soon after his victory at Bennington, Gen. Stark joined the main army, and Gen. Gates assigned to Gen. Lincoln the command of the forces to the eastward of the Hudson, including those which had been left in the new state, as well as such as had been summoned from Massachusetts who were to rendezvous at Bennington.

About the middle of September, an attempt was made under the direction of Gen. Lincoln, to cut off Burgoyne's communications with Canada by capturing some of the posts in his rear, in which Col. Herrick's rangers bore a prominent part. Col. Johnson with several hundreds of Massachusetts militia, was sent to threaten Ticonderoga from the Vermont side of the lake. Col. Brown with five hundred men, composed largely of the Vermont rangers, was to fall upon the enemy's post at the north end of Lake George, and if circumstances promised success, to unite with Johnson in an attack upon Ticonderoga. Col. Brown's part of the plan was well executed. With but trifling loss he succeeded in releasing over one hundred prisoners who had been captured at Hubbardton, and in taking two hundred and ninety-three of the enemy, destroying one hundred and fifty bateaux lying below the falls in Lake Champlain, and fifty above the falls in Lake George, including seventeen gunboats and one armed sloop.

About daylight of the morning of Brown's attack, Capt. Ebenezer Allen with his company of rangers made the perilous ascent of the steep and craggy rocks of Mt. Defiance, surprising and driving the garrison from its summit, just as a gunner was about to discharge a cannon on the assailants. Allen pointed the gun towards the old fort and fired it in token of his success. Col. Brown sent a summons to the commander of Ticonderoga demanding its surrender, but without effect; and not being in a condition to attack it, he returned with his men by water to Skenesborough, bringing off a considerable quantity of captured ammunition and military stores.

About this time Gen. Lincoln with most of the militia and also Col. Warner's continental regiment joined the main army under Gen. Gates, and military operations to the eastward of the Hudson were suspended. It was however reserved for the troops of the new state of Vermont to witness the *finale* of the grand expedition that had a few months previously, in great power and splendor ascended Lake Champlain. After the fate of Burgoyne became known in Canada, Gen. Carleton ordered all the posts south of the province line to be abandoned, and Ticonderoga was evacuated about the middle of November. The rear of the retreating garrison was overtaken by a portion of Herrick's rangers, with the result related in the following letter from the president of the Vermont council to Gen. Gates.

"State of Vermont. In Council.
BENNINGTON, 22 Nov., 1777.

"Dear General: I have the pleasure to inform your honor of the success of our Green Mountain rangers, in harrassing the enemy's rear on their retreat from Ticonderoga, in which Capt. Ebenezer Allen, with fifty rangers, has taken forty-nine prisoners, upwards of one hundred horses, twelve yokes of oxen, four cows and three of the enemy's boats, &c., &c.

"Major Wait, who was sent to take possession of Mount Independence, found nothing of consequence, excepting several boats which the enemy had sunk, in which there were some provisions. All barracks, houses and bridges were burnt, cannon to the number of forty broken and spiked up. He was so fortunate as to take one French sutler, with rum, wine, brandy, &c. * * * * * I have the honor to be, by order of the council, your honor's most obedient, humble servant,

THOMAS CHITTENDEN, President.

Hon. Major General Gates."

Thus ingloriously to the British arms terminated the campaign of 1777, in the northern department.[1]

[1] *Jour. Cong.*, vol. 2, p. 232, 276. *Everett's Life of Stark*, p. 80, 81. Minutes of Council of Safety in *Slade*, p. 197 to 240. And in *Stevens Papers*, vol. 3. Letters of Lincoln, Brown and Chittenden, in *Sparks's Rev. Cor.* vol. 2, p. 256–535. *Ira Allen's Vermont*, p. 103–106. Among the prisoners captured by Capt. Ebenezer Allen on this occasion was a negro woman named Dinah Mattis, and her infant child Nancy, whom he, "being conscientious that it is not right in the sight of God to keep slaves," declared

At the close of the preceding chapter it was stated that printed copies of the resolutions of congress of the 30th of June, 1777, had been forwarded by the New York council of safety for distribution in the "insurgent district." These resolutions it will be remembered disclaimed in strong language any participation of congress in the movement for a new state, and sharply censured Dr. Young, of Philadelphia, for promising a vote of congress in its favor. Several packages containing these resolutions, directed to friends of New York in the district, reached Fort Edward, a few days after Gen. St. Clair, with his retreating forces had arrived at that place, and when the country was in the highest state of alarm and confusion from Burgoyne's invasion. Gouverneur Morris, who was at that place as one of a committee of the New York council to confer with Gen. Schuyler on public affairs, after obtaining his advice and that of Gen. St. Clair, took the responsibility of opening the packages, and detaining their contents until he should receive further orders from the council. In his justification, he wrote (July 21) at considerable length to the council, expressing strong apprehension that the distribution of the resolutions at that critical juncture might prevent the inhabitants of the New Hampshire Grants from rendering efficient aid against the common enemy, which aid he deemed it of the utmost importance to retain. Feeling as Mr. Morris did, it was perhaps a proper act of prudence on his part, though there was really no occasion for his distrust of the patriotism of the people of the new state. The resolutions had doubtless already reached them, and if they had any effect, it was only to stimulate them to still greater exertions, in order that they might show themselves worthy of the independent position they had assumed, and of the confidence and countenance of their brethren in the other states. On the 31st of July, the council of safety of Vermont issued an address to their constituents, commenting on these resolutions, and showing that they did not in any way comply with the demands of New York as set forth in the papers their delegates had laid before congress, and did not condemn the measures that had been taken to form a new state, but only declared that congress had nothing to do with them.

---

to be forever free, and caused his certificate of her freedom to be recorded in the town clerk's office of Bennington, where the record is now found. Capt. Allen's deed of freedom, which bears date at Pawlet, Nov. 28, 1777, though claiming no merit as a literary performance, breathes in its language as warm and pure a spirit of philanthropy as the later and more important proclamation of President Lincoln. For a copy of the deed, see *Deming's Vermont Officers*, p. 184, and *Hollister's Hist. Pawlet*, p. 13.

This address was published in the *Connecticut Courant* of Aug. 18, and to it were appended, as evidence of the correctness of their interpretation of the resolutions, copies of the several New York documents before mentioned.

The constitution which had been framed by the convention of July, 1777, provided for the holding of an election under it in the following December, and for the meeting of the assembly in January; but owing to "the troubles of the war and the encroachments of the enemy," it was found impracticable to have it printed and circulated in season for such an election. The council of safety, in consequence requested the president of the convention to call the members together again on the 24th of December. This was accordingly done, when the time for the first election was postponed until the first Wednesday in March, and the assembly was required to meet at Windsor, on the second Thursday of the same month.

The constitution which was now finally completed, was preceded by a preamble in which the reasons for separating from New York and forming a new government, were stated in some detail, but which, as they have already been substantially given, will not now be repeated.

The constitution was in the main a copy of that of Pennsylvania, which had been earnestly recommended as a model by Dr. Thomas Young, the early friend of Vermont, and which was also understood to have the approval of Dr. Franklin and other eminent statesmen. In some important particulars, the Vermont constitution was an improvement upon that of Pennsylvania. This was especially the case in the first section of the declaration of rights, which announced in formal terms, the natural rights of man, to life, liberty, and the pursuit of happiness. The convention added to this "glittering generality" a clause as follows: "Therefore, no male person born in this country, or brought from over sea, ought to be holden by law, to serve any person as a servant, slave or apprentice, after he arrives to the age of twenty-one years, nor female in like manner, after she arrives to the age of eighteen years, unless they are bound by their own consent, after they arrive to such age, or bound by law for the payment of debts, damages, fines, costs, or the like." Vermont was thus the first of the states to prohibit slavery by constitutional provision, a fact of which Vermonters may well be proud.

The form of government was strongly democratic in its character. The elective franchise was given to "*every man* of the full age of twenty-one years" who had resided in the state for one year. Every such person was also eligible to any office in the state. The legislative power was vested in a single assembly of members chosen annually by ballot by the several towns in the state. Each town was to have one representative, and those towns having more than eighty taxable inhabitants, were entitled to two. The executive authority was in a governor, lieutenant governor and twelve councillors elected annually by ballot of the whole freemen of the state. The governor and council had no negative power, but it was provided that "all bills of a public nature" before they were finally debated in the general assembly should be laid before the governor and council "for their perusal and proposals of amendment," and also "printed for the information of the people," and that they should not be enacted into laws until the succeeding session of the assembly. From this provision was excepted "temporary acts" which in cases of "sudden emergency" might be passed without being delayed till the next session. The difficulties of a literal compliance with this article were so great that it was found necessary, in the first instance, to treat nearly all laws as temporary, and at the succeeding session to declare them permanent. In practice under this clause of the constitution, bills were allowed to originate in the council as well as in the house of assembly and in cases of disagreement between the two bodies upon any measure the matter was usually discussed in grand committee composed of both, the governor presiding. And although the final disposition of any measure was according to the pleasure of the house, the advisory power of the council had a strong tendency to prevent hasty and inconsiderate legislation. This article continued a part of the constitution until it was revised in 1786, when the provision for printing and postponing the passage of laws was expunged, and in addition to the advisory power of the governor and council, they were authorized to suspend the operation of a bill passed by the house until the next session of the legislature, when in order to become a law it must be again passed by the assembly.

This article in the original constitution in regard to the mode of enacting laws had been copied literally from the constitution of Pennsylvania, as was also a section which provided for the election by the freemen of the respective counties of "judges of inferior courts of common pleas, sheriffs, justices of the peace and judges of probate," who were to hold their offices "*during good behaviour* removable by the general assembly upon proof of maladministration." The mode of choosing judges of superior courts was left to the discretion of the legislature, and they were always elected *annually* by joint ballot of the council and assembly; and on the revision of the constitution in 1786, it was provided that county officers should also be annually chosen in the same manner. This frame of government thus modified, continued in operation long after the state became a member of the federal union, furnishing the people with as much security for their persons and property as was enjoyed by those of other states, and allowing to each individual citizen all the liberty which was consistent with the welfare of others. [1]

---

[1] For the constitution of 1777, see *Slade,* 241. For that of 1786, see statutes of 1787. For a history of the formation of the first constitution, see *Chipman's Life of Chittenden.* See also *Slade,* 81, 222, and 511.

CHAPTER XXIV.

Full Organization of State Government.

1778.

Military operations in 1778 — Troops raised and forts built by Vermont to protect the frontiers — Alarms and ravages by the enemy — Overtures by New York in relation to land titles — Their unfair character strengthens the opposition to New York — Election of state officers — Thomas Chittenden, governor, his character — Confiscation of tory lands — Return of Col. Ethan Allen from captivity — Trial of David Redding and his execution for "inimical conduct" — Union of sixteen New Hampshire towns with Vermont and its dissolution — Controversy with New Hampshire.

THE military operations in the northern department during the year 1778, were not of great importance in the revolutionary struggle. A winter expedition was, indeed, planned by the board of war, of which Gen. Gates was president, and was sanctioned by congress, to destroy the enemy's shipping at St. Johns, and perhaps to advance farther into Canada. The command was at first assigned by congress to Gen. Stark, but Gen. Lafayette was afterwards selected by the board of war, and appears to have been assured by Gen. Gates that a force of not less than twenty-five hundred men, including a body of Green Mountain Boys, would be in readiness for him at Albany, properly prepared for the expedition. When he reached that place on the 17th of February, he found scarcely twelve hundred men, and those, from want of suitable clothing and supplies, were in no condition for a winter campaign. There being no prospect that the deficiency of men and means could be supplied in time to take advantage of the strong ice on the lake, the expedition, by general consent, was abandoned. Gen. Lafayette appears to have been dissatisfied with the manner in which he had been hurried into the command, when no adequate preparations for the expedition had been made; and there certainly appears to have been peculiar neglect, or ignorance of the actual state of things on the part of the board of war. Although the attempt upon the shipping at St. Johns had been contemplated early in December, it was not until the 10th of February that the council of safety of Vermont was informed of it and was requested to furnish aid. The council immediately issued orders for raising a battalion of six companies of fifty men each, under Col. Herrick, and offered extra bounties and pay for their speedy enlistment. Within two weeks afterwards, before the men could be mustered, notice was received that the project of invading Canada had fallen through, and the men who had been enlisted were employed in state service to guard the frontiers.[1]

The frontier position of Vermont rendered her territory liable to sudden incursions of the British and their savage allies, for which great facilities were afforded by their full command of Lake Champlain. A feeling of insecurity very generally prevailed, rendering precautionary measures indispensable. In April, Col. Warner's regiment was ordered to Albany, and the other regular troops at that place were sent to the south, leaving the inhabitants of the new state to their own resources for protection. As a means of defence, a stockade fort was erected at Rutland covering two or more acres of ground, with a block house of hewn logs forming one end of it, raised two stories high. At this fort a constant garrison was maintained, and from it scouts traversed the country to the northward. Reports of expected attacks by the enemy were not infrequent, when bodies of militia were called out and marched to the frontier, perhaps to find there had only been a false alarm. These alarms kept the people in constant uneasiness, and were extremely annoying and burdensome. The inhabitants who had settled to the northward of Rutland had generally withdrawn from their possessions on Burgoyne's invasion. Some of them had, however, returned, trusting for their security either to the promises or to the humanity of the enemy. In November, 1778, a large British force came up the lake in several vessels, and thoroughly scoured the country as far south as Ticonderoga. "Such of the men," says Judge Swift, in his *History of Addison County*, "as had the temerity to remain on their farms, they took prisoners, plundered, burned and destroyed their property of every description, leaving the women and children to take care of themselves as they could, in their houseless and defenceless condition. Not a town in the county, where any settlement had been made, escaped their ravages. The only building in Middlebury, not wholly destroyed, except two or three in the southeast part of the town, which they seem not to have found, was a barn of Col. John Chipman, which had been lately built of green timber, which they could not set on fire, and which they tried in vain, with their imperfect tools, to cut down. The marks of their

---

[1] *Secret Jour. of Cong.*, vol. 1, p. 57 – 61, 65. *Sparks's Washington*, vol. 5, p. 264, 530. *Sparks's Rev. Cor.*, vol. 2, p. 72. *Irving's Washington*, vol. 3, chap. 28 and 29. *Minutes of Vt. Council*, Feb. 10 and Feb. 25, 1778. *Slade*, p. 232, 233, 234.

hatchets on the timbers are still to be seen." This is believed to have been the last actual incursion of the enemy during that year.[1]

We now recur to the civil affairs of the new state. Hitherto the men in authority in New York had represented the conduct of the inhabitants who were disaffected towards her jurisdiction as altogether factious and unreasonable, styling their claims under the New Hampshire charters as "unjust and iniquitous," and their complaints against the colonial government of New York, as "frivolous pretences." Their unconditional submission to her authority, which carried with it a surrender of their lands to the New York claimants, had been uniformly demanded. But the approbation and applause with which the noble exertions of the people of Vermont, during the campaign of 1777, had been received in the other states, and the steadiness with which they were progressing towards the establishment of a regular independent government, produced an apprehension in New York that such unconditional submission was not likely to be obtained. This apprehension was manifested in February 1778, by the appointment of a joint committee of the senate and assembly of that state, to take into consideration "the unhappy situation of the good subjects of the state in the eastern district," and by the action of the two houses on the subject. This joint committee reported a series of resolutions, proposing certain terms of accommodation with the inhabitants of that district, in regard to their land titles, which terms were declared to be offered as an inducement to them to submit quietly to the jurisdiction of the state. The resolutions were adopted by both houses, and were made known to the inhabitants by proclamation of the governor bearing date the 23d of February, 1778. They were drawn up with great skill and ingenuity and with a seeming candor and fairness, well calculated to produce an impression on those not familiar with the subject, that New York had generously offered all that could reasonably be demanded of her, and that her proffers, if acceded to, would quiet the titles of all the settlers under New Hampshire charters. In this light they have been viewed by some modern writers. Thus Wm. L. Stone, in his *Life of Brant*, speaks of the proclamation of the governor reciting those resolutions, as "conceived in the most liberal spirit," and of the resolutions themselves, as "offering to confirm all the titles which had previously been in dispute."

---

[1] *Minutes of Vermont Council. Pay Rolls* in the office of the secretary of state, Montpelier. *Swift's History of Addison County*, chap. 8.

But notwithstanding this appearance of liberality, the resolutions in reality offered no security whatever to the claimants under New Hampshire. They were preceded by a preamble in which the grievances under which the disaffected inhabitants had suffered by the oppressive acts of the colonial government in relation to their land titles, were either directly or tacitly admitted. The resolutions then contained proposals that confirmatory grants upon the payment of specified patent fees, should be issued by New York to certain classes of settlers under New Hampshire; but the language was so studied and so carefully guarded that the proposals only applied to a mere fractional part of the lands in controversy. The proposals did not purport to apply to any lands but such as were in the actual possession of claimants under New Hampshire. Of course all lands not yet occupied, however fairly or dearly they might have been purchased, would belong to the subsequent New York patentees. But the proffer to confirm the titles to lands, actually possessed, was limited to such *as were so possessed at the time grants of them had been made by New York*. Now, as most of the grants of New York had been made at an early day, and as settlements from that time up to 1778 had continued to be made under the previous grants of New Hampshire, notwithstanding such New York grants, the lands to which this proffer would apply, would be but a small portion of those in actual cultivation at the time of the passage of the resolutions. Not one-tenth, perhaps not one-twentieth part of the lands actually occupied under the New Hampshire title in 1778 came within the scope of these resolutions. The other nine-tenths, or nineteen-twentieths, being unprovided for, would of course, with all their improvements, be taken possession of by the New York claimants, whenever the jurisdiction of that state should be established. But this is not all. There was an inherent defect in the resolutions which rendered them utterly valueless, even in regard to the small portion of the lands to which they applied.

It was then a principle of law as well settled as at the present day, that a grant once made could not be recalled by the grantor. If the authority of New York to grant the lands were admitted, she had already parted with her title to them and had no power to regrant them to others. The confirmatory grants which she proposed to make to the New Hampshire occupants, would be of no avail to them as a defence to suits brought against them by the first grantees. The New York courts would declare them utterly null and void. This matter was well understood by the settlers. They had, indeed, been informed in the favorable report of the English board of trade, of

December, 1772, that it was out of the power of the crown, or of the government of New York, to annul the patents which had already issued, and in consequence the board had proposed to the king to recommend to New York to grant other lands to her former patentees in lieu of those which were possessed by purchasers under New Hampshire. The overtures of New York did not propose to make any such indemnity to the first grantees; and they were rendered the more suspicious in this respect by the fact that the resolutions as originally reported, did contain a guarantee of such indemnity, which provision was stricken out in the assembly, by a large majority. This vote seemed to indicate that it was not the intention of the assembly to carry out in good faith even the limited propositions which they had thought good policy required them to make.

The insufficiency of these resolutions to meet the real matter in dispute, and their deceptive character were well understood by the claimants under New Hampshire, and were clearly exposed in newspaper publications and also in a pamphlet by Ethan Allen published the following summer. Their defects became so apparent to the public that it was thought expedient by the New York assembly to pass explanatory resolutions, in which after stating that their former resolves "had been misrepresented by some and misunderstood by others," and declaring that "it was impossible to establish any general principle for the determination of all disputes," arising under the conflicting grants, but that "each case must be determined according to its particular merits," proceeded to propose to submit each case "to such persons as the congress of the United States should elect or appoint for that purpose." This proposal, with another of no importance in relation to lands which had not been granted by New York, was made known by proclamation of the governor, dated October 31, 1778. But this, if carried into effect, would involve every individual settler in a lawsuit before a foreign tribunal, the cost of which, even if the result should be favorable, would be likely to prove his ruin; and it was only regarded as an additional evidence of the continued insincerity and hostility of the New York government. In fact these explanatory resolves, as well as the original overtures of New York, instead of strengthening her interest in the new state, tended greatly to impair it, inasmuch as they showed very clearly that no security for the titles under New Hampshire was to be expected from that government, and that the only course for the inhabitants to take, in order to preserve their property, was to abide by and maintain their new state organization. This, by invalidating the New York patents, would at once cut the gordian knot by which their titles were bound, and which it was now, more than ever, demonstrated that the New York government never would allow to be untied.

It is difficult to conceive that these New York overtures could have been proposed in good faith by the land claimants, by whom they were doubtless concocted, who from their familiarity with the subject, must have known that they would be valueless to those whom they proposed to relieve. They were considered by the Vermonters as an artful attempt of their old enemies, the land traders, by holding out terms of conciliation apparently liberal, to make a favorable impression upon the public mind in other states, in order to strengthen the interest of New York in the general congress, which the government of that state desired should interfere in the controversy.[1]

It should be added that the legislature of New York, in March, 1778, had passed an act repealing the riot act of the colonial assembly of 1774, by which offenders on the New Hampshire Grants had been made subject to the punishment of death without trial; but as the original act had been limited in its operation to two years, which had long expired, and as it was universally regarded as a dead letter, its repeal was deemed a matter of no importance whatever. And an act of the New York legislature passed at the same session, granting a pardon for past offences against that government was considered as equally valueless.

At the first election under the constitution of the state, Thomas Chittenden was chosen governor by a large majority. He was born at Guilford, Conn., the 6th of January, 1730, but in early life became an inhabitant of Salisbury in that colony, where he resided until the spring of 1774. He then removed to Williston on the New Hampshire Grants, having become the purchaser of a considerable tract of land in that township. This he was obliged to abandon, on the retreat of the American forces from Canada, in 1776. The next year he purchased a farm in Arlington, where he remained till sometime after the close of the war, when he returned again to Williston and resided there until his death, which took place August 25, 1797. He had been an influential inhabitant of Salisbury, had represented the town in the colonial assembly for six or seven years, and was colonel of a regiment of militia. He had been brought up a farmer and his education was quite limited; but he had availed

[1] For the New York resolutions of February, 1778, see *Slade*, 82, and *Doc. Hist. N. Y.*, 951. Resolutions of Oct. 1778, *Conn. Courant*, Dec. 15, 1778, and February 2, 1779. *Allen's Animadversary Address*, Aug., 1778. *E. Allen's Vindication*, 1779. This has both sets of resolutions, page 13 to 44.

himself of opportunities in later life to acquire considerable information upon public affairs. His perceptions were quick and keen, and his mind so comprehensive as to enable him to take a full view of any subject however complex, and apparently by intuition, to make a correct decision. He had great tact in penetrating into the designs and characters of men, and he early acquired the position of leader in civil affairs on the New Hampshire Grants, and in the new state; and he continued through life to enjoy the confidence of the people in a very high degree. To his sagacity and almost unerring judgment must be attributed in a great measure, the successful progress and termination of the long and bitter controversy with the government of New York.

The legislature met at Windsor on Thursday, the 12th of March, when it was found that no person had received a majority of all the votes for either lieutenant governor or treasurer, and Col. Joseph Marsh of Hartford, was chosen by the assembly to the former office, and Ira Allen to the latter. The assembly divided the state into two counties by the range of the Green mountains, that on the west side being called Bennington, and that on the east, Cumberland. Each county was divided into half shires, for which special courts consisting of five judges each, were appointed, to continue in office until county officers could be elected as provided for by the constitution.

One of the most important measures of the session related to the disposition of tory lands. The council of safety had the previous year, as has been before stated, taken possession of the personal property of those who had gone over to the enemy, and disposed of it for the benefit of the state. But they had not meddled with their lands, otherwise than in some instances to lease them, for limited periods. It was now resolved (March 25th) by the assembly, that the whole subject of the confiscation of the estates of "inimical persons," and in relation to the claims of their creditors, should be referred to the determination of the governor and council, or to such persons as they should appoint. The governor and council thereupon ordered that the lieutenant governor and six members of the council who resided on the east side of the mountain, should be a court, with power "to confiscate and order the sale to be made of all such lands and estates as should, by sufficient evidence, appear to be forfeited in the county of Cumberland," and that the governor and members of the council residing west of the mountain should have the same authority in the county of Bennington, the proceeds of all sales to be paid into the treasury of the state. From minutes of the court of confiscation for the county of Bennington, now in the office of the secretary of state, it appears that the court on the 23d of April, "after several adjournments from day to day," during which the evidence in each case was examined, adjudged that one hundred and sixty-two persons named by them, residing or having estates in the towns on the west side of the mountain, had by their "notorious treasonable acts committed against the state and the United States of America, forfeited their whole estate to the state," and ordered the same to be confiscated and sold. A large portion of these persons were doubtless without much property, and the cases of some others were probably reconsidered, but quite a number of them were possessed of valuable lands which were sold. Estates were also confiscated and sold in Cumberland county, though the records of the court for that county have not been found. The income derived from this source was very considerable, sufficient to cover, for some time, a great portion of the state expenditures. It is proper to say that measures for confiscating the property of tories were pursued in all the states, though as before remarked, Vermont is believed to have been the first of the number to commence it.[1]

The legislature, after a session at Windsor of two weeks, adjourned to meet at Bennington on Thursday, the 4th of the ensuing June.

On the evening of the last day of May, four days before the legislature was to assemble, Col. Ethan Allen, who had been a prisoner with the enemy from the 25th of September, 1775, but who had just been exchanged for Col. Campbell of the British army, returned to Bennington, and the next day was one of great rejoicing. The people flocked into town to welcome him, and an old iron six-pounder, which in 1772, had been transported from the fort at East Hoosick, for defense against an apprehended invasion of Gov. Tryon of New York, at the head of a body of land claimants and British regulars, was brought out, and notwithstanding a great scarcity of powder, was fired fourteen times, "once for each of the thirteen United States, and once for young Vermont."

Allen, after his exchange, having visited the American camp at Valley Forge, Washington had written to the president of congress in regard to him as follows:

"I have been happy in the exchange and a visit from Lieut. Col. Allen. His fortitude and firmness seem to have placed him out of the reach of misfortune. There is an original something in him,

[1] *Ms. Journals of the Council,* March 25, 1778. *Minutes of Court of Confiscation,* March 25th and 26th, and April 23. *Slade,* p. 267.

that commands admiration; and his long captivity and sufferings have only served to increase, if possible, his enthusiastic zeal. He appears very desirous of rendering his services to the states and of being employed; and at the same time he does not discover any ambition for high rank. Congress will herewith receive a letter from him, and I doubt not they will make such provision for him, as they may think proper and suitable." Upon the receipt of this and Allen's letter the congress, May 14th, resolved, "that a brevet commission of colonel be granted to Ethan Allen, in reward of his fortitude, firmness and zeal in the cause of his country, manifested during the course of his long and cruel captivity, as well as on former occasions."

Allen had returned home to find his old friends as unreconciled as ever to British rule, and if possible, still more hostile to tories than they had previously been to Yorkers. They were at that time under great excitement about a tory by the name of David Redding who had been detected in acting as a spy for the enemy and in carrying off, for the use of the tories, a number of muskets from their place of deposit in Bennington. For these acts he had been brought to trial before the special court for the shire of Bennington for "inimical conduct," and having been found guilty, had, in accordance with the demand of public opinion, been sentenced to be hung on the 4th of June, the day appointed for the meeting of the legislature. The governor and council assembling in the morning of that day an application was made to them for a new trial, on the ground of irregularity in the proceedings against him, and it appearing that he had been convicted by a jury of only six men, and the governor and council being of opinion that he ought to have been tried by a jury of twelve, granted him a reprieve until "Thursday next, at two o'clock in the afternoon," adding in their order; "This council do not doubt in the least, but that the said Redding will have justice done him to the satisfaction of the public." The reprieve had been granted too late to prevent the assembling of a large concourse of people to witness the execution of one whom they, as well as the court, had already condemned as a traitor and spy. When the multitude found that the execution was not to take place, they were clamorous over their disappointment, and there were some indications that another tribunal, since personified as "Judge Lynch," might take the matter in hand. Whereupon Col. Allen suddenly pressing through the crowd, mounted a stump and raising his hand, exclaiming in his loudest voice, "attention the whole," proceeded to announce the reasons which had produced the reprieve, advised the multitude to depart peaceably to their homes and to return the day fixed for the execution in the act of the governor and council, adding with an oath, "you shall then see somebody hung, for if Redding is not hung, I will be hung myself." Upon this assurance, the uproar ceased and the crowd dispersed. Redding in accordance with Allen's prediction, was hung on the 11th of June, the day to which his execution had been postponed by the council, he having on the 9th been tried and convicted by a jury of twelve, Allen, by appointment of the governor and council, acting as attorney for the state.[1]

The government of Vermont now found itself involved in a new and very troublesome difficulty. Hitherto a good understanding had existed between the people of New Hampshire and those formerly included in her territory to the westward of Connecticut river. The government of that state had, in fact, in its official correspondence, repeatedly addressed those in authority, as officers of "the state of Vermont," had virtually acknowledged her independence, and was confidently expected to use its influence to have her independence acknowledged by congress. But this favorable prospect was soon clouded by the conduct of some people near Connecticut river in New Hampshire, who were ambitious to have a state formed, which should include such territory as would bring the seat of government to that river. At the first meeting of the assembly at Windsor, a committee from sixteen towns east of the river in New Hampshire, presented a petition representing that their towns "were not connected with any state with respect to their internal police," and praying that they might be admitted to constitute a part of the new state. They did not complain of serious grievances, either past or prospective. The argument used by them was, that New Hampshire had been originally granted as a province, to John Mason, and by his grant only extended sixty miles inland from the sea, that all the territory to the westward of the sixty mile line, had been annexed to it by virtue of royal commissions to the governors of the province, and that the royal authority having been overthrown, the people of the annexed territory were released from all obligations to continue in the New Hampshire government; and were left at perfect liberty to determine what jurisdiction they would be under. But the authority of the crown to determine the extent and boundaries of his royal governments, by his orders and

---

[1] *Slade,* 269. *Council,* June 4 and 9, 1778. *Allen's Narrative of his Captivity.*

commissions, had always been recognized and admitted in all the colonies, and it was obvious to all who were informed on the subject, that the territory between Mason's line and Connecticut river, was as legally a part of New Hampshire as that to the eastward of that line; and that the principles advocated by the petitioners would unsettle the boundaries of all the other colonies and states, and throw their governments into confusion and anarchy.

The legislature was at first inclined to reject the petition, but it was pressed with great earnestness; and some members from towns in Vermont, near Connecticut river, threatening to withdraw from the legislature and unite with the people east of the river and form a new state, it was at length resolved to refer the consideration of the petition to the freemen of the several towns, who should instruct their representatives in regard to it, the decision to be postponed to the next meeting of the assembly. During the recess the party in favor of the New Hampshire proposals were extremely diligent and active in securing a majority of the members, and when the legislature again assembled in June it was found that thirty-seven of the forty-nine towns represented had decided in favor of the union with the New Hampshire towns. An act was accordingly passed, authorizing the sixteen petitioning towns east of Connecticut river, to elect and send members to the assembly; and it was resolved that other towns on that side of the river, might also be admitted into the union, on producing a vote of a majority of the inhabitants, or on their sending representatives to the assembly.

In order to obtain the consent of the legislature to this union, it had been represented that the inhabitants of the towns which applied for it were almost unanimous in its favor, and that New Hampshire as a state would not object to the connexion. Neither of these representations turned out to be correct. Meshech Weare, president of New Hampshire, in August following, addressed a letter to Gov. Chittenden complaining of the conduct of Vermont in admitting those towns into its jurisdiction, informing him that a large minority in them were opposed to the union with Vermont, and that they claimed the aid and protection of New Hampshire. He averred that those towns had been settled and cultivated under grants from the government of New Hampshire, that they were within the boundaries of the state prior to the present revolution, that most of them had sent delegates to the convention of the state in the year 1775; had applied to that state for assistance and protection, and had received it at a very great expense; that the statement that "the sixteen towns were not connected with any state with respect to their internal police was an idle phantom, a mere chimera without the least shadow of reason for its support." And he added "that Boston in Massachusetts and Hartford in Connecticut, might as rationally declare themselves unconnected with their respective states, as those sixteen towns their not being connected with New Hampshire." President Weare also wrote to the New Hampshire delegates in congress, informing them of what had been done, and asking them to take the advice of the members, and to endeavor to obtain the aid of that body in the matter. The governor and council of Vermont, being aware that an application would be made to congress, sent Col. Ethan Allen in the month of September to Philadelphia, to ascertain in what light their proceedings were viewed by that body.

Col. Allen made a written report on the subject of his mission to the newly elected legislature which assembled at Windsor in October, the substance of which was, that papers had been read in congress from both New Hampshire and New York, against Vermont, and that in his opinion, New York alone would never be able to muster sufficient force in congress to prevent the establishment of the new state; but that the union with the New Hampshire towns was viewed with general disapprobation, and that unless the state receded immediately from such union, the whole power of the confederacy of the United States would be exerted to annihilate the state of Vermont and vindicate the right of New Hampshire. Only ten of the sixteen New Hampshire towns were represented in the assembly. These however insisted that in order to have the benefit of the laws and the protection of the state it was necessary that they should either be erected into a new county or annexed to the contiguous county to the westward of them; and this was certainly but reasonable, if they were to remain under the jurisdiction of the state. After long and earnest debate a vote was taken in the assembly, by which it was determined that no change should be made in the old counties, and that no new county should be formed. This was virtually a declaration against the continuance of the union, and was so received by the minority who made a written protest against the proceeding; and the representatives from the New Hampshire towns, together with fifteen members from some of the towns along the west side of the river, withdrew from the assembly. This left that body with barely a quorum, but the session was continued until the necessary public business was completed.

The members who had withdrawn from the assembly met together and gave a formal invitation to the towns on both sides of the river to meet and unite in a convention at Cornish in New Hampshire on the 9th of December 1778. The proceedings of this convention, in which only eight towns on the Vermont side of the river were represented, indicated very clearly that the main object of those concerned in it, was to form a state whose capital should be on Connecticut river; for they not only manifested a willingness to unite with Vermont as had been before attempted, but voted that they would "consent that the whole of the Grants" (Vermont) should connect with New Hampshire and become with them one entire state," either of which would be likely to effect the desired object. They appointed a committee to confer with the New Hampshire legislature on the subject.

To rid themselves of a connexion which had occasioned so much trouble and danger, the assembly of Vermont on the 12th of Feb., 1779, passed a formal vote declaring that "the said union should be considered as null from the beginning." Although this attempt at union with the New Hampshire towns was now at an end, it had served to engender an unfriendly feeling in the government of that state towards the independence of Vermont, the ill effects of which continued for years.

When the New Hampshire assembly met in March, a committee from the Cornish convention presented a memorial, which among other things, took the responsibility of making "an offer of the whole of the Grants [Vermont] to New Hampshire." A committee of the assembly thereupon made a report recommending that the state of New Hampshire should "lay claim to the jurisdiction of the whole of the New Hampshire Grants lying to the westward of Connecticut river," but that the state should exercise jurisdiction no farther west than the west bank of that river "until the dispute is settled by congress." This report was postponed until the next session of the legislature, when on the 24th of June it was taken up and adopted.[1]

---

[1] *Slade,* p. 89-105. *Ira Allen's Vindication,* 1779. *Williams's Vt.,* vol. 2, p. 177-185. *Ira Allen's Vt.,* p. 112-123. *Belknap's N. H.,* p. 385-389. *Hall's Eastern Vt.,* p. 325-328.

CHAPTER XXV.

PROGRESS OF THE CONTROVERSY WITH NEW YORK.

1779.

Military affairs in 1779 — Forts built by Vermont on the frontier — Men raised by the state to defend it — The levying of men in Cumberland county, by the advice of Gov. Clinton resisted — The property of delinquents seized for fines and rescued — Posse called out, many of the rescuers seized, tried, convicted as rioters and fined — Proclamation of pardon to others — Applications of the New York government to Congress — A committee of Congress appointed to visit Vermont — Mr. Witherspoon and Mr. Atlee of the committee at Bennington and their proceedings there — Answer of Governor Chittenden to their written queries, respecting the land and other difficulties with New York — Their attempt to bring about a reconciliation unsuccessful — Messengers sent by Vermont to obtain information from congress — Protest of Gov. Chittenden against resolutions of congress of June 16th, 1779.

THE military situation of Vermont, during the year 1779, was similar to that during the previous year. All the continental troops and supplies had been withdrawn from the state and her people were left to their own resources for protection against the common enemy. The ravages of the enemy on the border of lake Champlain, in the fall of 1778, had served to show both the exposure of the frontier and the disposition of the enemy to take advantage of its weakness. The best preparation in the power of the state for the security of its inhabitants was made. On the 25th of February, 1779, the general assembly, by resolution, constituted the governor and council "a board of war, with full power to raise any number of men that they should think necessary for the defence of the frontiers and to make any necessary preparations for the opening campaign." On the 12th of March, the board resolved that "the west line of Castleton and the west and north lines of Pittsford to the foot of the Green mountain be established as a line between the inhabitants of the state and the enemy," and all the inhabitants to the north of the line were directed to remove with their families to the south of it. Picket forts were to be built in Castleton and Pittsford near the centre of each town, and it was recommended "that the women and children should be removed to some convenient place south of the forts, and that the men with such part of their stocks as might be necessary, should remain on their farms, and work in collective bodies, with arms." Small garrisons were kept in these forts and a larger body of troops at Fort Ranger in Rutland, which continued to be the head quarters of the state forces. In order to maintain these forts and protect the frontier, drafts from the militia were frequently made, and bodies of the militia were sometimes called out *en masse.*[1]

At the session of the general assembly held in February, 1779, a code of laws, embracing the general subjects of legislation, was adopted and published. By the act for regulating the militia it was provided, that when the captain of a company should be directed by proper authority to furnish from his company a portion of his men, he might draw up a list of all whom he had a right to command, and divide the persons thus enrolled into as many classes as he wanted men. Each class thus formed was obliged to furnish a soldier. In case of a refusal to comply with this requirement, the captain was directed to hire a man for the class, pledging the faith of the state for his recompense. He was then to divide the cost of hiring the soldier among the members of the delinquent class, and upon a warrant issued for that purpose to levy upon their goods and chattels and sell the same at public auction, the money thus obtained to be used in paying the sum engaged to the hired soldier. This mode of raising men was generally approved, but in carrying the law into effect, the Vermont officers met with serious opposition from some of the friends of New York.

From the first organization of the state government, there had been a number of persons in the south-eastern part of the state who were opposed to its jurisdiction. They had been in constant correspondence with Gov. Clinton of New York, who, as early as July, 1778, had written them, earnestly recommending "a firm and prudent resistance to the draughting of men, the raising of taxes and the exercise of any act of government under the ideal Vermont state." They claimed to be and probably were a majority in four or five of the towns, in which, and in two or three others, committees of safety had been named who styled themselves a county committee. Gov. Clinton had issued commissions for forming a militia regiment in that section of the state, and it was claimed that it numbered nearly five hundred men. In April, 1779, in conformity to a request from Gen. James Clinton, commander-in-chief of the northern department, the board of war directed a levy of men "for the service of the state and of the United States in guarding the

[1] *Minutes of the Board of War,* in the office of the secretary of state at Montpelier.

frontier," and the captain of a company in Putney, in accordance with the law divided his men into classes, of which James Clay, and two others, known as active friends of New York, constituted a class. Refusing to furnish their man for the service, one was obtained to represent them, and they were informed of the sum to which they had subjected themselves, but they declined to pay it. Whereupon the sergeant of the company, having his proper warrant for the purpose, levied upon two cows the property of the delinquents and posted them for sale. On the 28th of April, the day they were to be sold, the friends of New York from that and some other towns, to the number of nearly a hundred under the lead of the New York colonel, assembled, and before the sergeant could be prepared for resistance, rescued the cattle and returned them to the parties from whom they had been taken.

A few days after this rescue, the New York colonel, becoming alarmed for the consequences which might follow this act, wrote to Gov. Clinton, informing him that Col. Fletcher, who commanded the new state's men, had gone over the mountain to their council at Arlington, and that it was apprehended Col. Ethan Allen with his Green Mountain Boys might be sent to aid in enforcing the Vermont authority. He asked the governor's advice, and suggested "the necessity of having the militia of Albany county held in readiness to attack them if they should gather with that design." A petition for protection against the Vermonters, signed by Samuel Minott as chairman of the New York committee, was also sent to Gov. Clinton. In answer to these applications, Gov. Clinton, under date of May 14th, recommended "firmness and prudence, and in no instance to acknowledge the authority of Vermont, unless there should be no alternative left between submission and inevitable ruin;" and he assured them that if he should discover that any attempt would be made to reduce the friends of New York by force of arms, he would "instantly issue his orders to the militia, who were properly equipped, and who would be led against the enemies of the state, whoever they might happen to be." It may be here observed that the letters of Gov. Clinton to the disaffected inhabitants in the vicinity of Brattleboro, were also on many subsequent occasions during the period of the controversy, quite lavish in their promises of protection by force of arms against the Vermonters, and that such protection was not only never afforded, but never even attempted. In fact the attempt would always have been vain. The government of New York, from its aristocratic character, had not any strong hold on the feelings of the masses of the people of the state, the want of which always enfeebled its efforts against the common enemy. Many of its people sympathized with their more democratic neighbors of Vermont, and could not have been brought to face them as enemies on the field.

It was impossible that the government of Vermont should overlook the public attack which had been made upon its authority, without, in effect, waiving its claim to an independent jurisdiction. Enlarged patriotism also seemed to demand that its authority should be vindicated. The men who claimed to act under the jurisdiction of New York had not been called upon by that state to render any military service whatever or to pay for any. All that was required of them was, to oppose Vermont. If their claim to exemption from service under Vermont should be admitted they would contribute nothing towards the common defence. The effect would be to encourage all who desired such exemption to unite with those who favored New York, and thus to weaken the power, not only of Vermont, but of the whole country.

The men administering the government of Vermont were prompt in determining upon decisive action. A session of the superior court of the state, having criminal jurisdiction, was soon to be holden by adjournment at Westminster. Early in May, the governor and council issued an order to Ethan Allen commanding him "in the name of the freemen of the state of Vermont to engage one hundred ablebodied effective men as volunteers in the county of Bennington, and to march them into the county of Cumberland seasonably to assist the sheriff of that county to execute such orders as he had or might receive from the civil authority of the state," previous to the said adjourned session of said court, which was to be held on the 26th of that month. In due time Allen, with his Green Mountain Boys, appeared in Cumberland county and uniting his men with a detachment of the militia of that county under Col. Fletcher, they succeeded in arresting between thirty and forty of those against whom warrants had issued, among whom were most of the leading New Yorkers in the county, including the colonel, lieut. colonel and major, and several of the captains and other officers of the New York regiment. They were soon brought to trial as rioters before the court at Westminster, and most of them convicted and fined in sums ranging from two to forty pounds each, according to their supposed influence as leaders or the contrary. Upon the payment of their fines, which considering the inflated state of the continental currency at the time, could have been little more than nominal, and satisfying the costs, they were all speedily discharged.

The legislature of the state met by adjournment, at Windsor, on the 2d of June, and the first day of their session, passed a resolution appointing a committee "to wait on his excellency the governor and the honorable council and give them the thanks of the assembly for their raising and sending the *posse comitatus* into Cumberland county, for the purpose of apprehending the rioters who were tried at Westminster."

The prompt action, and threatening and boastful language and manner of Allen in making his arrests seem to have had their intended effect of continuing, if not increasing the terror and alarm with which his hostile movements had long been regarded by the partizans of New York. It does not, however, appear to have been the desire of the Vermont government to deal harshly with its opponents, but rather, after vindicating its authority, to conciliate them. The views of those having the management of its affairs are doubtless fairly expressed in a letter written from Cumberland county at the time by Ira Allen to Col. Bellows of Walpole. "It is not our design," he says, "to treat the inhabitants of this county with severity, but with as much lenity as the nature of the case will admit. Yet the authority of this state must be supported, for commissions from two different states can no longer subsist together. We mean not to boast of our victory over those gentlemen who were in favor of New York in this county, but hope to make them our friends, and have the pleasure of treating them as such. We mean this movement as a defiance to the old government of New York, with whom we have long contended for our properties."

To show that they were not disposed to deal unkindly with the offending "Yorkers," the governor, on the 3d of June, a few days after the adjournment of the court, by the advice of his council, issued a proclamation granting a free pardon to all riotous offenders against the state jurisdiction, excepting only those persons who had been already convicted.[1]

While the inhabitants of Vermont had been striving to perfect and strengthen their state organization, the efforts of the New York government to procure the aid of congress to overthrow it, had been untiring. New York had always been represented in congress by some of her ablest men, but they had not succeeded in accomplishing much against the Vermonters. The delegates chosen by the legis-

---

[1] *Laws of Vermont*, 1779. *Slade*, 106-108, 309, 556. *Doc. Hist. N. Y.*, 957-976. *Ethan Allen Papers*, 289. *Williams's Vermont*, 247-250. *Hall's Eastern Vermont*, chap. XIII.

lature, the 16th of October, 1778, were James Duane, Gouverneur Morris, Philip Schuyler, William Floyd and Francis Lewis, all of whom had already been members of that body, Mr. Duane during the whole period of its existence. But notwithstanding this formidable array of talent it was deemed advisable, in reference to the Vermont difficulty, to strengthen it still further.

By the constitution of New York, the chancellor and judges of the supreme court were prohibited from holding any other office "excepting that of delegate to the general congress, upon *special occasions*." The legislature having resolved that "the disorders prevailing in the northeastern part of the state," furnished "a special occasion," proceeded on the 10th of November, to choose John Jay, who was chief justice of the supreme court, an additional delegate. Mr. Jay sustained a high reputation, both as a lawyer and a statesman, and it might well be supposed that his talents and influence would add strength to the claims of New York in that body. He took his seat in congress the 7th of December, and three days afterwards, on the resignation of Mr. Laurens, was elected its president, which place he held until September 28, 1779. But notwithstanding these advantages of character and official position, it was several months before Mr. Jay, with the cooperation of his associate delegates, could make much progress in the business for which he had been specially selected. He found, as he states in his final report to Gov. Clinton, great reluctance in congress to take up the subject. For this reluctance he assigned several causes, the most prominent of which were an alleged want of authority in congress to meddle with the internal affairs of a state; the apprehension, from the warlike and determined character of the Vermonters, that it would be difficult to enforce an order against them, and that if driven to extremities they might be induced "to join the enemy and increase their force;" and the favorable feeling of some of the members towards the claims of the inhabitants to independence, especially among those of New England whence the territory had been peopled.

It was not until the 22d of the ensuing May, that any movement appears to have been made in congress on the subject. On that day the New York delegates introduced a series of resolutions, declaring in substance, that the extent and boundaries of the several thirteen states were the same as during their previous existence as colonies, and that "no part of any one of them should be permitted to separate therefrom, and become independent thereof, without the express consent and approbation of such state." If these resolutions should be adopted, the whole matter would at once be decided in favor of New York, and without any hearing on the part of Vermont. The resolutions were referred to a committee of the whole, and the ensuing Saturday (the 29th) was named for their consideration. On that day the New York delegates presented a letter from Gov. Clinton, enclosing the communications to him before mentioned from Cumberland county, which contained an account of the rescue of the cattle from the Vermont sergeant by the friends of New York. Gov. Clinton's letter expressed strong apprehensions of further disturbances, and urged the speedy and decisive interposition of congress as the only means of preventing a serious conflict of arms. These papers, with some others in relation to the controversy, being also referred to the same committee of the whole, the subject was taken up and discussed on Friday the first of June, when the congress came to the following resolution :

"Whereas, divers applications have been made to congress on the part of the state of New York and of the state of New Hampshire, relative to disturbances and animosities among the inhabitants of a certain district known by the name of the New Hampshire Grants, praying for their interference for the quieting thereof; congress having taken the same into consideration,

"*Resolved*, That a committee be appointed to repair to the inhabitants of a certain district known by the name of the New Hampshire Grants, and inquire into the reasons why they refuse to continue citizens of the respective states which heretofore exercised jurisdiction over the said district; for that as congress are in duty bound, on the one hand, to preserve inviolate the rights of the several states; so on the other, they will always be careful to provide that the justice due to the states does not interfere with the justice which may be due to individuals :

"*Resolved*, That the committee confer with the said inhabitants, and that they take every prudent measure to promote an amicable settlement of all differences, and prevent divisions and animosities so prejudicial to the United States."

A committee of five members was accordingly chosen, any three of whom were empowered to act.

On the 7th of June Gov. Clinton addressed a long letter to the president of congress, giving an account of the further outrages which had been committed by Col. Allen and his associates in arresting and imprisoning the New York officers in Cumberland county. He also complained bitterly of the measure of sending a committee to confer with the inhabitants of the disturbed district, and of other acts of disrespect towards the state of New York which congress, as he alleged, had shown in relation to the revolters from her authority. On the 16th of June a committee to whom this letter had been referred, reported resolutions which were adopted, declaring, that the officers acting under the state of New York who had been restrained of their liberty on the New Hampshire Grants " ought to be immediately liberated;" and that the several other matters of complaint made by Gov. Clinton should be referred to the committee appointed to visit the district, and that further action should be postponed until their report should be made. The resolution for releasing the persons who had been arrested by Allen, was of course inoperative, they having been already discharged.

Only two members of the committee, Mr. Witherspoon of New Jersey and Mr. Atlee of Pennsylvania, visited Vermont. On reaching Bennington they had an interview with Gov. Chittenden and others in authority in the state, and undertook to reconcile the difficulties which had arisen in relation to the furnishing of men for military service, by entering into an agreement with Gov. Chittenden that the adherents of New York should voluntarily contribute their fair proportion, with others, for the raising of men to guard the frontier, and that so long as they did so, they should not be molested by the Vermont officers. On the 23d of June, Messrs. Witherspoon and Atlee addressed a letter from Bennington to Samuel Minott, the chairman of the New York committee at Brattleboro, informing him that they had been sent from congress " for the express purpose of endeavoring to bring about an amicable settlement of the differences between the state of New York and the inhabitants of the New Hampshire Grants, who had formed themselves into a state called by them the state of Vermont;" stating the agreement they had made with Gov. Chittenden, and recommending that the friends of New York should voluntarily and freely raise their full proportion of men to guard the frontier, whenever their neighbors were called upon for that purpose, "either by Continental officers or the new state." The letter concluded as follows: " This we are confident you will readily comply with, as otherwise people will be tempted to impute your conduct to disaffection to the cause of the United States. We hope you will understand that the protection and forbearance which is promised in your behalf is to be considered as on the condition of your cordially complying with our request, and in every respect behaving quietly and orderly while the measures for pacification are on foot."

On the same day Gov. Chittenden wrote to a Vermont officer in Cumberland county, informing him of the arrival of the committee of congress at Bennington, for the purpose of endeavoring to make an amicable settlement of their difficulties, concluding his letter as follows: "From the situation of present affairs and the pressing necessity of securing our frontier inhabitants, together with the advice of the committee aforesaid, transmitted in a letter, I presume the inhabitants will readily turn out in defence of their country, agreeable to orders, and in the meantime I would recommend, while they continue to do their proportion in the present war, the suspending of all prosecutions in the law against those who acknowledge themselves subjects of the state of New York (except capital offences), until congress make a determination of the matter."

On the 11th of June, some time before the arrival of the committee, Gov. Chittenden had issued an order for raising men for service on the frontier, and after the committee had left Bennington, he received information that the property of some delinquents in Cumberland county had been sold under such order in conformity to the law of the state, which information he at once communicated to them by letter, in which he stated that as this "was occasioned wholly by reason of those persons neglecting to do their proportion of duty in the present war, they would readily perceive it could not be construed to be any breach of the engagement which agreeably to their advice, he had entered into with them." In their answer, dated at Albany the 28th of June, they say they were "not willing to consider it a breach of the agreement," but expressed great apprehension that "it might be the means of defeating all their endeavors for promoting peace," and gave it as their opinion that the agreement would be wholly frustrated unless a stop was put to further proceedings of the kind, and restitution made to the people whose cattle had been thus seized.

This last proceeding had taken place in ignorance of the agreement with the committee. There is no doubt it would have been fairly carried out by Gov. Chittenden, as all that had been asked of those adhering to New York, was to do their proportion of service or pay for it voluntarily, and save the necessity of coercive measures. The proposed treaty was disapproved by the Cumberland county adherents of New York, and would have been most certainly rejected with indignation by Gov. Clinton, for impliedly, if not directly, admitting the existence of such a jurisdiction as that of the state of Vermont.

Before the gentlemen of the committee left Bennington, they submitted to Gov. Chittenden sundry queries, to which he returned written answers, the substance of which was as follows: that there was a large body of land in the state which had not been granted by either New Hampshire or New York, previous to the king's prohibitory order of 1767; that no lands had been granted by Vermont, but many petitions for grants were on file, waiting for a settlement of the public disputes; that there was a large quantity of land granted under New Hampshire, and regranted to other persons under New York that was not yet occupied by either of the grantees; that some old patents under New York were said to extend over some parts of the townships of Pownal, Bennington, and Shaftsbury, which were possessed under grants from New Hampshire of later date; that there were a few persons living in Vermont upon New Hampsire rights who had large property in lands in different townships not yet improved, and many that owned small quantities; that there were a few persons in actual possession of lands under the New York title, to which others had a prior right under New Hampshire; that the proclamations of the governor of New York of the previous year would by no means secure the property of the inhabitants in the soil — that they were "only a *shadow* without any principal substance, calculated to answer sinister purposes;" that their language excluded the most valuable lands in the state, and that it was out of the power of the legislature of New York to confirm the lands which had been previously granted to others. To the question, whether "if the property in the lands were perfectly secured to you would you be willing to return under the jurisdiction of New York," Gov. Chittenden answered as follows: "We are in the fullest sense as unwilling to be under the jurisdiction of New York, as we can conceive America would be to revert back under the power of Great Britain (except a few disaffected inhabitants who say they will become willing subjects of this state on the approbation of congress) and we should consider our liberties and privileges (both civil and religious) equally exposed to future invasions."

He further stated that experience had convinced him that a union with New York would impede the settlement of Vermont; that the proceedings in Cumberland county against those claiming to be under the jurisdiction of New York, had been wholly occasioned by their refusal "to do their tour of military duty in guard ing the frontiers of the state and of the United States of America against the common enemy, agreeable to the orders of the board of war of the state, issued in pursuance of advice from Brigadier General James Clinton for that purpose;" and that the people of the state would be willing to submit the long continued differences between the state and the state of New York, to the determination of congress on their being allowed equal privileges with that state in supporting their cause.

On the 13th of July, Mr. Witherspoon and Mr. Atlee presented to congress a written account of their proceedings, embodying the matters already related, in which they also stated that they were treated by the people they had visited with great courtesy and respect and were solemnly assured by them all, that they did not mean to break the union of the states or give encouragement to the common enemy. As these two gentlemen did not constitute a quorum of the committee, their written statement could not be considered as an official report, and it does not appear that any action was taken upon it by congress. Their mission to Vermont, though it probably had the effect to give to congress some additional light on the nature of the controversy, wholly failed of accomplishing anything in the way of reconciling it.[1]

In those days, before the powers of steam and electricity had been brought into use, and in the absence of regular mails, information traveled slowly. About the middle of June, the governor and council of Vermont having learned something of the action of congress of the first of that month, appointed Ethan Allen and Jonas Fay to repair to Philadelphia "to transact any business that concerned the state." They appear to have been at that city, or on the way there, while Mr. Witherspoon and Mr. Atlee were at Bennington. The principal object of their visit, seems to have been to give that body correct information in regard to the measures which had been adopted towards the adherents of New York, and in cementing and strengthening the state government. For this purpose they addressed a letter to the president of congress, which was presented on the 2d of July, transmitting a printed hand bill which contained Gov. Chittenden's order of the 6th of May, for calling out the *posse;* an extract from the proceedings of the court in the trial of the persons arrested, and the governor's proclamation of pardon, and also transmitting "a book containing the code of laws of the state of Vermont," which had been enacted the previous February.

Being convinced, after the return of these gentlemen, that a strong effort was about to be made to induce congress to adopt hostile measures towards the state, the governor and council deemed it advisable to obtain the fullest information in their power, in regard

[1] *New York Assembly Jour.*, Oct. 16, 21, and Nov. 10. *Jour. of Congress,* vol. 3, p. 128, 147, 148, 151, 285, 295, 297, 298, 308. *Slade,* 108, 110. *Doc. Hist. N. Y.*, p. 967, 986. *Williams's Vt.*, 247, 250. *Hall's Eastern Vt.*, chap. XIII. *Clinton Papers,* No. 2428.

to the actual state of the case before that body. They, therefore, towards the last of the month of July, instructed Jonas Fay and Paul Spooner, who had previously been appointed agents for the state to congress, to go to Philadelphia and obtain copies of all papers they should deem important, which had been presented to that body in relation to Vermont, with the reportsand resolutions thereon; in which mission they were successful. By these gentlemen Gov. Chittenden took occasion to address a letter to congress, bearing date August 5th, protesting against their resolution of the 16th of June, by which, he said, the authority of Vermont "had been impeached and censured before the facts and circumstances could have been particularly known to congress;" and affirming that the men who had been arrested in Cumberland county had been guilty "of a high-handed breach of the peace" in resisting the levy of men for the defence of the frontiers, but that notwithstanding their offence, they had been liberated before the passage of the resolution of congress. He further declared that many of them were "able-bodied, effective men of considerable property who were averse to taking up arms against the common enemy," and who had taken advantage of the dispute between New York and Vermont "to screen themselves from service;" and who had always refused whenever applied to, to furnish their quota of either men or money, in defence of their own frontier. He offered, in behalf of the people of Vermont, to pay their full proportion of the expense of the war with Great Britain whenever required to do so, although they had for a long time at their own cost of men and means, maintained their frontier defences. Referring to Gov. Clinton's letter to congress of May 29th, in which he had stated that he should "issue his orders to the militia and make the necessary arrangements for marching to repel the outrage" which had been committed in Cumberland county, Gov. Chittenden said, "I have issued like orders to the militia of this state, and notwithstanding I am far from countenancing a measure so disagreeable in its nature, yet the free born citizens of this state can never so far degrade the dignity of human nature, or relinquish any part of that glorious spirit of patriotism, which has hitherto distinguished them in every conflict with the unrelenting and long continued tyranny of designing men, as tamely to submit to his mandates, or even to be intimidated by a challenge from him." [1]

[1] *Jour. Cong.*, vol. 3, p. 317, 342. *Ethan Allen Papers*, 283, 293. *Vermont Council Jour.*, 269, 270. *Gov. Chittenden's Letter*, state department, Washington. *N. Y. Doc. Hist.*

CHAPTER XXVI.

ENGAGEMENT OF CONGRESS TO HEAR AND DECIDE THE CONTROVERSY.

1779-1780

Efforts of the New York Assembly to obtain the interposition of Congress against Vermont — Resolves of Congress engaging to hear and decide the controversy and enforce their decision — Measures of the Vermont government in vindication of the right of the state to independence — Agents of the state appear in Philadelphia and protest against the jurisdiction of Congress — The hearing of the controversy postponed.

ON the 8th of September, 1779, the delegates from New York laid before congress certain instructions of their legislature, of the 27th of the preceding month, directing them to make use of all possible exertions to obtain the speedy and effectual interposition of congress in behalf of the state against the Vermonters as the only means of preventing a resort to military force. The instructions stated that the principal business of the meeting of the legislature at that time was "to deliberate upon that momentous subject;" that the legislature would continue in session, without adopting any coercive measures, "until they were favored with the sentiments of congress," and "in case congress should decline to interpose by an express recommendation in favor of the state," Mr. Jay, who had the business in special charge, was directed "immediately to withdraw" from congress and report to the legislature. These instructions were accompanied by a memorial from the New York committee of Cumberland county, which also asked for the interposition of congress against the measures of Vermont. Circumstances favored the efforts of New York. New Hampshire, which had formerly been friendly to Vermont, had become hostile. In order to secure the quiet submission to her authority of her uneasy inhabitants on her western border, who were ambitious for a new state with its capital on Connecticut river, and with some hope of extending her territory to the westward of that river, by the action of congress, she had laid before that body a claim to the whole of Vermont. And now that the subject was brought before that tribunal the delegates from Massachusetts deemed it advisable to put in the ancient claim of that commonwealth to the southern part of the new state. Thus Vermont was deprived of the sympathy of a large portion of the members from New England, on which she had heretofore relied. Her treatment of the disaffected in her midst was loudly complained of, and some laws which had been enacted by Vermont, probably for the mere purpose of inspiring terror, for no attempt was ever made to execute them, subjecting those who opposed her authority to severe and degrading corporal punishment, were used to produce an unfriendly feeling against the managers of the new state government. They doubtless had such an effect, for though corporal punishment for acknowledged crime was then in common use in all the states, its threatened application to persons of respectable standing in society, for a political offence which many would justify, was very generally disapproved. Many months had been spent by Mr. Jay and his associate delegates, in preparing the minds of the members for active measures; and now that there was little or no hope left that a reconciliation of the several parties to the controversy could be effected, and an armed collision being apparently imminent, it was difficult to resist the appeal to congress to undertake its adjudication. The papers presented from New York were referred to a committee of five members, who on the 17th made their report, which was taken into consideration by congress, and on the 24th a series of resolutions on the subject was adopted.

The resolutions were preceded by a preamble, in which it was recited that applications had been made to congress, by the states of New York and New Hampshire, "relative to disturbances and animosities among the inhabitants of a certain district known by the name of the New Hampshire Grants;" and that a majority of the committee which had been appointed by resolution of the first of June last to visit the district, had not been able to meet; that such animosities were likely to disturb the peace of the United States, which rendered it "necessary for congress to interpose for the restoration of quiet and good order;" that the states of New Hampshire, Massachusetts and New York, claimed the said district, either wholly or in part, against each other, and against the people inhabiting it, and that the said people denied the jurisdiction of either of said states. For these alleged reasons, congress resolved as follows:

"*Resolved unanimously*, That it be, and hereby is most earnestly recommended to the states of New Hampshire, Massachusetts Bay and New York, forthwith to pass laws expressly authorizing congress to hear and determine all differences between them relative to their respective boundaries, in the mode prescribed by the articles of confederation, so that congress may proceed thereon by the first day of February next at the farthest; and further that the said states of New Hampshire, Massachusetts Bay and New York, do, by express laws for the purpose, refer to the decision of congress all differences or disputes relative to jurisdiction, which they may respectively have with the people of the district aforesaid, that congress may proceed thereon on the first day of February next; [and also to authorize congress to proceed to hear and determine all disputes subsisting between the grantees of the several states aforesaid, with one another, or with either of the said states, respecting title to lands lying in the said district, to be heard and determined by commissioners or judges to be appointed in the mode prescribed by the 9th article of the confederation aforesaid:[1]] and further to provide that no advantage be taken of the nonperformance of the conditions of any of the grants of the said lands, but that further reasonable time be allowed for fulfilling such conditions.

"*Resolved unanimously*, That congress will and hereby do pledge their faith to carry into execution and support their decisions and determinations in the premises, in favor of whichsoever of the parties the same may be, to the end that permanent concord and harmony may be established between them, and all cause of uneasiness removed.

"*Resolved unanimously*, That congress will, on the said first day of February next, proceed, without delay, to hear and examine into the disputes and differences relative to jurisdiction aforesaid, between the said three states respectively, or such of them as shall pass the laws before mentioned on the one part, and the people of the district aforesaid who claim to be a separate jurisdiction on the other; and after a full and fair hearing will decide and determine the same according to equity; and that neither of the said states shall vote on any question relative to the decision thereof. And congress do hereby pledge their faith to execute and support their decisions and determinations in the premises.

"*Resolved unanimously*, That it is the duty of the people of the district aforesaid, who deny the jurisdiction of all the aforenamed states, to abstain in the meantime from exercising any power over any of the inhabitants of the said district, who profess themselves to be citizens of, or to owe allegiance to any or either of said states; but that none of the towns, either on the east or west side of the

[1] This clause included in brackets was substituted by resolution of congress of October 2, for one repealed, which repealed clause is here omitted.

Connecticut river, be considered as included within the said district, but such as have heretofore actually joined in denying the jurisdiction of either of said states, and have assumed a separate jurisdiction which they call the state of Vermont. And further, that in the opinion of congress, the said three states aforenamed, ought, in the meantime, to suspend executing their laws over any of the inhabitants of said districts, except such of them as shall profess allegiance to, and confess the jurisdiction of the same respectively. And further, that congress will consider any violences committed against the tenor, true intent and meaning of this resolution as a breach of the peace of the confederacy, which they are determined to keep and maintain. And to the end, that all such violences and breaches of the public peace may be better avoided in the said district, it is hereby recommended to all the inhabitants thereof, to cultivate harmony and concord among themselves, to forbear vexing each other at law or otherwise, and to give as little occasion as possible to the interposition of magistrates.

"*Resolved unanimously*, That in the opinion of congress, no unappropriated lands or estates which are or may be adjudged forfeited or confiscated, lying in the said district, ought, until the final decision of congress in the premises, to be granted or sold.

"*Ordered*, That copies of the foregoing resolutions be sent by express to the states of New York, New Hampshire and Massachusetts, and to the people of the district aforesaid, and that they be respectively desired to lose no time in appointing their agent or agents, and otherwise preparing for the hearings aforesaid."

These resolutions were considered by the New York delegates as a virtual engagement of congress to decide the controversy in her favor, and if necessary, to carry its decision into effect by force of arms. The claims of both Massachusetts and New Hampshire were regarded by them as clearly unfounded, and, as it would seem, not without reason. That of Massachusetts had been decided against her in 1739 by the crown, the then acknowledged umpire, and that of New Hampshire in favor of New York by the same authority in 1764; and both decisions had been ever afterwards acquiesced in by the colonies against which they were made. Vermont was viewed as a mere nominal party. The states named in the resolutions were first to give their assent to a hearing of the controversy by congress, but the consent of Vermont was not asked. Her jurisdiction was denied in advance by requiring her to forbear granting unappropriated lands, and confiscating the lands of tories; and to abstain from the exercise of authority over a portion of the inhabitants within her limits, and to permit the exercise of the authority of either of the contesting states over any of the inhabitants who should choose their jurisdiction. She was indeed to be allowed to attend at the trial, but only, according to Mr. Jay, to prevent clamor, and to give the decision which was to be made against her the greater weight. In his report to Gov. Clinton, in explanation of the resolutions, dated the day after their passage, his language on this point was as follows; "You may ask why Vermont is made a party? the reason is this, that by being allowed a hearing, the candor and moderation of congress may be rescued from aspersions, and that the people, after having been fully heard, may have nothing to say or complain of, in case the decision of congress be against them, *of which I have no doubt.*"[1]

These resolutions were viewed in a similar light by the men administering the government of Vermont. They had been passed without their knowledge, and were believed by them to be the result of an understanding between the delegates of New Hampshire and New York for a division of the territory, in which understanding it was feared the delegates from Massachusetts had also participated.

Neither of these New England states, it was thought, could, upon any legal or equitable principles, make even a plausible case before congress, but their aid would be most essential to the success of New York, and when that was obtained a distribution of the spoils could be made. That there was some ground for this belief, at least so far as New Hampshire was concerned, will be seen hereafter.

"It was impossible," says Dr. Williams in his history, "that Vermont should comply with the resolves of congress. To have four separate jurisdictions existing at the same time, in the same territory, as the resolutions recommended, would at any time have been absurd and impossible; least of all was it to be admitted or attempted after the people had declared themselves to be a free and independent state, assumed the powers of government, and exercised them in all cases, and in every part of the state. They had already formed their constitution, enacted a code of laws, erected courts of justice, and fully exercised all the powers of government. The plan of four separate jurisdictions, which congress proposed, was incompatible with any state of society, and the more dangerous as New York was constantly aiming to break up the government of Vermont, by granting commissions to her adherents, encouraging informers and promoting disaffected persons in every part of the territory."

---

[1] *Doc. Hist. N. Y.*, p. 981, 987. *Jour. Cong.*, vol. 3, p. 350, 365, 366, 371. *Jay to Clinton*, September 25, 1779. *Life of Jay*, p. 88 to 95.

Vermont must therefore be content to submit quietly to the overthrow of her authority by the adjoining states, and the appropriation by them of her territory, or prepare to support with firmness and resolution her independent jurisdiction. She chose the latter.

The third annual election for state officers, had taken place on the first Tuesday of September, and on the second Thursday of October, the time fixed by the constitution, the legislature assembled at Manchester. The resolutions of congress having been fully discussed by the council and assembly in committee of the whole, it was unanimously resolved, that "the state ought to support their right to independence, at congress and to the world, *in the character of a free and independent state*," and it was recommended to the general assembly "to make grants of all, or any part of the unappropriated lands within their jurisdiction, that should not interfere with any former grants, as their wisdom might direct." It was further resolved, "That five persons be chosen by ballot, agents in behalf of the freemen of the state, to appear at the congress of the United States of America, on the first day of February next." Any three of them were authorized to vindicate the right of the state to independence, before that body; to agree upon articles of union and confederation in behalf of Vermont with the United States, and to transact any other political business of the state "as an independent state" at congress. The agents chosen, were Ethan Allen, Jonas Fay, Paul Spooner, Stephen R. Bradley and Moses Robinson.

The presentation of a claim to congress by Massachusetts, had not been anticipated, and Gen. Ethan Allen was appointed to visit the general court of that state and ascertain the character and extent of the claim. He was the bearer of a letter from Gov. Chittenden to the president of the Massachusetts council, making the inquiry, complaining of the oppressive conduct of New York, and earnestly affirming the justice and equity of the claim of Vermont to independence. The legislature of Massachusetts neglected to pass an act submitting her claim to the decision of congress, but the president of the senate, in reply to Gov. Chittenden's letter informed him that the claim of Massachusetts extended from the well known southern boundary of that state to a line of latitude running through a point three miles north of the source of the Merrimac river, and reached for that width west to the Pacific ocean, thus including southern Vermont and central and western New York, as well as a vast territory across the continent to the west. Of this claim congress was also officially informed, the government of Massachusetts thus placing itself in a somewhat equivocal position in regard to the controversy. It is probable that this claim of Massachusetts was made, not so much for the purpose of interfering with the rights of the new state, as by way of asserting her own ancient title to lands within the acknowledged jurisdiction of New York, to the westward of Vermont; which title she afterwards maintained with some success, as has been seen in a previous chapter. The states of New York and New Hampshire promptly passed acts submitting the decision of the controversy to congress, in compliance with the resolution of that body, and preparations were made by all parties for the contemplated hearing the succeeding February. Mr. Jay having been appointed by congress minister to Spain, vacated his office of president, and Samuel Huntington of Connecticut was chosen his successor. Mr. Jay also resigned his place as delegate, and Robert R. Livingston then chancellor of New York, was appointed special delegate in his stead, and with the other delegates from the state, was directed to act in her behalf in the management of the controversy. Samuel Livermore, with one or more of the other delegates from New Hampshire, was authorized to act for that state.[1]

Active and energetic measures were taken by the government of Vermont to enlighten the public mind in other states, in regard to the claim of the state to independence. In the preceding month of August an elaborate pamphlet had been prepared by Ethan Allen with the official approbation of the governor and council, setting forth the original title of New Hampshire to the territory of Vermont, the granting of its lands by that province and their settlement under that title, the order of the king transferring the jurisdiction to New York, the subsequent regranting of the lands by the latter province to city speculators, the attempts of the new patentees by the aid of that government to oust the settlers from their possessions, their forcible and successful resistance to the unfriendly and hostile measures of both the colonial and later rulers of New York towards the inhabitants.[2] At the time of the meeting of the legislature, this pamphlet had just been published, and pains was taken to have it extensively circulated among the leading men of the country. Col. Ira Allen

---

[1] *Williams's Vt.*, 113-116. *Slade*, 113-116. *Vt. Assembly Jour.*, Oct. 19, 20, 21 and 22, 1779. *Jour. Mass. Assembly.* *Wells's Life of Samuel Adams*, vol. 3, pp. 144-147. *Jour. Cong.*, vol. 3, pp. 368, 429, 430. *Jour. N. Y. Assembly*, Oct. 18 and 21, 1779.

[2] The following is a copy of the title page of the work: "A vindication of the opposition of the inhabitants of Vermont to the government of New York, and of their right to form an independent state. Humbly submitted to the consideration of the impartial world. By Ethan Allen. Printed by

was appointed by vote of the assembly to visit the legislatures of the states of New Jersey, Pennsylvania, Delaware, and Maryland; and by conference with their members and by distribution of "the vindication" to endeavor to produce an impression favorable to the interests of Vermont. Mr. Allen appears to have conducted the business of his mission with skill and ability, and with considerable success, and to have joined the agents of the state to congress at Philadelphia, prior to the expected hearing of the controversy by that body.[1]

By the adoption of the resolutions by congress, providing for the adjudication of the dispute, and by the addition of New Hampshire and Massachusetts as parties to it, new questions were presented for the consideration of that body and the public, which were thought to require special notice from the government of the new state. A pamphlet of fifty pages on the subject, was drawn up, under the direction of the governor and council, by Stephen R. Bradley, Esq., then a young lawyer, who had recently removed from Connecticut to Vermont, and who afterwards occupied a prominent position among the public men of the state. It was entitled "*Vermont's appeal to the candid and impartial world;* containing a fair stating of the claims of Massachusetts Bay, New Hampshire and New York; the right of the state of Vermont to independence; with an address to the Honorable American Congress, and the inhabitants of the thirteen United States." It was published at Hartford, by Hudson & Goodwin, in December, 1779. This appeal, after showing the weakness and invalidity of the claims of Massachusetts and New Hampshire to the territory in question, and treating of the unjust and oppressive conduct of New York, which rendered resistance to her authority a public necessity, proceeded in a clear and spirited manner to advocate the right of the state upon revolutionary principles, to maintain her independent jurisdiction.

Alden Spooner, 1779, Printer to the state of Vermont." On the second page was inserted a copy of a resolution, as follows:

"State of Vermont. In Council, Arlington 23d August, 1779. Resolved, that the following vindication be forthwith published, and that a number of the pamphlets be sent to the congress of the United States, and to the general assembly of every of these states; and that a number be likewise sent to the generals and other principal officers of the continental army, for their consideration. Per order of the governor and council.

JOSEPH FAY, Secretary."

The pamphlet covered one hundred and seventy-two pages.

[1] *Jour. Vt. Assembly,* October 21, 1779. *Ira Allen's Vt.*, p. 134. *Ira Allen to Penn. Council,* January 20, 1780, *in Penn. Archives,* 1779 – 1781, p. 89.

In immediate reply to the resolutions of congress, the appeal declared that the government of Vermont could not view themselves as holden either in the sight of God or man, to submit to the execution of a plan which they had reason to believe was commenced by neighboring states; that the liberties and privileges of the state of Vermont, by said resolutions, were to be suspended upon the arbitrament and final determination of congress, when in their opinion they were too sacred ever to be arbitrated upon at all, and what they were bound to defend at every risk; that the congress of the United States had no right to intermeddle with the internal police and government of Vermont; that the state existed independent of any of the thirteen United States, and was not accountable to them, or to their representatives, for liberty, the gift of the beneficent Creator; that the people of Vermont were not represented in congress, and could not submit to resolutions passed without their consent, or even knowledge, and which put everything that was valuable to them at stake; that there appeared a manifest inequality, not to say predetermination, that congress should request of their constituents power to judge and determine the cause, and never ask the consent of thousands whose all was at stake. It also declared that they were, and ever had been, ready to bear their proportion of the burden and expense of the war with Great Britain, from its first commencement, whenever they were admitted into the Union with the other states, but that they were not so lost to all sense and honor, that after four years war with Britain, in which they had expended so much blood and treasure, they should now give up everything worth fighting for, the right of making their own laws, and choosing their own form of government, to the arbitrament and determination of any man or body of men under heaven."[1] Copies of this pamphlet were furnished to the several members of congress prior to the expected hearing before that body, and were extensively distributed among the other public men of the country.

Jonas Fay, Moses Robinson, and Stephen R. Bradley, agents of the state of Vermont, were in attendance at Philadelphia on the first day of February, and presented to congress their credentials, together with "Vermont's appeal" and "a book containing the constitution and code of laws as established by the freemen of said state." In their letter to the president of congress, they announced their readiness to unite with that body in placing Vermont on the same footing with the other states of the confederation, but declared that they had no authority to close with the terms of the resolutions

---

[1] *Vermont's Appeal*, 38–40. *Williams's Vermont*, p. 253.

of the 24th of September preceding, and that the people of the state they represented did not deem themselves under obligation to do so. They further declared that if congress should determine to proceed under those resolutions, a postponement of the hearing would be indispensible to the rights of Vermont; that they had the strongest reasons to believe they should be able to show, if sufficient time were allowed them, "that in consequence of their remonstrances and petitions to the court of Great Britain, that power had made a distinct government of the territory now comprehending the state of Vermont, and appointed Gov. Skene to preside over the same previous to America's denying its supremacy;" that such evidence would overthrow the titles, under the crown, of the other claiming states, and "would oblige every man, even those interested, to acknowledge that Vermont had an equal right with the other American states to assume an independent government," and that until they should have had time to obtain and publish such evidence in support of their cause, they would never by reason of any partial adjudication "voluntarily surrender the liberties God and nature had vested them with."

The delegates from the claiming states were also in attendance upon congress, but the subject does not appear from the journals to have been mentioned in that body on the day appointed for its consideration. On the 8th of February, papers in relation to the controversy were read in congress, but no action was taken in regard to them. On the 2d of March, the succeeding Tuesday was assigned by congress for the consideration of the subject, but the matter seems to have been passed over, without further notice, until the 21st of that month, when it was ordered "that the same to be postponed, nine states exclusive of those who are parties to the question, not being represented in congress."

A majority of the members for various reasons, some of which will be noticed hereafter, were undoubtedly averse to coming to a decision of the controversy. Mr. Folsom, one of the delegates from New Hampshire, writing from Philadelphia, on the 17th of April, to Josiah Bartlett, says: "As to Vermont, there were several violent attempts by the delegates of New York and New Hampshire to bring the matter before congress, but without the least appearance of success. I have no expectation of any settlement till after the war is over, if I can believe the present members." The agents of Vermont had sometime before this returned home.[1]

[1] *Ira Allen's Vt.*, 134. *Williams' Vt.*, 254. *Jour. Cong.*, vol. 3, p. 430, 438, 439, 444. *Clinton Papers*, No. 2714. *B. H. Hall's Manuscript.*

CHAPTER XXVII.

THE HEARING OF THE CONTROVERSY IN CONGRESS.

1780.

Negotiations between New Hampshire and New York for dividing the territory of Vermont between them, with the ridge of the Green Mountain for a boundary — Vermont notwithstanding the resolutions of Congress of Sept., 1779, confiscates tory estates, grants unappropriated lands and compels Yorkers to contribute to the defence of the frontier — Congress by resolution of June 1780 censure the conduct of Vermont and fix upon the second Tuesday of September for the hearing of the controversy — Protest against the resolutions by the governor and council of Vermont — Proceedings at the hearing — Obstacles in the way of the success of the claiming states — Many of the members of congress favorable to Vermont — Congress resolve to postpone the subject.

THE many obstacles encountered by the New York delegates, in their efforts to obtain the efficient action of congress against Vermont, seem to have induced them to look favorably upon a proposal from the New Hampshire delegates for a division of the disputed territory between the two states. There was little doubt, if congress could be brought to a decision of the controversy between the two states, that it must be in favor of New York. New Hampshire had appealed to that body to prevent encroachments by Vermont on her territory east of Connecticut river, and probably, with little hope of making her title good against New York to the westward of it. If the danger to her territory from that source should be removed or overcome, as it was liable to be, she would have but small desire to continue the prosecution of a claim which was likely to result in the aggrandizement of her antagonist. The manners and institutions of the inhabitants of Vermont were similar to those of New Hampshire, and there is no doubt that the people of the latter state would have been much better pleased to see Vermont, to the westward of Connecticut river, an independent state, than to have the territory form a part of New York. But without the zealous cooperation of New Hampshire with New York, it was doubtful whether congress could be induced to come to a decision of the controversy; and the continuance of such cooperation could not be depended on unless some other inducement to action should be presented. The ridge of the Green mountain, which divides Vermont into two nearly equal parts, by a north and south line, might form a natural and convenient boundary between two states, and the eastern portion would greatly add to the wealth and power of New Hampshire. The idea of such an ultimate division was undoubtedly suggested at the time of the passage of the resolutions of September, 1779, and might have contributed to the unanimity with which they were passed.

A design of this character, which sought to bargain away the right of large bodies of people to choose their own form of government, could not be publicly avowed. But that it was seriously entertained, if not fully agreed upon, there is no doubt.

It appears from Mr. Jay's report to Gov. Clinton, dated the day after the passage of the resolution of the 24th of September, 1779, that there were some reasons that induced the passage of those resolutions which he was not "convinced of the prudence of committing to paper." It is probable they related to this matter. In a letter of the 7th of October, two weeks afterwards, Mr. Jay proceeded to prepare the mind of the governor for such an arrangement as follows:

"One of the New Hampshire delegates seems much inclined to make the ridge of mountains instead of Connecticut river the boundary between us; and that the soil between the mountain and the river should remain the property of those to whom it had been granted, either under New York or New Hampshire. He observed, and I think with propriety, that this line, by dividing the disaffected between the two states, would render the reduction of them to good order less difficult, and by interesting both states in their allegiance, prevent their again acting in a body, or easily uniting their councils for purposes injurious to government. My reply to this, gentlemen, was, that I had no authority to say any thing on this subject, that I knew the state of New York to be sincerely disposed to cultivate harmony with her neighbors, and was persuaded that no settlement founded in justice and mutual convenience will be disagreeable to them. To you, however, I must confess that the line he proposes does not appear to me to be impolitic. We have unquestionably more territory than we can govern, and the loss of that strip, would not in my opinion, overbalance the advantages resulting from it. On the contrary, unless I am much mistaken, exclusive of other considerations, the less our people have to do with Connecticut river the better. I would rather see the productions of our country go to sea by another route."

On the 9th of February following, after several unsuccessful attempts to induce congress to proceed to a hearing of the controversy in accordance with their previous resolutions, the New York delegates addressed a formal letter to Gov. Clinton, recommending an accommodation of the dispute with New Hampshire. The letter, which with other papers that accompanied it, was transmitted by the governor to the assembly, is not now to be found in the archives of the state, but there is no doubt from other sources of information, that it contemplated a division of the Vermont territory, by the line suggested by Mr. Jay. The letter of the delegates, with the accompanying papers, was referred by the two houses to a joint committee, of whom Mr. Townsend, who had been admitted as a representative in the assembly of the friends of New York in Cumberland county, was chairman. He was an intelligent lawyer of good character, possessing the entire confidence of the men he represented, and he had much influence in the body of which he was received a member. The letter of the delegates had been laid before the assembly the 21st of February, and on the 8th of March, Mr. Townsend reported from the committee the draft of a letter, in answer to it, which was adopted by the legislature, and transmitted to the delegates. The answer of the assembly, after stating that they conceived "it ineligible at that time to attempt an accommodation with New Hampshire in the mode proposed" by the delegates, continued as follows:

"We forbear to assign particularly the motives which influenced both houses in their determination upon this important question. Let it suffice to observe that after numberless applications to congress for their interposition, the business is at length in a course of decision, and it is deemed prudent at least for sometime, to wait the result, and you are desired by every means in your power to press for a speedy trial and determination. At a future day, possibly the measure may appear not only expedient but necessary, and if from obstructions to a trial or any other causes, you should continue or be more confirmed in the sentiment of a separate settlement with New Hampshire, it is the wish of the legislature that in such case one of the delegates should attend them at
on the of next, to which time and place they are adjourned, in order that they may be fully possessed of information upon this momentous subject."

This proposed division of the Vermont territory would not probably have been very distasteful to most of the land claimants under New York, whose grants which interfered with those of New Hampshire were almost exclusively on the west side of the Green mountain; but it was earnestly objected to by Mr. Townsend in behalf of the friends of New York to the eastward of the mountain, who, after their extraordinary exertions and sacrifices in endeavoring to establish the jurisdiction of their favorite state, were quite unwilling to be abandoned by it, to the mercy of those with whom they had long been in controversy. This opposition may perhaps have been the principal obstacle to the adoption of the proposal at that time.

It does not appear from the answer of the legislature, that its members were troubled with any scruples about the justice and propriety of thus bargaining away the people of Vermont without their knowledge, but only regarded it as a question of expediency, which they might be at perfect liberty to answer differently thereafter. It was long believed in Vermont that a full arrangement had been entered into between the two states, by which after a decision by congress in favor of New York, the eastern section of the state was to be relinquished to New Hampshire.[1] That this was not the finale of the project for dividing the territory of Vermont between the two adjoining claimants, will be seen hereafter. It seems to have been long entertained by delegates from New Hampshire, and not always unfavorably listened to by those of New York. There were, however, difficulties in carrying it into effect, which there never came a suitable time to overcome.

The legislature of Vermont, considering the resolutions of congress for adjudicating the dispute between New York, New Hampshire and Massachusetts as a virtual denial of her separate jurisdiction, and believing that any trial under them would be a mere mockery so far as the new state was concerned, had, as before stated, resolved, without regard to the injunctions of congress, to continue the full exercise of her authority as an independent state. She had accordingly, disposed of tory estates, granted vacant and unappropriated lands and levied troops to guard the frontiers, requiring the friends of New York as well as others to furnish men for that purpose. A full and perhaps in some respects an exaggerated account of the measures and conduct of the Vermonters having been sent by the friends of New York to Gov. Clinton, was by him transmitted to the delegates of the state in congress, who laid it before that body. Congress having already resolved to hear and decide the controversy, and having enjoined Vermont from exercising, in the mean time, the before mentioned acts of authority, could not well refuse, on the

---

[1] *Life of Jay*, vol. 1, p. 88. *Clinton Papers* in Albany State Library, No. 2540, 2791, 2806. *Jour. N. Y. Assembly* of Feb. 21, 22, and March 8, 1780. *N. Y. Assembly Papers*, Miscellaneous, vol. 1. *Slade*, 112, 127.

urgent demand of New York to condemn their violation. Accordingly congress, on the 2d of June, 1780, adopted a series of resolutions, which after stating by way of preamble that the inhabitants "of the district of country commonly known by the name of the New Hampshire Grants, in violation of the injunctions of congress had proceeded as a separate government to make grants of lands and sales of estates by them declared forfeited, and had also, in divers instances, exercised civil and military authority over the persons and effects of sundry inhabitants within the said district, who professed to be citizens of and to owe allegiance to the state of New York," declared such acts to be "highly unwarrantable and subversive of the peace and welfare of the United States," and strictly required the inhabitants of said district to forbear all further acts of such authority, either civil or military, until the controversy should be heard and determined by congress. The resolutions also declared that the disputes should be taken up and decided as soon as nine states, exclusive of those who were parties, should be represented in that body. On the 9th of June congress by resolution assigned the second Tuesday of September following for the hearing of the controversy under the resolution of the previous year.

Copies of these several resolutions, enclosed in a letter from the president of congress were received by Gov. Chittenden about a month after their passage, to which he by advice of his council, returned a spirited protest. It bore date July 25th, 1780, and after stating that the resolutions of the 2d and 9th of June, were considered by the people of Vermont as "subversive of the natural rights which they had to independence, as well as incompatible with the principles on which congress grounded their own right to independence," controverted the authority which congress had assumed by them, in the following logical language: "Vermont, being a free and independent state, have denied the authority of congress to judge of their jurisdiction. Over the head of all this, it appears that congress by their resolutions of the 9th ultimo, have determined that they have power to judge the cause, which has already determined the essence of the dispute; for if Vermont does not belong to some one of the United States, congress could have no such power without their consent, so that consequently, determining they have such power, has determined that Vermont have no right to independence; for it is utterly incompatible with the rights and prerogatives of an independent state, to be under the control or arbitrament of any other power. Vermont have, therefore, no alternative; they must submit to the unwarrantable decree of congress, or continue their appeal to heaven and to arms."

The governor then referred to the supposed understanding between New York and New Hampshire for dividing the territory between them, likening it to the then recent iniquitous division of Poland between three European sovereigns. He alluded to the maintenance of posts on the northern frontier by Vermont, not only for the protection of her own territory but also for the security of her three opposing neighboring states; he declared that their conduct in thus guarding the frontiers, had secured the friendship of private gentlemen and yeomanry whose representatives seemed to be seeking their destruction, and that having the general approbation of disinterested states, the people were undoubtedly in a condition to maintain government; "but should they be deceived in such connections," continued the governor, "yet, as they are not included in the thirteen United States, but consider themselves to be a separate body, they would still have in their power other advantages; for they are, if necessitated to it, at liberty to offer, or accept terms of cessation of hostilities with Great Britain, without the approbation of any other men or body of men; for on proviso, that neither congress nor the legislatures of those states which they represent will support Vermont in her independence, but devote her to the usurped government of any other power, she has not the most distant motive to continue hostilities with Great Britain, and maintain an important frontier for the benefit of the United States, and for no other reward than the ungrateful one of being enslaved by them." The governor admitted that Vermont had "dealt with severity towards the tories, confiscated some of their estates, imprisoned some, banished some, and hanged some, and kept the remainder in good subjection," and that "they had likewise granted unto worthy whigs, in the neighboring states, some part of their unappropriated lands; the inconsiderable avails of which had been faithfully appropriated for the defence of the northern frontiers." He claimed that the state of Massachusetts having passed no law in compliance with the resolutions of congress, could not be longer considered as a party to the controversy; that the claim of New Hampshire was too weak to entitle her to be considered as a real party, and "as a bar against the right of New Hampshire to a trial for any part of Vermont," he transmitted to congress a pamphlet entitled, *A Concise Refutation of the Claims of New Hampshire and Massachusetts Bay to the Territory of Vermont.* This pamphlet, of about thirty pages, had been prepared with care and ability, by Ethan Allen and Jonas Fay, and published under the direction of the governor and council.

The governor's protest against the resolutions concluded in the following language:

"Notwithstanding the usurpation and injustice of neighboring governments towards Vermont, and the late resolutions of congress, this government, from a principle of virtue and close attachment to the cause of liberty, as well as a thorough examination of their own policy, are induced, once more, to offer a union with the United States of America, of which congress are the legal representative body. Should that be denied, this state will propose the same to the legislatures of the United States, separately, and take such other measures as self-preservation may justify."

This protest of Gov. Chittenden was committed to the care of Ira Allen and Stephen R. Bradley, who were directed by the governor and council to repair to Philadelphia and attend to the political affairs of the state before congress. Luke Knowlton of Newfane was also in attendance on that body in behalf of the friends of New York, in Cumberland county. The party who were for a state whose capital should be on Connecticut river, either by the division of Vermont by the range of the Green mountain, or by annexing the whole to New Hampshire, as should be found most feasible, were represented by Peter Olcott of Newbury. Preparations were also made for the contemplated hearing by the delegates of the two contesting states of New York and New Hampshire.

On the 12th of September, the day fixed upon for the hearing, Messrs Allen and Bradley presented their commission as agents of Vermont, and accompanied it with the before mentioned protest of Gov. Chittenden, and a copy of the pamphlet therein referred to. The credentials of Mr. Olcott and a communication from those he represented, were also presented, which, together with the commission of Allen and Bradley, and the protest of Gov. Chittenden, appear to have been read in that body on that day. But nine states exclusive of those who were parties to the controversy, not being represented, further proceedings were postponed.

On the 19th of September, the secretary of congress was directed to notify Messrs. Allen and Bradley, Mr. Knowlton and Mr. Olcott, to attend the hearing at six o'clock that afternoon. All of them were present and their several credentials were read. The further proceedings of congress on that day and the next are stated in their journal as follows:

"The delegates of New York, as agents for the state, delivered in sundry papers, which were read, with an intent to prove that the land known by the name of the New Hampshire Grants, west of Connecticut river, is within the limits of the state of New York; and that the state of New Hampshire have acknowledged this, and that the people on the said tract had been represented in the legislature of New York, since the year 1764."

"September 20, 1780.

"Congress proceeded to the order of the day, the parties being present as yesterday except the delegate for the state of New Hampshire, who was absent through sickness, when the state of New York, by its delegates, proceeded in stating evidence to prove that the inhabitants of the tract of country known by the name of the New Hampshire Grants, west of Connecticut river, as part of the state and colony of New York, were duly represented in, and submitted to the authority, jurisdiction and government of the congress and convention of said state, till late in the year 1777; and that therefore the people inhabiting the said tract of country, have no right to a separate and independent jurisdiction." The evidence and argument on the part of New York being completed, the hearing in behalf of New Hampshire was postponed to the succeeding week.

At this stage of the proceedings, the agents of Vermont withdrew, and determined to attend the hearing no further. The following account of the proceeding is given in the language of Mr. Allen, one of the agents.

"The claims of New Hampshire and New York were put in, and both these states plead that Vermont had no pretensions to independence, but belonged to them. The agents of Vermont though present, were not considered or treated by congress as the agents or representatives of any state or people invested with legislative authority. Parts of two days were spent in hearing the evidence exhibited by New York, to show that the people on the New Hampshire Grants belonged to and of right were under the authority and jurisdiction of New York, and therefore had no right to a separate jurisdiction; a day being assigned to hear the claim and evidence of New Hampshire. During this time the agents of Vermont retained minutes of the proceedings of congress, and of the evidence exhibited by the agents of New York, that they might the better be prepared to remonstrate against them, as they had no idea of submitting the independence of Vermont to the arbitrament of congress, or, of objecting in any way to the evidence adduced against Vermont, however irregular or provoking. The principles on which the agents of Vermont went, were to remain quiet, let the business be conducted as it would; the worse, the more advantage they would have in remonstrating. They concluded it not advisable to attend and hear the claim and evidence of New Hampshire when it should be taken up by congress, therefore sent in their remonstrance to that body, and declined attending. Mr. Thompson, secretary of congress, called on and requested them to attend, which they refused. He then requested to know what report he should return to congress, when he received for answer, that while congress sat as a court of judicatory authorized by the claiming states *ex parte*, and Vermont was not put on an equal footing, they should not again darken the doors of congress."

The remonstrance of the agents earnestly complained of the mode of trial adopted as partial and unfair, declaring that the state of Vermont could not accede to it without denying itself, and argued at some length against the alleged injustice of the proceeding. The agents, nevertheless, professed their readiness on the part of the state of Vermont "to return to congress the number of the inhabitants of the state liable to do military duty; and that the state should from year to year, during the continuance of the war with Great Britain, furnish their full proportion of troops with the other states, allowing congress to determine their quota, and that at the close of the war the dispute should be settled by the mediation of sovereign powers," and that such arrangement should not "be construed to take away the right any of the United States claim to have in or over Vermont." They further stated that they were willing to agree that some one or more of the legislatures of the disinterested states should act as mediators and settle the dispute. Or that congress should interfere to prevent the effusion of blood; but that "they reprobated every idea of congress sitting as a court of judicature to determine the dispute, by virtue of authority given them by the act or acts of the state or states, that make but one party." The remonstrance concluded as follows: "It gives us pungent grief that such an important cause at this juncture of affairs, on which our *all* depends, should be forced on by any gentlemen professing themselves friends to the cause of America, with such vehemence and spirit as appears on the part of the state of New York; and shall only add that if the matter be thus pursued, we stand ready to appeal to God and the world, who must be accountable for the awful consequences that may ensue."

This remonstrance bore date the 22d of September, and on the 27th the hearing was resumed, as appears by the following entry upon the journal.

"Congress proceeded in the order of the day respecting the jurisdiction of the tract of country, commonly called the New Hampshire Grants, all the parties being present, except Ira Allen and Stephen R. Bradley, who being notified, declined to attend; when the agent of the state of New Hampshire proceeded to state the evidence tending to prove that the tract of country, known by the name of the New Hampshire Grants, was within the state of New Hampshire, and that therefore the people inhabiting the said tract of country, have no right to a separate and independent jurisdiction. The gentlemen [Messrs Knowlton and Olcott] appearing in behalf of sundry inhabitants of the said Grants, having nothing to add, and pressing congress to come to a determination, withdrew."

"*Resolved*, That the further consideration of the subject be postponed."

The principal argument at this hearing, in behalf of New York, was made by Mr. Duane, the veteran leader on that side of the controversy. It was very elaborate, and, as written out by him, has been preserved in the archives of the New York Historical Society, and of which there is a copy in the office of the secretary of state at Montpelier. In regard to the original right of New York and the transactions of the settlers during the colonial period, the argument is substantially the same as that found in "The State of the Right," which had been prepared by him in 1773, and of which full notice has been before taken. The additional argument before congress was based upon the alleged acquiescence of the inhabitants of the Grants, more especially those to the eastward of the Green mountain, in the authority of New York, at a later date. This has also been already sufficiently noticed.

Of the argument made in behalf of New Hampshire, no particular account has been found. Judging from the statements in a letter from Gen. John Sullivan, the delegate having the matter in charge, to president Weare, dated Sept. 16, three days before the hearing commenced, the managers for New Hampshire must have relied for success more on grounds of policy than on those of a legal or equitable character. Gen. Sullivan says, "I have assisted the Yorkers in establishing the fact of an utter aversion of those people [the Vermonters] to live under their jurisdiction, and at the same time have taken care to maintain the harmony which has ever subsisted between them and New Hampshire. This I find is likely to have the effect intended; the members begin to see that if the lands are judged to New York the continent must be involved in a war to enforce the determination of congress, which can only be averted by adjudging it to New Hampshire, and I am convinced this will finally turn the scale in favor of New Hampshire."

It is probable that this apprehension of difficulty in enforcing a decision in favor of New York, was very unfavorable to her claim, but that it tended to strengthen that of New Hampshire is more doubtful. A determination in favor of the independence of Vermont would have equally avoided the danger of a civil war, but that as well as a decision in favor of New Hampshire, would have grievously affronted New York. All difficulty would be most effectually avoided by congress, by forbearing to make any decision.

Vermont had warm friends in Congress, who believed the oppression of New York fully justified her people in opposing the jurisdiction of that state, and political considerations also operated in her favor, with other members. The question in relation to the disposition of the vacant western lands which were claimed by Virginia and several other states, to the exclusion of the residue, had long agitated and divided congress, and had hitherto prevented the adoption of the articles of confederation by all the states. Of these claims, that of Virginia was the most extensive and important. It reached west to the Mississippi, and indefinitely to the northward, including the present six states of Kentucky, Ohio, Indiana, Illinois, Michigan and Wisconsin. North and South Carolina and Georgia, also claimed west to the Mississippi. New Jersey, Pennsylvania, Delaware and Maryland were among the states whose rights to the avails of the lands was denied, and they, with apparent reason, claimed that those lands wrested from the crown of Great Britain by the common exertions of all the states, should be appropriated for the common benefit. The articles of confederation, which contained no provision in regard to those lands; had been agreed to by some of the states under protest that the adoption of them should not be considered a waiver of their right to a proportionate share in their proceeds. But the state of Maryland, had absolutely refused to sign the articles, until an amendment should be inserted providing for a fair participation of all the states in them. New York had set up a vague claim to western territory by way of inheritance to the six nations of Indians, and her delegates acted with those of Virginia and the other claiming states. If Vermont were declared to be a part of New York, her power and influence would be increased, but if admitted a member of the confederation, another vote would be added in opposition to such exclusive claims. The question in regard to these lands doubtless influenced the action of many of the members, and operated with other considerations to prevent a decision in favor of New York.

Some of the difficulties encountered by the delegates of New York in their efforts to obtain the action of congress in their favor, may be seen from the following extract of a letter written by John Morin Scott, one of their number, to Gov. Clinton, dated September 26th. He says: "New Hampshire, represented by Gen. Sullivan, seems too favorable to the people of the Grants, and countenances an idea too prevalent in congress, that the dispute between New Hampshire and New York should be settled by a court of commissioners constituted agreeably to the articles of confederation. The in view is evident. It is to create delay and thereby to dis- age the subjects of our state, and strengthen the Vermonters. have, however, gone through with the evidence on our own part * *. I am at a loss what is best to be done. If we push r a determination we may gain it by a bare majority, and even nis depends upon the prospect we have of New Jersey. Mr. Duane is of opinion that Maryland will be with us. I differ with him. In short it seems to be the system of the smaller states to compel the larger (the western bounds of which are undefined) to large concessions. This they expect to effect by embarrassing us with respect to the settled parts of the country. Gen. Sullivan is sick which has suspended business for a few days. * * * I am of opinion the sooner we press the matter to its crisis, the better; for I fear the interest against us is growing. Not that I imagine a majority will express it by deciding against us, but that it may continually be done by procrastination."

To this letter Gov. Clinton returned an immediate answer, hoping that congress would be pressed to a decision, even if it should be carried "by only the vote of a single state." But all efforts of the New York delegates to obtain a decision in their favor were ineffectual. On the 29th of November, Mr. Duane wrote to Gov. Clinton, that the Vermont business remained quiet, but that he foresaw there must be a rehearing in consequence of the changes in several delegations.[1]

Dr. Williams, writing when the memory of this hearing before congress was fresh, thus speaks in regard to it in his history:

---

[1] *Clinton Papers*, Nos. 2856, 2865, 2981, 3181, 3215, 3240, 3258, 3393. *Jour. Cong.*, vol. 3, p. 462, 464, 465, 513, 518, 520, 526. *Slade*, 118, 124. *Ira Allen's Vermont*, p. 140-146. Ms. of B. H. Hall. *Cong. Doc.*, in state department at Washington, No. 40, vol. 1. *Journals of Vermont Assembly*, Oct. 14, 1780. *Williams's Vermont*, p. 257.

"At no time had the spirit of parties run higher than at this period. During the whole of this trial, it does not appear that either of the contending parties, had any idea of conciliatory measures; all seem to have been determined to effect their purposes. And although Vermont was not admitted to appear as one of the parties before congress, her expectations and prospects had at no time been so high. She well understood the ground, on which she stood, and it was generally believed in the other states, that some of her leading men would incline to join with Canada, and make the best terms they could with the British government, if no alternate was held out, but submission to the government of New York. In this state of the parties it was as dangerous to the American c to decide against Vermont, as against New Hampshire or New Y Congress felt and wisely endeavored to avoid the difficulty. question was made whether congress had the power to form a r state, within the limits of the union. Those who remember t virulence of these parties, and the precarious situation of th American contest at that time, will not wonder that congress found reasons to avoid coming to any decision at that period, for no decision could have been made, that would not have proved highly irritating to some of these states, already too much inflamed by the violence and duration of the contest."

CHAPTER XXVIII.

Invasion from Canada, a Truce, and Preparations for the Future Defence of the State.

1780-1781.

Military events of 1780 — Frontier forts garrisoned and militia in readiness for service — Their promptness commended by Gov. Clinton — Invasion from Canada in October and Capture of Fort George and Fort Ann on the New York frontier, and the destruction of Royalton, Vermont — Great alarm and flight from the New York border — Gen. Ethan Allen's truce with the enemy by which their farther ravages in New York and Vermont are prevented, and they retire to Canada — Accusations and complaints against Allen — He vindicates himself before the Vermont assembly, who approve of his conduct — Vermont assembly obtain provisions for the supply of troops for the ensuing year by assessing the several towns for their delivery in kind, and raise money and add to the power of the state by grants of land — The governor of Vermont, by circulars to the adjoining states, demands a relinquishment of their claims to her territory, and proposes a union with them for mutual defence against the common enemy — Massachusetts relinquishes her claim.

THE military events with which Vermont was connected in the year 1780 cannot be passed over without a brief notice. All the Continental troops being withdrawn from her territory, she was left entirely to her own resources and exertions for protection against the enemy in Canada. The forts at Rutland, Castleton and Pittsford were strengthened and were continually occupied by small garrisons of militia levies, and measures were taken to have the body of the militia held in readiness to turn out *en masse* when required. Two companies of rangers were also kept in constant service, for patrolling the frontiers and keeping watch for approaches of the enemy. The promptness and activity of the Vermonters against the common enemy was such, on one occasion, as to extort praise from the governor of New York. In the month of May Sir John Johnson, with a body of tories and Indians, made an unexpected irruption from Canada into the Mohawk valley and ravaged the country in the vicinity of his former residence at Johnstown. Gov. Clinton, with some militia from Albany, hastened to Lake George for the purpose of intercepting him on his return. At the south end of the lake, before crossing it, he dispatched a request to the commanding officer at Castleton to meet him at Ticonderoga with such force as he could muster. The next day after the call was received, Major Ebenezer Allen, of the Vermont rangers, wrote him that he had reached Mount Independence, with over two hundred men, and was in the immediate expectation of being joined by one hundred more, but that he had no boats, which he trusted the governor would furnish to enable him to cross over to Ticonderoga. Sir John by passing farther north and striking Lake Champlain at Crown Point made his escape. But Gov. Clinton, writing to the New York delegates in congress, was constrained to say that "the punctuality and readiness of the militia of the Grants in complying with his request with about two hundred and forty men, did them great honor."[1]

No serious invasions of the enemy were made during the summer, but early in October, Major Carleton came up Lake Champlain with a fleet of eight large vessels, containing upwards of one thousand men, regular troops, loyalists and Indians. Fort Ann was invested by a large force, and its garrison of fifty men was compelled to surrender. Captain Chipman commanded a part of Warner's regiment about eighty in number, at Fort George. On the morning of the 11th, he dispatched an express to Fort Edward for provisions, of which the post was nearly destitute. While on the way this person was fired upon by a party of twenty-five men, but he escaped and returned to the fort. Captain Chipman, supposing the party to consist of a scout from the enemy, sent out all his garrison except fourteen men. This detachment met the enemy a short distance from the fort, where a conflict ensued, in which almost every man was either killed or taken. The enemy then marched to Fort George, which, after a short resistance was surrendered by capitulation. On their way to Fort George they had burnt and destroyed all before them, and after demolishing the two forts which they had captured, they kept up continued demonstrations of making farther advances.

This invasion justly created great alarm. The militia of Vermont were called out and ordered to rendezvous at Castleton, under the command of Brig. Gen. Ethan Allen. Gov. Chittenden also sent to the militia of Berkshire county, Mass., for aid. The assembly, which was sitting at Bennington, adjourned for several days to enable the members to take the field. Gov. Clinton wrote from Albany to Gov. Chittenden, for assistance, and was answered on the 18th of October, that the militia of the state were at the north, but that he would send him those which were expected from Berkshire

---

[1] *Clinton Papers*, May 29 and June 1, 1780, No. 2973. *Life of Brant*, vol. 2, p. 81.

as soon as they should arrive, adding that the state over which he presided "were always ready to cooperate in any measures for the defence of the frontier." In northern New York there was a perfect panic, and few men could be rallied against the enemy. On the 18th, Col. Webster wrote Gov. Chittenden from White Creek (now Salem) that the enemy were in large force at Ticonderoga, that they had burned Ballstown and were on their way to Stillwater or Saratoga or Fort Edward, and earnestly asked for help. Gen. Schuyler on the 20th, wrote to Gov. Clinton in a similar strain of alarm, and a few days later Fort Edward was abandoned, the garrison retiring to Saratoga.

Simultaneously whit this invasion under Carleton, a party of about three hundred, most of whom were Indians, under the command of one Horton, a British lieutenant, had proceeded from Lake Champlain up Onion river and through the woods to Royalton on White river, which they reached the 16th of October. There they killed two persons, took about thirty prisoners, burnt twenty houses, killed a large number of cattle and committed other serious depredations. This irruption was a complete surprise, and before a sufficient force could be rallied to attack them the raiders had made their escape with their prisoners and such booty as they could carry off. At the same time Sir John Johnson, with a large force, principally Indians, was traversing the valley of the Mohawk, dooming the lives and property of the inhabitants to destruction. These three marauding expeditions were doubtless several parts of one concerted plan of the enemy.

Carleton's forces had passed to the westward of the Vermont settlements without molesting them. This forbearance was no doubt designed. The British ministry were aware of the position of Vermont towards New York and were desirous of profiting by the controversy. As early as March, 1779, Lord George Germain had written to Gen. Haldimand, who commanded in Canada, to give encouragement to the Vermonters. Similar directions had been subsequently repeated, and he had resolved to try the effect of a conciliatory policy towards them. There were citizens of Vermont, who had been captured by the enemy and were prisoners in Canada, and their friends had applied to Gov. Chittenden to effect their release. Among them were some officers of Col. Warner's regiment. He had accordingly, by the advice of his council, written to Gen. Haldimand, on the 27th of September, proposing a cartel for the exchange of prisoners. Gen. Haldimand had written a letter in

41

answer, acceding to the proposal, which letter Maj. Carleton, accompanied by one from himself, sent to Gen. Allen under a flag. Maj. Carleton's letter, dated October 26th, informed Gen. Allen that he had authorized the bearer of it, Capt. Sherwood, to treat with him or the governor on the subject, and proposed a cessation of hostilities during the continuance of the negotiation. To this proposal Gen. Allen assented, insisting, however, that the northern frontier of New York should be included in the armistice. "This additional territory," says Ira Allen in his history, "produced some altercation; for on the part of Maj. Carleton it disappointed his expedition; on the part of Gen. Allen it would have been exposing Vermont to many difficulties, had her general consented to a truce, and left the frontiers of a neighboring state exposed. However, in consideration of future prospects, Gen. Allen's proposition was admitted and a truce settled including the frontiers of New York to Hudson's river." The principal force of the enemy had by this time retired to Ticonderoga and Crown Point. On the 31st of October, when a quorum of the Vermont assembly again met, all the correspondence of Gen. Allen with the British officers and others while in command at Castleton, was laid before them by the governor, whereupon it was resolved "that this assembly do approve of the captain general and commander-in-chief's making proposals to his excellency Gen. Haldimand for settling a cartel for the exchange of prisoners, and further advise and command him to appoint and empower some suitable person or persons to further negociate the settlement of a cartel with Maj. Carleton agreeable to Gen. Haldimand's proposals for that purpose." It was also resolved, "that the captain general be and hereby is requested to discharge the militia and volunteers raised for the defense of the northern frontier." Although the New York officers had been informed by Gen. Allen of the arrangement for the cessation of arms, the alarm on their part continued. Rumors, apparently well founded, reached them that Carleton had received reenforcements from Canada, and was returning to renew his attacks. The conduct of Gen. Allen appeared suspicious, and apprehensions were entertained that by the withdrawal of the Vermont troops New York was to be left to the mercy of a cruel enemy. Under date of the 31st of October, Gen. Schuyler wrote from Saratoga to Gov. Clinton, that the conduct of some people at the eastward was alarmingly mysterious; that a flag under a pretext of settling a cartel with Vermont had been on the Grants, that Allen had disbanded his militia, and that the enemy in number upwards of sixteen hundred were rapidly advancing upon the New York frontier. He requested the governor to "entreat Gen. Washington for new continental troops," and begged him to hasten himself to Saratoga. Gen. Schuyler also wrote the same day to Gen. Washington giving an account of the capture of Fort George, the ravages of the enemy, and the conduct of the Vermonters, so far as it had come to his knowledge, stating his belief, that the sending of a flag for the exchange of prisoners was a mere cover to some design of the enemy, and expressing the strongest apprehensions that they would be unable to raise a sufficient force to resist their attacks. The next day Schuyler wrote to Clinton that the militia at Fort Edward had all left, and that Col. Gansevoort would probably be obliged to abandon it, that the enemy were approaching Skenesborough, and that the people were in a panic and removing their families. The alarm was unfounded. The enemy made no further demonstrations against the frontier, and soon returned down the lake to Canada.

The transactions of Gen. Allen with the invading enemy on this occasion excited much comment throughout the country, often of an unfavorable character. There was nothing in the fact of negotiating a cartel for the exchange of prisoners which was out of the common course of events, Col. Gansevoort of the New York forces being at the same time in correspondence with the British officers for the like purpose. But the armistice seemed a mystery which many were not disposed to have solved by the mere fact of the existence of a desire on the part of the enemy to detach the Vermonters from the American cause, without also connecting with it a willingness on their part to be detached. Surely there was no necessity for this additional motive in order to account for the measure. The cessation of arms, offered by the enemy, would save the frontiers from the invasion and ravages of a powerful army and would prevent for the time being the effusion of blood, and it was, in all respects, highly advantageous, to the inhabitants of the state. These advantages certainly furnished a sufficient, good, and commendable motive for acceding to it, without looking about to find a bad one.

But notwithstanding the palpable benefit of the measure to the state, suspicions were entertained that something wrong had been done, and the desire for a public investigation of the matter was very general. Charges were made against Allen in the assembly. On the 3d of November, three days after the militia had been discharged, a remonstrance against him was presented to that body by Capt. William Hutchins, and the next day another by Simeon Hathaway. The precise character of these cannot now be ascertained, the papers not having been preserved. That they charged him with misconduct in entering into the armistice there is no doubt.

The most satisfactory account that can now be given of the proceeding will be furnished by a copy of all that appears on the journal of the assembly in relation to it. The following is such copy.

" Friday, November 3, 1780.

A remonstrance signed William Hutchins was handed to the speaker and ordered that the consideration of the remonstrance be deferred till to morrow morning, nine o'clock.

" Saturday, Nov. 4.

The remonstrance of Captain Hutchins, which was referred to this day was read and after some debate was dismissed; after which Gen. Allen made a speech in the house to the assembly in which he observed there was uneasiness among some of the people upon account of his conduct, etc., and that he would resign his commission, and if the assembly thought best to give him the command at any time he would endeavor to serve the state according to his abilities.

" Saturday, Nov. 4, 2 o'clock, P.M.

Resolved, That this assembly will take the matter of the remonstrance signed Simeon Hathaway for himself and others unto consideration at some convenient time."

Afterwards on the same day, " Ordered that the consideration of the remonstrance signed " Simeon Hathaway for himself and others " be postponed until 2 o'clock in the afternoon, Monday next.

Resolved, That the resolution passed for dismissing the remonstrance signed by Capt. Wm. Hutchins, be and is hereby reconsidered, and thereupon ordered that said remonstrance be taken into consideration on Monday next, 2 o'clock, afternoon.

" Monday, Nov. 6, 2 o'clock P. M.

"The remonstrance signed by Capt. Hutchins, and the remonstrance signed by Simeon Hathaway for himself and others, which were referred to this day were taken into consideration. And Capt. Hutchins's remonstrance was read, and the other read and while reading Gen. Allen rose up and said he would not hear any more of it as it was beneath his character to sit there and hear such false and ignominious assertions against him, and went out of the house. After some debate a member of the house was desired to notify him that the assembly would proceed to take the matter of Capt. Hutchins's into consideration and would hear the parties. Gen. Allen accordingly attended and requested to know of the house whether they would proceed to hear the remonstrance of Mr. Hathaway, and if they did he would not attend to either, and being answered that they both would be taken into consideration he went out of the house. And after some debate and taking the evidence of Joseph Fay and Stephen R. Bradley, Esquires, the matter was postponed till to-morrow.

"Tuesday, Novr 7.

"The remonstrance signed Simeon Hathaway which was referred to this day was read and after some debate was referred until this afternoon, 2 o'clock. Adjourned until 2 o'clock, afternoon.

"Met according to adjournment. The remonstrance which was signed Simeon Hathaway, &c., which was referred until this afternoon was taken under consideration and after some debate,

"*Resolved*, That the remonstrance signed Simeon Hathaway for himself and others be dismissed by reason of the undue form thereof.

"*Resolved*, That Capt. Hutchins have liberty to withdraw his remonstrance against Gen. Ethan Allen.

"*Resolved*, That a committee of two be appointed to return the thanks of this house to Gen. Ethan Allen for the good service he has done this state since his appointment of brigadier general, and that this house do accept his resignation as brigadier general according to his offer made this house on Saturday last.

"The members chosen were Mr. S. Robinson and Mr. Jones."

Messrs. Fay and Bradley, whose evidence was taken, had been on the staff of Gen. Allen while at Castleton, and their testimony seems to have satisfied the house that nothing improper had been done by him.[1]

The legislature at this session adopted active measures for recruiting the finances of the state, and for providing for its future defence against the common enemy. The depreciated and uncertain value of the floating Continental currency, and the almost entire absence

---

[1] *Clinton Papers*, No. 3277, 3281, 3282, 3324, 3328. *Ethan Allen Papers*, p. 331–337, 355. *Haldimand Papers*, vol. 1, p. 515, 517. *Jour. of Vermont Assembly*. *I. Allen's Vermont*, p. 151, 152. *Life of Brant*, vol. 2, p. 129–135. *Thompson's Vermont*, p. 69, 70. *Life of Warner*, p. 75. *Sparks's Washington*, vol. 7, p. 179, 180, 269. Gen. Allen was rechosen brigadier general of one of the brigades of militia, April 11, 1781, but declined to accept the appointment, upon which Gen. Samuel Safford was elected.

of specie, together with the confusion incident to the frontier position of the state, and its controversies with its neighbors, rendered it inexpedient, if not impracticable, to raise money for state purposes by direct taxation. But an efficient law was passed for collecting in kind large quantities of beef, pork, flour, and other articles of provisions, for the supply of the troops for the ensuing year, which were to be delivered to the commissary general by the several towns, according to their respective quotas designated in the act. In order to raise money for the payment of troops, and to meet the other expenses of the government, provision was made for an extensive disposition of ungranted lands.

As early as the June session of the assembly in 1779, Ira Allen had been appointed surveyor general, and directed to procure at the expense of the state copies of all charters of lands lying in the state from whatever government they might have been issued, and to make a general plan of the state, showing what lands had been granted and what not. In undertaking to perform this duty he met with much embarrassment. The record book of charters granted by New Hampshire had been taken to England by Gov. John Wentworth, when he fled from the colony at the beginning of the revolution, and many of the original charters had been carried to New York, either for confirmation or in protest against new grants from that colony, and with the city, were in possession of the enemy. From those which could be procured from the towns and other sources, and from the information that could be otherwise obtained, Mr. Allen made a plan of the state, which was presented to the legislature at this session. Notwithstanding the opposition of New York and New Hampshire to the independence of Vermont and the equivocal position of congress, confidence in the firm and permanent foundation of its government, was very general throughout the country, and the office of the secretary of state was flooded with applications for grants of land from persons residing without the state; as well as from those within it. The whole subject was referred to a joint committee of the council and assembly, who made a report (Nov. 4), that from an examination of the multiplicity of the petitions in the secretary's office and the several claims to the same lands which had appeared since their appointment, and of the plan returned by the surveyor general, they found "that it was impracticable at that time to grant the prayer of each petition, partly for want of proper surveys, and partly, as the committee conceived, for want of unappropriated lands in the state whereon to make such grants." The committee, however, recommended the granting of forty-eight townships, for most of which charters were soon afterwards issued. Each charter included about thirty-six square miles, or twenty-three thousand and forty acres, divided into sixty-five to seventy-five shares, which were granted to that number of individuals designated by name, besides five shares for public purposes, viz: One for a college in the state and one for a county grammar school, these two to be disposed of under the direction of the legislature; one share for the first settled minister; one for the support of a gospel ministry; and one for the support of schools in the town. Each share would therefore cover something over three hundred acres. By these grants a considerable sum was obtained for the use and defense of the state. Ira Allen, in an address to the public in 1786, speaking of the grants, says: "this mode of procuring money made the state many firm and interested friends abroad, amongst which were some of the first characters in the United States." It may be added that among the grantees were many of the officers and soldiers of the Continental army. In making these grants the lands which had been patented by New York after the king's prohibition of 1767, were treated as vacant and unappropriated.[1]

Congress not having acceded to the offer of Vermont to become a member of the federal union, the administration of the state now prepared to act upon the measure indicated by Gov. Chittenden at the close of his letter to the president of that body, of the 25th of July preceding, viz: that of applying for such union to the governments of the states separately. Circulars, making such offer, and enclosing his letter to the president of congress, were accordingly addressed by him to the governors of New Hampshire, Massachusetts, Connecticut, and New York. To the three first named of them, he presented the proposition of a union with Vermont for the purposes of defence, and in support of it stated that it was probable the enemy in Canada would be reenforced before the conclusion of the next campaign; that owing to the greater advantages of navigation by the lakes which they possessed, they could suddenly bring their whole force into Vermont; that this would no doubt be the object of the next campaign unless measures should be taken to prevent it; and that in such an event the people of Vermont would either be sacrificed, or be obliged to retire into the interior parts of the United States for safety, or be under the disagreeable necessity of making such terms with the British as might remain in their power. Of

[1] *Jour. Vt. Assembly*, June 3, 1779, Oct. 21, 1779, Oct. 25, and Nov. 4, 1780. Ira Allen in *Vermont Gazette*, Aug. 7, 14, and 21, 1786.

New Hampshire and Massachusetts it was demanded that, prior to such union, they should abandon their claims of jurisdiction over every part of Vermont. To this demand it does not appear that New Hampshire made any special reply, but the legislature of Massachusetts resolved to relinquish their claim of sovereignty over the state, provided congress should acknowledge her to be an independent state and admit her into the union. The government of Connecticut was understood to be favorable to the independence of Vermont, but no definite response to Gov. Chittenden's request is found. The proceedings of New York on the application of Gov. Chittenden require a more full consideration.[1]

---

[1] *Letter of Gov. Chittenden to Gov. Clinton* of November 22, and to the other governors of December 12, 1780. *Journals of Mass. Senate and Assembly,* March 8, 1781.

CHAPTER XXIX.

Governor Clinton prevents a Settlement of the Controversy with Vermont by threatening to prorogue the Assembly.

1780--1781.

Letter of Gov. Chittenden to Gov. Clinton, demanding the relinquishment by the legislature of New York, of their jurisdiction over Vermont, and proposing a union of the two states for defence against British invasions — Circumstances favorable to the success of the proposal — Gov. Clinton's hostile message transmitting the letter to the assembly — Resolutions of the senate looking to the acknowledgment of the independence of Vermont — The resolutions taken up in the House — Message of Gov. Clinton threatening to prorogue the assembly if they persisted in considering the resolutions — The governor's action prevents further proceedings.

THE demand by Gov. Chittenden of the governor and legislature of New York, for the relinquishment of the claim of jurisdiction of that state over the territory of Vermont, and his offer of a union with that state for mutual defence against the common enemy, was couched in the following direct language.

"State of Vermont,
In council, Arlington, Nov. 22, 1780.

"Sir: Inclosed I transmit your excellency a copy of my letter to congress of the 25th of July last, and on a full examination of the controversy between the state of New York and this state, and duly considering the present peculiar circumstances of both states, I am inclined to make a positive demand on the legislature of the state over whom you preside, to give up and fully relinquish their claim to jurisdiction over this state; and also propose to them to join in a solid union with this state for mutual defence against the British forces which invade the American states, particularly such part as make incursions on the frontiers of the two states from the province of Quebec.

"Such a union for the reciprocal advantage of both governments, I am willing to ratify and confirm on the part of this state.

"Colonel Ira Allen who delivers this, waits your answer to these proposals.

"In behalf of the council and general assembly, I have the honor to be with great esteem your excellency's

Very obedient humble servant,

THOMAS CHITTENDEN.

"His Excellency George Clinton Esq.,
Governor etc., of the state of New York,
To be communicated to the legislature thereof."

It could not have been entirely without some hope of success that this communication was made. Many circumstances favored the application; New York had recently had a full hearing before congress, in which her claim had been presented to that body with great earnestness and ability. All her efforts to procure a decision in her favor had resulted in disappointment, and there was no reasonable prospect that congress could ever be induced to enforce the submission of the Vermonters. The idea of compelling their submission by the power of New York alone, though sometimes suggested in threatening language by Gov. Clinton, and perhaps by others, could never have been seriously entertained. The aristocratic government of New York was weak in the affections of her own people, and many of them who were acquainted with the origin and nature of the controversy, sympathized with the revolters, rather than with their adversaries. A coercive experiment, as has already been seen, had been tried during the colonial period, under more favorable circumstances than the present, and had proved a complete failure. There was much less hope of success now.

During the four years that the New Yorkers had been vainly importuning congress to interfere in their behalf, Vermont had been in the actual exercise of an independent jurisdiction, and her affairs had been conducted in such manner as to inspire general confidence in the strength and permanency of her institutions. Her power to protect, not only her own frontier, but that of New York also, from invasions of the enemy, had been recently shown by the promptness with which she had mustered an imposing force on the northern border, as well as by her diplomatic skill in inducing the enemy to retire without attempting contemplated ravages; while on the other hand the weakness and imbecility of New York had been exhibited in the utter inability of her officers to assemble her militia for frontier protection. "A solid union for mutual defence against the British force," such as was proposed by Gov. Chittenden, must have appeared quite desirable, at least to that large portion of the inhabitants of New York who were exposed to invasions from Canada.

The legislature of New York was to meet at Albany on the 2d of January, 1781. Thither Col. Ira Allen repaired to deliver Gov. Chittenden's letter. But Gov. Clinton was not there until sometime after that date, and a quorum of the two houses for the transaction of business was not formed until the last day of that month. Mr. Allen, however, remained in Albany and made the object of his mission known to such of the senators and members as were in attendance and to the public. The proposal met with much favor, and a compliance with it was undoubtedly desired by the mass of the people in the northern part of the state. A petition to the legislature at this session adopted at a meeting of the inhabitants of Schaghticoke after enumerating many other grievances concluded as follows: "It is thought very essential by the people of this district, to have a reconciliation formed with the people of the eastern district of this state which would contribute greatly to the safety of the frontiers." A petition of the committees of the several districts of the county of Albany prepared and signed at a meeting held at Kinderhook was still more explicit on this subject. It declared it to be a serious grievance, "That the district of country called the state of Vermont, notwithstanding their manly firmness and attachment to the freedom and independence of America, have been opposed by this state in obtaining the benefit of a confederation with the United States to the great disadvantage of the frontiers of this state in their general defence against the common enemy."

But the proposal of Vermont encountered the decided and earnest opposition of Gov. Clinton.

On the 5th of February he transmitted Governor Chittenden's letter to the assembly, with the following characteristic message:

"Gentlemen: You will receive with this message a letter from Thomas Chittenden dated the 22d of Nov. last, making a positive demand on the legislature to give up and fully relinquish the jurisdiction of this state over the part thereof generally distinguished by the name of the New Hampshire Grants, with a copy of his letter to congress of the 25th of July last.

"Nothing but the desire of giving you the fullest information of every matter of public concern, could induce me to lay before you a demand, not only so insolent in its nature and derogatory to the honor of the state, and the true interests of your constituents but tending to subvert the authority of congress (to whom the determination of the controversy is solemnly submitted) and establish a principle destructive in its consequences to the power and happiness of the United States.

"George Clinton.

"Albany, Feb. 5, 1781."

This message, with the accompanying letters, was referred in the house to a committee of nine members and in the senate to a committee of the whole.

On the 21st of February the subject was considered in the senate, Robert R. Livingston, chancellor of the state, who had been appointed by the legislature a special delegate to attend to the controversy in congress and who had represented the state at the hearing before that body the previous September, was called before the committee and examined in relation to the matter. After due deliberation, the committee reported a series of resolutions looking to an adjustment of the controversy, on the basis of recognizing the New Hampshire Grants as an independent state. The resolutions, which are too long for insertion here, after affirming the right of New York to the government of the territory in dispute, declared, in substance, that it was inexpedient further to insist upon such right, and provided for the appointment of commissioners to confer with commissioners from Vermont, with full powers to adjust and settle the terms upon which the state would make a cession of her jurisdiction over that district. This report of the committee was adopted the same day by the senate with but one dissenting vote, and sent to the house of representatives. In that body after the consideration of the resolutions had been once or twice postponed, they were made the special order of the day for the 27th of February. On that day the entry on the assembly journal is as follows, viz :

"The order of the day being read, for taking into consideration the resolutions of the honorable the senate, relative to the tract of country commonly called the New Hampshire Grants, Mr. Speaker put the question, whether the house will now proceed to take the said resolutions into consideration. Debates arose and it was carried in the affirmative."

Upon the declaration of this vote, the governor's private secretary, who, it seems, had been waiting the result, announced a message from his Excellency which was immediately read. In his message the governor stated that he had received information "in a manner that claimed his credit, that certain resolutions, originating in the senate, had been sent to the assembly for concurrence, proposing the relinquishment of jurisdiction to that part of the state commonly designated by the name of the New Hampshire Grants," and declaring that "if the house should agree to carry those resolutions into effect, the duties of his office would oblige him to exercise the authority vested in him by the constitution and *prorogue them.*"

This message, threatening to put an abrupt end to the session of the assembly, in case they should proceed to concur with the senate in the passage of the resolutions, had its intended effect of preventing their adoption. But for this extraordinary threat to exercise an odious power, which has since been expunged from the constitution, there is every reasonable probability that the controversy would have been brought to a speedy and happy close, and all the troubles and heart burnings which resulted from it, for several succeeding years, would have been thereby prevented. Gov. Clinton, not only on this occasion, but on all others, during the whole period of the controversy, manifested an obstinate determination that no terms, short of absolute submission to the authority of New York, should be entertained. It is not doubted that Gov. Clinton possessed many commendable qualities as a citizen and a patriot. A friendly biographer says of him, that "his patriotism was undoubted," that he possessed frankness and amiability in private life; was kind and affectionate in his personal relations, warm in his friendship and decided in his enmity." There needs no stronger proof that he was "decided in his enmity," than that which is furnished by his uniform and untiring hostility to the claims of the Vermonters. But for this very "decided enmity," there is little room for doubt that their independence would have been acknowledged by New York, and the state admitted a member of the Confederation ten years earlier than its actual occurrence in 1791.[1]

Gen. Schuyler was a member of the senate and took an active and leading part in the proposed measure of conciliation. His residence at Albany and Saratoga in the vicinity of the disputed district and his extensive intercourse with its inhabitants while in the military command of the northern department, together with the knowledge he had acquired of the disposition of the members of the continental congress during his former and recent service in that body, had undoubtledly made him better acquainted than any other public man of the state, with the true nature and character of the controversy. He had no confidence that congress would effectually interfere in behalf of New York. The hatred of the Vermonters to the government and institutions of that state, embittered by a controversy of fifteen years duration, in which they believed they were contending for their dearest rights, rendered any thought

---

[1] *Assembly Papers*, Albany. *Clinton Papers*, No. 3384 and 3616. *Journals of N. Y. Senate and Assembly*. *Street's Council of Revision*, p. 111.

of undertaking to subdue them by force of arms out of the question; and any effort to reclaim them by proffers of conciliation, which they ever distrusted, equally so. Despairing of any other means of reconciliation, and fearing that if the hostility of New York towards them was allowed to continue, they might be driven to resort for aid to the common enemy, Gen. Schuyler appears to have entered heartily into the measure of providing for the acknowledgment of their independence. On the 21st of February, 1781, the day on which the conciliatory resolutions were adopted by the senate, he wrote Gen. Washington that he had made a motion in that body looking to the creation of "a new state," and on the 4th of May following he wrote Washington again in relation to the Vermonters, saying: "I was anxious for ceding the jurisdiction beyond a twenty mile line from Hudson's river, that their independence might be immediately acknowledged, and they made useful to the common cause; but the governor put a stop to the business, 'as the affair was referred to the decision of congress.' I sincerely wish they would speedily decide, acknowledge them independent and admit them into the union." Chancellor Livingston who was examined before the senate, and many other prominent men of New York are presumed to have concurred with Gen. Schuyler in this movement. That it was founded in wisdom and enlightened statesmanship appears to be established and confirmed by subsequent events.[1]

The course taken by Gov. Clinton was not justified by the terms of the constitution and was clearly unparliamentary. He had the power by the constitution to prorogue the legislature. But to undertake to influence the deliberations of either house upon a measure properly before it, by a formal threat to put an end to the session if it was proceeded with, was a direct attack upon the freedom of debate, and a palpable breach of legislative privilege. Such was probably the light in which it was viewed by the senate. On the 12th of March that body on motion of Mr. Schuyler proceeded to the consideration of the governor's threatening message, when it was resolved to present him an address "on the subject matter" of it, and it was ordered that Mr. Schuyler and Mr. Platt should prepare and report a draft of such address. This was about two weeks before the close of the session, and nothing further is found on the journal in relation to it.

---

[1] *Sparks's Rev. Cor.*, vol. 3, p. 213. *Sparks's Washington*, vol. 8, p. 43.

Gov. Clinton, in a letter addressed to Gen. McDougall, one of the New York delegates in congress, under date of April 6th, attributes the neglect of further action on the subject by the senate, to an official letter from that delegate to him of the 12th of March, in which it was in substance stated, that the recent cession by New York of western territory to the United States, had removed the cause of the opposition to New York with the delegates of several of the states; and that a decision in her favor might soon be expected. It is scarcely necessary to say that this expectation was delusive. Gov. Clinton speaks of the effect of the letter as follows: "Your official letter informing that there was reason to hope for a speedy and just decision of the controversy by congress, arrived very opportunely. It changed the sentiments of some, and for the present stopped the mouths of all, and occasioned the laying aside of a long address moved in the senate in consequence of my message to the assembly, but not yet agreed to."

Gov. Clinton in his letter, admits that the measure of reconciliation proposed by the senate, was approved by "the greater part of the citizens of Albany and Schenectady, and the inhabitants of the northern frontier," and that his "message to the assembly declaring his intentions to prorogue them, was unpopular in Albany." He says, however, that "if the measure had succeeded, it would have reflected lasting ignominy and disgrace upon the state." Twenty years later he might, perhaps, have looked upon the matter in a different light.[1]

During the early part of these proceedings at Albany the legislature of Vermont was in session at Windsor. In order to be in readiness to act upon any favorable response to the application of Gov. Chittenden, the assembly on the 17th of February chose, by ballot, Col. Ira Allen and Major Joseph Fay "agents to wait upon the legislature of the state of New York at Albany, to agree upon and establish the line" between the two states. A committee was appointed to join from the council to prepare and report instructions for the agents. Five days afterwards, as the assembly was about to adjourn, the whole subject of instructing the agents and of agreeing upon and settling the boundary was committed to the governor and council. On the 7th of March, after the receipt of information of Gov. Clinton's threatening message and the suspension thereupon of further action on the subject by the New York assembly, the council at a meeting at Arlington, voted "not to send

---

[1] *N. Y. Senate Journals. Clinton Papers,* No. 3575, 3616.

the agents to Albany or to write any further to the general assembly of New York at present." [1]

The failure of this attempt to put a happy end to the controversy which for a time promised to be entirely successful, and the arbitrary and abrupt manner in which it was defeated, served to exasperate still further the feelings of the Vermonters towards the government of New York, and furnished them with an additional apology for the retaliatory measure to which they soon afterwards resorted.

---

[1] *Vermont Assembly Journals,* Feb. 17 and 22, 1781. *Council Journals,* Feb. 22 and March 7, 1781.

CHAPTER XXX.

ENCROACHMENTS OF VERMONT ON THE TERRITORIES OF NEW YORK AND NEW HAMPSHIRE.

1780-1781.

Attempts of the friends of New York in Eastern Vermont, to form a new state in the valley of the Connecticut — Annexation of New Hampshire towns west of Mason's Grant to Vermont on their application — Petition of inhabitants of New York to the eastward of Hudson's river, for a union with Vermont — Proposals accepted and union formed.

WHILE the events of which an account has been given in the preceding chapter, were occuring to the westward of Vermont, others of no less importance were in progress on the other side of the state. The inhabitants along the two sides of Connecticut river had settled their lands under New Hampshire charters, were similar in their character and habits, and had like notions of government. Although many of them were satisfied with the different governments to which they respectively belonged, others were desirous of entering into some new organization of a state whose seat of government would be established upon that river. This object would be accomplished, either by annexing the whole of Vermont to New Hampshire, or by dividing Vermont by the ridge of the Green mountain, and uniting the eastern part with that portion of New Hampshire lying west of Mason's grant. Either of these would have Connecticut river nearly in the centre of the territory, and ensure the placing of the state capital upon its bank. The same result would doubtless be effected by attaching the territory in New Hampshire west of the Mason line to the whole of Vermont, as much the largest part of the new jurisdiction would be east of the Green mountain. All these projects had their friends, as had also the plan of annexing the eastern half of Vermont to New Hampshire; and when the resolve of congress, of the 27th of September, 1780, declining, after a full hearing, to decide the long pending controversy, became known, the subject of a new state organization was extensively agitated.

Among the earliest to move in the matter were the supporters of the New York jurisdiction in the southeastern part of Vermont. They had struggled long and earnestly to maintain their favorite jurisdiction, in the hope of eventual aid from congress. This hope they felt had failed them. New York was powerless to protect them, and there seemed no chance left for them but to submit quietly to the government of Vermont, or to connect themselves with some other state organization. They resolved to attempt the latter alternative. A convention of the New York committees of the several towns in that section of Vermont was called for the 31st of October, at which a committee of thirteen, consisting of Luke Knowlton, Hilkiah Grout, Oliver Lovell, John Sargeant, Micah Townsend, Jonathan Hunt, Simon Stevens, Charles Phelps, Benjamin Henry, James Clay, Elkanah Day, Thomas Cutler and Barzilla Rice, was appointed to take into consideration the feasibility of a new government, and to meet and consult with committees or conventions of the inhabitants on both sides of Connecticut river. The object of the meeting at which this committee was appointed was declared to be, to devise such measures as should be calculated "to unite in one political body all the inhabitants from Mason's grant on the east to the height of land on the west side of Connecticut river." The chairman of this committee was Luke Knowlton, who had represented the Vermont friends of New York at the recent hearing before congress, and who had lately returned from Philadelphia. All the others had, up to this time, been active and prominent adherents of the New York jurisdiction. Conventions for a comparison of views, and for consultation were soon afterwards held at Charlestown and Walpole, on the New Hampshire side of the river. At this latter convention the report of a committee was approved in favor of uniting all the New Hampshire Grants on both sides of the river under one state jurisdiction, and it was declared that "from the best authority that could be obtained, it appeared that the agent of the state of New Hampshire was endeavoring to confirm a division of the Grants, contrary to their true interests; which had given the people on the Grants just occasion to rouse and exert themselves in support of an union of the whole." It was then recommended as the means of preserving harmony and arriving at a proper result that a convention from every town in the Grants should be held at Charlestown, on the third Tuesday of the ensuing January, at which the whole subject should be considered and finally acted upon. All parties appear to have acquiesced in this suggestion.

Forty-three towns, situated on the two sides of Connecticut river, were represented in this convention. Much pains appears to have been taken by influential men in New Hampshire to obtain a majority in favor of attaching either the whole or the eastern part of Vermont to that state. But after full discussion, a large majority of the convention was found to be in favor of joining the already established government of Vermont. Upon which, twelve of the delegates protested against the proceedings, and withdrew from the convention, most of whom were members of the New Hampshire legislature. The convention then appointed a committee to confer with the assembly of Vermont, which was to hold a session at Windsor early in the ensuing month, and adjourned to meet at the same time at Cornish on the Connecticut river opposite Windsor.

On the 10th of February, the Charlestown committee made application to the Vermont legislature for a union of the towns west of Mason's grant with that state. About the same time a petition was presented by sundry inhabitants living to the westward of Vermont for a like union with the state, of the territory lying to the eastward of Hudson's river. The petitioners prayed for protection against the enemy in Canada, declaring that they were left to the mercy of the enemy by New York, and that unless Vermont would receive them into union "they should be obliged to remove with their families and effects into the interior parts of the country for safety."

The propriety of complying with these two applications was discussed in a joint committee of the whole council and assembly, and the views of the committee were embodied in a report, in which a concise history of the origin and progress of the hostile proceedings of the people and governments of the adversary states towards the inhabitants of Vermont was given, tending to show that the extension of the jurisdiction of the state to the east and west, as asked for, had become a necessary measure of self-defence against the unjust claims of those states, which were striving by every possible means to increase their territories and power by the extinguishment and annihilation of Vermont. Such extensions of jurisdiction were also declared to be just to those who asked for them, and necessary to the adoption of proper means for the defence of the frontiers against the common enemy. In conclusion the committee recommended, "that the legislature of the state do lay a jurisdictional claim to all the lands situated east of Connecticut river, north of Massachusetts, and south of latitude forty-five, and that they do not exercise jurisdiction for the time being." It was also recommended that a like jurisdictional claim, but not to be exercised for the time being, should be made to all the land situate north of the north line of Massachusetts, extended to the Hudson, and to the east of that river. These recommendations were approved by the legislature, and a joint resolution making the claims of jurisdiction was adopted.

In accordance with this resolution, negotiations were immediately entered into with the Cornish convention for settling the terms upon which the eastern union should be consummated, which in a few days were mutually agreed upon. They were in substance, that the constitution of the state of Vermont should remain unchanged until it should be altered in the mode therein pointed out; that as soon as circumstances should permit, the legislature of the state should apply to congress to be admitted into the confederation, and that after such admission, congress might determine questions of disputed boundaries; that the expenses and losses of the several towns on both sides of Connecticut river, occasioned by the war, should thereafter be equitably adjusted; and that a general act of amnesty and oblivion should be passed by the legislature for all offences and acts of trespass committed against the authority of the state by persons under a claim of being subjects of New York, and all suits, prosecutions and judgments against them, should be discharged and annulled. Other provisions of less importance were made, and it was agreed that the question of forming the union on such terms, should be submitted to the several towns in the state of Vermont, and to the towns to about twenty miles east of Connecticut river, and that if two thirds of the towns on each side of the river approved of the union, it should be considered as ratified and completed. The assembly then adjourned to meet again at Windsor on the first Wednesday of the ensuing April.

At the April session it appeared that the requisite number of towns on both sides of Connecticut river had voted for the union, and it was accordingly declared to be consummated. Thirty-five members, representing twenty-eight towns east of the river, then took seats in the assembly.

It has already been seen that at the first organization of the state in 1778, it had been divided into two counties, Bennington on the west side of the Green mountain and Cumberland on the east. At the session of the assembly in February, 1781, a new division had been made. Bennington county was circumscribed to its present limits, and the towns to the northward of it were formed into the county of Rutland. Cumberland county was made to constitute three counties, viz: Windham, Windsor and Orange, the two former having about the same extent as at present, and the latter embracing all the territory to the northward of the county of Windsor. At the April session of 1781, the towns on the east side of the Connecticut opposite to the counties of Orange and Windsor, were annexed to those counties respectively, and the towns opposite the county of Windham, were erected into a new county by the name of Washington. Provision was also made for transferring the suits which were pending in the New Hampshire counties of Cheshire and Grafton to the proper counties organized under the Vermont authority.

Other necessary measures for perfecting the eastern union having been taken, the legislature turned its attention to the subject of that which had been proposed to the westward of the state.[1]

Additional petitions for a union with Vermont, having at this session been received from inhabitants residing between the west line of the state and Hudson's river, the subject was again discussed in committee of the whole, and a report was made in which the petitioners were designated as "the people inhabiting that part of the former government over which Gov. Philip Skene was to preside, to which the legislature at their session in February last laid a jurisdictional claim." The report recommended to them to choose members to attend a convention at Cambridge, on the second Wednesday of the ensuing May, to consider and act upon the subject. It advised the legislature to appoint a committee to meet the convention with power to agree upon articles of union, the articles to be submitted to the several districts of the territory, and that if approved, they should choose members to represent them in the assembly of the state. This report appears to have met with considerable opposition from members of towns near Connecticut river, and especially from those lately admitted to a union from the east side of it. It was, however, approved and adopted by 48 ayes to 39 nays. A joint committee from the council and assembly was appointed to attend the Cambridge convention, who agreed upon the terms of a union, and reported the same to the legislature at its session holden at Bennington, on the second Wednesday of June following.[2]

The situation of the inhabitants of this district was peculiarly alarming. They formed the northern frontier of New York, but that state had failed to protect them from invasions of the enemy. Their memorials to the legislature for aid had been ineffectual. They had the previous winter hoped for the settlement of the controversy with Vermont, and were greatly dissatisfied with the conduct of Gov. Clinton in preventing it. In point of fact, the state government of New York, by reason of its unpopularity and the general distress, was utterly unable to furnish them any adequate

[1] *Hall's E. Vt.*, p. 400–402, 424, 4. *Slade*, p. 128–137, 427, 428. *Journal of Assembly*, Feb. 7th, 10th, 14th, to 21st, 1781, and April 5th. *Williams's Vt.*, p. 258. *I. Allen's Vt.*, p. 149.

[2] *Jour. Vt. Assembly*, April 11th, 1781. *Slade*, 138.

security against the ravages of the enemy from Canada. Of this there is no doubt. Col. Stone, a writer friendly to New York, in his *Life of Brant*, represents the condition of affairs in the state at this period as truly deplorable. "So wretchedly supplied," he says, "were the small garrisons from Albany northward and westward, both in respect to food and clothing, that it was only with the utmost difficulty that the officers could keep the soldiers upon duty. Ravaged as the Mohawk country had been the preceding summer and autumn, no supplies could be drawn from the diminished and impoverished inhabitants remaining in those settlements; and it was equally difficult to procure supplies either at Albany or below, or eastwardly beyond that city."

So great and universal was the distress for provisions, that Gen. Clinton, on the 29th of March, wrote to the governor, "I am hourly under apprehensions that the remaining different posts occupied for the defence of the frontiers of this state will be abandoned, and the country left open to the ravages of the enemy." On the 5th of May Gen. Clinton again wrote the governor, "From present appearances, I am convinced that the troops will abandon the frontier." * * * "I have repeatedly called for assistance from every quarter, but could obtain none." "Great blame," says Col. Stone, "was imputed to congress, and likewise to the state government, for allowing the commissariat to come to such a deplorable pass. The resources of the country were known to be abundant for the comfort and sustenance of a much larger army than was at that time in the field." In the midst of this distress the Mohawk country was threatened by the Indians. Information was also received that the enemy had come up Lake Champlain in great force, and an immediate invasion was apprehended. On the 21st of May, Gen. Schuyler wrote from Saratoga that he had "been informed from very good authority, that the enemy's morning and evening guns at Ticonderoga had been distinctly heard near Fort Ann for three or four days past." And on the 24th he wrote again still more confidently of the enemy's approach. "Capt. Gray," he says, "is returned. He has not been near enough to determine the enemy's force, but sufficiently to discover by their fires that they are numerous." But in addition to all other evils, Col. Stone says, "Treachery was at work, and from the temper of great numbers of the people, the carriage of the disaffected, and the intelligence received by the means of spies and intercepted dispatches, there was just cause to apprehend that should the enemy again invade the country, either from the north or the west, his standard would be joined by much larger numbers of people than would have rallied beneath it at any former period. The poison was actively at work even in Albany." Mr. Stone further says, "that from the tenor of the intercepted dispatches the conclusion was irresistible, not only that a powerful invasion was about taking place from the north, but that very extensive arrangements had been made in Albany, and the towns adjacent, for the reception of the invaders, whose standard the disaffected were to join, and whose wants they were to supply." "Under all these circumstances of internal and external dangers," continues Mr. Stone, "with but slender garrisons at the points of greatest exposure, and those so miserably provided that the soldiers were deserting by dozens, showing dispositions not equivocal of going over to the enemy, without provisions or the means of procuring them, and scarcely knowing whom to trust among their own people, lest the disaffection should prove to be more extensive than recent disclosures had taught the officers to suppose; the spring of 1781 may well be considered as the darkest period of the revolution." [1]

If Mr. Stone had sought for the causes of the weakness and imbecility of the New York government, he might have found one of its principal elements in its inappropriateness to the wishes and aspirations of a republican people. It is doubtless true that New York originally contained a greater proportion of tories than any other of the thirteen states, South Carolina perhaps excepted, and it is probably equally true that their numbers had been continually on the increase in consequence of the unsatisfactory manner in which the state government had been constituted and administered. A large portion of those who were strongly whig in sentiment and feeling, looked upon the rulers of the state with jealousy and distrust, as constituting an established aristocracy, having interests separate and distinct from those of the great body of the people; men in whose election they had no part, over whom they had no control, and who were administering the government for the benefit of a class, rather than for the common good. Whoever will take the trouble to read the numerous memorials presented to the legislature from time to time, from different parts of the state, and especially those at the previous winter session, which are still preserved in the archives at Albany, cannot fail to perceive that such feeling was very extensive and general. Among the matters complained of as grievances were the restricted property qualification of voters, by which a large por-

[1] *Stone's Life of Brant*, vol. 2, p. 142, 145, 146, 151, 153.

tion of the people were excluded from any share in the government; and also the participation in the administration of public affairs of the ordinance members and senators who comprised over one-third of the legislature. These had been appointed by the convention of 1777 as nominal representatives of the southern portion of the state in possession of the enemy, were then in the fifth year of their service, and were to hold their places while such possession of the enemy continued; except in case of vacancies which, when occurring, were to be filled by vote of one or the other of the two branches of the legislature. To these evils in the organization of the government the memoralists added as their supposed natural products, partial legislation, plurality of offices in the same person or family, office holding by members of the assembly, official corruption and general suffering and distress.

This, not altogether unreasonable dissatisfaction of the people of the northern frontier with the ruling authorities of New York, in connexion with their failure to furnish security against the apprehended ravages of the common enemy, if they do not afford a proper justification, will at least be sufficient to account for the desire of such people to unite themselves with a more democratic government, whose power was deemed adequate to their protection.[1]

The articles of union agreed upon at Cambridge, were substantially the same as those which had been adopted on the formation of the eastern connexion. They, however, met with opposition from a portion of the eastern members, who were desirous of retaining the preponderating power of the state on their side of the Green mountain. With this desire, the annexation of the New York territory would interfere, as it would leave the state as heretofore about equally divided by the mountain. The articles were adopted by a vote of fifty-three ayes to twenty-four nays. Acts were then passed organizing the newly acquired territory into townships for purposes

[1] Among the memorials at the winter session of 1781, was one from the committees of Charlotte county, assembled at White Creek, now Salem, which after enumerating several other grievances, declared that their exposure to the incursions of the enemy was such that if protection was not afforded them by the state, they would be obliged to abandon their habitations and remove into the interior of the country. Petitions from the inhabitants of Schaghticoke and the committees of Albany county have already been mentioned, in which among other grievances complained of, was the conduct of the government of New York, in opposing the independent jurisdiction of Vermont. See assembly papers in the office of the secretary of state, Albany. Also *Legislative Papers* and *Clinton Papers* in the N. Y. State Library.

of representation and local government, and to ensure to its inhabitants, the due administration of justice and equality of taxation. On the 18th of July Gov. Chittenden issued a proclamation announcing the annexation of the territory to Vermont.

Thus while New Hampshire and New York were extending their claims over the whole of Vermont and striving by every means in their powers to annihilate her jurisdiction, her statesmen, by resorting to a similar policy, were making alarming encroachments upon their territories, and this, on the application of their own dissatisfied citizens. By the two unions thus formed Vermont had greatly weakened the power of her adversaries and had added to herself an extent of territory fully equal to that over which she had originally claimed jurisdiction. No measures could have better exhibited the genius of her statesmen, and none could have more effectually contributed to sustain her independence. By this bold and decisive policy, she had augmented her resources, compelled the respect of her enemies, gained upon the confidence of her friends, and at the same time had quieted in a great degree the most serious disaffection at home.[1]

---

[1] *Jour. Vt. Assembly*, April 11, and June 15 and 16, 1781. *Slade*, p. 138-141, and p. 430-432. *Williams*, p. 259, 260. *I. Allen's Vt.*, p. 156, 157. *Legislative Papers*, N. Y. State Library, No. 2429.

CHAPTER XXXI.

Proceedings of Congress favorable to Vermont.

1781.

Gen. Ethan Allen's communication to congress of Col. Beverly Robinson's letters inviting the Vermonters to unite with the crown and become a separate government — Letter of President Weare of New Hampshire complaining of encroachments by Vermont read in congress and referred to a committee — First report of committee recommitted and final report adopted, for the appointment of a committee to confer with agents that might be sent from Vermont — Vermont agents arrive and after conference with them the committee report a resolution in favor of the admission of Vermont on her relinquishment of her recent claims on New Hampshire and New York — The resolution adopted by the vote of all the states except New York — The legislature of New York protest against the resolution, and that of Vermont declines to accede to it.

BESIDES the effect upon the public mind of the enlargement of the territory of Vermont at the expense of New York and New Hampshire, there were other circumstances and events which tended to produce a feeling in the country and in congress favorable to her state independence. Among these, not the least perhaps, was the increasing apprehension, that if Vermont were allowed to be driven to extremities by her hostile neighbors, she might be induced to seek for her defence the aid of the common enemy This apprehension it was not for her interest wholly to counteract. It has already been seen that the controversy with New York in which the people of Vermont had long been involved, was well understood by the British ministry; that the British officers had been instructed to encourage the separation of Vermont from New York, and that with the view of drawing her people over to the crown, the commander of the forces in Canada had the previous autumn, consented to a truce, highly favorable to them.

Further evidence of the efforts of the king's officers in the same direction had been furnished to congress in the spring of this year (1781) by the transmission to that body by Gen. Ethan Allen of two letters received by him from Col. Beverly Robinson, a prominent loyalist of New York city and a confidant of Sir Henry Clinton, the British commander-in-chief. The first of these two letters bore date at New York March 30, 1780. It stated that the writer had been informed that he (Gen. Allen) "and most of the inhabitants of Vermont were opposed to the wild and chimerical scheme of the

Americans in attempting to separate the continent from Great Britain, and that they would willingly assist in uniting America again to Great Britain." If this information were correct he wished Allen would write him, and stated that any proposals he should make would be faithfully laid before the commander-in-chief and he flattered himself "he could do it with as good effect as any person whatever." On the return of the people of Vermont to their allegiance he did not doubt they could obtain "a separate government under the king and constitution of England," and intimated that he and his Vermont friends would be allowed the honors and principal management of the new government. The second letter was dated February 2, 1781, and covered a copy of the former, under the apprehension that the original had not been received. In this the former offers were renewed with greater confidence, under the assurance that he now wrote by authority, and that the terms then suggested would be granted "provided he and the people of Vermont took an active part with the crown." The letter of Gen. Allen transmitting these to congress, is characteristic of the writer, and illustrates the spirit of the time. It is as follows:

"SUNDERLAND, 9th March, 1781.

"Sir: Enclosed I transmit your excellency two letters which I received under the signature thereto annexed that they may be laid before congress. I shall make no comment on them, but submit the disposal of them to their consideration. They are the identical and only letters I ever received from him, and to which I have never returned any manner of answer, nor have I ever had the least personal acquaintance with him, directly or indirectly. The letter of the 2d of February, 1781, I received a few days ago with a duplicate of the other, which I received the latter part of July last past, in the high road in Arlington, which I laid before Gov. Chittenden and a number of the principal gentlemen of the state, within ten minutes after I received it, for advice. The result after mature deliberation, and considering the extreme circumstances of the state, was to take no further notice of the matter. The reasons for such a procedure are very obvious to the people of this state, when that congress have previously claimed an exclusive right of arbitrating on the existence of Vermont as a separate government. New York, New Hampshire and Massachusetts Bay, at the same time, claiming this territory either in whole or in part, and exerting their influence to make schisms among her citizens, thereby, in a considerable degree, weakening this government, and exposing its inhabitants to the incursions of the British troops and their savage allies, from the province of Quebec.

"It seems that those governments, regardless of Vermont's contiguous situation to Canada, do not consider that their northern frontiers have been secured by her, nor of the merits of this state in a long and hazardous war, but have flattered themselves with the expectation that this state could not fail (without their help), to be desolated by a foreign enemy, and that their exorbitant claims and avaricious designs may, at some future period, take place in this district of country.

"Notwithstanding these complicated embarrassments, Vermont during the last campaign defended her frontiers, and at the close of it opened a truce with Gen. Haldimand, who commands the British troops in Canada, which continued near four weeks in the same situation, during which time Vermont secured the northern frontiers of the state of New York, in consequence of my including them in the truce, although that government would have but little claim to *my* protection.

"I am confident that congress will not dispute my sincere attachment to the cause of my country, when I do not hesitate to say, I am fully grounded in opinion that Vermont has an indubitable right to agree on terms of cessation of hostilities with Great Britain, provided the United States persist in rejecting her application for a union with them; for Vermont of all people would be the most miserable, were she obliged to defend the independence of the United claiming States, and they at the same time at full liberty to overturn and ruin the independence of Vermont.

"I am persuaded when congress consider the circumstances of this state, they will be more surprised that I have transmitted them the enclosed letters, than that I have kept them in custody so long; for I am as resolutely determined to defend the independence of Vermont as congress that of the United States, and rather than fail will retire with the hardy Green Mountain Boys into the desolate caverns of the mountains, and wage war with human nature at large.

"I am with respect and esteem,
Your excellency's most obedient servant,
ETHAN ALLEN.

"His Excellency,
Samuel Huntington, Esq.,
President of congress."

Although congress took no direct action on this communication of Gen Allen, yet his bold and determined character as well as his patriotic services and sufferings in the cause of his country, were well known, and it was doubtless remembered, and probably exerted an influence in shaping the future measures of that body.[1]

On the 22d of June, immediately after the formation of the western union, the legislature of Vermont had appointed Jonas Fay, Ira Allen and Bazaleel Woodward, agents to congress, with full authority to negotiate the terms of a union with the United States, and on the ratification of such terms to take seats in congress, as delegates from the state. Messrs. Fay and Allen resided within the original limits of Vermont, and Mr. Woodward in the newly acquired territory from New Hampshire. Although these agents were thus early appointed, they did not repair to Philadelphia until some time in the ensuing month of August. When they arrived there they found that very important measures in relation to Vermont, had been entered upon by congress.[2]

Ever since the hearing of the controversy by congress, the previous September, there had been a growing disposition in that body to recognize the independence of Vermont. Her people had always shown a patriotic devotion to the common cause of the country, performing with alacrity and skill, as well as bravery, their full proportion of military service with their brethren of the adjoining states. They were evidently in earnest in their opposition to the claims of New York and New Hampshire, and as determined to maintain their independence of those states, as congress was that of the United States against Great Britain. Their recent encroachments upon the territories of those claiming states, were evidence of both the power and the popularity of their state government. It had already been in successful operation for more that four years, and to overthrow and break it up by outside pressure, and compel its inhabitants to submit to a jurisdiction which they detested, was an undertaking in which few were willing to engage, and which many would deem altogether impracticable.

---

[1] *Ethan Allen Papers,* p. 327, 345, 347. *Ira Allen's Vt.,* p. 153. *Williams's Vt.,* p. 262. Copies of these letters to Gen. Allen and of his to the president of congress, which latter had been written under the advice of the governor and council, were laid before the Vermont assembly on the 12th of April and their proceedings were by vote of that body approved.

[2] *Jour. Vt. Assembly,* for June 22, 25 and 27. *Livermore to Weare,* Aug. 21, 1781.

On the 9th of July the delegates from New Hampshire had laid before congress a letter from Pres. Weare, complaining of the extension of the Vermont jurisdiction to the eastward of Connecticut river; stating that New Hampshire had been reduced to such a condition by defection in her western borders, that unless the evil were stopped, he feared the state would be "very soon ruined in a great measure, and would be unable to contribute further towards the war." This letter, with accompanying papers, was referred to a committee consisting of Messrs. Sherman of Conn., McKean of Del., Carrol of Md., Varnum of R. I., and Madison of Va. While the matter was pending before this committee an intercepted letter from Lord George Germain the British minister to Sir Henry Clinton, commander of his majesty's forces in New York, was laid before congress, and soon afterwards published in the *Pennsylvania Packet.* It bore date the 7th of the preceding February, and contained a clause in the following language:

"The return of the people of Vermont to their allegiance, is an event of the utmost importance to the king's affairs; and at this time if the French and Washington really meditate an irruption into Canada, may be considered as opposing an insurmountable bar to the attempt. Gen. Haldimand, who has the same instructions with you, to draw over those people, and give them support, will, I doubt not, push up a body of troops to act in conjunction with them to secure all the avenues through their country into Canada; and when the season admits, take possession of the upper parts of the Hudson's and Connecticut rivers and cut off the communications between Albany and the Mohawk country. How far they may be able to extend themselves southward or eastward, must depend on their numbers and the disposition of the inhabitants."

This letter was conclusive evidence that the British generals in New York and Canada had orders to receive and support Vermont, and that the ministry were persuaded of the disposition of those people to join the king's government. In this latter particular the ministry were clearly mistaken, having been deceived by the adroitness of the Vermont leaders, as will fully appear hereafter. Lord Germain's letter, however, when considered in connection with Allen's letter and the rumors in regard to the truce between Gen. Haldimand and the Vermonters, and the frequent flags that were said to have passed between them, was well calculated to favor the cause of Vermont in congress. It furnished her friends, already numerous, and probably a majority, with the resistless argument against the claim of New York, that the public safety demanded the relinquishment of that claim.

The successful encroachment of the Vermonters upon the territory of New Hampshire, had made the government of that state quite willing to acknowledge the independence of Vermont, provided the latter could be restricted to her original limits. Massachusetts, as has already been seen, had withdrawn her claim on condition that Vermont should be admitted into the federal union. And from the favorable proceedings of the New York legislature towards Vermont, the previous winter, it was in the absence of the New York delegates, who were not then in attendance on congress, confidently expected that she also could be induced to make a like relinquishment on her part, and that the independence of Vermont might thus be recognized by the concurrent assent of all the claiming states.

With a view to bring about this desirable object, the committee, on the 31st of July, made a report recommending to the legislatures of New York and New Hampshire to relinquish their several jurisdictions over the state of Vermont, and to consent to her independence according to her former extent. But the arrival of Messrs. Duane and L'Hommedieu, as delegates from New York, put an abrupt end to this plan of adjustment. The land claiming influence had again resumed the control of the New York legislature. Three days after the report was made to congress, and before it was acted upon, they presented to that body a memorial in which, after referring to former resolutions and engagements of congress to determine the controversy, they declared "that they were expressly instructed by the legislature of the state of New York to urge congress, agreeably to those said resolutions and engagements, to decide the controversy so long subsisting respecting the claim of independent jurisdiction set up under the pretended state of Vermont, and to take measures in the mean time for restraining the encroachments of the said inhabitants, at least within the bounds which they themselves have, till the late extraordinary extension, considered, represented and claimed as comprehending the New Hampshire Grants." Upon the presentation of this memorial the report was recommitted to the same committee.

This committee, in accordance with the request and demand of the New York legislature and delegates proceeded to take measures for deciding the controversy, not indeed as had been hoped by them by the establishment of the claim of New York, but in favor of the independence of Vermont.

The following account of the proceedings of Congress on the report of this committee is copied from the journal of Aug. 7, 1781.

"Congress took into consideration the report of the committee, consisting of Mr. Sherman, Mr. McKean, Mr. Carroll, Mr. Varnum and Mr. Madison, to whom was recommitted their report on a letter of the 20th of June, from the president of New Hampshire, together with a motion relative to the subject, and thereupon came to the following resolutions:

"Whereas the states of New Hampshire and New York have submitted to congress the decision of the disputes between them and the people inhabiting the New Hampshire Grants, on the west side of Connecticut river, called the state of Vermont, concerning their respective claims of jurisdiction over the said territory, and have been heard thereon; and whereas the people aforesaid claim and exercise the powers of a sovereign, independent state, and have requested to be admitted into the federal union of the United States of America; and in order thereto, and that they may have an opportunity to be heard in vindication of their said claim:

"*Resolved*, That a committee of five be appointed to confer with such person or persons as may be appointed by the people residing on the New Hampshire Grants, on the west side of Connecticut river, or by their representative body, respecting their claim to be an independent state, and on what terms it may be proper to admit them into the federal union of these states, in case the United States in congress assembled shall determine to recognize their independence, and thereof make report:

"And it is hereby recommended to the people of the territory aforesaid, or their representative body, to appoint an agent or agents, to repair immediately to Philadelphia, with full powers and instructions to confer with the said committee on the matters aforesaid, and on behalf of the said people, to agree upon and ratify terms and articles of union and confederation with the United States of America, in case they shall be admitted into the union, and the said committee are hereby instructed to give notice to the agents of the states of New Hampshire and New York to be present at the conference aforesaid.

"*Resolved*, That in case congress shall recognize the independence of the said people of Vermont, they will consider all the lands belonging to New Hampshire and New York respectively, without the limits of Vermont aforesaid, as coming within the mutual guarantee of territory contained in the article of confederation; and that the United States will accordingly guarantee such lands and the jurisdiction over the same, against any claims or encroachments from the inhabitants of Vermont aforesaid."

The committee chosen under the foregoing resolutions were Mr. Boudinot of New Jersey, Mr. Van Dyke of Delaware, Mr. Carroll of Maryland, Mr. Montgomery of Pennsylvania, and Mr. Randolph of Virginia.

James Madison, who was a member of the committee which reported the foregoing resolutions, and who as a delegate from a *large* and a *southern* state had always been opposed to the admission of Vermont into the confederation, gave a brief account of the proceedings of congress on the subject at this period and of the causes which operated to produce the result to which that body came, in a letter to his friend Edmund Pendleton, which is deemed worthy of insertion here.

The letter is as follows:

"PHILADELPHIA, August 14, 1781.

"Dear Sir: The controversy relating to the district called Vermont, the inhabitants of which have for several years claimed and exercised the jurisdiction of an independent state, is at length put into a train of speedy decision. Notwithstanding the objections to such an event, there is no question but they will be established into a separate and federal state. A relinquishment made by Massachusetts of her claims; a despair of finally obtaining theirs on the part of New York and New Hampshire, the other claimants on whom these enterprising adventures were making fresh encroachments; the latent support afforded them by the leading people of the New England states in general from which they emigrated; the just ground of apprehension that their rulers were engaging in clandestine negotiations with the enemy; and lastly, perhaps, the jealous policy of some of the little states, which hope that such a precedent may engender a division of some of the large ones, are the circumstances which will determine the concurrence of congress in this affair."

Messrs. Fay, Allen and Woodward, who, as has been seen, had been appointed agents to congress by the legislature of Vermont, the previous June, arrived in Philadelphia about the middle of August, and were there first informed of the existence of the resolutions of the 7th of that month. Their credentials were submitted to the committee appointed under those resolutions; but it appearing that they had been chosen to represent the state of Vermont as recently enlarged by its eastern and western unions, and not the people on the New Hampshire Grants only, as contemplated by the resolutions of the 12th of August, the committee did not feel authorized to confer with them. The matter was accordingly referred to congress, who directed the conference to proceed with those gentlemen.

The conference took place on the 18th of August, and was carried on by questions proposed by the committee, to which the agents made answer. By the written answers of the agents, the committee were informed that if Vermont should be admitted into the federal union, her people would bear such a proportion of the expenses of the war with Great Britain as should be mutually judged equitable; that her government in settling the titles of land granted by New Hampshire, or by New York previous to the present revolution, had it "in contemplation to adopt such modes as the circumstances arising out of each case, might justify, without adhering to the strict rules of law;" that in regard to those persons who had not performed the conditions of settlement of the lands granted them, it was the intention to allow them "a further reasonable time for fulfilling such conditions;" that the numbers of the inhabitants of Vermont, not including the eastern and western unions, were estimated at thirty thousand, and that the quantity of land in the same extent of territory was estimated at five millions of acres. To the question as to what applications had been made, either publicly or privately, by the enemies of the United States or their adherents, to draw off the people of Vermont from their affection to the United States, the agents replied that the committee were possessed of copies of Beverly Robinson's letters and of Brig. Gen. Allen's letter communicating them to congress, and that "any private offers they could not avouch for." The agents in answer to the question as to what aid, in men and provisions could be raised in the state of Vermont, in case of invasion by the enemy, replied, that there were within the limits of the state as before circumscribed, a body of seven thousand militia, that they were in general "well armed and accoutred," and had ever shown themselves "spirited in case of alarms;" that as regarded provisions, the country was fertile, but new; that emigrations from the other states were frequent; that the legislature had at their session in October last, levied a tax on the inhabitants sufficient to victual fifteen hundred troops in the field for twelve months, and that a larger store of provisions could probably be collected during the ensuing autumn.

At the same time the agents presented to the committee their proposals for the admission of Vermont as one of the United States. The terms on which they desired admission were, that the state according to its original limits to the westward of Connecticut river should be admitted a member of the confederation, that delegates from it should be allowed to take their seats in congress as soon as the union should be completed; that the claims of New Hampshire and New York, to the eastern and western unions should be determined by a court of commissioners constituted in the mode prescribed by the article of confederation, and that Vermont should have the same right as any other state on application to congress, to be heard in the settlement of the controversy.

These proposals were disapproved by the committee, who on the 20th reported to congress and recommended the adoption of the following resolution :

" *Resolved*, That it be an indispensable preliminary to the recognition of the independence of the people inhabiting the territory called Vermont, and their admission into the federal union, that they explicitly relinquish all demands of lands or jurisdiction on the east side of the west bank of Connecticut river, and on the west side of a line, beginning at the northwest corner of the state of Massachusetts, thence running twenty miles east of Hudson's river, so far as the river runs northeasterly in its general course ; then by the west bounds of the townships granted by the late government of New Hampshire to the river running from South bay to Lake Champlain, thence along the said river to Lake Champlain, thence along the waters of Lake Champlain to the latitude of forty-five degrees north, excepting a neck of land between Massiskoybay and the waters of Lake Champlain."

This resolution was understood and treated as a virtual engagement on the part of congress to acknowledge the independence of Vermont and admit her a member of the federal union, whenever she should consent to restrict her boundaries to the limits therein prescribed, which were in substantial accordance with her original claim of territory. On the question of agreeing to the resolution, the yeas and nays were taken, when twelve states, being all except New York, voted in the affirmative. The only delegates who voted in the negative were Mr. Duane and Mr. L'Hommedieu from New York, and Mr. Matthews one of three in attendance from North Carolina.[1]

[1] *Jour. of Cong.*, Aug. 3, 7, 8, 17 and 20th, 1781. *Continental Congress Papers*, State Dep., Nos. 40 and 191. *Madison Papers*, vol. 1, p. 96. *Clinton Papers*, Nos. 3862, 3870, 3878, 3916, *B. H. Hall's Ms. Williams's Vt.*, p. 273. *I. Allen's Vt.*, p. 176. *Slade*, p. 157 - 160. *Letters of Sullivan to Weare*, of July 10, July, 17, and Aug. 21, 1781. *Haldimand Papers*, vol. 1,

On being furnished with copies of the foregoing resolutions of congress, Gov. Clinton addressed a letter to the New York delegates arguing at great length that congress had no authority under the articles of confederation, to recognize the independence of Vermont and admit her a member of the federal union, and insisting that a decision in her favor in the manner contemplated by congress would be a mere nullity. This argument, which seems to have been approved by the delegates, was in a subsequent letter, by him, restated and amplified; and when the legislature met in November following, the subject was taken up and on the 19th of that month a very long report was adopted, reiterating the same view of the subject, and protesting in the most decided language against any such unauthorized "assumption of power" by congress. The amount of all this argument, stripped of its technicalities and special pleading, was, that congress under the submission to them had full authority to decide the controversy in favor of New York, but none whatever to determine it in favor of Vermont.

If this view of the case were correct, it is apparent that Mr. Jay and his associate delegates from New York must have practiced a fraud upon the friends of Vermont and upon congress in procuring the passage of the submission resolutions of September, 1779, those resolutions having been advocated by them and universally understood as providing for a full hearing of the controversy and for its decision in favor of whichsoever of the contending parties it should be deemed right and proper. No such fraud could have been contemplated. Undoubtedly the New York delegates expected a decision in their favor and were under no apprehension whatever that it could possibly be against them. They therefore meant to offer and did offer to Vermont the opportunity to be heard before a tribunal having full authority to decide in their favor, in order as stated by Mr. Jay in his account of the resolutions to Gov. Clinton that "congress might be rescued from aspersions," and that the Vermonters "after having been fully heard, might have nothing to say or complain of, in case the decision of congress should be against them," of which he adds, "I have no doubt."

---

p. 439. This resolution is entered on the journal of congress of the 20th of August and is not mentioned on that of the next day. It appears however from the report of a committee found on the journal of the 17th of April, 1782, that it was reconsidered and reaffirmed on the 21st of August. This will account for its being sometimes referred to as a resolution of the 20th and at others as of the 21st and again as of both dates.

It is true that the articles of confederation did not provide for the determination of a dispute between a people claiming a separate jurisdiction, and a state of the confederacy claiming them as its subjects, and for that very reason the resolutions of congress called on the contesting states to pass laws expressly conferring such authority on congress. New Hampshire and New York responded to the call, the law of New York enacting, among other things, that congress might "determine the question of jurisdiction between the people on the west side of Connecticut river and New York, either by themselves, or by commissioners under the ninth article of the confederation." There was, therefore, no foundation whatever for the denial by the governor and legislature of New York of the power of congress to decide the controversy in favor of Vermont.

The annual election for state officers in Vermont took place two weeks after the passage of the resolution of congress of the 20th of August, before it could have been known to many, if indeed to any, of the electors. The legislature, in obedience to a resolve of the previous assembly, met at Charlestown on the east side of Connecticut river, on the second Thursday of October. The assembly consisted of one hundred and thirty-seven members, representing one hundred and two towns. Of these, sixty members from forty-five towns were from the territory which had lately united with the state from New Hampshire. Of the twelve councilors, two were from the same territory. Thomas Chittenden had been reelected governor, but there being no choice of lieutenant governor, Elisha Paine, from the New Hampshire side of the river, was chosen by the legislature. When the resolution of congress, of the 20th of August, which was in effect an offer to admit Vermont into the federal union according to the original extent of her territorial claim, was laid before the general assembly, its members were not prepared to accede to it. Those from the eastern union were anxious to remain annexed to Vermont, and many on the opposite side of Connecticut river sympathized with them. Those who would have been glad to accept the terms offered by congress, felt under obligations to their new friends and were unwilling to insist upon an abrupt separation from them.

After a full discussion, a plan, in connexion with certain proposals to be made to the two adjoining states, was agreed upon by general consent, for adhering to the two unions. The proposals to New Hampshire were that the legislatures of that state and Vermont should, by committees appointed for that purpose, mutually agree "upon five or more judicious and unprejudiced persons," to whom all questions of boundaries between them should be submitted, and whose determination should be final and conclusive. The like proposition was to be made to New York. The legislature then appointed commissioners to treat with the two contesting states in regard to boundaries, and also passed a resolution declaring their willingness, whenever Vermont should "become united with the American states" to submit all disputes with other states to congress. The proceedings of the legislature on this subject, which were concluded the 19th of October, were directed to be officially transmitted to congress by the governor.

After a session of about three weeks, the legislature adjourned to meet at Bennington on the last Thursday of the ensuing January. Thus the end of the year 1781 found the legislature of Vermont unprepared to accept the favorable terms offered her by congress, and the legislature of New York protesting against the validity of the action of congress.[1]

---

[1] Gov. Clinton to delegates, Aug. 25 and Sept. 18, 1781. *Legislative Papers*, State Library, Albany, No. 2435, 2442. *Slade*, p. 160 to 166. *Life of Jay*, vol. 1, p. 92. *Jour. of Cong.*, Sept. 24, 1779. *Journal Vermont Assembly*, Oct. 16, 17, 18, 19 and 27th, 1781. *I. Allen's Vermont*, p. 193–200.

CHAPTER XXXII.

NEGOTIATIONS WITH CANADA.

1781.

THE subject of the negotiation of the Vermonters with the British authorities will now be resumed. Hitherto the matter has been considered only in the light in which it appeared to the public and to congress, from the letters of Col. Beverly Robinson to Gen. Ethan Allen and his communication transmitting them to congress; from the forbearance of Gen. Haldimand to molest the territory of Vermont in his invasion of the northern frontier and his granting a truce to Gen. Allen; from the intercepted letter of the British minister in which he spoke of "the return of the people of Vermont to their allegiance" as an event either already accomplished, or about to be; and from the suspicions which the mysterious interchange of flags between Vermont and Canada, aided by common rumor, had occasioned. We are now to go behind the curtain which seemed to be drawn by the Vermonters around their transactions, for the purpose of ascertaining what were their real dealings with the enemy, by what motives they were governed, and what was the effect of their proceedings on the affairs of the state and on the common cause of the country.

Within a few years past, copies of all the papers of Gen. Haldimand in relation to the negotiation have been obtained from England, and are preserved in two manuscript volumes in the office of the secretary of state at Montpelier. These, in connection with the facts before known and especially with the account given of the negotiation by Dr. Williams and Ira Allen in their histories of Vermont, furnish very full materials for such examination. The subject in all its details might occupy a volume. Its character and effects may however be sufficiently seen by a more general outline.

In the letter of Gen. Haldimand to Gov. Chittenden, which was sent to Gen. Allen by Major Carleton in October 1780, he expressed some unwillingness to comply with the governor's request for an exchange of prisoners, but said, "if you will send me a proper person with full powers, to Major Carleton at Crown Point or St. Johns to confer upon this business I shall authorize the major to receive him." In Maj. Carleton's letter to Gen. Allen, enclosing this, he stated that he had authorized Captain Sherwood to treat with Governor Chittenden on the subject.[1] These two letters having been read before the Vermont Assembly, on the 31st of October, the application of the governor to Gen. Haldimand for an exchange of prisoners was approved and the governor was advised "to appoint and empower some suitable person or persons to negotiate the settlement of a cartel with Major Carleton, agreeable to Haldimand's proposals." In pursuance of this vote of the assembly the governor by the advice of his council, two days afterwards, commissioned Col. Ira Allen and Major Joseph Fay for that purpose. They proceeded immediately on their mission, and having met Capt. Sherwood and Mr. George Smith, who had been appointed commissioners on the part of the British, they all agreed to go into Canada together. When they arrived at East Bay they found that the ice, which was already forming, obstructed their way. After spending several days in endeavoring to break through the ice, it was agreed on account of the condition of the lake, that Messrs. Allen and Fay should return to Vermont, and that they should see that commissioners should repair to Canada as soon as circumstances would admit. During the time the commissioners were together, "much political conversation and exhibits of papers," says Ira Allen, "took place." [2] This "political conversation" having been reported to Gen. Haldimand, he was undoubtedly led to believe there was a fair prospect of his being able, by offering suitable inducements, to detach the Vermonters from the American cause, and bring them over to the support of the crown. Accordingly, under date of December 20th, he prepared written instructions to his commissioners for that purpose, authorizing them to offer to the people of Vermont a separate government under the crown, with extensive popular privileges, and special rewards to those who should be instrumental in bringing about the change.[3] But the obstacles to a winter communication between Vermont and Canada were such as to postpone any further negotiations until the ensuing spring. Dr. Jonas Fay was, indeed, commissioned by the governor of Vermont to go on the business during the winter, but after proceeding on the ice of the lake as far as Split Rock, he found it insufficient for further traveling and was obliged to return.

The situation of the state on the opening of navigation on the lake, of which the enemy had the complete command, would be one

---

[1] *Steven's Papers,* vol. 6, p. 369.

[2] *Ira Allen's Hist.,* p. 152, 153. *William's Vt.,* 265.

[3] *Haldimand Papers,* vol. 1, p. 193–121. *Ira Allen's Hist.,* p. 153.

of extreme peril. The force in Canada from an apprehended invasion had been increased, and was altogether too large to be resisted by any body of troops that Vermont could keep in the field. The state would be constantly exposed to sudden invasion and ravage by a cruel enemy, and although a frontier to both New York and New Hampshire, they were each claiming her territory, and in order to weaken her, were apparently quite willing she should encounter the enemy alone. Congress, by the influence of those claiming states, as was believed, had withdrawn from her territory all continental troops and munitions of war, and had declined to furnish either provisions or pay for the men of the state who were guarding her frontier. Left alone to her own resources, which were clearly insufficient to enable her to make successful resistance to the common enemy, by force of arms, her statesmen were compelled for their defence " to resort to policy in the room of power."

In April Col. Ira Allen was commissioned to continue the negotiation for the exchange of prisoners, and he was specially instructed by "the governor and his cabinet council" to make use of every possible means to prevent further hostile attacks from the enemy, which it was well understood could only be done by making their commander believe that Vermont, at no very distant day, would conclude with him a separate peace and submit to the authority of the crown.

Col. Allen reached the Isle aux Noix (a few miles north of Canada line) about the 8th of May and spent seventeen days in conference with the British commissioners. The negotiation on the part of Col. Allen was mainly verbal, though he found it necessary, in order to obtain the confidence of Gen. Haldimand to transmit him various papers showing the proceedings of the state government and the relations in which it stood to congress and the neighboring states. A daily journal of the conference was kept by the British commissioners, of which a copy covering twenty manuscript pages is found in the Haldimand papers, and an account of it is also given by Ira Allen in his history.

It was proposed by the British commissioners, in accordance with Gen. Haldimand's instructions, that the territory of Vermont should be a colony under the crown, with privileges equal to those enjoyed by any other colony, and that those who assisted in effecting such an event should be duly honored and rewarded. It was further proposed that two loyal battalions should be raised in Vermont to be officered and commanded by such men as the Vermont leaders should designate, who should be entitled to the British half pay provision; that a force of not less than three thousand men should be sent to cooperate with them against the other states, to advance as far as Albany and engage in such other offensive operations as circumstances should permit. They wished to conclude a treaty at once. Allen's object was delay. To obtain which and to keep the British forces inactive, he represented that although the principal men in the Vermont government, in consequence of the hostility of the neighboring states and of congress, were desirous of returning to their allegiance, yet that a very large portion of the people, who had always been ardent whigs, were by no means ready for the change; that time must be given to prepare their minds for it; that by granting a cartel for the exchange of prisoners and an armistice, their feelings would be conciliated and they would appreciate the advantages of a reunion with Great Britain, and be induced to unite in the measure. He further stated, that he had no authority to conclude a treaty, and that such authority could only be given by the legislature, which was to meet about the middle of the ensuing June; that at such meeting the eastern and western unions with the state would be further consolidated, by which it was expected Vermont would be greatly strengthened, and made the more ready to enter into the proposed treaty; that every exertion would be made by him and his associates in the government of Vermont to induce the legislature to appoint commissioners to enter into a treaty, though he could not positively engage that success would attend their efforts; but that a full report of their proceedings should be made to Gov. Haldimand by the 20th of July ensuing. Upon these assurances the British commissioners consented to a cartel for the exchange of prisoners and made "a verbal agreement that hostilities should cease between the British and those under the jurisdiction of Vermont until after the session of the legislature, and until a reasonable time afterwards for a commissary of prisoners to go on board the Royal George in Lake Champlain, and even longer if prospects were satisfactory to the commander-in-chief." [1]

On Allen's return home he gave a full account of his negotiation to Gov. Chittenden and those of his advisers who were associated in the measure; and in order that they might all share in its dangers and responsibility, he took from them a certificate in writing as follows:

---

[1] *Haldimand Papers*, vol. 1, p. 67-103, 203-241, 273-277, 287, 289. *Ira Allen's Hist.*, 161-171. *Life Chittenden*, 266. *Williams's Vt.*, 266.

STATE OF VERMONT, June, 1781.

Whereas Col. Ira Allen has been with a flag to Quebec for the purpose of settling a cartel for exchange of prisoners, and has used his best policy by feigning or endeavoring to make them believe that the state of Vermont had a desire to negotiate a treaty of peace with Great Britain — thereby to prevent the immediate invasion or incursion upon the frontiers of this state, as appears by the letter he sent to Gen. Haldimand dated May 8, 1781, enclosing a copy of Col. Beverly Robinson's letters to Gen. Allen and Gen. Allen's letter to congress, and the resolutions of the assembly of Vermont approbating the same, as also the circular letter to the several states delivered to Dundas according to his verbal report made to us this day. We are of the opinion that the critical circumstances this state is in, being out of the Union with the United States and thereby unable to make that vigorous defence we could wish for — think it to be a necessary political manœuver to save the frontiers of this state.

JONAS FAY,	THOMAS CHITTENDEN,
SAMUEL SAFFORD,	MOSES ROBINSON,
SAMUEL ROBINSON,	TIMOTHY BROWNSON,
JOSEPH FAY,	JOHN FASSETT.[1]

These men were among the most ardent patriots of the state who during the whole revolutionary period and afterwards, so long as they lived enjoyed the full confidence of the people and were called by them to occupy the most honored and trustworthy positions in their gift. They had no idea of submitting to British authority; but under the circumstances in which they were placed deemed it proper to resort to stratagem, always practiced and deemed justifiable in war, to ward off the expected blows of an enemy.[2]

The frequent exchange of flags with Canada had excited strong suspicions in the country, in Vermont as well as in other states, that something wrong was on foot. Rumor proclaimed that the Vermont leaders were making a treaty of peace, and forming an alliance with the British government. To such treaty nine-tenths of the people of the state would be deadly opposed. The subject of Col. Allen's mission would come before the legislature which was to meet

[1] *Stevens Papers*, vol. 7, p. 179. *De Puy's Ethan Allen and the Green Mountain Boys*, p. 411.

[2] See Biographical notices of these several persons in the Appendix, No. 1.

at Bennington on the 13th of June, when the difficult task would be imposed on those who had been concerned in the negotiation of satisfying the general assembly and the whig public, that nothing of the kind had been in contemplation, and at the same time to have it understood by the friends of Great Britain, that the consummation of such a treaty, at no very distant day, was extremely probable. This difficult task, was, however, by the skillfulness of Gov. Chittenden and Col. Allen, performed with a considerable degree of success.

On the 19th of June the council and assembly, in accordance with a resolve of the preceding day, met in committee of the whole, the governor in the chair, for the purpose of making an "inquiry into the grounds of the report of a treaty with Canada." The governor stated that in consequence of application from several persons praying that some measures might be taken to procure the exchange of their friends who were prisoners in Canada, he had, in the recess of the legislature, with the advice of his council, authorized Col. Allen to go to the Isle aux Noix, to settle a cartel for the exchange of prisoners; that Col. Allen had met the British commissioners and with difficulty had completed the business in behalf of Vermont, that no such exchange had taken place with the United States or any other state in the northern department, and he referred the committee to Col. Allen for any further explanation which they might wish. Col. Allen then gave such an account of his transactions as satisfied the legislature that no such treaty had been made, and that nothing had been done inconsistent with the interest of the state. It is stated by Col. Allen in his history, that in the audience there were intelligent whigs from other states who came to ascertain the character and extent of the negotiation and who as well as the legislature, were persuaded that all was patriotic and right on his part, and that spies were also in attendance from Canada to learn what report he would make of his transactions with the British commissioners, and that they were equally well satisfied. But however satisfactory Col. Allen's exposé may have been to those who heard him, it was not sufficient to allay the suspicions which extensively prevailed in the other states and in congress, that there was something in the negotiation unfriendly to the common cause of the country; and it also required much further explanation to keep Gen. Haldimand well assured that good faith had been observed towards him.[1]

---

[1] *Ira Allen's History,* p. 172–174. *Haldimand Papers,* vol. 1, p. 277, 293, 313. *Assembly Jour.,* June 18th and 19th.

No steps having been taken by the legislature of Vermont towards the appointment of commissioners to enter into a treaty with Gen. Haldimand, as he had been led to expect, some explanation of the reasons for the omission seemed indispensable, for otherwise he would be likely to consider the armistice at an end, and commence hostilities at once. It was therefore deemed advisable by Gov. Chittenden and his cabinet council, for Col. Allen to address him a letter on the subject, which was done under date of the 10th of July. The letter was intended and well calculated to produce delay in his warlike operations, by making him believe there was still a strong probability that the Vermonters would accede to his proposals. Some of its most important statements were to the effect, that congress still continued hostile to Vermont; that three agents had been appointed to apply to congress for the admission of the state as lately enlarged, one of whom was from the eastern union; that the application would be rejected, which would greatly increase the dissatisfaction of the Vermonters with that body; that emissaries from other states had been in attendance upon the legislature watching and endeavoring to influence its proceedings; that on a political scrutiny of the members it was found that a majority of them were whigs, and that it would not only be premature and useless, but dangerous to final success to introduce the subject of a treaty to them as a body; that the frinds of a treaty were therefore obliged to work in some degree "under the rose;" that their numbers and strength had however been increased; that the three brigadier generals of the militia lately appointed, and also the commanding officer on the frontier were acquainted with his proceedings at the Isle aux Noix; that in the eastern and western unions were many strong friends of Great Britain; that although the people were not yet ripe for a treaty, every exertion was making to prepare them for it; that the agents, of which the writer was one, would start for congress about the first of August; and finally that at their annual election which would take place early in September, "in all human probability a large majority of the then officers of government would be well disposed, and that then by the advantage of another denial from congress, and having the reins of government in their hands for one year, they would make a revolution so long looked for by many." [1]

The reasons and motives for dispatching this letter are stated in a written document delivered to Col. Allen by his associates in the negotiation, of which document the following is a copy:

---

[1] *Hald. Papers,* vol. 1, p. 291.

"STATE OF VERMONT, 10 July, 1781.

"Whereas this state is not in union with the United States although often requested, etc.

"This the British power are acquainted with and are endeavoring to take advantage of these disputes thereby to court a connexion with this state on the principle of establishing it a British province. From various accounts we are well assured that the British have a force in Canada larger than this state can at present raise and support in the field, and this state have no assurance of any assistance from any or either of the United States however hard the British forces may crowd on this state from the province of Quebec by the advantage of the waters of Lake Champlain, etc. Although several expresses have been sent by the governor of this state to several of the respective governors of the United States with the most urgent requests to know whether any assistance would be afforded in such case, yet no official answer has been made by either of them.

"Wherefore we the subscribers do fully approbate Col. Ira Allen sending a letter dated Sunderland, July 10, 1781, and directed to Gen. Haldimand, and another letter to Capt. Justice Sherwood, purporting an intention of this state's becoming a British province, etc. This we consider a political proceeding to prevent the British forces from invading this state, and being a necessary step to preserve this state from ruin, when we have too much reason to apprehend that this has been the wishes of some of our assuming neighbors, in the mean time to strengthen the state against any insult until this state receives better treatment from the United States or obtain a seat in congress.

"THO^s^. CHITTENDEN. JONAS FAY.
JOHN FASSETT. SAM^L^. ROBINSON.
TIM^Y^. BROWNSON. JOSEPH FAY."[1]

Col. Allen's letter was committed to the care of Maj. Joseph Fay, who was commissioned by the governor to carry out the arrangement which had been made the previous May for the exchange of prisoners on board the Royal George on Lake Champlain. Thence the letter was dispatched to Gen. Haldimand at Quebec, where it was received by him about the first of August. He appears to have

[1] *Stevens Papers*, vol. 7, p. 225. See also *De Puy's Ethan Allen and Green Mountain Boys*, p. 412.

been greatly disappointed at the inaction of the Vermont government on the subject of a treaty, and to have strongly distrusted the sincerity of Allen and his associates in their intercourse with him. In a letter to Sir Henry Clinton at New York, of the 2d of August, he complains that the flag promised by the 20th of July had but just arrived, and of Col. Allen's letter he says: "It is fraught with much sincerity or much duplicity, the latter I fear is the real sense of it, which I am the more inclined to think from his not coming with the flag." The general, however, concluded to wait and hear what Maj. Fay had to offer on the subject.[1]

It required the utmost exertions of Major Fay to remove the suspicions which were entertained by Gen. Haldimand and his commissioners against the good faith of the Vermonters, in which he seems, after a skillful labor of over two weeks, to have only partially succeeded. It was, however, finally agreed that commissioners from Vermont should meet the British commissioners at Skenesborough by the middle of September, to complete the exchange of prisoners, and that they should then report the result of the new application to congress, Mr. Fay engaging that certain important papers and documents relating to the affairs and proceedings of Vermont should then be furnished, and in the meantime hostilities against the state were to be suspended.[2]

Col. Ira Allen and Major Joseph Fay met the British commissioners at Skenesborough, according to agreement, and furnished them with copies of sundry papers relating to Vermont affairs, among which were the letter of President Weare of New Hampshire to congress of June 20th, the questions of the committee of congress to the Vermont agents of the 18th of August, and their answers thereto; the terms offered by the agents for the admission of the state into the union, and the resolution of congress of the 20th of that month, by which the terms were rejected. The character of these documents, and the apparent frankness and candor of the Vermont commissioners in communicating them made a favorable impression, but their position was peculiarly embarrassing. Gen. Haldimand had been led to believe by Col. Allen's letter of the 10th of July, and Major Fay's confirmatory statements in August, that at the election which was to take place in September, and which had just then passed, a majority of the officers elected

---

[1] *Hald. Papers*, vol. 1, p. 313.

[2] *Ira Allen's Hist.*, p. 175. *Life of Chittenden*, p. 214, *Hald. Papers*, p. 313, 319–343, 345–369.

would be favorable to a treaty, and that when the legislature came together in October, commissioners would be appointed to conclude it. There could not have been the least expectation on the part of the Vermonters that such would be the case, but the probability of such a result had been held out to Gen. Haldimand and his commissioners as the only practicable means of obtaining a prolongation of the armistice. If any or all of the men who had been privy to the negotiation should venture to propose the measure of entering into such a treaty, they very well knew that it would be rejected by an overwhelming majority of the legislature, and that those who favored it would be deserted by the people, and treated as enemies of the state and country. The meeting of the legislature was just at hand, and a like expedient to that in June, of having no movement made in that direction could not be repeated with any hope of success. Such a failure of the legislature to act would be pretty sure to convince the already wavering mind of Gen. Haldimand of the bad faith of the Vermonters, and to result in an immediate commencement of hostilities.

The only mode of avoiding this difficulty was by shifting the risk and responsibility of making the first public proposal of a treaty from the Vermont legislature to Gen. Haldimand. This would save the leaders in the negotiation from exposure to their own people, and might have the effect to continue the inaction of the British forces to the end of the campaign.

With these ends in view, Messrs. Allen and Fay represented that although they and their associates in the Vermont government were anxious to bring about a reconciliation, yet that a very large portion of their people would be opposed to a separate treaty, and from the best information they could then obtain, they felt compelled to express the opinion that if they should propose and advocate the measure in the coming session of the legislature they would be likely to be defeated in their efforts. As a last resort for accomplishing the desired object, and as the best means of effecting it, they proposed that Gen. Haldimand should issue a proclamation embodying the offers he had made to them of a separate charter government, embracing their territory in its largest extent from Hudson's river to Mason's line, securing them in their land titles and in the choice of their own officers, except the governor, and in all the privileges enjoyed by the most favored colony under the crown; that the proclamation should be committed to the care of the British commissioners, who at the proper time should send it by a flag, under seal to the commanding officer at Castleton, directed to the speaker of the assembly, to whom it would be immediately forwarded. It was represented that a suitable time for sending the proclamation would be soon after the rejection by the legislature of the terms offered by congress, when the members would be likely to be in an unfriendly mood towards that body, but of the proper time the Vermont commissioners were to give notice by a flag. The contents of the dispatch would be unknown until it was opened by the speaker and laid before the house, and it was alleged by Messrs. Allen and Fay that this mode of introducing the subject would enable the friends of the measure to exercise a much greater influence in its favor than if they should in the first instance publicly commit themselves to the measure by proposing it. Gen. Haldimand appears to have hesitated about acceding to this proposal, on account of the uncertainty in regard to the temper with which his proclamation might be received. In answer to certain written queries to the Vermont commissioners they stated that their proposal coincided with the opinion of the governor and such of his council as wished for a British government, that the proclamation would lay a good foundation for the action of the legislature, that under the circumstances in which it would be presented there was the highest probability of its success, and that even if it should be rejected they were confident it would not injure the prospects of a reunion, but would "add to the number of those who would still pursue the grand object."

This plan was finally agreed upon and the form of a proclamation was prepared, of which a copy is found in the Haldimand papers. The Vermont legislature was to meet the second week in October, and Gen. Haldimand determined to send about that time with his proclamation a strong force to Crown Point, to encourage the efforts of the friends of the crown and to act according to circumstances. He also directed strong parties from Niagara to appear on the Mohawk river and on the frontier of Pennsylvania to harrass the Americans, to distract and divide their forces and to diminish their supplies.[1]

Gen. St. Leger at the head of the British army from Canada ascended Lake Champlain as far as Ticonderoga, General Enos having the command of the troops of Vermont on the frontiers with his head quarters at Castleton. The several officers under him, among whom were Colonels Samuel Fletcher and Ebenezer Walbridge, were fully acquainted with the Canada negotiations. Notwithstanding

---

[1] *Haldimand Papers*, vol. 1, p. 465, 469, 471, 477, 361, 367–505. *Ira Allen's Vt.*, p. 184, 189. *Williams's Vt.*, p. 266.

the agreement for the cessation of arms, it was necessary to keep up the mimicry of war, by sending out scouts to observe the movements of the enemy. One of these scouts fell in with one of St. Leger's, shots were exchanged, and Sergeant Tupper who commanded the Vermont scout was killed on the spot, and his men retreated. General St. Leger caused the body of the sergeant to be decently buried, and sent all his clothes with an open letter to Gen. Enos expressing his regret for his fate and making an apology for his death. The dispatch and apparel were openly delivered to Gen. Enos, and caused considerable excitement among the troops. What followed will be related in the language of Col. Ira Allen.

"Gen. Enos and Colonels Fletcher and Walbridge wrote letters and sent immediately an express to Gov. Chittenden at Charlestown, announcing the arrival at Ticonderoga of the British army; wherein they blended public matters and private negotiations. Mr. Hathaway, the messenger, not being in the secret, failed not to proclaim the extraordinary message of Gen. St. Leger through the streets of Charlestown, till he came to the governor, which happened in the recess of the legislature, and occasioned crowds of people to follow him to hear the news. The governor and others were sitting in a large room, among whom were some persons that were eager to learn about the negotiations which were generally supposed to be carried on between the British in Canada and Vermont, to make an ill use thereof. The governor opened all of the letters and thought it prudent to peruse them himself before he allowed them to be publicly read. The letters were found to contain both public and private information, which occasioned some change of letters between the governor and Messrs. Brownson and Fassett, who were in the secret and were next to the governor. In this confused moment, Major Runnals [who was in command of some New Hampshire troops stationed at Charlestown], came in and inquired of Col. Allen what was the reason that Gen. St. Leger was sorry that Sergeant Tupper was killed? Mr. Allen said he could not tell. Mr. Runnals repeated the question; and Mr. Allen observed, that good men were sorry when good men were killed, or met with misfortune, which might be the case with Gen. St. Leger. This answer enraged Mr. Runnals, and he again loudly inquired what reason could possibly induce a British general to be sorry when his enemy was killed, and to send his clothes to the widow? Col. Allen then requested Major Runnals to go at the head of his regiment and demand the reason of his sorrow, and not stay there asking impertinent questions, eating up the country's provisions, doing nothing when the frontier was invaded.

Very high words passed between the Major and Col. Allen, till Mr. Runnals left the house. This maneuver drew all the attention from the letters. It was then proposed that the board of war should be convened, and the governor summoned the members of the board to appear as soon as possible in his chamber, leaving Mr. Hathaway to detail the news to the populace, the board of war all being in the secret. New letters were made out from Gen. Enos and Cols. Fletcher and Walbridge's letters, and for the information and satisfaction of the public, read in council and assembly for the originals, and then returned to the governor. These letters contained every thing but the existing negotiations which prudence and policy dictated to be separated from other parts of the letters." [1]

Gen. Haldimand, who as has been seen, had entered into the plan of making an offer to the Vermonters by proclamation with some reluctance, from the fear that it might be unfavorably received, appears to have left the time of its publication wholly to the discretion of the Vermont commissioners. They were of course in no hurry to have it forwarded while the enemy could be otherwise kept quiet. The legislature of the state did not complete their consideration of the proposal of congress of the 20th of August until the 19th of October, when as had been anticipated, its terms were declined, and commissioners were appointed to negotiate with the claiming states as before related. It had been agreed to delay the issuing of the proclamation till such legislative action had taken place. Events at the south furnished a sufficient excuse for not having it forwarded at all. The army of Lord Cornwallis had been besieged at Yorktown for some weeks by the combined American and French forces under Washington, and had actually surrendered on the 19th of October. News in those days traveled slowly. Towards the latter part of the month a report of the surrender, which had indeed been for some days expected, reached Charlestown. Upon which Col. Allen addressed a letter to the British com-

[1] The dispatches were committed by Gov. Chittenden fcr revision to Nathaniel Chipman then a rising young lawyer who had been admitted into the secret of the negotiation, who afterward became a senator in congress and chief justice of the state, and whose patriotism was never doubted. He was learned and eminent in his profession. His work on the principles of government, evinces a knowledge of constitutional law and a power of reasoning that would have done honor even to Daniel Webster. He is justly entitled to rank among the most profound and able jurists of the country. See his life by his brother Daniel Chipman generally, and particularly pp. 37, 70, also *Chipman's Reports*, Rutland, 1793, *Principles of Government*, Burlington 1833. *Allen's Biography.*

missioners, enclosing copies of the proceedings of the legislature on the resolutions of congress, stating the report of the capture of Cornwallis, and adding that whether true or false it would have an effect upon the people unfavorable to the negotiation, and that in the then critical situation of affairs it would be altogether improper to publish the proclamation. The package containing this letter appears to have reached the British commissioners at Ticonderoga about the first of November, upon which the troops and military stores were embarked, and were soon on their way to Canada, thus ending a campaign which had threatened carnage and desolation to the whole northern frontier, with the loss of only a single life, and with only a small expenditure of means.[1]

---

[1] *Haldimand Papers*, vol. 1, p. 519, vol. 2, p. 127 - 139, 153 - 155, 122 - 127. *Life of Stark*, p. 285. *Life of Brant*, vol. 2, p. 201 - 3. *Ira Allen's Vt.*, p. 189 - 192. The account in the text, especially in relation to the proclamation, differs in some respects from that of Mr. Allen, but appears to be fully sustained by the correspondence and reports found in the *Haldimand Papers*.

CHAPTER XXXIII.

Favorable Effects of the Canada Negotiations on the State and Country.

1781-1782.

Gen. Stark at Saratoga in command of the northern frontier without the means of defence — The author of the life of Brant condemns the Canada negotiation, but admits that it saved New York as well as Vermont from invasion and carnage — Letter of Gov. Chittenden to Gen. Washington on the negotiation and the affairs of Vermont — Civil war threatened in the territories newly acquired from New York and New Hampshire — Washington's reply to Chittenden, urging the relinquishment of the eastern and western unions and assuring him of the consequent admission of the state into the federal union — The legislature of Vermont complies with his advice, and appoints agents and delegates to Congress.

DURING the year 1781, while the negotiations of which an account has been given were going on, the frontiers of New York as well as those of Vermont, had been greatly exposed to incursions from the enemy, without any adequate means of defence. On the 25th of June Gen. Washington wrote Gen. Stark, then at his home in New Hampshire, requesting him to assume the command in northern New York, with his headquarters at Saratoga, informing him that the operations of the campaign made it necessary to recall the continental troops from that quarter; that his principal force would be a body of militia from Berkshire county, Massachusetts, and "the militia and state troops of New York;" and that he relied upon him to use his utmost exertions "to draw forth the force of the country from the Green mountains," which, from his "unlimited influence with those people," he trusted he would be able to do. On the 15th of July, Stark wrote Washington from Derryfield that he should set out for Saratoga the beginning of the next week, and on his way there would "hold a treaty with the Green Mountain Boys, but," he added, "not having seen or been acquainted with those turbulent sons of freedom for several years I am at a loss to determine my reception, but hope it will be such as shall lead to the general good."

On the 9th of August, he again wrote Washington from Albany, that he had been at Bennington and made a visit to the governor, who together with the leading men of the country, had promised him every assistance in their power to repel the common enemy; and, he added, "I have reason to believe from their conduct that their promises are not fallacious; for before I came to Bennington, Major McKinstry, who has command of the troops at Saratoga, sent an express to apprise them of the enemy's advance for his post. The alarm was spread and in a few hours one hundred and fifty men on horseback, marched to his assistance. The alarm proved false, and next day they returned but not until they had visited Saratoga." As further evidence of the good disposition of these people, he stated that on the Monday previous, a party of eleven men principally tories, had been discovered in the south-east part of Bennington, who had made prisoner of Esq. Bleecker of the New York government and were taking him to Canada, that they were pursued and captured by the Vermonters and their prisoner released. Gen. Stark suggested that they might be treated as spies, but referred the disposition of them to Gen. Washington who afterwards wrote him to consider them as prisoners of war. It may be added that Gen. Enos, who was in command of the Vermont troops, placed himself under the military direction of Gen. Washington, and his subordinate United States officers, and that he was in continued correspondence with Gen. Stark, and always in readiness to render him assistance and obey his commands.[1]

Gen. Stark, at Saratoga found himself in command of an extensive frontier, without any proper means of defending it against any serious attack of the enemy. The imbecility which characterized the efforts of the New York government in the early part of the season, of which an account has already been given, continued to a great extent to prevail. Want of men and destitution of supplies of every description were the constant complaints of the general; and Gov. Clinton's best exertions, from the disaffection of his people and the consequent weakness of his authority, were insufficient to furnish adequate relief. In cases of alarm, which from the known strength and mysterious movements of the enemy in Canada and on Lake Champlain were not unfrequent, calls on the militia, if not wholly disregarded, were but tardily and partially responded to. There is no doubt whatever that the British force in Canada which at several times made hostile demonstrations from St. Johns, but which was kept at bay by the negotiation of the Vermonters, was sufficient to have made a successful inroad upon the

---

[1] *Life of Stark*, p. 211, 215, 275, 277, 282. *Rev. Cor.* vol. 3, p. 353. Correspondence of Gen. Enos with Washington, and Enos and Col. Walbridge with Stark, in the *Washington Papers*, U. S. State Department, vol. 53.

exposed northern frontier of New York, with a fair prospect of extending its ravages as far south as Albany. Col. Stone, in his interesting life of Brant, has given a detailed history of the military preparations and movements in the northern department during this campaign, together with some account of the Vermont troubles, in which he takes the New York view of the controversy, and attributes the worst of motives to the Vermont leaders. He nevertheless admits that the invasion of northern New York was averted, not by the military preparations for her defence, but by what he calls the treasonable negotiations of the Vermonters with the enemy.[1]

Mr. Stone is among the few writers of history who have charged the Vermont leaders with the serious intention of surrendering their state to the British crown. The evidence on which he appears to rely in support of this charge consists of the affidavits laid before the New York legislature early in 1782, by Gov. Clinton, of two persons who had been in Canada and had learned that Allen and Fay were there negotiating with the enemy for uniting Vermont to the British crown, together with information obtained and furnished the governor by an intelligent gentleman then lately in New York city, stating what were understood to be the terms of the treaty. It will be perceived that this proves nothing more than what has been fully stated in the preceding pages and has always been admitted, viz: that the Vermont leaders in answer to the advances made to them by the British officers, persuaded those officers that they were desirous of entering into such a treaty, whenever they could induce their people and legislature to concur in the measure. The question remains, what were the motives and objects of the Vermonters in these proceedings? Was the negotiation, as they always insisted, an act of dissembling on their part to secure their state from the invasion and ravage of a public enemy, or were they really intending to surrender it to that enemy? That the motive which they assigned for their conduct was amply sufficient to account for it, without seeking for any other, cannot be questioned. And when their acts are well explained by the patriotic motive under which they profess to have acted, it seems unjust, as well as unnecessary, to undertake to convict them of others less pure, which they altogether disclaim and deny.

Mr. Stone, while charging the Vermont leaders with the design of delivering their state into the hands of the enemy, concedes that

---

[1] *Life of Brant*, vol. 2, chap. 6 and p. 196, 197, 203. *Life of Stark*, p. 215, 286.

"there was never any intention on the part of the Vermontese to listen to the British proposals," and that "it was very certain from the conduct of the people of the Grants when they heard of St. Leger's regrets for killing the sergeant, that they were prepared for no such arrangement." In point of fact, there were doubtless fewer friends of Great Britain among the people of Vermont than in any other part of the country, of equal population. Their patriotism had been tried by the fiery ordeal of Burgoyne's invasion, during which the tory element had been sifted out. Most of those who had feared his power or could be allured by his promises, had passed within his lines and had not been allowed to return. His known sympathizers who had remained had been generally banished and their property, as well as that of those who had fled, confiscated. The state had thus been almost entirely purged of its tories, who had indeed, been more harshly dealt with, than those of any other state. Dr. Williams, in his history says: "So odious were the British proceedings and government at that time to the people of America, that it was with difficulty, the people of Vermont could be kept quiet, under the idea of a correspondence carried on with the British, though known to be designed for their protection. Once or twice there were small insurrections to demand explanations; and nothing but the well known strong attachment of the gentlemen concerned, to the independence of Vermont and of America, could have preserved them from open violence and destruction."

Whatever the adversaries of the Vermont leaders may have alleged against their patriotism, their foresight and sagacity was never called in question. These qualities are sufficiently attested by the masterly skill and ability with which, for a series of years, they managed the affairs of their people to the discomfiture and defeat of the host of eminent and adroit politicians and statesmen of other states, by whom they were on every side assailed. These men well knew that any attempt to transfer the allegiance of their people from their common country to Great Britain would be wholly unavailing, and that whosoever should undertake it, however much they might have been formerly honored, would be at once deserted and discarded by them. That such men should deliberately enter upon a measure which they could clearly see must end in their own disgrace and consign them to infamy, is altogether incredible. They were not fools and could never have been guilty of such folly. While the insidious advances of the enemy to the Vermonters were adroitly used by them for protecting their territory against invasion, they could not have been unwilling to discover that the negotiation was likely to have another favorable effect upon their interests; that by operating on the fears of congress, its tendency was to induce its members the more readily to listen to their application for admission into the union of the states. This had been the long continued object of their ambition, by which they would be fully secured against all danger of ever being brought again under the oppressive and detested jurisdiction of New York. The favorable effects of these fears in congress on the claims of Vermont have already been noticed.[1]

The acts of St. Leger, before mentioned, showing his regret for the death of Sergeant Tupper, tended strongly to confirm the suspicions which already prevailed to a considerable extent, of the existence of a treaty between the British and the Vermonters, unfavorable to the common cause of the country. Gen. Stark, at Saratoga, wrote to Gov. Chittenden under date of Nov. 5th, stating that being in command of the northern department, he felt it his duty to ask of him the perusal of the original letter of the British commander respecting the deceased sergeant, and the fullest information on the subject, that he might report the same to the commander-in-chief. Gen. Stark, in his letter, spoke of the alacrity with which the militia of Vermont had "taken the field on every requisition," and stated that on receiving the news of the surrender of Cornwallis, he had caused the glorious event to be announced "by a discharge of fourteen cannon and of a like number of platoons, in honor of the United States of America," the fourteenth discharge being for Vermont. Gov. Chittenden did not decline an explanation, but made it directly to Gen. Washington, and so informed Gen. Stark.

The explanation, which gave the real character and object of the negotiation, was not entirely new to Washington. An official copy of the resolutions of congress, of the 7th of the preceding August, which it will be remembered, invited the Vermonters to appoint agents to repair to Philadelphia and consult with a committee of congress on the subject of the admission of their state into the federal union, had been committed to the general to be forwarded to Vermont. It was dispatched by a special messenger, Capt. Ezra Heacock, with a verbal message from Washington to Gov. Chittenden, the object of which was to learn whether the people of Vermont would be satisfied with the independence suggested by those resolu-

[1] *Life of Brant*, vol. 2, p. 197, 203, note. *Life of N. Chipman*, p. 37–61, *Sparks's Life of Ethan Allen*. *Hildreth's U. S.*, vol. 3, p. 408. *Street's Council of Revision*, p. 104. *Lossing*. *Williams's Vermont*, p. 272.

tions, or whether they seriously contemplated joining the enemy and becoming a British colony. Gov. Chittenden entered into a free conversation with the messenger on the subject of the affairs of Vermont, assuring him that the negotiation with Canada was resorted to as the only means of securing their state against invasion from the enemy, that their people were zealous supporters of the independence of the United States, and desirous that their state should become a member of the federal union; but that under no circumstances would they be subject to the jurisdiction of New York. This conversation Gov. Chittenden requested Capt. Heacock to report to Gen. Washington.

The letter of Gov. Chittenden to Washington of which a copy will be found in the Appendix, No. 10, bore date Nov. 14, 1781. It contained a comprehensive history of the efforts of the people of the state to gain admission into the federal union, and to maintain their independence against the aggressive claims and attacks of the neighboring states, of their patriotic and noble exertions and sacrifices in the cause of their country, and it gave a detailed account of their negotiations with the enemy, made necessary for their defence, in consequence of the hostility of the adjoining states and their neglect to furnish them aid. The letter expressed the utmost confidence in the wisdom and patriotism of Gen. Washington, and was in effect an able and manly appeal to him to use his great influence in favor of their claim to independence.[1]

The frontiers of Vermont were scarcely relieved from apprehended invasion by the withdrawal of the British forces to Canada, when serious troubles from conflicting claims of jurisdiction arose in both the eastern and western unions. In some places to the eastward of Connecticut river, justices, sheriffs, and constables, appointed by both Vermont and New Hampshire, were exercising or attempting to exercise jurisdiction over the same persons. In one instance a New Hampshire sheriff in undertaking in obedience to the direction of the New Hampshire assembly, to release two prisoners from Charlestown jail, was himself arrested and imprisoned by the Vermont sheriff. The latter being sent by the authorities of Vermont to Exeter as one of a committee "to agree on measures to prevent hostilities" was arrested and thrown into prison at Exeter and there held as a hostage for the release of the New Hampshire sheriff. The militia of both states were ordered to hold themselves in readi-

---

[1] *Sparks's Rev. Cor.*, vol. 3, p. 440. *Ira Allen's Vt.*, p. 220. *Williams's Vt.*, p. 276.

ness to march to sustain their respective jurisdictions. But the New Hampshire assembly issued a proclamation, allowing forty days to their revolted citizens to return to their allegiance, by which a conflict of arms was, for the time being, happily averted.

The danger of an armed collision was still more imminent in the territory of the western union. Col. John Van Rensselaer, whose residence was near San Coick, now North Hoosick, acting under the authority of New York, appears to have arrested at New City (Lansingburg) a person having a colonel's commission under Vermont, but who, after some riotous proceedings, effected his escape. Afterwards, about the first of December, Col. Van Rensselaer was himself arrested with several others and taken to Bennington, where, he says in a letter to Gen. Gansevoort, he was "treated like a gentleman and discharged." Other arrests were soon afterwards made by both sides, each party gathering its adherents in arms, who for several days encamped against each other in the vicinity of San Coick. On the 12th of December, Col. Yates wrote from San Coick to Gen. Gansevoort at Albany, informing him that the favorers of the Vermont jurisdiction appeared desperate, that he had only about eighty men and the insurrectionists one hundred and forty-six; that the rioters were secured in a block house; that a field piece and artillerymen were wanted to dislodge them, and that speedy reenforcements were required, and urging him to come immediately and take the command. Hitherto none but residents to the westward of the twenty mile line had taken part in the controversy. But Gov. Chittenden, having tried in vain to effect a temporary reconciliation, by a mutual release of prisoners, and a forbearance of further arrests until he could call the legislature together, saw no other means of preventing bloodshed, than by calling out a sufficient force from the original territory of Vermont to render it necessary for the New Yorkers to disperse at once. The regiment of Col. Walbridge from Bennington and its vicinity was accordingly ordered to march to San Coick, upon which as had been anticipated, Col. Yates with his small force retreated. Gov. Clinton, who was at Poughkeepsie, had instructed Gen. Gansevoort to raise the necessary force and quell the insurrection. The final result will be related in the words of Mr. Stone in his *Life of Brant:* "On the 16th Gen. Gansevoort took the field himself, repairing in the first instance to the headquarters of Gen. Stark at Saratoga, in order to obtain a detachment of troops and a field piece. But the troops of Stark were too naked to move from their quarters; and it was thought improper for him to interfere without an order from Gen.

Heath. Gansevoort then crossed over to the east side of the river, in order to place himself at the head of such militia as he could muster in Schaghticoke and Hoosick; but was soon met by Col. Yates, in full retreat from the house of Col. John Van Rensselaer. He had been able to raise but eighty men of Col. John Van Rensselaer's regiment to put down the insurgents; and on arriving at San Coick he discovered a force of five hundred men advancing from the Grants to the assistance of the rebels. Gansevoort retired five miles farther, in order to find comfortable quarters for his men, and then attempted, but without success, to open a correspondence with the leaders of the insurgents. Calls had been made upon four regiments, viz: those of Cols. Yates, and Henry K. Van Rensselaer, as heretofore stated, and upon Col. Van Vechten, and Major Taylor. But from the whole no greater force than eighty men could be raised. Of Col. Van Vechten's regiment, only himself, a few officers and one private could be brought into the field. Under these discouraging circumstances, the general was compelled to relinquish the expedition, and the insurgents remained the victors, to the no small terror of those of the inhabitants who were well disposed, inasmuch as they were apprehensive of being taken prisoners and carried away, as had been the case with others, should they refuse taking the oath of allegiance to the government of Vermont." [1]

Notwithstanding the success of the Vermont government in vindicating its authority in the territory recently claimed from New York and the temporary restoration of quiet in that from New Hampshire, the position of the state was not entirely such as could be desired. While the states of New York and New Hampshire were seeking to appropriate her territory, and annihilate her jurisdiction, and congress was apparently giving countenance to their efforts, she might perhaps have been justified by the law of self defence, or excused by that of retaliation, in extending her claims over portions of their territory. Under such circumstances her measures of annexation doubtless tended to increase her power and resources, and if no change had occurred in those circumstances, public opinion in other states might have permanently sustained and sanctioned the proceeding. But when congress voluntarily offered to acknowledge the jurisdiction of Vermont over all the

[1] *Life of Brant*, vol. 2, p. 205-207. *Clinton Papers*, Nos. 4071, 4124, 4161, 4206, 4213, 4217, 4219, 4223, 4225, 4230, 4238, 4245, 4246, 4269. *Life of Stark*, p. 296, 300, 301, 302. *Ira Allen's Vt.*, p. 200-203. *Williams's Vt.*, p. 279, 280. *Belknap's N. H.*, p. 391, 392.

territory which had been originally claimed for her, and all for which her people had been for years contending, and to guaranty such territory to her against those adverse states, her government found itself placed in a new and unexpected position, one which it was difficult to vindicate by sound argument. This was attempted in a pamphlet of sixteen pages, published at Hartford in January, 1782, entitled: *The Present State of the Controversy*, etc. The writer presents very strong, if not conclusive reasons for the original extension of jurisdiction; but his argument is much less satisfactory on the question of its continuance in the altered state of affairs. His principal objections to the overture of congress were the want of power in the Vermont legislature to dissolve the connexions which they had formed with the new territories, and the apprehension that congress might not live up to their engagement and admit the state into the federal union, after she should have weakened herself by relinquishing the additional territory. This last objection was doubtless entitled to some consideration, and though such a violation of faith could not be reasonably anticipated, yet if it were actually to occur it would place congress so clearly in the wrong before the world as to add greatly to the moral strength of the cause of Vermont. Even in that event it might possibly be wise to accede to the proposition, for the maxim that "it is better to suffer wrong than to do wrong," is not only sound morality, but may often be the dictate of sound policy.

Although the legislature of Vermont, on the first announcement of the proposals of congress, had declined to accede to them, the people were by no means unanimous for their rejection. Probably a majority of the inhabitants of the original territory of the New Hampshire Grants west of Conecticut river, would from the first have gladly accepted the overture of congress, but for the entangling obligations in which they were involved towards those who had so recently united with them. The sentiment of the friends of Vermont in other parts of the country was undoubtedly in favor of such acceptance.

But whatever objections might have been entertained by the people of Vermont and those administering their affairs to the offer of congress, they were in great measure removed by an appeal to their reason and patriotism in a letter from Gen. Washington, written in answer to that from Gov. Chittenden to him before mentioned. It bore date January 1, 1782, and urged in the strongest terms, a relinquishment of their recently acquired territory, in compliance with the wishes of congress. In the letter Washington says:

"It is not my business neither do I think it necessary now to discuss the origin of the right of a number of inhabitants to that tract of country, formerly distinguished by the name of the New Hampshire Grants, and now known by that of Vermont. I will take it for granted that their right was good, because congress by their resolve of the 7th of August imply it, and by that of the 21st, are willing fully to confirm it, provided the new state is confined to certain described bounds. It appears therefore to me, that the dispute of boundary is the only one which exists, and that this being removed all further difficulties would be removed also; and the matter terminated to the satisfaction of all parties. You have nothing to do but withdraw your jurisdiction to your old limits and obtain an acknowledgment of independence and sovereignty, under the resolve of the 21st of August, for so much territory as does not interfere with the ancient established bounds of New York, New Hampshire and Massachusetts. I persuade myself you will see and acquiesce in the reason the justice and indeed the necessity of such a decision. In my private opinion, while it behoves the delegates of the states now confederated to do ample justice to a body of people sufficiently respectable by their numbers and entitled by other claims to be admitted into that confederation, it becomes them also to attend to the interests of their constituents, and see, that under the appearance of justice to one they do not materially injure the rights of others. I am apt to think this is the prevailing opinion of congress, and that your late extension of claim has, upon the principles I have above mentioned rather diminished than increased the number of your friends, and that if such extension should be persisted in, it will be made a common cause, and not considered as only affecting the rights of the states immediately interested in the loss of territory, a loss of too serious a nature not to claim the attention of any people."[1]

The legislature of Vermont, at its October session, had adjourned to meet at Bennington on the last day of January; but a quorum for the transaction of business did not assemble until the 11th day of February, when the governor laid before them, among other papers, the foregoing letter of Gen. Washington, and another of the 17th of January, on the same subject, from Gen. Oliver Wolcott, one of the delegates in congress from Connecticut. On the 16th, the subject of the relations of the state towards congress and the

---

[1] *Sparks's Washington*, vol. 8, p. 220. *Williams's Vt.*, 281, *I. Allen's Vt.* p. 221–225.

claiming states was taken up in committee of the whole, the governor in the chair, and discussed from day to day until the 21st, when the legislature without a division, resolved to dissolve the eastern and western unions and to apply to congress for admission to the Union on the terms indicated by the resolutions of congress, of the 7th and 21st of the preceding August.

In pursuance of this determination, Jonas Fay, Moses Robinson, Paul Spooner, and Isaac Tichenor were appointed agents of the state to settle with congress the terms of admission of the state into the federal union, any one or two of them being authorized to take their seats in that body as delegates, as soon as the union should be consummated. They were instructed to proceed immediately to Philadelphia, and it seemed now that the long continued troubles of Vermont with her neighboring states and with congress were at an end, and that she might hereafter peaceably and quietly enjoy her independent jurisdiction.[1]

---

[1] *Journal of Assembly*, February 11, 16, 18, 19, 20, 21, 22, 26, and 28th. *Slade*, 168-170. *Williams's Vermont*, 282. *Ira Allen's Vermont*, 214-217.

CHAPTER XXXIV.

PROCEEDINGS OF CONGRESS FAVORABLE TO VERMONT.

1782.

Proceedings of Congress in relation to the non-compliance of Vermont in October 1781, with the resolves of the previous August — And also on the acceptance in February, 1782, by Vermont of the terms of those resolves and the relinquishment of her late claims of jurisdiction over new territory — A committee of congress report fully in favor of Vermont, but the report is not acted upon.

WE now return to the proceedings of congress in relation to Vermont. On the 17th of December 1781, a letter from President Weare, to the New Hampshire delegates in congress, with accompanying papers, giving an account of the late disturbances in the western part of that state, growing out of the claim of jurisdiction by Vermont, was read and referred to a committee of five, of whom Mr. Carroll of Maryland, was chairman. Sundry papers relating to similar troubles in north-eastern New York were afterwards referred to the same committee. On the 7th of January, 1782, the committee made a report which after being discussed on several occasions, was on the 21st recommitted to another committee of five of which Mr. Ellery of Rhode Island, was chairman: This committee reported on the 25th of January, and after debate on that day, and on the 28th, the whole subject was referred to a grand committee of one delegate from each of the thirteen states. A few days afterwards Jonas Fay and Ira Allen, who, with Elisha Paine and Abel Curtis, had been appointed by the governor and council of Vermont to repair to Philadelphia, and watch over the interests of the state, arrived and presented their credentials to congress. They had, Mr. Allen says, "repeated interviews with committees and members of that body, who appeared very much dissatisfied with the legislature of Vermont, for not complying with their resolves of the 7th and 20th of August." The agents in justification of the extension of the state jurisdiction, alleged that they were driven into the measure as a means of self preservation against the prior hostile acts and claims of the two adjoining states; that the orders of Governor Chittenden for calling out the militia both against New Hampshire and New York had the salutary effect intended, of preventing the effusion of blood, and of averting civil war, by making it apparent that opposition for the time being would be fruitless; that the legislature had appointed commissioners to adjust with commissioners from those states the boundaries between them, but that they would not enter into any negotiation on the subject. On the 6th of Feb., they presented a memorial to Congress embodying the grounds of their justification in some detail, but without apparently producing any favorable impression. The grand committee on the 19th of February submitted their report from which it clearly appeared that the non-compliance of Vermont with the terms offered by congress, was viewed with strong disapprobation.

The report, after reciting the resolutions of congress of the 7th and 20th of August, the failure of the Vermonters to comply with them, and their attempts to establish their jurisdiction beyond the limits therein prescribed, proposed the adoption of resolutions in substance as follows:

1. That the boundaries of the territory of the New Hampshire Grants were and should be as described in the resolution of 20th of August.

2. That in case the inhabitants of the said territory, in one month after notice given of these resolutions to Thomas Chittenden, Esq., should relinquish their claim to all territory without those boundaries and accede to the articles of confederation, their district should be acknowledged as a free and independent state and admitted into the union.

3. That in case the said inhabitants should not comply with the foregoing terms within the time specified, their neglect should be considered as a manifest indication of designs hostile to these United States, and that thereupon the forces of those states should be employed against them; and further that in such case congress would consider all the lands within the district to the eastward of the ridge of mountains as belonging to the state of New Hampshire and all to the west of the ridge to New York.

Another resolution was in these words:

"*Resolved*, That in case of the neglect or refusal of the inhabitants residing within the district aforesaid, to comply with the terms prescribed in the resolutions aforesaid, the commander-in-chief of the armies of these United States, do without delay or further order carry these resolutions as far as they respect his department into full execution."

This report, after debate on the day of its presentation, was again taken up on the first of March, when after an unsuccessful motion to amend the second resolution, another was made to strike out the whole of it, and on the question shall the resolution stand? only six states of the thirteen voted aye, and the resolution was in effect rejected. A vote was then taken on recommitting the report for further consideration, which was also lost; these several votes very clearly indicating that congress, at that time, were averse to any action on the subject. If intelligence in those days could have traveled by electricity or even by steam, as at present, the debates and votes on this report would have been altogether unnecessary, the legislature of Vermont having seven days previous (February 22), dissolved both the eastern and western unions, and resolved to accede to the proposals of congress. The Vermont agents left for home the 2d of March, and met the news of the action of their legislature on crossing the Hudson at Fishkill.

The appointment by the Vermont legislature of Jonas Fay, Moses Robinson, Paul Spooner and Isaac Tichenor as agents to announce to congress the readiness of the state to accede to the proposals of that body, has already been mentioned. They bore a letter from Gov. Chittenden to Gen. Washington, thanking him for the kind notice he had taken of the affairs of Vermont, informing him of the compliance of the legislature with his advice in withdrawing their claim to the old limits of the state, and expressing "the highest expectation" of the speedy admission of the state into the federal union. The letter also called Gen. Washington's attention to the local situation of the state "as an extended frontier awfully exposing these infant plantations to the power and fury of the common enemy," and referred him for a more particular account of its situation, to the bearer of the letter.[1]

Having arrived in Philadelphia, the agents on the 31st of March, addressed a communication to the president of congress, stating that in consequence of the resolution of that body of the 20th of August last, the state of Vermont had invariably pursued every measure in order to comply with it, in a manner that was consistent with the obligations she was under to the people inhabiting the east and west unions, and maintaining the peace and harmony of her citizens with those inhabitants. The letter enclosed an official copy of the resolutions of the legislature, declaring their compliance with the said resolution of congress, and also a duplicate of their commission

[1] Papers of Continental congress in State Dept., Washington, No. 40, vol. 2. and No. 186. *Stevens' Papers,* vol. 8, p. 121–153. *Jour. Cong.,* Jan. 25, 28, Feb. 19, and March 1, 1782. *Williams's Vt.,* 285. *Rev. Cor.,* vol. 3, p. 492. *Ira Allen's Vt.,* 208–213. Mr. Allen expresses strong regret at this action of the Vermont legislature, but few will probably agree with him.

under the great seal of the state empowering them in behalf of the state of Vermont, to subscribe the articles of confederation. This letter of the agents was read in congress the next morning, and together with all papers on the files, relating to the same subject, received since the said 20th of August, was referred to a committee consisting of Messrs. Clymer of Pennsylvania, Carroll of Maryland, Clark of New Jersey, Livermore of New Hampshire, and Law of Connecticut. On the question of commitment the yeas and nays were called, and the states of New York, Virginia and Georgia voted No, and South Carolina was divided, indicating that the compliance of congress with its overture of the 20th of August, was to meet with serious opposition.

The opponents of Vermont being dissatisfied with the manner in which the notice of the letter of the agents had been stated on the journal, Mr. Madison of Virginia, on the 3d of April moved to amend the record by entering upon it a copy of the proceedings of the Vermont legislature in October, 1781, declining to accede to the resolution of the 20th of August, and the protest of the legisture of New York of the 19th of the preceding November. The motion failed, but the papers having been copied into Mr. Madison's motion, appear on the journal as a part of it.

On the 17th of April, the committee, to whom the letter of the Vermont agents and other papers were referred, presented their report. It recited the resolution of the 20th of August, stating that it had been adopted by the vote of nine states, and reconsidered and reaffirmed on the 21st, and that in the opinion of the committee, the competency of congress to enter into the resolution was full and complete, notwithstanding the protest of the legislature of New York of the preceding November.

The following is the residue of the report, viz:

"That on the day of the people residing in the district called Vermont, in considering the said act of congress of the 20th and 21st of August, did reject the propositions therein made to them, as preliminary to an acknowledgment of their sovereignty and independence and admission into the federal union, as appears by their proceedings on the files of congress; but that on a subsequent day, the aforementioned resolution of the 20th and 21st of August, being unaltered and unrepealed, and the proposition therein contained, in the opinion of your committee still open to be acceded to, the said people did, in their general assembly on the 22d of February last, enter into the following resolutions:

"That the west bank of Connecticut river, and a line beginning at the northwest corner of the commonwealth of Massachusetts, from thence northward twenty miles east of Hudson's river, as specified in the resolutions of August last, shall be considered as the east and west boundaries of this state. And that this assembly do relinquish all claims and demands to, and right of jurisdiction in and over any and every district of territory without said boundary lines.

"That in the sense of your committee, the people of the said district, by the last recited act, have fully complied with the stipulation made and required of them in the resolutions of the 20th and 21st of August, as preliminary to a recognition of their sovereignty and independence, and admission into the federal union of the states, and that the conditional promise and engagement of congress, of such recognition and admission, is thereby become absolute and necessary to be performed; your committee therefore submit the following resolution:

"That the district of territory called Vermont, as defined and limited by the resolutions of congress of the 20th and 21st of August, 1781, be, and it is hereby recognized and acknowledged by the name of the state of Vermont, as free, sovereign and independent; and that a committee be appointed to treat and confer with the agents and delegates from said state, upon the terms and mode of the admission of the said state into the federal union."

On the presentation of this report, Mr. Scott of New York, seconded by Mr. Livermore of New Hampshire, moved that the first Tuesday of October be assigned for its consideration. For which motion only the states of New York and Virginia voted. Mr. Montgomery of Pennsylvania, seconded by Mr. Ellery of Rhode Island, moved that it be considered on the third Tuesday of June, in favor of which only the two states of Pennsylvania and Rhode Island could be obtained. Upon which, Mr. Middleton of South Carolina, seconded by Mr. Bee of the same state, moved that it be taken up on the following Monday, but only the two states South Carolina and Georgia voted for that day. The subject was then dropped. The proposal of congress of the 20th of August, to acknowledge the independence of Vermont had been made by the vote of nine states, and it was understood, that in accordance with the articles of confederation, that number would be required to complete her admission into the union. Although a majority probably concurred with the committee in their report, it was obvious from the votes on these several motions that the friends of Vermont could not count on the requisite number to adopt it, and were, therefore, not ready to fix upon a time for taking it into consideration. Mr. Madison a few days afterwards, in writing to Mr. Pendleton, says, "The committee on the last application from Vermont have reported fully in their favor. The consideration of their report will not be called for, however, until the pulse of nine states beats favorably for it. This is so uncertain that the agents have returned." Mr. Madison, with the other delegates from Virginia, had voted for the resolution of the 20th of August, but they were now, from political considerations, opposed to carrying it into effect. Such was also understood to be the case with other southern delegates. The grounds of this opposition, together with some account of the intrigues in congress that operated unfavorably to Vermont will be given hereafter.

The Vermont agents, disappointed at this result, immediately prepared to leave Philadelphia, addressing, before their departure, a brief letter on the subject to the president of congress, which letter, showing the unpleasant position in which the failure of congress to perform its engagement had placed the state, is deemed worthy of insertion. It is as follows:

"PHILADELPHIA, April 19, 1782.

"Sir: The situation in which congress has been pleased to leave the business of our mission, as agents and delegates from the state of Vermont, renders our attendance at present unnecessary.

"As the representatives of an independent and virtuous people, we esteem it our duty to inform congress that, in consequence of their faith pledged to us, in and by a resolution of the 20th of August last, and by official advice from sundry gentlemen of the first respectability in America, the legislature of Vermont have been prevailed upon to comply, in the most ample manner, with the resolution aforesaid.

"On the 31st ult. we officially acquainted congress with the said compliance, together with the powers vested in us, in full confidence that, from the integrity and wisdom of that honorable body, no obstacle could prevent our confederation and union with them.

"We are disappointed by the unexpected delay of congress, in executing, on their part, the intent and spirit of the resolve above cited.

"We would not wish to urge the attention of the grand council of America from matters of more consequence than merely the happiness of a state; but the critical situation Vermont is reduced to, by casting off a considerable portion of her strength, in being exposed, as a forlorn hope, to the main force of the enemy in Canada, and destitute of the aid of the United States, in whose cause, at an early period, she freely fought and suffered, will, we presume, sufficiently apologise for being thus urgent, that unnecessary delay may not deprive us of the benefits of the confederation.

We purpose to leave this city to-morrow morning, and expect to be officially acquainted when our attendance will be necessary, and have the honor to be, sir, your most obedient and humble servants,

JONAS FAY,
MOSES ROBINSON,
ISAAC TICHENOR."

"His excellency the
President of Congress.[1]

[1] *Jour. Cong.* April 1, 3 and 17. *Madison Papers,* vol. 1, p. 121. *Slade,* p. 172.

CHAPTER XXXV.

Disturbances in Windham County, and Military Affairs.

1782.

Opposition to the Vermont authority in the south east corner of the state is encouraged by Gov. Clinton who appoints civil and military officers and advises them to resist the Vermont officers by force, which they do — Laws of Vermont enforced against them — The military used against the Yorkers as a *posse comitatus* — The New York sheriff and regimental officers arrested, tried, convicted and banished the state, not to return under the penalty of death — Military affairs and further overtures from Canada.

IT was evident from the proceedings of congress that no dependence could be placed on the performance of their engagement, to admit Vermont into the union, and that the state curtailed of her enlarged territory by the deception that had been practiced upon her, must rely in future solely on her own separate exertions and resources to maintain her independence. Her situation was indeed critical. The relinquishment of the claim of territory to the eastward of Connecticut river, had caused much dissatisfaction among its inhabitants, with whom a considerable number along the west bank of that river sympathized; and intrigues were set on foot, and for sometime continued to induce the inhabitants to the eastward of the Green mountain to separate from Vermont and unite with New Hampshire, which intrigues were countenanced and encouraged by, at least, a portion of the men concerned in the government of the latter state. In the southeast part of the county of Windham, new troubles soon arose with some of the old friends of New York. On the formation of the eastern union in February, 1781, a general amnesty in favor of all who had previously denied the authority of the state had been granted by the legislature, and all open opposition to its jurisdiction had ceased. Many who had formerly been disaffected, took the oath of allegiance to the state; the towns of Brattleboro, Guilford and Halifax, in which had been their principal strength, had been ever since represented in the general assembly, and all had remained quiet. Even Gov. Clinton had apparently ceased to stimulate them to resistance. The civil and military officers whom he had several years previously commissioned, had long forborne to act, and no attempt to exercise authority under the New York jurisdiction, had been made for more than a year. But the dissolution of the union with the New Hampshire territory, was the occasion of considerable dissatisfaction, with some of the former New York opponents of the Vermont jurisdiction; and when it became known that congress had failed to admit the state into the union, after her compliance with the resolutions of the preceding August, the opposition became earnest and active.

On the 30th day of April, a petition prepared by Charles Phelps, was addressed to Gov. Clinton, by persons styling themselves "a committee of the towns of Brattleboro, Guilford and Halifax in the county of Cumberland;" complaining of the Vermont government and asking that a regiment might be raised "in the county of Cumberland" under the authority and pay of New York, and that probate judges, justices, coroners and all other officers might be commissioned under that state, and that the worst criminals might be carried to Albany or Poughkeepsie for trial. In answer to this petition, Gov. Clinton (May 6), promised to use his best endeavors to obtain commissions for the officers required, as soon as the council of appointment could be convened; and referring to the resolutions of Congress, of Sept. 24, 1779, and ignoring those of August, 1781, by which they had been superseded, declared that "if any person should under pretence of authority from the assumed government [of Vermont] attempt to enforce these laws," "*resistance by force*," was "in every point of view justifiable."

The legislature of Vermont, at its session in Feb., 1782, had passed an act for "raising three hundred able bodied effective men for the ensuing campaign," to be apportioned among the several towns "according to the common list of each town." In case of non-compliance, the selectmen of any town might divide the inhabitants into as many classes as there were men to raise, and if a class failed to furnish its man they were directed to hire one and collect the sum paid of its delinquent members, by levy on their property under a warrant issued for that purpose. On the receipt of Gov. Clinton's letter, declaring "resistance by force" to be justifiable, the disaffected inhabitants of Guilford assembled and voted "to stand against the pretended state of Vermont with their lives and fortunes." A few days afterwards the execution of a warrant for the levy of fifteen pounds against the members of a delinquent class in that town, in the hands of a sheriff's deputy for the county of Windham, was resisted, and a cow which had been seized, was rescued from the possession of the officer by a mob.

Another petition was now prepared, and was dispatched to Gov. Clinton at Poughkeepsie by Charles Phelps, who for several years was a leading spirit in the opposition to the Vermont authority. The object was to hasten the appointment of civil and military offices, that the jurisdiction of New York might be resumed and established, to which end it was deemed of the highest importance by Mr. Phelps that Chief Justice Morris of the New York supreme court should speedily, with the county judges to be newly appointed, hold "a court of oyer and terminer in the county of Cumberland" before which the offenders against the New York authority might if it should be deemed advisable be brought for trial. No project could possibly be wilder than this. The court house and jail were in possession of the Vermont authorities, and nine-tenths of the population of the county were opposed to the New York jurisdiction, which, indeed, had not for a long time been either exercised or claimed. Mr. Phelps failed to convince either Judge Morris or the governor of the feasibility of holding his desired criminal court, but obtained from Gov. Clinton commissions bearing date June 5, for the necessary complement of civil and military officers for the ideal county of Cumberland.[1] The officers thus commissioned were three to adminster oath of office, seven justices of the quorum and of the court of oyer and terminer, and fifteen justices of the peace, Mr. Phelps holding one of each of these several offices. Timothy Phelps his son, was sheriff, and the regimental officers were Timothy Church Colonel, William Shattuck first major, Henry Evans second major, and Joel Bigelow adjutant. The field officers were directed to nominate those of inferior grade whom the governor soon afterwards commissioned, and he also engaged to appoint judges of the court of common pleas and other county officers whenever their services should be needed.[2]

The government of Vermont was aware of the preparations that were making to resist its authority, and resorted to energetic mea-

---

[1] Mr. B. H. Hall, whose sympathies were with the adherents of New York, speaks of their strength at this period as follows: "The friends and supporters of the government of New York who, until the year 1780, had composed a large portion of the population of the towns in the south eastern part of Vermont, had been gradually decreasing in power and numbers. At this period a majority of the inhabitants of Guilford, and a minority of the inhabitants of Brattleboro and Halifax, the family of Charles Phelps in Marlboro, and here and there an individual in Westminister, Rockingham and Springfield, and a few other towns, represented their full strength." *Hall's E. Vt.*, p. 423.

[2] *Clinton Papers*, No. 4482, 4527, 4565, 4574. *Doc. Hist. N. Y.*, vol. 4, 1010-1012. *Slade*, 183, 184, 446. *Hall's Eastern Vt.*, p. 420-432.

sures for enforcing it. The legislature which assembled at Windsor on the 13th of June, passed "an act for the punishment of conspiracies against the peace, liberty and independence of the state," by which all persons who conspired against its jurisdiction and forcibly resisted its authority, were made liable to imprisonment or banishment, in the discretion of the supreme court; and any person returning from such banishment, without leave of the general assembly, was, on conviction, to suffer death. An act was also passed authorizing the governor to raise any number of men he might deem necessary, and appoint officers to command the same and cause them to be marched into any part of the state "to assist the sheriffs in their respective counties in the due execution of their offices." But before resorting to force, it was deemed advisable to see what could be done by conciliatory means. With that view, the assembly passed a resolution, "requesting Isaac Tichenor, Esq., to repair to the towns of Brattleboro, Halifax and Guilford, and explain the proceedings of congress to the disaffected in a true light, and that he use his utmost exertions to unite the people in those towns to the government of the state." Mr. Tichenor, then under thirty years of age, was a native of New Jersey, a graduate of Princeton, and a lawyer by profession. He was afterwards, for long periods, a judge of the supreme court, and governor of the state, and for more than one term a senator in congress. He was a ready speaker, and noted for his fascinating manners and great persuasive conversational powers. Although he executed his mission with prudence and ability, it was in a great degree unsuccessful. The opposition to the Vermont authority, led and stimulated by the newly appointed civil and military officers under New York, grew still more determined. On the 10th of July, Charles Phelps wrote Gov. Clinton, urging him to obtain an order from Gen. Washington for four small field pieces to be sent from Springfield to Brattleboro, to be used against the Vermonters, and to have the governor at the same time issue his printed proclamation, assuring the friends of New York, that they would be protected in their opposition by a competent military force; General Washington's approval of the cause of New York, thus publicly shown, would, he argued, in connexion with the proclamation, so intimidate the Vermonters, as to prevent any further proceedings on their part. If Gov. Clinton confided in the efficacy of these measures, he probably very well knew that Gen. Washington, after the friendly advice he had recently given the Vermonters, and which they had followed into the very difficulties they were now encountering, was not likely to countenance any such proceeding against them. At any rate no application was made to him for cannon, nor was any proclamation issued. A few days afterwards, a committee of the hostile inhabitants of those towns addressed a formal petition to Gov. Clinton, asking for military aid in their opposition to Vermont, and for information and advice in regard to the proper measures to be adopted by them. To this petition the governor returned a long answer, in which he informed them that in his opinion congress would never decide in favor of the independence of Vermont, and he feared they would not in favor of New York; that the legislature of New York would never relinquish their claim to the territory in question, "unless impelled thereto by the most inevitable necessity;" that though "it was not in his power positively to stipulate that any body of troops or militia should march to their defence," yet he "did not wish to be understood as discouraging them in their opposition to the usurpation" of the Vermont government. This letter, though it did not give certain assurance of immediate aid, was calculated to inspire confidence in the ultimate triumph of the New York jurisdiction, and to strengthen the determination of its friends to resist the Vermont authority. On the receipt of this answer, the adherents of New York openly boasted that they expected assistance from the government of that state, and a considerable number of them, in a formal and solemn manner, pledged themselves to each other "to oppose the state of Vermont even to blood."

Opportunities to resist the Vermont authority were not wanting. A judgment in a civil suit had been rendered by a Vermont justice against Timothy Church of Brattleboro, the recently appointed colonel under New York, and the execution was placed in the hands of Jonathan Hunt, sheriff of Windham county, for collection. Towards the latter part of August, the sheriff in attempting to execute the process, was resisted by Church and his friends, and an arrest prevented. The sheriff without further effort, reported the facts to Gov. Chittenden. Other hostile demonstrations against the authority of the state were also made, rendering it indispensible for the government, either to abandon its claim to jurisdiction, or to take effectual measures to maintain it.

On the 2d of September, Gov. Chittenden, in accordance with the advice of his council, issued a commission to Gen. Ethan Allen, empowering and directing him to raise two hundred and fifty volunteers out of the two regiments of Col. Walbridge and Col. Ira Allen in Bennington county, "...... and have them equipped with horses, arms, and accoutrements, and march them into the county of Windham, as a *posse comitatus* for the assistance of the civil authority within said county." The men were mustered at Bennington, and very early on Monday morning of the 9th of September, they left that place for the scene of their intended operations. While this force had been gathering, the passes across the mountain had been guarded to prevent a knowledge of the preparations from reaching the disaffected towns. When the party reached Marlboro, twenty-five miles from Bennington, detachments were sent to different points to arrest offenders, Allen at the head of the main body taking his course to Guilford, the stronghold of the friends of New York. On reaching that place some show of opposition was made, but Allen aware of the terror which his name and threatening language was wont to inspire advanced without molestation, and in his stentorian voice made proclamation to the people as follows: "I Ethan Allen, do declare that I will give no quarter to the man, woman or child who shall oppose me, and unless the inhabitants of Guilford peaceably submit to the authority of Vermont, I swear I will lay it as desolate as Sodom and Gomorrah." This proclamation, backed by the strong force of armed men, with which it was accompanied, had the desired effect of deterring resistance and preventing the effusion of blood. During the day the Vermont force had been increased to four or five hundred, by additions from the militia of Windham county. The whole party rendezvoused at Brattleboro in the evening, when it was found that of the disaffected, some twenty or more had been made prisoners, among whom were Timothy Phelps, the New York sheriff, Col. Timothy Church, and Majors William Shattuck and Henry Evans of the New York regiment. Charles Phelps, the most untiring and irrepressible of the New York leaders, though closely pursued, made his escape and fled to Poughkeepsie to carry the news of the demonstration of the Vermonters to Gov. Clinton. The next day the prisoners were sent under a strong guard to Westminster, and placed in jail.

On the 11th a special term of the superior court was held at Westminster for the trial of the prisoners. The court consisted of Moses Robinson, chief judge, and Dr. Jonas Fay, John Fassett and Paul Spooner, side judges. Stephen R. Bradley was the prosecuting attorney. Indictments were found against the prisoners and they were put upon trial. In most of the cases there was little dispute about the facts, and verdicts of guilty were readily obtained. The four principal leaders, viz: Timothy Church, Wm. Shattuck, Henry Evans, and Timothy Phelps, were considered as deserving the extreme penalties of the law. The judgment of the court in these cases was, that each of them "be taken from the bar of the court back to the common jail of the county, there to remain in close imprisonment until the 4th day of October next, and that they be then taken by the sheriff of the county from the common jail and carried without the limits of the state; and that they be then and there forever banished from the state, not to return thereunto, on the penalty of death; and that all their goods, chattels and estates be condemned, seized, sold and forfeited to the use of the state." On the other offenders fines were imposed. The goods of some of the delinquents against whom warrants had issued and who had fled, were seized and confiscated to the use of the state. The session of the court lasted four days. On the 17th of September a special session of the same court was held at Marlborough, where Samuel Ely, an uneasy and troublesome person, then recently from Massachusetts, was tried for denying and defaming the authority of the state, and was sentenced to banishment for eighteen months; and fines were imposed on a few others. Thus closed for this occasion the judicial proceedings of the state against the Yorkers. Charges of unnecessary cruelty were made by them against the Vermonters which from the hostile and excited feeling of the accusers, should be taken with some degree of allowance. It is said that Allen himself acknowledged that the method which had been pursued by him "was a savage way to support government." In the situation in which the Vermont government was placed, it was indispensable, unless it meant to abandon entirely its claim to an independent jurisdiction, to take strong and decisive measures against its adversaries, and perhaps those which were pursued were not more harsh and violent than the exigency required.[1]

Some notice must now be taken of the military affairs of the state during the year 1782.

Although the capture of the army of Lord Cornwallis in the autumn of 1781 was viewed by the Americans as decisive of the want of ability in the British government to subdue them, it was not known whether it would be so accepted in England, or whether still further desperate efforts to conquer the country might be looked for. In this uncertainty preparations were earnestly made by congress for another campaign. The legislature of Vermont, in order

---

[1] *Slade*, p. 454. *Clinton Papers*, Nos. 4447, 4654, 4655, 4697, 4680 *Vt. Council Jour.*, for Aug. 29 and Sept. 2, 1782. *Doc. Hist. N. Y.*, vol. 4, p. 1010. *Williams's Vt.*, p. 290, *Ira Allen's Vt.*, p. 233. For a more particular account of the transactions in Windham county at this period, see *B. H. Hall's Eastern Vt.*, p. 420 - 455.

to guard as far as was within their power, against an invasion from Canada, had, as has been before stated, directed the raising of three hundred men for permanent service in garrisoning the frontier posts. They had also provided for the collecting of supplies for a much larger force, partly by a tax on the polls and estates of the inhabitants payable in provisions, to be stored in the several towns for preservation, and for use as needed.[1] The British had a force of several thousand regular troops, besides large bodies of royalists and Indians at their command, and until quite late in the season an attack upon the northern frontier was very generally apprehended, not only in Vermont, but by the neighboring states.

Notwithstanding the abrupt termination in the fall of 1781 of the efforts of the enemy in Canada to seduce the Vermonters from their allegiance to the revolutionary cause, they were still disposed to continue their exertions in that direction. The ensuing winter they were extremely anxious to learn the effect which the surrender of Cornwallis had produced on the minds of the people of the state. On the 28th of February, 1782, one of the British agents wrote as follows: "My anxiety to hear from you, induced me to apply to his excellency [Gen. Haldimand] for leave to send the bearer with this, which having obtained, I earnestly request you to send me in the most candid, unreserved manner, the present wishes and intentions of the people and leading men of your state, respecting our former negotiations, and what effect the late catastrophe of Lord Cornwallis has on them. Will it not be well to consider the many chances and vicissitudes of war? However brilliant the last campaign may appear, the next may wear a very different aspect. Add to this the great probability of your being ruined by your haughty neighbors, elated by what they call a signal victory, and I hope you will see as I do, that it is more than ever your interest to unite yourselves with those, who wish to make you a free government. Will there be a proper time to send the proclamations? I repeat my request, that you will tell me without reserve, what may be expected in future."[2] It does not appear that any response was made to this inquiry.

On the 15th of April, 1782, Gen. Haldimand received a despatch from the British minister (Lord George Germain) dated the 2d of January, in which he was directed "to make the recovery of Vermont to the king's obedience, the primary object of his attention," and informed him that whatever expense he might incur in effect-

[1] *Slade*, p. 440, 446.
[2] *Williams's Vt.*, 267. *Haldimand Papers*, vol. 2, p. 81, 219.

ing it would not be grudged. He also expressed the hope that Gen. Haldimand notwithstanding the misfortune of Cornwallis, would "be able to carry with him early in the spring a much larger body of troops than Mr. Washington could spare from his army to go against them." A few days after the receipt of these instructions, on the 22d of April, the British agents wrote again to Vermont, as follows: "In confidence we take this opportunity to acquaint you, by the authority of Gen. Haldimand, that he is still inclined to treat amicably with the people of Vermont; and these his generous and humane instructions, are now seconded by much stronger powers from his majesty, than he has hitherto enjoyed for that purpose. We do in confidence officially assure you, that every article proposed to you in his excellency's former offers as well as the confirmation of the east and west unions in their utmost limits, will be amply and punctually complied with. We hope your answer may be such as to unburden our anxious minds." [1] Extremely fearful about the result, and impatient at not receiving an answer, on April 30th they wrote again, carrying their offers and promises to a still greater extent. "His excellency has never lost sight of his first object, and I am happy to be able in this, to inform you that the general has lately received by the way of Halifax full powers from the king to establish Vermont government, including the full extent of the east and west unions, with every privilege and immunity formerly proffered to you; and he is likewise fully authorized, as well as sincerely inclined, to provide amply for * * * and to make * * * brigadier general in the line, * * * * * * * field officers, with such other rewards as your sincerity and good services in bringing about the revolution, may in future merit. In short the general is vested with full power to make such rewards as he shall judge proper, to all those who distinguish themselves in promoting the happy reunion. And as his excellency has the greatest confidence in you, and * * *, much will depend on your recommendations." [2]

But notwithstanding the liberal offers which Gen. Haldimand allowed his agents to make, it would seem from his correspondence with Sir Henry Clinton that he had not much expectation they would be favorably answered. In a letter to General Clinton dated April 28th, after speaking of the difficulties of his situation, and intimating that his encouragement to the Vermonters which had been

---

[1] *Williams's Vt.*, p. 268.

[2] *Williams's Vt.*, p. 269.

ineffectual before the misfortune of Lord Cornwallis, was not likely to prove successful now, he writes as follows: "The crisis is arrived when coercion alone must decide the part Vermont will take, and that measure should be determined upon from the minute the troops directed by Lord George to appear upon their frontiers shall take post, and must be carried into execution as far as possible, after giving them sufficient notice, by laying waste their country, if they do not accept the terms offered.[1] Reports from Canada foreshadowed this intended invasion, and excited much alarm in the frontier states. The month of June appears to have been fixed upon as the time for entering Vermont with a hostile army, but the difficulty of procuring supplies for the troops produced unexpected delays, and it was not until considerably later in the season that the contemplated force for the expedition could be mustered at the Isle aux Noix.

Early in July, Col. Ira Allen was sent again into Canada, with a letter from Gov. Chittenden to Gen. Haldimand, requesting the release of two officers, belonging to Vermont, who were then prisoners in that province. The British agents were extremely anxious to bring their negotiations with Vermont to an immediate decision. All the arts of negotiation were employed, on the one hand, to make it appear to be for the interest of Vermont to declare herself a British province, and on the other, to avoid this step, without bringing on a renewal of hostilities. On the 11th of July, Col. Allen at Quebec addressed a very long letter to Gen. Haldimand, in which a variety of political matters, more or less connected with the affairs of Vermont, were discussed with diplomatic skill and ability, the object being to inspire the general's confidence in the friendly disposition of the Vermonters towards Great Britain, and in their hostility to congress; the logical inference from all which was that Vermont wished and ought to be a British province, but that the present was a most unpropitious and dangerous time to attempt its consummation.[2]

A secret treaty was offered by the British agents and much urged. But in the event, Gen. Haldimand agreed to continue the suspension of hostilities, and wrote a very friendly letter to Gov. Chittenden, bearing date August 8th, fully complying with his request for liberating the prisoners, and announcing his pacific disposition towards Vermont, in this unequivocal manner: "You may rest assured that I shall give such orders, as will effectually prevent

---

[1] *Haldimand Papers*, vol. 2, p. 221.

[2] *Willivms's Vt.*, p. 269. *Haldimand Papers*, vol. 2, p, 283–299.

hostilities of any kind being exercised in the district of Vermont, until such time as a breach on your part, or some general event may make the contrary my duty. And you have my authority to promulgate in such manner as you shall think fit, this my intention to the people of the said district, that they may without any apprehension continue to encourage and promote the settlement and cultivation of that new country, to the interest and happiness of themselves and their posterity." [1]

It was doubtless believed by the Vermont leaders that the forbearance of Gen. Haldimand to invade their state was owing wholly, as that of the previous year had unquestionably been, to their adroitness in encouraging his overtures for a renewal of their allegiance to the British crown. It is now, however, quite certain that such was not the case. The people of England had become sick of prosecuting a war which was loading them with an enormous debt, and of which they saw no prospect of a favorable termination. Lord North had resigned and a new ministry had been appointed who were sincerely desirous of peace, even at the cost of acknowledging the independence of their revolted colonies. Sir Henry Clinton had been recalled from New York, and Sir Guy Carleton appointed to the chief command in America, with instructions which prohibited him from undertaking further offensive operations.[2] On the 21st of June, before Col. Allen reached Canada, Gen. Haldimand received a dispatch from Carleton, communicating the pacific intentions of the new ministry, and the next day he wrote that general in answer, expressing his gratification at the unavoidable delay which had prevented his hostile movement into Vermont, and stating that he should continue to collect the troops and supplies at the Isle aux Noix, which had been intended for the expedition, where they would be in readiness, " should the laudable disposition and indications for peace now existing prove ineffectual, and offensive measures be unhappily renewed." [3] The extraordinary diplomatic labors of Col. Allen at Quebec to prevent an invasion of Vermont were therefore altogether unnecessary, the intended expedition against the northern frontiers having, in consequence of secret instructions from England, been already forbidden. Thus while Allen was endeavoring to delude Haldimand into the belief that Vermont was wishing an alliance with the crown, he himself was allowed to act under the

[1] *Williams's Vt.*, p. 270.

[2] For Carleton's instructions, see *Sparks's Washington*, vol. 8, p. 296–298, note.

[3] *Haldimand Papers*, vol. 2, p. 253–261.

false assumption that his state was in great danger of being ravaged by the enemy. The concentration of a body of several thousand men at the north end of Lake Champlain, near the Canada border, continued to produce alarm in the northern department during the greater part of the season. From the opponents of Vermont within the state, and in New York and New Hampshire, many letters were addressed to delegates in congress, to Gen. Washington and to others, stating their belief of an intended invasion, and not unfrequently expressing the apprehension of a contemplated cooperation of the Vermonters with the invaders.[1] This apprehension, though industriously propagated, does not appear to have been credited by intelligent persons. Gen. Washington, to whom the motives and policy of the Vermonters, in their Canada negotiations had been fully disclosed, and who was also better informed than the public in general, in regard to the objects of the enemy, does not appear to have given credence to these reports. In a letter addressed by him to Gov. Clinton, under date of Oct. 19, 1782, he says, "I do not consider the late reports of the enemy being in force at the Isle aux Noix to indicate anything farther than an attention to their own security."[2] All apprehensions of invasion from Canada were not long afterwards happily removed by provisional articles of peace which were signed at Paris on the last day of November, 1782.

---

[1] For these unfriendly reports against Vermont, see *Clinton Papers; Stevens Papers,* also *Madison Papers,* vol. 1, p. 151, 184, 214, 215.

[2] *Sparks's Washington,* vol. 8, p. 361.

CHAPTER XXXVI.

Resolves in Congress Hostile to Vermont.

1782.

Congress in regard to Vermont is influenced by other questions pending before it, particularly by the controversy about the western lands — Account of the claims of Virginia and other states to those lands, and of the opposition to them in congress — New York, by the cession of her claims to the United States, acquires friends and support against Vermont — Mr. Madison on the state of parties on the Vermont question in May, 1782 — Phelps, Shattuck and Evans, refugees from Vermont, supported by Gov. Clinton, go to Philadelphia and complain against the government of that state — Hostile resolutions passed by congress against Vermont, December 5, 1782 — Copy of the resolutions, and an explanation of their practical operation.

IF we would undertake to account for the indecision and changing conduct of congress, in relation to the claim of Vermont to an independent jurisdiction, we must look beyond the actual merits of her claim into the supposed effect of its admission or rejection upon other measures in which the members, or a portion of them, felt a deeper and stronger interest. It has already been stated that on the hearing of the respective claims of New York and New Hampshire in the year 1780, the disposition of congress towards Vermont, was influenced in a considerable degree by the effect which her admission unto the union as a separate state would be likely to have on the determination, in that body, of the question in regard to the western lands. These lands were claimed by Virginia and some other large states as their exclusive property, the claim of Virginia being the most important, including besides the present state of Kentucky, all the land in the United States lying to the northward of the Ohio river and east of the Mississippi. These exclusive claims were denied by the other states, by which it was insisted that the lands, at the commencement of the revolution, were not assigned to any particular province, but belonged to the crown, and that when they were wrested from the crown by the common exertions of all the states, they ought to be disposed of for the common benefit. At the time of the hearing before mentioned, several of the states that were opposed to these exclusive claims, and among them New Jersey, Pennsylvania, Delaware and Maryland, were disposed to favor the claim of Vermont, with the view of obtaining an additional vote against the pretensions of Virginia and the other claiming states. By a change of circumstances, and by the skillful management of the delegates from New York, Vermont had now lost a portion of the support which she had received from that quarter, and it had been turned against her.

There being no tribunal to which an appeal could be made for the determination of the controversy in regard to these western lands, congress, as the best means of bringing about an adjustment, had recommended to the states claiming them, to make liberal cessions of them to the United States, the territory ceded to be formed into new states of convenient size and the lands to be disposed of for the general benefit. New York was the first state to move in the matter, by the passage of an act, in Feb., 1780, authorizing her delegates in congress, by a proper instrument by them to be executed, to restrict the boundaries of the state in its western parts, in such manner as they should deem expedient. The claim of the state was generally deemed to be of a shadowy character, and her proffered cession appears for a considerable time to have been little noticed. It was not until March, 1781, that a deed was executed in congress, and it was a long time thereafter before it was accepted by that body.[1] Of the claim of New York thus relinquished, Mr Madison said that it was "very extensive but her title very flimsy," and that she urged it "more with the hope of obtaining some advantage or credit by its cession, than of ever maintaining it."[2] The advantage here referred to, no doubt related to her claim to the territory of Vermont, which she expected would be greatly strengthened by the favor with which her cession would be received. A few days after the execution of the deed (March 12) Mr. McDougal, one of the New York delegates, wrote to Gov. Clinton, "that the cession of New York had removed the cause of opposition of Maryland," and other states, and that the question of the New Hampshire Grants would soon be favorably decided.[3] But these expectations were not fully realized. In fact the members from the other states were slow to perceive that the cession was of much importance to the United States, though it did eventually serve to increase the number of the supporters of New York in congress to some extent, sufficient indeed to enable her delegates, with the aid of other influences, to procure the adoption of threatening though as it turned out, inoperative resolutions against Vermont.

[1] *Jour. Cong.* March 1, 1781, vol. 3, p. 582-586. Also vol. 4, p. 100.

[2] *Madison Papers*, vol. 1, p. 121.

[3] *Clinton Papers*, No. 3575.

The claim of Virginia extended to all the vacant lands that could be expected to be made available for a considerable period of time, and was the great obstacle in the way of an adjustment of the dispute. In January 1781, her legislature under the extreme pressure of Arnold's invasion, agreed upon a cession of the territory northeast of the Ohio, but it was clogged with so many conditions and reservations as to render it unsatisfactory to a large majority of congress. The state of Connecticut, which claimed a narrow belt of land extending west to the Mississippi, had proposed a cession of all beyond Lake Erie. These cessions with that of New York, and the claims of certain land companies for lands west of the Alleghanies, were referred to a committee, who, against the solemn protest of the delegates of Virginia, went into a hearing of the evidence in support of all other claims, and made their report on the 3d of November, 1781 — the Virginia delegates declining to elucidate their title. The report denied any right in Virginia to the lands described in her deed of cession, and set up that of New York against it, which it was argued embraced the valley of Ohio, and was maintainable and valid against Virginia by way of the succession of New York to the title of the Six Nations of Indians. It recommended the acceptance of the cession of New York, and that Virginia and Connecticut should reconsider their acts and make more liberal and satisfactory relinquishments of their claims.

With the view of giving the legislature of Virginia an opportunity to make their proposed cession more acceptable, the report was suffered to lie until the coming spring, when it was taken up for consideration and discussed with great earnestness and warmth, so much so as to call away the attention of congress from almost every other subject. It was the misfortune of the claim of Vermont to admission into the union, to be overshadowed and put aside by this all-absorbing question. On the 16th of April, 1782, the report on the western lands was debated, but without any vote being taken. The next day (the 17th), the committee, of which Mr. Clymer of Pennsylvania was chairman, made their report in favor of the admissiom of Vermont into the confederation, on the terms proposed by congress the preceding August, and the failure of congress to fix upon a time for taking it into consideration, took place, as before stated. The next day, the debate on the report of the committee on the cessions of Virginia and the other states, was resumed, and was continued again on the first, second and sixth of May, when the order of the day for its consideration was postponed by a vote of all the states present except Virginia and South Carolina. This vote was considered as a virtual rejection of the Virginia cession as then proposed, and it disposed of the subject for the time being.[1]

Mr. Madison, who took an active part in the debates in favor of the claim of Virginia and against the admission of Vermont, has left a record of his views on the state of parties in congress at this period in relation to both these subjects, which is deemed of sufficient importance to be inserted in full. In assigning the motives by which he alleges the delegations of the several states were governed in their action upon the Vermont question, it cannot but be noticed as a remarkable circumstance that no intimation is given that a single state or member was or could in any degree be influenced by a consideration of the real merits of the Vermont claim to independence. Whether the inhabitants of Vermont had a sufficient cause for separating from the jurisdiction of New York or not, or whether the resolutions of August, 1781, imposed an obligation on congress which it would be a breach of faith to violate, or otherwise, were entirely ignored. Each of the states, according to Mr. Madison, appear to have been governed solely by the supposed effect which the admission or rejection of the Vermont claim, would have upon their individual state interests, irrespective of the merits of the claim itself.

Mr. Madison's account of the state of parties at this time, is dated May 1. 1782, and is as follows :

"The two great objects, which predominate in the politics of congress at this juncture, are *Vermont* and the *Western Territory*.

"I. The independence of Vermont and its admission into the confederacy are patronized by the eastern states (New Hampshire excepted) first, from an ancient prejudice against New York, secondly, the interest which citizens of those states have in lands granted by Vermont; thirdly, but principally, from the accession of weight they will derive from it in congress. New Hampshire having gained its main object by the exclusion of its territory east of Connecticut river from the claims of Vermont, is already indifferent to its independence, and will probably soon combine with other eastern states in its favor.

"The same patronage is yielded to the pretensions of Vermont by Pennsylvania and Maryland, with the sole view of reenforcing the opposition to claims of western territory, particularly those of Virginia, and by New Jersey and Delaware with the additional view of strengthening the interests of the little states. Both of these con-

[1] *Jour. Cong.*, vol. 4, p. 11, 13, 14, 20-25, 55, 68-70, 82, 83, 100, 101, 265.

siderations operate also on Rhode Island, in addition to those above mentioned.

"The independence of Vermont and its admission into the union are opposed by New York for reasons obvious and well known.

"The like opposition is made by Virginia, North Carolina, South Carolina and Georgia. The grounds of this opposition are, first, habitual jealousy of a predominance of eastern interests; secondly, the opposition expected from Vermont to western claims; thirdly, the inexpediency of admitting so unimportant a state, to an equal vote, in deciding on peace, and all the other grand interests of the union now depending; fourthly, the influence of the example on a premature dismemberment of the other states.[1] These considerations influence the four states last mentioned in different degrees. The second and third, to say nothing of the fourth, ought to be decisive with Virginia.

"II. The territorial claims, particularly those of Virginia, are opposed by Rhode Island, New Jersey, Pennsylvania, Delaware and Maryland. Rhode Island is influenced in her opposition, first, by a lucrative desire of sharing in the vacant territory as a fund of revenue;[2] secondly, by the envy and jealousy naturally excited by superior resources and importance. New Jersey, Pennsylvania, Delaware and Maryland are influenced partly by the same considerations, but principally by the intrigues of their citizens, who are interested in the claims of land companies. The decisive influence of this last consideration is manifest from the peculiar and persevering opposition made against Virginia, within whose limits these claims lie.

"The western claims, or rather a final settlement of them, are also thwarted by Massachusetts and Connecticut. This object with them is chiefly subservient to that of Vermont, as the latter is with Pennsylvania and Maryland to the former. The general policy and

---

[1] In August 1781, a petition from over one thousand inhabitants of Kentucky for a new state had been presented to congress, to which there was an unwillingness on the part of Virginia, to accede. A similar feeling in favor of a new jurisdiction was known to prevail among the settlers on the Tennessee to the westward of North Carolina, and South Carolina and Georgia were not unlikely to be exposed to like dangers when the country to the west of them should be occupied by emigrants. *See Hildreth*, vol. 3, p. 469, 539. *Madison Papers*, vol. 1, p. 164. *Papers* in State Department, Washington.

[2] Doubtless a similar "lucrative desire" to that which prompted Virginia to wish to monopolize the whole of the "vacant territory" as an exclusive "fund of revenue."

interests of these two states are opposed to the admission of Vermont into the union; and if the case of the western territory were once removed, they would instantly divide from the eastern states in the case of Vermont. Of this, Massachusetts and Connecticut are not insensible, and therefore find their advantage in keeping the territorial controversy pending. Connecticut may likewise conceive some analogy between her claim to the western country and that of Virginia, and that the acceptance of the cession of the latter would influence her sentiments in the controversy between the former and Pennsylvania.

"The western claims are espoused by Virginia, North Carolina, South Carolina, Georgia and New York, all of these states being interested therein. South Carolina the least so. The claim of New York is very extensive, but her title very flimsy. She urges it more with the hope of obtaining some advantage or credit by its cession, than of ever maintaining it. If the cession should be accepted, and the affair of Vermont terminated, as these are the only ties which unite her with the southern states, she will inmediately connect her policy with that of the eastern states, as far at least as the remains of former prejudices will permit."[1]

It will be perceived from this view of Mr. Madison, of the state of parties in congress, which was doubtless in the main correct, that sectional feeling operated strongly against Vermont, and that the four southern states of Virginia, North Carolina, South Carolina and Georgia, on that account as well as on the ground of their claims to western lands, were opposed to her independence, although they had all voted for the resolutions of the preceding August, specifying the terms on which she should become a member of the federal union, which terms had been fully complied with. With these four states and New York opposed, it would of course be impossible to obtain nine of the thirteen states in her favor. This the agents of Vermont, who were in attendance when congress on the 17th of April, 1782, had declined to consider the report of the committee in favor of their state, plainly saw. It was evidently useless for Vermont to continue longer knocking at the door of congress for admission. The agents had accordingly left Philadelphia, addressing a letter to the president, informing him that they should expect to be officially notified if their attendance should again become necessary, as has been before stated. No such notice was ever given to them or their

[1]For this sketch of Mr. Madison's views, see *Madison Papers*, vol. 1, p. 122, and *Sparks's Washington*, vol. 8, p. 547.

state, and whatever proceedings were afterwards taken in congress against Vermont, were wholly *ex parte.* In regard to these subsequent *ex parte* measures, it may be observed in general, that though brought about by the influence of New York, they were of no advantage whatever to that state, and only served to prolong the existence and increase the bitterness of an unprofitable controversy. Though sometimes annoying and troublesome to Vermont, they were much more so to the few friends of New York, within her limits, who were thereby encouraged to keep up a fruitless and to them a damaging resistance to the Vermont jurisdiction.

Gov. Clinton and his associates in the government of New York, were untiring in their exertions to obtain the aid of congress. In addition to the proposed relinquishment of their alleged claim to western territory, they sought to conciliate the favor of the members by a new show of fairness and liberality towards the inhabitants of Vermont. An act was accordingly passed on the 14th of April, 1782, granting pardon and amnesty to her people for all past offences against the New York authority. On the same day, another bill entitled "an act for quieting the minds of the inhabitants in the northeastern part of this state" became a law. By this act all charters granted both by the colony of New Hampshire and the "assumed government of Vermont" prior to any grant of the same land by New York, were declared to be valid, and parties occupying lands in opposition to prior New York titles were to be quieted in their possessions — all on condition that the people submitted themselves to the New York jurisdiction. Notwithstanding the comprehensiveness of the language of this act, it left a very large portion of the equitable claims against the New York title unprovided for, as might be readily shown. [1] But there was an inherent defect in the measure which deprived it of its power of protection — the want of authority in the legislature to invalidate the titles it proposed to set aside. The constitution of New York had declared the grants of the colonial governors in the name of the crown to be valid, and the grantees had acquired a property under that government in their

[1] Among the inequitable New York claims which this act would allow to be valid, would be the million and a half of acres that had been patented to the city land jobbers in known violation of the king's prohibitory order in council of July, 1767, which patents had been properly treated as void by the Vermont government and disregarded in their subsequent grants. See *Jour. of Vt. Assembly* for Oct. 25, 1780, when it was resolved unanimously that such patents "should not be considered a sufficient bar against granting the same lands to respectable and worthy petitioners."

grants of which the legislature could not deprive them. The New York courts, upon the acknowledged principle that a grant once made, could not be recalled at the option of the grantor, would undoubtedly decide in favor of the titles of the New York patentees. But the establishment of a new state would invalidate the New York patents. This was well understood.

The act was without influence in Vermont, and appears not to have been much regarded in congress. On the 21st of May, the two acts of the New York legislature were presented and read in congress, when it was moved by Mr. Scott from New York, and seconded by Mr. Middleton of South Carolina, that they "be committed to a special committee to report thereon," but the motion was decided in the negative, and nothing further in regard to them appears on the journal.[1]

The subject of the western lands occupied much of the attention of congress during the residue of the year, and parties ran high in regard to it. The finances of the country were in a deplorable condition, the continental currency had become worthless, the confederation was deeply in debt, and being without power to levy contributions on the people or the states, their credit was wholly exhausted. Under these circumstances a large majority of the members looked upon the western lands as a source from which the public credit might perhaps be resuscitated. A grand committee of a member from each of the states, made a report in July, recommending a liberal relinquishment of those lands by the claiming states, and declaring that they would thereby constitute "an independent fund for the discharge of the national debt." This report was discussed from time to time with much warmth, but without definite result. The great obstacle in the way of making use of these lands for the benefit of the United States, being the tenacity with which Virginia adhered to her extensive claims. If Virginia should cede her claim, her example would be likely to be followed by the states to the south of her, which cessions of those four southern states would include all the waste lands within the territory of the United States. Tired of waiting for the compliance of Virginia, a majority of the members came to the determination to set up and maintain the claim of New York against it. It was held that Virginia was wholly without title, and though that of New York, which comprised an indefinite portion of the valley of the Ohio, and clashed with that of Virginia, was not deemed as strong as was claimed by her delegates, it could

[1] *Jour. Congress*, vol. 4, p. 31, 32, 33, 34. *Slade*, 173-176.

nevertheless be made to appear plausible and even equitable as against a party having no title whatever. With the view of using it to supplant the claim of Virginia, or at least to induce that state to make a more liberal cession, it was on the 29th of October, voted to accept the cession of New York as already made, the state of Virginia alone voting in the negative, the delegates of both North and South Carolina being divided. [1]

Mr. Madison, a few days after this vote (Nov. 5), wrote from Philadelphia to Edmund Randolph as follows:

" Besides the effect which may be expected from the coalition with New York, on territorial questions in congress, it will I surmise, prove very unfriendly to the pretensions of Vermont. Duane seems not unapprized of the advantage which New York has gained, and is already taking measures for a speedy vote on that question. Upon the whole, New York has, by a fortunate coincidence of circumstances, or by skillful management, or by both, succeeded in a very important object. By ceding a claim, which was tenable neither by force nor by right, she has acquired with congress the merit of liberality, rendered the title to her reservation more respectable, and at least damped the ardor with which Vermont has been abetted." [2]

About two weeks after the acceptance of the New York cession the Vermont question came again before congress. It has already been stated that when the sheriff of Windham county with his military *posse* arrested several of the newly appointed New York officers, Charles Phelps, one of the most active of them, had made his escape, and fled to Poughkeepsie to make report to Gov. Clinton. From that place, contrary to the governor's advice who seems to have distrusted Phelps's discretion, he went to Philadelphia, where he arrived early in October. He presented a memorial to congress, setting forth in his peculiar, involved and inflated language, the grievances of himself and politicial friends. He was not long afterwards joined by Shattuck and Evans who also memorialized congress, giving an account of their arrest, trial, and banishment for opposing the authority of Vermont. Gov. Clinton had written earnestly to the New York delegates to insist upon the immediate interposition of congress for the relief of the fugitives, and for the vindication of the New York claim of jurisdiction. All the papers on the subject had been referred to a committee, before which Mr. Phelps had been allowed several hours to present his case, and he had been very busy

[1] *Jour. Congress*, vol. 4, p. 100.

[2] *Madison Papers*, vol. 1, p. 470.

for weeks in exhorting and importuning individual members, in which for a portion of the time he had the assistance of Messrs. Shattuck and Evans.[1]

A committee to whom these papers had been recommitted made a report which was taken up for consideration on the 14th of November. It ascribed the measures complained of in the papers referred to them to "the state of New York having lately issued commissions, both civil and military, to persons resident in the district called Vermont," and recommended the state of New York to revoke the commissions; to the government of Vermont to make satisfaction to the sufferers and to allow them to return unmolested to their habitations; and to both governments to adhere to the resolves of congress of September 24, 1779, in the exercise of their jurisdictions, until a decision of the controversy should be made by congress. Several votes were taken on questions in relation to the report which indicated that a majority of the members were not satisfied with it, though it was not, definitely disposed of.[2] Mr. Madison, in a memorandum of this day's proceedings, says: "The temper of congress on this occasion, as the yeas and nays show, was less favorable to Vermont than any preceding one, the effect probably of the territorial cession of New York." [3]

The exertions of the New York delegates, aided by the zealous importunities of Mr. Phelps, to obtain the action of congress against Vermont were actively continued and were eventually in some degree successful. On the third of December, the report of the committee was postponed to make way for a set of resolutions still more hostile to that state, introduced by Mr. McKean of Delaware. Under this day's date Mr. Madison says: "The proceedings on this subject evinced still more the conciliating effect of the territorial cession of New York on several states, and the effect of the scheme of an ultra-montane state within Pennsylvania, on the latter state.[4] The only states in congress which stood by Vermont were Rhode Island, which is supposed to be interested in lands in Vermont, and New

---

[1] *Papers* in state department Washington, No. 40, vol. 2. *Clinton Papers*, No. 4761, 4762, 4772, 4773, 4796, 4802, 4809, 4825, 4828, 4831, 4833, 4842, 4850, 4857, 4858, 4862. *Hall's Eastern Vt.*, Chapter 456-470.

[2] *Jour. Cong.*, vol. 4, p. 105, 106.

[3] *Madison Papers*, vol. 1, p. 198.

[4] There was at this time a movement on foot for the formation of a new state beyond the Alleghanies to include portions of Virginia and Pennsylvania, against which the legislature of the latter state was taking strong measures. *Madison Papers*, vol. 1, p. 475, 500.

Jersey whose delegates were under instructions."[1] These instructions deprecated coercive measures against Vermont after her compliance with the resolutions of congress of August 1781, as improper and unjust. (For this instruction see Appendix, No. 11).

On the 5th of December, the resolutions which had been presented by Mr. McKean, were seconded by Mr. Hamilton of New York, and were adopted by the vote of seven of the thirteen states. The resolutions were as follows:

"*Whereas* it appears to congress by authentic documents that the people inhabiting the district of country on the west side of Connecticut river, commonly called the New Hampshire Grants, and claiming to be an independent state, in contempt of the authority of congress, and in direct violation of the resolutions of the 24th of September, 1779, and of the 2d of June, 1780, did, in the month of September last, proceed to exercise jurisdiction over the persons and properties of sundry inhabitants of the said district, professing themselves to be subjects of, and to own allegiance to the state of New York, by means whereof divers of them have been condemned to banishment, not to return on pain of death and confiscation of estate; and others have been fined in large sums, and otherwise deprived of property; therefore,

"*Resolved*, That the said acts and proceedings of the said people, being highly derogatory to the authority of the United States and dangerous to the confederacy, require the immediate and decided interposition of congress, for the protection and relief of such as have suffered by them, and for preserving peace in said district, until a decision shall be had of the controversy, relative to the jurisdiction of the same;

"That the people inhabiting the said district, claiming to be independent, be and they are hereby required, without delay, to make full and ample restitution to Timothy Church, Timothy Phelps, Henry Evans and William Shattuck, and such others as have been condemned to banishment and confiscation of estate, or have otherwise been deprived of property since the first day of September last, for the damages they have sustained by the acts and proceedings aforesaid; and that they be not molested in their persons or properties on their return to their habitations in the said district.

"That the United States will take effectual measures to enforce a compliance with the aforesaid resolutions, in case the same shall be disobeyed by the people of the said district.

---

[1] *Madison Papers*, p. 215.

"That no persons holding commissions under the state of New York, or under the people of the said district, claiming to be independent, exercise any authority over the persons and properties of any inhabitants in the said district, contrary to the forementioned resolutions of the 24th of September, 1779, and the 2d of June, 1780.

"That a copy of the aforegoing resolutions be transmitted to Thomas Chittenden, Esq., of Bennington, in the district aforesaid, to be communicated to the people thereof."

By the articles of confederation a majority of all the thirteen states was necessary to carry any measure, and these resolutions were adopted by the vote of seven states — a bare majority only. Among the seven were the two states of New York and New Hampshire, whose delegates do not appear to have had any hesitation in voting, although the resolutions of congress of the 24th of September, 1779, which it was now proposed to enforce by military power, had declared that neither of the states interested in the controversy "should vote on any question relative to the decision thereof." The other five states voting for the resolutions were, Pennsylvania, Delaware, Virginia, and North and South Carolina. Rhode Island and New Jersey voted in the negative, and the four states of Massachusetts, Connecticut, Maryland and Georgia, not being sufficiently represented, did not vote.[1]

That the passage of these resolutions by congress was mainly owing to the before mentioned causes assigned by Mr. Madison is doubtless true, though it is not improbable that the extravagant and ill-founded statements made by Mr. Phelps and his associate refugees, of the great strength of their friends in Vermont, and of the weakness of its government, as well as the alleged design of its officers to enter into a treaty with the public enemy; all of which were industriously propagated by them and by other enemies of the state at that time, might have operated to influence the action of individual members. It is difficult to account for the votes of the New Hampshire delegates in favor of the resolutions, but upon the hypothesis of their expectation that if they should be enforced by military power, the territory of Vermont would be divided by the ridge of the Green mountain, and the eastern half assigned to their state. It seems incredible that they could have hoped for a decision in their favor against the claim of New York, which their province had for years acknowledged. They had long since pro-

[1] *Cong. Jour.*, vol. 4, p. 112, 113, 114. *Slade*, 177, 178.

posed such a division, as has been seen, and a grand committee of congress, the preceding winter, had threatened it against Vermont, in case she should not speedily comply with the terms of the resolutions of that body of August, 1781. There can be no doubt that the people of New Hampshire would much rather have seen Vermont an independent state, with her boundaries restricted as they had been by her own act to the west bank of Connecticut river, than to allow her territory to have increased the extent and power of New New York.[1]

These resolutions were of an extraordinary character; based on a principle subversive of all regular and peaceful government. Congress, in their resolves of September, 1779, had invited the states claiming the territory of the New Hampshire Grants to pass acts authorizing that body to hear and decide the controversy between them and the people inhabiting the territory, and between each of the claiming states, promising to come to a determination of it, the ensuing February. It had been three years since both New York and New Hampshire had enacted laws submitting the decision to congress; more than two years since both those states had been fully heard on their claims before that body, and more than one year since congress had, in effect, decided the controversy against both of them,

---

[1] Such a division of Vermont was for several years the subject of occasional negotiations between officials of the states of New Hampshire and New York, though it is not probable that any treaty was ever consummated. It appears by a letter from Mr. Floyd, one of the New York delegates, to Gov. Clinton, dated February 18th, 1783, that a formal proposal for a compromise had been made to New York on the part of New Hampshire *the previous summer*, of which Mr. Floyd urged the speedy acceptance by the New York legislature.—(*Clinton Papers*, No. 4934.) A compromise with New Hampshire was spoken of with favor by Alexander Hamilton, in letters to Clinton, written in the spring of 1783, and in July of that year, as the only way by which New York could acquire any part of the Vermont territory.—(*Life of Hamilton*, vol. 2, p. 198–200. *Life of Gov. Morris*, vol. 1, p. 214.) Gov. Clinton wrote Hamilton he would submit to a division of the territory by the summit of the mountain "for the sake of peace."—(*Ibid.*) Such a division of Vermont was also earnestly mentioned by the New Hampshire delegates to President Weare in letters of Dec. 11, 1782, and Jan. 16, 1783, as a proper matter for special legislative instruction. (Volume of *Papers Relating to Vermont* in the office of the secretary of state, New Hampshire.) The impracticability of carrying into effect such an arbitrary measure, for which no claim of right could be set up, probably prevented its being actually attempted. On the last vote taken in congress on the Vermont question, the two states of New Hampshire and New York voted together, all the other states against them. *Jour. Cong.*, June 3, 1784.

by resolving to acknowledge the independence of Vermont, on her acceding to certain terms which she had accepted. In the resolutions of September, 1779, when a speedy decision was contemplated, it was declared to be the duty of the people of the New Hampshire Grants, "to abstain, *in the mean time*, from exercising any power over any of the inhabitants of the district who professed themselves to be citizens of, or to owe allegiance to, any or either of said states;" and the several claiming states were required in the like manner to suspend executing their laws upon any of the inhabitants of the district, "except such of them as should profess allegiance to and confess the jurisdiction of the same, respectively." Here were three independent jurisdictions to be extended over the same territory, each to be exercised over such persons only as should voluntarily consent to come under its authority. If the government of Vermont desired to exert its authority over any individual, he might readily avoid it by professing allegiance to New York or New Hampshire. If, for instance, a creditor should wish to collect a debt, the defendant in a suit before a Vermont court might nullify the proceeding at once by professing allegiance to one of those states, and as neither of them had courts in the territory before which legal proceedings could be instituted, the mere declaration of his allegiance to another jurisdiction effectually deprived the creditor of all remedy. If a party were arrested on a Vermont warrant for theft or burglary or any other crime, and the accused should solemnly profess allegiance to New York, the court would be bound by the resolutions of congress to discharge him at once. Of course, if the resolutions were obeyed, contracts would be disregarded and crimes would be committed with impunity. The debtor or the criminal had only to profess allegiance to a jurisdiction, other than that under which he was charged, and he would go free. So when any service or contribution for the defence of the country or the public benefit was required, the lawless, the unpatriotic, and the parsimonious might readily take advantage of the provisions of these pliant resolves to screen themselves from liability. Hence the resistance to the levies of men for the protection of the frontier, and to taxation for public purposes. It would seem also from the terms of the resolutions that a party might change his profession of allegiance from one jurisdiction to another, as might suit his interest or convenience. Such appears to have been their practical construction, by those who had lately been fined and banished by the Vermont courts, the greater part of whom had for sometime admitted the jurisdiction of that state and quietly submitted to its authority. Timothy

Church and William Shattuck, the highest field officers of the New York regiments, who were two of the five persons that had been banished, had both voluntarily taken the oath of allegiance to the Vermont government, months before receiving their commissions from Gov. Clinton. Church soon after his appointment signalized his change of allegiance by collecting his friends together and resisting the sheriff of the county when he came to levy an execution issued to enforce a judgment which had been rendered against him for debt by a Vermont justice. Shattuck had participated in an armed resistance to the execution of the laws of Vermont for levying men for the defence of the frontier, and when sentenced to banishment, had repaired to Philadelphia to claim the protection of congress against the laws of a government which he had solemnly sworn to support and maintain.[1]

By the practical operation of the resolutions of congress of 1779, society would be resolved into its original elements, where any person, so far as his individual power extended, might do just exactly as he pleased, without being accountable for his conduct to any government or law whatever. Such a state of society never did and never could exist in any community for any long period of time, without producing lawlessness and anarchy too intolerable to be borne. Congress had at first prescribed it as a temporary expedient, but now, after its unsuccessful trial for more than three years, these resolutions of December 5, 1782, proposed to march an army into Vermont, and establish it permanently by military force.

---

[1] *Hall's Eastern Vt.*, p. 425, 438, 439, 477, 482. *Slade*, p. 184.

CHAPTER XXXVII.

VERMONT AND CONGRESS ON THE RESOLUTIONS OF DECEMBER, 1782—THEY ARE NOT TO BE ENFORCED.

1782-1783.

The Vermont legislature in October, 1782, appoints agents to negotiate a union with the confederation—The Vermonters are surprised at the *ex parte* December resolves of congress, and will not submit to them—Letter of remonstrance of Gov. Chittenden to the president of congress, and its subsequent confirmation by the general assembly—Gen. Washington alarmed at the prospect of a collision of arms, transmits his correspondence with Gov. Chittenden to congress, and earnestly objects to the employment of the army against Vermont—Gov. Clinton and the New York delegates urge speedy and decisive action, but congress will not use force, and forbears to act.

ON the 10th day of October, 1782, a few weeks after the trial of Gov. Clinton's officers and their associates, for resisting the authority of Vermont, the general assembly commenced its session at Manchester. Aside from matters of ordinary legislation, the principal object of discussion was the relation of congress towards the state. Nothing had been heard from that body since the departure of the agents of the state from Philadelphia, the preceding April, when they had informed the president that they should expect to be officially notified whenever their attendance should again become necessary. There was not much hope of obtaining the favorable action of congress, and the question was raised and debated whether or not it was advisable to appoint agents to that body. But that nothing might be wanting on their part, to bring about an amicable union with the other states, it was finally resolved, "That it is expedient to choose persons to attend congress, to transact the business of the state, if necessary;" and Moses Robinson, Paul Spooner, Ira Allen and Jonas Fay, were chosen for that purpose. Instructions were prepared for their government, which "vested them or any two of them, with powers as plenipotentiaries to negotiate the admission of the state into the federal union of the United States, and to agree upon and to ratify terms of confederation in behalf of the state, whenever opportunity should present therefor." They were required "when directed by the governor and council to repair to the American congress."[1] No prospect appearing that an application to congress would prove successful, the agents did not act under their appointment.

While the legislature of Vermont was thus manifesting a friendly disposition towards congress, the enemies of the state in that body aided by outside importunities were actively preparing hostile measures against it, which, a few weeks later, found expression in the resolutions of the 5th of December, before recited. After some discussion in congress in regard to the manner in which those resolutions should be communicated to the Vermonters, they were finally enclosed in a letter from the president, dated the 11th of December, and committed to the commander-in-chief of the army for transmission to Gov. Chittenden. They were received by him towards the latter end of the month, and evidence of their delivery to him was furnished congress on the 15th of January, 1783, in a letter from Gen. Washington.[2]

These resolutions it will be recollected, required the government of Vermont to indemnify for their losses, certain persons who had been punished for resistance to its authority and to restore them to their former conditions, and also to submit to the establishment of two independent jurisdictions, besides its own, within the territory of the state. This *ex parte* proceeding was received by the people of Vermont, with great surprise, not unmingled with indignation, at what was considered a flagrant breach of faith, pledged to the state by congress, in their resolutions of August, 1781. No serious thought of complying with the resolutions appears to have been entertained.[3]

The communication from the president of congress, having by Gov. Chittenden been submitted to his council, he, in accordance with their advice, returned a spirited answer, remonstrating in strong and decided, but respectful language against the unexpected proceedings of that body. The remonstrance, which bore date January 9th, 1783, began by stating that the subject would be laid before the legislative authority of the state, whose adjourned session would be held on the secend Thursday of the ensuing February. It then "reminded congress of their solemn engagement to the state in their public acts of August 7th and 21st, 1781," which were recited at length, and gave an extract from the letter of Gen. Washington of

[1] *Assembly Jour.*, Oct. 10, 16, 17, 18 and 21. *Council Jour.*, Oct. 17 and 21.

[2] *Madison Papers*, vol. 1, p. 228, 229, 240.

[3] *Hall's Eastern Vt.*, 478, 479, and *Clinton Papers*.

the first of January, 1782, in which he declared that Vermont had "nothing to do but to withdraw her jurisdiction to the confines of her old limits and obtain an acknowledgment of independence and sovereignty under the resolve of the 21st of August." It then stated that "confiding *in the faith and honor* of congress" proffered in those acts, and having "*great* confidence" in the assurances of Gen. Washington, the legislature of the state had circumscribed their claim of jurisdiction in compliance with the terms offered them by congress; and had informed congress of their compliance by agents appointed for that purpose; that a committee of congress to whom the matter had been referred, had reported "that the conditional promise and engagement of congress" to recognize the independence of the state and to admit it into the federal union had "thereby become absolute and necessary to be performed;" that congress, having delayed action on this report, the agents had returned home, but that others had been appointed at the last October session of the legislature with full powers to negotiate the admission of the state into the union, whenever congress should be ready to consider the subject; that the inhabitants of the state having thus secured as they supposed, the friendly disposition of congress, could not be otherwise than alarmed on receiving their late hostile resolutions. It was then insisted in the remonstrance that the resolves of September, 1779, and June, 1780, on which those of December 5th, 1782, were predicated, were by their terms only to continue in force until congress should act upon and decide the controversy between the claiming states and Vermont; that the resolves of August, 1781, engaging to admit the state into the union on certain conditions, which had become absolute by a compliance therewith, could not be otherwise considered, than as a decision of the dispute in favor of Vermont, and consequently as putting an end to the operation of those prior resolutions, and rendering them null and void. It was further insisted that congress, under the articles of confederation, had no authority whatever to control the internal police of any of the states; much less that of Vermont, whose inhabitants had lived in a state of independence from their first settlement, governing themselves, until their state government was formed in Jan., 1777, by committees and conventions in the manner afterwards followed in the other states on their first separation from the British government. It was argued at some length and with great force of reasoning, that the execution of the threatening resolutions of the 5th of December, passed at the instance of their old New York enemies, would be equally arbitrary and unjust with the measures attempted to be enforced by the English crown on the colonies, and that congress ought not to demand submission to them. In regard to the measures which had been adopted by the Vermont goverment to enforce its authority, Gov. Chittenden's remonstrance proceeded as follows:

"Although this state is not amenable to the tribunal of congress for the management of their internal police, I nevertheless will give them a brief narrative of facts, relative to those delinquents, in whose behalf congress in their resolution of December last have interfered. At the session of the general assembly of this state in February, 1781, they made a general act of amnesty in favor of all persons within this state, who had previously made opposition to its authority; upon which they unanimously submitted to this government, and all opposition to it ceased for more than a year, when the legislature having ordered a certain quota of men to be raised in the several towns throughout this state, for the defence of the frontiers, evil minded persons in the town and vicinity of Guilford, in the southerly part of the county of Windham, opposed the raising and paying of them, and Gov. Clinton of the state of New York, by letters to them and otherwise, interfered in their behalf, which caused a second insurrection in this state, and though every prudent and lenient measure was taken by the government to reclaim the offenders, they proved ineffectual. In the meantime Gov. Clinton gave commissions, civil and military, to sundry of those disaffected persons, and they had the effrontery to attempt to exercise the laws of New York, over citizens of this state, when a military force, was by direction of the government sent to assist the sheriff of Windham county, in the execution of the laws of this state; and the procedure of the court, relative to the five criminals, who were banished, and to sundry others who were amerced in pecuniary fines, was in due form of law. The notorious Samuel Ely, who was a ringleader of the late seditions in the state of Massachusetts, a fugitive from justice, was one of the banished. He had left that state, and was beginning insurrection in this, when he was detected, and carefully delivered to the sheriff of the county of Hampshire, in the state of Massachusetts, who, as I have been since informed, has secured him in jail at Boston, to the great satisfaction and peace of that state.[1]

---

[1] Dr. J. G. Holland, in his *History of Western Massachusetts*, vol. 1, p. 230, treating of the disturbances in that state in 1782, thus speaks of this person: "The earliest and most inveterate demagogue in the field was Samuel Ely. He was a cast-off, irregular clergyman, who had acted as a minister of the gospel in Somers, Ct. He was a vehement, brazen-faced declaimer, abounding in hypocritical pretensions to piety, and an industrious

This same Samuel Ely, Timothy Church and William Shattuck, who were three of the banished, had previously taken the oath of allegiance to this state, and so had a greater part of those who were fined; and many of the towns in which they resided, had for several sessions of the assembly, previous to their insurrection, been represented in the legislature of this state."

On this state of facts, it was claimed that the offenders, having previously submitted to the government of Vermont, were even by the resolutions of 1779 and 1780, under obligation to obey that government, and could not escape from its authority by merely changing their professions of allegiance to that of New York, and that consequently their punishment could be no violation of those resolutions. After some severe remarks on the character and conduct of Charles Phelps, at whose instigation it was supposed the resolves of the fifth of December had been passed, the remonstrance of Gov. Chittenden concluded by a renewal of the offer of Vermont to become a member of the federal union. This remonstrance was transmitted to the president of congress, and was laid before that body on the 4th of February. It was also published in pamphlet form and extensively circulated among the leading men of the country, and especially among the officers and soldiers of the army, that they might have some knowledge of the merits of the controversy, in case they should be called upon to enforce the hostile resolutions of congress.[1]

On the presentation of this document to congress, Mr. Hamilton of New York moved that it be referred to a committee, which motion was seconded by Mr. Dyer of Connecticut. "Mr. Wolcott of Connecticut wished to know the object of the motion for commitment, upon which Mr. Hamilton said his view was to fulfil the resolutions of congress which bound them to enforce the measure," "Mr Dyer

---

sower of discord, and he delighted in nothing more than arousing jealousies between the poor and the rich." . . . "In the month of April, 1782, he succeeded in raising a mob of sufficient force to disturb the holding of the supreme court and court of common pleas at Northampton. For this offense he was indicted and convicted and imprisoned in the jail at Springfield." He was rescued from jail by a mob and fled to Vermont, there to be dealt with as stated in the text.

[1] The title page of the pamphlet publication of Gov. Chittenden's communication was as follows: "A copy of a remonstrance of the council of the state of Vermont against the resolutions of congress of the 5th of December last which interfered with their internal police. Hartford, printed by Hudson and Goodwin, 1783." A copy of the pamphlet is in the archives of the Vermont Historical Society. It is also inserted in *Slade*, p. 178 to 185.

said his was, that so dishonorable a menace might be as quickly as possible renounced. He said General Washington was in favor of Vermont; that the principal people of New England were all supporters of them, and that congress ought to rectify the error into which they had been led, without longer exposing themselves to reproach on this subject. It was committed without dissent."[1]

The remonstrance of the governor and council of Vermont, having referred to the letter of Gen. Washington of the 1st of January, 1782, he deemed it advisable for his own justification, to lay before congress, a copy of the whole correspondence between himself and Gov. Chittenden, which was accompanied by a letter from him to the president of that body, as follows:

"HEAD QUARTERS, NEWBURG, 11th Feb., 1783.

"Sir: Within these few days I have seen printed copies of 'a remonstrance of the council of the state of Vermont,' against the resolutions of the 5th of December last, addressed to your excellency, in which are several extracts from a letter of mine.

"Duty as well as inclination prompts me to lay before congress the whole of that letter, and the one to which it was an answer.

"If it should be necessary, a committee of congress, with whom I was in conference on these matters in the course of last winter, can give such further information on this subject as I doubt not will be satisfactory.

I have honor to be, &c.,
G. WASHINGTON."[2]

The committee of congress referred to in this letter, with whom Washington had been in conference, consisted of Messrs. Carroll of Maryland, Cornell of Rhode Island, Clark of New Jersey, Jones of Virginia, and Middleton of South Carolina, to whom had been committed the complaints of New Hampshire and New York against the enlarged claims of jurisdiction by Vermont.[3]

Under the same date with his letter to the president of congress, Gen. Washington wrote at some length to Mr. Jones, reminding him that the committee of which he was a member had approved of his answer to the letter of Gov. Chittenden "to the effect that it was given," and arguing earnestly against the use of coercive mea-

---

[1] *Madison Papers,* vol. 1.

[2] *Washington's Ms. Letters,* state department, Washington.

[3] *Letter Books of Washington* in state department. *Papers of the old Congress,* state department, No. 40, vol. 2, and No. 186.

sures against the Vermonters. After stating that he supposed the army would be expected to enforce a compliance with the resolutions, and that he was sure the Vermonters had a powerful interest in the New England states, he says, "Let me ask by whom that district of country is principally settled? And of whom is your present army (I do not confine the question to this part of it but will extend it to the whole) composed? The answers are evident — New England men. It has been the opinion of some, that the appearance of force would awe those people into submission. If the general assembly ratify and confirm what Mr. Chittenden and his council have done, I shall be of a very different sentiment; and, moreover, that it is not a trifling force that will subdue them, even supposing they derive no aid from the enemy in Canada; and that it would be a very arduous task indeed, if they should, to say nothing of a diversion which may and doubtless would be made in their favor from New York, if the war with Great Britain should continue." Again he says, "It may be asked, if I am acquainted with the sentiments of the army on the subject of this dispute. I answer no, not intimately. It is a matter of too delicate a nature to agitate for the purpose of information. But I have heard many officers of rank and discernment, and have learned by indirect inquiries that others express the utmost horror at shedding blood in this dispute; comparing it in its consequences, though not in its principles, to the quarrel with Great Britain, who only thought she was to hold up the rod and all would be hushed. I cannot at this time undertake to say that there would be any difficulty with the army, if it were to be ordered on this service, but I should be exceedingly unhappy to see the experiment. For, besides the reasons before suggested, I believe there would be a general unwillingness to imbrue their hands in the blood of their brethren."[1] This letter was doubtless written with the intent that other members of the congress besides Mr. Jones should be availed of his views on the subject, and with the hope of preventing so dire a calamity as a civil war among those who had heretofore battled together against the common enemy.

The foregoing letter of Gen. Washington to the president of congress, with its enclosures, was read in that body on the 17th of February, and referred to the same committee to whom had been committed the remonstrance of Gov. Chittenden. On the 4th of March the delegates from New York presented to congress a letter from Gov. Clinton, accompanied by sundry affidavits showing that

---

[1] For this letter at length see *Sparks's Washington*, vol. 8, p. 382.

the Vermonters, instead of complying with the late resolutions of that body, were wholly disregarding them, by arresting and imprisoning such of the banished persons named in those resolutions as had returned to the state, and by other acts manifesting their intention to continue the independent exercise of their authority over all inhabitants within the limits of their territory. The letter of Gov. Clinton earnestly appealed to congress for speedy action on the subject. On the 14th of April, a letter from Gov. Chittenden, enclosing another to the president of congress signed by the speaker in behalf of the general assembly of Vermont, was laid before that body. It embodied the views of the legislature of the state in regard to the resolves of the previous December, and reaffirmed the principles set forth in the previous remonstrance of the governor. In denying the right of congress to meddle with the internal affairs of the state, the following language was used: "The citizens of this state have ever entertained the highest opinion of the wisdom and integrity of congress, and have manifested their confidence in that body, by a spirited exertion in the prosecution of every measure against the common enemy, at the risk of life and fortune. We still are ready to comply with every reasonable requisition of congress; but when congress require us to abrogate our laws, and reverse the solemn decisions of our courts of justice, in favor of insurgents and disturbers of the public peace, we think ourselves justified to God and the world, when we say we cannot comply with such their requisitions." The document concluded with a request that congress would "execute on their part the intent and spirit of their resolution of the 21st of August, 1781," by which the state would become a member of the federal union.[1]

No report having been made on any of the papers which had been received in relation to the December resolutions, they were all on the 28th of April, referred to a new committee consisting of Mr. Carroll of Maryland, Mr. Gorham of Massachusetts, Mr. Lee of Virginia, Mr. White of New Hampshire, and Mr. Mercer of Virginia. This committee having had the whole subject before them made their report the 25th of May, the substance of which was that before taking any other steps in relation to the matters mentioned in the different papers referred to them, congress ought first to determine "whether the inhabitants of that district of country commonly called Vermont" should be admitted into the union as a separate state. No action was taken on the report, and it appears to have been the

[1] *Slade*, p. 185.

last proceeding in congress in relation to Vermont during the year 1783.[1] Whatever may have been the intentions of those who had voted for the threatening resolutions of the previous December, it had become obvious, since the decided attitude against their execution which had been taken by Vermont, and the views of Gen. Washington on the subject had become known, that a majority of the members had no thought of employing the army to enforce them.[2]

---

[1] *Journals of Congress* and *Papers of Congress* in State Department.

[2] *Papers of the old Congress,* Washington State Department.

CHAPTER XXXVIII.

End of Resistance to the Authority and Independence of Vermont.

1783-1784.

Encouraged by the December resolves of congress and by letters of Gov. Clinton, Timothy Church and Timothy Phelps return from banishment to defy the authority of Vermont—They are seized and committed to Bennington jail—Are released on their promises of submission to the laws—Fresh disturbances—Charles Phelps and William Shattuck arrested and sent to Bennington jail—The Yorkers subdued by military force—Phelps pardoned, and Shattuck discharged, on submission—Urgent appeal of the New York legislature to congress to decide against Vermont—Sharp letter of Gov. Chittenden to the president of congress on the inconsistent and unfair conduct of New York—Report of congress committee May 29, 1784, against the appeal of New York and in favor of the independence of Vermont, being the last proceeding of the confederation congress in relation to the controversy—Final end of resistance to the Vermont jurisdiction.

WHILE the resolutions of December 1782 added nothing to the strength of the cause of New York in congress, they were of serious detriment to the adherents of that state residing in Vermont. From the language of the resolutions and the continued assurances of protection given by Gov. Clinton, the activity and violence of the opponents to the government of Vermont were increased, which only served to prolong a troublesome and hopeless resistance, and bring upon themselves an increased severity of treatment. Soon after the passage of the resolutions the persons who had been banished the previous October, returned to their former residences, to defy the authority of the state, and continue their disturbances. Timothy Church, the New York colonel, being found in Brattleboro towards the latter end of December, was arrested and committed to the jail in Bennington. Early in February while the supreme court of Vermont was sitting at Marlborough, Timothy Phelps who held Gov. Clinton's commission as sheriff of Cumberland county, entered the court room and in a loud voice with presumptuous arrogance proclaimed his own pretended official authority, and ordered the court to disperse. He was immediately arrested by order of the court and sent to Bennington jail. Both Church and Phelps were liable by the laws of the state to be indicted and tried for returning to the state after banishment, and on conviction, to suffer death.

Rumors that they were thus to suffer prevailed and were probably not discountenanced by the Vermont authorities, though no steps appear to have been taken in that direction. The prisoners were allowed the free use of their pens, of which they seem to have availed themselves without stint in writing letters, denouncing the sheriff, jailer and other Vermont officials; laboring to excite popular sympathy in their favor, and vainly soliciting protection from Gov. Clinton. The government of Vermont seem to have been anxious to reclaim them, and others of the disaffected, by lenient measures. At the session of the general assembly in February 1783, a special act was passed in relation to Timothy Church, which recited that he had petitioned for relief "setting forth his hearty penitence and determination to behave orderly and submissive in case of pardon," and then declared him to be "pardoned and discharged from the sentence passed against him in the supreme court, on his paying all costs of suit and of his confinement in consequence thereof." Another act was passed at the same session authorizing the governor and council to grant pardons on their proper submission to the other persons who had been banished. On the 15th of May, Church after an imprisonment of nearly five months, having complied with the terms of the act in his favor was released, and Timothy Phelps on a similar compliance with the general act was discharged the 24th of June following.

But the submission of these persons was rather formal than real. Soon after his discharge, Church repaired to Poughkeepsie, and made an affidavit against the Vermonters, declaring among other things, contrary to the fact of his having taken the freeman's oath, and notwithstanding his late submission, that he "never did acknowledge himself to owe allegiance or subjection to the pretended state of Vermont." On his return home, Gov. Clinton, under date of the 24th of June, furnished him with a letter of advice in which he encouraged him to expect that congress would soon decide the controversy in favor of New York, and counselled him, in case the Vermonters should attempt to execute their laws against adherents of that state, to call out his regiment and resist their execution by force of arms. No immediate outbreak, however, took place, though the threats and hostile attitude of the Yorkers, instead of subsiding, continued to increase until they became so serious as to require the decisive action of the government. At the session of the legislature in October, an act was passed which recited that "a number of persons living in the southern part of the county of Windham, to the great disturbance of the public peace, had banded together, to oppose sheriffs, constables and collectors in the execution of their offices, and in many instances had proceeded to outrageous abuses, which threatened the ruin of the government unless speedily remedied, which evil to prevent," it was enacted that one hundred able bodied effective men, properly officered, should be immediately raised for the term of six months, unless sooner discharged, to be commanded by Col. Benjamin Wait, and stationed in that part of the state to aid the civil authority in the due execution of the laws. In order to induce submission without the use of force, the governor in pursuance of a resolve of the assembly, issued a proclamation "offering a free and ample pardon for all offences committed against the state by any persons in the southern part of Windham county, who had theretofore opposed the government," upon their taking the oath of allegiance to the state before any justice of the peace, within thirty days. At the same session a retaliatory act was passed, which reciting that by a law of New York, persons living in Vermont were not allowed to commence suits at law in the courts of that state without taking the oath of allegiance to its jurisdiction, enacted that no inhabitant of New York should be permitted to prosecute a suit in Vermont, so long as such New York law should continue in force.

A considerable number of the former friends of New York, availed themselves of the benefit of Gov. Chittenden's proclamation, and took the oath of allegiance. This appears to have been very generally the case with the people of Halifax, where there had hitherto been a strong party of Yorkers. But others continued their opposition, and some of them did not confine themselves to defensive measures. About 2 o'clock in the morning of the 6th, of November, a party of armed men to the number of ten or more, headed by Francis Prouty of Brattleboro, forcibly entered the house of Luke Knowlton of Newfane, and making him their prisoner conveyed him across the line into the state of Massachusetts; but more than a hundred men being speedily rallied in pursuit, Knowlton was released and allowed to return home.

Efforts were now made by the Vermont authorities to arrest the leading Yorkers — those who were engaged either in making or promoting disturbances. William Shattuck, who had been banished was made prisoner on the 25th of December, by Oliver Waters a constable of Brattleboro, and taken to Bennington jail. Charles Phelps was arrested on the 4th of January, 1784, and on the 8th Francis Prouty was captured and taken to prison. Several other arrests were made. The activity of constable Waters had made him quite obnoxious to the Yorkers. He lodged at the public house of

Mr. Arms in Brattleboro, which on the night of the 16th of January was assaulted by some twenty or thirty men, who discharging their muskets through the doors and windows wounded one man in the leg and shot a traveler through the thigh. Having forcibly entered the house they seized Waters and conveyed him into Massachusetts, intending to take him to Gov. Clinton at Poughkeepsie. He was, however, overtaken at Northampton by a party in pursuit, rescued and brought safely back to Brattleboro.

On the seizure of Waters the most vigorous measures were adopted for subduing the Yorkers. Bodies of militia numbering several hundreds joined the small state force under Col. Wait at Brattleboro; the strongholds of the Yorkers were visited and some of the insurgents taken prisoners, while others fled across the state line into Massachusetts, whither they were not pursued. In a few days, all open defiance of the Vermont authority ceased and the militia were discharged, only a few state troops being left in Guilford to secure the continuance of quiet. A term of the supreme court was held at Westminster early in February for the trial of the prisoners, on most of whom small fines were imposed; some were released without trial, while a few received more severe punishment. Francis Prouty was sentenced to pay a fine of forty pounds and costs and be "imprisoned in close confinement for forty days;" and until the fine and costs were paid. Charles Phelps the most active and untiring opponent of the Vermont jurisdiction, was by the judgment of the court "attainted of treason; was sentenced to sixty days imprisonment and all his estate real and personal was forfeited to the use of the state." While the militia had been engaged in subduing the Yorkers in January the only blood which had been shed was that of Silvanus Fisk, a sergeant of the militia, who had been so severely wounded by a musket ball discharged by the insurgents at Guilford, as eventually to cause his death. After the dismissal of the militia, the party of state troops at Guilford, apprehensive of a night attack from the fugitives in Massachusetts, kept sentinels posted on the avenues to that town near the state line. On the night of the 5th of March two men were dimly seen approaching from the south, who being hailed by the sentinel turned and fled. Upon which they were fired upon and one of them, David Spicer, was mortally wounded. He was a citizen of Massachusetts, but his companion was one of the leading Yorkers of Guilford, going to the residence of his family. The two men were not the advance of an invading party as had been feared.

Information of this occurrence was immediately dispatched by the officer in command of the state troops to Gov. Chittenden at Bennington, where the legislature was holding an adjourned session. Gen. Samuel Fletcher, who was a member of the state council, and commanded the brigade of militia of Windham county, was directed by the assembly to repair to the scene of the disturbances, and was vested with discretionary powers to adopt such measures as he should deem advisable for the restoration of peace and quiet. Under his direction all the state troops were, during the month of March, gradually withdrawn and dismissed, and no further outbreaks took place.

During the session of the legislature, which commenced the 19th of February and continued until the 9th of March, a new "act against high treason and misprision of treason" was passed, by which any resident of the state for levying war against the state, or aiding or assisting any enemy at open war against the state, was, on conviction, to suffer death; and his estate was to be confiscated to the use of the state; and any citizen who should endeavor to join the enemies of the state, or knowingly conceal such attempt of others, was made liable to fine and imprisonment in the discretion of the court — such imprisonment not to exceed ten years. By another act, discretionary power was conferred on the governor and council, to grant pardons on such terms as they should deem expedient, during the recess of the legislature, to any persons in the county of Windham, who had opposed the authority of the state, and who should appear "penitent and desirous of returning to their duty." At this session, Charles Phelps, who was confined in the jail at Bennington, under his recent sentence, petitioned the legislature to be released from prison, promising thereafter to submit peaceably to the jurisdiction and laws of the state. The legislature thereupon promptly passed an act declaring that he "be immediately discharged from his imprisonment, and that no part of his estate, which had been seized and confiscated by order of the supreme court, should be sold or disposed of, until further order of the assembly." On the 27th day of February, the day of the passage of the act, as appears by the journal of the council, "the said Charles Phelps, being admitted to a personal appearance before the council, did voluntarily take the oath of allegiance and fidelity to the state of Vermont." A petition of William Shattuck, who was also in Bennington jail, was less favorably received, and he continued in prison until sometime in April, when, on his compliance with certain terms, he was released by the governor and council. Thus, for the present at least, if not finally, the independent jurisdiction of the state appeared to be vindicated.[1]

Up to the time of the adjournment of the assembly in March, 1784, no proceedings had taken place in congress in relation to Vermont, since the making of the report of the committee of the 26th of May, 1783, of which an account was given at the close of the preceding chapter. The legislature of New York appears also to have been for some time quite passive. But now, early in this year (1784), the appeals of the friends of New York residing in Vermont, for relief against the vigorous measures of the government of that state, were so urgent as to require an earnest effort by the New York legislature in their favor. The sufferers had been encouraged by the New York government to continue their resistance to Vermont, and now in their deep distress, had strong claims upon it for assistance. The idea of employing the state militia for their protection does not appear to have been entertained, and the only resort of the legislature was a new appeal to congress.

On the 2d of February, Mr. Duane, the old foe of the Vermonters, as chairman of a committee of the senate which had been appointed to prepare instructions to their delegates in congress "respecting the rights of the state to the district of country commonly called the New Hampshire Grants," made an elaborate report which among other things declares "that the leaders of the district in question have actually raised troops and now employ them to reduce other inhabitants, resident in said district, and acknowledging themselves citizens of this state to submit to their assumed government;" that the state of New York "is in the disagreeable situation of having hostilities commenced against her citizens, but that if she must recur to force for the preservation of her lawful authority, the impartial world will pronounce that none of the bloodshed, disorder or dissention, which may ensue, can be imputable to this legislature," and further that the delegates inform congress, that "the legislature conceive themselves to be urgently pressed by the great duty of self-preservation to prepare for the worst," and that if congress for the space of two months after nine states should be represented there, should not pronounce their decision of the controversy, their neglect

[1] See *Clinton and Legislative Papers* in the New York state library, and papers in the office of the secretaries of state at Albany and Montpelier. *Journal of Assembly and Council. Slade,* p. 467, 470, 475, 476, 483, 490. For a more full account of the occurrences in Windham county during the period embraced by this chapter, see *B. H. Hall's History of Eastern Vermont,* chaps. 17, 18 and 19.

would "be considered as a denial of justice." Further instructions of a similar import urging a speedy decision of the controversy, were prepared by a joint committee of the two houses, and on the 2d of March the whole being adopted by both branches were forwarded to the delegates. On the 24th of April Messrs. De Witt and Paine, the New York delegates, presented to congress a written representation of the claim and demands of New York founded on their instructions, which was referred to a committee consisting of Mr. Read of South Carolina, Mr. Sherman of Connecticut, Mr. Ellery of Rhode Island, Mr. Hardy of Virginia, and Mr. Beatty of New Jersey.[1]

The journals of the New York senate showing the adoption of Mr. Duane's report, having been published, Gov. Chittenden by the advice of his council addressed a letter to the president of congress, in relation to it, and to the position then occupied by the state of New York in regard to the controversy, which is deemed worthy of insertion at length. The letter presents the unfair and inconsistent conduct of New York in a clear light, and for close logical argument and cutting sarcasm, it will be difficult to find a state paper which is its superior. It is as follows:

"State of Vermont,
Arlington, April 26, 1784.

"Sir: With that respect for congress which the citizens of this state have ever maintained, I beg leave to transmit to your excellency the sentiments of the council of this state, on the late proceedings of the senate and assembly of the state of New York respecting this state, that your excellency may lay the same before congress, for their consideration.

"On the 21st of October, 1779, the legislature of the state of New York passed a special law empowering congress to hear and determine the controversy between that state and this, not upon the principles of the confederation, but according to equity; and on the 7th and 20th of August, 1781, congress proposed preliminaries of a settlement of the said controversy, to this state, which were accepted and fully complied with by the legislature of this state at their session in February, 1782.

"The legislature of the state of New York, in the November preceding (1781) had spiritedly remonstrated against the prelimi-

[1] *Jour. N. Y. Senate and Assembly. History of Eastern Vermont,* p. 522-525.

nary settlement of congress aforesaid, an extract of which remonstrance is as follows:

"'*Resolved*, That in case of any attempt of congress to carry into execution their said acts of the 7th and 20th of August last, this legislature with all due deference to congress, are bound in duty to their constituents, to declare the same an assumption of power in the face of said act of submission of this state, and against the clear letter and spirit of the second, third, ninth and eleventh articles of confederation, and a manifest infringement of the same, and do therefore hereby solemnly protest against the same.'

"But of late it appears, the senate and assembly of the state of New York are again urging congress to decide their controversy with this state. It seems they are willing congress should settle the dispute as *they* have a mind, but not otherwise.

"It appears from the late journal of the senate of the state of New York, 'That the delegates be further instructed to press congress for a decision in the long protracted controversy respecting the right of this state to the district commonly called the New Hampshire Grants;' and further, 'But that if she must recur to force for the preservation of her lawful authority, the impartial world will pronounce that none of the bloodshed, disorder or dis-union which may ensue, can be imputable to this legislature.' As to this *bloody proposition* the council of this state have only to remark that Vermont does not wish to enter into a war with the state of New York, but that *she will act on the defensive*, and expect that congress and the twelve states will observe a strict neutrality, and let the two contending states settle their own controversy.

"As to the allegation of the state of New York against the conduct of this state in bringing a few malcontents to justice and obedience to government, whom they have inspired with sedition, I have only to observe that this matter has been managed by the wisdom of the legislature of this state, who consider themselves herein amenable to no earthly tribunal.

"Before I conclude this letter I beg leave to remind your excellency that it appears to the council of this state improper that the states of New York and New Hampshire, who are competitors for the jurisdiction thereof, should vote in congress on any motion which respects Vermont, and also contrary to the express resolution of congress of the 24th of September, 1779, in the words following: 'And that neither of the said states shall vote on any question relative to the decision thereof;' that is, relative to the independence of Vermont, although it appears from the journals of congress that those claiming states have ever since voted on all matters in which the interest of this state has been concerned.

"Sir: I conclude this letter with the satisfaction of reminding congress that this state is still desirous of a confederation with the United States.

"I have the honor to be, etc.,
THOMAS CHITTENDEN

"His Excellency,
The President of congress."

This letter was read in congress the 17th of May, and referred to the same committee to which had been committed the representation of the New York delegates and other papers relating to the disturbances in Vermont. This committee reported the 29th of May, fully in favor of Vermont, reciting the resolutions of congress of August, 1781, which offered preliminaries of settlement, and their acceptance by Vermont, affirming and declaring the binding obligation of congress to acknowledge the independence of the state, and concluding with a resolution as follows:

"*Resolved*, That the district of territory lying on the west side of Connecticut river, called Vermont, within the limits and boundaries described in the act of congress of the 20th of August, 1781, and the people inhabiting the same, be, and they are hereby recognized and declared to be a free, sovereign and independent state, by the name of the state of Vermont. That the said state of Vermont, being within the limits of the United States, shall be considered a part of the confederacy, on the same principles as the new states, who shall have established permanent governments agreeably to the act of congress of the 23d of April last, until it shall accede to the articles of confederation and be admitted into the federal union of these states."

In regard to the sufferings of individuals by banishment and confiscation of property, etc., complained of in the papers submitted to them, the committee reported that "if congress should judge it expedient to take any further order respecting those matters, it would be proper again to commit those papers." The papers were not again committed. It was now well understood that a majority of the states were favorable to Vermont, but it required the concurrence of nine of the thirteen to acknowledge her independence and admit her into the union, and as that number could not be obtained, her friends in that body were averse to coming to a vote on that question. On the 3d of June, a few days after the report was made, the delegates of New York moved to postpone another matter which was under consideration, for the purpose of taking up this report, but only the states of New York and New Hampshire voted in favor of the motion.[1]

This appears to have been the last motion made, and the last vote taken on the Vermont question in the Continental congress. From this time forward, Vermont was allowed to pursue the even tenor of her way, without any interference on the part of the government of the confederation.

With the month of March, 1784, all active opposition to the jurisdiction of Vermont ceased. At the session of the general assembly in October following, many of the disaffected persons presented petitions for relief from the penalties for which they were liable, and an act was passed granting twenty-six of them by name, a free pardon, and ordering any property of theirs which had been seized by the authority of the state, and not disposed of, to be restored to them, on condition that they should within three months appear before some justice of the peace for the county of Windham, and take the oath of allegiance to the state. Of these persons, seven were from Brattleboro, eighteen from Guilford, and one from Marlboro. At the same session, Charles Phelps petitioned the legislature for a pardon, and for a reversal of the sentence of the supreme court, attainting him of treason and confiscating his property. The committee, to whom the petition was referred, reported that the petitioner "had been meritorious in his former opposition to the regranting of lands by New York," and "in opposing the uniting and associating of the people of Cumberland county with New York," and had been "very servicable to his country by procuring and selling, without profit to himself, a quantity of arms, ammunition and salt;" but that "he had been for a number of years past exceedingly obstinate against and troublesome to the state." On the whole the committee, "on account of his former merit, his advanced age and the bad circumstances of his family," recommend that a full pardon be granted him, and that all his estate which had been confiscated, and not disposed of for the use of the state, should be restored to him, on his payment of the sum of thirty-five pounds lawful money "towards defraying the extraordinary cost that the government had been at on account of the exertions of himself and his associates against it." An act was

---

[1] *Papers of the old Congress* in the state department at Washington, No. 40, vol. 2, p. 465 and No. 186. *Jour. of Cong.*, June 3, 1784.

passed in accordance with this report, and Mr. Phelps continued a peaceable citizen of the state during the remainder of his life, which terminated in April, 1789, in the seventy-third year of his age. His descendants have been numerous and respectable, and some of them have occupied very honorable positions in the state and country.[1]

The Windham county sufferers in the cause of New York, afterwards petitioned the legislature of that state for compensation for their losses, alleging in substance that they had been occasioned by the confidence they had placed in the assurances of congress and the government of New York, of eventual support and protection against the jurisdiction and authority claimed by the Vermonters, in which they had been disappointed. In 1786, the legislature, in response to their petition, appropriated a township of land eight miles square, for their benefit, situated on the Susquehanna river, since known as the town of Bainbridge, which was divided among more than one hundred claimants, in supposed accordance with their proportionate losses, the largest quantity assigned to any one person being three thousand eight hundred and forty acres, and the smallest ninety acres.

Many of the leading friends of New York removed from Vermont, while others remained and became quiet and peaceable supporters of the government.[2]

---

[1] *Jour. Vermont Assembly* for Oct. 23, 26, 1784, and *Slade*, p. 494, 495.

[2] *Hall's Eastern Vermont*, p. 541-546, and Appendix K, p. 757. *Doc. Hist. N. Y.*, vol. 4, p. 1014-1022.

CHAPTER XXXIX.

FROM THE PEACE WITH GREAT BRITAIN UNTIL THE ADMISSION OF VERMONT INTO THE UNION.

1784 - 1791.

Vermont after the peace is practically independent — Exercises sovereign authority from necessity — Such as prescribing a standard of weights and measures, regulating the value of coins, and in the establishment of Post Offices — In common with other states, coins copper.—Free from the embarrassments of the confederation, is not anxious to become a member of it — Movements in New York by Hamilton, Jay, Schuyler and others for the admission of Vermont into the Union — After the adoption of the constitution of the United States, commissioners are appointed by New York and Vermont, who agree upon terms, securing the Vermont land titles; and upon an adjustment of the controversy, the state is admitted into the Union in 1791.

BY the definitive treaty of peace, signed at Paris, September 3, 1783, and ratified by congress the following January, Vermont was included in the territory acknowledged by Great Britain to belong to the United States. Though claimed by New York her jurisdiction over it was merely nominal. For all practical purposes Vermont was independent of every other government. The confederated congress could, indeed, be scarcely considered a government. Its powers from the beginning had been almost exclusively of an advisory character, depending for their execution upon the separate will of each individual state. In the early stages of the contest with the mother country, the requirements of congress of the states had been received and treated with respect. But as the war progressed jealousies sprung up among its members and among the states, and its requisitions became continually less and less regarded; and when the pressure from without was withdrawn by the restoration of peace, little or no attention was paid to them. The paper currency which congress had emitted had become worthless, their revenues were exhausted, the public creditors were full of complaints against their proceedings, and they were without resources to answer the numerous demands that were perpetually made upon them. Their wisdom, as well as power, was very generally distrusted, and incapable of relieving themselves from their embarrassments, congress was daily sinking into insignificance and contempt.

The United States had contracted an immense debt in the prosecution of the war, and congress was making constant, though almost useless calls upon the states and their people to furnish the means for its payment. From these annoying calls Vermont, in consequence of having been refused admission into the union, was exempt. The several states were also deeply in debt. But the government of Vermont, by the disposition of her public lands, the imposition of taxes payable in provisions for the supply of her troops, and by her policy of deluding the enemy into inaction, had come out of the contest with but few outstanding obligations. Much of her territory was yet ungranted, and settlers from other states, invited to her territory by the mildness, as well as the efficiency of her government, the comparative lightness of her taxes, the fertility and cheapness of her public lands, annually made large accessions to her population and resources. The confidence which the people of Vermont originally had in the wisdom and ability of congress, had been greatly impaired by the evasive and vacillating conduct of that body towards the state, and they were now well prepared to share in the general want of respect with which their irregular and imbecile proceedings were viewed. They could not fail to see and feel that while their own condition was gradually improving, that of their neighbors was constantly growing worse. Under these circumstances, it cannot be matter of wonder that their admission into the federal union should cease to be an object earnestly sought after, or even very much desired. On this subject, the people of Vermont became content to remain passive for several years, cultivating a friendly feeling and intercourse with the neighboring states, and ready to unite with them on equal terms in any measure that should promise to be of general public benefit.

A great evil under which the people of Vermont labored at the close of the war grew out of their defective land titles. Until after the organization of the state government in 1779, there was no office in which conveyances of land were recorded, and consequently no place to which a purchaser could resort to ascertain the validity of a title. The New Hampshire charters had then been granted fifteen years or more, during which period numerous frauds had been practiced by base men who had made it a business to obtain the confidence of persons wishing to purchase, and to deed them lands to which they had no manner of claim. By this means very many of the settlers found themselves occupying land of which they could not show a chain of conveyances from original proprietors, but on which they had in good faith made extensive and valuable improvements. By the common law, formed for a very different state of things, they were liable to be turned out of their possessions by any stranger who could show a legal title, without receiving any compensation for their improvements, although they may have increased the value of the property four or even ten fold. The legal owner had voluntarily, perhaps designedly, neglected to make an early claim to the land, and it would be manifestly in the highest degree unjust, to allow him thus to reap the fruits of the labor and expenditures of another. This was clearly seen, but there was no precedent for a remedy, and the lawyers with a professional bias against change, were not in general disposed to aid in devising one. After several legislative suspensions of all land trials, and the consideration of various projects, a bill by the efficient aid of Nathaniel Chipman, one of the best jurists of his time, was framed for that purpose and enacted into a law at the session of the general assembly in October 1785. By this act a proceeding was pointed out by which after a judgment in ejectment for the plaintiff, any defendant who had purchased a title supposing it to be good in fee, and had entered into possession of the land and made improvements upon it, might have the value of such improvements ascertained by the verdict of a jury, and unless the plaintiff in ejectment should pay for them, he was not to be availed of the benefit of his judgment. This law, though novel in its character, was founded on the clearest principles of natural justice. It has always been popular in the state, and several of our sister states, availing themselves of our invention and experience have adopted the same system.[1] The act concluded with a section declaring that no action whatever for the recovery of lands should be prosecuted, where the cause of action had accrued previous to its passage, unless such action should be commenced within three years from the first day of the preceding July. The whole act was well adapted to the condition of titles and of society at the time of its passage. This act when spoken of in reference to its first provisions, which, secured to the occupant compensation for the improvements he had made in good faith, was usually denominated the Betterment act, and in reference to its latter provision, the Quieting act.

The government of Vermont during this period of her independence exercised all the powers of sovereignty which her isolated political situation seemed to require. Among them were those of

[1] *Slade's State Papers*, p. 500, also p. 388, 405, 488, 494, 392, 411, 443. *Life of Nathaniel Chipman*, by Daniel Chipman, p. 62, 65.

prescribing a standard of weights and measures, and of regulating the fineness and value of coins. These powers however, for the want of any action of congress in relation to them, had in like manner been exercised by states of the confederation. Vermont also provided for the coinage of copper. In 1785 an act was passed granting to Reuben Harmon, Jr., of Rupert, the exclusive privilege of coining copper for a limited period. In 1786 an additional act was passed extending the time for the exercise of the privilege, and prescribing more particularly the weight and devices of the coins. This power of coining copper appears to have been likewise exercised during the period of the confederation by Connecticut and other states. In 1784 an act was passed by the Vermont legislature under which post offices were established, and a post master general appointed to superintend their management; and to the post riders was given the exclusive right of transporting letters and packages, "the rates of postage to be the same as in the United States." [1]

These powers were exercised from necessity, rather than from a disposition to disregard any proper measures of congress. The revised constitution of the state of 1786 provided for the annual election of delegates to congress, though none ever had occasion to attend it, and in accordance with the spirit of the fourth article of the confederation, the legislature declared by law that all the citizens of the United States should be equally entitled to all the privileges of law and justice, with those of Vermont.[2] The people of Vermont, though temporarily estranged from the confederation were connected with the states which composed it in feeling and interest, and considered themselves as forming a part of the same nationality.

While the government of Vermont remained in a great degree inactive, in regard to obtaining an acknowledgment of her independence by congress, it became a subject of serious consideration in New York whether it would not be to the advantage of the whole country, including that state, to have Vermont become a member of the confederation. All well informed men had become convinced that any further attempt to recall her people to the jurisdiction of New York, would be altogether ineffectual, and worse than useless; that

---

[1] *Vermont Laws* edition of 1787, p. 105, 161. In regard to the coining of copper by Vermont and other states, see *Appleton's Cyclopedia* article coins. *Slade,* 509. *Thompson's Vt.*, p. 135. *N. Y. Hist. Mag.* for January, 1868, p. 32. *Vt. Hist. Gazetteer*, p. 227. Anthony Haswell of Bennington was appointed post master general. See *Slade*, p. 498, and *Council Minutes,* March 5, 1784.

[2] *Slade,* 449. *Acts of* 1787, p. 31.

their independence was a fixed fact that could not be changed. The interest of the state in the general affairs of the country was similar to that of New York, and her votes in congress would naturally favor that interest. Why then persist in keeping her out of the political fold, where her influence and action was quite sure to be beneficial? It was difficult to give a sensible answer to this question. Although Gov. Clinton had manifested a uniform and untiring hostility towards Vermont, and by the efficient aid of his land claiming friends, had always (except in a single instance as previously related), been able to carry the legislature with him, there had long been prominent men in that state who did not concur in his views. Gouveneur Morris, early in the year 1778, and repeatedly afterwards, had written Clinton earnestly protesting against his policy of resisting the claim of Vermont to independence, which claim he insisted must prove successful.[1] Gen. Schuyler, as has already been seen, had long favored Vermont's independence. Alexander Hamilton, a few days after entering congress, and while the subject was in a degree new to him, had advocated the passage of the hostile resolutions of the 5th of December, 1782, but he very soon afterwards became satisfied that the measure had been a mistaken one, and he thereafter urged a friendly adjustment of the matter.[2] Mr. Jay and other leading statesmen of New York, had also abandoned their early views on the subject and become favorable to Vermont independence.

In the spring of 1787, Mr. Hamilton, who was a member of the New York assembly, introduced into that body a bill "to authorize the delegates in congress to accede to ratify, and confirm the independence and sovereignty of the people inhabiting the district of territory commonly called Vermont." The bill made no provision in regard to land titles, under New York patents, but left the claimants to their remedy under the articles of confederation. These claimants, who principally resided in New York city, where the assembly was sitting, having had a meeting on the subject, presented a petition to the assembly, asking to be furnished with a copy of the bill and to be allowed to be heard in regard to it, by counsel. Both requests were granted, and Wednesday the 28th of March was assigned for the hearing. On that day, Richard Harrison, a lawyer of distinguished learning and ability, was heard at the bar of the house in opposition to the bill. He argued at length against the

[1] *Letter*, 4th of March, 1778, and *Life of Morris*, vol. 1, p. 211 – 215.

[2] *Life of Hamilton* by his son J. C. Hamilton, vol. 2, p. 198 – 204.

necessity and policy of the measure; against the constitutional power of the legislature to consent to the dismemberment of the state, and also against the injustice of thereby depriving the petitioners of their property without compensation, and alleged that the remedy which they might have by the organization of a court under the articles of confederation would be entirely valueless, because "it would be attended with such an enormous expense as the petitioners could by no means sustain, and to which sovereign states alone would be found equal." He was answered by Mr. Hamilton, who argued with great power and ability in favor of the propriety and policy of conceding the independence of Vermont, which had now become fully established, and which it was beyond the power of New York to overthrow; and he claimed that public necessity often justified governments in curtailing their former limits. He insisted that the state was not under a strict obligation to make compensation to the losing claimants. "The distinction," he said, "is this — if a government voluntarily bargains away the rights, or dispossesses itself of the property of its citizens in their enjoyment, possession, or power, it is bound to make compensation for that of which it has deprived them; but if they are actually dispossessed of those rights or that property by the casualties of war or by revolution, the state, if the public good require it, may abandon them to the loss without being obliged to make reparation." New York, he claimed, had done all in her power to preserve the rights of the petitioners, by striving for years to maintain her jurisdiction over the controverted district without success, and now, in yielding to the stern law of necessity, would only cease to keep up a vain claim to territory of which she was actually dispossessed, and which she could never recall. The bill was debated for several days and finally passed the house on the 11th of April by a vote of twenty-seven ayes to nineteen nays. It however failed to pass the senate.[1]

A few weeks after this action of the New York assembly, (May 14th) the convention that framed the constitution of the United States assembled at Philadelphia. In September following the result of their labors was communicated to congress, and the constitution, by order of that body, was transmitted to the several states for their consideration. From that time till the middle of the following summer the public mind was greatly absorbed by the discussion of

[1] *Jour. N. Y. Assembly*, March 15, 24, 28, April 11. For Mr. Harrison's argument see *N. Y. Daily Advertiser*, for April 3, 1787. For Hamilton's reply, see *Works of Hamilton*, vol. 2, p. 374-390. See also J. C. Hamilton's *Republic of the U. S.*, vol. 3, p. 228, 235.

the new frame of government, and by the action of the several state conventions in regard to it; and during the year 1788 no movement in the New York legislature appears to have been made in relation to Vermont. The convention which formed the constitution had dedeclared by resolution, that as soon as it should be ratified by nine states, congress should fix a day on which electors should be appointed by the states ratifying it, a day on which the electors should assemble to vote for the president, and the time and place for commencing proceedings under the constitution. Early in July 1788, congress at the city of New York, where its sessions had been held since January 1785, received official information of the ratification of the constitution by eleven of the thirteen states, and immediately took up the subject of putting it in operation. But the question in regard to the place where the new government should be first organized, elicited such diverse views and such warm discussions that it was not until the 13th of September, after often repeated debates, during which the yeas and nays were taken over twenty times, that the city of New York was finally designated. The electors were to be appointed the first Wednesday of January 1789, were to assemble for the choice of president the first Wednesday in February, and proceedings under the constitutions were to commence on the first Wednesday of March.[1]

The controversy in regard to the seat of government was in a great degree sectional, and if the then existing relative position of the states could be preserved the people of New York had strong hopes of continuing it in their city. Kentucky, with the assent of Virginia, had applied to congress for admission into the union as a new state, and the application, in July 1788, had been postponed for the consideration of the new government. There was no doubt that Kentucky would become a member of the union at an early day, and unless Vermont could also be admitted the preponderance in the states would be clearly against New York. For this reason, to say nothing of other influences in operation, many of the citizens of New York became quite anxious for the acknowledgment of the independence of Vermont.

In February, 1789, a bill was introduced into the New York assembly declaring the consent of the legislature to the erection of the district called Vermont into a separate state, which passed that body by a vote of forty yeas to eleven nays, but like that of 1787

[1] *Jour. Congress*, September 28, 1787, and from July 3, to September 13, 1788, vol. 4, p. 776-782, and 828-867. Appendix to vol. 4 of *Journal*, p. 28 to 61.

for the same object, it was defeated in the senate.[1] But at a brief session of the legislature in July following, the advocates of Vermont were more successful. On the 6th of that month a bill was introduced into the assembly, providing for the appointment of commissioners to negotiate with the Vermonters in regard to their independence. On the 8th, a petition of John Jay and fifty-seven others was presented, stating that although the petitioners were interested in the lands in the district of Vermont under New York patents, they were nevertheless extremely desirous, on public considerations, for the admission of the district into the federal union as an independent state, and were willing for their land claims, "to receive justice in any manner which the nature of the case and the situation of public affairs might point out as most expedient." How much influence this petition had on the action of the legislature is not known.[2] But on the 14th of that month, a bill became a law, appointing seven commissioners with full powers, "on such terms and conditions and in such manner and form, as they should judge necessary and proper, to declare the consent of the legislature" to the erection of the district of Vermont into a new state. It was however provided, that nothing in the act contained should be construed to give any person claiming lands in such district to be erected into an independent state, any right to any compensation whatever from this state."[3]

An official copy of this act, having been transmitted by the commissioners therein named to governor Chittenden, he laid it before the legislature at their session in October following. By this time the new government of the United States under the constitution had been put in operation, a system of laws for its practical administration had been adopted, with decided indications that it would rescue the country from the embarrassments under which it had been laboring, and establish its nationality on a firm and creditable basis. Gen. Washington, in whom the people of Vermont had the most perfect confidence, and whom they had always considered as specially friendly to them, was now at its head as president, and this improved condition of affairs offered new and additional inducements for the state to become a member of the Union. With the assent of New York, which now seemed almost, if not quite assured, the only obstacle in the way of such Union was the condition of their land titles. While the state remained wholly independent,

---

[1] *Assembly Jour.*, February 27.

[2] *Clinton Papers.*

[3] *Laws of N. Y.*, 13th Sess. p. 2.

the inhabitants were safe against the New York claimants, but whether they would be so under the federal government, might perhaps be questioned. By the new constitution the federal courts would have jurisdiction in all the states, between citizens of different states; and the claimants under New York would be at liberty to institute suits in Vermont before such courts for the recovery of the lands they claimed. If such suits should be successful, a large portion of the inhabitants would be deprived of their property and homes, and the great object for which they had for years been contending would be thereby defeated. Although such a decision in favor of the claims of New York after her jurisdiction had been discarded and successfully overthrown by revolution, was extremely improbable, yet there was too much at stake to allow any risk to be run in relation to them.

This matter had been the subject of correspondence the previous year between Nathaniel Chipman of Vermont and Alexander Hamilton, in which the latter had admitted the propriety of providing against such a contingency, and had suggested as a means of doing so, that Vermont should by a convention called for that purpose "ratify the constitution upon condition that congress should provide for the extinguishment" of the New York claims. This plan, which depended for its execution upon the uncertain disposition of congress, and under the most favorable circumstances that conld be anticipated, was likely to be attended with great delay, does not appear to have been seriously entertained on the part of Vermont. The readiest and most feasible mode of accomplishing the object in view seemed to be for the state of New York to provide for the extinguishment of the claims of her own grantees, by making some compensation to the claimants, towards which the government of Vermont on an amicable adjustment of the matter might properly be called upon to contribute.

The New York act, in regard to her colonial land claims, was unsatisfactory to the Vermont legislature; but by entering into negotiation with the commissioners appointed by it, explanations might be made to them that would lead to further legislation by that state which would be acceptable. The legislature of Vermont therefore, on the 23d of October, 1789, passed an act appointing commissioners with authority "to treat with commissioners that now are *or hereafter may be appointed*, by the state of New York," and granting them full powers "to ascertain, agree to, ratify and confirm a jurisdictional or boundary line between the state of New York and the state of Vermont, and to adjust, and finally determine, all and every matter or thing which in any wise obstructs a union of the state with the United States." The act further declared that every act or agreement of the commissioners appointed by it, made and entered into with "certain commissioners that now are, *or hereafter may be* appointed by the state of New York should be as effectual to every purpose as if the same had been an immediate act of the legislature." The only limitations to the powers of the commissioners were, that they could not lessen or abridge the then existing jurisdictional limits of the state, or oblige any claimants to lands under grants from New Hampshire or Vermont to relinquish their claims, or "in any wise subject the state of Vermont to make any compensation to different persons claiming under grants made by the late province, and now state of New York, of lands situate and being in the state of Vermont and within the jurisdiction of the same." The commissioners appointed by the act were Isaac Tichenor, Stephen R. Bradley, Nathaniel Chipman, Elijah Paine, Ira Allen, Stephen Jacob, and Israel Smith, any four of whom were authorized to perform the duties assigned to the whole.[1]

The commissioners of the two states met in the city of New York in February 1790, when after spending several days in the interchange of views and proposals, it became apparent that the New York commissoners had no authority under the act appointing them to make any satisfactory stipulations in regard to their colonial land patents, and the negotiation was consequently broken off.[2] But the legislature of the state was then in session at Albany and a bill was soon introduced repealing the former act, and conferring additional powers on commissioners for the adjustment of the controversy, which bill on the 6th of March became a law. By this act full power was conferred on the commissioners, not only to relinquish the jurisdiction of New York over the territory of Vermont, but also to provide in such manner and form as they should deem proper for securing the titles to lands therein "against persons claiming the same lands under grants from the state of New York while a colony or since the independence thereof." And the act further provided that any compensation that should be received by the state by the agreement of the commissioners for the relinquishment of the jurisdiction of the state over the territory of Vermont, or of the claims of New York grantees to lands therein, should be for the use of such land claimants and not for the use of the state. The commissioners appointed by this act were Robert Yates, Robert R. Livingston, John Lansing

[1] *Slade*, p. 192.

[2] *Ms. Correspondence of Coms. and Reprot of Vt. Commissioners to the assembly* of October 21, 1790.

Jr. Gulian Verplanck, Simeon De Witt, Egbert Benson, Richard Sill and Melancton Smith. It is perhaps worthy of remark that Gov. Clinton's unrelenting hostility to Vermont, as well as his characteristic obstinacy, was shown in a vain attempt to defeat this measure for an amiacable adjustment of the long continued controversy. When the bill reached the council of revision he filed written objections against it and moved its rejection, but he was overruled by his associates, Chancellor Livingston and Judges Yates and Hobart. It thus escaped a veto, and became a law.[1]

The commissioners of the two states agreed upon a meeting at Stockbridge on the 6th of the ensuing July, but owing to the sickness of two of those of New York no meeting was held. But on the 27th of September following, the commissioners came together in the city of New York, and on the 7th of October, their negotiation was completed by a satisfactory arrangement, depending only for its final consummation upon the favorable action of the Vermont legislature. The New York commissioners entered into a formal written stipulation, declaring "the consent of the legislature of the state of New York that the state of Vermont be admitted into the Union of the United States of America, and that immediately on such admission, all claim of jurisdiction of the state of New York, within the state of Vermont should cease;" and further declaring, "the will of the legislature of the state of New York, that if the legislature of the state of Vermont should, on or before the first day of January, 1792, declare that on or before the first day of June, 1794, the said state of Vermont would pay to the state of New York the sum of thirty thousand dollars, that immediately from such declaration by the legislature of the state of Vermont, all rights and titles to lands within the state of Vermont under grants from the late colony of New York, or from the state of New York, should cease," those only excepted, which had been made in confirmation of former grants under New Hampshire. The requisite act for the payment of the thirty thousand dollars to the state of New York was passed by the Vermont legislature on the 28th of the same October, in which act it was also declared that "all grants, charters, or patents of lands lying within the state of Vermont made by or under the government of the late colony of New York," with the exception of the before mentioned confirmatory grants, were "null and void and incapable of being given in evidence in

---

[1] *Street's Council of Revison,* p. 418. *Laws* 13th Session, p. 13.

any court of law within the state."[1] At the same session a convention was called to meet at Bennington on the 6th of the ensuing January, to act upon the question of the adoption of the United States constitution, which on the 10th of that month was ratified by a vote of one hundred and five yeas to two nays. The legislature holding an adjourned session at the same time and place, appointed Nathaniel Chipman and Lewis R. Morris, commissioners to attend upon congress and negotiate the admission of the state into the union. They immediately repaired to Philadelphia and laid before the president the proceedings of the convention and the legislature of Vermont, and on the 18th of February 1791, congress passed an act which declared "that on the 4th day of March 1791, the said state, by the name and style of the state of Vermont, shall be received into this union as a new and entire member of the United States of America." This act was passed without debate or objection, and thus was happily terminated by the free consent of all parties a controversy which had existed and been attended with more or less bitterness and violence for over a quarter of a century.[2]

This work has now reached the close of the period of which the author proposed to treat. In his investigations he has sought for the original and most authentic sources of information, and has endeavored to state the facts of history in their true light. He thinks it satisfactorily appears that the early inhabitants of Vermont were under the necessity of uniting together in a separate and distinct community, and in forming an independent state, in order to maintain their titles and preserve their property, and were fully justified in their resistance to the oppressive measures of New York, and in their revolt against its authority; and that they conducted their public affairs, both against New York and the common enemy, with a patriotic energy and consummate ability, that commanded the respect of their contemporaries, and which entitles them to the honored remembrance of their posterity.

---

[1] For an account of the distribution of the sum paid by Vermont among the New York land claimants see Appendix No. 13.

[2] *Jour. N. Y. Assembly. Ms. Correspondence of the Com. Report of the Vt. Commissioners to the Assembly,* Oct. 21, 1790. *Slade,* p. 192-194. For a copy of the instrument executed by the *N. Y. Com.,* of Oct. 7, 1790, see the *Vermont Gazetteer* for Oct. 25, 1790.

APPENDIXES.

APPENDIX NO. 1.

Biographical Sketches of the Principal Persons mentioned in this Work.

Major Ebenezer Allen.— Ebenezer Allen was born at Northampton, Mass., October 17, 1743, emigrated to Poultney, Vt., in 1771, was a lieutenant in Col. Warner's regiment of Green Mountain Boys in 1775, removed to Tinmouth and was a delegate from that town to the several conventions of the New Hampshire Grants in 1776, and of those that declared the state independent and formed the state constitution the succeeding year. In July 1777, he was appointed a captain in Col. Herrick's battalion of state rangers, and distinguished himself in the battle of Bennington. In September following at the head of forty of his men he took possession by night assault, of Mount Defiance, and on the retreat of the enemy from Ticonderoga captured fifty of their rear guard, all of which is more particularly related in the body of this work. Among the prisoners on the latter occasion was Dinah Mattis a negro slave with her infant child, and he, being as he declares, " conscientious that it is not right in the sight of God to keep slaves," gave her a written certificate of emancipation, and caused it to be recorded in the town clerk's office at Bennington, where the record may now be seen. It bears date " Head Quarters Pawlet 28th November, 1777," and is signed " Ebenezer Allen Captain." Allen was afterwards promoted to a majority in the rangers and rendered other valuable services, showing himself to be a brave and successful partisan leader. In 1783, he removed to South Hero, where he resided till the year 1800 when he went to Burlington and died there March 26, 1806.— See *Deming's Vt. Officers* p. 183-4, and *Hollister's Pawlet*, 13, 83.

Ethan Allen.— So much has been said of Gen. Allen in the body of this work, that little remains to be added, especially as he is already widely known to the reading public. Ethan Allen was the oldest son of Joseph Allen and Mary Baker, who were married at Woodbury, Conn., March 11, 1736, and he was born at Litchfield, January 10, 1737. The other children of Joseph and Mary Allen were Heman, Lydia, Heber, Levi, Lucy, Zimri and Ira.

Ethan Allen came from Salisbury where he had resided for several years, to the New Hampshire Grants, now Vermont, about 1769, and had his residence here until his decease, living first at Bennington then at Arlington and Sunderland, and finally at Burlington. He was active in preparing for the defence of the ejectment suits brought against the settlers by the New York claimants, and attended the trials which took place at Albany in June, 1770. The titles of the settlers being declared invalid, they resolved to defend their possessions by force, if necessary, and Allen became their most prominent leader. With his corps of men styled Green Mountain Boys, he was successful in resisting the Yorkers, and also in the capture of Ticonderoga from the British, he and his men acquiring in both cases from Lieut. Gov. Colden, the name of the Bennington mob. In September, 1775, failing in an attempt with a volunteer force of Canadians, to capture Montreal, he was taken prisoner, sent to England in irons and treated with great indignity and cruelty. After remaining a prisoner over two years and some months he was exchanged and liberated in May, 1778. On the 14th of that month, congress, by resolution, granted him a brevet commission of lieutenant colonel " in reward of his fortitude, firmness and zeal in the cause of his country, manifested during his long and cruel captivity, as well as on former occasions." He was afterwards brigadier general in the militia of Vermont, and rendered the state essential and important services, both in a military and civil capacity.

In a letter from his brother, Ira Allen, to Dr. Samuel Williams in 1795, it is stated that Ethan began to prepare for college, but that the death of his father left the family in such circumstances that the design was not pursued. His early education was evidently defective, but he acquired much information by reading and observation, and held the pen of a ready, though an unpolished writer. His meaning was, however, always clear, and there was a peculiar boldness and quaintness in his language which attracted and fixed the attention of his readers, and was well calculated to inspire confidence in his sincerity of purpose and in the justice of the cause he advocated. He wrote largely on the subject of the New York controversy, first in several articles in 1772, mostly published in the *Connecticut Courant* and *New Hampshire Gazette*, and some of them printed in hand bills. They were very effective, and exerted an important influence on the public mind unfavorable to the New York land speculators and to the colonial government that sustained them. In 1774 he published a pamphlet of over two hundred pages against the validity of the titles of the New York claimants to lands on the New Hampshire Grants, and in answer to " The state of the right of New York," which had appeared the year previous under the sanction of the assembly of that province. In this, many historical facts were brought to bear against the claim of New York to extend easterly to Connecticut river prior to the king's order in 1764; and the oppressive conduct of the government towards the settlers under New Hampshire was strongly exhibited. It also embraced the answer of himself and his proscribed associates, to the outlawry act of New York of that year. In 1778 he published a pamphlet of twenty-four pages, entitled *An Animadversory Address*, in which he exposed the deceptive and unsatisfactory character of the overtures contained in Gov. Clinton's proclamation of the 23d of February of that year. In 1779, a pamphlet of one hundred and seventy-two pages prepared by him entitled " A vindication of the opposition of the inhabitants of Vermont to the government of New York, and of their right to form an independent state; humbly submitted to the consideration of the impartial world," was published under the authority of the governor and council. He was also the author of other publications in pamphlets, in hand bills, and in the newspapers, during the subsequent controversies of the state with New York and New Hampshire, all of which evinced his accurate general knowledge of the political situation of the state and country, and his ability to present his views in a clear and forcible manner. "A narrative of Col. Ethan Allen's captivity" prepared by him, was printed in Philadelphia, 1779, which was extensively read, and acquired great popularity, numerous editions of it having since been published. In 1784 appeared his theological work, a book of 477 pages, printed for the author at Bennington. The purport of it is sufficiently indicated by its title which was "Reason the only oracle of man, or a compendious system of natural religion." It is said to be more polished in style than his other writings. Its sale was quite limited, and the principal effect of it was to bring upon the author the sharp displeasure of the religious public.

Allen like other men was not free from defects of character, but his merits greatly predominated. Rev. Zadock Thompson in a well considered lecture justly sums up his character as follows: "The conspicuous and commendable traits on which his fame rests, were his unwavering patriotism, his love of freedom, his wisdom, boldness, courage, energy, perseverance, his aptitude to command, his ability to inspire those under him with respect and confidence; his high sense of honor, probity and justice, his generosity and kindness, and sympathy in the afflictions and sufferings of others. Opposed to these good qualities were his self-sufficiency, his personal vanity, his occasional rashness, and his sometimes harsh and vulgar language. All of these characteristic traits might be abundantly proved by well known facts and authentic anecdotes."[1] Jared Sparks towards the conclusion of his interesting life of Allen published in the first volume of his American Biography says of him; "His character was strongly marked, both by its excellencies and defects; but it may be safely said, that the latter were attributable more to circumstances beyond his control than to any original obliquity of his mind or heart. The want of early education, and the habits acquired by his pursuits in a rude and uncultivated state of society, were obstacles to his attainment of some of the higher and better qualities, which were not to be overcome. A roughness of manners and a coarseness of language, a presumptuous way of reasoning upon all subjects, and his religious skepticism, may be traced to these sources. * * * Yet there is much to admire in the character of Ethan Allen. He was brave, generous and frank, true to his friends, true to his country, consistent and unyielding in his purposes, seeking at all times to promote the best interests of mankind, a lover of social harmony, and a determined foe to artifices of injustice, and the encroachments of power. Few have suffered more in the cause of freedom, and few have borne their sufferings with a firmer constancy or loftier spirit."

Gen. Allen died at Burlington, in a fit of apoplexy, Feb. 12, 1789, and was interred with military honors, his former military associates from

---

[1] *Vermont Quarterly Gazetteer*, No. 6, page 560, 569.

other parts of the state, some of them from Bennington one hundred and twenty miles distant, attending his funeral. In obedience to an act of the legislature passed in 1855, a monument has been erected over his remains at Burlington, near Winooski Falls. It consists of a Tuscan column of granite, forty-two feet in height and four and a half feet diameter at its base, with a pedestal six feet square, in which are inserted four plates of white marble, having the following inscriptions to wit — on the west side " Vermont to Ethan Allen, born in Litchfield, Ct., 10th Jan. 1737, O. S., died in Burlington Vt., 12th Feb., 1789, and buried near the site of this monument." On the south side, " The leader of the Green Mountain Boys in the surprise and capture of Ticonderoga, which he demanded in the name of the Great Jehovah and the Continental Congress." By act of the legislature a commanding statue of Allen representing him in the attitude of demanding the surrender of Ticonderoga, has since been placed in the portico of the capitol at Montpelier. It is of Vermont marble designed and executed by our native artist L. G. Mead, and is equally creditable to its subject and the artist.

Gen. Allen was twice married. First to Mary Brownson, of Woodbury, Ct. By her he had one son and four daughters. The son died at the age of 11 years, while his father was in captivity. Two of the daughters died unmarried. One of them, Parmelia, married Eleazer W. Keyes, Esq., she and her husband both residing and dying in Burlington. The other daughter Lucy married the Hon. Samuel Hitchcock, of Burlington, and was the mother of Gen. Ethan A. Hitchcock now living and of eminent distinction in the military history of the country. She died in 1842. His second wife was Mrs. Fanny Buchannan, by whom he left a daughter and two sons. After his death the daughter entered a nunnery in Canada and died there. The sons, Hannibal and Ethan A. Allen, both held offices in the United States army, and both died many years ago at Norfolk, Va. The latter left a son bearing his own name still living in New York city.

Heman Allen.—Heman Allen, brother of Ethan, was born at Cornwall, Conn., Oct. 15, 1740, was an intelligent and respectable merchant at Salisbury, at the commencement of the revolution, served in Canada as captain in the regiment of Green Mountain Boys in the campaign of 1775, was agent of the Dorset convention of January 1776, and presented their petition to congress to be allowed to serve in the common cause of America under other officers than those named by the Provincial congress of New York, lest they should be prejudiced in their land titles, by acknowledging that jurisdiction. He made a report of his mission to Philadelphia to the convention held at Dorset, July 24th, 1776, was a delegate from Rutland to the convention of January 15, 1777, which declared the independence of the state, and from Colchester to that which formed the state constitution in July of that year. Ira Allen in his history, page one hundred and one, thus speaks of his decease. " Heman Allen, Esq., a member of the council of safety of Vermont, went to the field of battle, [of Bennington] the weather being hot, and his fatigue great, he caught a violent cold, and died of a decline on the 18th of May following " (1778).

Ira Allen, who bore a distinguished part in the early affairs of Vermont, as has been shown in the body of this work, was the youngest of the family of brothers of which Ethan Allen was the oldest, and was born in Cornwall, Conn., May 1, 1751. He must have received in his youth a good English education, as he was early a practical surveyor; and in later life a clear and forcible writer in politics and history. He was scarcely twenty-one years of age when he became the proprietor of lands under the New Hampshire charters of Burlington and Colchester; and from the year 1772, he was active and earnest in his opposition to the claims of the New York patentees.

He was a lieutenant in Warner's regiment of Green Mountain Boys, and served in Canada in the campaign of 1775; was a member from Colchester in all the conventions of the New Hampshire Grants in 1776 and 1777, and took a prominent part in the framing of its constitution. He was a leading member of the council of safety which carried the state triumphantly through the trying campaign of 1777; was a member of the council and treasurer of the state for nine years after the first organization of its government in 1778, and was surveyor general for about the same number of years. On almost all occasions during the revolutionary period he acted, either alone or with others as agent of the state in their transactions with the Continental congress and with the governments of New Hampshire and New York, and those of other states. He was the principal manager of the negotiations with Gen. Haldimand to ward off invasions from Canada, in which he was entirely successful. He was a man of decided talent, and having an imposing presence and a pleasing address, his qualifications as a diplomatist were of a high order, and they were frequently exerted to the advantage of the state.

He was the author of numerous publications in defence of the state during the controversies with New York and New Hampshire, some of which were printed in newspapers and hand bills, and others in pamphlets. Among the latter class of publications was a pamphlet of some forty or fifty pages in answer to one published by the convention of New York of October 4, 1776. It was entitled *Miscellaneous Remarks*, etc. He was also the author of another pamphlet with a similar title, published in October, 1777, against later proceedings of the New York convention, and especially against the constitution of that state, which had then been recently published. In 1779, he published a pamphlet of forty-eight pages, entitled "A Vindication of the conduct of the general assembly of the state of Vermont," in dissolving their union with the sixteen New Hampshire towns. He was also the author of many of the official state papers from 1778 to 1786. He was active in the foundation of the Vermont University at Burlington, to which he made liberal donations in lands.

In 1796, he went to France and purchased of the French republic twenty-four brass cannon and twenty thousand muskets, ostensibly for the supply of the militia of Vermont. The vessel named the Olive Branch, a neutral bottom in which they were shipped from Ostend for this country, was captured by a British man of war and carried to England, where the cargo was libelled for forfeiture. After a contest of seven or eight years in the English courts, he succeeded in obtaining a restoration of his property, but the delay and the enormous expense of the proceedings rendered its release of little value to him. He published a volume of over four hundred pages, in London in 1798, and another still larger in Philadelphia, in 1805, giving an account of his purchase and the proceedings against him in England.

There seems to be some mystery about the real object of his purchase. While in England he wrote and published in London his *History of the state of Vermont, one of the United States of America*, etc. In his preface he speaks of the capture of the Olive Branch and of the libel for the forfeiture of the cargo, and says: "In the course of this cause the character of the people of Vermont and that of the claimants, were frequently called in question, which operated as a stimulus to this publication." He makes an apology for inaccuracy of dates and other imperfections, arising from the absence of original documents.

He is not uniformly accurate, but his work contains much valuable and reliable matter which is not found elsewhere. To some extent he follows Dr. Williams, whose history had been previously published.

Mr. Allen resided in Philadelphia during some of the latter years of his life, where he died January 7, 1814.

Remember Baker.—Remember Baker, whose active and earnest opposition to the New York claimants, in connexion with Allen, Warner and others, has already been quite fully related, was born at Woodbury, Ct., in 1737. He was cousin to Ethan Allen, his father being a brother of Allen's mother. He had served as a soldier at Lakes George and Champlain in the French war, and had thus acquired a knowledge of the lands on his route there and in their vicinity. He settled in Arlington in 1764, and built in the east part of the town the first grist mill on the New Hampshire Grants north of Bennington. After the attempt of Justice Munro to take him to Albany jail, when he was treated with great harshness, and of which an account has been given in the text, he appears to have been generally desirous of inflicting severer punishment on the Yorkers than most of his companions. He was with Allen, having the rank of captain, at the taking of Ticonderoga May 10, 1775; and afterwards when Gen. Schuyler took command in the northern department, he was employed by him to obtain information of the military situation of the enemy on the Canada border, and was unfortunately killed in a skirmish with some Indians in the neighborhood of St. Johns in August following.

Goldsbrow Banyar—Whose claims to Vermont lands exceeded the quantity of six townships, was clerk of the New York colonial council during the whole period in which land grants were made by that province in the district of the New Hampshire Grants, giving him great facilities as a land speculator. He appears to have been a man of much shrewdness and to have occupied a sort of neutral position during the revolution. He died at Albany in 1815, at the great age of 91, leaving a large estate to his descendants.

Joseph Bowker was an early settler in Rutland under the New Hampshire title, and participated in the opposition to the New York patent of Socialborough, which covered the land of the township, though he was not named in the outlawry act of that province. He was one of the trusted men of the town and state in their early days, was president of the several conventions for the formation of a new state held in 1776, and of those that declared the state independent and framed the state constitution in 1777. He was afterwards a member of the governor's council and held other honorable and responsible positions. He died at Rutland in 1784.

Stephen R. Bradley was born in Wallingford, Ct., Feb. 20, 1754; graduated at Yale College in 1775, studied law, and came to Vermont about 1778 and settled at Westminster. He drew up "Vermont's appeal" published by the state council December, 1779, and from that time was actively engaged in various capacities in the affairs of the state. He acted for a long time as prosecuting attorney of the county, was colonel and afterwards general of the militia, and often a representative in the general assembly. He was one of the commissioners named in the act of the Vermont assembly of 1789, and as such participated in the final adjustment of the controversy with New York. After the admission of Vermont into the union, he was three times elected United States senator, serving in that capacity over fourteen years. His death occurred Dec. 9, 1830. For a more extended biography of him see *Hall's Eastern Vermont*, page 593.

James Breakenridge was of Scotch-Irish descent, and came early to Bennington from Massachusetts. He was one of the defendants in the Albany ejectment suits, and his farm being adjoining the twenty mile line, was the scene of many disturbances between the New York and New Hampshire claimants, as related in the text. Mr. Breakenridge was a very quiet man and was never personally engaged in any riotous proceedings, though he was often denounced by the Yorkers as a rioter, and was one of the proscribed persons in the famous New York riot act of 1774. He was sent to England with Jehiel Hawley of Arlington as agent of the settlers in 1771, and was otherwise favorably noticed by them. He had been chosen lieutenant of the militia company formed in Bennington in 1764, and in accordance with the custom of the times, was usually designated by his military title. Mr. Breakenridge was a man of exemplary moral and religious character, and died April 16th, 1783, aged 62, leaving numerous descendants, one of whom, a grandson, John Breakenridge, still occupies the old homestead.

Silvanus Brown, who had the honor of being named and proscribed in the New York riot act of 1774, was a farmer and an early resident of Rutland. He is described in the act as "Silvanus Brown late of Socialborough, yeoman." His offence was, resisting the survey of his farm by the New York claimants, he having a title under New Hampshire, ten years earlier than that under the patent of Socialborough.

Gideon Brownson, from Salisbury, Ct., was one of the first settlers in Sunderland, early in 1765 — was a captain in Warner's regiment of Green Mountain Boys, and served in Canada, in the years 1775 and 1776. In 1777 he was commissioned a captain in Warner's continental regiment, and served through the war, having been promoted to the rank of major.

He was the first town clerk and represented the town several years in the legislature.

Timothy Brownson, also of Sunderland, was a prominent man in the early civil affairs of the state. He was a member of the governor's council from the first organization of the state government in 1778 until 1795, and was one of the most trusted and confidential advisers of Gov. Chittenden during the whole period of his perilous and successful administration. He was one of the first who was concerned in the famous Canada negotiation, and his long tried and well known integrity and love of country was such, that no one who knew him would doubt that the motives which actuated him were pure and patriotic.

Nathaniel Chipman, one of the commissioners on the part of Vermont for the adjustment of the controversy with New York, and agent of the state to congress for obtaining its admission into the union, was one of the most eminent jurists and able statesmen of his time. Some notice has already been taken of him in the body of this work in connection with the dispatches from Gen. Enos to Gov. Chittenden on the occasion of the death of Sergeant Tupper in 1781. In addition, it is proper to state that he was born at Salisbury, Conn., November 15, 1752, was a graduate of Yale college in 1777, served as a lieutenant in the army at Valley Forge and other places for more than a year, studied law, and took up his residence at Tinmouth, Vt., in 1779, whither his father had previously removed. He was a judge of the supreme court of the state for several years, was afterwards in 1791, appointed by Gen. Washington, judge of the district court of Vermont, but resigned in 1796. He was senator in congress for six years from the 4th of March, 1797, and chief justice of the supreme court in 1813 and 1814. His judicial opinions and other writings are evidence that he possessed a high order of talent, and statesmanlike views. He died the 13th of February, 1843, in the ninety-first year of his age. See his life by Daniel Chipman, and *Allen's Biographical Dictionary*.

Thomas Chittenden.—The formation of the territory of Vermont into a separate state, the successful progress of its government, and its final establishment against the powerful opposition of other governments, were owing in a great degree to the almost unerring foresight, unhesitating firmness and sound judgment of Thomas Chittenden. He was chosen one of the council of safety by the convention that formed the state constitution in July, 1777, and became at once the president of that body; was chosen the first governor of the state in March, 1778, and from that date until 1797, he was annually reelected to that office, with the single exception of the year 1789, when there being no choice, Moses Robinson was elected by the legislature. The next year Gov. Chittenden was rechosen by a large majority. During the whole period of his administration, he exerted a powerful and healthy influence over the affairs of the state, and had the pleasure of witnessing the triumphant success of his earnest efforts, in the prosperity and happiness of a grateful people, whose political affairs he had for years been greatly instrumental in guiding. He resigned the office in the year 1797, on account of failing health.

Gov. Chittenden was born in Guilford, Conn., January 6, 1730, removed in early life to Salisbury, and became a leading inhabitant of the town, representing it in the assembly of the colony for several years, and holding the office of colonel of the militia. He became a land holder in Williston on the New Hampshire Grants, and settled in that town in 1774. He was, however, obliged to abandon his habitation on the approach of the enemy in the fall of 1776, and from that time he took up his residence in Arlington until after the close of the war, when he returned to Williston, where he died the 25th of August, 1797. His descendants are numerous, several of whom have occupied high political positions in the state and country.— See his life by Daniel Chipman; and also ante p. 276.

Nathan Clark was active and prominent in the early period of the land controversy with New York, was frequently chairman of the general committee and conventions of the settlers, and was a member from Bennington and speaker of the first general assembly of the state in 1778. In 1776 he was chairman of the Bennington committee of safety and received the thanks of Gen. Gates for his promptness in supplying the army at Ticonderoga with flour. He came to Bennington from Connecticut as early as 1762, and died in that town the 8th of April, 1792, at the age of 74. One of his sons, Nathan Clark, Jr., lost his life in the battle of Bennington. Another son Isaac Clark, familiarly known as "Old Rifle," was a colonel in the war of 1812, and distinguished as a partisan leader.

George Clinton, governor of New York in 1777, and during the whole subsequent period of the controversy of Vermont with that state, was born in the county of Ulster, New York, the 26th of July, 1739. He was admitted to the bar in that colony in 1764, and was a member of the colonial assembly from 1768 till its final dissolution in 1775. He was chairman of the committee of that body which reported the resolutions of the 5th of Feb., 1774, offering large rewards for the apprehension of Ethan Allen and seven others, and which were made the foundation for the famous outlawry act against them of the 9th of the ensuing month. From this time forward, during the whole period of the controversy, he exhibited on all occasions, as has already been seen, the most bitter animosity towards the people of Vermont, always advocating the most violent measures against them, and opposing with all his might, all efforts of others for an adjustment of the controversy. It would seem from an original letter to him found in the Clinton Papers, from Cavendish, Vt., informing him that his lands in that town were about to be sold for taxes, that he was a land claimant under the New York title, but to what extent is not known. He was distinguished for the tenacity, not to say obstinacy, with which he adhered to any view once taken of a subject; but whether his uniform hostility towards the Vermonters was owing wholly to his early commitment against them, while a member of the colonial assembly, or in part to his being interested in the controversy as a land claimant, is not known. Gov. Clinton continued to be the chief magistrate of New York until 1795, when he declined a reelection. During his administration he undoubtedly rendered very important services to his state and country. In 1801, he was again elected governor and held the office for three years. In 1805 he was elected vice president of the United States, and again in 1809, and while in that office he died April 20th, 1812. *Journals of the Colonial Assembly*, *Slade's State Papers*, page 37, *Street's Council of Revision*, page 85 to 112, *Doc. Hist. N. Y.* vol. 4, p. 869. There was another George Clinton who was governor of New York under the crown for the years from 1743 to 1753, and who returned to England at the end of his term with an immense fortune derived principally from fees received for land grants. He made the first announcement that New York extended east to Connecticut river, in a correspondence with Gov. Wentworth in 1750.

Robert Cochran, was one of the eight persons named in the New York act of assembly of 1774, who without trial were condemned "to suffer death without benefit of clergy." He came to Bennington on the New Hampshire Grants from Coleraine, Mass., about the year 1768, but soon afterwards removed to Rupert, where he held lands under the New Hampshire charter of that town. In the fall of 1771, some persons undertook to occupy his land under the New York title, but they were promptly driven off. From that time he was an active associate with Allen and others in opposing the New York land claimants, for which he incurred the hot displeasure of the government of that province. He held the rank of captain in the corps of Green Mountain Boys organized previous to the revolution, and on being informed of the massacre by the tories at Westminister, in March, 1775, he appeared at that place within forty-eight hours, at the head of over forty men from the west side of the mountain, and with twenty-five of them assisted in conveying the tory prisoners to Northampton jail. He held the rank of captain in the expedition to Ticonderoga in May following, and was with Warner at the capture of Crown Point. He soon afterwards entered the service in Col. Elmore's regiment, in which he held the rank of captain until July 29th, 1776, when by resolution of congress he was promoted to a majority in the same regiment; John Brown, Esq., of Pittsfield, who had been active in the Ticonderoga expedition, being its lieutenant colonel. In October following, the regiment, four hundred and forty strong, was on the frontier in Tryon county, New York, Maj. Cochran being in command of Fort Dayton. In November of that year, a new arrangement of the New York regiments took place under the direction of the convention of that state. The field officers of the third regiment commissioned the 21st of that month, being Peter Gansevoort colonel, Marinus Willett lieutenant colonel, and Robert Cochran major. Among the recommendations of Maj. Cochran, was one from Jellis Fonda, Esq., who says he was "an active good soldier, true to the cause" and that he would "choose to be in the rangers, as he is well used to the business and understands the woods as well as any man." He served with reputation in the campaign of 1777, and was probably on the staff of Gen. Gates, for a portion of the time, as he appears to have been the bearer from him to the Vermont council of safety, in September, of important despatches, some of which were to be forwarded to the adjoining states. In 1778 he was sent by the commanding officer in the northern department, into Canada, to obtain information of the military condition of the province, where he had a very narrow escape from arrest and execution as a spy. Mr. Lossing gives the following account of the adventure. "His errand being suspected, a large bounty was offered for his head. He was obliged to conceal himself, and while doing so at one time in a bush heap, he was taken dangerously ill. Hunger and disease made him venture to a log cabin in sight. As he approached he heard three men and a woman conversing on the subject of the reward for his head, and discovered that they were actually forming plans for his capture. The men soon left the cabin in pursuit of him, and he immediately crept into the presence of the woman, who was the wife of one of the men, frankly told her his name and asked her protection. That she kindly promised, and gave him some nourishing food and a bed to rest upon. The men returned in the course of a few hours, and she concealed Cochran in a cupboard, where he overheard expressions of their confident anticipations that before another sun they would have the rebel spy, and claim the reward. They refreshed themselves and set off again in quest of him. The kind woman directed him to a place of concealment some distance from her cabin, where she fed and nourished him until he was able to travel, and then he escaped beyond the British lines. Several years afterwards, when the war had closed, the colonel lived at Ticonderoga, and there he accidentally met his deliverer, and rewarded her handsomely for her generous fidelity in the cause of suffering humanity." In September, 1778, Maj. Cochran was in command of Fort Schuyler, and he was in active and reputable service on the Mohawk frontier during the remainder of the war, becoming a lieutenant colonel in 1780. Like most of the patriotic officers of the revolution, he came out of the contest in poverty. On the occasion of the separation of the officers of the army at Newburgh, in 1783, the following anecdote of Baron Steuben and Maj. Cochran is related in the life of the former, found in *Sparks's American Biography*. "On the day that the officers separated, the Baron's attention was directed to Col. Cochran, whose countenance showed marks of deep distress. Steuben said what he could to comfort him, but with little effect. 'For myself,' said Cochran, 'I care not; I can stand it. But my wife and daughters are in the garret of that wretched tavern. I know not where to carry them, nor have I the means for their removal.' 'Come,' was the answer, 'I will pay my respects to Mrs. Cochran and your daughters, if you please.' Maj. North says he followed the party to the loft, and that when the Baron left the unhappy family, he left hope with them, and all that he had to give."

After the war Col. Cochran resided at Ticonderoga, and lastly at Sandy Hill. He died at the latter place, and was buried at Fort Edward. His remains are near the grave of the lamented Jane McCrea, who was so inhumanly murdered by Burgoyne's Indians in 1777. In Lossing's *Field Book of the Revolution*, at page 102 of volume 1, is a representation of his tomb stone, with the following inscription: "In Memory of Col. Robert Cochran who died July 3, 1812, in the 74th year of his age; a Revolutionary officer."

My authorities for this sketch, besides those mentioned in the body of the work in connection with the name of Cochran, are *Hall's Eastern Vt.*, 225, 226, 236. *Petitions of Cochran to Gov. Clinton for land in* 1797, *in*

Assembly Papers at Albany, vol. 14, p. 513. *American Archives*, vol. 6, p. 941; vol. 1, p. 712, and vol. 3, p. 292, 577, 614, 314, 814. *Lossing's Pictorial Field Book of the Revolution*, vol. 1, p. 102. *Stevens's Papers*, vol. 3, p. 715, 721, 870. *Slade*, 213. *Stone's Life of Brant*, vol. 1, p. 357, note on 404; vol. 2, p. 148, 149. *Annals of Tryon County*, p. 122, 160. *Sparks's American Biography*, vol. 9, p. 76.

Cadwallader Colden, so often mentioned in this work, was of Scotch parentage and born in Ireland in February, 1688. He came first to Philadelphia and afterwards in 1718, to New York, became a member of the provincial council in 1722, and soon afterwards surveyor general of the province. From the year 1761, he acted as chief magistrate of the colony at different periods, by virtue of his office of lieutenant governor, for a large portion of the time until the beginning of the revolution, during which time he amassed a large fortune in the business of issuing land patents. To his exertions more than those of any other individual, was owing the transfer of the jurisdiction of the present territory of Vermont from New Hampshire to New York; and he was the first to inaugurate the unjust and oppressive policy of regranting the lands which had been included in the previous charters of New Hampshire. Lieut. Gov. Colden was a man of considerable learning and talent, and doubtless rendered many valuable services to the colony. He was a tory of the deepest dye, but his fortune was saved to his descendants by his decease prior to the passage of the New York attainder acts. His death took place at his residence on Long Island, September 21, 1776. He was the author of several valuable works, the most noted of which is the *History of the Five Nations of Indians*, first published in 1727.

The Rev. Jedediah Dewey, was the first minister of Bennington and was settled there in the fall of 1763. He had the honor of being indicted as a rioter by the court at Albany, though he was never engaged in any riotous proceeding. He is said in the *New York Narrative* of 1773, to have advocated in town meeting forcible resistance to the execution of the judgments of the New York courts in the ejectment suits, which was probably the case. In 1772 he held a correspondence in behalf of the settlers with Gov. Tryon, with a view to an adjustment of the land controversy, but without any favorable result. He died much regretted, December 24, 1778, after a prosperous pastorate of fifteen years.

Lord Dunmore, administered the government of New York under the crown, from the 19th of October, 1770, till the 9th of July, 1771, during which time he was able to amass a handsome fortune in money from the fees of office, and to acquire a claim to a large quantity of lands granted by himself, fifty-one thousand acres of which, were on the New Hampshire Grants. He was a greedy, unprincipled Scotch tory, and died in England in 1809. See more about him, *ante* pages 100–103.

John Fassett, was one of the nine or ten persons who were first concerned in the Canada negotiation of 1781. His name is attached to he two certificates given to Ira Allen, approving of the part he had taken in endeavoring to prevent Gen. Haldimand from invading the state. He was born in Hardwick, Mass., June 3, 1743, and came to Bennington with his father, John Fassett senior, in 1761, and removed to Cambridge, Vt., in 1784, where he died. He was a member of the state council from 1779 until 1796, with the exception of the years 1785 and 1786, and a judge of the supreme court for eight years from 1778. He had numerous influential family connections, who with himself were well known for their attachment to the cause of their country, and it would have been extremely difficult to make any person who knew him believe that he could ever have been influenced by any other than patriotic motives. This may also be said of the other persons who were associated with him in approving the Haldimand negotiation.

Dr. Jonas Fay, was born at Hardwick, Mass., January 17th, 1737, and removed to Bennington, in 1766. He occupied from an early day a prominent position among the settlers on the New Hampshire Grants, as well in the contest with New York as in that with the mother country, and also in the organization of the state government. In 1772, when Gov. Tryon invited the people of Bennington and its vicinity to send agents to New York to inform him the grounds of their complaint, he with his father Stephen Fay, was appointed for that purpose. He was clerk to the convention of settlers that met in March, 1774, and resolved to defend by force Allen, Warner and the others who were threatened with outlawry and death by the New York assembly, and as such clerk, certified their proceedings for publication. At the age of nineteen he had served in the French war during the campaign of 1756 at Fort Edward and Lake George, as clerk of Capt. Samuel Robinson's company of Massachusetts troops, and he served as surgeon in the expedition under Allen at the capture of Ticonderoga. He was continued in that position after the Green Mountain Boys were relieved by the arrival of Col. Elmore's Connecticut regiment, and he was appointed by the Massachusetts committee who were sent to the lake in July, 1775, to muster the troops as they arrived for the defence of that post. He was also surgeon for a time in Col. Warner's regiment.

In January, 1776, he was clerk to the convention at Dorset that petitioned congress to be allowed to serve in the common cause of the country as inhabitants of the New Hampshire Grants and not under New York, and also of the convention which was held at the same place in July following. He with Thomas Chittenden, Reuben Jones, Jacob Bayley and Heman Allen were appointed by the convention which declared the state independent in January, 1777, delegates to prepare and present to congress a declaration and petition announcing the fact and the reasons for it, of which declaration Dr. Fay was the author and draughtsman. He was secretary to the convention that formed the constitution of the state in July, 1777, and was one of the council of safety then appointed to administer the affairs of the state until the assembly provided for by the constitution should meet; was a member of the state council for seven years from 1778, a judge of the supreme court in 1782, judge of probate for five years from 1782, and he attended the continental congress as agent of the state on not less than four different occasions, from 1777 to 1782.

Dr. Fay was a man of extensive general information, decided in his opinions and bold and determined in maintaining them. His education was such as to enable him to draw with skill and ability, the public papers of the period in which he was in active life, of many of which besides the declaration of independence before mentioned, he was the reputed author. He was on terms of friendship and intimacy with Gov. Thomas Chittenden, the Allens, Warner and the other founders of the state. Dr. Fay resided in Bennington, in the practice of his profession, when not in the public service, from 1766 until after the year 1800, when he removed to Charlotte for a few years, and afterwards to Pawlet, but returned again to Bennington, where he died March 6, 1818. He was twice married and has left numerous descendants.

Joseph Fay, son of Stephen and brother of Jonas Fay, was born in Hardwick, about 1752, and came to Bennington a member of his father's family in 1766. He was secretary of the council of safety and perhaps also a member of that body in 1777, and secretary of the state council from 1778 till 1784. He was the associate of Ira Allen in conducting the famous negotiation with Gen. Haldimand, by which the operations of the enemy were paralyzed and the northern frontier protected from invasion during the last three years of the revolutionary struggle. His talents and acquirements were very respectable, and possessing a fine personal appearance and agreeable manners and address, he was well calculated to manage such a diplomatic adventure with adroitness and ability. He removed from Bennington to New York city, where he died of the yellow fever in 1803. He married in early life a daughter of the Rev. Jedediah Dewey, the first minister of Bennington, of whom Theodore S. Fay of literary distinction, and late minister of the Uuited States to Switzerland, is a grandson.

General Samuel Fletcher was born at Grafton, Mass., in 1745, settled in Townshend prior to 1775, was in the battle of Bunker hill, was a captain in the militia in 1776, was at Ticonderoga with his company when it was abandoned by St. Clair in 1777, became a major and continued in the service until after the capture of Burgoyne. In 1781, he was chosen by the assembly of the state a brigadier general, and he afterwards became major general. He took an active part in the formation of the new state of Vermont, was a member from Townshend of the conventions of October 30th, 1776, and January 15, 1777, and was a member of the assembly 1778 and 1776; and in 1780 he became one of the council, which office he held for nine years. In 1788 he was chosen sheriff of the county of Windham, and continued in that office for eighteen years in succession. He was also judge of the county court for four years. He was much respected for his courage, integrity and business capacity; and his manners were peculiarly pleasant and agreeable. He died at Townshend September 15, 1814. One of his daughters was the mother of Epaphroditus Ransom, who became governor of Michigan. For further in regard to Gen. Fletcher, see *Hall's Eastern Vermont*, p. 640, and *Thompson's Gazetteer*, Townshend.

Col. Samuel Herrick was an active and prominent man in the early military affairs of the state. He came to Bennington about the year 1768, but left the town and state soon after the close of the revolutionary war, removing to Springfield, Montgomery county, New York, and nothing is known of his previous or subsequent life. He served as captain at the taking of Ticonderoga in 1775, and on the evacuation of that post by St. Clair in 1777, he was appointed colonel of a regiment of rangers raised by the Vermont council of safety. In the battle of Bennington at the head of the few rangers then enlisted and a body of local militia as a separate detachment, he led the attack on the rear of Baum's right, and was distinguished for his bravery and skill in both engagements of that day. Gordon, in his history, in giving an account of the battle, speaks of "the superior military skill" of Colonels Warner and Herrick, as being of great service to Gen. Stark. Col. Herrick was subsequently in command of the south-western regiment of militia of the state, and in that capacity as well as in command of his corps of rangers was in active service in several occasions during the war.

Stephen Jacob, who was one of the commissioners named in the act of the Vermont legislature of 1789, for adjusting the controversy with New York, was a native of Connecticut, and graduated at Yale College in 1778. On the 16th of August, 1778, the first anniversary of the battle of Bennington, he attended a celebration of the victory in that town, and read a patriotic poem, in honor of the event. It is still extant and has considerable merit. He afterwards settled in Windsor in the practice of law, represented the town in the assembly for several years and was a judge of the Supreme Court, for four years from 1803. He died at Windsor in February, 1817, at the age of 61. Noah Smith, a classmate of Mr. Jacob, and who afterwards also became a judge of the Supreme Court, delivered an address at the above named celebration of the battle of Bennington in 1778, which it still preserved.

Dr. Reuben Jones was an active and prominent whig in the early period of the revolution, and was also earnestly engaged in the organization of the state, and in maintaining its independence. That he was a man of intelligence, is proved by his *Relation of the Proceedings of the People of the County of Cumberland and Province of New York*, connected with the Westminster Massacre. At the meeting of the committees of Cumberland and Gloucester counties held at Westminster, the 11th of April, 1775, for the purpose of devising means to resist the progress of oppression, Dr. Jones served as clerk, and he was often chosen to similar positions on other important occasions. He was a delegate from Rockingham to the conventions held at Dorset, on the 25th of September, and the 30th of October, 1776, and also in that at Westminster, the 15th of January, 1777, which declared the state independent. At this convention he was chosen one of the agents to present the declaration and petition for a new state to the Continental congress, and his name is appended to such declaration, with those of Jonas Fay, Thomas Chittenden, and Heman Allen. He represented the town of Rockingham in the general assembly in 1778, 1779 and 1780, and was a representative from Chester in 1781. Neither the time or place of his birth or death has been ascertained. *Slade*, p. 55, 60, 66, 68, 70. *Hall's Eastern Vt.*, 753, 754.

John Taber Kempe, one of the leading antagonists of the early settlers on the New Hampshire Grants, was attorney general of the province of New York from 1758 to the revolutionary period, when he adhered to the crown, and was attainted and his property confiscated. He was proprietor under the New York title of one-third of the grant of Princetown, covering lands in Arlington, Sunderland and Manchester, and also of other lands on the New Hampshire Grants, to a large, but an unknown extent. He was associated with Duane in the prosecution of the ejectment suits against the settlers, of which an account has already been given. He went to England after the close of the war.

Sir Henry Moore was governor of New York from November 12th, 1765, to the time of his death, which occurred September 11, 1769. He made few grants of land that were troublesome to the New Hampshire settlers, and so far as is known neglected to make large grants for his own personal benefit, which can scarcely be said of any other New York governor. For further in regard to him see ante page 83 - 97, also *Doc. Hist. N. Y.*, vol. 3, p. 584 - 608, and *Col. Hist. N. Y.*, vol. 8, p. 197, note.

John Munro, who for several years was very troublesome to the New Hampshire settlers, was a Scotchman, an agent of Duane and Kempe, a New York justice of the peace, and resided in Shaftsbury within a few rods of the New York line. After the year 1772, the threats of the Green Mountain Boys appear to have kept him quiet. But on the approach of Burgoyne in 1777 he joined the enemy, and his personal property in Vermont was confiscated. It appears from a long and very melancholy letter, which he wrote to his friend Duane, dated at Springfield in December, 1786, that he was then on his return to Canada from England where he had been prosecuting his claims on the British government for his services and losses as a loyalist; but that the greater part of his claim had been rejected, because of " the New Hampshire claims covering the most part of his property." It would seem from this letter that the English commissioners did not consider the New York grants as constituting a valid title against those of New Hampshire. The letter further stated that in consequence of such rejection of his claim he was returning to his family "penniless, without money, friends or interest," and he appealed strongly to his old friend and employer for sympathy and aid, with what success is unknown. *Munro's letter to Mr. Duane*, Dec. 24, 1786.

Elijah Paine, was one of the commissioners named in the act of the Vermont legislature in October, 1789, for adjusting the controversy with New York. He was a graduate of Harvard College in 1781, and was a senator in congress for six years from 1795. In 1801, he was appointed by President Adams, judge of the district court of Vermont, which office he held until his death, which occured at Williamstown, Vt., April 21, 1842. As a judge and citizen he was much respected. He was father of Charles Paine, who was governor of Vermont in 1841 and 1842.

Moses Robinson, son of Samuel, senior, was born March 26, 1741, married Mary daughter of Stephen Fay, and after her death Susannah Howe, and died at Bennington, May 26, 1813. He was the first town clerk of Bennington, chosen in March, 1762, and held the office nineteen years. He became colonel of the militia, and was with his regiment at Mount Independence on its evacuation by St. Clair, in 1777; and was a member of the famous council of safety that carried the new state successfully through the bloody campaign of that year. On the first organization of the supreme court in 1778, he was appointed chief justice, which office he held until 1789, when he became governor of the state for one year. He was also a member of the state council for seven years. He was one of the first senators elected to congress from this state in 1791, which office at the expiration of about five years, he resigned in 1795. He was one of the tried friends of the state and country, who in 1781, with Thomas Chittenden, Samuel Safford, Jonas Fay, Joseph Fay, Samuel Robinson, Timothy Brownson, and John Fassett, certified their approval of the conduct of Ira Allen, in preventing the invasion of the state from Canada, by making the commanding general believe that the people were about to return to their allegiance to the king. No person who was acquainted with this band of patriots, would think of accusing them of motives unfriendly to the cause of the country.

Samuel Robinson, Senior, was the pioneer settler of the township of Bennington in 1761, and agent of the settlers on the New Hampshire Grants in 1766, to present their petition to the king for relief against the government of New York. So much has been said of him in the body of this work that little remains to be added. (See chapter IX.) He was born at Cambridge, Mass., in 1705, removed to Hardwick in 1735, from which place he emigrated to Bennington. He had served with reputation for not less than three campaigns in the French war, as captain, and was at the head of his company in the battle of Lake George in September 1755, when the French were defeated. He was commissioned a justice of the peace by Gov. Wentworth, February 8, 1762, being the first person appointed to a judicial office within the limits of the state. He left for England late in the year 1766, and died in London of the small-pox, in October 27, 1767. Of his high character and commendable and partially successful efforts in England, a full account has been given in the text. He left six sons and three daughters, all born at Hardwick, all of whom became heads of families and all of them have numerous descendants. The names of the children were Leonard, Samuel, Moses, Silas, Marcy, Sarah, David, Jonathan and Anne. Marcy, the eldest daughter, married Joseph Safford, brother of Gen. Samuel Safford; Sarah married Benjamin Fay, son of Stephen, and Anne married Isaac Webster. Of the sons, Leonard and Silas, after the war removed from Bennington to Franklin county, where they died. David became United States marshal of the district of Vermont, and Jonathan, chief judge of the supreme court and senator in congress, and both died in Bennington. The other two sons were active public men during the period of which this work treats, and of them separate notices are given.

Col. Samuel Robinson, son of Samuel senior, was born August 15, 1738, and died at Bennington, May 3, 1813. He was active in the early New York controversy, and he commanded a company of militia in the battle of Bennington, was "overseer of tories," a member of the board of war and held various other honorable and responsible offices both civil and military, during the revolutionary period. Col. Robinson possessed good natural abilities, was enterprising, upright and honorable, was noted for his unflinching courage, and beloved for the kindness, generosity and nobleness of his nature and conduct. He was one of the eight persons, who in 1781, certified in writing their approval of the efforts of Ira Allen, to prevent the invasion of the state by *finesseing* with Gen. Haldimand. His patriotism was never doubted.

Samuel Safford, was born at Norwich, Conn., April 14, 1737; was one of the early settlers in Bennington, and died there March 13, 1813. When the committees of the several towns met at Dorset in 1775, to nominate officers for the battalion of Green Mountain Boys, recommended by congress, he was named as major under Warner, and he served in the corps with him in Canada. When Warner's continental regiment was raised in 1776, he was commissioned by congress its lieutenant colonel and served as such, in the battles of Hubbardton and Bennington and throughout the war. In June, 1781, he was chosen a brigadier general of the militia; he represented Bennington several years in the general assembly, was one of the state council, and for twenty-six successive years, ending in 1807, he was chief judge of the county court for Bennington county. He was upright and intelligent, of sound judgment and universally respected. He was concerned with Chittenden and others in the Canada negotiations, and his patriotism was never questioned.

Israel Smith, was one of the commissioners in the Vermont act of 1789, for settling the controversy with New York. He was born at Suffield, Conn., April 4, 1759. He graduated at Yale college in 1781, studied law and was admitted to the bar in this state in 1783. He resided first at Rupert, but removed to Rutland about 1791, when he was elected a representative in congress, and he was reelected in 1793. He was also again elected in 1801. He was chosen senator in congress in 1803, which office he resigned on being elected governor of the state in 1807. Soon after his election as governor, his health began to decline and he died at Rutland, December 2, 1810.

John Smith, who was sentenced to death without trial by the New York riot act of 1774, is described in the act as "John Smith late of Socialborough, yeoman." He had settled in Rutland under the New Hampshire charter of 1761, and when the New York claimants under the patent of Socialborough issued in 1771, in disobedience of the king's order, came to take possession of his farm, he resisted them, for which offence he was thus condemned to execution. He was the first town clerk and the first representative of Rutland in the general assembly, and was a respectable and peaceable citizen.

Paul Spooner, was a physician, his early residence in the state being at Hartland, from which he removed to Hardwick after the year 1790. He was a member of the state council four years from 1778, then lieutenant governor until 1786, judge of the Supreme Court for nine years ending in 1788, and was an agent of the state to the continental congress in 1780, and again in 1782. He enjoyed the confidence and respect of his contemporaries, but a particular account of him has not been obtained. He is believed to have been well educated, and to have had a good professional reputation.

Gen. John Stark.—Gen. Stark's connexion with the revolutionary history of Vermont has been quite fully stated in the preceding pages and will not be again repeated. Nor is it intended to give more than a very brief notice of him. He was of Scotch descent and was born at Londonderry, New Hampshire, August 28, 1728. He served with reputation as a partisan leader in the Indian and French wars, fought bravely at the head of his regiment of militia at the battle of Bunker Hill, and commanded the van of the right wing at the battle of Trenton. After the battle of Bennington in 1777, he was commissioned brigadier general by congress. He continued in active service through the war, and in 1781 commanded on the northern frontier with his head quarters at Saratoga, as already stated in this work. He died at Derryfield, now Manchester, N. H., May 8th, 1822, at the advanced age of 93.

Peleg Sunderland, is described in the New York riot act of 1774, of which he was an intended victim, as "late of Socialborough in the county of Charlotte, yeoman." He was a noted hunter and had been active with Allen, Warner and others, in resisting the New York claimants. In J. H. Graham's *Descriptive Sketches of Vermont*, published in London, in 1797, he gives the following account of the naming of Onion river. "A Mr. Peleg Sunderland in 1761, in hunting for beaver on this stream lost his way, and was nearly exhausted with fatigue and hunger, when a party of Indians fortunately met him, and with great humanity relieved his wants, and saved him from perishing. Their provisions were poor; but what they had they freely gave, and their kindness made amends for more costly fare. Their whole store consisted of onions, and Mr. Sunderland then gave to the stream, near which he was so providentially preserved, the name of Onion river, which it has retained ever since." Mr. Thompson in a note to page 197 of his *Gazetteer*, makes the name to be derived from the Indian word Winooski, which signified Onion. I do not pretend to decide which is correct in regard to the origin of the name, or whether either is. When John Brown, Esq., in the early spring of 1775, was sent to Canada by the Boston committee of safety, for the purpose of guarding against danger from that quarter in case of the commencement of hostilities by the British forces at Boston, which was speedily anticipated, he obtained from the committee of the New Hampshire Grants, the assistance of two companions and guides, of whom Peleg Sunderland was one. Of his services on that occasion we have an authentic account. At the session of the legislature commencing in February, 1787, he, describing himself as of Manchester, presented a petition in which he stated among other things, "that sometime in the month of March, 1775, he was called upon and requested by the grand committee at Bennington to go to Canada as a pilot to Maj. John Brown, who was sent by the provincial congress as a delegate to treat with the Indians in that province respecting the then approaching war, which service the petitioner performed at his own expense and charge, and was out in said service twenty-nine days, and has never received any compensation therefor, and has no place to look for redress except it be to your honors." Upon this part of Mr. Sunderland's petition, the committee of the assembly reported as follows: "It is sufficiently proved to your committee that the petitioner did go to Canada by order of the authority, to pilot the said Maj. Brown, as set up in said petition, therefore it is the opinion of your committee that the petitioner receive out of the state treasury, eight pounds and fourteen shillings, in hard money orders, for his services." The report was accepted and a bill was passed accordingly. Maj. Brown in a letter from Montreal dated March, 29, 1775, says, "two men from the New Hampshire Grants accompanied me over the lake, the one was an old Indian hunter acquainted with the St. Francis Indians and their language, the other was a captive many years among the Caughnawaga Indians." The former was doubtless Sunderland, and the other was probably Winthrop Hoyt. (About Hoyt see *Am. Archives*, vol. 2, p. 734 and 892, fourth series, and *Doc. Hist. N. Y.*, vol. 4, p. 896.) From this letter it appears that these guides of Maj. Brown were of essential service to him in communicating with the Indians. Sunderland was as true to the cause of his country against the common enemy, as he had been to the settlers against New York.

Ira Allen in his history gives the following account of an occurrence in which he bore a part. "In the spring of 1782, a loyalist officer, out of Canada, having raised seventeen recruits in the county of Albany, set out to conduct them to Canada; he supposed it was safer to pass through Vermont than to continue in the state of New York. They were furnished with some stores at the Roaring branch in Arlington. As they were putting them into their knapsacks in the silent watches of the night, Lieut. William Blanchard passing that way fell in amongst them; they made him prisoner. On their march towards Canada, they also fell in (at Manchester) with Sergt. Ormsby, who shared the same fate with Blanchard. To prevent alarm they struck off the road immediately, and took to the woods. The next morning early, Maj. Ormsby was apprised of the situation of his son and his fellow prisoner, and the route the enemy had taken. The major despatched an express to Col. Ira Allen to inform him of the circumstance, as the colonel at that time commanded a regiment of militia in that neighborhood. In the meantime, the major directed Capt. Sunderland to pursue the enemy with a party of men. The captain took his hounds with him, who by their scent, followed the tracks of the enemy and thus proved faithful guides to the party. Col. Allen on the receipt of this intelligence posted full speed to Manchester, sent to Capt. Eastman of Rupert to raise a party of men and waylay in a certain pass in the mountain, where he took the whole party and released Lieut. Blanchard. Capt. Sunderland came up a few moments after, when the sagacity of his hounds was amazingly perceptible, by their going up and smelling to the feet of the prisoners." The account then states that the prisoners were brought before the governor at Sunderland, and ordered to Bennington jail, from which they were afterward sent to Canada and exchanged for Vermonters who were prisoners with the enemy. *Allen's History*, p. 230, 231.

The Hon. John S. Pettibone, now living in Manchester, remembers when quite young, to have seen Sunderland, who he thinks was a man of influence and of good standing and character. In a letter to the author he speaks of him as follows: " He was a great hunter, and feared neither bears nor tories. I am sure he took as much pleasure in chasing and capturing the latter as the former. I should think a bear would come down from the tree when he found Sunderland was there, as readily as the coon would at the name of Capt. Martin Scott." Judge Pettibone had often heard the story of the capture of the tories from the mouths of those concerned in it, and which substantially agrees with that of Mr. Allen. Jonathan Ormsby, the young sergeant who was made prisoner by the tories was afterwards killed by the smugglers in the Black Snake encounter near Burlington in 1808. See *Thompson's Vt.*, p. 95.

An examination of the Manchester records shows Captain Sunderland to have resided in that town until the year 1791, to have been the owner of real estate and other property and to have possessed the confidence of his townsmen. In 1787 he was appointed at the head of a committee of three to draw instructions for the town representatives to the assembly. On another occasion he was one of a committee on the subject of the school lands of the town, and his name appears on the records on other important occasions. The date of his removal from Manchester, or the time and place of his death has not been ascertained. He was evidently a man of intelligence, as well as of activity and enterprise, and of respectable standing in society.

Isaac Tichenor, who was prominent in the latter part of the New York controversy, was born at Newark, N. J., February 8, 1754, and educated at Princeton College, then under the presidency of the celebrated Dr. Witherspoon, for whom and whose memory he always had the highest veneration. He graduated in 1775, and while pursuing the study of law at Schenectady, N. Y., he was early in 1777 appointed assistant to Jacob Cuyler, deputy commissary general of purchases for the northern department, having for his field of service an extensive portion of the New England states. In the performance of his official duties he came to Bennington the 14th of June, 1777, and was there superintending the collection of supplies for the army during the principal part of the summer of that year. On the 13th of August, he left Bennington with a drove of cattle for Albany, and returned the 16th by way of Williamstown, arriving on the battle ground about dark, just as the fighting had ceased. From this time his residence was in Bennington when not in actual service in the commissary department. About the close of the war he commenced the practice of law and soon became active in public affairs. He represented the town in the general assembly in 1781 and for the succeeding three years, was agent of the state to congress in 1782, and was the same year appointed by the legislature to visit Windham county and advocate the claims of the state with the friends of New York in that section, in which enterprise he was in some degree successful. He was a member of the state council for five years from 1787, was one of the commissioners named in the act of 1789, for adjusting the controversy with New York, was a judge of the supreme court for five years from 1791, and in 1796 was chosen a senator in congress to supply the vacancy occasioned by the resignation of Moses Robinson, and also for the succeeding six years, which place he resigned on being elected governor in October, 1797. He held the office of governor for ten consecutive years until October 1807, when Israel Smith was his successful competitor. He was however elected again in 1808, making his whole term of service in the executive chair eleven years. In 1814 he was again chosen senator in congress, which office he held for six years, terminating March 3, 1821, when he retired from public life. Gov. Tichenor died December 11, 1838, leaving no descendants. He was a man of good private character, of highly respectable talents and of accomplished manners and insinuating address. His fascinating personal qualities acquired for him at an early day the sobriquet of the " Jersey Slick," by which he was long designated in familiar conversation. He was a federalist in politics, and his popularity was such that he was elected governor for several successive years after his party had become a minority in the state.

Sir William Tryon, succeeded Lord Dunmore as governor of New York July 8, 1771, and held the office until the king's government was superseded by that of the revolution. He was however absent from the province on a visit to England from April 7th, 1774, to the 25th of June, 1775, during which time, Lieutenant Governor Colden exercised the office. The character and conduct of Gov. Tryon prior to and during the period of his actual administration have been sufficiently described in the body of the work. See pages 103-109, 138-148, 166-168, 157, 158, 180.

He left New York and went on board a man of war in the harbor, in October 1775, but returned to the city on its evacuation by Gen. Washington in September 1776, and continued the king's nominal governor until March 1780, when he resigned his commission and went to England. While he continued to hold the office of governor, he was promoted to the rank of brigadier-general, and in his military capacity commanded several marauding expeditions to Connecticut, burnt Norwalk and Fairfield, and committed many other depredations in which he fully maintained the reputation which he had already acquired of having the propensities and feelings of a savage barbarian. He died in London, January 27, 1788.

Ebenezer Walbridge was born at Norwich, Conn., January 1, 1738, settled in Bennington about 1765, where he died October 3, 1819. He was a lieutenant in Col. Warner's regiment of Green Mountain Boys before Quebec in the winter of 1776, was an officer in the battle of Bennington, was colonel of the regiment of militia of that town and vicinity in 1781, was with his regiment at Castleton, in October, 1781, on the threatened invasion by St. Leger, and with the other principal military officers, was entrusted with a knowledge of the secret negotiations with Canada, of which the conduct of St. Leger relating to the death of Sergeant Tupper, was a consequence. He also commanded the troops before whom the militia of New York fled from San Coick, December following. He was afterwards brigadier general. He was two years a representative in the assembly, and for eight years, commencing in 1780, a member of the state council. He was an enterprising business man, and was concerned in erecting and putting in operation the first paper mill that was built in the state, in 1784.

Col. Seth Warner was born in Roxbury, then Woodbury, Conn., May 17, 1743, came to Bennington to reside in January, 1765, and remained there until the summer of 1784, when being in failing health he returned to his native town where he died the December following, in the forty-second year of his age. The life of Warner is so interwoven with the early history of Vermont, that little need be added to what has been already said of him in the body of this work. In the controversy with the New York land claimants, he was always active, and uniformly successful in whatever he undertook. As a military leader he was honored and confided in by the people of the state, above all others, and his bravery and military capacity appear to have been always appreciated by intelligent officers from other states with whom he served. In the disastrous retreat from Canada in the spring of 1776, he brought up the rear, and he was in command of the rear guard on the evacuation of Ticonderoga, by which he was involved in the action at Hubbardton. At Bennington he was with Stark for several days before the battle, and was his associate in planning the attack upon Baum's entrenchments and in carrying it into execution; and it was by his earnest advice, and contrary to Stark's first impression, that Breyman was immediately opposed, without first retreating to rally the scattered American forces. Stark, in his official account of the battle, was not the man to overlook the valued services of his associates. In his official letter to Gates he says that Warner marched with him to meet the enemy on the 14th, and of the battle of the 16th: "Warner's superior skill in the action, was of great service to me." Contemporaneous histories confirm the account given by Stark. Gordon, in his *History of the Revolution*, takes a similar view of the services of Warner, and Dr. Thatcher in his journal, in commencing his account of the action, says: "On the 16th, Gen. Stark, assisted by Col. Warner, matured his arrangements for the battle," and then describes it conformably to Stark's account of it.

The late Hon. D. S. Boardman of Connecticut, who in his youth often saw Warner, speaks of him as follows: "Col. Warner was of noble personal appearance; very tall, not less than six feet two inches; large framed, but rather thin in flesh, and apparently of great bodily strength. His features were regular, strongly marked, and indicative of mental strength, a fixedness of purpose, and yet of much benevolent good nature, and in all respects both commanding and pleasing. His manners were simple, natural and in all respects entirely free from any kind of affectation, social, and at once both pleasing and dignified; and when engaged in relating the events of his life, both military and ordinary, he displayed no arrogance, but interwove in his narrative a notice of such incidents as showed love of adventure, and at the same time his love of fun." See *N. Y. Historical Magazine*, vol. 4, p. 201.

Warner was distinguished for his cool courage, and perfect self-possession on all occasons, and for the entire confidence with which he always inspired his associates and those under his command.

It is to the credit of the state of Connecticut that its legislature has caused a neat and substantial granite monument to be erected over Warner's remains at Roxbury. It is an obelisk about twenty-one feet in height with appropriate base, plinth, die and mouldings, with the following inscriptions:

East (front) side.—"Col. Seth Warner of the army of the revolution, born in Roxbury, Conn., May 17, 1743; a resident of Bennington, Vt., from 1765 to 1784; died in his native parish December 26, 1784."

North side.—"Captor of Crown Point, commander of the Green Mountain Boys in the repulse of Carleton at Longeueil and in the battle of Hubbardton; and the associate of Stark, in the victory at Bennington."

South side.—"Distinguished as a successful defender of the New Hampshire Grants; and for bravery, sagacity, energy and humanity, as a partisan officer in the war of the revolution."

West side.—"His remains are deposited under this monument, erected by order of the general assembly of Connecticut, A.D. 1859."

Col. Warner came to Bennington a single man, was married a year or two afterwards to Hester Hurd of Roxbury, and settled in the north-westerly part of the town. He was a near neighbor of James Breakenridge, his house being on the corner opposite the present district school house, at Irish Corner. The house erected by him was standing though in a very dilapidated condition until the fall of 1858, when it was destroyed by fire. This residence of his was to the westward of that of Breakenridge and within less than a mile of New York line, on the outskirts of the settlement, where he appears to have lived in security throughout the New York controversy, notwithstanding numerous indictments were found against him as a rioter and large rewards were offered for his apprehension. This freedom from attack is to be accounted for by the terror with which his boldness and resolution and that of his brother Green Mountain Boys inspired his land claiming enemies, coupled with the well known fact that a great majority of the inhabitants of the bordering county of Albany sympathized with him in his hostility to the unjust demands of the speculators, and would sooner aid in his rescue, than in his capture.

Warner was for so long a time engaged in the defence of the New Hampshire Grants, and in defence of his country in the revolutionary war, that his attention appears to have been wholly diverted from his own private concerns, and he died insolvent leaving his family destitute. It is scarcely necessary to say that a sensational story published in *Harper's Magazine*, some years since, and extensively copied in other publications, to the effect that Gen. Washington had generously relieved the homestead of the colonel's widow from the incumbrance of a mortgage of over nine hundred dollars, is pure fiction. The writer must have been imposed upon by some pretender. In October 1787, on the petition of Mrs. Warner representing her destitute condition, the legislature of Vermont granted to her and her children two thousand acres of land in Essex county, which was then supposed to be valuable, but which turned out to be of little worth. See a copy of Mrs. Warner's letter to Dr. Williams, and her petition to the assembly of October, 1787, in the appendix to the address of George F. Houghton, Esq., before the legislature of Vermont, Oct. 28, 1848. See further in regard to Col. Warner in that address, and also in the life of Warner by Daniel Chipman, Middlebury, 1848.

William Williams, held the rank of colonel in the militia in 1777, and with a portion of his regiment was at the battle of Bennington, and is entitled to a share in the honors of the victory. He is mentioned by Stark in his official letter to Gates, as marching with him to meet the enemy. He was an early settler in Marlborough, but in 1777 resided in Wilmington. He afterwards removed to Canada where he died in 1823. He had served with reputation in the French war, and appears to have enjoyed the confidence and respect of his fellow citizens, both in military and civil capacity.

James, Duke of York, to whom New Netherland was granted in 1664, was son of Charles the first, who was beheaded by his subjects in 1649, was younger brother of Charles the second, and was born October 15, 1633. He was an exile on the continent with his brother and returned with him to England on his restoration in 1660. On the death of his brother the 6th of February, 1685, he succeeded to the crown with title of James the second. Being a Roman Catholic, and attempting the establishment of that religion in England, he was almost universally distrusted by all other denominations, who united in inviting William, Prince of Orange, from Holland, who landing in England with a powerful army, was welcomed by the people, and with Mary his wife, a daughter of James, were crowned king and queen in February, 1689. James had previously fled to the continent, and he died in France, September 16, 1701. On his accession to the throne in 1685, the province of New York which had been his private property while he was duke of York, became, by the operation of law, annexed to the crown, and was ever afterwards treated like other national domain. See *ante* p. 17 and 18.

James Duane, the leading antagonist of the settlers and claimants under the New Hampshire title, and of whom much has been said in the body of this work, was born in the city of New York, February 6, 1733, studied law and became eminent in his profession. He married a daughter of Col. Robert Livingston, the proprietor of Livingston's Manor, and thus became identified with the landed aristocracy of the province. He held the New York title to large tracts of lands which interfered with the previous grants of New Hampshire, and was attorney for most, or all of the other New York claimants. He was very active in his endeavors to overthrow the New Hampshire title, and thus incurred the severe displeasure of the settlers. He espoused the whig cause in the revolution, was a delegate in congress from New York during nearly its whole period, and in that body exerted an unfavorable influence against the Vermonters, and a like influence in the New York legislature of which he was also a member. In 1784, he was appointed mayor of the city of New York, and in 1789 judge of the United States district court of New York, which office he resigned in 1794, and removed to Schenectady where he resided until his death, which took place February 1, 1797. See a biographical notice of him in the 4th volume of the *Documentary History of New York*, page 1063.

APPENDIX NO. 2.

[See page 45.]

EXTRACT FROM THE COMMISSION OF KING GEORGE THE SECOND TO GOV. WENTWORTH, DATED JUNE 3, 1741, SHOWING THE EXTENT OF THE PROVINCE OF NEW HAMPSHIRE AND THE GOVERNOR'S AUTHORITY TO GRANT LANDS.

"And further, know ye that we reposing special trust and confidence in the prudence, courage and loyalty of you the said Benning Wentworth, of our special grace, certain knowledge and meer motion have thought fit to constitute and appoint you the said Benning Wentworth to be our governor in chief of our province of New Hampshire within our dominions of New England, in America, bounded on the south side by a similar curve line pursuing the course of the Merrimack river at three miles distance on the north side thereof, beginning at the Atlantic ocean, and ending at a point due north of a place called Pautucket Falls, *and by a straight line drawn from thence due west across the said river till it meets with our other governments.* And bounded on the north side by a line passing up through the mouth of Piscataqua harbor, and up the middle of the river into the river Newickwannock, part of which is now called Salmon Falls, and through the middle of the same to the farthest head thereof, and from thence north two degrees westerly until one hundred and twenty miles be finished from the mouth of Piscataqua harbor aforesaid, or *until it meets with our other governments*, and by a dividing line parting the Isle of Shoals and running through the middle of the harbor between the said islands to the sea, on the southerly side, the south westerly point of the said islands to be accounted part of our province of New Hampshire, with all and singular the powers and authorities hereby granted to you for and during our will and pleasure. * * * * *

"And we do hereby likewise give and grant unto you full power and authority by and with the advice of our said council to agree with the inhabitants of our said province for such lands and tenements and hereditiments as now are or hereafter shall be in our power to dispose of and them to grant to any person or persons for such terms and under such moderate quit rent, services and acknowledgments, to be thereupon reserved unto us, as you by and with the advice aforesaid shall think fit; which said grants are to pass and be sealed by our seal of New Hampshire, and being entered on record by such officer or officers as you shall appoint thereto shall be good and effectual in law against us, our heirs and successors."

A true extract from Gov. B. Wentworth's commission as entered and recorded in the secretary's office, State of New Hampshire.

Attest, JOSEPH PEARSON,
Deputy Secretary.

APPENDIX No. 3.

[See page 48.]

ORDER OF THE KING IN COUNCIL, DIRECTING NEW HAMPSHIRE TO SUPPORT FORT DUMMER.

{ Seal } At the court at Kensington, the 6th day of September, 1744.—
Present,

The King's most excellent Majesty,

Lord President.	Lord Delawar.
Lord Privy Seal.	Mr. Speaker.
Earl of Winchester.	Mr. Vice Chamberlain.
Lord Cathcart.	

WHEREAS, William Shirley, his majesty's governor of the province of Massachusetts Bay hath by his letters to the Lord President of the council and to the Duke of Newcastle one of his majesty's principal secretary's of state (which have been laid before his majesty at their Board), complained of his majesty's province of New Hampshire for neglecting to take possession of and to provide for a Fort, called Fort Dummer, which was built by the Massachusetts government about twenty years since upon the then western frontiers of that province and been hitherto garrisoned by them, *but is lately fallen within the limits of said province of New Hampshire, by the settlement of the boundary line* between the two provinces, and which Fort is represented by the said governor to be at this time of very great consequence to all his majesty's subjects in those parts in regard it is situated within three or four days march at furthest from a very strong fort built within these few years by the French at Crown Point, which will be a place of constant retreat and resort for the French and Indians in all their expeditions against the English settlements, and therefore requesting that his majesty will be graciously pleased to give such directions in relation thereto as may prevent the said Fort from falling into the hands of the enemy, the Massachusetts government not thinking themselves obliged to provide for a fort which no longer belongs to them.

His majesty in council this day, took the same into consideration, together with a report made thereupon by the Lords of the committee of council and hath been thereupon pleased to order that the said Fort and the garrison thereof should be supported and maintained, and that the governor or commander-in-chief of New Hampshire should forthwith move the assembly in his majesty's name to make a proper provision for that service, and at the same time inform them, that in case they refuse to comply with so reasonable and necessary a proposal his majesty will find himself under a necessity *of restoring that fort with a proper district contiguous thereto to the province of the Massachusetts Bay who cannot with justice be required to maintain a Fort no longer within their boundaries*, and that the said governor should transmit to his majesty at his Board with all convenient speed an account of his proceedings together with the final resolution of the assembly thereupon. But his majesty considering the importance of the said Fort and the great mischiefs that may happen to his subjects in those parts in case the same should in the meantime fall into the hands of the enemy, doth therefore think it proper hereby to order and require the governor of the Massachusetts Bay to represent to the assembly of that province the necessity of continuing to provide for the security of Fort Dummer until a final answer can be obtained from New Hampshire, and his majesty's pleasure be further signified herein.

WM. SHARPE.[1]

Extract from the Report of the English attorney and solicitor generals, dated August 14, 1752, *on a case stated by the king in council, for their opinion, with respect to certain tracts of land granted by the governments of Massachusetts Bay and Connecticut in New England.*

"There are also about 60,000 acres of land situated *on the west side of Connecticut river* which were purchased by private persons from the government of Connecticut, to whom that land had been laid out by the government of the Massachusetts Bay, as an equivalent for two or three townships which the Massachusetts Bay purchased from Connecticut government. This tract of land by the determination of the boundary line in 1738, *is become part of New Hampshire*, but the proprietors of it are subject to no conditions of improvement, and the land is waste and uncultivated." [2]

APPENDIX NO. 4.

[Referred to at page 5 and 58.]

PROCLAMATION OF LIEUT. GOV. COLDEN, ANNOUNCING THE KING'S ORDER MAKING CONNECTICUT RIVER THE BOUNDARY BETWEEN NEW YORK AND NEW HAMPSHIRE.

By the Hon. Cadwallader Colden, Esq., his Majesty's lieutenant governor and commander-in-chief of the province of New York and the territories depending thereon in America.

WHEREAS, I have received his Majesty's order in council of the 20th day of July last, establishing the boundary line between his province of New Hampshire and this his province of New York, with directions to cause the same to be made public, which is in the words following:

---

[1] (*Mass. Archives* in the office of the Secretary of that State, vol. 72, p. 698).

[2] From *Mass. Archives*. See *Stevens Papers*, 1730-1775, p. 14, and *Doc. Hist. N. Y.*, vol. 4, p. 542.

{ Seal } "At a court at St. James, the 20th day of July, 1764.—
Present,

The King's most excellent Majesty.

Lord Steward.	Earl of Hillsborough.
Earl of Sandwich.	Mr. Vice Chamberlain.
Earl of Halifax.	Gilbert Elliot, Esq.
Earl of Powis.	James Oswald.

Earl Harcourt.

"WHEREAS, there was this day read at the board, a report made by the right honorable the lords of the committee of council for plantation affairs dated the 17th of this instant upon considering a representation from the lords' commissioners for trade and plantations, relative to the disputes that have for some years subsisted between the provinces of New Hampshire and New York concerning the boundary line between those provinces. His majesty taking the same into consideration was pleased with the advice of his privy council to approve of what is therein proposed, and doth accordingly hereby order and declare the western banks of the river Connecticut from where it enters the province of Massachusetts bay, as far north as the forty-fifth degree of northern latitude to be the boundary line between the said two provinces of New Hampshire and New York. Wherefore the respective governors and commanders-in-chief of his majesty's said provinces of New Hampshire and New York for the time being and all others whom it may concern are to take notice of his majesty's pleasure hereby signified and govern themselves accordingly.

WM. BLAIR.

I have therefore thought proper to publish and notify his majesty's said order in council by this proclamation, to the end that all his majesty's subjects within this province may conform thereto and govern themselves accordingly.

Given under my hand and seal at arms at Fort George in the city of New York in council this 10th day of April, 1765, in the fifth year of the reign of our sovereign lord, George the third, by the grace of God, of Great Britain, France and Ireland, king, defender of the faith, etc.

CADWALLADER COLDEN.

By his Excellency's command,
G. BANYAR, Deputy Secretary.

APPENDIX NO. 5.

[See page 94.]

ORDER OF THE KING IN COUNCIL FORBIDDING THE GOVERNOR OF NEW YORK TO MAKE GRANTS OF LANDS LATELY CLAIMED BY NEW HAMPSHIRE.

At the court of St. James the 24th day of July, 1767, Present,

The King's most excellent Majesty,

Archbishop of Canterbury.	Earl of Shelburne.
Lord Chancellor.	Viscount Falmouth.
Duke of Queensbury.	Viscount Barrington.
Duke of Ancaster.	Viscount Clare.
Lord Chamberlain.	Bishop of London.
Earl of Litchfield.	Mr. Secretary Conway.
Earl of Bristol.	Hans Stanley, Esq.

WHEREAS, There was this day read at the board, a report from the Right Hon. the lords of the committee of council for plantation affairs dated the 30th of last month in the words following viz:

"Your majesty having been pleased to refer unto this committee the humble petition of the incorporated society for the propagation of the gospel in foreign parts, setting forth among other things, that Benning Wentworth, Esq., governor of New Hampshire in New England made several grants of large tracts of land lying on the west side of Connecticut river, which were incorporated into about one hundred townships, and several shares were reserved in each of the said grants to the petitioners for a glebe for the church of England and for the benefit of a school; that the government of New York having claimed the said lands and the jurisdiction thereof, granted great part of those lands without reserving any shares for the above mentioned public uses; and therefore the petitioners pray that the grants made by the government of New Hampshire may be ratified and confirmed, or such order made thereupon as to your majesty should seem meet. And your majesty having been likewise pleased to refer unto this committee the humble petition of Samuel Robinson of Bennington in North America, on behalf of himself, and more than one thousand other grantees of lands on the west side of Connecticut river, under certain grants issued by the said governor of New Hampshire — setting forth amongst other things, that the said governor made grants to the petitioners of several tracts of land lying as aforesaid on the western side of the Connecticut river, which were incorporated into above one hundred townships and supposed to be within the government of New Hampshire, whereupon the petitioner's expended large sums of money in settling and cultivating the same. That on the 20th of July, 1764, the said lands having been declared by your majesty to be within the government of New York, the lieutenant governor of that province made grants of parts of the said lands included within the petitioner's grants, which being of infinite prejudice to them; they therefore most humbly pray (amongst other things) that their said several grants made by Gov. Wentworth may be ratified and confirmed under your majesty's royal order. The lords of the committee in obedience to your majesty's said order of reference, have taken the said petitions into their consideration, together with a report made by the lords commissioners for trade and plantations upon the former of the said petitions, and do thereupon agree humbly to report as their opinion to your majesty, that the most positive orders should be immediately sent to the governor of New York, to desist from making any grants whatsoever of any part of those lands, until your majesty's further pleasure shall be known."

His majesty taking the said report into consideration, was pleased with the advice of his privy council to approve thereof, and doth hereby strictly charge, require and command that the governor, commander-in-chief of his majesty's province of New York for the time being, do not, (upon pain of his majesty's highest displeasure) presume to make any grant whatever of any part of the lands described in the said report, until his majesty's further pleasure shall be known concerning the same.

W. SHARPE.[1]

APPENDIX NO. 6.

[See page 118.]

BILL OF EXCEPTIONS IN THE LEADING EJECTMENT TRIAL AT ALBANY.

Peter Quiet, *ex dem.*
John Small
vs.
Josiah Carpenter.

Memorandum, that on the 28th day of June, A. D. 1770, before Robert R. Livingston, Esq., and George Duncan Ludlow, Esq., justices of our lord the king, for the trial of causes arising in the county of Albany, and brought to issue in the supreme court of judicature for the province of New York, the defendant in the above cause offered to give in evidence to the jury, sworn and empaneled in the above cause, an instrument under the great seal of the province of New Hampshire [the charter of the township of Shaftsbury], which they alleged to be a grant of the lands in question, which same instrument is dated the 20th day of August, A. D. 1761, and in the first year of the reign of King George the Third, with the several endorsements thereon, *prout* the said grant and endorsements, to which the plaintiff's counsel objected, for that no evidence had been given to the court and jury aforesaid, to prove that the said province of New Hampshire ever included the lands in question, or that any authority

---

[1] *Doc. Hist. N. Y.*, vol. 4, p. 609.

had ever been vested in any governor of New Hampshire to grant the said lands or to exercise any powers whatsoever there, but that on the contrary, it appeared to the court that the lands in question were within the province of New York, and prayed that the instrument aforesaid might not be received in evidence. And thereupon the said justices did declare and give it as their opinion that the same was not legal evidence, and did preclude the said defendant from giving the said instrument and the endorsements thereon in evidence to the said jury. Whereupon the counsel for the defendant did request of the said justices, according to the form of the statute in such cases provided, the present bill, which the said justices, at the request of the said counsel for the defendant, signed at Albany, the day and year first above written.

ROBERT R. LIVINGSTON,
GEO. D. LUDLOW.

SILVESTER of counsel for the defendant,
J. T. KEMPE of counsel for the plaintiff.[1]

APPENDIX NO. 7.

[See pages 150 and 151.]

THE NEW YORK ARGUMENTS IN FAVOR OF THE CONNECTICUT RIVER BOUNDARY CONSIDERED.

The claim of New York to extend eastward to the Connecticut river prior to and independent of the king's order of July, 1764, was elaborately advocated in a report made by a committee of the colonial assembly of the province on the 10th of March, 1773, which is found on the journal of that body of that date. It was published at the time with *A Narrative of Proceedings* and *An Appendix*, and was extensively circulated in vindication of the title of New York to the territory of the New Hampshire Grants, and as a defence of the New York government against the complaints of the settlers.

As stated in the text it was prepared with great care by James Duane, a learned and skilful lawyer of New York city, who as a large land claimant, had a deep personal interest in the establishment of the New York title. It is entitled *A state of the right of the colony of New York with respect to its eastern boundary on Connecticut river, so far as it concerns the late encroachments under the government of New Hampshire.*

This document embodies all the arguments that have at any time been adduced in favor of the New York title, and presents it in a very plausible and imposing light. It has been received by some historical writers, without inquiry into the truthfulness of its statements, as a full and complete

---

[1] From papers of the old congress in the state department, Washington, No. 40, vol. 1.

vindication of the early right of New York to the territory in question, and as a satisfactory defence of the conduct of the government of that province towards the settlers. In that light it appears to have been viewed by Benjamin H. Hall, author of the *History of Eastern Vermont*, who without any apparent suspicion that any thing could be wrong in this official manifesto, has rested the theory of his work, so far as it relates to the New York controversy, upon its supposed correctness, and has consequently treated the New Hampshire claimants as wholly in the wrong throughout his entire work, thereby making his book an apology for the unfeeling avarice and cupidity of their oppressors. If he had looked upon the matter of this paper as open to inquiry and criticism, and had applied to it the like thorough investigating talent which he has happily displayed upon other subjects, he would most certainly have discovered that instead of being a reliable historical document it was so largely tinctured with misrepresentation and falsehood as to be clearly unworthy his confidence.

This paper of Mr. Duane is unreliable, not so much because the facts stated are absolute falsehoods, though some of them are unfounded, as that most of them are unimportant to a right understanding of the real question in controversy, the main facts upon which the proper solution of that question depends, being either carefully omitted or so distorted and discolored as to make them convey erroneous impressions.

The subject of the ancient eastern boundary of New York has been very fully discussed in the preceding chapters, and it is not proposed to restate the facts and arguments therein adduced, but merely to notice some of the most important assumptions in this official manifesto, which seem to conflict with the view already taken of the New York claim.

1. The report commences with the statement of a variety of historical facts tending to show that the Dutch were the first to discover and occupy Connecticut river, and that New Netherland originally reached to that river, leaving it to be inferred that such was its boundary at the time of its conquest under the grant of King Charles to the Duke of York. Upon this supposed inference as a basis, the author builds an argument in favor of the extension of New York to that river, by virtue of its succeeding to the rights of New Netherland. It is undoubtedly true that the duke's charter was designed to embrace the Dutch territory of New Netherland, and the argument would be quite conclusive if it were only founded upon fact. But the whole of it is a bold attempt at deception, and could have been no otherwise understood by Mr. Duane, for he must have well known the fact that more than thirteen years prior to the charter to the duke and the surrender of New Netherland to the English, the eastern boundary of the Dutch colony had been solemnly agreed upon by treaty between Gov. Stuyvesant and the New England commissioners at Hartford to be a line drawn from the west side of Greenwich bay on Long Island Sound, northerly twenty miles up into the country and afterwards indefinitely so that it "come not within ten miles of Hudson's river." This treaty as we have already seen (chap. 2) had some years prior to the duke's charter been solemnly ratified by the States General of Holland, and was a line so well established and understood by the Dutch, that when they made a temporary reconquest of the country in 1673, the commission which was

issued to their governor Colve described the colony as bounded easterly, not by Connecticut river, but by such treaty line. This attempt at deception by suppressing an important historical fact, which overthrows and annihilates the whole argument of the author, and turns it directly against himself, is calculated to cast a damaging suspicion upon the whole report, sufficient at least to justify and require a thorough examination of it before assenting to its correctness. The grossness of this attempt at deception is made most palpable by the fact that the author refers to and relies largely upon the letter of Gov. Stuyvestant to Col. Nicolls of September 2, 1664, in answer to his demand for the surrender of New Amsterdam, to prove the eastern extent of the province to Connecticut river. In that very letter, although the Dutch governor claims that New Netherland *originally* included that river, he yet mentions and recognizes the treaty of Hartford of 1650, by which that river boundary had been relinquished and the new one above mentioned established. For the letter at length see *Smith's History of New York*, vol. 1, p. 20 – 26.

2. In endeavoring to make the settlement of the eastern boundary of New York with the colony of Connecticut appear consistent with the claim of the province to reach Connecticut river to the north of that colony, the author not only ignores the fact of the existence of the Hartford treaty of 1650 with the New England commissioners, by which the Dutch abandoned all claim to extend eastward to that river, but also the fact that any commissioners of the king accompanied the expedition for the conquest of the New Netherlands, or made or attempted to make any adjustment of boundaries with Connecticut at the time of the conquest, slurring over all that matter with a general declaration that during the first year of the administration of the duke's governor Nicolls "a fruitless attempt was made for establishing a boundary between New York and Connecticut." Now this "fruitless attempt" of the author of this report was a solemn adjudication made by the king's commissioners, of whom the duke's governor Nicolls was one, assented to by commissioners from Connecticut (as has already been seen) and was well understood at the time and afterwards by the New York authorities, as fixing upon a twenty mile line from the Hudson as the boundary, though by a mistake in the written award the line was made to take such a direction that it would eventually cross the Hudson, instead of running parallel to its general course. The settlement of 1683, mentioned in the report as an original adjustment was but a confirmation of the spirit and intention of that of 1664, as may be seen by a report of the English board of trade on the subject in vol. 4 of the *Colonial History of New York*, p. 625. See also *Smith's N. Y.*, vol. 1, p. 35 – 38, and also *ante*, chap. 3, where the matter is fully explained.

3. A large portion of this *State of the Right* is taken up with what purports to be an account of the transactions between the governments of New Hampshire and New York, in regard to the boundary, after the controversy arose, that can have little or no bearing upon the question of right which the document purports to discuss; and with a recital of the original charters of New Hampshire showing that by those charters the province extended inland from the Atlantic only sixty miles, not reaching by many miles to Connecticut river. This nobody ever disputed, and the only effect of introducing it would be to draw away the attention of

the reader from the real question in the case, viz: what was understood by the king to be the eastern boundary of New York in 1741, when he declared in his commission to Gov. Wentworth that his province extended westerly "to his majesty's other governments." It is not deemed necessary to take any further notice of this part of the report.

4. The government of New York never having made any settlements to the eastward of a twenty mile line from the Hudson, it was quite important for the author of this manifesto to produce if possible some evidence of an early claim to territory beyond such line. This he attempted to do by referring to sundry grants made by that government of lands alleged to be situated, not indeed upon Connecticut river nor any where near it — but towards it, and a little beyond a twenty mile line. The force of this evidence must depend wholly upon the intent of the governors of the province in making the grants. In order to have any weight whatever it must appear that the grants were made with the knowledge that the lands were beyond such line, and with the understanding that the territory covered by them was within the province. If the grants were issued under misapprehension or without the knowledge of the granting officer of their eastern extent, they would of course have no tendency to prove the point which the author sought to establish. In order to judge of the weight which ought to be given to this evidence it seems necessary to have some understanding of the general character of the early New York patents.

Perhaps this may be sufficiently shown by quoting the language of Surveyor General Colden, found in a report made to Gov. Cosby in 1732, upon the state of the lands in the province. He speaks of these grants as follows:

"There being no previous survey to the grants, their boundaries are generally expressed with much uncertainty, by the Indian names of brooks, rivulets, hills, ponds, falls of water, etc., which were and still are unknown to Christians. * * * * This has given room to some to explain and enlarge their grants according to their own inclinations by putting the names mentioned in their grants to what place or part of the country they please, of which I can give some particular instances where the claims of some have increased many miles, in a few years, and this they commonly do by taking some Indians in a public manner to show them places as they name to them, and it is too well known that an Indian will show any place by any name you please for the small reward of a blanket, or a bottle of rum." *Doc. Hist. N. Y.*, vol. 1, p. 383.

The grants which are named in Mr. Duane's *State of the Right*, as covering lands in the disputed territory are the following, viz: 1. The Manor of Rensselaerswick, granted in 1685. 2. Westenhook in 1705. 3. Hoosick in 1688. 4. Wallumscoick in 1739; and 5. The patent to Godfrey Dellius in 1696.

An examination of each of which will form the subject of the residue of the present paper.

The only one of these five grants in which the descriptive words give any intimation that any part of the land might be situated eastward of a twenty mile line from the Hudson is that of the manor of Rensselaerswick, and the language of that was considered so equivocal that it was for some time understood as reaching only twelve miles from that river. The patent bears date Nov. 4, 1685, and grants and confirms a tract of land "beginning at Barent's Island in Hudson river and extending northward on both sides of said river unto a place called the Kahoos or the Great Falls of said river, and extending itself east and west all along from each side of said river backward into the woods twenty-four English miles." The early construction of these words appears to have been that the whole extent of the patent was twenty-four miles across the river, twelve miles each side of it. It is spoken of in ancient documents as being a tract twenty-four miles square, with Albany in the center.

The patent of Rensselaerswick was not, however, an original English grant, but was made by Gov. Dongan *in confirmation* of previous Dutch grants, and in pursuance of one of the articles of the capitulation of the country by Gov. Stuyvesant to the English, of September 6, 1664, which declares "that all people shall continue free denizens, and shall enjoy their lands, houses, goods, wheresoever they are within this country, and dispose of them as they please." The grants of which this is a confirmation, were made to Killian Van Rensselaer, in 1630 and 1637 prior to the boundary treaty of Hartford, which fixed upon a line less than twenty miles from the Hudson as the eastern boundary of New Netherland, when the Dutch pretensions had scarcely any limit to the eastward. This is fully stated in the New York *State of the Right*, which we are now considering, as follows: "The Rensselaer family are not indebted to the government of New York for their estate; they continue to enjoy it by an act of justice, and not of favor. It was originally a Dutch colony of itself, granted to their ancestors by the Dutch West India company, who held it as a part of New Netherland, under the States General." The confirmation of the Dutch title in accordance with ancient description, can hardly be considered as setting up a very strong claim for the province to reach eastward to Connecticut river, especially as the governor's inclination to criticise particularly the extent of the grant into an unknown wilderness, may be supposed to have been somewhat blunted by the receipt of two hundred pounds, which he afterwards admitted was advanced him by Mr. Van Rensselaer at the time of making it.[1]

It seems that no settlements were ever at any time made under New York upon this manor or indeed upon any other grant east of a twenty mile line upon the borders of Massachusetts, for Gov. Tryon in writing to Lord Dartmouth July 1, 1773, says: "There are four tracts of land affected by the partition [the settlement of the Massachusetts line], the manor of Rensselaerwick granted in 1685, the manor of Livingston in 1686, the patent of Hoosick in 1688, and the patent of Westenhook in 1708, and I do not learn there are any possessions under either of them to the eastward of the line agreed upon by the commissioners." *Col. Hist. N. Y.*, vol. 8, p. 381.

2. The patent of Westenhook is stated in the New York manifesto to have been granted "on the 6th of March, 1705, and that its eastern bounds are about 30 miles from Hudson's river."

---

[1] *Brodh. N. Y.*, 762, 202, 267. *Col. Hist. N. Y.*, vol. 3, p. 412, and vol. 4. p. 823. *Colden's letter to Board of Trade*, Oct. 11, 1764, in *N. Y. Historical Society archives.*

This is a grant belonging very clearly to the class of those described in the representation of Surveyor General Colden from which an extract has been given, the location and extent of which is subject to great uncertainty and very conveniently liable to expansion. The position it occupies and the distances to which it reaches depend upon a very long, indefinite and confused description, from which it appears to extend along sundry "creeks," over several "plains" and to and from several "rifts or waterfalls," etc., etc., all of them with long and seemingly unpronounceable Indian names. No mention is made of Hudson's river and it could probably be located in the manner mentioned by Mr. Colden in almost any place in the province which the proprietors should choose. In 1775 a petition of persons claiming to be proprietors of Westenhook was presented to Gov. Tryon who forwarded it to the English board of trade as evidence of a claim of the petitioners to certain lands which had been asked for by some reduced officers. The lords of trade in a representation to a committee of the privy council, thus speak of this patent:

"The other claim to which we beg leave to refer your lordships is founded upon a grant to certain inhabitants of New York in the year 1705, commonly called the West hook patent, the circumstances of which grant will more fully appear to your lordships from the annexed copy of a petition presented to Gov. Tryon by the proprietors of that patent and by him delivered to us. But we beg leave to observe to your lordships that upon the fullest consideration of this claim, and of every thing which has been offered to us in support of it, we cannot think it ought to have any weight in this consideration, there being no evidence whatever that the lands supposed to be conveyed thereby were ever taken up at any time *or indeed that they ever could have been taken up, as the description of the limits in the grant itself, has no reference whatever to any places or point of determination at present known or to be found within the district in question.*" *Col. Hist. N. Y.*, vol. 8, p. 576.

Such an unintelligible description cannot surely be considered as asserting any claim whatever to territory reaching to Connecticut river!

3. The patent of Hoosick bore date June 2, 1688, and was issued to three persons without any specification of quantity and was described as follows:

"All that tract of land with its appurtenances situate, lying and being above Albany, upon both sides of a certain creek called Hoosick, beginning at the bounds of Schackoock, and from thence extending to the said creek to a certain fall called Quequick, and from the said fall upwards along the creek to a certain place called Nachawickquack, being in breadth on each side of said creek two English miles, that is to say two English miles on one side of the creek, and two English miles on the other side of said creek, the whole breadth being four English miles and is in length from the bounds of Schackoock to the said place called Nachawickquack."

The beginning of the tract was probably about six miles from the Hudson, and it is evident from the description that Gov. Dongan in New York city could not have made the grant with any view of extending the province more than twenty miles from that river, for he could not know that it would reach half that distance, and it therefore has no tendency to prove a claim of jurisdiction over any part of the disputed territory.

The Hoosick river rises in Berkshire county, Mass., and running in a north-westerly direction, crosses a corner of Vermont in the town of Pownal, and pursues its course for a considerable distance, nearly parallel to the twenty mile line, and then turning almost at right angles reaches the Hudson from the north-east. From the starting point near Schaghticoke, the tract four miles in width must extend not less than twenty miles up the river in length before reaching such line. The terminus of the tract, "a certain water fall called Nachawickquack," might doubtless have been located, in the mode pointed out by Surveyor General Colden, wherever the claimants pleased. It was however, never reached by any survey, and its position remains unascertained and unknown to this day.

4. The patent of Wallumscoick, dated the 15th of June, 1739, was a grant to six persons, and purports to have been made upon a survey and to contain twelve thousand acres, "beginning at a certain marked tree, which is 147 chains distant from the dwelling house of Garrett Cornelius V'n Ness, measured on a line running south 75° east from the south-east corner of the said house to the said tree, and running from the said marked tree, north 13° 30′ west 90 chains and 40 links, thence 40° 15′ east, 220 chains, then north 77° east, 90 chains, then south 31° 40′ east, 604 chains, then south 65° west, 92 chains, then north 44° 30′ west, 150 chains, then north 75° west, 129 chains, then north 20° west, 146 chains, then south 60° west, 173 chains, then north 4° west, 76 chains, to the place where this tract of land first began, containing 12,000 acres, and the usual allowance for highways."

There is nothing about the grant indicating that it extended more than twenty miles to the eastward of the Hudson, and it could not therefore have been designed to claim jurisdiction beyond that distance. It did however begin some three or four miles to the westward of a twenty mile line, and following the windings of the creek, a branch of the Hoosick, which has since borne the name of the patent, reached about the same distance to the eastward of it, into the town of Bennington.

But apparently the most formidable ancient claim of jurisdiction over the disputed territory brought forward in Mr. Duane's *State of the Right*, was that of a patent to one Godfrey Dellius.

This patent, as appears from the New York records, bears date September 3, 1696, and purports to have been issued "by his excellency Benjamin Fletcher, his majesty's governor and commander-in-chief of the province of New York and the territories depending thereon in America," and to grant "to our loving subject the Rev. Godfrey Dellius, minister of the gospel at our city of Albany," some eight or ten hundred thousand acres of land lying on the east side of Hudson's river — "he yielding, rendering and paying therefor yearly and every year unto us, our heirs and successors, on the first day of our blessed Virgin Mary at our city of New York the annual rent of one raccoon skin, in lieu and stead of all other rents, services, duties and demands whatsoever." This grant together with another still more extraordinary of lands on the Mohawk river made by the same governor to the same reverend gentleman, were three years afterwards, in 1699, set aside and annulled by act of the New York assembly, approved by the crown, as having been obtained and issued by fraud, and the reverend Mr. Dellius, by the same act was declared to be suspended from further exercising his ministerial functions.

The following is the statement of the claim made in the New York document under consideration.

"So long ago as 1796, a grant passed the great seal of this colony to Godfrey Dellius for a tract extending from the north bounds of Saratoga (which lies both sides of Hudson's river, about thirty miles north of the city of Albany) to the Rock Rosian, a station indisputable, and which is well known to lie on Lake Champlain and above twenty miles to the northward of Crown Point. This tract extends twelve miles east from Hudson's river *and the same distance east from Wood creek, and the waters to the northward;* and it is worth a remark that such was its value and importance at that early day that the legislature conceived the grant to be too great a favor for one subject,and passed a law in 1699, repealing it as extravagant."

This account of the Dellius grant, by which it is declared to include a tract of land in Vermont twelve miles in width, lying on the east side of Lake Champlain, and extending some fifty miles in length from Fair and West Haven on the south to Charlotte on the north, has hitherto been regarded as historical truth. It has been referred to as such in historical works and on a map of Lake Champlain and the bordering territory published in the first volume of the *Documentary History of New York* in 1849, its supposed northern boundary in Vermont has been designated and dignified by a special *red line.* The reader will no doubt be surprised to learn that upon no rational construction of the language of the grant, can it possibly be made to include a single acre of Vermont territory. The importance which has been given to this grant by the advocates of the New York title demands that it should be fully examined.

The patent which is found on the *Albany Records*, vol. 7, p. 53, describes the land in the following words: "A certain tract of land lying upon the east side of *Hudson's river* between the northernmost bounds of Saratoga and the Rock Retsio, containing about seventy miles in length and goes backwards into the woods from *Hudson's river*, twelve miles until it comes into *Wood creek*, and so far as it goes be it twelve miles more or less from *Hudson's river* on the east side, and from said creek by a line twelve miles distant from *said river*." Precisely the same description is found in the act annulling the grant in *Van Schaick's Statutes*, p. 32, except that the name of the rock is printed *Rosian* instead of *Retsio.*

It is impossible by any intelligible reading of this description to carry any part of the tract to the eastward of the waters of Lake Champlain. Unless its language is violently distorted from its natural meaning the land it describes is bounded all the way on the west by Hudson's river, all the way on the east by a twelve mile line from the Hudson, except that Wood creek, "so far as it goes" forms a part of the east line, whether it be more or less than twelve miles from that river. The only objection that could be urged to this construction would seem to be, that if the tract followed the course of Hudson's river, even to its source, it might not reach as far north as the latitude of Rock Rosian, and at all events its east line of twelve miles from that river would be a very long distance to the west, or southwestward of that rock, which rock, according to Mr. Duane, "is a station indisputable and well known to be on Lake Champlain about twenty miles to the northward of Crown Point." That such would be the position of the land in reference to Rock Rosian, now known as Split Rock, if it were now surveyed by the actual course of the river, in conformity to our construction, is not denied, and yet it by no means follows that we should reject either the rock, or the river as substantial parts of the description. The language of the grant is to be construed in accordance with the intent of the parties and in reference to their geographical knowledge and belief at the time it was made.

It should be borne in mind that the northern branch of Hudson's river was understood for nearly a century after the grant to Dellius, to take its rise nearly as far north as latitude 45 degrees, and to run in a southerly direction about parallel to Lake Champlain. It is so laid down in the early maps. In 1750, half a century after the Dellius grant, John Henry Lydius, an intelligent Indian trader, gave his affidavit before the mayor of Albany in which he stated that "he had always heard that the purchase made by Godfrey Dellius in the year 1696, was commonly esteemed to extend to the Rock Regio." * * "and the deponent further says that he well knows the northern branch of Hudson's river extends at least twenty leagues further north than Crown Point." This affidavit was taken at the request of Gov. Clinton and transmitted by him to the board of trade in London. (*Col. Hist. N. Y.*, vol. 6, p. 561, 569, 577.) As late as 1768, Gov. Moore writes to Lord Hillsborough that the rivers Hudson and Connecticut had never been traced to their sources. Gov. Tryon in 1774, in a report to the English board of trade says, "Connecticut river extends beyond and Hudson's river takes its rise a little to the southward of the forty-fifth degree of latitude. (*Ibid.* vol. 8, p. 107, 436.) We must suppose then that Hudson's river at the time of the grant was understood to reach considerably further north than the Rock Retsio, otherwise written Rosian or Regio.

In the description of the tract, the Hudson river is beyond question a controlling boundary and can not be dispensed with, without making the language altogether unintelligible. If any other part of the description cannot be literally followed, it must give way to that part which is indispensible. But there is no need of discarding any portion of it. It is not necessary to the description that the Rock Retsio should be a point with which the tract should come in actual contact. It will be sufficient if it be considered as a well known mark situated as far north as the land should be allowed to extend along the Hudson. Thus full effect will be given to every word of the description, and there will be little trouble in ascertaining its meaning.

The other points mentioned in the Dellius grant were pretty well known. The "northernmost bounds of Saratoga" were the Battenkill, which falls into the Hudson from the east, Saratoga which had been previously patented, extending across and east of the Hudson six miles along said kill. Wood creek takes its rise between the south end of Lake Champlain and the Hudson, and running north easterly some fifteen or twenty miles falls into that lake at Whitehall. It was the early route from Albany to Canada, and is now that of the northern New York canal. If any one with these explanations will read over the description in the patent, he will

HUDSON'S RIVER AS ANCIENTLY BELIEVED.

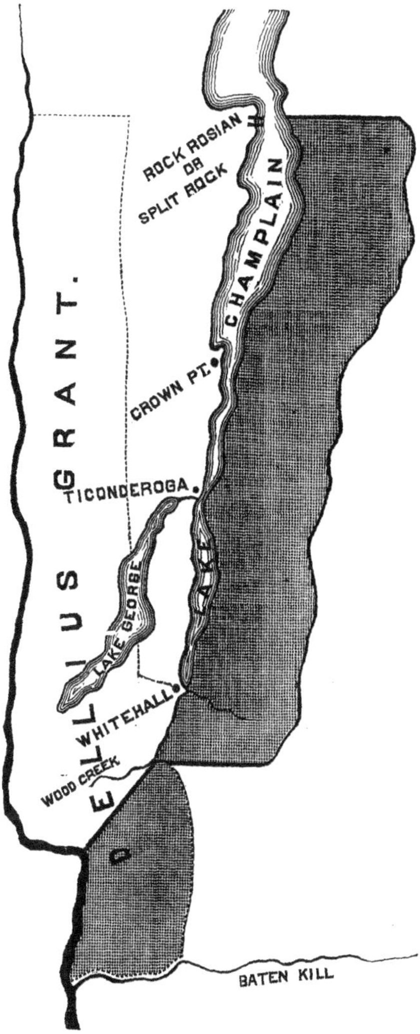

DELLIUS GRANT.

ROCK ROSIAN OR SPLIT ROCK

CHAMPLAIN

CROWN PT.

TICONDEROGA.

LAKE GEORGE

LAKE

WHITEHALL

WOOD CREEK

BATEN KILL

The shaded part represents the Dellius Grant in two parcels, as erroneously claimed by Mr. Duane.

SARATOGA.

The Dellius Grant of 1696, bounded West by the Hudson, North and South by dotted Lines, and East by dotted lines and Wood Creek.

have no difficulty in understanding what was meant by it. It grants to Dellius a tract of land extending from the Battenkill on the south as far to the northward as the Rock Retsio is situated, bounded *all the way of its length on the west by Hudson's river*, and extending eastward into the woods twelve miles from that river, except that for a few miles of its length its eastern boundary is Wood creek, " be it twelve miles more or less from said river."

No step can be taken towards sliding the west boundary of this grant over to the eastern shore of Lake Champlain without wresting the language of the grant from its clear and obvious meaning, and any attempt to do it would show the perfect absurdity of such a construction. The eastern line of the tract, beginning at its southern boundary runs parallel to Hudson's river at a distance of twelve miles from it for some fifteen miles or more " until it comes unto Wood creek." Of this there can be no dispute. According to the natural construction of the language, the eastern boundary of the tract continues along Wood creek " so far as it goes." But according to Mr. Duane the eastern boundary stops at Wood creek, and the creek then takes the place of Hudson's river and becomes at once the western boundary, and the eastern boundary is consequently shoved twelve miles further to the eastward. This it will be perceived divides the domain of Mr. Dellius into two separate and distinct parcels, the north east corner of the southern parcel merely touching the south west corner of the northern at a single point. The absurdity of this construction may be clearly seen by the subjoined plan, the dark ground representing the tract or tracts according to Mr. Duane, and the dotted lines in connexion with the Hudson river showing the form of the grant as really intended to be made.

Dr. Fitch in his interesting and valuable history of Washington county, published in the *Transactions of the New York Agricultural Society* for 1848, speaks of the Dellius grant as covering " *about half the land in Washington county, and a still larger quantity in the present state of Vermont.*" He then gives correctly the descriptive words of the grant, but appears in great doubt about its measuring. He is not satisfied with Mr. Duane's explanation of it, apparently for the reason that he extends the tract far to the northward of Wood creek, *along the waters of Lake Champlain*, whereas no mention is made of the lake as one of its boundaries. This is certainly a very formidable objection, one that it is difficult to overcome. In order to get rid of it Dr. Fitch asserts that Crown Point " was commonly regarded by the French as the head of the lake and the mouth of Wood creek," and adds that " this document, though extremely vague, appears to contemplate this topic in the same light." He thus extends the Wood creek boundary of the track as far north as Crown Point. But this stops twenty miles short of " Rock Retsio," and the same difficulty still remains. This he overcomes by conjecturing that Mr. Duane's well-known " indisputable station " may not after all have been Split Rock, but some undiscovered rock near Crown Point, at the mouth of his imaginary Wood creek. This conjectural location of the tract it will at once be perceived, leads into at least two insurmountable difficulties. First, it transfers Wood creek from the eastern to the western boundary of the tract, leaving it, as in Mr. Duane's description, in two distinct parcels;

and secondly, by extending Wood creek to the northern limit of the tract, the important closing words of the description are ignored and rejected as unmeaning, viz: the words "and from said creek by a line twelve miles distant from said [Hudson's] river." If Dr. Fitch, instead of endeavoring to make the description conform to the idea that a large portion of the tract was in Vermont, had merely sought to ascertain from its language where it was really intended to be located, he would probably have found no difficulty in perceiving that Hudson river formed its whole western boundary, and that Wood creek "so far as it goes," in connexion with a twelve mile line from that river, constituted its eastern. That the Rock Retsio, sometimes written Rosian, Rodgio, Rogeo and Rogio, was "the Great Rock" afterwards known as Split Rock, situated some twenty miles to the northward of Crown Point, there is no manner of doubt. (*See Colonial History of N. Y.*, vol. 3, p. 802, vol. 4, p. 748, vol. 6, p. 569.)

Whether the merit of extending this Dellius claim eastward into the territory of the New Hampshire Grants, is due to the inventive genius of Mr. Duane or to that of some of his land claiming contemporaries, is perhaps doubtful. In a report made January 6, 1772, by a committee of the New York council, of which Mr. Smith the historian was chairman, in opposition to the validity of the French Grants on Lake Champlain, certain recent patents by the New York government, to reduced officers and soldiers, and also this ancient Dellius patent are mentioned as interfering with those grants, and the report recommended the preparing of a map by the surveyor general "exhibiting the French Grants and the English patents to the northward of Crown Point to be laid before his majesty with all convenient speed." The map found in the first volume of the *Documentary History of New York*, at page 572, is presumed to have been made in pursuance of this report. It exhibits with a *red line* what purports to be the northern boundary of the Dellius patent running east from Split Rock, but is silent in regard to its other boundaries. Doubtless for the reason that the surveyor general was unable to find them east of the lake. Under date of the 5th of January, 1773, Gov. Tryon, in a letter to Lord Dartmouth denying the validity of the French claims, says this Dellius grant "comprehends a large tract extending from Saratoga along Hudson's river, the Wood creek and Lake Champlain *on the east side* upwards of twenty miles to the northward of Crown Point." A few weeks later the idea is incorporated into Mr. Duane's *State of the Right* in the language before recited. Nothing indicating such a construction of the language of the patent is found prior to these dates. The grant is referred to in a report to the crown by the English board of trade in 1690, and in other official papers of a subsequent date, and also by Mr. Smith in his history of New York, and is always treated as bounded on the west by the Hudson river, and never as lying east of Wood creek or Lake Champlain. (*See Col. Hist. N. Y.*, vol. 4, p. 391, vol. 5, p. 11, 22, and *Smith's N. Y.*, vol. 1, p. 155, *Doc. Hist. N. Y.*, vol. 1, p. 567 - 571, 576.)

It is thus seen, that this famous grant which has so long been claimed as evidence of the exercise of ancient jurisdiction by New York over the territory of Vermont, cannot by any conceivable process be made to reach eastward to its western boundary. Having thus gone through with the list of New York patents which are claimed to cover lands to the eastward of a twenty mile line from the Hudson, or eastward of Lake Champlain, we have seen that only one of them could possibly have been supposed from its language, at the time it was made, to extend beyond that line, and that the language of that was of doubtful construction; and further, that the grant was made under such circumstances as to deprive it of all force as a claim of jurisdiction, whatever may have been its meaning. Indeed the fact that the New York government for a period of one hundred years from 1664, abstained from making grants to the eastward of a line coming so near their settlements on the Hudson as twenty miles, furnishes very strong evidence that such line and not Connecticut river, had during all that period been regarded by that government as the eastern limit of the province.

APPENDIX NO. 8.

[See page 169.]

Col. John H. Lydius.

John Henry Lydius, the land claimant mentioned in the text, was the son of a Dutch minister, was born at Albany, in 1694, and lived to the very great age of 98. He became an Indian trader and went to Montreal about 1725, abjured the protestant faith and declared himself a catholic. He there married a half-breed woman, became familiar with the French and Indian languages, and was active in his intercourse with the Indians. His sincerity as a catholic was eventually doubted; he was suspected of being concerned in carrying on an illicit trade with the English, and in 1730, was tried as a spy and banished. (*Col. Hist. N. Y.*, vol. 9, p. 19, 1021.) He returned to Albany, where his intercourse with the Indians continued. Under date of February 1, 1732, he obtained a paper purporting to be a deed with the names and marks of certain Mohawk Indians attached, of two separate parcels of land of most extravagant dimensions. One of the tracts was wholly in the present limits of Vermont, and extended southerly sixty miles from the mouth of Otter creek, by twenty-four miles in width, containing over nine hundred thousand acres; the other, more than half as large, embraced a great portion of Wood creek, and extended twenty miles down the east side of the Hudson. In a pamphlet published at New Haven, Conn., in 1764, under the auspices of Lydius, the consideration of the deed is stated to be the eminent pious services of his father "a minister of the gospel at Albany," in instructing the Mohawks, and the continuation of such instructions by the son. At a council with the Six Nations in 1755, at which Lydius was present, an Oneida sachem addressed Col. Johnson, the Indian superintendent, as follows: "Brother, you promised us that you would keep this fire place clean from all filth, and that no snake should come into this council room. That man sitting there, (pointing to Col. Lydius) is a devil, and has stole our lands. He takes Indians slyly by the blanket, one at a time, and when they are drunk, puts some money into their bosoms and persuades them to sign deeds of their lands." This was in reference to a deed of lands on the Susquehanna. (*Col. Hist. N. Y.*, vol. 6, p. 984.) It is not likely that the mode in this case differed much from that in relation to the lands on Wood and Otter creeks. In regard to these lands and especially those on Otter creek, it is by no means certain that the Mohawks ever claimed that they were within their hunting grounds. In a representation of the New York council to Gov. Monckton, in Jan., 1763, it is denied that the Mohawk Indians had any claim at the date to either of the tracts. However that may be, Lydius some years after the date of the deed became a confidant of Gov. Shirley of Massachusetts, assisted him in his transactions with the Six Nations and in his controversy with Col. Johnson, and obtained from him a commission as colonel of the Indians. He also procured from him a paper bearing date August 31, 1744, purporting to be a confirmation of his Indian deed, and an absolute conveyance to him of the lands it described in fee, "*in obedience to his majesty's special command of the 5th of October last.*" This was altogether out of the ordinary mode of making grants by the king, and from the character and needy circumstances of Gov. Shirley, there is no reasonable doubt that he was induced to issue the document without any authority whatever. If there had been any such command of the king, it would have been in writing, and a copy of it would undoubtedly have been given in the pamphlet before referred to. But no such writing was ever exhibited — or ever claimed to be in existence.

About the time of Shirley's deed, Col. Lydius appears to have built a house on his Wood creek tract near Fort Edward, and to have afterwards resided there a portion of the time for several years. (*Col. Hist. N. Y.*, vol. 9, p. 1101-2, vol. 10, p. 42, 144, 146. No. 49 on map in *Col. Hist. N. Y.*, vol. 1, p. 556. *Dr. Fitch's History of Washington Co.*, p. 903.) Immediately on the close of the French war in 1760, he seems to have taken active measures to dispose of his Shirley lands. Calling the Otter creek tract fifty-eight miles in length by twenty-four in breadth, he divided it (on paper) into thirty-five townships, of about thirty-six square miles each, numbering and giving names to each of the townships. No. 7 is called Durham, which perhaps embraces the same land afterwards patented by New York by that name. He also plotted in a similar manner his Wood creek claim. In the New Haven pamphlet before referred to, it is stated that Lydius, "in the year 1760, gave out several townships of land, the first to Connecticut people, and others to those of New York and Rhode Island, on the moderate rent of five shillings sterling per hundred acres, improvable land; first payable twenty years after the date of his leases." If we suppose two thirds of the Otter creek tract to be *improvable* land, and to be leased at the above rate, it would produce an income of about three thousand dollars per annum. But as the first rent was not payable till the end of twenty years, and the title long before the expiration of that time became utterly worthless, it is not probable that he realized much from the grant. He is supposed however to have carried on a lucrative trade with the Indians for a series of years, and he might perhaps have been in good pecuniary circumstances. He was in England in 1767, soliciting the government for aid in a controversy with the New York government and perhaps for compensation for services alleged to have been rendered in America, in which he was probably unsuccessful. (*Ms. Diary of Wm. Samuel Johnson.*)

He never returned to America but died near London in 1791. The *Gentleman's Magazine* for April of that year contains a biographical notice of him, written, it would seem, by a scrivener, who had known him for some time previous to his death, and who was called upon to write his will. His account of the deceased, by the extravagance of its statements imposes a heavy tax on our credulity. The writer among other things says he was shown by the deceased an "Indian deed with a great number of seals and uncouth Indian names." Also "another writing for a large tract of country containing many millions of acres, the consideration he paid for it being 11,000 pounds," equal to 55,000 dollars. "The extent of his territory reached from sea to sea." Holland was the country of his ancestors, where he had been made a baron. "As a christian he was firm and sincere." "His humanity he amply evidenced by settling 2700 families with habitations, and when he left America strictly commanded his children to support and succor them in his absence, as the means to obtain the blessing of heaven." It appears from this account that one of his daughters had married and died in England, and that another the wife of a Col. Cuyler, was then living in America. This daughter is mentioned by Dr. Fitch in his history of Washington county (p. 904) as having afterwards died at Greenbush, N. Y.

It is difficult to determine the precise character of Col. Lydius. That his manners and address were prepossessing, and that he was well stocked with the kind of talent that fitted him for an Indian trader and land speculator there can be no doubt. He incurred the displeasure of Sir Wm. Johnson and other New York officials, who give him an unfavorable character. His land claims certainly have a bad odor.

See further in relation to him, *Stone's Life of Sir Wm. Johnson*, vol. 1, p. 159, 272, 289, 291, 464, 502, 504; vol. 2, p. 187. Index to the *Colonial History of New York*, title *Lydius.*

APPENDIX NO. 9.

[See pages 239, 246.]

The Name Vermont, and Dr. Thomas Young.

In giving a copy of the declaration of independence by the convention of January, 1777, at page 239, I have not inserted the words "alias Vermont," after those of New Connecticut, from a conviction, after a careful examination, that they do not belong there. These words are found in *Slade's State Papers* (p. 70), and in *Williams's History of Vermont*, and also in the manuscript copy in the possession of James H. Phelps; but I think they must have been inconsiderately added to the journal or an early copy of it, by way of explanation, after the name Vermont had been adopted in lieu of New Connecticut, and afterwards, in transcribing, erroneously taken as a part of the original. My reasons for believing that the "alias Vermont," was not in it, are the following:

1. The very great improbability, not to say absurdity, of supposing that the convention would have specified two names for their new state, allowing either of them to be used, or that both should be used, the latter preceded by an *alias*.

2. In the rendue of the journal of the convention, not found in Slade, but in a copy in the possession of Mr. Phelps, the new state is twice called by the name of New Connecticut, and the name of Vermont is not again mentioned. Thus, in the journal, we read as follows:

"12th, voted that the declaration of New Connecticut be inserted in the newspapers."

"14th, voted that Dr. Jonas Fay, Col. Thomas Chittenden, Dr. Reuben Jones, Col. Jacob Bayley and Capt. Heman Allen be the delegates to convey the remonstrance and petition to the Honl Continental congress, and further to negotiate business in behalf of New Connecticut."

3d. In the supplementary declaration published by the June convention in the *Connecticut Courant* of June 30, 1777, where the name Vermont was officially adopted, the reason for the change is stated to be that when the name New Connecticut was given to the state, it was unknown to the convention that there was already a territory of that name on the Susquehanna river, and it is then declared that "instead of New Connecticut, the said district shall ever be known by the name of Vermont," which language excludes the idea that the name Vermont could have been mentioned in the former declaration.

4. Ira Allen who was a member of the January convention and was familiar with all the proceedings in forming the new state, in his history (page 78 and 79) inserts what purports to be the declaration, in which he gives the name of New Connecticut only, omitting the *alias*.

5. In the declaration and petition of the agents of Vermont to congress presented April 8, 1777 announcing their formation of a separate state, no name for the state is mentioned, probably for the reason that the agents had learned that the name of New Connecticut was already appropriated to another territory. If the name Vermont had been in the original declaration they would very likely have used it.

All accounts concur that the name of Vermont was given to the state by Dr. Thomas Young of Philadelphia. Ira Allen says in his history that "the name Vermont was given to the district of the New Hampshire Grants, as an emblematical one, from the French *Verd-mont*, Green mountain, intended to perpetuate the name of the Green Mountain Boys, by Dr. Thomas Young," etc. In a petition to the Vermont assembly in behalf of the widow of Dr. Young, signed by Thomas Chittenden, Ethan Allen and Joseph Fay, in 1785, they speak highly of Dr. Young's services in establishing the independence of the state, and say that "to him we stand indebted for the very name of Vermont."

The first appearance of the name in print was, without doubt in the letter of Dr. Young dated the 11th of April, 1777, addressed "to the inhabitants of *Vermont* a free and independent state." At the date of the letter the agents appointed to present the declaration and petition for a new state, to congress, Jonas Fay, Thomas Chittenden, Heman Allen and Reuben Jones, were in Philadelphia, where they doubtless learned what had been unknown to them in January, that there was already a *New Connecticut* on the Susquehanna river, and that it would therefore be necessary to find another name for the state. That of Vermont being proposed by Dr. Young was no doubt approved by those gentlemen, and was thus announced in his letter under the expectation that it would be adopted by the convention that was to assemble in June following, as was then actually done by a unanimous vote. This seems to be a natural explanation of the origin of the name, and of the reason for its adoption, and I cannot entertain any doubt that only the name of New Connecticut was in the original declaration.

The services and influence of Dr. Young in promoting the independence of our state and in forming its first constitution were doubtless very considerable. His letter "to the inhabitants of Vermont" before mentioned, besides the paragraph which had incurred the censure of congress, contained a brief argument in favor of a constitution having but a single legislative body, with an advisory power only in the executive, and recommended the constitution of Pennsylvania as a model, and this recommendation was followed. He was an old acquaintance of Ethan Allen, they having resided near each other for some time, the one in Dutchess county, New York, and the other at Salisbury, Conn. Dr. Young had also resided in Albany, and afterwards in Boston, and had removed to Philadelphia about the beginning of the revolution. He was an active and ardent patriot at an early day, and a political writer of some note. He was associated with James Otis, Samuel Adams, Joseph Warren, and other distinguished whigs of Boston, in their resistance to the oppressive measures of the crown, and his name is found with theirs on most of their committees, for several years before the breaking out of the war. On the day of the destruction of the tea, he with Samuel Adams addressed the great public meeting in favor of the resolution that no tea should be allowed to be landed, and he was doubtless aware of the manner in which it was to be destroyed. John Adams, speaking of Paine's notions of government as shown in his *Common Sense*, says they flowed from ignorance "and a mere desire to please the democratic party of Philadelphia, at whose head were Mr. Matlock, Mr. Cannon and Dr. Young." He further says that Matlock, Cannon and Young had influence enough to get the plan adopted in substance, in Georgia, Vermont and Pennsylvania," and adds, "these three states found them such systems of anarchy, if that expression is not a contradiction in terms, that they have altered them and made them more conformable to my plan." (*Diary* 507, 508, and *Jour.* 476, 1000.) This remark is scarcely true of Vermont. Our constitution has been changed by adding a second legislative body, but the executive has still only advisory power. The word anarchy has no proper application to the effects of our first system. Dr. Young is believed to have died in Philadelphia, in the latter part of the year 1777. Ira Allen in his history says of him, that he greatly interested himself in behalf of the settlers of Vermont; that "by several publications, he was highly distinguished as a philosopher, philanthropist and patriot, and for his erudition and brilliancy of imagination," and that "his death was universally regretted by the friends of American independence, as one of her warm supporters, and by the republic of letters as a brilliant ornament." For the whole of Dr. Young's letter. (See *Thompson's Vt.*, 106. See also *Vt. Q. Gazetteer* No. VI, p. 568. *Bancroft*, vol. 8, p. 478, 485, and *Life and Times of Joseph Warren.* Index Thomas Young.)

APPENDIX NO. 10.

[See page 378.]

LETTER FROM GOV. CHITTENDEN TO GEN. WASHINGTON.

"State of Vermont, Arlington 14th November, 1781.

"Sir: The peculiar situation and circumstances with which this state for several years last past has been attended, induce me to address your excellency on a subject, which nearly concerns her interest, and may have its influence on the common cause of the states of America.

"Placing the highest confidence in your excellency's patriotism in the cause of Liberty, and disposition to do equal right and justice to every part of America, who have by arms supported their rights against the lawless power of Great Britain, I herein transmit the measures by which this state has conducted her policy for the security of her frontiers; and as the design and end of it were set on foot, and have ever since been prosecuted on an honorable principle (as the consequences will fully evince) I do it with full confidence that your excellency will not improve it to the disadvantage of this truly patriotic, suffering state; although the substance has already been communicated by Captain Ezra Hedcock, employed by Major Gen. Lincoln, by your excellency's particular direction, and who arrived here with the resolutions of congress of the 7th day of August last, which appeared in some measure favorable to this state.

"I then disclosed to him the measures this state had adopted for her security, which I make no doubt have by him been delivered to your excellency; and, though I do not hesitate that you are well satisfied of the real attachment of the government of this state to the common cause, I esteem it nevertheless my duty to this state, and the common cause at large, to lay before your excellency, in writing, the heretofore critical situation of this state, and the management of its policy, that it may operate in your excellency's mind as a barrier against the clamorous aspersions of its numerous, and in many instances, potent adversaries.

"It is the misfortune of this state to join on the province of Quebec and the waters of the Lake Champlain, which affords an easy passage for the enemy to make a descent with a formidable army on its frontiers, and into the neighborhood of the several states of New York, New Hampshire and

Massachusetts, who have severally laid claims in part or in whole, to this state, and who have used every art which they could devise to divide her citizens, to set congress against her, and finally to overturn the government and share its territory among them. The repeated applications of this state to the congress of the United States to be admitted into the federal union with them, upon the liberal principles of paying a just proportion of the expenses of the war with Great Britain, have been rejected, and resolutions passed *ex parte* tending to create schisms in the state, and thereby embarrass its efforts in raising men and money for the defence of her frontiers, and discountenancing the very existence of the state. Every article belonging to the United States, even to pickaxes and spades, has been by continental commissaries ordered out of this state, at a time when she was erecting a line of forts on her frontiers. At the same time the state of New York evacuated the post of Skenesborough for the avowed purpose of exposing this state to the ravages of the common enemy.

"The British officers in New York, being acquainted with the public disputes between this and the claiming states, and between congress and this state, made overtures to Gen. Allen in a letter, projecting that Vermont should be a colony under the crown of England, endeavouring, at the same time, to draw the people of Vermont into their interest. The same day Gen. Allen received this letter (which was in August, 1780), he laid it before me and my council, who, under the critical circumstances of the state, advised that no answer, either oral or written, should be returned, and that the letter should be safely deposited till further consideration, to which Gen. Allen consented. A few months after, he received a second letter from the enemy, and the same council advised that Gen. Allen should send both letters to congress, inclosed in a letter under his signature; which he did, in hopes that congress would admit Vermont into the Union; but they had not the desired effect.

"In the fall of the year 1780, the British made a descent up the Lake Champlain, and captured the Forts George and Anne, and appeared in force on the lake. This occasioned the militia of this state, most generally, to go forth to defend it. Thus the militia were encamped against the enemy near six weeks when Gen. Allen received a flag from them, with an answer to my letter dated the preceding July to Gen. Haldimand, on the subject of an exchange of prisoners. The flag delivered a letter to Gen. Allen, from the commanding officer of the enemy, who were then at Crown Point, with proposals for a truce with the state of Vermont, during the negotiating the exchange of prisoners. Gen. Allen sent back a flag of his to the commanding officer of the British, agreeing to the truce, provided he would extend the same to the frontier posts of the state of New York, which was complied with, and a truce took place, which lasted about three weeks. It was chiefly owing to the military prowess of the militia of this state, and the including the state of New York in the truce, that Albany and Schenectady did not fall a sacrifice to the ambition of the enemy that campaign.

"Previous to the retiring of the enemy into winter quarters, Col. Allen and Major Fay were commissioned to negotiate the proposed exchange of prisoners. They proceeded so far as to treat with the British commissioners on the subject of their mission, during which time they were interchangeably entertained with politics, which they treated in an affable manner, as I have been told. But no cartel was settled, and the campaign ended without the effusion of blood.

" The cabinet council, in the course of the succeeding winter, finding that the enemy in Canada were about seven thousand strong, and that Vermont must needs be their object the ensuing campaign, circular letters were therefore sent from the supreme executive authority of this state to the claiming states before mentioned, demanding of them to relinquish their claims to this state, and inviting them to join in a solid union and confederation against the common enemy. Letters were also sent to your excellency and to the states of Connecticut and Rhode Island. Each of these letters stated the extreme circumstances of this state, and implored their aid and alliance, giving them withal to understand, that it was out of the power of this state, to lay in magazines, and support a body of men, sufficient to defend this state against the force of the enemy. But to these letters there has been no manner of answer returned.

" From all which it appeared that this state was devoted to destruction by the sword of the common enemy. It appeared to be the more unjustifiable, that the state of Vermont should be thus forsook, inasmuch as her citizens struck the first offensive blow against British usurption, by putting the continent in possession of Ticonderoga, and more than two hundred pieces of cannon; with Crown Point, St. John's, and all Lake Champlain; their exertions in defeating Gen. Carleton in his attempt to raise the seige of St. John's; their assisting in penetrating Canada; their valor in the battles of Hubbardton, Bennington and at the landing, near Ticonderoga; assisting in the capture of Gen. Burgoyne; and by being the principal barrier against the power of the enemy in Canada ever since.

" That the citizens of this state have by nature an equal right to liberty and independency with the citizens of America in general, cannot be disputed. And that they have merited it from the United States by their exertions with them in bringing about the present glorious revolution, is as evident a truth as any other, which respects the acquired right of any community.

" Generosity, merit, and gratitude, all conspire in vindicating the independence of Vermont. But notwithstanding the arguments, which have been exhibited in sundry pamphlets in favor of Vermont, and which have been abundantly satisfactory to the impartial part of mankind, it has been in the power of her external enemies to deprive her of union, confederation or any equal advantage in defending themselves against the common enemy.

" The winter was thus spent in fruitless attempts to form alliances, but no advantages were procured in favor of this state, except that Massachusetts withdrew her claim, on condition that the United States would concede the independence of Vermont; but that if they would not, they would have their snack at the south end of its territory. Still New York and New Hampshire are strenuously opposed to the independence of Vermont; and every stratagem in their power, to divide and subdivide her citizens, are exerted, imagining that their influence in congress and the certain destruction, as they supposed, of the inhabitants of this state by the common enemy, could not fail of finally accomplishing their wishes.

"In this juncture of affairs, the cabinet of Vermont projected the extension of their claim of jurisdiction upon the states of New Hampshire and New York, as well to quiet some of their own internal divisions occasioned by the machinations of those two governments, as to make them experience the evils of intestine broils, and strengthen this state against insult. The legislature, accordingly, extended their jurisdiction to the eastward of Connecticut river to the old Mason line, and to the westward to Hudson's river; but, in the articles of Union, referred the determination of the boundary lines of Vermont, and the respective claiming states, to the final decision of congress, or such other tribunal as might be mutually agreed on by the contending governments. These were the principal political movements of the last winter.

"The last campaign opening with a gloomy aspect to discerning citizens of this state, being destitute of adequate resources, and without any alliance, and from its local situation to Canada, obliged to encounter the whole force of that province, or give up its claim to independence and run away, Vermont being thus driven to desperation by the injustice of those who should have been her friends, was obliged to adopt policy in the room of power. And on the first day of May last, Col. Ira Allen was sent to Canada to further negotiate the business of the exchange of prisoners, who agreed on a time, place, and other particulars relating to the exchange. While he was transacting that business, he was treated with great politeness and entertained with political matters, which necessity obliged him to humor, in that easy manner that might save the interest of this state in its extreme critical situation, and that its consequences might not be injurious to the United States. The plan succeeded, the frontiers of this state were not invaded; and Lord George Germain's letter wrought upon congress and procured that from them, which the public virtue of this people could not.

"In the month of July last, Maj. Joseph Fay was sent to the British shipping, on Lake Champlain, who completed an exchange of a number of prisoners, who were delivered at Skenesborough in September last; at which time and place Col. Allen and Maj. Fay had a conference with the British commissioners. And no damage, as yet, had accrued to this, or the United States from this quarter. And in the month of October last, the enemy appeared in force at Crown Point, and Ticonderoga; but were maneuvered out of their expedition, and are returned into winter quarters in Canada, with great safety, that it might be fulfilled which was spoken by the prophet, 'I will put my hook in their nose and turn them back by the way which they came, and they shall not come into this city (alias Vermont) saith the Lord.'

"It remains that I congratulate your excellency, and participate with you in the joy of your capturing the haughty Cornwallis and his army; and assure your excellency that there are no gentlemen in America, who enjoy the glorious victory more than the gentlemen of this state, and him who has the honor to subscribe himself your excellency's devoted and

"Most humble servant,

THOMAS CHITTENDEN."

APPENDIX NO. 11.

[See p. 413.]

INSTRUCTIONS OF THE LEGISLATURE OF NEW JERSEY TO THE DELEGATES OF THE STATE IN CONGRESS, PASSED NOVEMBER 1, 1782.

"To the Hon[l] Elias Boudinott, John Witherspoon, Abraham Clark, Jonathan Elmer and Silas Condit, Esquires, delegates representing this state in the congress of the United States.

"Gentlemen: Application having been made to the legislature for instructions on the important subject of disputes subsisting between the states of New York, New Hampshire and the people on the New Hampshire Grants, styling themselves the state of Vermont, which is under consideration of congress, they are of opinion (as far as they have documents to direct their inquiry) that as the competency of congress was deemed full and complete at the passing of the resolutions of the 7th and 20th of August, 1781 (each of those states having made an absolute reference of the dispute to their final arbitrament), those acts may be supposed to be founded on strict justice and propriety, nine states having agreed to the measure, and that great regard might be had to any determination of congress, when no new light is thrown upon the subject, or weighty matters occur to justify a reversion of such their decision, and more especially, as it appears that the people on the New Hampshire Grants, have, by an act of their legislature, on the 22d of February last, in every instance complied with the preliminaries stated as conditional to such guarantee.

"The legislature taking up the matter upon general principles are further of opinion, that congress considered as the sovereign guardians of the United States, ought at all times to prefer the general safety of the common cause to the particular separate interest of any individual state, and when circumstances may render such a measure expedient, it ought certainly to be adopted.

"The legislature know of no disposition in congress to attempt to reduce the said people to allegiance by force, but should that be the case, they will not consent to the sending any military force into the said territory to subdue the inhabitants to the obedience and subjection of the state or states that claims their allegiance.

"They disclaim every idea of imbruing their hands in the blood of their fellow citizens, or entering into a civil war among themselves at all times, but more especially at so critical a period as the present, conceiving such a step to be highly impolitic and dangerous.

"You are therefore instructed to govern yourselves in the discussion of this business by the aforesaid opinions, as far as they may apply thereto."—*Madison Papers*, vol. 1, p. 489.

APPENDIX NO. 12.

[See page 201.]

COMMISSION FROM THE MASSACHUSETTS COMMITTEE OF SAFETY TO BENEDICT ARNOLD TO ENLIST MEN AND CAPTURE TICONDEROGA.

"To Benedict Arnold Esq., commander of a body of troops on an expedition to reduce and take possession of the fort of Ticonderoga.

Sir: Confiding in your judgment, fidelity, and valor, we do, by these presents, constitute and appoint you, colonel and commander-in-chief over a body of men not exceeding four hundred, to proceed with all expedition, to the western part of this and the neighboring colonies, where you are directed to enlist those men, and with them, forthwith, to march to the fort at Ticonderoga, and use your best endeavors to reduce the same, taking possession of the cannon, mortars, stores, etc., upon the lake; you are to bring back with you such of the cannon, mortars, stores, etc., as you shall judge may be serviceable to the army here, leaving behind what may be necessary to secure that post, with a sufficient garrison. You are to procure suitable provisions and stores for the army, and draw upon the committee of safety for the amount thereof, and to act in every exigence, according to your best skill and discretion, for the public interest, for which this shall be your sufficient warrant.

BENJAMIN CHURCH, JR.

For the committee of safety.

"By order,

WILLIAM COOPER, Secretary.

Cambridge, May, 3, 1775."

The above is from the journals of the provincial congress and committee of safety of Massachusetts, page 534. By the same journals the following dates and facts appear.

1775.

April 29, Capt. Arnold had reached Cambridge with a company from Connecticut, p. 527.

30, He reported to the committee of safety the condition of Ticonderoga, p. 529, 695.

The same day (April 30th) the committee wrote to the New York congress for leave to capture Ticonderoga, but did not wait for an answer. *Jour.*, p. 695.

May 2, A sub-committee was appointed to confer with Arnold, and on the same day the provincial congress was desired to furnish him with horses, ammunition, etc., for the expedition, p. 531, 523.

May 3, The above commission was issued to Arnold. At this date the men from Connecticut and Pittsfield had reached Bennington, and Allen was mustering the Green Mountain Boys.

APPENDIX NO. 13.

[See page 449.]

Distribution of the Thirty Thousand Dollars paid by Vermont among the New York Land Claimants.

On the 6th of April, 1796, the legislature of New York passed an act by which Robert Yates, John Lansing, Jr., and Abraham Van Veghten, were appointed commissioners to examine and decide upon the claims of all persons to lands under New York grants, which had been ceded by that state to Vermont, and to make "a just and equitable distribution" of the money which had been paid into the treasury by the latter state. The commissioners in compliance with the provisions of the act, having given the requisite public notice to the claimants, met in the city of Albany on the 10th of July, 1797, and continued their sittings from time to time until the 23d of April, 1799, when they made their final report, dividing the thirty thousand dollars among seventy-six different claimants, assigning to them proportionate shares according to the number of acres to which they had respectively shown themselves entitled. The whole number of acres to which the New York title was held by the commissioners to have been proved was 600,100, for which the claimants would receive $49.91 for every thousand acres, or a very small fraction less than at the rate of five cents per acre.

The quantity of Vermont lands which had been granted by New York besides confirmatory grants, exceeded two millions of acres, more than three times the quantity for which allowances were made by the commissioners. This deficiency in the allowance of claims was owing to several causes. First, to the length of time, from twenty to thirty years, which had elapsed since the making of the grants, during which, from the deaths and removal of parties and changes in business, the knowledge of the existence of a portion of the claims or of the evidence of them would be likely to be lost. Secondly, the smallness of the amount which could be expected under the award of the commissioners would induce many, from various motives, to withhold their claims. Thus some were doubtless withheld in the hope of obtaining a greater allowance from the liberality of the New York legislature, to which many petitions were presented — some with a view of prosecuting them before the federal courts, in which suits were repeatedly threatened, while the politicians who had taken an active part in opposing the independence of Vermont might omit presenting their claims, to avoid the imputation of having acted from personal motives. But thirdly, a very large portion of the deficiency may be accounted for by the fact that most of the original grants were made for the benefit of government officials, and their favorites and friends, a majority of whom joined the enemy in the revolution, and generally left the country at the close of the war. Many of them had indeed been attainted by the New York government, and their claims had thus become forfeited to the state. Of this latter class were Governors Dunmore and Tryon, and Attorney General Kempe, whose extensive claims have already been mentioned. Many other officials and government favorites were also attainted and their property confiscated, including no less than seven of the twelve members of the governor's council, whose claims were probably large. It seems not improbable that one-third of the original claims were held by the adherents of the crown, and in consequence were left unpresented.

The commissioners kept a journal of their proceedings, in which were entered the date and description of the patents, and of the several conveyances under which the claimants derived their titles, by which the purpose and character of the original grants can to a considerable extent be ascertained.[1] This journal has been frequently referred to in the body of this work, and the character of several of the grants, founded on the facts it discloses, has been sufficiently stated.

A further examination of the report of the commissioners and their journals, shows very clearly in accordance with our former account, that the great mass of the grants was obtained, not as the *form* of the applications to the governor stated, " with intent to cultivate the same," but for mere purposes of speculation. With very few exceptions, the claimants were residents of New York city, mostly lawyers, merchants and professional land jobbers.

Of the 600,100 acres for which allowances were made, over 500,000 acres were granted to nineteen of the seventy-six claimants, whose average quantity exceeded 26,000 acres each. The claims of eight parties covered 376,000 acres, nearly two thirds of the whole, the smallest quantity of this number being 22,000 acres. A brief notice of these eight claims will serve to explain and illustrate the character of the whole.

Taking these in their alphabetical order, the first claim is that of Samuel Avery, who was for a considerable time a resident of Westminster, in Cumberland county. He appears to have been one of the favored inhabitants of the New Hampshire Grants, to whom patents were freely issued by the New York government. His grants were of a late date when it had become an object for the earlier city speculators to strengthen their interest in the territory, in order to overcome the formidable resistance of the settlers to their iniquitous claims. One of Avery's claims was founded on a patent issued to him and twenty-three associates for 24,000 acres, bearing date August 16th, 1774. On the 17th and 18th of the same month, these twenty-three associates conveyed their shares to him. Another claim was for 28,000 acres, patented to Humphrey Avery and twenty-seven others, in September, 1774, all of whom on the 29th of that month, conveyed their titles to him, thus vesting in him the whole 52,000 acres, and showing very clearly that the grants were made for his sole benefit. These two tracts adjoined each other, and were in the easterly part of the present county of Addison. These with a claim for 200 acres in Durham and 1,000 in another town of which Samuel Avery was a grantee, made up the 53,200 acres, for which he was allowed the sum of $2,655.03. These grants were made by Lieut. Gov. Colden. Avery continued his applications for land, for some months into the revolutionary period, and on the 28th of October, 1775, obtained a patent for 40,000 acres from Gov. Tryon, after he had fled for safety on board a British man-of-war lying in New York harbor. The land was situated in the vicinity of his former

---

[1] The original journal is found in the office of the secretary of state at Albany, and there is a copy in the secretary of state's office at Montpelier.

grants, but his claim for it was disallowed by the commissioners, for the reason that it was made after the date which had been prescribed in the New York constitution, as the time when the colonial grants should cease to be valid.[1] To Goldsbrow Banyar, in his own name and that of his son William, for 150,800 acres of land, was awarded the sum of $7,528.36, being over one quarter of the whole amount paid by Vermont into the New York treasury. Banyar was secretary to the governor and council during the whole period in which grants of Vermont lands were made. His grants were in numerous patents, made in the names of other persons from whom he at once took conveyances.[2]

The next claim in order is that of William Cockburne for 30,070 acres for which he was allowed $1,495.95. He was a resident of New York, and a deputy surveyor general under Alexander Colden, son of the lieutenant governor; was arrested and dealt with by the Green Mountain Boys for attempting to survey lands under New York patents, that had been previously granted by New Hampshire, and by threats prevented from completing that of Socialborough, as related in the previous part of this work. His allowance was for lands in several different tracts, and it is unnecessary to state, were entirely of a speculative character.[3]

The claim of James Duane was for 52,500 acres, for which his heirs were allowed the sum of $2,621.29. It was for 10,400 acres in the patent of Princetown, 15,000 in Socialborough, 4,741 in Durham, 12,750 in Chatham and the residue in Eugene, the two last being selected by him in satisfaction of military warrants, which he had purchased. All these grants were of lands which had been previously chartered by New Hampshire, and all the patents except that of Princetown, were issued in violation of the king's order of July, 1867, forbidding any further grants.[4]

To the executors of Simon Metcalf, a New York surveyor, was allowed $1,417.47 for 28,400 acres, all but about three thousand of it being in the patent of Prattsburg, granted July 6, 1771 in violation of the king's prohibitory order, covering lands in Swanton and Highgate, both of which had been chartered by New Hampshire in 1763.[5]

The next claim is that of William Smith for 23,600 acres for which he was allowed $1,181.69. He was a member of the New York council from 1778 to the end of the colonial government, and participated in the advice of that body given Lieutenant Governor Colden on the 20th of October 1769, under which the order of the king, forbidding further grants of land in the controverted district, was ever afterwards violated. A few weeks after giving the advice (November 13th) he became the proprietor of 6000 acres of land in the patent of Royalton, and he continued, from time to time to obtain further grants, until he acquired the New York title to the quantity for which the above allowance was made. Mr. Smith, who was the author of the history of New York, became a tory at the revolution, was called before the council of safety in June 1777 and ordered to be confined to the Manor of Livingston. Being connected by marriage with the powerful Livingston family, he escaped being included in the attainder act; and more

1 *Albany Records, Land Patents*, vol. 16. *Jour. of Com'rs*, p. 10, 11, 12, 13, 64, 121, 130.
2 *Land Patent Records*, vols. 14 to 17, and *Jour. of Commissioners*. Index, Banyar.
3 Albany Patent Records, *Journal of Com's*, p. 61, 62, 63.
4 *Journal of Coms.*, p. 42, 45, 85, 88.
5 *Journal of Coms.*, p. 53, 54, 90, 91, 124, 130.

fortunate than most of his associate members of the council, was in consequence enabled to share in the distribution of the sum received from Vermont for the benefit of the land claimants. Mr. Smith was sent within the enemy's lines at New York, where he remained until the evacuation of the city in 1783, when he repaired to England. He was afterwards appointed chief justice of Canada, and died there in 1793.

Besides the above quantity of land a patent was issued May 3, 1770, to the same William Smith and others, for 25,000 acres called Mooretown, 22,000 acres of which were for his special benefit, and of which he received conveyances from his nominal associates. This 22,000 acres he conveyed in 1788, to his son-in-law John Plenderleaf of Scotland, and for which Plenderleaf was allowed by the commissioners the sum of $1096.68.[1]

A claim was allowed to Brook Watson of $1197.76 for 24,000 acres, as assignee in trust for one William Kelley to whom in his name and twenty-three others the tract had been patented May 10, 1770, by the name of Gageborough. Kelly was a resident of New York city, and Brook Watson an English merchant, who has been previously mentioned (p. 216) as figuring in New York and Canada, in the character of a deceitful and bitter enemy to the American cause.[2]

There were six other allowances which exceeded 10,000 acres each, and fifty of the seventy-six exceeded 1,000 acres each. Few or none of the claimants, for either large or small quantities, ever expected or desired to occupy their lands. Their grants were all, with trifling exceptions, if any, of a purely speculative character. The applicants to the New York governors knew that the lands were either already occupied or rapidly settling under grants from New Hampshire, which they had been taught to believe were defective, and they sought the New York title, for the large gains they expected to obtain by the sale of it to the New England emigrants or to others, wholly regardless of any equitable claims to the lands which parties might have who wished to cultivate them.

Some claims were presented to the commissioners, which for various reasons were disallowed, one of which was of sufficient magnitude to deserve a brief notice. It was a claim of John Kelly, an Irish lawyer of New York city. Kelly was a tory within the enemy's lines, during the war of the revolution, but was lucky enough to escape being attainted, and thereby to save his land claim from forfeiture. His claim, included in numerous tracts, was for 115,119 acres, 78,619 of which were presented in his own name, and 36,502 in the names of Robert Troup and four others as assignees for the benefit of Kelly's creditors, his excessive land speculations, by the failure of his Vermont titles, having rendered him insolvent. His original title to the lands does not appear to have been controverted, but the whole claim was rejected; that part of it presented by his assignees, for the reason that he had stated in his assignment that he had received a grant of other lands in Vermont in lieu of those assigned, and the larger claim in his own name was disallowed, because he had also averred in his assignment that he was "not seized or possessed of any real estate," other than that included in the assignment. See the manuscript report of the commissioners. Index to the names of the claimants.

[1] *Jour. of Coms.* *Smith's N. Y.*, vol. 1, Introductory Memoir. *Col. Hist. N. Y.*, vol. 7, p. 909.

[2] *Jour. Coms.*, p. 27.

The following Table shows the names of the claimants among whom the $30,000 *paid by Vermont was distributed by the New York commissioners, by their final report, April* 23, 1799, *together with the sums awarded each, and the quantity of land for which each claimant was allowed. See Documentary History of New York, vol.* 4, *p.* 1024.

No.	Names of Claimants.	Sum Allowed.	No. of Acres to each.
1	Samuel Avery,	$2,655 03	53,200
2	James Abeel,	548 93	11,000
3	Goldsbrow Banyar,	7,218 94	144,600
4	John Bowles,	745 26	14,900
5	Catharine Bowles,	49 91	1,000
6	James Beeckman,	72 56	1,450
7	William Banyar,	309 42	6,200
8	Thomas B. Bridgen,	162 65	3,260
9	Samuel Bard,	149 72	3,000
10	Robert Bowne,	49 91	1,000
11	William Cockburn,	1,495 95	30,070
12	Ebenezer Clark,	37 42	750
13	James McCarra,	24 93	500
14	Alexander Cruickshank,	37 00	750
15	Executors of Cadwallader Colden,	449 15	9,000
16	Richard Cary and wife,	122 92	2,460
17	Henry Cruger,	149 72	3,000
18	Thomas Clark,	237 05	4,730
19	Archibald Campbell.	49 91	1,000
20	Archibald Currie,	9 98	200
21	William McDougall,	37 42	750
22	Heirs of James Duane,	2,621 29	52,500
23	Gerardus Duycking, jr.,	49 91	1,000
24	John Delancey,	49 91	1,000
25	Obadiah Dickinson,	49 91	1,000
26	Alexander McDougall,	34 93	750
27	George Etherington,	98 32	2,000
28	Thomas Etherington,	74 11	1,700
29	James Farquhar,	99 81	2,000
30	Jillis A. Fonda,	49 90	1,000
31	John Galbriath,	99 81	2,000
32	James Guthrie,	37 42	750
33	William Giles,	5 49	110
34	Joseph Griswold,	147 73	3,000
35	John Goodrich,	199 63	4,000
36	Charles Hutchins,	9 98	200
37	Jonathan Hunt,	948 23	19,000
38	John Hensdale,	49 91	1,000
39	John Johnson,	124 77	2,500
40	Luke Knowlton,	249 53	5,000
41	Peter Kemble,	199 63	4,000
42	Abraham Lott,	698 69	14,000
43	John Lawrence,	49 91	1,000
44	Robert Lewis,	119 78	2,400
45	Joel Lyman,	49 91	1,000
46	Elijah Lyman,	49 91	1,000
47	Executrix of Simon Metcalf,	1,417 47	28,400
48	Catharine Metcalf,	99 81	2,000
49	Th's Norman & wife, heirs of Crean Brush,	718 60	14,400
50	Jane Nesbit,	12 48	250

Table continued.

No.	Names of Claimants.	Sum Allowed.	No. of Acres to each.
51	Elias Nixon,	$24 95	500
52	Barbara Ortley,	134 75	2,700
53	Eleazer Porter,	49 91	1,000
54	John McPherson,	99 81	2,000
55	Isaac Rosevelt,	399 25	8,000
56	Peter Sim,	37 42	750
57	Samuel Stevens,	653 63	13,000
58	William Smith,	1,181 69	23,600
59	Jacob Shefflin,	97 32	2,000
60	Francis Stevens,	199 63	4,000
61	Diana Smith,	49 91	1,000
62	Executrix of Michael Schlatter,	99 81	2,000
63	John M. Scott,	49 91	1,000
64	John Titts,	9 98	200
65	Samuel Thatcher,	149 71	3,000
66	Peter Van Schaick,	199 63	4,000
67	William Wickham,	149 72	3,000
68	Brook Watson,	1,197 76	24,000
69	Gerard Walton,	49 91	1,000
70	John Watts,	99 82	2,000
71	William Walton,	199 63	4,000
72	George Wray,	39 92	800
73	Staltham Williams,	199 63	4,000
74	John Bard,	449 15	9,000
75	John Plenderleaf,	1,096 68	22,000
76	Samuel Partridge,	49 91	1,000
	Total,	$30,000 00	600,100

INDEX.

ERRATA.

Page 4, line 7, for western, read *eastern*.

" 7, line 32, for natives, read *nation*.

" 20, line 20, for such, read *new*.

" 20, line 26, the words "corresponding with the length of Delaware bay" should be read after the words "lower portion of it" in the next line.

" 22, line 22, for on read *in*.

" 23, line 19, for west, read *out*.

" 29, in the caption of the chapter, for and, read *on*.

" 30, line 18, strike out the word *not*.

" 52, line 3, after Long Island, read *sound*,

" 61, line 23, for points, read forests.

" 68, line 24, for resources, read *revenue*.

" 69, line 11, the words "should constitute a board" should be read before the words "who were to set out lands."

" 93, line 10, for rested, read *vested*.

" 150, line 26, for No. 6, read *No.* 7.

" 186, line 12, for run, read *river*.

" 321, line 12, for whit, read *with*.

" 481, Appendix No. 6, the defendant's name should be *Isaiah* instead of Josiah.